Śree Lalitā Mahātr

श्री ललिता सहस्रनामम्

Sree Lalita Sahasranama

(1000 holy names of the divine Mother – With Transliteration of Samskrit verses/ names - a lucid rendering and commentaries in Engish)

*

A translation of the book written in Tamil by *Śree*. S. Gaŋapatisubramaŋian and *Śree* M. Sundararaman mainly based on "*Soubhāgya Bhāskaram*" the commentary in Samskrit by *Śree Bhāskararāya*.

*

Translated into English by

RAMAMURTHY NATARAJAN

M.Sc., B.G.L., CAIIB, CCP, DSADP, CISA, PMP, CGBL, 6σ-Black-Belt

*

2013

*

Name of the Book: *Sree Lalita Sahasranama* (1000 holy names of the divine mother - With Transliteration of Samskrit verses/ names - a lucid rendering and commentaries in English)

First Edition: April 2011
Second Edition: July 2013

Author: **Ramamurthy Natarajan,** Chennai.
http://ramamurthy.jaagruti.co.in/

ISBN: 978-93-82237-15-0

Number of Pages: 737

*****

Table of Contents

*****

P.M. Venkatasubramanian,
Chairman,
M/s Royal Sundaram Alliance
Insurance Company Limited,Chennai.
(Retired Managing Director of GIC of India)

1A/3, Third Main Road,
Vijay Nagar, Velacherry,
Chennai - 600 042.
15th September 2009

Foreword-1

The author is a perfect example of the good old saying '**Where there is a will, there is a way**'. Even most of the profound literary scholars would have demurred at the thought of undertaking the herculean task of translating the ever increasing popular Tamil edition of *Lalitā Sahsranāmam* to English. But the author has taken this as an opportunity and a divine blessing and has managed to complete it almost with perfection. His qualities are comparable to that of *Arjuna's* dedication, *Yudhishṭra's* righteousness, *Veda Vyāsā*'s knowledge and *Hanuman's* mighty power. Rightfully he is named after the legendary god *Ram* himself.

The author with all his capabilities, devotion and the divine blessings of *Śree Mātā*, managed to complete the translation within 9 months. He has used modern day tools like laptop and internet for extensive research in an effort to reproduce the Tamil version and at the same time retain its originality and flavour.

The Hindu religious philosophy is so vast and contains so many masterpieces and treatises where each one is a deep ocean in itself. But there are many linkages between these gems of literary and divine masterpieces. In this work the authors of the original and translated versions have tried to provide some sneak preview into these linkages so that the readers, if not able to understand it fully, at least would be able to appreciate the essence.

As Lord *Śree Krişhŋa* himself said in *Śreemad Bhagavad Gita*, it takes several births before one is born as a human being by virtue of his past deeds, which brings him closer to God. As human beings, so blessed we are that we are one step closer to Devine which we can attain if we whole heartedly devote ourselves to God during our life time.

By giving way to transient pleasures knowingly or unknowingly, we however move farther from God and salvation. It is therefore imperative upon every one of us to purify ourselves and for this, as mentioned in *Lalitā Sahsranāma* itself, there is no better way than uttering the divine names of *Śree Lalita*. It would even be more potent and effective, if we understand and import behind these divine names of *Śree Lalitā* while chanting. It is towards this end that the author has made an effort to bring this rare work of art, where literature and divinity confluence and has translated into various languages from the Language of Gods, themselves - Samskrit.

He had steadfastly worked on this spread over the past 9 months – not only translating the Tamil version into English but also finding out equivalent English words wherever Samskrit words themselves were used in the original Tamil version. I am quite confident that this work is going to benefit a larger audience with different religious background through the medium of English and not being confined to Hindus only as the great work of *Lalitā Sahasranāma* is meant to be for the welfare of the universal family (*Vasudeva Kudumbam*) as per the great Hindu tradition) !!!

Śree Mātre Namah

P.M.Venkatasubramanian

*****

Telegram :

Telex No. : 41-6376 UNOM IN

UNIVERSITY OF MADRAS

(Established under the ACT of Incorporation XXVII of 1857: Madras University Act 1923)

(State University)

DEPARTMENT OF SAMSKRIT

MARINA CAMPUS, CHENNAI-600 005

DR. SINIRUDDHA DASH
PROFESSOR AND HEAD
DIRECTOR, NCC PROJECT

Phone : 28449518/23/24

Fax : 91-44-25366693.

"Learning Promotes Natural Talent"

10th December 2009

Foreword-2

There are various *Sahasranāma* hymns about each of the Hindu Gods. Among them only two *Sahasranāmas* on *Vişŋu* and *Lalitā*, are very famous. *Vişŋu Sahasranāma* forms part of *Mahābhārata* and it was told by *Bheeshma* to *Yudhishtira* and others.

Lalitā Sahasranāma forms part of the *Brahmāŋḍa Purāŋa* and it was told by *Śree Hayagreeva* to Sage *Agastya*. In this hymn itself, it has been stressed more than once that it is a very secret one and should not be told to ineligible persons. Hence this is not very popular like *Vişŋu Sahasranāma* among the common people. However, it is well known to those who follow *Śākta* principles and *Devee* worshippers.

Śree Adi Śaṇkara first wrote commentary in Samskrit to *Vişŋu Sahasranāma*. *Śree Bhāskararāya* wrote the commentary in Samskrit to *Lalitā Sahasranāma*. These commentaries are not just meanings, but research theses on those hymns.

I went through the commendable work done by Śree Ramamurthy on *Śree Lalitā Sahasranāma* with its English rendering. The specialty of this laudable work is a complete rendering into English of the Tamil work of *Śree*. S. Gaŋapatisubramaŋian and *Śree* M. Sundararaman. This Tamil work was in turn based on the famous book *"Soubhāgya Bhāskaram"*, the commentary on *Śree Lalitā Sahasranāma* in Samskrit by *Śree Bhāskararāya*.

The introduction and study part of the present work is unique and gives more details about the work and its implied meanings – not usually found in other publications. It is aimed at common audience and not necessarily scholarly readers.

Every name in this *Sahasranāma* is loaded with a lot of inner *mantras*. These cryptic inner meanings are explained in detail with comparison to other *Purānas, Upanishads, Śree Bhagavad Geeta*, etc.

The *Phalaśruti* part of this *Sahasranāma* explains in detail about various results or fruits that can be reaped by chanting these names. But if they are chanted, after understanding the inner meanings of them, definitely more benefits can be reaped. It is generally enjoined in the *Upanishads* that the performance of a *brahmavidya* or any other *vidya* is better done when performed after knowing its meaning as in *"yo nāchiketam agnim chinuyāt ya evam veda"*, etc.

This book helps the readers, to clearly understand the meanings, traditions/ methods of performing worship, etc., in simple English. It also elaborates the details about *Devee* worship, *Śreechakra, Śreevidya*, etc. Especially the *Paribhāsha* verses are astonishing ones – the way they explain the unique method of splitting the verses into names.

I understand, Śree Ramamurthy conceptualised this initiative in December 2008 and has completed the mammoth task in a matter around 9 months. It is not only translating from Tamil to English, but from Samskrit to English, since most of the Samskrit words are used, as they are, in Tamil.

May *Śree Devee* shower **Her** blessings on him.

Professor and Head
Department of Samskrit
University of Madras, Chennai

Dr. *Siniruddha Dash*

*****

श्रीः

Dedication

Śree Devee's blessings can be the only factor instrumental in reproducing the book in its current form.

However, there have been many worldly supports in this cause and I take this opportunity in conveying my heartiest appreciations to them.

The 1000 divine names of *Lalitā* start with *Śree Mātā* (mother of universe) and the point where my journey of life started is at my mother Smt. *Alankaravalli*. Hence it would be apt to thank her for giving me the most important resource required in this cause – a healthy body and a clear conscience. She suffered a lot in her life in upbringing us and though she is not physically present with us now, she continues to live within our hearts, through all our actions and continue to shower her blessings. It is her dedication and hard work which forms the foundation of our core values and it is because of her that we stand at where we are at present. I dedicate this cause and as a result this book to her.

Fittingly one of the two authors of the Tamil edition *Śreemān*. S. Gaŋapatisubramaŋian is my maternal uncle (younger brother of my mother). I got inspired in *Vedas* in general and Samskrit in particular from him and he is a sort of *mānaseeka guru* for me like *Dronacharya* to *Ekalavya*. He was never short of ideas and it was his vision and dream to bring this book in English. Though he is also physically not available now to see this book in English, I am confident that his blessings are another source for me to complete this task. I dedicate this book to him also.

Śreemān S. Srinivasan, a cousin of *Śreemān*. S. Gaŋapati Subramaŋian, conceptualised this task of translating into English. However, on account of various reasons he could not pursue. But he gave his full support in all possible ways to me especially in printing and bringing out this book in this form. My hearty thanks to him.

My sincere thanks to Smt. Neeta Agrawal, who has beautifully designed the cover, which has come out in a nice way as it is in your hands.

I just cannot move out by saying thanks to Sri. P.M. Venkatasubramanian (PMV as he is affectionately called as) and Dr. Sinirudha Dash who have written the forewords – nice words about me. I hope I am worthy of them.

As always, my family has been very supportive and helpful, without whom this cause would not have been successful. My family members helped me a lot in reviewing and reducing the mistakes. I pray to *Śree Lalitā* for their wellbeing and continued support in future endeavours.

Chennai
June 2011

RAMAMURTHY N

*****

श्रीः

Preface

"Avanarulāleye Avan Tāl Vanangi" – to worship his feet with his own blessings is a famous Tamil saying.

I am elated for the simple reason that the whole journey of writing this book was completed within 9 months from the time the idea was firmed up. But the fact is that we are all just a medium for **Her,** it was **Her** wish and thus it was destined to happen. It was **She** who has done it and **She** has used me as a tool.

The original Tamil edition written by learned scholars, *Śree* S. Gaŋapati Subramaŋian and *Śree* M. Sundararaman of Gnana Bhāskara Sangam, at the behest of their Guru (*Śreemati Prakaasambaa Sametha Śree Chidānanda Nātha*) was first published in the year 2000. Since then it continued to have increasing popularity among the Tamil-knowing public especially those who have passion towards religion. But all its way through there were repeated requests to the author/ publishers from several quarters that the Tamil edition be translated into English for the benefit of the larger audience in mind. This formed the crux of this enthralling journey.

There were so many roadblocks to overcome on the way some of which are worth mentioning for the reason that these could provide an insight and also a motivating factor for many a people who have passion to indulge in similar activities but are still thinking where or how to start.

A lot many Samskrit words are used in Tamil as they are. In most of the sentences only the verb was in Tamil otherwise the subject, predicate and adjectives were all Samskrit words. Hence it ended up translating the words to English not only from Tamil but also from Samskrit. This was the biggest challenge. It is always difficult to translate the divine Samskrit language to convey the exact sense because of the fact that English is not exhaustive as Samskrit, whereas Samskrit is complex. As Mathew Arnold explained about the difficulties in translating the Bible from Hebrew to English, here also some of the expressions and phrases are notoriously untranslatable. In most cases, English is found wanting for communicating exactly some of the expressions or feelings, but similar limitations in Samskrit is a lot lesser. For instance there are no words/

phrases communicating the exact meaning of the word *Dharma*. Hence a lot of search, research is required to convey the true sense for some of the words.

Using tools like computers for directly translating instead of hand writing has helped in more ways than one. It has done a little part towards saving the Mother Nature by saving huge amount of paper work. Also the process of reviewing was much easier and so did the proof reading and subsequent corrections. Any number of such reviews and corrections were easily possible.

I believe that justice has been done to whatever little possible work I have done and I do hope that the original book has been translated without losing its flavour.

I have tried to maintain simple and easily understandable English throughout this edition keeping in mind an average reader. Hence I request the readers to take cognizance of any good messages conveyed rather the language used for it. Also I request them to notify of any mistakes so that it could be corrected in future editions.

Of course, to read this book, the readers may have to have a little knowledge of Samskrit, which could not be avoided entirely. But the effort required for learning and understanding it is miniscule when compared to the virtues we are getting out of it. So let us all put that small effort and seek **Her** blessings.

Om Tat Sat

*****

श्रीः

Introduction

Of all the means of realising God, the easiest is chanting the name with fervor – *Rāmakrişhŋa Paramahamsa.*

Lalitā Sahasranāma is a unique hymn in that *Śreedevee* who is extolled is not a sectarian deity, but the universal spirit who is the ultimate guiding principle of this universe. All the names are mellifluous and if chanted with an understanding of their meanings, they enable the devotees to attain remarkable peace and bliss. Sage *Pathanjali* says, *Tat Japatas Tatartta Bhavanam* – the name of a God has to be told after understanding the meaning and enjoying the same. A CD player plays the chant perfectly, but it will continue to remain as CD player and will never become divinised. Only a person who chants with faith knowing its meaning and focusing the awareness makes progress. *Śree Bhāskararāyā*'s commentary helps the devotees to have an insight into the deep significance of each name.

There are many books which provide meanings for *Lalitā Sahasranāma* in English. Then what is the specialty of this book? This is not **just another book**. In this page I try to explain in a nutshell, how different this book is and the research which has gone into this book.

Śree Bhāskararāya was the first to write the *bhāshyam* (commentaries in Samskrit) for *Lalitā Sahasranāma*. The magnum opus of the Tamil book was primarily based on this commentary, which has now been translated into English verbatim.

The best feature of this book is that every name is compared with the corresponding meanings/ analogies in 20+ Upanishads, various *mantras, Brahmasūtram, Devee Bhāgavatam, Mahā Shoḍanyāsam, Nityā Shoḍashikārnavam,* different *Sutrās, Shiva* and other *Puranas, Soundaryalaharee, Śree Durgāsaptasatee, Śree Lalitā Trishatee, Śree Lalitopākhyānam, Śree Varivasyā Rahasyam, Sreemad Bhagavad Geeta, Sreevidyā saparyā paddhati, Sruti* and *Smrutis, Vişhŋu Sahasranāmā* and what not.

Just to mention the references, it has taken more than half the page. Hence to compare every name with these is more than enough proof to understand the effort that has gone into.

For instance 712th name *Ee* has explanations/ references' running for 5 pages and the irony is that this is the smallest name and has got the longest explanation. The inner cryptic meanings, interpretations, etc., are also explained in detail. This stands as a testimony to the effort that has been put into bringing the best possible correct and truthful information.

In addition to the commentaries for the 1000 names, the Tamil book has lot of information, must know details for every pious individual. Hence I have chosen to translate and provide here the entire introduction part including the publisher's note, preface, etc., of the Tamil edition.

Every one of the thousand names has got loaded with so much of *mantra*s and inner meanings. The forty verses called *Paribhāshā stotras* is a self-contained research paper on *Lalitā Sahasranāma*. It is perfect allegory. At the outset the surface meaning of these verses is as praising and bowing *Śreedevee*. But the deep meaning is that, it explains the structure of all the thousand names – how many names contain how many letters, the following names start with which letter, the starting letter of every hundredth name, etc. It is a delight to read these 40 verses. However, it is very difficult to understand by oneself, without the detailed interpretations/ explanations given in this book. This is because the numerals are denoted by Samskrit letters and in cryptic method.

Every human being must recite the *Lalitā Sahasranāma*, failing which he has not attained the fruit of his/ her birth. This has been mentioned in *Lalitā Sahasranāma* itself. I have made an effort to understand this so that people can appreciate it further and get the blessings of *Śreedevee*.

<u>Conventions</u> – All the wordṣ in Samskrit when transliterated in English have been written in *Italic* form. While transliterating the Samskrit words into English, most of the international convention of diacritical marking has been followed, but not in its entirety. For example - *Krişna* has continued to be written as *Krishna* – for easy reading. 'Ā' has been used wherever 'aa' pronounciation is required. But 'ee' has been used in the place of 'ī'. The important reason for the same is that the author does not Intend scholarly readers but expects a very common audience for this

book. However most of the internationally accepted markings have been used. The diacritical marks used in this book and the corresponding pronunciations are as below:

ā	-	as in August or author
ḍ	-	as in do or industry
ĕ	-	as in seen, or been
ŋ	-	as in Kannan
ş	-	as in push
ś	-	as in Shankar or Shyamala
ţ	-	as in tea

Śreedevee wherever mentioned implies *Śree Lalita*. Also it is mentioned in bold letters as **She, Her, etc.,** to indicate *Śree Lalita*. The entire 1000 names have been listed in the alphabetical order in Appendix 1. The Samskrit words which cannot be translated directly into English as a single word, have been explained in Appendix 2.

The names are written in *Devanāgari* also to make the reading easy for those who can read Samskrit.

The *Lalitā Sahasranāma shlokas* or verses have been given in Annexure 1 to this book for completeness taking a minor deviation from the Tamil book.

Om

*****

Dedication - as in Tamil Edition

Most of our life has been spent in worldly affairs like family and profession. An iota of virtue in the previous births has led to some devotion to Gods, able to reach some good teachers in this line, got initiated in *mantras* and could involve ourselves in chanting and other actions. But still we are not yet relieved from worldly affairs.

In these circumstances, a good friend of ours and also known to our teacher Śree K. Sundararaman (retired from a high post from M/s Chemplast) suggested that he wanted to read the commentary of *Śree Bhāskararāya* for *Śree Lalitā Sahasranāma* alongwith some of his friends. We informed him that the book with Tamil meanings published by Kumbakonam Śree Gaŋesa Iyer would be of much help in this regard. However, we are not getting that book for years.

We felt that if that book is printed again it would be of great help to the devotees of *Śree Lalita*. But we could not find out from whom we have to get permission, where are they, etc., to re-publish it. We dropped this idea, since publishing without proper approval will be against ethics and also will be illegal.

Hence, Śree K. Sundararaman, requested our teachers to bring out a fresh Tamil translation that would be suitable for the current day worldly men. He requested, "Your society, coming in the race of *Śree Chidānanda Nātha* and not interested in fame or glory and really involved in the service of *Śreedevee*, has to do it". Our teachers also accepted this request and decided that this has to be done as a mark of respect to *Śree Chidānanda Nātha* and entrusted the task to us.

Though we wanted to do this task, which would satisfy our teachers, we hesitated that we do not have adequate knowledge and capacity to own this responsibility. Out teachers have ordered that "you two have to do this by any means". How can we disobey our teachers? In addition to that order, to encourage us they blessed that "there were a lot of great learned in our *guru paramapara* (lineage of teachers). They would show us a good path for us, who are following a good tradition. They would support us with adequate knowledge and capacity. They would also bless us with good messages to come to our mind".

With the strength of their blessings as the only support and as per their orders, we started this task on 09th May 1997. By October 1998 (*sarath Navarāthri*) period, the task has almost been completed. In the meantime on account of our ill health and on account of our family and professional chores, we could not complete it in a full-fledged way. Whenever our mind and body became tired, our teachers encouraged us and got this task completed. Even after completion of writing, the printing took some time. This work also got completed in July 1999 (during *Vārāhi Navarāthri*) period.

To write this Tamil meaning, the works of Śree Gaŋesa Iyer, *Śree Radha Krişhŋa Sāstrigal* and the English translation of *Śree Ananda Krişhŋa Sāstrigal* were all of much help. Our sincere thanks to them.

When there is a lot of crowd, the father used to lift his child above his head to show any function; the child will also be very happy thinking that he has seen the function, which has not been seen by others. We are also in the state of that child. With the blessings of our lineage of teachers, we could fathom the depth (*gambheera*) of the commentary of *Śree Bhāskararāya*. (Isn't he the son of *Śree Gambheera rāya*?)

Sir Isac Newton, a famous scientist from west, also has conveyed almost a similar message. "If I have seen further than others, it is because I have stood on the shoulders of giants".

This Tamil commentary has been written with the unlimited compassion of *Śreedevee*. As per the route shown by *Śree Ādi Śaņkara*, we offer back **Her** own words;

Pradeepa Jvālābhir Divasakara Neerājanavidhi:
Sudhāsootesh Chandropala Jalalavairarghya Rachanā I
Svakeeyairambhobhi: Salila Nidhishouhityakaraŋam
Tvadeeyābhir Vāgbhistava Janani Vāchām Stutiriyam II *Soundaryalaharee* – 100

Even if there are any mistakes, we seek the blessings of *Śreedevee*, with the help of *Kālidāsā*;

Amba Staveshu Tava Tāvadakartrukāni Kuntee Bhavanti
Vachasāmapi Kumpha Nāni I
Dimpasya Me Stutirasāvasamanjasāpi Vātsalya Nighna
Hrdayām Bhavateem Dhinotu II

(*Ambā Stavam*)

Again we follow *Kālidāsā*;

Vidhe Vedye Vidye Vividhasamaye Veda Kulike
Vichitre Vishvādye Vinayasulabhe Veda Janani I
Shivajne Sulasthe Shivapadavadānye Shivanidhe
Shive Mātar Mahyam Tvayi vitara Bhaktim Nirupamām II

(*Sakala Jananee Stavam*)

With utmost care, we have tried to avoid the printing and word mistakes. However, in such a voluminous book some mistakes could have crept in. According our previous generation people's sayings;

Gachchata: *Skhalanam Kāpi Bhavatyeva Pramādata*: I
Hasanti Durjanāstatra Samādadhati Sajjanā: II

Those good people who read this book are requested to take only the good things, like a Swan bird and ignore the flaws.

With a prayer to our teachers and to *Śreedevee* to bless us with the eternal devotion, we dedicate, with regards, this book in Tamil to our lineage of teachers and to *Śreedevee*, who is in the form of spiritual teachers.

Āshrayeham Guruvarān Prakāsha-chid-guhānandān I
Ātma-prakāsha-vimala-shānta-poorŋān Devyabhedān II

Chennai
28th July 1999

S. Gaŋapatisubramaŋian
M. Sundararaman
(Gnāna Bhāskara Sangam)

*****

Publisher's Note

(as in Tamil edition)

The book called *Śree Lalitā Sahasranāma* is a treasure house, which contains within itself, whatever *tatva* relating to *Śreedevee*, in sacred writings, scriptures, *Vedas* and *Upanishads*. It is like ocean of milk containing nine gems. No other hymn can be equated to this hymn.

Though the Supreme Being is frozen in many a form, worshipping it in the form of mother is the best and easy too. For everyone at all times, chanting of *Śree Lalitā Sahasranāma* is the best and great tool to reach salvation. The great person called Śree Bhāskararāya, who was an ardent worshipper and great learned man, has written the commentary for *Śree Lalitā Sahasranāma* in Samskrit, titled *Soubhāgya Bhāskaram*. Our teachers have given us an opportunity to publish this book in Tamil based on this book. We submit our grateful regards in their feet.

Śree Gaŋapatisubramaŋian and Śree Sundararaman have their profession as Accountants and have an indepth knowledge of Samskrit, great worshippers of *Śreedevee*, devotion to gods and teachers, but so simple to look at. They, according to our requests, most obedient to as a mother and giving respect to our words, have taken the task of writing this book as a sincere one and have brought out most of the rare matters, which were not been published so far. Especially they have completed this rare task with so much of hard work, amidst their busy schedules.

This book has come out successfully, after a series of tasks like, purchase of papers, proof correction, incorporating beautiful pictures on the cover page through computers, compiling and quoting various evidences for the secret statements mentioned in the names, not only making it as a combination of words but also making it as interesting as possible to all types of readers to enjoy depending on their capacity and to fulfill their wishes.

The authors, in spite of their ill health, considering the task on hand as God, have completed it in a fantastic manner. We seek to *Śreedevee*, who is in the form of *Gurumaŋḍala*, to provide all her blessings like long and healthy and fulfillment of all the eight types of desires to these two authors.

Amidst busy work schedule, *Brahmasree Goda G Venkateshvara Sāstrigal* has set apart his valuable time for writing the Foreword for this book with so much of poetic taste. Our hearty and sincere thanks to him. He has also helped in another way to the authors, in this regard. He gave a discourse on *Soubhāgya Bhāskaram* every Sunday for five years in our society. This has kindled the interest on us, with the blessings of our teachers.

Our unlimited thanks are due to Associated Printers who have brought out this book in a great grand manner at a very less cost. Our thanks are due to Śree V Hariharan, promoter of Adview Crafts, for artistically and beautifully designing the pictures on the cover and other pages.

The commentary on *Śree Lalitā Sahasranāma* has come in search of your house. The objective of publishing this book is to propagate devotion on God and teachers among all. We request our teachers, who always bless us in a subtle form, to make this goal fulfilled. We request all the readers to read this book and become eligible for the limitless compassion of *Śree Rājarājeshwaree*. We seek *Śree Lalitā*, to bestow her blessings, matured knowledge and great wealth to all those who have worked hard to bring out this book successfully.

15th October 1999

Śree Chitānandanātapādarenu
Śreemati Rājammal

*****

Foreword
(to the Tamil edition)

The learned have said: *'Mokshaika Hetu Vidyā Śreevidyāiva Na Samshaya:'*

The wants of human beings are many. The most common among them is about salvation. Salvation means, getting rid of all the sorrows, suffering presently and moving to the stage of Supreme Bliss. This has been clearly mentioned in *Vedas*. The evidences like *Svetasvatara Upanishad* (II-3,8) that self realisation is an important tool to this; *Gnānādeva Tu Kaivalyam Tameva Viditvā Ati Mrutymeti*. Still it is very difficult for everyone to get that self realisation. That can be reached only by getting the *Vedānta* books like *Upanishads, Śreemad Bhagavad Geeta, Sūtras* of *Vyāsa* and their commentaries, etc., hearing them read by teachers, thinking about them and meditating on them. Further maturity, determination, control of organs, control of mind, passion, peace, patience and interest on salvation are all very important. Getting eligible for this from and out of normal family life is very difficult.

For this purpose only, *Vedas* have prescribed the routes of worship (*upāsana*) and devotion for the medium level people. Because of this worship the mind becomes focused, get drenched in the benign look of good teachers, get the opportunity to hear *Vedāntas* in this birth itself and be useful to get salvation. It will not be a great loss for them, even if they do not get self realisation in this birth itself. Because, after death, they reach the world of *Brahma* called *Śreepuram*. There they get taught the self *tatva* by *Sanaka* and other sages and reach soul salvation early. Hence they do not have re-birth again and enjoy the supreme form. This is the important usage of worship path. For those who do not follow this path, *Vedas* have prescribed the path of actions. That is, actions like – *Sandhyāvandanam*, chanting of *mantras* (*japa*), *homa* (conducting sacrificial fires), doing *poojas, Agnihotram, Chātur māsya, Darsa, Vājapeyam, Ashvamedham*, etc. *Sāstra* says that for those who do these actions without specific interest on the results, but still do them only for satiating the Supreme Being, get their mind purified and enter into the worship path or the knowledge path, which is above it.

Tametam Vedānuvachanenena... Vivitishanti.
Brahadāraŋyaka Upanishad (44-22)

Vedas mention such worship in many ways. They are, *Prateeka* worship, *Sampat* worship and *Aham Graham*, etc. In the section of *Veda* called *Āraŋyakam* the methods of such worship have been clearly mentioned, the rules prescribed, the regulations to be followed, etc. They are mentioned in Upanishads also then and there.

Our ancestors and sages have all in general followed the worship path only. It was easy for them to follow the worship path because they have learnt the *Vedas* and have understood the meanings also. The worship method started to fade away on account of passage of time and since most of the people did not understand the meaning of *Vedas*. At this stage, the great incarnation *Śree Ādi Śaṇkara* wanted to clearly show this path and have identified and evolved six important worshipping methods. That is why he got the title as *Shanmatha Pratishtāpanāchāryar* (establisher of six religions). Like him some more great people have also explained the worshipping methods. However, only the methods established by *Śree Ādi Śaṇkara* prevail in this world. Those six methods are; *Gānapatyam, Koumāram, Souram, Saivam, Vaishnavam* and *Śāktam*.

For each of these the *Sūtras*, commentaries, worshipping methods, etc., have been prescribed. The great persons like *Śree Bhāskararāya*, who came after *Śree Ādi Śaṇkara* have expanded these methods as easily understandable by all and followed the traditions.

The six methods mentioned above are all of equal status. However, worshipping of *Śreedevee* has been considered as a great one and has been followed by many people right from early days. For *Śree Ādi Śaṇkara* also, internally liked path is worshipping of *Śreedevee* only. That is the reason, he has specifically mentioned in his commentaries on *Śree Bhagavad Geeta* as; *Shakti Shaktimatoh abeda*: This is clearly mentioned in the 14th chapter. Hence let us see some nuances about worshipping *Śreedevee*.

We read about worshipping *Śreedevee* in *Veda* and others. *Rig Veda* (5-47-4) says; *Chatvāra Ĕm Pipratikshemayanta*: The verses beginning with *Emānukam* in *Yajur Veda* describe about *Śreechakra* and *Kunḍalinee* and other energies in our body. Many *Upanishads* forming part of *Atharva Veda* like *Tripuropanishad, Devee Upanishad, Tripura tapinee Upanishad, Pāvanopanishad* and *Buhvrucha Upanishad* explain worshipping

Śreedevee. The books called *tantras* are in the form of discussions between *Paramashiva* and *Śreedevee*. They form the basis for this worship. There are 64 in number and the important among them are – *Tantra Rāja Tantram* and *Svatantra Tantram*. These are must read books for all the worshippers.

Sūtras: The *Sūtras* which form the basis for *Śreevidyā* are all done by *Parasurāma*. Hence they are called *Parasurāma Kalpasūtras*. It has 10 sections. The second section describes about worshipping *Gaŋapati* and all the other describe about worshipping *Śreedevee*. One famous *Meemāsaka* called *Rameshwara Soori* has written commentary for this in a convincing and clear way. His most liked disciple is our *Śree Bhāskararāya*.

Purāŋas: *Śree Vyāsa* has clearly shown in his *purāŋas* about the greatness of worshipping *Śreedevee*. Particular mention has to be made about *Śreedevee Bhāgavatam, Brahmānḍa Purāŋam, Mārkaŋḍeya Purāŋam, Skanda Purāŋam* and *Padma Purāŋam*. The famous *Durgā Saptashatee* is a subset of *Mārkaŋḍeya Purāŋam*. The hymn *Śree Lalitā Sahasranāma* forms part of *Brahmānḍa Purāŋa*. *Lalitopākhyāna* explains in detail about the plays of *Śreedevee* like destruction of *Bhanḍāsura*.

Stotras: There are many verses describing the methods and greatness of worshipping *Śreedevee*. Important among them are; *Śreeshubakotaya Stuti, Shakti Mahimnā Stotra* authored by sage *Doorvāsa, Durgāchandra Kalā Stotra, Soundaryalaharee* authored by *Śree Ādi Śaṇkara, Panchadashee Stotra* and *Tripurasundaree Mānaseeka Pooja*.

The greatest among the worshippers of *Śreevidyā*, is *Śree Parameshvara* himself. Next in the order is *Śree Hayagreeva, Agastya, Lopāmudra, Indra, Kubera*, Sun, Cupid, *Kālidāsa*, etc. It is understood that *Śree Lalitā Sahasranāma* hymn was told to sage *Agastya* by *Śree Hayagreeva*. *Parasurāma* and other incarnations also are worshippers of *Śreedevee*. In that process this worship goes on and on in the form of the teacher-disciple race from deities, to *Siddhās*, to sages and to human beings. An important person in this race is *Śree Bhāskararāya*, who lived in 1690 - 1785 C.E. He is such a great man, that he has written many books like *Varivasyā Rahasyam, Setubandham, Soubhāgya Bhāskaram* (commentaries for *Śree Lalitā Sahasranāma* hymn) and *Drusabhāskaram*. He followed the path of *Vedas*. However, he performed various sacrifices and worshipping of *Śreedevee* without fail and showed this path to his disciples. In the same manner, *Avalānanda Nātha* alias *Ārthor Avalōn*, a Westerner, has published a number of scholarly treatises and helped this world. Thus, this worship has spread throughout the country. In the last century a great person called *Śree Chitānanda Nāda* got initiated into this worship from *Śree Guhānanda Nāthar* in Allahabad (who has sacrificed everything including his dress) for many years, practiced it, got the experience and initiated it to many of his disciples. Many of his disciples are spread across the country. He has translated lot of books, which are the roots for *Śreevidyā* in Tamil. They are *Varivasya Rahasyam, Kāmakala Vilāsam, Shakti Mahimnā Storam,* commentaries for *Trishatee, Subramanya Tatva* and *Nityāhnikam*.

A great work done by him is the worshipping procedure called *Śreevidyā Saparyā Paddhati*. This has been formulated in an excellent manner based on the treatise called *Nityotsavam* by *Umānanda Nātha, Varivasya Prakāsam* and *Varivasya Rahasyam* by *Śree Bhāskararāya, Parasurama Kalpasūtra* and *Paramānanda Tantra*. There is no doubt that the worshipping method followed by all in India as well as abroad is this method only. He approached many learned people, compiled various matters and made clear very subtle nuances. He himself has given discourse on this. In the same way, he made my teacher (*Ātma Vidyā Bhooshaŋam Vidyāvāridhi Sāstraratnākaram*) *Brahmasree Injikollai Jagateeshwara Sāstrigal* to give discourse in Tamil on the books called *Śree Lalitā Sahasranāma, Setubandam, Kāmakala Vilāsam* and *Varivasyā Rahasyam* and helped the then living disciples. These books are very difficult and can be understood only by those who have solid in-depth knowledge on 3 or 4 *sāstras*. Many books have subsequently been published on the methods of worship and *Nityāhnikam*. However, it is surprising that, there is no value addition by adding something new or making the method easier.

There are four important methods in this worship of *Śreevidyā* viz., *Samayāchāra, Vāmāchāra, Dakshiŋāchāra* and *Koulāchāra*. Out of these *Samayāchāra* and *Dakshiŋāchāra* are based on *Veda* path. Whatever be the method, everyone can get *Śreedevee*'s blessings, by following what was instructed by the teacher.

<u>Eligible candidates for worshipping *Śreedevee*</u>: Only men or couples are eligible to do many rites or rituals mentioned in *Veda*. Ladies have

become ineligible to do them. According to the saying; *Na Gāyatryā: Paro Mantra:*, only males are eligible to chant the *Gāyatree mantra* itself and the same is the case with other *mantras* also. The only route to reach the *Dharma* for those not belonging to the three castes is to serve all others. Hence the route of action (*karma mārga*) has become unapproachable for many. On the contrary worshipping *Śreevidyā* has become a method that can be easily followed by all at all times.

Śree Krişhŋa said in *Śreemad Bhagavad Geeta* (9-32); *Striyo Vashyā: Tat Soodrā: Tepi Yānti Parāmgatim*. Accordingly this method can be followed by all.

This method can be followed easily by children, youth, elderly people, those who are with family, widows or widowers.

Equanimity: Equanimity is the first prerequisite that is needed for the worshippers of *Śreevidya*. This advice is the best in *Traipura Siddhāntam* rules, even before initiating the *mantras*. One should have a feeling that the method followed by him in worshipping *Śreedevee* is the best. At the same time he should not denounce the other methods or deities. The living beings in the world follow the methods of their own liking, which in turn are the results of actions done in previous births and according to their mental maturity. However, everyone should one day or other may come to worship *Śreedevee*. Hence it is a crime to denounce other worshippers.

In the same manner, all the 64 arts are games of *Śreedevee* only. All those arts are forms of *Śreedevee* only. (235th) *Chatu- shshashţiyupacārādhyā* and (236th) *Chatushshashţikalāmayee* are **Her** names. Hence the other arts like music, dance, drawing, etc., cannot be ridiculed. In addition to understanding devotion to teachers, the worshippers of *Śreevidyā* have to understand one other important matter - that is self realisation. The author of the *Sūtra, Parasurama*, has clearly mentioned this. Hence each one has to do the hearing, chanting and meditation as much as possible. Lack of interest is not in order in the path of knowledge.

Śree Lalitā Sahasranāma is the one which has to be chant by worshippers of *Śreedevee*. A number of commentaries/ translations have been written for this. Some of the important ones are;

1. *Śree Soubhāgya Bhāskaram* by *Śree Bhāskararāya*.
2. *Jayamangala* by *Bhatta Nārāyaŋa*
3. *Parimalam* by Simamputla Ramamurthy Sastry
4. *The Ocean of Tranquility* by C. K. Jaisimha Rao

Even out of these the first one is incomparable. We read lot of translations for this book. The important one among them is the Tamil meaning by Śree G.V.Gaŋesa Iyer. In the same way, *Śree* S V Radha Krişhŋa Sastry also has clearly translated in Tamil. Still lots of issues, mentioned by *Śree Bhāskararāya* in Samskrit in secret way, have not been cleared. They are to be obtained through teachers or those learned in *sāstras* and great worshippers, who have experienced it. The 1000 names in this hymn are like 1000 *mantras*. A message, conveyed once, has not been repeated again or in any other name. Hence, *Śree Bhāskararāya* has clarified through *Salākshara Sūtra* about the cryptic letters for these 1000 *mantras*. In the same way some of the inherent meanings also have not been cleared in the above mentioned books.

I did through discourses, by the blessings of teachers and *Śreedevee*, from 1982 onwards, every Sunday, in *Śree Gnānabhāskara* Society about various books on *tantra, mantra, sāstra* and commentaries on *Vedas*, followed by *Soubhāgya Bhāskaram* of *Śree Bhāskararāya* in detail in Tamil. This book is mainly published by taking notes from those discourses. Hence the question, that why a new Tamil translation, when already done by Gaŋesa Iyer and all, does not arise. In the same way, something more than what is mentioned in the commentary of Śree *Bhāskrarāya* has been discussed in the discourse from the *tantras*, as mentioned in other books like Jayamangala, Ārthur Avalōn and C. K. Jaisimha Rao and from the commentaries of *Vedas*. It has to be noted that the authors have included some of them in this book.

The time spent in compiling this book by me and by the members of the society is worthwhile in our life. An important use is that we had the focused mind on *Śreedevee* during those days. The mental resolve of *Śree Chidānandanātha* to propagate the plays (*leelas*) and greatness of *Śreedevee* to this world is also another reason for the same. I pray with prostration in the lotus feet of the teacher, that in the same way other books also should be published in Tamil. Let the blessings of mother of this universe (*Jaganmātā*) be showered on all.

Advaita Vedānta Prachāramaŋ Sāhitya, Meemāmsā, Nyāya,
Vedānta Siromaŋi Vidyāvāriti, Advaita Siddh Ranākara
Dr. Goda Venkateshvara Sastri
M.Sc., Ph.D, CAIIB

Chennai 02nd October 1999.

*****

श्रीः

Preface

(As in the Tamil edition)

I – Some important aspects of this book:

1. This section lists down briefly the various aspects of *Śree Lalitā Sahasranāma* and especially in this publication. The aim of it is to give a high level idea of the specialties of this book, for the first time readers; through this they should get an interest in their mind in reading this book. Though these specialties have been elaborated in the concerned places, at the cost of duplication some of them are being mentioned here as reiteration.

2. This *Śree Lalitā Sahasranāma*, as indicated by the name, is a hymn mentioning 1000 names of *Śreedevee*. According to our tradition, for each of the deities we worship, we have 100, 300 and 1000 names listed down. These are used to chant as well as doing *archanā* to the respective deities. It is a specialty of our religion to have 1000 names to worship, *Śreedevee*, who is the earlier most *Shakti* without any form. The fundamental message within this is that the entire universe originated from sound. That sound is in the form of letters. Hence any sound or letter either directly or symbolically indicates the Supreme Being – hence limitless hymns. LiFCO themselves have published 1000 names about at least 35 deities. These are all taken from various *purāŋas*. *Śree Vişhŋu Sahasranāma* is taken from *Mahābhārata* as told by *Bheeshma*. *Śree Lalitā Sahasranāma* is taken from *Brahmānḍa Purāŋa*. In this series, the *Trishatee* (300 names) on *Parameshwara* alone is taken from *Vedas* in the form *Rudranamakam*. *Śree Gaŋapati Sahasranāma* is seen in *Vināyaka Purāŋa*. It is conveyed by *Śree Gaŋapati* himself. *Śree Parameshwara*, when he started for killing the demon *Tripurā*, he forgot to worship *Śree Gaŋapati* and hence he lost the battle. Hence, as suggested by *Nāradā*, he worshiped *Śree Gaŋapati* and again ventured for the battle. At that time the 1000 names on *Gaŋapati*, was conveyed by *Gaŋapati* himself to *Shiva*. The hidden meaning of this is the direct explanation of the statement in Tamil that *"Avanarulāleye Avan Tāl Vanangi"* – to worship his feet with his own blessings. In the same manner, this *Lalitā Sahasranāma* also was communicated by eight *Vāgdevees* with the own orders of *Śreedevee* only. They are; *Vasinee, Kāmeshvaree, Moodhinee,*

Vimalā, Aruṇā, Jayinee, Sarveshvaree and *Koulinee* – the secret *Yoginees* residing in the seventh hall of *Śreechakra*. *Śreedevee,* herself says about them in the first part of this hymn as "on account of my blessings, you have great capacity of speech. Further you have been appointed to provide the capability of speech to my devotees. You always think of my names". Hence compile a hymn symbolically with my names, so that my devotees can pray and get my blessings.

3. The supreme being, which do not have any form has been given names to –

- Worship with thousands of names.
- Imagine hand, feet and other organs and give oblations to it.
- Describe it as having various characters and indicate them with the concerned names to bow it.
- Assume that it has done various actions and communicate those actions through different stories and worship with names concerning to those stories.

In this the number 1000 is not just a measurement, but to indicate it is infinite.

4. In the later part it has been mentioned that there are crores of 1000 names about *Śreedevee*. They are *Ganga, Gāyatree, Shyāmalā, Lakshmee, Kali, Bālā, Lalitā, Rājarājeshvaree, Saraswatee* and *Bhavani*. This *Lalitā Sahasranāma* hymn is the greatest among all of them.

5. Let us consider the important reason for this. In official matters, if we need to get some work done, don't we praise that concerned officer? The one issue in this regard is that there do not exist a single official who can solve all our problems. Further our request or praising is not concerning that official – it is just because he has the capacity to solve our problem. Hence the respect and devotion is to the capacity of that official only. This is what we accept as worshiping the *Shaktis* (energies). This method is worshipping the capacity with each of the deities, by separating the capacity from the deity. Hence each name consist these *shaktis*. In some of the names this has been explicitly mentioned. However, in most of the names it is mentioned through secret root letters (*beejāksharas*), *mantras* or cryptic sounds. This is individual specialty of this hymn. That is the reason why it is enough if one chants this hymn.

There is nothing else needed for the development of human beings. This has been repeatedly mentioned in the results part of this hymn.

6. The greatness of Samskrit language is mentioned in the name itself (Samskrutam – done in a perfect way). Each word has lots of meanings. In the same manner splitting of each word differently will provide different meanings. This makes different people split the words differently and convey different meanings. Though it can be taken that this does not affect heavily, this hymn exactly has 1000 names – not even a single more or less. Hence if splitting of words is not done properly and the names read individually, then count of 1000 may change. That is the reason, to split the words properly, *Salākshara Sūtras* were first formulated. Because this is not available now *Paribhāshā Maṇḍalam,* with 40 verses, was written by the teacher of the author of this book. All these have been explained in this book.

7. In the same manner, there are 51 letters in Samskrit – out of which the specific 19 letters have been left out and the remaining 32 letters only have been used to begin the 1000 names in this hymn. This and number of names beginning with each of the letters have all been calculated. The 25th name *Shuddha Vidyānkurākāra Dvijapakti-dwayojjwala* seems to explain the reason why only these 32 letters have been used.

8. Further each of the verse in the *Paribhāshā Maṇḍalam* is about *Śreedevee* and indicates the beginning letters of the names and the number of letters in each name as well.

9. Further the beginning letters of each of the hundredth name (101st, 201st, ...) has also been mentioned in one of these verses. All these convey the message that the splitting of words has to be done very carefully. So much care has been taken that even if a small mistake happens, it may affect greatly. This much care is needed because this hymn forms part of *Brahmāṇḍa Purāṇa* as a continuous verse and since the written format was not earlier available it was passed on by word of mouth to the disciples by the teachers.

10. One other specialty of this hymn is that the main part of 182.5 verses, we cannot read any fillers or any word which does not have any

meaning. That is, there are no filler words or meaningless words like *Cha, Vai, Tu, Hi, Eva,* etc.

11. There is no repetition of names. If such duplication is seen, by properly splitting the names those names can be considered as a new one. Hence there is no flaw of such duplication of names.

12. As mentioned earlier, each of the names contain *mantras*, only if this hymn is learnt through a proper teacher its complete meaning can be understood and enjoyed. That is the reason, the secret meanings and *mantras* are not explained explicitly in this book.

13. One other surprising aspect is seen in many names. If 3 or 4 names are contained in a half verse, individual meanings can be taken for them. If those 3 or 4 names are read in a combined manner, even then we get a complete meaningful sentence. For instance;

i. *Sudhāsāgaramadhyasthā Kāmākshee Kāmadāyinee*
(61st, 62nd and 63rd names)
61 – One who dwells in the midst of the ocean of the nectar.
62 – One who has beautiful eyes.
63– One who fulfills all the desires.

When these names are read in a combined manner it gives the meaning that **She**, who has beautiful eyes and by residing in the midst of the ocean of nectar, fulfills all the desires of **Her** devotees.

ii. *Gāyatree Vyāhruti: Sandhyā Dvijavrunda Nishevitā*

420 – One who is in the form of *Gāyatree*.
421 – One who is in the form of invocations.
422 – One who is in the form of twilight.
423 - One who is well worshipped by the groups of twice born.

When these names are read in a combined manner it gives the meaning that **She,** in the form of *Gāyatree*, is worshipped in the twilight, with invocations like *Bhoo:*, *Bhuva*: and *Suva*:, by the groups of twice born.

iii. *Kleemkāree Kevalā Guhyā Kaivalyapadadāyinee*
622 – One who is the personification of the letter *Kleem*.
623 – One who is the Absolute devoid of all attributes.

624 – One who is the most secret.
625 – One who bestower of the solitary abode.

When these names are read in a combined manner it gives the meaning that *Śreedevee*, in the form of the Kleem root letter, as an individual who is devoid of all attributes, if worshiped in secret form bestows the salvation.

Thus these are some of the combination of names.

14. Thus *Śreedevee*, having ordered the *Vāgdevees* to compose such a hymn, was once seated in her palace throne. At that time, in order to worship *Śreedevee*, crores of *Brahmas* with their consorts *Brahmanis*, *Nārāyaŋās* with *Lakshmees*, *Rudras* with *Gowrees*, *Shaktis* like *Mantriŋee* and *Ḍanḍinee*, *Devas*, *Mānavā*, *Siddhās* and countless groups of *shaktis* had visited the hall. They all took their seats after having a sight of *Śreedevee*. Then, *Śreedevee*, by her benign look itself ordered *Vāgdevees* to read the hymn composed by them. Immediately they got up and with bowed hands started to praise *Śreedevee* with this hymn. When this hymn was exhibited, *Śreedevee* and everyone assembled there got very much satisfied. *Śreedevee* ordered those assembled there, that they have to chant this hymn in order to satisfy **Her**. Hence from that day onwards, all the *Devas* including *Brahma*, *Vişhŋu*, *Rudra* and all started reading this hymn with devotion. In the first part, which describe this, the verbs (describing the order of *Śreedevee* and all others started reading this hymn) are used in the present tense. This means that the order the reading the hymn happen even today continuously.

15. It has been reiterated in more than once, in the beginning as well as at the end that this hymn is very secret and has to be learnt through proper teacher. Isn't that *Śree Hayagreeva*, has not told this to *Agastya* easily? How many questions and replies for this purpose were discussed? Then only *Śree Hayagreeva* told this to *Agastya*. This itself is enough to convey the greatness of this hymn.

16. The last part explains the various results/ fruits that can be reaped and also the methods of chanting this hymn. The method of chanting this hymn, specifically to get a particular wish satiated, is also mentioned. Further it has been mentioned that the worshipper has to chant it as a daily chore, without any specific wish. The interesting fruit

of this hymn is that it acts as expiation for all kinds sins done. But, if a flaw is found in doing one particular action that also needs expiation. Thus, if this hymn is chanted as expiation for other sins and a flaw is found during that chanting, which can be the expiation for this? The chanting of this hymn acts as expiation for various sins including the flaws that happen during the chanting of itself. This is the specialty of this hymn. That is to clear off all dirt we use in water – however to clear the dirt in the water also, we use water.

17. Among all the worships of *Shaktis*, *Śree Lalitā* is predominantly main. With **Her** order only we got this hymn. According to various *purāŋas*, different form of *Devees* have different places – for instance, Kāncheepuram for *Kāmākshee*, Madurai for *Meenākshee*, *Kāsi* for *Visālākshee*, etc. But, there is a doubt that *Śree Lalitā*, who is above all these forms of *Devees*, does not seem to have a dedicated place for **Her**. Surprisingly we got the answer to this question, by the time we finished writing this book. After getting *Śree Lalitā Sahasranāma* and *Śree Lalitā Trishatee* told by *Śree Hayagreeva*, *Agastya* got excited and asked "Where I can have sight of *Śree Lalitā*"? *Śree Hayagreeva* replied to this question that there is a temple for *Śree Lalitā* at the holy place called *Thirumeeyachoor*, wherein *Aruŋan* (chariot driver of Sun) and Sun worshipped her. If you go there you can be fortunate to have a *darshan* of *Śree Lalita*. Accordingly, Agastya visited *Thirumeeyachoor* and had worshipped *Mikurā Aruŋeshvara* and *Lalitā* with this hymn and got satisfied, says the history of *Thirumeeyachoor*. This village called *Thirumeeyachoor* is at a distance of one kilometer from Peralam, in Nannilam Taluk, Tiruvāroor District. This very old temple is being renovated (excerpts are available from the magazine called *Śree Amman Darisanam*, May 1998 edition).

18. The meaning of the 927th name, *Storapriyā*, is that *Śreedevee* is interested in getting praised. While explaining this name *Śree Bhāskararāya* gives many a meaning to the word *Stora*. They are given in six types – bowing, blessing, telling a story, describing the greatness, felicitating and praying. *Śree Bhāskararāya* himself has quoted instances for each of the varieties:

Trijagadvandyā (627)	–	bowing
Svastimatee (448)	–	blessing
Mithyājagadadhishţhānā(735)	–	telling a story

Bhaṇḍāsurendranirmukta Shastrapratyastravarshiṇee (79) – describing the greatness
Ichchāshaktijnāshaktikriyāshaktisvaroopiṇee (658) – felicitating
Sāmrājyadāyinee (692) – praying

We wanted to classify all the 1000 names in the above six types. But being afraid of the volume of the book, we did not attempt it.
In addition, some of the specific specialties of the individual names are explained then and there. We request that this secret hymn with such greatness be read thinking on the meanings by all by properly learning it and be eligible for the blessings of *Śree Lalita*.

II. Some of the specialties of this publication:

1. In the previous part we saw some of the specialties of this hymn. Further, we indicate some of the specialties of this publication. Ordinarily the speakers used to mention one thing – "those who talked before me have explained everything in this regard. What is there more for me to convey?" We thought such a statement is appropriate for this book also. We started this task, with a hesitation that what is that differently we can write, after the great learned like *Śree Bhāskararāya* has explained and further so many worshippers have written with their blessings? When the task progressed by compiling the essences from all the other books and whatever intuited to our small knowledge with the blessings of our teachers, this publication has shaped – as evidenced by *Śree Ādi Śaṇkara* in his *Subramaṇia Bhujanga* verses;

Chitekā Shatāsyā Hruti Tyotateme Mukānnissarante
Kirachchāpichitram.

2. An important aspect of this book is that it has to be read repeatedly, think aloud in the mind and enjoy the reading. To enable this, this book has been written in a smooth and easy flow and easily understandable even by laymen and in the Tamil which is acceptable to this generation of people. Isn't that the people who wrote this are lay men?

3. It is very difficult to understand the *Paribhāshā Maṇḍalam*, which is written to split the verses and get the 1000 names properly. Further, though the earlier verses *Salākshara Sūtras* are not available at present, the available one or two Sūtras have been explained in simple language

in this book – this is a new aspect. Such an elaborate discussion is just to describe how carefully our ancestors have accessed in the matter of splitting these names from the verses.

4. Two sections describing the philosophy of *Śreevidyā* and the method of worship have been added, to enable those who want to progress in the path of worship by having this book as a support. In addition, the unison of worshipping of *Śreevidyā* and *Vedānta*.

5. As far as possible the concerned quotes from various other books have given in an elaborate manner. Also the root of it is also quoted to enable further reading in detail.

6. Importantly it is a very difficult task to completely to adopt and comprehend *Soubhāgya Bhāskaram* of *Śree Bhāskararāya*. Because there is no other book, which was not handled by him for his commentaries. Further in most of the places he has cryptically indicated the meanings. It is very difficult to identify and explain it. Still, an attempt has been made to give a clue of it for those who read this book. We have not explained which were not understood by us and which are secret. To our best we have given it not Deviating from the commentaries of *Śree Bhāskararāya*. In some of the places, some more stuff has been added.

7. To explain easily some of the matters have been given in table format.

8. Not to be difficult for reading and also not to be a strain for eyes, effort has been taken in composing and printing.

9. Further where the Samskrit letters are written in Tamil, it has subscripted as 2 or 3 or 4, to avoid mistakes in pronunciations.

10. It has been an attempt first of its kind to provide the drawn paintings as below:

   a. *Śree Hayagreeva* advising *Agastya* - to explain the origin of this hymn
   b. *Vasinee* and other seven *Vāgdevees* in front of *Śree Lalitāmahātripurasundaree* in **Her** assembly hall as an exhibition of the first time composing this hymn.

11. We hope that this book with such specialties will be useful for the devotees.

*****

Śree Vidyā

1. Some of the important aspects of *Śreevidyā* have been compiled in this section, based on various books on *Śreedevee*. We hope this will be helpful to more clearly understand the meaning of this *Sahasra- nāma*.

I. *Happiness is the one everyone wants*:

2. Everyone in this world wants only happiness. This is called *purushārttam*. The happiness is of two types. One is self-imagined. Hence it is perishable. This is indicated by the name *kāmam* (wish). This is unreal. The other one is salvation, which is eternal and indestructible.

Both these are reached through *Dharma*. But Dharma is reached through economic (*artha*) means viz., wealth.

In general all these four, that is, *Dharma*, economic wealth, wish and salvation, are in a combined form called as *purushārthas*.

To enjoy the eternal salvation, *Paramashiva* has prescribed various *vidyās – Veda, sāstra, smruti, purāŋas*, epics, etc. These depend on various differences in human beings and the purity of their minds. Hence they are all means of getting correct knowledge only. There are no Inter-*se* gradations among them. The followers of one method should not denounce the other. But at the same time, we read in a *sāstra* praising a presiding deity and denounce other deities. The inherent truth in this is to bring interest and confidence to those who follow that *sāstra*. Denouncing of other *sāstras* is not to degrade or ridicule them. But, the intention is, that those who are not competent should not enter into it.

This is what is advised in *Koulopanishad* as; *Lokān Na Nindyāt*, in *Para-surama Kalpasūtra* as; *Sarva Darshana Anindā* and in *Śreemad Bhagavad Geeta* as; *Na Buddhibedam Janayet*.

The salvation is to recognise by experience that the soul that is imagined as 'self' is actually the form of eternal supreme being only and the body and the universe are all perishable. This truth has been hidden by ignorance (illusion). *Vedas*, etc., help in re-recognising the truth and to identify the real form.

II. The form of Supreme Being:

3. *Veda* itself could not define the form of the Supreme Being. They only give a negative description that "this is not supreme Being and that is not, etc. *Veda* says that the Supreme Being is beyond the realm of mind and speech; *Yato Vācho Nivartthante Aprāpya Manasā Saha*. In reality, *Veda* says, that realising the union of the soul with Supreme Being, which is without any qualities, or any flaws or any form, is called salvation. The great statements like *Tatvamasi* also advise the same. To realise this many *vidyās* (*Maduvidyā, Bhoomā Vidyā*, etc). without any qualities, have been advised by *Vedas*. But only some people can follow this.

We worship, with devotion, the supreme being, which is not a male or female or neutral and does not have any attributes, by assigning a form to it. We also assign some attributes to that form. Hence this is called *Saguŋopāsana* (worshipping with attributes). The name and form are created according to the will and pleasure of the individuals based on the maturity of their minds.

Śree Ādi Śaṇkara established six religions, by streamlining and systemising the existing practices of worshipping with attributes and removing any flaws in them. One among them is *Śreevidya*.

Since the supreme being is without any attributes, or flaws and the supreme spirit is the source of all sensations with periodic cessation activities, there is no thought of 'self' for it. It is a witness to all without any limitations or attachments. The feeling of 'I'-ness occurs to it only through energy. In that case it acquires attributes and flaws. *Kāmakalā Vilāsam* says that *Paramashiva* who is without any limitations and is in the form of knowledge, acquires the feeling when sees in a mirror on account his reflection he gets the feel of 'I'-ness' when looking into the mirror of reasoning.

Sāstras say that this form of *Paramashiva,* without any limitations and full of knowledge, is called *Kāmeshwarā* and the reflected form seen in the mirror is called *Kāmeshwaree* or *Lalita.*

Since it is the 'One-ness' (*Ahantā*) of *Parameshwarā* as a combined form of souls, it is called *Parāhanta*. Because of this *Parāhanta* only

Parameshwarā gets the feel of the need for creation; *Sa Ikshata Bahu Syām Prajāyeya.*
Hence *Śreedevee* is the cause of creation of this world. Since *Paramashiva* gets such quality of actions called as *Dharmas*, he is called as *Dharmee*. Those *Dharmas* are called as *Tripurasundaree, Shakti* and *Devee*. Though addressed through different names both are one and the same. The unified form of both is called the supreme being. Hence when *Śreedevee* is addressed as supreme being, **Her** form is called as the *Prakāsha Vimarsha* (manifest and unmanifest) and *Sāmarasya* (equal without any superior or inferior).

III. Mother and God:

4. *Veda* advises as; *Mātru Devo Bhava* – the mother has to be seen as God. By reversing this, we see the God as mother in *Śreevidya*. We move closely and friendly with mother. We can be affectionate to her. The affection of mother over her children is the greatest. She does not mind the mistakes done by children, forgives them and do lot of help.

5. Thus worshipping the God in the form of a woman is also in practiced in other countries. The researchers say that such worship was in vogue in Egypt and other countries in ancient days. In Rome in Europe, before the Christianity was spread, worshipping *Devee* was in practice. She has been described as having sandal jewels in forehead, wearing garlands and with long hair. She says about herself as below;

> "I am she that is the mother of all things Mistress and governess of all elements The initial progeny of the worlds The chief of the powers divine, The Queen of Heaven; the principal of the Gods celestial, the light of the Goddesses..."

My name, my divinity is adored throughout the world, in diverse manners, in variable customs and in many names, for the Phrygians call me the mother of the Gods; the Athenians Minerva; the Empyreans Venus; the Canadians Diana; the Sicilians Droserpina; the Eleusians Ceres; some Juno, others Bellona, other Hecate; and principally the Ethiopians who are excellent in all kinds of Ancient doctrines and by their proper ceremonies accustomed to worship me Queen Isis".

It seems the tribal people called *Koul* in Britain and ancient people in France were worshippers of *Devee*. It seems, by the triangles drawn by them and mapping the Sun, Moon and fire to those triangles, Jews were involved in worshipping *Devee*.

It is also seen that such worship in vogue in China and Japan.

(Reference – the foreword in English, written by Śree K.M.Panickar for the book titled *Śreevidyā Mantra Bhāshyam* by *Brahmaśree Perunkulam Veerarāgava Sāstry*).

IV. Ancient and praised by *Vedas*:

6. The worshipping method is very ancient. There are evidences for this in *Vedas* and *purāŋas*. For instance, these are about *Śreedevee - Śree Sooktam, Durga Sooktam, Sundaree Tāpinee Upanishad, Pāvanopanishad, Rātre Sooktam, Devee Sooktam, Devee Upanishad, Tripuropanishad, Bahvroshopanishad, Koulopanishad, Guhyopanishad, Mahopanishad, Sarasvatee Rahasyopanishad, Soubhāgya Lakshmi Upanishad* and *Śreechakra Upanishad.*

In *Śree Rudram*, we read as;

Yā Te Rudra Shivā Tanoos Shivā Vishvāhabeshajee I
Shivā Rudrasya Beshjee Taya No Mruḍa Jeevase II

In *Purusha Sooktam*, we read as; *Hreeshcha Te Lakshmeeshcha Patnyou*

Kenopanishad says that *Uma Devee* came in person to advise I*ndra*.

The *Kāmakala Beeja, 'Ĕm'*, which is very important in worship of *Devee* has been mentioned in *Srutis*. For instance;

Ya: *Prāneeti ya Ĕm Shrunoti Yateem Shrunotyalakam Shrunoti*
Ya Em Chakāra na So Asya Vedā Chatvāra Ĕm Piprati Kshemayanta:

So many learned and elders have followed this method of worship. The notable among them are; *Vashisţar, Sanakar, Sanātanar, Sanatkumārar, Sukhar, Durvāsar, Agastyar,* his wife *Lopamudra, Kālidāsar, Gowḍapādar* and *Śree Ādi Śaṇkara*.

V. Books about *Śākta*:

In addition to *Vedas*, mention has been made in many *purāŋas* also about worshipping *Devee*. Most important among them are – *Devee Bhāgavatam, Brahmaŋḍa Purāŋam, Mārkaŋḍeya Purāŋam, Skānḍam* (*Soota Samhitā* part), etc.

The principles and methods of worshipping have been mentioned in many a *tantra*. The goal of this worship is to make the worshipper feel through experience the *Vedānta* statement that self and the supreme being is one and the same. Everyone can experience this only by his own efforts. Hence the practicing methods have been explained in these *tantra* books. There are some contradicting views between them. However, since they have a single goal, they have to be taken as correct and the method which is best suitable for the individuals should be followed.

These *tantras*, are mainly in the form of dialogue between *Parameshwara* and *Parameshwaree*. Their names may change like *Bhairava, Bhairavee*, etc.

In addition, some learned people, have compiled the practices during their time and published books about it.

Some important books on *Śākta* explaining about the *Śreedevee* worship are:

- *Tantra Rāja Tantram,*
- *Vāmkeshwara Tantram* (a part of which is *Nityā Shoḍashikārnavam*),
- *Rudrayāmalam, Kulārnavam, Gnānārnavam, Tattātreya Samhita, Sharadā Tilakam*
- *Prapancha Sāram* (written by *Śree Ādi Śaṇkara*),
- *Paramānanda Tantram,*
- *Kālidāsā's Chitkagaŋa Chandrikā*and *Panchastavam* (a group five small verses),
- *Durvāsā's Shakti Mahimnā Stotram* and *Lalitā Stavaratnam* (also called as *Āryātvichati*),
- *Parasurama Kalpasūtra, Tripurā Rahasyam,*
- *Śree Vidyā Ratnā Sūtras* by *Śree Gouḍapata*

- *Soundaryalaharee* written by *Śree Ādi Śaṇkara* and its various commentaries
- *Varivasyā Rahasyam* by *Śree Bhāskararāya*
- *Kāmakalā Vilāsam*
- Various books written by Sir John Woodroffe (Arthur Avalon) – particularly – *Shakti* and *Shāktha*, The Serpent Power and The Garland of Letters.
- *Śree Vidyārnava Tantram*
- Books written by *Śree Chidānanda Nātha* – the list is given in his biography section.
- *Tirumantiram* by *Tirumoolar*, Some songs by *Maŋickavachagar* and Some songs by various *Siddhās*.

VI. Who is eligible for this worship? Who can take it?

7. Anybody who has ardent wish to reach the salvation is eligible for this worship. No bar on sex, caste, etc. The eligibility is based on good conduct, devotion, passion, control of organs, purity (both of mind and body), faithfulness and devotion towards the teacher.

We often experience that though we have heard of the *Vedānta* principles many a time that do not stick to our mind permanently. This worship will be of utmost help for those who are in this stage. We can consider them as the fittest.

Most people do this worship with the temporary goal in mind like (childbirth, curing of diseases, etc). and not the eternal knowledge or salvation in mind. They would get the results they wanted. In due course they themselves would get interest in knowledge and salvation.

VII. The method of worship has to be learnt only through a teacher.

8. Whatever be the intellect, it will give its fruits only if it is obtained through an appropriate teacher. It is not correct to think that we can get the knowledge through reading from the books. Such an intellect got only through the books will not give fruits on the other hand may land up in some side effects.

The importance of a teacher has been stressed in *Vedas*, *Smrutis* and *Tantra Sāstras*.

Mainly, *tantras* do not cover about this worship – many important principles, methods and *mantras*. Further, more than the methods mentioned in *tantras*, the method traditionally followed by the lineage of teachers is better placed. If there is a controversy between *sāstra* and tradition, only the tradition prevails. Traditions are to be learnt through a proper teacher.

Those who are interested should reach to an appropriate teacher and request him to initiate. One important caution has to be noted in this regard.

The relationship of teacher-disciple is the best. The disciple surrenders to the teacher and request to bring him up. Hence before finalising one person as a teacher, the disciple has to completely understand about the teacher. It is a general rule that once finalised, he cannot change the teacher. Nowadays, we hear that, the teachers demand a lump sum as a fee to initiate any *mantras*. It does not seem to be a new matter. Rameshwarar, who wrote the commentaries for *Parasurama Kalpa Sūtra*, has quoted the below one even at his time;

Guravo Bahava: *Santi Shishya Vittāpahārakā*: I
Durlabhoyam Gurur Devee Shishya Santāpahārakā: II

Devee! There are many teachers who appropriate the wealth of the disciples. It is very rare to see the teachers who remove the sufferings or sorrows of the disciples.

However, this caution has to be carefully followed. That is one has to decide on a teacher, with good qualities. *Sāstras* have in detail explained the characters of a good teacher. The important ones among them are – peaceful, pure, one who perform his actions properly, one who has knowledge of *sāstras*, one who has control of his organs, one who has good mind, one who does not have ego, one who has compassion, one who hails from a good teacher-disciple race, one who is not greedy, one who is capable of clarifying the doubts of his disciples and one who has passion towards development of the religion.

It is very rare to have one person who has all these qualities. One who has most of these qualities can be considered.

The teacher also tests the disciple, decides on his qualification and advise and initiate accordingly.

The duties of a disciple are – have full faith on the teacher, do service as for as possible, act according to his advises and chant the *mantras* taught by him.

VIII. This *Sahasranāma* can be chant only those who got initiated.

9. The first part of this hymn (44th verse) says that this hymn has to be sung for satiating *Śreedevee* after doing *archana* for the *Śreechakra* and chanting *panchadashee mantra*. In the next verse **She** says, "even if *archana* is not done for me and even if my *mantra* is not chanted, this hymn has to be sung for my satisfaction" – it has to be taken that, this has been mentioned to reiterate the importance of this hymn. This has further been made clear in the last part (verses 5 and 6). Accordingly, after taking bath in the morning, finishing the oblations like *Sandhyā vandanam* (both *vaidheeka* and *tāntreeka*), etc., according to the individual's tradition, the prayer room has to be entered and worship to the *Śree Chakra* has to be done first. The *mantra* has to be chanted for 100 or 300 or 1000 times. And then only this secret hymn has to be read.

In the same last part (verses 81, 82 and 83), it has been mentioned that this hymn should not be told to those who do not have *Śreevidyā mantra*. If this rule is violated, *Yoginees* get angry and may land up in ill effects.

Hence, those who want to chant this hymn with devotion have to reach an appropriate teacher, get initiated and then only this has to be chant. What to do till such time? The reply is available in the same part (verses 48 and 49) – this hymn has to be written in a book and that book has to be worshiped.

One need to have the faith that *Śreedevee* herself will lead to a proper teacher. **She** herself has the names *Gurupriā*, *Gurumoorthi*: and *Gurumaŋḍalaroopiŋee*.

IX. *Śreechakram* and *Meru*:

10. A deity can be worshipped on an idol or picture. This is the physical form of that deity.

In a metal sheet if some lines are drawn according to the prescribed rules that is called *yantra*. This is the subtle form of the deity.

It is a habit to wear this *yantra* as a casket.

The combination of some sounds is called *mantra*. This is still subtle form of the deity than *yantra*. All the 51 verses of *Kandar Anuboothi*, talk about various *yantras*. Similarly each of the verse of *Soundaryalaharee* has one *yantra* corresponding to it. The *yantras* relating to other deities are also in vogue.

An important *yantra* relating to *Śreedevee* is *Śreechakra*. It can be noted that only this *chakra* has a prefix *Śree*.

Śreechakra has four upward triangles, five downward triangles and a *bindu* in the centre. This *yantra* has Lotus with eight or sixteen petals, three girdles and three border lines. (In some schools it is two border lines. *Śree Bhāskararāya* says that, in his book called *Setu Bandam*, both the versions are evidenced). In the *Śreechakra* in vogue in South India the gates of the border lines will be open.

Looking at this *Śreechakra* in a different dimension, we see *Bindu*, eight triangles, two polygons of ten corners each, polygon of 14 corners, eight petals, sixteen petals and three border lines. Thus we get nine halls (*Āvaranams*). (It is not the practice to treat girdles as *Āvaranam*).

The upward triangles are treated as pertaining to *Shiva* and the five downward triangles pertaining to *Shakti*. The same *Śreechakra* is rotated 180 degrees, making the *Shiva* triangles downward then it is called *Shiva chakram*.

If this Śreechakra is made as a three dimensional figure (with length, breadth and height), then it is called *Meru*. This *Meru* is of three types, depending on the imagination of the worshippers.

If it is imagined as unified with 16 *nityā Devees* it is called *Meru Prastāram*, when unified with 51 letters it is *Kailāsa Prastāram* and when unified with *Vāgdevees* it is *Bhooprastāram*.

We saw that there are nine *Āvaranams* in *Śreechakra*. *Āvaranam* means curtain or fence or compound or fort.

There is a separate worshipping method for *Śreechakra*. The deities, *Siddhis* and *Chakreshwaree* in each of the *Āvaranās* have to be worshipped. By getting their permission, we have to move to the next *Āvarana*.

The method of starting from the border lines and ending with *Bindu* is called destructive (*laya*) method. On the other hand starting from the *Bindu* and ending with border lines is called creative method. Mostly only the *laya* method is in practice.

Special *tatvas* (philosophies) for each of the *Āvarana* of *Śreechakra* have been mentioned in *tantra sāstras*. *Śree Chidānanda Nātha* has explained this in detail in his book called *Saparyā Padhati Vāsanai*. For the fear of volume, the explanation has not been discussed here. However, a list prepared by himself detailing the qualities of each of *Āvaranas* has been given here.

11. Further the main emotions and the taste as described in the book called *Kāmakalā Vilāsam* and in 51st verse of *Soundaryalaharee* are added in the list below.

Āvaranam	***Tatva***	**Prevailing Sentiments**	**Main Emotion**
1.	Earth	*Rathi*	Love
2.	Moon	Happiness	Heroic
3.	Eight forms	Sorrow	Compassion
4.	*Mahāmāyā*	Fear	Fearful
5.	Ten incarnations	Disgust	Disgust
6.	*Vaishvānaran*	Furious	Furious
7.	Nature	Comedy	Comedy
8.	Three qualities	Surprise	Wonder
9.	*Brahmam*	Equality	Peace

X. Different stages in *Śreevidyā*:

13. There are different stages in *Śreevidya*. The important ones are *Bālai*, *Panchadashee* and *Shoḍashee*. Imagining *Śreedevee* as nine years

old girl and is the worship of *Bālā Tripurasundaree*. The *mantras* pertaining to this get expanded a little and reach the other two stages.

There are 12 types of *Panchadashee mantras*. The *mantra* originated from each sage is one *Panchadashee*. The sages of the 12 *mantras* are: *Manu*, Moon, *Kubera*, *Lopamudra*, Cupid, *Agastya*, Fire, Sun, *Indra*, *Skanda*, *Shiva* and *Krodha Bhattārakā* (*Durvasa*).
Further it seems, there are *mantras* pertaining to *Nandikeshwar*, *Hari* and *Yama*.

The most famous among the *Panchadasheemantras* are the *Kādhividyā* originated by Cupid (starting with the letter *ka*) and *Hādividyā* originated by *Lopāmudra* (starting with the letter *ha*). Even among these two, only the *Kādhividyā* is in practice. It is said that this is the greatest. The reason for such a conclusion is *Lalitā Trishatee* is based on *Kādhividyā* and only the *Kādhividyā* has been merged with other *beejas* in *Mahā Shoḍasee mantra*. Further in the first part of this hymn (verse 17) it has been mentioned as; *Śreevidyāiva Tu Mantranām Tatra Kādhir Yatā Para*.

Śree Bhāskararāya mentions 14 different meanings for the *Kādhividya*. (His book called *Varivasyā Rahasyam* may be referred). In recent times, Śree Veeraraghava Sastrigal from Kerala has given 80 different meanings. It has been told this has got the approval of *Śree Abhinava Nṛsimha Bhāratee swamijee* of *Shringeri Sharada Peeṭa*. (The book called *Śreevidyā Mantra Bhāshyam* written by *Śree Veeraraghava Sastrigal*, published by *Vāvilla Ramaswamy Sastrulu* at Chennai in 1960).

Devee Upanishad has cryptically been described in *Kādhividyā*, *Chaṇḍi Navākisharee mantra* and *Bhuveshwaree mantra*.

XI. Different forms of *Śreedevee*:

14. There are many forms for *Śreedevee*. **She** has a name also as *Bahuroopa*. It is said that **She** has many 1000 names.

It is told that for administering this universe while imagining doing different tasks, **She** is told to take different forms. Further depending on different places the forms also change. Again various people worship imagining *Śreedevee* with different colours, depending on the wish they want to get fulfilled.

In a famous way, **She** is worshipped as *Devee, Mahātripurasundaree, Rajarajeshwaree, Kāmeshwaree, Lalitā, Kāmākshee, Bhuvaneshwaree* and *Kalee*. In general there is a feeling that *Kalee* has a fierce form. The pictures also describe her in such a form. The picture poses are - naked, with garland of skulls and killing a demon with a trident. All the forms of *Śreedevee* are with compassion. By destroying the evil habits of the demons, **She** shows good path to him also. *Saptashatee* also says; *Chitte Krupā Samara Nishturatā Cha Drushta*. We worship the demon *Mahishan* also, who was killed by *Śreedevee*, in the *Chaṇḍikā Parameshvaree Āvarṇa Pooja*.

In *Skānda* also it has been mentioned that *Soorapadman*, after he is killed, he becomes a peacock and made the vehicle of Lord *Muruga*.

XII. Different methods of worship.

15. Worshipping of *Śreevidyā* is mainly of two paths – *Samaya* and *Koula*. The *Samaya* path has two sub-divisions – *Dakshiṇa* and *Vāma*. Within each sub-division there are three methods viz., *Bāhyā* (without tools) and *Āntara* (worshipping without any tools) *Parāpara Pooja* (both the methods mixed).

Only the *Bāhyā* method is used in *Koula* path. Even in principles, the *Koula* and *Samaya* paths differ. The principle of *Samaya* path is that in the *Sahasrāra Kamala*, the *Kunḍalinee* energy merges with *Shiva* and the supreme bliss is enjoyed through the nectar rain falling from it.

Koula path is of two types viz., *Poorva* (East) and *Uttara* (West). According to this path the principle is that the triangle in the *Sahasrāra* is the dwelling place of *Śreedevee*. The opinion of the followers of East *Koula* path is that the salvation is awakening of the *Kunḍalinee*. They perform the *Bāhya* worship in *yantras*. The worshipping practice of the followers of West *Koula* path physically includes worldly happiness like alcohol, fish, meat and ladies. The *tantras* explaining this method mention that the worshipper has to imagine himself as *Kāmeshwara* and his consort as *Kāmeshwaree*. It has to be imagined that the Supreme Bliss comes out through their union. It can be thought that this method makes the addicts of alcohol, etc., as offering them to *Ĕshwar* and consume the same with the mind treating them as *prasadam*. The real meaning is that, in due course of time, the worshippers get their mind changed and will reduce the consumption and as time passes may drop the habit itself once and for all. The addicts who follow this method say that this method is correct when looked at in a psychological way. But they fall below the expectations. Instead of improving themselves, they reach the state of unrecoverable sorrow state. This is equal to walking on the sharp edge of a knife. It is so fearful similar to embracing the neck of a tiger or having a snake around one's neck.

Krupāna Tārākamanāt Vyāgrakantāvalambanāt I
Bujangatāranānnoonam Asakyam Kulavarttanam II

Those who follow *Koula* path should have special qualities. The ordinary people without those qualities cannot follow this path. If they still try to follow they may land up in some ill effects. Considering the *Koula* path only, it has been said about worshipping *Śreedevee* is; *Tarala Karaṇānāmasulabha*.

In this method, since there are methods against the righteousness, demeanor and sacred rules, some humility for *Śreevidyā* itself.

This method can be successfully followed only by those, who have worshipped the other deities with the concerned methods, one who has matured inner-self and who has controlled his five senses.

Śree Lakshmeedara, in his commentary for the 41st verse of *Soundaryalaharee* have mentioned some other methods followed by *Koulas* and says, "There are lot of things to be mentioned here. But since they are all against *Vedas*, I have left them. Some of the methods have been indicated here just to give an impression. The idea behind it is to prevent people from following the *Koula* path.

The *Samaya* path is so soft. The importance is given to righteousness, demeanor and sacred rules. In this method the worship starts with the feeling that self is the soul and *Śreedevee*, different from self is the supreme being. That is, in the beginning there is a duality thinking that self and the worshipped deity are different. By performing worship many a time, chanting the *mantras* and by reading or hearing the scriptures relating to *Shakti*, little by little this duality mind set is changed to non-duality mind.

Only the *Samaya* method is appropriate for most of the people. That too, those who are somewhat lower grade according to mental status, physically use the alcohol, fish and meat. Instead of these three some soft representatives have to be used.

The five things whose beginning letters are *'Ma'* are called as *Pancha Makāram*. The real philosophy behind this is as follows;

Śreedevee has one name as *Panchatanmātrasāyakā*(11th name). The five arrows are the essence of sound, touch, form, taste and smell. The *Śākta tantras* mention this as *kula* things. *Kula* means *moolādhara* and other five bases. In all these six bases, these five elements are there respectively - earth, water, fire, air and ether. The mind to understand the *panchatanmātras* is also another *kula* thing. These are all symptoms of the supreme being in the form bliss.

Only these *kula* things were mentioned above, for the lower grade people, as alcohol, etc., by the *tantras*. These *tantras* are not recognised by the knowledge *kāṇḍa*.

If observed keenly, it can be understood that this worship itself is like a sacrifice. The five *makārās* are the oblations in the sacrificial fire. The higher grade people have to be identified as below;

Alcohol – the fire *tatva* – the *Brahmatmaikya Akaṇḍākāra Vruddhi* - the fall that spreads from *Sahasrāhāra*.
Fish – the water *tatva* – that controls and makes the outward looking organs to revert and look inwardly.

Meat – the earth *tatva* – cuts with the knife of maturity, the animal form controlled by the righteousness and the wickedness. This makes the self-form integrated with the supreme being.

Hand Signs– the air *tatva* – to flame all the bad habits in the fire called *Brahma Vidya*.

Union – the ether *tatva* – the unison of *Shiva* and *Shakti*. Those who want to know more about *pancha makāra* can read *Śree Chidānanda Nātha*'s book called *Saparyā Pattadi Vāsanai*, or *Kulārnava Tantra* or Sir John Woodroffe (Arthur Avalon)'s *Shakti* and *Shāktha*).

There are two types in *Samaya* path viz., right and left. These depend on the individual's mind set. This has been explained in the 912th name *Savyapasavyamārgastha*.

It has been told that in both these methods the method of worshipping is of three types. Worshipping with tools like flower, fruits and other things – *Apara* (*Bāhya*) method is used when the worshipper does not have any knowledge of non-duality. Fit for medium grade people.
Entirely not having the duality mind is called *Parā* worship. Assuming all the actions done as worship is called *Parā* method. This is the greatest one. Fit for higher grade worshippers.

Parāpara method is to convert the duality mind set to non-duality through practice. Fit for medium grade worshippers. By starting with *Apara* method, the complete meaning has to be reminded in every stage of worship. Little by little the non-duality mind has to be reached. Later the stage of doing *Parā* worship also has to be reached.

XIII. *Śreevidyā* is very secret:

16. *Tantras* say that *Śreevidyā* has to be worshipped by keeping it as a most secret, since it is so great and it gives the salvation, which is the ultimate wish of human kind. Other *Vidyās* are like bitches, who are visible to all, but *Śreevidyā* is like a family lady who is visible only to husband who has a right over her.
Parasurama Kalpa Sūtra says;

> *Veshashyā Iva Prakattā: Vedādi Vidyā:*
> *Sarveshu Darshneshu Gupteyam Vidyā* II

Kulārnava Tantra says;

> *Anyāstu Sakalā Vidyā: Prakatā Ganikā Iva* I
> *Iyam Tu Shāmbhavee Vidyā Guptā Kulavadhooriva* II

Hence it is mentioned that, this *Śreevidyā* has to be protected as very secret. If it anyone tells this to ineligible people, he will fall into hell. Hence it has been prescribed that the worshipper of *Śreevidyā* has to hide his worship from others;

Koulopanishad says; *Anta*: *Shākta*: *Bahi*: *Shaiva*: *Loke Vaishnava*: II
Kālee Vilāsa Tantra says;

> *Anta*: *Shāktā*: *Bahi*: *Shaivā*: *Sabhāyām Vaishnavā Madā*: I
> *Nānāmoorttidarā*: *Koulā*: *Vicharaŋti Maheetale* II

The intrinsic message is that worshipping *Shakti* should be known only to inner self mind. In practice, the *kumkum* as a *prasadam* of *Śreedevee*, should be worn in between the eye brows and also should be hidden by other *Saiva* symbols like *Viboothi*, etc. The hand signs of *Śreevidyā* should not be shown in public and also one should not advertise that he is a worshipper of *Śreevidya*.

Since *Śreedevee* and *Vişhŋu* are one and the same, talking about the greatness of *Vişhŋu* is equal to talking about the greatness of *Śreedevee*.

In Christianity also it has been told that worshipping has to be kept as secret. The below quote from Bible, St. Mathew – 6, evidences this:

(5) And when thou prayest, thou shall not be as the hypocrites are; for they love to pray standing in the synagogues and in the corners of the streets, that they may be seen of men. Verily I say unto you, they have their reward.

(6) But thou, when thou prayest, enter into thy closet and when thou hast shut thy door, pray to thy Father which is in secret; and thy Father which seeth in secret shall reward thee openly.

XIV. The results of worshipping:

17. *Śreedevee* is in the form of guileless compassion. **She** bestows compassion without expecting anything in return. She is the mother of all the worlds. Hence however we, being **Her** children, worship her. **She** accepts it and bestows her blessings with compassion. Only the devotion and passion are important. **She** does not expect much of actions. (But, they help us in focusing the minds). **She** does not even expect us to understand the inner meanings of the actions. (However, if we know them it would fetch us the result early. Hence, in the next sections, we discuss about creation – seven creations and half creation).

Śreemad Bhagavad Geeta (IX – 26) also advises us;

Patram Pushpam Phalam Toyam Yo Me Bhaktyā Prāyachchati I
Tadaham Bhaktyupahrutamashnāmi Prāyatātmana: II

Worship of *Śreedevee* can also be carried out without straining the body. The body is called as a temple (*Deho Devalaya Prokto*). Further *Śreedevee*, is being worshipped in the form of bliss and as a liker of eroticism – as *Lalitāmbikai. Nityā Shoḍashikārnavam* says that the worshipper has to decorate himself beautifully and perform worshipping with a smile in his face.

Similarly, for those who worship with a feeling of surrendering to **Her**, **She** bestows both the enjoyment as well as salvation.

Mangala Rāja Stavam in *Rudrayāmala* says;

Yatrāsti Bhogo Na Cha Tatra Moksha: I
Yatrāsti Moksho Na Cha Tatra Bhoga: I
Śreesundaree Sātaka Punkavānām I
Bhogashcha Mokshashcha Karasta Eva II

989th name *Vājnchitārthapradāyinee* says that **She** bestows what is sought for. But, *Śree Ādi Śaṇkara* says one step further in his *Soundaryalaharee* (4th verse) that **She** bestows more than what is sought for; *Dātum Phalamapi Cha Vānchāsamadhikam*. **She** only saves from all dangers. Elders say that "What is to be done while in crisis? Just think about the feet of *Śreedevee*. What will do that type of thinking? It makes even *Brahma* and others as servants";

Āpati Kim Karaŋeeyam Smaraŋeeyam Charaŋayugakamampāyā
Tat Smaranam Kimkurute Brahmhādeenapi Kinkaree Kurute II

In *Saptashatee* also we read as;

Durge Smrutā Harasi Beetimashesha Janto: I
Svastai: *Smrutā Matimateeva Shubhām Dadāsi* II
Dāridriya Dukkha Bhaya Hāriŋee Kā Tvadanyā I
Sarvopakāra Karanāya Sadārdra Chittā II

Again in 12th chapter of *Saptashatee, Śreedevee* has promised to save from all dangers.

We all continue to do one or other mistake. While enquiring about the expiation, it is understood that thinking of the feet of *Śreedevee* is the only way out. 743rd name *Pāpāraŋyaḍavānalā* also conveys the same message.

Brahmānḍa Purāŋa says;

Krutasyākilasya Pāpasya Gnānatognānatopivā I
Prāyashchittam Param Proktam Parāshakte: Padasmruti: II

It is enough if we worship *Śreedevee* after surrendering with her and with determined and focused mind and with devotion. We need not ask anything. **She** herself will bestow us what is good for us including the four types of wishes.

XV. The knowledge of creation, which will help in dissolution:

18. The goal of a good worshipper is to be happy with the understanding that he is not different from the Supreme Being by his own experience.

If it is understood that how we and the universe originated, it would be easy to retrace in the same path to reach the Supreme Being. Hence it is necessary to know the creation of this universe.

Vedas say the creation of this universe as below.

Aitreya Upanishad (**I**-1-1) says – there was only one soul in the beginning. Nothing else was there. It wanted to create the worlds – it created;
Ātmā Vā Itameka Eevākra Āseen Nānyat Kinchanamishat I
Sa Eekshata Lokānnu Srujā Iti Sa Imān Lokānasrujata II

Taitreeya Upanishad (**I**-2-6) says – That supreme being, from which the ether and other things originated, desired to expand very much and grow (as world with name and form). It did penance with this desire and spread the light of knowledge. By doing that penance it created all the things whatever is available now;

Sokāmayata I *Bahusyām Prajāyeyeti* I *SaTapo'tapyata* I
Sa Tapas Taptvā I *Idam Sarvamasrujata* II

Chāndogya Upanishad (VI-2-3) says – It created the light by saying "I will become many and grow in a huge way". According to the saying "I will become many", the *Sat* in the form of that light created water;

Tataikshata Bahu Syām Prajāyeyeti Tattejosrujata Tatteja
Ikshata Bahu Syām Prajāyeyeti Tadapo'srujata II

Brahadāraŋya Upanishad (I-4-3) says – That *Virāt Purush* did not enjoy the wealth individually. Hence, since it cannot enjoy the wealth alone, wanted a second. That *Virāţ Purush* became male and female and became a form of tight embracing. Later split his form into two. From that originated the male and females;

Savainaiva Reme Tasmātekkee Na Ramate Sa Tviteeamacchat
Sahaitāvānāsa Streepumāmsou Samparishvaktou
Sa Imamevātmānam Tvetā' Pātayat Tata:
Patishcha Patneechāpavatām II

Taitreeya Upanishad (III-10-6) says – I am the only who originated before this world, which is so beautiful and structured. I am prior to *Devas*. I am neutral of the eternal post;

Ahamasmi Pratamajā Rudāsya I
Poorvam Devebhyo Amrutasya Nā Pa Ĕ II

Muŋḍako Upanishad (I-1-8) says – By the penance (of knowledge), the *Brahmam* (with the goal of creation) grows. From this originated the un-manifested food. From this originated the *Hiraŋyagarbhā* in the form of breath, mind, the five elements which seem to be truth, the worlds (actions) and from actions the results (liked as nectar);

Tapasā Seeyate Brahma Tato'nnamabijāyate I
Annāt Prāno Mana: *Satyam Lokā*: *Karmasuchāmrutam* II

XVI. Creation of this universe – as told by *tantra sāstras*:

19. The same message is described in *tantra sāstras* with poetic taste. This is described in two dimensions viz., seven and half.

The *Brahmam*, which is without origin and eternal, shines in two ways viz., with and without qualities. This is called as *chit* (pure consciousness).

It has unlimited powers. It contained within itself the things which can originate at any point of time. (That is, they later originated from it). The natural quality of it is to show itself.

From its form with attributes (called as *Sat Chit Ānandam* - Existence, knowledge and bliss absolute) the energy originated. From the energy originated the sound and from sound the *mahābindu* (the great point).

A movement happened in the *mahābindu* and very subtle sound waves (called as *mātrukās*) originated. When a stone is thrown in a tank, water waves are created and hit each other. In the same manner, due to these sound waves the *mahābindu* was split into three (*bindu, nātham* and *beejam* [seed] – this *nātham* is different from the one mentioned earlier). From the *mātrukās*, originated the sound what we hear (letters, words and sentences). *Tantra sāstras* mention that *Bindu* is *Shiva,* the *beeja* is *Shakti* and *Nātha* is the union of *Shiva-shakti*. This *Shiva-shaktitatva* does not come apart even during the time of dissolution. *Nātham* is called as *Sat* (existence) (this is explained as *Sātākya* = *Satākyayata*:). *Śreevidyā tantras* say that these *Bindu, Beejam* and *Nātham* are mentioned respectively as *Prakāsha, Vimarsha* and *Misra* (bright, dark and soothing). These are also called as *Sukla, Rakta* and *Mishra* (*Mahābindu* is called as fourth *Nirvāna* feet). These three, in a combined manner, are called as three *bindus*. *Tantra sāstras* mention these three in various ways like, Moon, fire and Sun or *Icchā, Gnāna* and *Kriya* or *Vāmā, Jyeshtā* and *Roudhree* or *Brahma, Vişhŋu* and *Rudra*.

These three *bindus* are imagined as three vertices of a triangle. The desire, knowledge and action of the *Brahmam* with attributes create this universe. In the commentaries of *tantra sāstra*, Sun is called as *Kāman* (Cupid) and Moon and fire jointly called as *kalā* (art). Hence the combined form is called *Kāmakala*. This triangle is also called as *Kāmakala*.

It is told that the universe originated from *Kāmakala*. From *Shiva -Shakti tatvas* originated the other 34 *tatvas* (detailed later). Hence the *tantra sāstras* say that the universe, in the form of 36 *tatvas*, originated only from the *Kāmakala*.

We saw that according to *Vedantas*, the supreme being got the idea creation – that word creation is indicated as *Ĕkshanam* (a look), *Kamam* (desires), *tapas* (penance) and *Vichikeersha*. This *Ĕkshanam* and *Kāmam* have another name as *Shāntā Shakti*. This *Shāntā Shakti* (energy) is the combined form of *Icchā*, *Gnāna* and *Kriya* energies. The action of *Icchā*, *Gnāna* and *Kriya* energies is this universe. This universe is in the form of 36 *tatvas* right from *Shiva* till earth, as mentioned in the *Śākta* (Kāshmeera) and *Saivasāstras*.

A *Tatva* has many roles for the enjoying souls, the enjoyed objects, the enjoyment, the causes of enjoyment and the feel of enjoyment, till dissolution.

Soota Samhita says;

> *Ā Pralayam Yattishtati Sarveshām Bhoga Tāyi Bhootānām* I
> *Tat Tatvamiti Proktam Na Shareera Kaţāti Tatvamata*: II

Some *sāstras* say the number of *tatvas* is 36, some other say that they are 24 and still some other classify differently. As per the *Śākta tantras*, we consider it as 36 for our discussion purposes.

These 36 *tatvas* are majorly classified as *Ātma*, *Vidyā* and *Shiva*.

The *Shiva tatva* is of the form of *ParaShiva*. The thought (or desire) of creation in *ParaShiva* is *Shakti Tatva*. The knowledge in the form of ego as 'self', the feeling that 'everything is my form' in the *SatChitĀnanda* form are called *Sadāshiva Tatva*. The knowledge with name and form is called *Ĕshwara Tatva*. *Shuddha Vidyā* is the knowledge that there is no difference between the souls and the universe.

These five *tatvas* in a combined manner is called *Shiva Tatva* or *Shuddha Tatva*. Also called as manufactured dirt and indicate the causal body. It is worth noting that the *Shiva Tatva* is animate. It has to be keenly noted that each of these five *tatvas* is contained in the previous one. In the same manner the *tatvas* that are going to be discussed later, one is contained in the previous one.

The *purusha tatva* is completely describing pure consciousness, bliss, desire, knowledge and action.

- *Kalā tatva* is reducing the energy of doing all actions.
- *Avidyā tatva* is reducing the energy of knowledge.

The *tatva* called *Rāgā* is reducing the energy of desire in the form of eternal satisfaction.

Kāla tatva is reducing the energy of eternity in the form of pure consciousness.

Māyā tatva is that gives an illusion that there is mutual difference between the universe and the soul.

These seven *tatvas* in a combined form is said as *Vidyā tatva*. They indicate the subtle body called as deceitful dirt. Since this is with self desires, it contains both the brightness (and mobility) that is reflected in this and the immobility that is to be discussed later as *Ashuddha tatva*. Since it contains shuddha and *ashuddha tatvas, Vidyā tatva* is also called *shuddhashuddha tatva*.
The *purusha* with consciousness is the soul. He is the doer and the beneficiary. The self form does not do anything and also does not enjoy anything. Only the illusion makes such a form the status of action and enjoyment. Hence it has to be kept in mind this is only an imagination.

Only the *Ĕkshanam* (a look), *Kāmam* (desires) and *Vichikeersha* mentioned in *Vedas* are the 12 *tatvas* mentioned above in different names.

The state of supreme being ready to exhibit itself is called the *prakruti* (nature) *tatva*. It equally has the three qualities viz., *satva, rajas* and *tamas*. From this originates the *Ahankāra* (ego) *tatva* with predominant *rajo* quality. The soul enjoys this universe only through this.

Bhuddhi (intellect) *tatva* with predominant *satva* quality originates. *Manas* (mind) *tatva* with predominant *tamas* quality originates.

The *Ahankāra, Bhuddhi* and *Manas tatvas* in a combined form is called inner-self (*antakkaraṇam*). To feel and enjoy these, further 20 *tatvas* originate in an orderly form. In short these are said to be - five organs of knowledge (eyes, ears, nose, tongue and skin), five organs of action (tongue that speaks, hands, legs, anus and the genital organs) five self-characteristics (sound, touch, form taste and fragrance) and five primary elements (ether, air, fire, water and earth).

That 24 *tatvas* beginning from *prakruti* (nature) till earth, in a combined form is called as *Ātma tatva*. This is also called atomic dirt. This indicates the physical body. These are tools for enjoyment. These, in a combined manner are called as *Ashuddha tatva*. These are static in nature.

The ego, manufactured and deceitful dirt hide the *Parashiva.* The *Shiva* with these curtains like bodies is the soul; one without these curtains is *Paramashiva.* The below verse in Tamil, of the learned make us easily understand how the three dirt hides the *Parashiva* ;

Maratthai Maraittatu Māmata Yānai
Maratthil Maraintatu Māmata Yānai
Paratthai Maraittatu Pār Mudal Bhootam
Paratthil Maraintatu Pār Mudal Bhootam

Splitting of *Mahābindu* into three (*bindu, nātham* and *beejam*) in a metamorphic way mentioned as *Kāmeshwaran* and *Kāmeshwaree* in *Śāktasāstras*.

XVII. *Kunḍalinee* energy:

20. There is a saying that what is available in the universe is also available in the body. The supreme being, which is omnipresent is also available in our body. *Tantra sāstras* say that, in this, the *Shiva* part is in the *Sahasrāram* and the *Shakti* part is in the *Moolādhāram* as a snake wound into 3.5 rounds, sleeping with its head inside the cavity. The principle of this *sāstra* is that this *Kunḍalinee* can be awakened and merged with *Shiva* in the *Sahasrāram*. If this is done, we can enjoy the supreme bliss by the nectar that flows and wets all the *nāḍis* (pulse). This is a common principle across some other *sāstras* also. *Yoga sāstras* mention the physical methods of awakening the sleeping *Kunḍalinee*. But, this is a dangerous one. If not done properly, it may have lot of side effects. Hence, the elders have advised that only the method of devotion is suitable to most of us (even if it is a little belated). (The book *Deivathin Kural*, 6th Volume may be referred).

Kunḍalinee energy is called as a subtle form of *Śreedevee*.

Those who want to know in detail about *Kunḍalinee* may refer to the book called The Serpent Power by Sir John Woodroffe. XVIII. Non-duality and *Śreevidyā Sāstra*:

(This part is a gist of pages 685 to 689 from the book called *Deivathin Kural*, 6th Volume).

21. Both have a common goal. That is, to be happy by getting the knowledge "I am the *Brahmam*" by experience, is the goal.

Though there is an agreement with the end status, there is some difference about creation. It has been said that non-dual *Vedanta* is unreal and *Śreevidyā* is transformation or evolution argument. Unreal means showing what is non-existent as existent and what is existent as non-existent. A rope being seen as a snake is unreal. Rope is real and the snake is a lie. There is nothing like two as rope and snake. The true rope seems to be a snake in the unreal sense. This is only for an instance. In the same fashion, the principle of the non-duality is that the real supreme being seems to be soul or universe.
Disorder means the brightness due to reflection. Sun reflecting in water is transformation. In the same way, the principle of *Śākta* is that the uncontrolled *Shiva shakti* is reflecting under control and seem to be soul and universe. The bright *Shiva* reflects in the genius *Shakti* and being shown as soul and universe.

One matter being changed to another is called evolution. The revolution argument says, for example milk getting converted into curd, in the same way the souls becoming the universe.

There is perennial argument between the followers of non-duality, transformation and evolution principles. Milk can become curd, but curd cannot become milk again. According to this the souls cannot again become supreme being. The important criticism of the followers of evolution principle is that this argument cannot be accepted. We are not entering Into this argument.

22. According to transformation principles, it is the act of illusion to show the non-existent as existent and vice versa. The illusion is without origin. It is told that it cannot be identified as such. The non-dual *Vedunta*

advises that only if illusion is removed, the knowledge of *Brahmam* can be attained.

Śree Kānchi Kāmakoṭl Paramāchārya has told that – *Śākta sāstras* say that only the *chit* (pure consciousness) plays by reflecting in different forms. They also say that by living in this same world, by having the external things in this world itself as tools we have to reach and merge with the true and eternal *Brahmam*.

Non-duality says that duality is the act of illusion. *Śākta* says that duality is also created by *Śreedevee*, who is the *Brahma Shakti*. By worshipping to *Parāshakti*and doing achievements according to *Śreevidyā sāstras*, the bondage with the illusion can be removed. *Śreevidyā sāstras* advise that by crossing the illusion, by integrating with the base energy (*ādhāra shakti*) and further integrating with the base peace (*ādhāra shantam*) with which the *ādhāra shakti* has merged – and in this route we can get integrated with the non-duality.

Only the *Brahmam* seems to be the soul by illusion: The non-duality *sāstras* say that by following the path of knowledge and removing the illusion, the soul becomes the *Brahmam*. It has been clearly accepted in *Śāktas* especially by *Srevidyā tantras* that basically the soul and *Shiva* are one and the same and again at the salvation they become one. Duality, special non-duality, *Saiva Siddhānta*, *Shiva* non-duality and Kashmir *Saivam* – in this order - started against non-duality and little by little come closer to it and the last one Kashmir *Saivam* becomes almost closest. Further non-duality – i.e. integration of the soul and the *Brahmam*, is mentioned only in *Śākta*. The difference between these two is only in the creation of non-duality and not in salvation (The book *Deivathin Kural*, 6th Volume).

On account of these reasons this *Lalitā Sahasranāma* has been mentioned as greater than other *Sahasranāmās*, because it explains the principles of *Śākta*.

Note: *Śree Bhāskararāya* himself has indicated in the below mentioned places about the evolution argument;

a) Commentaries for 735th name *Mithyājagadadhishṭhāna*.
b) Commentaries for the 3rd verse of *Varivasya Rahasryam*.

c) Explanation for 5th verse, 4th chapter of *Nityā Shoḍashikārnavam; Tasyām Parinatāyām Tu Na Kashchit Para Ishyate.*

It can be noted that *Śree Ādi Śaṇkara* also in his commentaries for *Brahma Sūtra* (II-1-14) mentions that Śreevyāsa himself during the course of his actions encourage the evolution argument. The readers who want more details can read the original books.

XIX. *Nityā Devees*:

23. Worshipping of *Nityā Devees* is an important part of *Śreevidyā* method. *Śreedevee* has taken the forms of the fifteen *Nityā Devees*. Further, it is the practice to mention that **She** herself is the sixteenth *Nityā Devee*.

Tantra Rāja Tantra explains in detail about *Tithi Nityā Devees*.

It has been told that *Tithi Nityā Devees* have connection to the subtle sound called *mātruka*. They are (alongwith 36 *tatvas*) the form of time. They are the vowels. They are the universe. Other *sāstra* books have mentioned them as having connection with the five base elements (ether, air, etc)., they are the letters of *Śreevidyā mantra* and alternate names for the nights of bright lunar fortnight (*Darshā, Drushtā*, etc). as mentioned in *Vedas*.

The meditation verses and worshipping methods of each of the *Nityā Devees* have been mentioned in *Tantra Rāja Tantra*. Depending upon the requested desires the meditation verses and the description of forms of *Devees* may change.

XX. The glory of *Parāshakti*:

24. We saw the thought of *Brahmam* for creation as *Shakti* (energy). From this is it clear that *Shiva* and *Shakti* are unified, equal status and equally treated. Even then the part of activities of the world depends on *Shakti*. In the same way the capacity of giving results for worships (with desire) lies with *Shakti*.

Hence, those who want easy and fast results worship the female i.e. *Shakti* part of the supreme being. Such worship prevails for a long time.

Sāstras have decided that *Gayatree Devee* is in the form of the supreme being and worshipping her by those who have been done with *Upanayanam*, is the same as worshipping the supreme being. Hence, it has been told that all the twice-born are *Śāktas* only and not *Saivas* or *Vaishnavas* since they worship *Gayatree*, who is the earliest *Devee* and mother of *Vedas*;

Sarve Dvijā: Shāktā: Proktā: Na Shaivā Na Cha Vaishnavā: I
Ādideveemupāsante Gāyatreem Vedamātaram II

XXI. The differences between *Shiva, Shakti* and *Viṣhŋu*:

25. We know from various evidences that there is no difference between *Shiva* and *Shakti*. It can be reminded that *Shakti* is the thought for creation of *Shiva.*

In the same manner different evidences have advised that there is no difference between *Shakti* and *Viṣhŋu*. These are as below;

The supreme being, in the form of pure intellect has split into two due to illusion as righteousness (*dharmam*) and the person who has the righteousness (*dharmee*). *Paramashiva* himself is *dharmee. Dharmam* has again been split into two – one male and the other female forms. The male form protects, in the form of *Vishnu*, the universe. The female form is the consort of *Shiva.* All these three forms put together is the broad *Brahmam*. Thus says the *Saiva* (*Śreekanta*) religion. This has been explained by *Śree Appayya Deekshitar* in his book called *Ratna Traya Pareeksha*. He has well established this in his own commentary through various quotes and evidences. Some of the important verses from that book (Mysore publications);

Nityam Nirdosha Gantam Niratisaya Sukam Brahma Chaitanyamekam
*Dharmo Dharmeeti Bhetatvayamayati Cha Prutakbhooya Māyāvachena*I
Dharmas Tatrānubhooti: Sakala Vishayiŋee Sarvakāryānukoolā
Shaktichchechāti Roopā Bhavati Guŋagaŋachchāchrāyastveka Eva II
Kartrutvam Tasya Dharmee Kalayati Jagatām Panchake Srushţi Poorve
Dharma: Pumroopamāptvā Sakala Jagatupātānapāvam Piparti I
Streeroopam Prāpya Divyā Bhavati Cha MahisheeSvāchrāyasyātikartu:
Proktou Dharmaprapetāvapi Nikamavatām Dharmivat Brahmakotee II

Śree Bhāskararāya has quoted this in many a place.

Even in this *Sahasranāma, Śreedevee* has been addressed as *Nārāyaŋee, Govinda Roopiŋee, Viṣhŋu Roopiŋee, Vaishŋavee, Mukundā*, etc. Again, since the supreme being is the root cause of both of them, they have been treated as brother and sister and *Śreedevee* has been addressed as *Padmanābha Sahodaree* (it can be reminded that they have been mentioned as brother and sister in the *Prātānika Rahasya*, which is read as part of *Saptashatee*).

Further, many names of *Śree Viṣhŋu Sahasranāma* are comparable with that of the names in this *Sahasranāma*. As far as possible this has been mentioned in this book. Thus the indifference between *Shiva, Shakti* and *Viṣhŋu* has been established.

But, in the last part of this hymn, it has been mentioned that there is no other *mantra* equal to *Śreemantrarāja* or there is no other deity equal to *Śree Lalitā* or there is no other *Sahasranāma* equal to this one. Further, the name of *Shiva* is greater than *Viṣhŋu Sahasranamā* and a single name from this hymn is greater than *Shiva Sahasranāma*. The details are given in the concerned verses. Let us see some important reasons here;

a) We call the supreme being with the thought of creation as *Shakti*. Hence *Śreedevee* is nearer to the supreme being than any other deities (it has to be construed that the duality principle is considered here, since this is based on many deities). The learned have shown to us that more than other practices like duality and special-non-duality, the *Śreevidyā* tradition is close to the non-duality principle (paragraph 22 may be referred).
b) The combined energy form of all the deities is *Śreedevee*.
c) The method of worship, the philosophy and principles about the presiding deity has been explained in this hymn. This has not been done in any other *sahasranāmas*. These policies and principles are the guide to get the knowledge of the supreme being.
d) This is the only *Sahasranāma* that has been composed by the order of the concerned presiding deity by *Vāgdevees* with **Her** own blessings. It has to be noted that though *Gaŋesha Sahasranāma* has been told by *Mahāgaŋapati* himself, the above mentioned specialties do not exist in it.

XXVI. The signets in worshipping *Śreevidyā*:

26. The mudra, signet, is one of the five important parts of *Śreevidya*. By combining the fingers and showing it in a particular form is called signet. Each signet, cryptically, indicates a message or an emotion. We all know that such signets are already shown during dancing. Those who know the signet can understand the message conveyed by it.

The origin of the word *mudra* (signet) can be explained in two different ways. One explanation is *mudam rāti* – i.e. giving happiness. This happiness is for both – one who shows the signet and to whom it is shown.

The second explanation is *Modanāt, Drāvanāt* – i.e. it is called as *mudra* since it makes the person to whom it is shown as happy and it drives away the sins of the person who shows it. The meaning of the word *Drāvanāt* has been given as that it drives away the universe from the mind of the worshipper – i.e. the mind set of duality.

There are signets relating to the concerned presiding deity and satisfying that deity in worships of all the deities. Some signets are common to all the deities - for example joining both the palms to bow. It is known to all of us that lots of signets are used in martial arts like goongfū, karate, etc.

There are many signets in worshipping *Śreevidyā* also. It is the practice to show the deer sign when chanting the *guru patukā* (chappals of teacher) *mantras* and immediately followed by the signs of *sumukha* (good face), *suvruddha* (good development), *mudgara* and *chaturasra* (fourth) and with the *yoni* sign to pray the teacher and *Gaŋapati* respectively in the left and right shoulders.

There are signs to be shown in *Navāvarŋa* worship during *Āvāhanam, Nyāsa, Pātrasādanam* and *Nivedanam*. The 122nd name *Shāmbhavee* is not accounted here since its fundamental meaning is consort of *Shambu*. Further *Shāmbhavee* signet has been mentioned in *yoga sāstra* and not in this method of worshipping. There are names in this *sahasranāma* with two names of signets.

In 979th name *Gnānamudra* has been mentioned. This is also called as *chinmudra*. It is to show the round symbol by joining the thumb and the forefinger of the right hand. *Paramashiva,* in the form of *Dakshiŋāmoorthi* by keeping silent teaches the unison of *Brahmam*-soul to *Sanakā* and other sages, through this signet. (*Śree Ādi Śaṇkara*'s *Dakshiŋāmoorthi Ashţakam* may be referred).

In 982nd name *Yonimudrā* has been mentioned. The teacher has to be bowed with this signet. In *Navāvarŋa* worship also at the end of every *Āvarŋa, Śreedevee* has to be bowed with this signet. This signet also indicates the unison of *Brahmam*-soul.

Ten signets, in a combined form, have been mentioned in 977th name *Dashamudrāsamārādhya*. It is easy to know these signets by seeing them in person when somebody shows it. These are shown in *Navāvarŋa* worship.

Each signet has to be shown by using all the fingers of both the hands and having them jointly in equal position. It has been mentioned that the five fingers of each hand indicates the five primary elements (earth, etc)., the right side and the right hand indicate the bright *Shiva* form and the left side and the left hand indicate the immaculate *Shakti* form. (It can be reminded that the left of the *Ardhanāree* is female form). While showing the signets by joining the hands, the unified form of *Shiva* and *Shakti* has to be imagined and the signets indicate the creation and other actions. It has been told that if the signets are shown properly the deities get satisfied else they get angry.
However, these signets are not to be shown in public places as seen by lay men. It can be reminded that more than once it has been stressed that *Śreevidyā* worship has to be kept secret. These signets can be shown only during worship times.

Further those who aim at salvation these signets should be shown through mental desire and others can show them through hands. The below statement is seen in *Parasuramakalpa Sūtra*, annexure 2 (1979 publication page 611);

> *Mānasaroopa Sankalpā Mudrā Mokshārthinām Vidu*: I
> *Itareshām Tu Sarveshām Hastābhyām Shasyate Budhai*: II

Out of these, while establishing *Śreedevee* during *Navavarŋa* worship in *yantra* (either in *Sreechakra* or *Meru*) the signet called *Trikhandā* is shown. The worshippers of *Shoḍasee*, while performing worship to *Bindu* after the ninth *Āvarŋa* show this signet. This can be taken as the combined form of all the signets. It can be noted that *Śreedevee* is called as *Trikhaŋḍeshee* in the 983rd name.

Śree Chidānandanāthar has mentioned in brief based on the *Deepikā* commentaries of *Amrutānanda Yogi* for *Yogineehrudayam* (the latter part of *Nityāshoḍashikārnavam*).

Āvarana	**Signet**	**Philosophy (*tatva*)**
1.	*Sarvasamkshobhiŋi*	Indicates the creation of the entire universe by the illusion of the static energy imagined from the pure conscious energy.
2.	*Sarvavidravinee*	Indicates the status of the universe (the status enjoyed by the five knowledge organs).
3.	*Sarvākarshinee*	Indicates the state of the mind with the knowledge (after the above enjoyment) in a subtle form (i.e. the remembering of the enjoyments).
4.	*Sarvavashankaree*	Indicates the matters that would be enjoyed by mind and the organs as well. The happiness and the sorrows of the enjoyer – i.e. the bliss status of the enjoyer (including the sorrows).
5.	*Sarvonmādhinee*	Indicating the careless state of the mind after the understanding that the worldly affairs would not provide eternal happiness, understand the flaws in them and the state of having an aversion to the experience of the universe – i.e. the state of determination in the mind.
6.	*Sarva Mahānkushā*	Even after having the determination, because of its previous experience the mind may turn out to the outward enjoyments. This indicates the focusing of the mind, at that time and making it looking inwardly. i.e. Meditating upon the self-realisation.
7.	*Sarvakhesaree*	Indicates the expansion of the mind that would involve in the broad supreme being. i.e. it can also be construed as remembering the great statements. (*Śree Bhāskararāya* says in his commentary that this can happen

Āvarana	Signet	Philosophy (*tatva*)
		only through compassion of the teacher and by learning the *tantras*, aimed at); *Sā Cha Gurudayālakshya Tantradhyayana Janya.*
8.	*Sarvabeejam*	The self-form is the only cause of the universe. Hence it indicates that only the soul is the dwelling place and the brightness for the entire universe. i.e. it indicates *nitityāsana.*
9.	*Sarvayoni*	Indicates the union of the soul with the *brahmam.* i.e. the state of *savikalpa samādhi* (the initial temporary state of the spiritual state of consciousness).
10.	*Sarvatrikhanda*	Indicate the salvation state of the soul.

By showing these signets the presiding deities in the concerned *Āvaranas*, the head of *chakras, Siddhis* and the *mudra Devees* get satisfied. They permit to move ahead to next *Āvaranas*. (i.e. they provide the mind set to move ahead).

27. This preface has become lengthier part of this *Lalitā Sahasranāma*, which explains the relationship between *Śreevidyā* and the knowledge of *Brahmam*, by including various matters that are necessary for worshipping *Śreevidyā*, the relevant meanings and philosophies, etc., with the concerned evidences. We believe that by reading this, the readers will become more knowledgeable and then when they read this *Sahasranāma* it will be convenient for them.

XXII. The philosophy of *Śree Lalitopākhyāna*.

28. The gist of a story in *Lalitopākyāna*, a part of *Brahmānḍa Purāŋa*, has been mentioned from 64th name *Devarshigaŋa Sanghāta Stooyamānātma Vaibhavā*till 84th name *Haranetrāgni Sandagdha Kāma Sanjeevanoushadhi:*. We give below in a nutshell what was told by *Śree Chidānandanātha* about the demons, *Balā, Shyāmalā, Vārāhi* and other *Shaktis*, the inherent meaning of all these, etc.

29. This miraculous explanation would be interesting for the readers.

Indra is a soul with pure inner-self, with ingenuity.

Cupid, who was burnt by *Paramashiva* was passionate towards the tools of enjoyments like flowers, sandal, ladies, etc.

Bhanḍasura is the form an impure soul with all the flaws. He was pride with ego in the form of *beeja*, eroticism, talking in air without experience, performing worship just to attract others as an outside drama. The pride is mentioned in Samskrit as *Dambhan*. If the letters in the word *Dambhan* is transposed we get the word *Bhanḍan*.

Vishanga is interested in sound, touching, etc.

Vishukran is the opposite state of *shukra*, the knowledge of lustre. It is the state of sorrow alongwith the idiotic thoughts.

The 30 sons of (starting from *Chaturbāhu* till *Upamāyan*) are the thoughts like ego, illusion, action, etc.

The 8 ministers of *Bhaṇḍa* (*Indrachatru*, *Vidyunmāli* and others) are the form of desire, anger, stinginess, greed, delusion, envy, enchantment and harmful.

The army of *Bhaṇḍa* is a group of duality, a tool for the thought of soul (and hence an obstruction to the knowledge of *Brahmam*).

Vighnayantra is a group that obstructs obtention of knowledge of non-duality. (These were destroyed by *Gaṇapati*. That is the reason, it is told, that the *mantra* of *Śree Gaṇapati* has to be initiated in worshipping of *Śreevidyā*).

The city of *Soonyaka* is ignorance. *Chitagni Kunḍa* is the tool that destroys the ignorance and its actions; *Śreelalitāi Aham Pata Lakshyārttha Roopa Ātmagnānam*. The *Śreechakrarāja* chariot is the universe, body or the pure inner-self.

The energies of *Śreechakra* are capable of destroying the ignorance of non-duality.

The details of self-improvement *Shaktis* of *Śreelalitāmbā* are:

No.	**Name of the energy**	**The organ or part of *Lalitā* from which it originated**	***Tatva* (philosophy)**
1.	*Parāmbā*	Heart	The meaning of non-duality
2.	*Shyāmala*	Intellect	Expansion of mind
3.	*Vārāhi*	Ego	Eternity
4.	*Vigneshwaran*	Smile	Happiness
5.	*Shaḍāmnāya Devatās*	*Moolādhāra* and the six *chakras*	Six knowledge groups like self independence, etc.
6.	*Pālai*	Games	The starting state of non idol thinking.
7.	*Sampatkaree*	Goad	*Yoga*
8.	*Ashvārooḍhai*	Noose	Control of internal organs.
9.	*Nakulee*	Palate	Hearing
10.	*Rashmimālā Devatās*	From *Moolādhāra* till *Brahmarandiram*	The base of the knowledge in the matters like sound, touch, happiness, sorrow, etc.

The summary of this story is that *Śreelalitā Devee* destroyed *Bhaŋḍa* and his army (the thought of non-soul and ignorance) with all **Her** *shaktis*. The philosophy of the battle between *Śreedevee* and *Bhaŋḍā* is the eternity with the character of the soul is grown, by destroying the thought of non-soul and ignorance.

All the bows aimed by *Bhaŋḍa* are the form of ignorance. The bows returned by *Śreedevee* are all in the form of knowledge that will cure ignorance.

In gist, the battle between *Śreedevee* and *Bhaŋḍa* is between soul and self-knowledge.

Further, the posterior form of *Śreedevee* was mentioned by killing of *Bhaŋḍāsura*. Again such a battle is happening everyday within every soul. Once the soul part called *Bhaŋḍa* is destroyed the complete form of *Śree Lalitādevee* is being unified with *Shiva* form. Such a great philosophy is explained in this story in a cryptic manner.

The same message was conveyed in the name *Chaŋḍamuŋḍā-suranishoodinee*. *Chaŋḍa* and *Muŋḍa* indicate the happiness and sorrow created by the desires and aversion. Only after removal of these the other bad qualities can be removed. The below verses in *Śreemad Bhagavad Geeta* also explain the necessity of removing the desires and aversion;

Āpooryamāṇamachalapratishṭam Samuḍramāpa: Pravishanti Yatvat I
Tatvatkāmā Yam Pravishanti Sarve Sa Shāntimāpnoti Na Kāmakāmee II-70
Kāma Esha Krodha Esha Rajoguṇasamudbhava: I
Mahāshano Mahāpāpmā Viddhyenamiha Vairiṇam II III-37
Veetarāgabhayakrodhā Manmayā Māmupāshritā: I
Bahavo Gnānatapasā Bhootā Madbhāvamāgatā: II IV-10
Adveshṭā Sarvabhootānām Maitra: Karuṇa Eva Cha I
Nirmamo Nirahankāra: Samadu:khasukha: Kshamee II
Santushṭa: Satatam Yogee Yatātmā Drudanishchaya: I
Mayyarpitamanobuddhiryo Madbhakta: Sa Me Priya: II XII–13 & 14

That is the reason, it seems this name has originated, though there were *Raktabeejan, Nishumban* and *Shumban* who are above *Chaṇḍa* and *Muṇḍa*, the destruction of them are considered less than that of *Chaṇḍa* and *Muṇḍa*.

Navāvarṇa Table

#	***Ākruti***	***Prakruti***	***Beejam***	***Chakara***	**Head of *Chakra***	***Yoginis***	**Deities**	***Siddhi***	**Signet**	**State of mind**	
1	Boopuram	*Am Ām Sou:*	*Lam* earth	*Trailokya Mohana*	*Tripurā*	*Prakata*	*Aṇima* and other - 10 *Brahmee* and other - 8 *Sarvasamkshobinee* and other – 10	*Aṇimā*	*Sarva Samkshobinee*	State of ignorance	Awaken

#	***Ākruti***	***Prakruti***	***Beejam***	***Chakara***	**Head of *Chakra***	***Yoginis***	**Deities**	***Siddhi***	**Signet**	**State of mind**	
2	16 petals	*Im Kleem Sou:*	*Sam* Moon	*Sarvāshā Paripooraka*	*Tripureshee*	*Gupta*	*Kāmākarshinee* and other 16	*Laghimā*	*Sarva Vidrāvinee*		Dream
3	8 petals	*Hreem Kleem Sou:*	*Ham Shiva*	*Sarva Sam Kshobhana*	*Tripurasundaree*	*Guptadara*	*Ananka Kusumāan*d other 8	*Mahimā*	*Sarvākarshinee*		Deep Sleep
4	14 angles	*Haim Hkleem Hsou:*	*Ĕm Kāmakala*	*Sarva Soubhāgya Dāyaka*	*Tripuravāsinee*	*Sampratāya*	*Sarva Sankhobine* and other 14	*Iṣṭva*	*Sarva Vashankaree*	State of knowledge	Thought of self desire of Ĕshwar
5	Outer 10 angles	*Hsaim Hskleem Hssou:*	*Aem Vişhŋu*	*Sarvārtha Sādhaka*	*TripurāŚree*	*Kulotteerna*	*Sarva Siddhiprata* and other 10	*Vaśtva*	*Sarvonmādinee*		Reaching a teacher on one's own
6	Ineer 10 angles	*Hreem Kleem Blem*	*Ram* fire	*Sarva Rakshākara*	*Tripuramālinee*	*Nikarpa*	*Sarvagnāan*d other 10	*Prākāmya*	*Sarvamahānkushā*		Hearing of holy stories

#	Ākruti	Prakruti	Beejam	Chakara	Head of Chakra	Yoginis	Deities	Siddhi	Signet	State of mind
7	8 angles	*Hreem Śreem Sou:*	*Kam Kāmeshwara*	*Sarvaroga Hara*	*Tripurāsiddhā*	*Rahasya*	*Vashinee* and other 8	*Bhuddhi*	*Sarva Kesaree*	Repeating of *mantras*
8	Triangle	*Hsraim Hsklreem Hsrou:*	*Nadam Trishakti*	*Sarvasiddhi Prada*	*Tripurāmbā*	*Atirahasya*	Weapons - 4 *Mahākāmeshwaree* and other - 4	*Ichchā*	*Sarvabeeja*	Satvāpatti, Asam*shakti* - Nitityāsanam
9	*Bindu*	Panchadashee, fourth *Vidyā*	*Bindu* supreme being	*Sarvānandamaya*	*Samasta Chakreshvaree* with *Mahatripurasundaree*	*Parāparā Atirahasya*	*Mahātripurasundaree Tureeyāmbā*	*Prāpti Sarvakāma*	*Sarvayoni Sarvatrikhandā*	Patārttābāvanā Turyakā - Savikalpa Samadhi Sāpekshika - Nirvikalpa Samadhi

Śree Gurubhyo Namā:
("Sir") Śree Chidānanda Nada

Śreenatimindi Subramaŋia Iyer, whose *Deeksha* name is *Śree Chidānanda*

Nada, incarnated in this century (20th century) to advise the greatness, worshipping methodologies and philosophies for the Tamil speaking people.

Aiming that the devotees of *Śreedevee*, who read this book, should know something about the great services rendered by him to *Śreevidyā*, this part has been included.

There is a small and beautiful village called Seppittankulam, around 24 miles south and 10 miles west of Tavalagiri hills, which is also called as while hills. Some centuries before, some *Vaidheekha* families, settled here from Seven Godavari delta, as a race were called *Natimindi*. A great person called *Narasayyā* was born in this race in *Gowdinya gotra*. He belonged to *Andhra Venki Nāddu* – son of the couple *Śree Venkatarāyalayya* and *Śreemati Kanakammāl*. He had *Vaidheeka* as profession. He was very much devoted to Lord *Muruga* of *Tirutani*. He was wedded to *Ammāyi Ammal* daughter of *Śree Kuppayyā* of *Pudupalayam Magadamedu*.

Once, *Śree Narasayyā* was suffering from heavy stomach ache. On account of severe pain, he went to *Nedunkunran* with thought of suicide. Enroute, Lord *Muruga* disguised as an elderly person gave a herbal medicine for the body sufferings and *shadākshara mantra* for the worldly sufferings. *Muruga* tested *Śree Narasayyā* in many ways. *Ammāyi Ammal* also expired. Even amidst various sufferings and tests he did not leave his devotion to lord *Muruga*. After some time *Śree Narasayya* married *Kāmākshee*, the third daughter of *Śree Kuppayya*.
The couple *Śree Narasayya* and *Kāmākshee* was blessed first with a daughter followed by a son. The son Subramaŋian born on 01-11-1882 was later shone as *Śree Chidānandar*.

Śree Narasayya himself taught *Vedas* for this child. For general studies, he also admitted him in a school. Subramaŋian learnt everything in a formal way. At the age of 16, he was wedded to *Śreemati Visalakshi*, a relation through his mother, belonging to Pazhavantangal of Chennai.

They started their life at *Kāncheepuram*. Subramaŋian lived there alongwith his two younger brothers *Venkataraman* and *Kuppusamy*. Out of his passion towards learning English, he also learned it.

Śree Narasayya expired in 1901. Since he had to support the entire family, he went through the teacher's training in 1904 and became a teacher of a corporation school in 1905. From 1913 onwards, he became the headmaster of the Corporation Model School in *Vallabha Agraharam*, Triplicane, Chennai. After serving for 25 years he retired from that job in 1937. He learnt painting while he was in the Teacher Training, by the encouragement of its head Rev. Father Mathew. He also became expert in Tamil literature by the fortunate meeting with *Venpapuli* T. S. *Velusamy Pillai* (all these helped him later). It helped in painting the picture of *Śree Guhananda*.

As per the wish of his mother, he travelled to North in 1911. On account of child birth, he could take his wife. He stayed with Bairava Sastry at Tarakanch *Shiva* Mutt at Allahabad. It was a holy time of *Mahodaya* coupled with *Kumba Mela*. He went to take bath in *Triveni Sangama* all along meeting various *Yogis* and *sadhus*. There he saw a great person with so much of lustre. At once, getting excited, he bowed to him and requested to save from the worldly affairs. That great person also thought a while. It seems, he, who knows all the three times, wanted to propagate the greatness of *Śreedevee* again accordingly to the present times, through this bowing South Indian. He ordered him to meet him again after 2 days on the *Mahodaya* day at Sun rise. On Monday morning in 1911, full Moon day, that great person with *deekshā* name as *Guhananda Nada* initiated *Śree Subramania Iyer*. He bathed him, advised *Mahā* sentence, *Hamsa mantra* and *Śreevidyā Shoḍasee mantras*. He also advised the lineage of teachers, traditional methods, *Pādukāmantra* and gave him the name *Chidānanda Nada*.

Śree Chidānanda Nada returned to the place where he was staying and explained everything to his mother. He also invited *Śree Guhānanda Nada* for the *pooja* performed at the residence of *Śree Sastry*. *Śree Chidānanda Nada* stayed with his teacher for 27 days from the very next day and learnt some important secrets of *Shiva vidyā*, Subramaŋia *Tatva*, subtle points of non-duality principle and other advises. He used to take food only after feeding his teacher and mother. At this juncture *Śree*

Guhānanda advised *Shakti Panchāksharee* and *Subramaŋia mantra* to *Kāmākshee Ammal* also.

Śree Guhananda Nada got ready to go to *Badrikāshramam* for *Shiva-ratree*. He ordered his disciple to return to South India and chant *Soota Samhita, Mahā Vākya Ratnāvali,* etc., secretly for 12 years. He blessed him that everything would be fine and you will get the self realisation. He also blessed that his subtle form can be seen in the *Muruga* idol at *Tirutani* on the full Moon day during January – February (even nowadays this can be seen).

As per the orders of his teacher, *Śree Chidānanda Nada* secretly worshipped for 12 years. He got the complete understanding of *Vedantas* from *Kallidaikuruchi Rājānga Swāmi. Vallimalai Śreekumara tuluvamar Tirupugazh* Society compiled all his Tamil writings and published as *Tirutanigai Prapanta Tirattu*. Further his book called *Kanda Purāŋa Sankraham* was also published in 1925. In this book *Śree Chidānanda Nada* has included, *Nirguŋa Subramaŋian Ashtotrashata Nāmāvali* written by his teacher *Śree Ātmananda Nātha*. This society conferred the title *Arutkavi* to him in 1933 in *Tiruvattesvarar* temple.

Śree Chidānanda Nada heard about *Śree Seshadri Swamy* of Tiruvaŋŋāmalai and was very much interested to meet with him. This got satisfied in the month on 20th May 1920. He could meet and bow to him by around 9:00 p.m. at *Kampattinaiyanar* temple. *Śree Seshadri Swamy* ordered him to come around 3:00 a.m. *Śree Chidānanda Nada* was keeping awake and waiting. Exactly at 3:00 a.m., *Śree Seshadri Swamy* arrived, *Śree Chidānanda Nada* bowed him and he gave *darshan* with red colour body. *Śree Chidānanda Nada* was standing almost unconscious and *Śree Seshadri Swamy* started talking to him with compassion – "look at me deeply. Got it? No doubt? This is the same thing what you have. Protect what is given to you". Immediately *Śree Swamy* left that place.

After this incident, *Śree Chidānanda Nada* met with *Ramana Maharishi*, who is called as Junior *Seshadri* and discussed about *Vedanta* for quite a long time.

After secret worship for 12 years in the year 1924 during *Shārada Navarātree* time on a full Moon day he performed *Śreevidyā Navavarŋa* worship on a *Śreechakra* in the *Kāmākshee* temple at *Kāncheepuram*. This worship was some reason obstructed. *Śree Chidānanda Nada* continued it on every full Moon day for 20 years, as per the orders of *Śree Kānchi Kāmakoṭi Paramāchārya*. Till date this worship is being pursued by disciple race of him.

Some 70-80 years ago, on account of improper worship of *Śreevidyā* by some people, it earned a bad name. On account this many a person hesitated to start this worship. At this juncture, *Śree Chidānanda Nada* established the proper worship of *Śreevidyā*, by clearly explaining its specialties and showing evidences from *Veda* and *purāṇas*. He initiated 1000s of disciples based on their capacity. He made 100s of people as heads of mutts and ordered to perform *Navāvarṇa* worship.

Since he was a teacher in a school, students used to call him with respect as "Sir". The disciples who were initiated by him also started to call him as "Sir". Even when they talk about him among themselves, he was addressed as "Sir". It has become a practice. Among those who were made as heads of mutts by him, there were some ladies (*Suvāsinis*). *Śree Chidānanda Nada* was the cause of them doing the *Navāvarṇa* worship in public.

In those days during worship of *Titi Nityā*, only males were deified as *Titi Nityā Devees*. He changed this practice and made initiated ladies (*suvasinis*) only to be deified as *Titi Nityā Devees*. He also defined an abridged method of *Bindu* offerings and learning the same.

He established *Śree Brahma Vidyā Vimarsini Sabha* (society) to research and to teach the secrets of *Śreevidya*. This society met every week and did research about various books. Many *Sāstra* experts in Chennai participated in these meetings.

As a result of this research many books were published. Some of them are:

1. *Śreevidyā Saparyā Pattadi*: This clearly explains the method of *Navāvarṇa* worship. This was compiled based on many books on *tantra*. Right from the day this book was published, only this method is being followed in Śaṇkara Mutts and other religious people. If we look at the other books published in recent times, these are all based on this book only. Some *nyāsās* and verses are suffixed or prefixed in them. Some other books are published in Tamil for those who do not know Samskrit.

2. *Śreevidyā Saparyā Vāsanai*: This explains the inner philosophies of each stage of *Navāvarŋa* worship. This explains how this worship helps in getting the experience of non-duality. This clearly evidences that *Śreevidyā* and the non-duality principle established by *Śree Ādi Śaṇkara* are one and the same. This book was published in English and Tamil. Naţarāja Iyer, who was secretary of this society has noted down the points of discussions. Those points helped in release of this book. For this service, the entire *Śreevidyā* society has to have gratitude to him.
3. *Guru Tatva Vimarsam*: This book explains the extreme philosophies of teacher. This was based on *Veda* and *Gurugeeta*. This clarifies the *beeja* letters of *Guru Pātukāmantra*.
4. *Śree Nagara Vimarsam*: This book was Tamil translation of *Lalitā Stavaratnam* and *Āryā Tvishatee* by sage *Durvāsa*. It explains various inherent meanings.
5. *Shakti Mahimna Stotram*: This book is also a Tamil translation of a book written by sage *Durvāsa*. It mentions various inherent meanings.
6. *Varivasya Rahasyam*: This is Tamil translation of a book written by *Śree Bhāskara Rāya* in the same name. It is based on the commentaries written by him.
7. *Śreevidyā Nityāhnikam*: This is a single window compilation of various actions, chanting, meditations and readings that are to be followed by worshippers of *Śreevidya*. The 15 *Katkamālāmantras* were first published in this book.
8. *Śreelalitopākyāna Vimarsam*: This is the *Lalitopākyānam* from *Brahmānḍa Purāŋa*.
9. *Ajapā Kalpam*: A guide explaining the *Ajapa* chanting.
10. *Maněshwa Panchakam*: Tamil translation of *Maněshwa Panchakam* written by *Śree Ādi Śaṇkara*.
11. *Lalitā Trishatee Bhāshyam*: Tamil meanings based on the commentaries of *Śree Ādi Śaṇkara*.
12. *Śree Subramaŋia Tatvam*: This book explains various secret philosophies learnt from *Śree Guhānanda* when he stayed with him. *Śree Chidānanda Nada*, dedicated this book in the feet of *Śree Guhānanda* and changed the name of the society also to *Śree Guhānanda Brahma Vidyā Vimarshinee Maŋḑalee*. In due course the name has become *Guhānanda Maŋḑalee*.
13. *Kāmakalā Vilāsam*: This book is the Tamil meaning based on meaning written by *Śree Nadanānanda Nātha* for the book written in Samskrit by *Śree Puŋyānandanātha* of Kashmir. Various subtle points about *Śreevidyā* have been explained in this. This is an important book in *Kādhividyā* tradition. This Tamil meaning was published during the 60th birthday occasion of "Sir". During that occasion, *Śree Kānchi Kāmakoţi Paramāchārya* conferred him with the title *Abhinava Bhāskarar*. Śreevatsa Somadeva Sarma, who wrote preface to this book, has astonished whether *Śree Ādi Śaṇkara* and *Śree Bhāskara Rāya* have together incarnated as *Śree*

Chidānanda Nada. In the greeting message sent by *Śree Vishuddānanda Teerta Swamy* of *Sringeri Mutt* also has mentioned *Śree Chidananda* as *Nava Bhāskarar*.

14. *Śreevidyā Geeta*: This is the Tamil meaning of *Tripurā Rahasyam*, which is part of *gnāna* (knowledge) *Kāṇḍa*.

In addition to the above, *Śree Chidānanda* has written some other books also. Some noteworthy among them are:

- *Gnāna Prakāsana* – this is a *Vedanta* drama.
- *Kamalāmbikā Mahātmiyam* – this is a book about *Śreedevee* in Tiruvarur. Some subtle philosophies from *Devee Mahatmiyam* (*Saptashatee*) and *Navāvarṇa Keertanas* of *Śree Muthuswamy Deekshitar*, have been clearly explained in this book.
- *Kamalālaya Kshetra Tatvam* – This book is based on *Muchukunda Sahasrananāma* and various other ancient books. This clearly explains the philosophy of the form of *Śree Thiagarāja* in this holy place. It advises that the heart of *Śree Thiagarāja* is the location of *Bindu*. It also clearly advises that the name *Veedhi Vidangan* indicates *Hamsa Mantra*.
- *Śree Panchanata Kshetra Tatvam* – This book advises that Tiruvaiyar, which is the holy place of five rivers, is the master place of the physical universe and the mental place in the form of order of the subtle body.
- *Chidambara Rahasyamum Naṭarājan Tatvamum*
- *Āryā Chataka* meaning of *Mooka Panchashati* – (included in the publication of *Kāmakoṭi Gocha Stanam*).
- The preface written to the book *Lalitopākyānam* by *Śreevatsa Somadeva Sarma*. The inner meaning of the battle with *Bhanḍāsura* has been explained in this book.
- The preface given to the *Lalitā Sahasranāma* of *Kumbakonam Śree Gaṇesaiyer*. This has been published as it is.
- Different verses and poems written in Tamil and Samskrit.

In 1946 he inaugurated the form of his teacher seen in *Śree Muruga* idol at Tirutani to be seen by public, during the new Moon day (the anniversary day of his initiation). Deifying of pots, worshipping of teacher groups, *Chaṇḍi* sacrificial fire, etc., will begin even on the previous day at the *Soorā Chetty* choultry in the bottom of the hill. This festivity is still being performed by the disciples of "Sir".

There is a worship of *Gaṇapati* in the form of *Uchchishta Gaṇapati*. There is a special and secret *sahasranāma* for this worship. By tradition this is being advised only to the eligible disciples. Many subtle things about

Śreevidyā have been mentioned in this. Śree Chidānanda Nada did know this secret *sahasranāma* also. He chants this in front of the head of *Sringeri mutt Śree Sachitānanda Shivābhinava Narasimha Bharatee Swamy* as per his order and got some of the mistakes in his understanding and some of the doubts clarified. At that juncture swamy discoursed the meaning of the last 2 names for nearly 30 minutes.

One of the main services done by *Śree Chidānanda Nada* to *Śreevidyā* is discoursing the commentary of *Śree Lalitā Sahasranāma* by *Śree Bhāskararāya* in Tamil.

Śree Chidānanda Nada had established *Śreechakra* or *Meru* in some of the *Siddhās* and great peoples' *samadhis* and performed *Navāvarŋa* worship.

In 1955 he started a periodical by name *Śreevidya*. It was planned that this issue should be available with the worshippers of *Śreevidyā* every year in each of the 4 *Navarāthris*. It had many great articles that are useful to the worshippers. On account of his ill-health and due to shortage of money (since the subscribers were not prompt), he could release 8 issues only. When the material for the ninth issue was ready, he expired. Some of his disciples released the 9th issue. But this was not continued further.

He left his physical body on sixth day of *Shārada Navarāthree* - September 1957 (on the day of *Mahā Vajresvari Nityā*). At that time *Śree Kānchi Kāmakoţi Paramāchārya* was performing his daily chore worship camping at Samskrit College, Mylapore, Chennai. He just stopped it for a minute and then continued it. The people around were rumbling and thought that whether they have done any mistake or did not gather any item for the worship, etc. At the end of the worship *Paramāchārya* explained "at that time a worshipper was welcomed at *Maŋi Dveepa* and I was enjoying it". This was mentioned to us by a close associate of *Paramāchārya*. He has also tied us that his name should not be revealed.

Though *Śree Chidānanda Nada* was in the family life he lived like an ascetic. Even during ill-health he worked hard for *Śreevidya*.

He taught important books to his disciples. He participated on time, even in those days when the transport facilities were not this high, for the *poojas* performed at the house of his disciples.

His character can be described in multiple dimensions as – gigantic form, had eyes and face with lustre, peaceful, an example of simplicity, full of compassion, one who corrects the mistakes firmly, with mercy, one who is interested in the religious growth of his disciples, faithful, dedicated himself and hardworking for *Śreevidyā*, unattached, greatly devoted to teachers, had deep knowledge of *Śreevidyā* and *Vedanta* and at the same time prompt in doing the *vaidheeka* ordained actions, one who has the capacity to see his deity of interest in all the things seen and read and one who has the broad mentality of utilising his intellect to be useful to all.

Śree Chidānanda Nada continue to be in *Śreepura* and guide us all. Let us bow his feet and reach salvation.

*****

Śree Lalitā Mahathripurasundaryai Nama:

(From the Tamil book of *Lalitā Sahasranāma* by *Śree G. V. Gaŋesaiyer*)

I. History of the book:

Śree Lalitā Sahasranāma is in the form of dialogue between *Śree Hayagreevā* and Sage *Agastya*, as part of *Lalitopākhyāna* in *Uttara Kānḍa* of *Sreemad Brahmānḍa Purāŋa*.

Śree Lalitopākhyāna has many divisions like *Mantra Kānḍa, Nyāsa Kānḍa, Poojā Kānḍa, Purashcharaŋa Kānḍa, Homa Kānḍa, Rahasya Kānḍa* and *Stotra Kānḍa*. In these, *Shyāmala* and *Vārāhi Sahasranāmas, Panchameestavarāja* and other *stotras* and this *Lalitā Sahasranāma* form part of *Stotra Kānḍa*.

This was compiled by *Vāgdevees* like *Vasinee, Kāmeshvaree* and others as per the orders of *Śreedevee* for the benefit of the devotees. The *Sāstras* have confirmed that if this hymn is read by the devotees after understanding the meaning and if *Śreedevee* is prayed and meditated upon, **She** gets much satisfied.

Brahmānḍa Purāŋa is the last among the 18 great *purāŋas*. The author *Vedavyāsa* has well included the matters relating to all the *mantras* and the form of *Brahmavidya*.

II. The philosophy of *purāŋas*:

Purāŋas originated to explain the nuances in *Vedas* to those who are not permitted to learn them and to explain the subtle points in *Vedas* through detailed descriptions. Hence *Purāŋas* are called as sub-*Vedas*. *Vedas* have been majorly classified into three *kāndas* (divisions) viz., *Karma* (action), *Upāsana* (worship) and *Gnāna* (knowledge). The sub-*Vedas* of *Karma Kānda* are *Dharma Sāstra* and *Smrutis*. The *Purāŋas* are the sub-*Vedas* of *Upāsana and Gnāna Kāndas*. Hence the gist of *Purāŋas* is only the form of *Brahmam* and nothing else.
Since this *Lalitā Sahasranāma* is also like a *Purāŋa*, its summary should also be the form of *Brahmam* only. The tool for a worshipper to understand the *Brahmam* not differently from him is *Brahmavidyā* or

Śreevidya. *Lalitā* in the form of *Śreevidyā* is also addressed as *Lalitāmbā, Tripurasundaree, Parai, Parāpattārikai, Parāhantā, Chitshakti, Samvit,* etc., all conveying one and the same meaning. A detailed description of *Śreevidyā* has been made in this book. It is necessary for the readers to read it leisurely.

III. *Lalitā Sahasranāma* resembles *Vedas*:

It was earlier mentioned that this *Lalitā Sahasranāma* was composed by *Vasinee* and other *Vāgdevees*. These *Vāgdevees* are only the speech form of *Śreedevee*. *Śreedevee*'s sublime forms are *Pashyantee, Madyama* and *Vaikharees*. As per the *Veda* statement *Yasya Vishvasitam Vedā:, Vedas* are the breath of *Parameshwaran*. The inhale and exhale breathes are due to the movement of oxygen.

Pashyantee, Madyama and *Vaikharees* speeches also related to breathe only. Though inhale and exhale are caused by the same movement of oxygen, there is some mutual difference in them: hence this *Sahasranāma* (composed by *Vāgdevees* explaining the glory of *Śreedevee*) and the *Vedas* (which are the inhale and exhale of *Parameshwara*) are equal: there is no difference between them. *Vedas* shine with anterior and posterior theories. In the same manner this *Sahasranāma* also shine with anterior – form of verses with attributes and posterior – form of verses without qualities, theories.

There is a formula defined for the *Veda* statements and sentences. In the same way there is an old formula called *Salākshara Sūtras* for this *Sahasranāma* also. The great man who wrote this formula is not known. We don't think that anybody would object for the thought that this could have been written by *Vāgdevees* themselves.

IV. The format of this *Sahasranāma*:

These *Salākshara Sūtras* are 24 in number. Some of these mention that the 1000 names of this *Sahasranāma* begin with such-and-such letters. All the names in this hymn begin only with 32 letters. This can be seen from the list of names given as an appendix to this book. As per the evidence of *Soota Samhitā* it can be understood that all the 1000 names begin only with one of the 32 letters;

Dvāttrimshadbhedabhinnā Cha Ya Tām Vande Varapradām I
Akārādikshakārāntai Varŋairratyanta Nirmalai: I
Asheshashabdairyā Bhāti Tāmāmodapradām Numa: II

The *Sūtra* also measures and conveys the number of names beginning with each of the letters.

The *Paribāshā Sūtras* – 40 in number – are in the form of description of *Salākshara Sūtras*, whose origin is not known. These were composed by *Śree Nrusimhānanda Yajvāva*. He is the teacher of *Śree Pāsurānanda Nada* alias *Bhāskaramaki*, who wrote commentary for this *Sahasranāma*. Some differences are found from the names currently being used and that are mentioned in the *Sūtras*. The *Sūtras* confirm that the names beginning with *Ā* are 10 in number, *Ja* – 19, *Sha* – 59 and *Sa* – 122. However, in practice the names beginning with *Ā* are 11 (one more) in number and *Ja* – 18 (one less). Hence it leads to the presumption that a name that was starting with *Ja* has changed to being with *A*. The (46th) name *Sinjjānamaŋimamjeera Maŋḍitasreepadāmbujā* has been included under *Sa* (*Si*) in the *Sūtras*. But it seems that it has to be included under *Sha* (*Shi*) serial. Further according to first verse of the *Sūtras Triguŋai*: - three names starting with the word *Guŋa* – *Guŋāteetā, Guŋanidhi*: and *Guŋapriya*. But there is no name as *Guŋapriya*. Instead we have a name as *Gurupriya*. This is one difference. We find very little differences like this – *Śree Bhāskara Rāya* himself has mentioned at the end of his commentaries that it is not a very big fault to have such minor differences.

These 1000 names are like *mantras*. Hence the *Sūtras* define the number of letters in each of the *mantras*. In addition to such definition it also explains the serial in which those *mantra*s occur. Hence it is quiet impossible to modify the serial in which the names occur, or to insert a new name or to delete an existing name or even to modify an existing name.

The names which are in the form of *mantra*s give the desired results to those who chant with devotion. This has been explicitly mentioned in the last part of the hymn.

The complete hymn of 1000 names is in the form of a garland of *mantras*. All the four castes are eligible to read this.

The meanings of these 1000 names are in a continuous form explaining the characters of the form of *Brahmam*. This cannot be over sighted by those who subtly do research on this hymn.

The character of the *Brahmam* has been mentioned in *Brahma Sūtra* called as *Sāreeraka Meemāmsa* as *Janmādyasya Yata*: for those who has thirst to know the *Brahmam*. Again in *Upanishads*, the same is mentioned as *Tajjalānitishānta Upāseeta*. *Purāŋas* are the meaning form of *Upanishads*, which are themselves *Brahma Kāṇḍas*. It has already been mentioned that this *Sahasranāmā* is a gist of all *purāŋas*. The first three names of this *Sahasranāmā* explain that *Śreedevee* (*Chitshakti*) only is the cause of the creation, protection and destruction of this universe. They are respectively – *Shreemātā*, *Shreemahārājnee* and *Shreemat-simhāsaneshwaree*. From the fourth name onwards till 999th name the fourth and fifth actions of *Śreedevee* viz., screaming from the impacts of material pleasure & displeasure (*Tirodhāna*) and blessings (*Anugraha*) are mentioned. The soul gets the bondage and salvation through *Tirodhāna* and *Anugraha*. Hence the tools for the removal of bondage and to seek the bliss, are described in detail in this hymn. The last name *Lalitāmbikā* describes the knowledge and realisation experience. This can be well read from *Śree Lalitānubhooti Prakaraŋa* of the book called *Svānubhooti Rasāyana* written by *Śreemad Paramahamsa Kotakanallur Sundara Swāmi*. In the meantime, some research on the names *Chidagnikuŋḍasambhootā* (4th) till *Shiva Shaktyaikya Roopiŋee* (999th) has been summarised in the below table:

No.	Serial Nos of the names	The subject dealt with
1.	4 and 5	Form of brightness
2.	6	Form of reflection
3.	7 to 51	Gross form
4.	52 to 54	Dwelling place of *Śreedevee*.
5.	55 to 63	*Śreepuram*, the city of *Śreedevee*.
6.	64 to 84	The actions of *Śreedevee* after being originated from *Chidagni*. Lot of secret glories of *Śreedevee* has been described.
7.	85 to 87	Subtle *mantra* form
8.	88 and 89	Subtle *kāmakalā* form
9.	90 to 112	Subtle *kuŋḍalinee* form

No.	Serial Nos of the names	The subject dealt with
10.	113 to 131	Tools to reach *Śreedevee*, who is in 5 different forms as – physical, sublime, subtle, minute and cosmic.
11.	132 to 134	Free from affectations
12.	135	Criticism of scientific school of religion
13.	136	Criticism of logical school of religion with evidences
14.	137	Criticism of vacoom profounder school of religion
15.	138	Criticism of logical school of religion
16.	139	Criticism of those who argue that *Brahmam* is with organs.
17.	141	Criticism of those who argue that *Brahmam* is with characters.
18.	147	Criticism of Cārvāka theories
19.	151	Criticism of duality theory
20.	153 to 256	The characters of the exceptional face of *Śreedevee*
21.	257 to 274	The form of *Śreedevee* as a savior of the souls suffering from five types of sorrows and the savior of five types of *Brahmams*.
22.	275 to 999	Description of the mental, daily chores, the inner and very inherent meanings of *mantrasāstra*, *yoga sāstra*, non-duality *sāstra*, *tantra sāstra*, devotion *sāstra*, etc.

If the continuity of the 1000 names right from the beginning till the end is keenly observed, it can be seen that it is arranged in very much similar to the four divisions *Brahma Sūtra* viz., *samanvaya* (integration of the diverse texts into a homogeneous total picture), *avirodha* (removing all possible objections and internal contradictions), *Sādhana* (the worshipping methods) and *Phala* (the results).

No.	Serial Nos of the names	The subject dealt with
1.	1 to 3	Neutral character
2.	4 to 131	*Samanvaya* (confirming that everything is in the form of *chitshakti*)
3.	132 to 256	*Avirodha* (nullifying the criticism of all the other schools)
4.	257 to 274	Tool for self-enquiry and realisation
5.	275 to 999	Doing mental realisation through various evidences of *sāstras* and other tools
6.	1000	Results of the form of knowledge of self realisation

1. The names relating to non-duality *sāstra*: *Ameyā, Ajā, Ātmavidyā, Ekākinee, Antarmukha Samārādhyā, Kevalā, Kooţasthā, Guŋāteetā, Chinmayee, Chiti:, Chidekarasa Roopiŋee, Chicchakti:, Chetanā-roopā, Jnānavigrahā, Tatpadalakshyārthā, Tat, Tvam, Ayee, Dvaita-varjitā, Deshakālaparichchinnā, Nirādhārā, Naishkarmyā, Brahmatmaikyasvaroopiŋee, Brahmaroopā, Parā, Bhoomaroopā, Mohanāshinee, Mithyājagadadhishţhānā, Muktidā, Muktinilayā, Vedavedyā, Vyāpinee, Shivā, Srutiseemanta Sindoorikrutapādābja Dhoolikā, Shivamkaree, Sarasvatee, Satyānandasva Roopiŋee, Sacchidānanda Roopiŋee, Sarvopanishadudghushţā*, etc.
2. The names relating to *mantra sāstra* and *Śreevidyā*: *Akulā, Ādishakti:, Icchāshakti Gnānashakti Kriyāshakti Svaroopiŋee, Ĕ, Umā, Oḍyānapeeţhanilayā, Kadambavanavāsinee, Kāmākshee, Kirichakrarathārooḍhadaŋḍanāthāpuraskrutā, Kāmeshwara Mukhāloka Kalpita Śreegaŋeshvarā, Karāmgulinakhotpanna Nārāyaŋadashakruti*: and *Kāmeshwarāstranirdagdhasabhaŋḍā Surashoonyaka*. These names are related to *Lalitopākhyānam* and *Devee Bhāgavatam* – *Gurumaŋḍala Roopiŋee, Gurupriyā, Manuvidyā, Chandravidyā, Chitkalā, Jnānamudrā, Jnānajneyasva Roopiŋee, Tatvāsanā, Trikoŋāntaradeepikā, Trikhanḍeshee, Trikoŋagā, Panchapretāsanāseenā, Panchakrutyaparāyanā, Pratipanmukhya Rāgāntatithimaŋḍalapoojitā, Pāshahastā, Panchasankyopachāriŋee, Bisatantutaneeyasee, Bindumaŋḍala Vāsinee, Balipriyā, Bindutarpaŋasantushţā, Bhagamālinee, Mahātantra, Mahāmantra, Mahāyantrā, Mahāyāgakramārādhyā, Merunilayā, Mantrasārā, Rahastarpaŋatarpitā, Vimarsharoopiŋee, Veeramātā, Śreevidyā, Śreeshoḍashākshareevidyā, Śreechakra-rājanilayā, Sarvamantraswaroopiŋi* and *Sāmarasyaparāyaŋa*.

This *Sahasranāma* gives room and supports all the extreme religions like *Samaya, Koula* and *Mishra*.

This includes the names like (a) *Samayācāratatparā* and *Samayāntasthā* which talk about religions and (b) *Koulamārgatatparasevitā, Kuleshvaree, Kulasanketapālinee and Kulāmrutaikarasikā* which talk about *Koula* religion.

3. Some names relating to *yoga*: *Moolādhāraikanilayā, Brahma-granthivibhedinee*, 101st to 110th names, *Vishuddhichakra Nilayā* (475) onwards 62 names, *Yoginee, Yogadā, Yogyā* and *Yogānandā*

relate to *Yoginee nyāsā* method. The above 101st name *Maŋipoorāntaruditā* relates to *Samaya* religion and explains the usage of purity. The format of *Kuŋḍalinee* and piercing through the knots are described in this name. The *yoga* has been explained both through religion and *koula*.

4. The names relating to *bhakti* (devotion) *sāstra* viz., *upāsanā kānḍa* of *Vedas*: *Bhaktigamyā, Bhaktivashyā, Bhaktasoubhāgyadāyiŋee, Bhaktipriyā, Kshipraprasādiŋee, Bhaktachittakekighanāghanā, Nāmapārāyaŋapreetā, Lopāmudrārchitā, Dhyānagamyā, Varadā* and *Kāmapoojita*.

5. The names relating to *karma* (action) *Kānḍa* of *Vedas*: *Krutajnā, Shishţeshţā, Shishţapoojitā, Svāhā, Svadhā, Shubhakaree, Sāmrājya-dāyinee, Deekshitā, Yajnaroopā, Yajnapriyā, Yajnakartree, Yajamānasvaroopiŋee, Dharmādhārā* and*Varŋāshramavidhāyinee*.

Thus when deeply read, it is very clear that there is nothing in this world which is not talked about in this *Sahasranāma*.

6. Furthermore, there are some names which are the essence of the meanings of all the *sāstras* – *Vishvaroopā, Pashupāshavimochanee, Parā, Moolaprakruti:, Parākāshā, Parātparā, Savyāpasavya Mārgasthā* and *Bisatantutaneeyasee*. Its greatness will be very clear while reading the commentaries.

Brahmam has been mentioned as a *Shakti* in this hymn. Only this is being described as various names like *Brahma Shakti, Ātma Shakti* and *Chitshakti*. However, it is nameless: and hence formless. Those who want to know more about *Chitshakti* can refer the *Śreevidyā* section in this book.

The *chitshakti* described in this hymn has no *Linga* and hence it is flawless. This *chitshakti* cannot be explained through speech; hence *Śreedevee* has been mentioned in masculine, feminine and neutral genders.

Among all the *Sahasranāmās* those relating to *Devee* are great. Among them the greater ones are ten in number viz., *Ganga, Gāyatree,*

Shyāmalā, Lakshmee, Kāli, Bālā, Lalitā, Rājarājeshvaree, Saraswatee and *Bhavāni*. This *Lalitā Sahasranāma* is the greatest among all of them.

These have been mentioned in the first section itself in detail. May be referred, if necessary.

V. The commentaries for this *Sahasranāma*:

1. *Vimarsānanteeyam* – This was written by *Vimarsānanda Nada*, disciple of *Śreemad Vimalananda Nada*. So far this has not gone for printing. The manuscript was found in *Kancheepuram* and it is available in the library at Adyar.
2. The commentary of *Śreevidyāraŋya Swamy*. It is available in the library at Jammu in Kashmir.
3. Another one written by one of the *Sankaracharyas* in the race of *Śree Ādi Śaṇkara*.
4. One written by *Śreebhāsurānanda*. This is the one greatly used in the present days. Many a scholar has accepted that there is no other commentary equal to this.

The biography of *Śree Bhāskararāya*, his living time, his religious philosophies, other books written by him, the temples consecrated by him, etc., have been detailed in the section called "Bhāskara and his glory". This may be referred.

VI. The author of translation of the commentary in Tamil for this *Sahasranāma*:

Śreeman G.V.Gaŋesaiyer B.A., B.L., helped the Tamil speaking world by translating the commentary of Śree Bhāskara*rāya* for this hymn in Samskrit. His translation was such that it did not deviate from the original in any account and also had relevant quotes from *Vedantas*, Logic *sāstra*, *Āgamās*, *Purāŋas*, *Sūtras*, etc.

It seems he had high knowledge in *Vedanta sāstra* and *Śreevidyā sāstra*. The flow of his Tamil translation was so clear and easily understood by everyone. Since he was an expert in English also he learnt the book Arthur Avalon written by Sir John Woodroffe and other books. It seems he belongs to the race of Tiruvaiyar Śreevidya.

He has also written a great Tamil meaning for the commentary of *Lakshmeedhara* for *Soundaryalaharee* written by *Śree Ādi Śaṇkara*.

Further he has written explanations in Tamil for the *Satakās* (100 verses) written by the ancient great poet *Mookakavi – ĀryāShatakam* and *KaţākshaShatakam*. All the books written by him were published by Śree Janartana Printing Works Limited, Kumbakonam. I owe him a lot and convey my sincere thanks for making me write a preface for his commentary for this hymn.

Even though I am in no way eligible to write the preface for the great book (meaning in Tamil) written by Śreemān Iyer, a great scholar and who has training and experience in *Adyātma sāstra*, but still I agreed to it as a pride task bestowed on me.

Something more has to be explained in the preface, but due to volume they have been left. It is a sad feeling in my mind that Śreemān Gaŋesaiyer is not available to see his book being published. Though his physical body has been lost, his pride body will not get destroyed.

We both wanted to mutually meet and discuss, but something has obstructed this and it never happened.

Since *Soundaryalaharee, Āryā Shatakam, Kaţāksha Shatakam* and *Lalitā Sahasranāma* are related to Śreevidyā, it is our primary duty to encourage these books.

Shivam

Śreebrahmavidyā
Vimarsinee Sabhā
Chennai

yours obedient

N. *Subramaŋia Iyer*

*****

Biography of Śree Bhāskara Rāya

Many years back the book called *Soubhāgya Bhāskaram*, commentary on *Lalitā Sahasranāma* was published 2 or 3 times. The biography of *Śree Bhāskara Rāya* was not written in detail in this book. It was mentioned that he was born in either in Sānkvee or Peet city in Maharashtra and he lived as leprosy patient or as a beggar and nothing else is known about him. Lot of incidents in the biography of *Śree Bhāskara Rāya* were first published in the preface of the book called *Varivasyā Rahasyam* published by *Śree Brahmavidyā Vimarisinee Sabha*, Chennai established by *Śree Chidānandanātha*, our teacher. *Śree Bhāskara Rāya* has specifically mentioned the completion dates of his books *Soubhāgya Bhāskaram* and *Setu Bandam* in those books themselves. In the commentary of *Sahasranāma* it is mentioned as *Motachchāyā Mitāyām*. If this is converted to numbers we get during Oct-Nov of 1785 C.E., ninth day of bright lunar fortnight, Wednesday. In the same manner in his books called *Setu Bandam*, which is the description of *Nityā Shoḍashikārnavam*, it is mentioned as *Shake Sharmachāpe* – i.e. the book was completed on the holy *Shivarāthree* day of 1733 C.E. The *Vikrama* calendar is mentioned in one book and the *Salivahana Sahaptam* was mentioned in the other. This indicates the difference in place of publishing. *Soubhāgya Bhāskaram* was written in Banaras, where in *Vikrama* era is being followed (even today), whereas *Setu Bandam* was written in Goa also called as *Śree Saptakoteeshvaram*. It seems *Salivahana* era is in vogue in this area. Hence it could have been mentioned in the book. *Salivahana* era is 134 years less than *Vikrama* era. From these 2 evidences we can consider the period of *Śree Bhāskara Rāya* as the early part of 18th century C.E. In addition his disciple *Jagannāta Paŋdit* (*Umānanda Nāda* after initiation) has explained a method of worship, with the permission of his teacher, in a book called

Nityotsavam. He himself has mentioned the completion date of this book as *Rasārnvakarveta Miteshu*. This means 4876 *kali* years – i.e. 1775 C.E. This also in a way helps to decide the period of *Śree Bhāskara Rāya*. In addition in his book called *Guptavati,* a description of *Chaṇḍi Saptashatee,* he has mentioned it as *Sādhuchchāyā Parimitaprmodavarshe Chidambare Tanutāt*. That means this book has been written in the place called Chidambaram in the year 1740 C.E. In the same manner, in another book written by himself called *Drusha Bhāskaram* we read that it has been written in 1708 C.E. From all these it can be derived that he has written 4 books between 1708 and 1740. In the year 1775 the book called *Nityotsavam* was completed by his disciple. From all these it can be calculated that his period is between 1690 and 1785. His biography has been written by *Śree Umanandanada* in an epic poetry form titled *Śree Bhāskara Vilāsa Kāvyam*. There is no mention about years in this book. Further even there is some difference in the names of the Tamil years as Keelaka, Promoda, Kalayukti, etc. Calculating backwards from the Tamil year *Vegudanya* (corresponding to the then current year 1998 C.E)., 1758 C.E. can correspond to Tamil year *Vegudānya*. The year of completion of the *Sahasranāma* was 1729 (Tamil year *Kalayukti*). But calculating backwards from 1758 (*Vegudānya*) – 1729 will correspond to Tamil year *Sādāraṇa*. In this way we find some differences in the names of the years. However, the count is correct – the reason for the same is not known. The below details are taken from the book called *Śree Bhāskara Vilāsa Kāvyam*.

Śree Bhāskara Rāya was belonging to *Viswamitra Gotra* (race). *Dukadeva* son of *Ekanada* was born in this race. His son was *Yamāji Paṇdit*. *Śree Gambirarāya* was born to him and his wife *Chandramamba*. Their race is *Bhagavata* race. Still he learnt the complete *Āgama sāstra* from his uncle *Āgamacharya Nārāyaṇa* who was belonging to the race *Sreevatsa Gotra*. He was living in Beejapur city itself. Once the king of *Vijayanagara* asked him to give a discourse on *Mahabharata* in his assembly. Having been happy and excited with his scholarly speech ability, he conferred him a title as *Bharati* for his entire race. He has translated the *Mahabharata* into the Parsi language. *Gambirarāya* has written the *Viṣhṇu Sahasranāma* in a verse format as *Padyaprasoonānjali*. He has detailed the story of his race in it. Once *Gambirarāya* visited the city called *Bagā* (later called as Hyderabad) alongwith his wife. There only *Śree Bhāskararāya* incarnated as an early morning Sun for this couple *Gambirarāya* and *Konamambu*. Even at the early childhood he got initiated with the *mantra* called *Vāgdevata* from his father and he got the knowledge of even tough books and *sāstras*, as a surprise to everyone. Later *Gambirarāya* moved to Banaras as holy visit with his family. There itself, he performed *Upanayana* to his son in a great grand manner. Later he made his son as a disciple to *Śree Narasimhayajvā* in the nearby village called *Lokapalli* near the town called *Nārāyaṇapet*. In a short duration *Śree Bhāskara Rāya* has well learnt all the *Vidyās*. Later he got initiated in the Śreevidyā worship through a teacher called *Shiva datta Shukla* (called as *Prasantanada* after initiation) in Gujarat. With the permission of his teacher, he started to go around Bharath to spread the matters relating to *mantra-sāstra*. Later he learnt *Gowḍa Tarka* (logic) *sāstra* from *Śree Gangadaravajapeyee* and became expert in it. Since learning *Atharva* was diminishing, he himself learnt it and taught to others also to publicise it. The learned readers might remember that recently *Śree Kānchi Kāmakoti Paramāchārya* sent one *Punḍdit* to Gujarat and asked him to learn *Atharva* from the only surviving teacher there and asked him to spread it in Tamilnadu. What a wonder - how these two great men had unique thought in supporting *Vedas*?

Śree Bhāskararāya later married a girl called *Ānandee* and initiated her also. Her initiation name was *Padmavatiammal*. Once when he visited Gujarat, there he won the debate with a great scholar in *Vallabha* tradition. Further he also won in a debate with a *Madhwa* saint while returning. Thorough this he married a lady called *Pārvatee*, who was a relative of this saint in his previous *ashrama*. Later he went to Banaras with his 2 wives and did a *Somayaga*. Then he lived in Banaras itself for some time.

By hearsay some interesting incidents have been heard to have occurred in his life during his stay at Banaras. During his time, it is usual for the *Vaidheekas* to make fun and find fault in worshipping paths. Some scholars thought that *Śree Bhāskararāya* belonged to rightist path and has to be criticized and hence waiting for the suitable opportunity. Having known this, *Śree Bhāskararāya* circulated a notice that he was planning to do a sacrifice and whoever wants to debate with him can come and attend. Some scholars accepted this challenge and visited the place of *yāga* (fire sacrifice) alongwith *Śree Paramahamsa Kunkumānanda nada*, a great scholar living in Banaras. *Śree Bhāskararāya* welcomed everyone and offered hospitality to all of them in a proper way. They all were stunned by the ability, debating capability and knowledge in *mantra-*

sāstra of *Śree Bhāskararāya*. They asked various questions to him, but he replied all of them with ease. Later those scholars asked him whether he can tell the names, origin and history of the 64 crores of *Yoginee Devees* mentioned in the 237th name *Mahāchatushshashţikoţi Yogineegaŋasevita*. Immediately *Śree Bhāskararāya* without any hesitation said "Ok I will start telling – note down" – and after meditating upon *Śreedevee*, started as a flow of water opened from a dam to tell about the *Yoginee Devees*. Those scholars became tired of writing the name and other details. *Kunkumānanda* told them that not to think of that person as an ordinary human being. He is a great devotee who has got the blessings of *Śreedevee*. **She** herself sat on his shoulders and replied your questions. Hence you people cannot win him. By saying he spread the holy water in their eyes and asked them to see. They also became fortunate to have a look at *Śreedevee*. They all bowed to *Śree Bhāskararāya* and sought his pardon.

Kunkumānanda mentioned here was a great knowledgeable person who had self realisation. When white *viboothi* is spread on his body it became red *kumkum* and this name to him.

Tānāji Jadav was the knight to the king *Sāhu* who was the grandson of *Sivāji* at Maharashtra. His son *Chandrasena Jadav* was the king of *Palakee* in Karnataka. He was a disciple of *Śree Bhāskararāya* with great respect and devotion. He has no children and hence he was very much worried. He came to see *Śree Bhāskararāya*, who visited near his place. He bowed him and conveyed his worry. *Śree Bhāskararāya* blessed him and said he would soon get a male baby and gave him *prasādam*. After the return of *Chandrasena* to his kingdom, as per the blessings of his teacher, his wife got pregnant. In the meantime *Nārāyaŋa Devar*, a worshipper, visited his Palki town. He is also a disciple of *Śree Bhāskararāya*. With the usage of *Śree Bhāskararāya*'s initiation itself, he got the high capability of speech. Not knowing these details, *Chandrasena* went and bowed him alongwith his wife. He asked him about the sex of the baby in the womb of his wife. He, by reflex, said that it would be a female child. *Chandrasena* was taken aback and he said "my teacher *Śree Bhāskararāya* said it would be male baby and you are saying this way". By hearing this *Nārāyaŋa Devar* got wild and said to *Chandrasena* "idiot, you are testing my teacher's words with me and have done disrespect. You have to suffer the fruits of it. You will get a baby who will be neither a male nor a female". By saying this, he started from that place after bowing to his teacher again and again through his mind. *Chandrasena* also felt that this situation has arisen on account of his own foolishness and returned to his place. After some time he got a eunuch baby. After some years *Śree Bhāskararāya* happened to visit that place. Chandrasena bowed his teacher alongwith his wife and child. By seeing the child with eunuch characters he asked *Chandrasena* about the incident. He bowed him, narrated the story of the curse of Nārāyaŋa Devar and said it all due to his sin. After hearing the story, though it was due the foolishness of *Chandrasena, Śree Bhāskararāya* thinking that his words should not go wrong, he took the child alongwith him with the intention of making him a male. He built an Ashram in the Coast of nearby Krişhŋa River. He stayed and performed a vow called *Trusārgyapradānam* aiming at Sun for the baby sake. Daily he used to come to the river, bowed to Sun and gave *argya* to him and prayed for manliness of the child called *Ramachandra Jadav*. After this worship he had to walk a long distance to his ashram in the hot Sun. On account of this his disciples were very anxious and gave an idea to their teacher that they can build the Ashram near the river. Hearing this the teacher said, why can't we bring the river near the Ashram? The disciples hearing this thought "the learned can do this also just by thought". The next day *Śree Bhāskararāya* meditated upon Sun just at the entrance of his Ashram itself. "I began your prayer in the Krişhŋa River, for the manliness of this *Ramachandra Jatav*. To help this you have to make the river flow near this ashram". Sun replied to this "Oh! Great worshipper, every object created by *Brahma* has some controls. Don't you know that they cannot Deviate from those controls? If you want to make this child a male, you should have asked it directly to me. Why are you asking me to divert the path of the river, etc.? Immediately *Śree Bhāskara* replied with anger that "Do you think I am a beggar? This child should get manliness through praying to you and worshipping *Drusabhāskara*. This will spread the greatness of worshipping Sun to this world. A person worth to be a God has the capacity to do a task or not to do or to do it in a modified manner. If you can't do this, leave it. I will get it done through any means". At once Sun blessed that "till the end of your life River Krişhŋa will flow through near your ashram". Thus *Drusabhāskara* worship was completed in a grand manner and *Ramachandra Jatav* became a complete man. As evidence to this – in the place called Munimedu there are two paths of Krişhŋa River – current one and the previous one. Further, *Śree Bhāskara* has written a book called *Drusabhāskaram* explaining this method of worshipping Sun.

754th name in this *Sahasranāma* is *Aparna*. This has been explained as "by worshipping which God the debts are cleared, **She** is called *Aparnā*". As a background to this, a hearsay story is being told – Once *Śree Bhāskararāya* owed some money to a person. Since he could not repay it on time, the debtor abused him. *Śree Bhāskararāya* regretted a lot and wrote a meaning to this name as *Apgatam Runam Yasyā*: *Sā Aparna*. Further *Śree Bhāskararāya* in his own book called *Deveestavam* he has written the below verse – this has been mentioned by himself while commenting the 754th name;

Ruŋamishţama Datvaiva Tvannāma Japato Mama I
Shive Kathamaparŋeti Rooḍhirbhārāyate Na Te II

That is, I am regularly worshipping you. How can you have the name *Aparnā*, without clearing my debt? It is said that, after this *Śreedevee* herself went in disguise as *Śree Bhāskararāya*'s wife and repaid the money to the debtor. There is no evidence other than the above verse for this story. It seems to be a real life one.

Later *Bhāskararāya* came to Tanjore as per invitation of the king coming in the race of Bosale. He was given a village to live as gift by the king. At that time Gangadhara Vajpeyee, who was his teacher for logic *sāstra*, was living in Tiruvalankadu, Kumbakonam, the South of Cauvery River. Having heard this *Śree Bhāskararāya* established a village called Bhāskararājapuram on the other side Cauvery and started living there. Another hearsay story - *Śree Bhāskararāya* imagined a Muslim lady belonging to Andhra as *Śreedevee* and did worship on her. For this purpose he brought her to his *Pooja* room with his yoga skills and would send her back to her place after the worship.

After some time, he came to a place called Madyārjunam, a village in Tiruvidaimarudhoor and started living at Mahādāna Street there. During that time, in the evenings, he used to sit in the front verandah of his house resting on the wall and placing his legs raised on a pillar. Daily, a saint from the nearby Veppatoor village used to go via that street to the Mahalinga Swamy temple at Tiruvidaimarudoor. Everybody in the street used to respect him by standing up when he passes by. But *Śree Bhāskararāya* ignored this saint. On account of this that saint got an enmity on him. Once during *pradosham*, incidentally, they both happened to meet. At that time the saint started to talk ill of *Śree*

Bhāskararāya in front of the entire public. But, *Śree Bhāskararāya* said to the saint that if he bowed him like other *grahastas*, then the head of the saint would have been broken into pieces and he did not bow him just to protect the saint only. To prove this, *Śree Bhāskararāya* kept the *daŋḍa* (a stick that is usually carried by a saint) and *kamaŋḍala* (a water jug) of the saint in a corner and bowed them. They both broke into pieces. Seeing this, the saint understood the greatness of *Śree Bhāskararāya* and sought pardon with him. From this incident, when the saint crosses his road *Śree Bhāskararāya* used to go inside his house, not to disrespect him. The reason for such greatness to *Śree Bhāskararāya* is due to *Mahashoḍānyasa* performed by him on a daily basis. The philosophy is that those people who perform *Nyāsa* regularly take the form of *Ardhanāreeshwara*.

Śree Bhāskararāya has written in total 42 books covering various subjects like *Meemāmsai, Vedāntam, Nyāsam, Mantrasāstram*, etc. That has been given in a list separately. He constructed many a temple and arranged for regular worship and other religious activities. Those temples are;

(i) *Śree Chakreshwara* temple at Banaras.
(ii) *Śree Pānduranga Swamy* temple at Moolahrata.
(iii) *Śree Gambeeranātaswamy* temple at Kokanam.
(iv) *Śree Vajreshwara* temple at RamEshwaram.
(v) *ŚreeChandralamaba Devee* temple at Samnadi. This is the family deity of *Śree Bhāskararāya* and also it is said that this temple is in the form of *Śreechakra*.
(vi) *Śree Kaholeshvara* temple at Kerala.
(vii) After his period his first wife *Padmavatee* constructed *Śree Bhāskareshvarar* temple in *Bhāskararājapuram* near the Cauvery River.

It is understood that this great person called *Śree Bhāskararāya Deekshita Bharatee* left this world and reached *Śreepuram* at the age of 95. From his writings it is very clear that he had high regards on *Śree Ādi Śankara* and *Śreemad Appaila Deekshita*. *Śree Umanandanada*, the primary disciple of *Śree Bhāskararāya*, in his book called *Śree Bhāskara Vilasa Kavya* mentions as below;

Yasyādrushto Nāsti Bhūmaŋḍalāmsho Yasyā Dāso Vityate Na Kshetĕshwai
Yasyāsādyā Nāsti Vidyā Kimanyair Yasyākāra: Sā Parāshaktireva II

There is no place in this world not seen by him, no king who has not become disciple of him and no *vidyā* not known to him – he is the form of *Parāshakti*.

In the biography of *Śree Ādi Śaṇkara*, there used to be a hearsay story stating the reason for him not writing the commentary for *Lalitā Sahasranāma*, but writing only for *Vişhŋu Sahasranāma*. With the intention of writing commentary, he asked a small girl to bring the *Sahasranāma* book (in general and not specifying). She brought *Vişhŋu Sahasranāma* book and this happened twice or thrice. With this *Śree Ādi Śaṇkara* thought that this is the intention of *Śreedevee* and wrote commentary only for *Vişhŋu Sahasranāma*. Due to this reason, *Śreedevee* wanted to have a good commentary for **Her** *Sahasranāma* by a great person and hence made *Śree Bhāskararāya* to originate and write this commentary. Having got this great good luck (*Soubhāgyam*) to write this commentary, he titled the book as *Soubhāgya Bhāskaram*.

There are differences of opinion about the religion of *Śree Bhāskararāya*;

(viii) **In *Vedanta***: Does he belong to *Vivartta* or *Parināma* (dimension) group? The reason for this doubt is that in the explanation for the 3rd verse, first part of *Varivasya Rahasya* he himself has mentioned that the *tāntrikās* (following the *tantras*) criticises the *Vivartta* argument of *Vedantees* (who is skilled in *Vedantas*) and supports *Parināma* argument. In this regard Śree Chidānanda Nada has written a detailed description that it is very clear that *Śree Bhāskararāya* supports the non-duality principle of *Śree Ādi Śaṇkara* and it is not fitting that that he supports any other philosophy.

(ix) **Worshipping method**: There was a wrong opinion that he was following rightist (*vāma*) method. He has just explained the rightist method in his *Setu Bandam* and other books. This could have led to this conclusion. In reality he followed only the leftist (*Savya*) method.

(x) He has followed the below verse written by *Appaiyya Deekshitar* in his book called *Ratnatrya Pareeksha* in his life and spread the same.

Nityam Nirdoshagandham Niratishayasukham Bruhma Chaitanyamekam I
Dharmo Dhurmeetibhe Dadvaya Miti Pruthagbhooya Māyāvachena II

The pure consciousness in form of bliss, which is eternal, does not even have an iota of ignorance, does not have anything else as equal or greater, is the *Brahmam*. Only that is being seen as *Dharmam* (righteousness) and *Dharmee*.

One other interesting matter – in the meaning for the 13th name *Champakāshoka Punnāga Sougandhikalasatkachā*, the word *Sougandhi* denotes one flower or good fragrance of all the flowers. Based on this meaning we can find the solution for the question in *Tiruvilayadal Purāŋa* – whether the hair of the ladies has fragrance on its own or on account the flowers adoring the hair. In the dispute, in this regard, between *Śree Parameshwara* and a devotee called *Nakkeera, Nakkeera* was burnt. He boldly told *Parameshwara* that even when you show your third eye, the fault is fault only and hence he was burnt. This story was mentioned by *Tetiyoor Brahmaśree Sastrigal* in his meaning for *Soundaryalaharee*. The below verse from *Hālāsya Māhātmiya* says that on account of this debate, he had to take one more birth before attaining salvation;

Ambāparadhato Muktim Nakkeero Naiva Gachchati I
Ambāparadhato Bhooya: *Muktimāpa Dhvijottama*: II

The author conveys two evidences through this verse. First - in the 43rd verse of *Soundaryalaharee, Dhunotu Dhvāntam, Śree Ādi Śaŋkara* conveys through the word *Sahajam* that the fragrance of the hair of *Śreedevee* is very natural. This clearly indicates that *Śree Ādi Śaŋkara* is the incarnation of *Śree Parameshwara*. The second – in the 13th name Śree Bhāskara*rāya* says that the fragrance is due to the flowered adoring *Śreedevee*'s hair. This indicates that he is the incarnation of *Nakkeera*.

List of books written by *Śree Bhāskararāya*:

No.	Subject	Book
I.	*Vedāntam*	1. *Chaŋḍa Bhāskaram* 2. *Neelāchala Sapetikā*
II.	*Meemāmsa*	3. *Vāda Goutoohalam* 4. *Pāttachandrodayam*
III.	*Vyākaraŋam*	5. *Rasikaranjanee*
IV.	*Nyāsam*	6. *Nyāya Mandanam*

No.	Subject	Book
V.	*Chandas*	7. *Chanḍobhāskram* 8. *Chandasgoustupam* 9. *Vruddachandrodayam* 10. *Vārddikarājam* 11. *Choteevruddhi*
VI.	*Kāvyam* (poetry)	12. *Chandrasālā* 13. *Maturāmlam* 14. *Bhāskarasubhāshitam*
VII.	*Vaidheekam*	15. *Vaidheekakosam*
VIII.	*Smruti*	16. *Smruti Tatvam* 17. *Sahasrabojanakanteekā* 18. *Sanguchakrangaŋaprāyachittam* 19. *Ekādashee Nirnayam* 20. *Pradosha Nirnayam* 21. *Drushabhāskaram* 22. *Kuntabhāskara*
IX.	*Stora*	23. *Shivastavam* 24. *Deveestavam* 25. *Shivadaŋḍakam* 26. *Shivāshtotarashanāma Stotra Vyākyānam*
X.	*Mantrasāstra*	27. *Gadyotam* (*Gaŋapati Sahasranāma Bhāshyam*) 28. *Chandralāmbāmāhātmyateekai* 29. *Nāthanavaratnamālā Manjushā* 30. *Pāvanopanishad Bhashyam Prayogam* 31. *Śreesookta Bhāshyam* 32. *Koulopanishad Bhāshyam* 33. *Tripuropanishad Bhāshyam* 34. *Śree Lalitā Sahasranāma Bhāshyam* (*Soubhāgya Bhāskaram*) 35. *Soubhāgyachandrodayam* (*Soubhāgya Ratnākara Bhāshyam*) 36. *Varivasyā Rahasyam* 37. *Tripurasundaree Bhāhya Varivasyā Rahasyam* 38. *Śree Ratnālokam* (*Parasurama Kalpa Sūtra Bhāshyam*)

No.	Subject	Book
		39. *Guptavatee* (*Devee Māhātmya Saptashatee Bhāshyam*) 40. *Shatashlokee* 41. *Mālā Mantroddhāram* (relating to *Katkamāla*) 42. *Setu Bandam*

The above list is based on the book *Varivasyā Rahasyam* published by *Śree Chidānandanada*.

*****

The Authors of the Tamil Edition

A brief about the publishers and the authors of the Tamil edition in their words follows:

The lineage of teachers of the authors of the Tamil Edition:

The beginning of any worship is searching and reaching a teacher. Getting initiated in the *mantras*, with his blessings is called worship. One more important matter is to know the lineage of teachers. The philosophy of teacher has been mentioned in 725th name *Dakshiṇāmoortiroopiṇee* of this *Sahasranāma*. One sense of this is that *Śreedevee* herself is in the form of a teacher. The other sense is that **She** is the first teacher and we are all disciples/ lineage of teachers of **Hers** follows till our teacher. Hence every disciple should know about at least three generations - his teacher (*guru*), teacher's teacher (*parama guru*) and his teacher (*parameshti guru*). There are separate *padukā mantras* for each of them. Further it would be great if one can know upto seven generations. Our teacher only showed us our lineage of teachers. That is:

Poorṇānandanātha
Sānthānandanātha
Vimalānandanātha
Prakāsānandanātha
Ātmānandanātha
Guhānandanātha
Chitānandanātha
Prakāsānandanātha alongwith his consort *Śreeprakāshāba*

We bow to them all and dedicate this book, which is being published by their blessings, in their feet.

Om Sarvachaitanya roopām Tāmātyām Deveemcha Deemahi I
Buddhim Yā Na: Prachodayāt II

About us:

Śree Ādi Śaṇkara's words – *Satsangatve Nissangatvam. Nissangatvam* – for this status of without any association, *Satsangatvam* – association with good people is the only route. It is the first step to eradicate association with bad things or people. Aiming this, some of the like-minded people joined together and formed an association called *Gnāna Bhāskara Sangam*. This is a kind informal group without minding about any legal formalities, without any income & expenditure accounts, president, secretary, etc. This had the residence of our teacher as its headquarters. It involved in some of benevolent activities for the past 15 years. Worships were performed during monthly and annual *parva* days. As a part of it learning about the books relating to *Śreedevee* on Sundays was one of the activities. In this regard *Brahma Śree Goda G Venkatesa Sastri* conducted discourse based on the book called *Soubhāgya Bhāskaram*, written by *Śree Bhāskararāya* on *Lalitā Sahasranāma*. This book is the result of the enjoyment of this discourse.

We pray that this *Sangam* to grow more and more and involve itself in charitable activities. Let our teachers' and *Śree Lalitā Mahātripurasundaree*'s blessings be showered on all, in this regard.

Vande Gurupatatvantvam Avānmanasa Gocharam I
Raktashukala Prapāmishram Atarkyam Traipuram Maha: II

*****

Paribhāshā Verses Detailing the Sequence of names In Śree Lalitā Sahasranāma Stotra

1. *Śreegambheeravipachchita: Piturabhoodya: Konamāmbodare*
*Vidyāshtādasakasyamarmabhidya:Śreenrusimhādguro:*I
Yachcha ŚreeShivadatta Suklacharaŋai:Poorŋābhishiktobhavat
Sa Tretā Tripurā Trayeeti Manute Tāmeva Nāthatrayeem II

a. *Śree Bhāskararāya*, who had *Śreegambheerarāya* as father and *Konamāmbha* as mother, *Śree Nṛsimhanātha* as teacher through whom he has learnt the secret of 18 *vidyās* and got complete initiation through *Śree Shiva datta Shukla*. He imagined three *nādās* as *Tretagnis, Tripuras* and *Trayees*.
b. *Śree Bhāskararāya* introduces himself in this first verse by mentioning lineage of his teachers. He bows to his birth teacher (father) was *Śreegambheerarāya*, education teacher was *Śree Nrusimhanandanātha* and initiation teacher was *Śree Shiva datta Shukla*.
c. The word *Trayee* has lot of meanings – three *agnis* viz., *Gārhapatyam, Āhavaneeyam* and *Dākshināgni*. *Trayee* also means three *Vedas* – *Rig, Yajus* and *Sāma*. *Tripurā* is explained in 626th name.

2. *Gurucharaŋasanātho Bhāsurānandanātho*
Vivrutim Atirahasyām Veeravrundair Namasyām I
Rasayati Lalitāyā: Nāmasāhasrikāyā:
Gurukrutaparibhāshā: Savivrunvan Ashesha: II

a. *Paribhāshā* verses were written by his teacher *Śree Nṛsimhanandanātha*, who was blessed by his teacher *Bhāsurānandanātha*. *Śree Bhāskararāya*, blessed by his teacher, explains in detail these verses, which are very secret and greatly worshipped by the group of devotees with respect.
b. *Bhāsurānandanātha* is the initiation name of *Śree Bhāskararāya*.
c. This *Lalitā Sahasranāma* has three great qualities. This exactly has 1000 names. One name is mentioned only once and there is no duplication. Further there are no fillers like *Cha, Tu, Hi, Ěva*, etc. The names, beginning from *Shreemātā* and ending with *Lalitāmbikā*, are contained in 182.5 verses. *id*entifying the individual names by splitting the verses is very difficult. That too it should be identified satisfying the above qualities. To help in this regard there were 74 verses called *Salākshara Sūtras*. Unfortunately, these verses

excepting 3 or 4, are not available now. Hence they are not known to anybody. Even if known, understanding the same is very difficult. For instance 2 Sūtras and their description are given at the end of this section. Since these verses are lost, *Śree Nṛsimhanandanātha* has composed 40 verses as an enabler to split the names. These are being explained here.

3. *Ashţābhir Vānmayānām Adhipatibhiramoghoktibhir Devtābhi*:
Mātrājnaptābhir Agriyam Yadarasi Lalitā Devya Nāmnām Sahasram I
Yadbrahmaŋeeramesa Prabhruti Divishadām Vismayā Dhānadaksham
Tatraikasyāpi Nāmna: *Kathamiva Vivrutim Mādrusha*: *Kartumeeshte* II

a. This *Sahasranāma* was composed by eight *Vāgdevees*, who are head of speech, as per the orders of *Śreedevee*. This hymn gave surprise to all *devas* like *Brahmani* (*Saraswatee*), *Viṣhŋu*, etc. For such a great hymn, how can a person like me write description even to a single name?

4. *Tathāpi Śreemātrā Daharakuhare Sootrdharayā*
*Samādishtā Vāsām Adhipatishu Kāpyanyatamikā*I
Madeedya Śreenathatrāyacharaŋa Nirŋejana Jalai:
Pavitre Jihvāgre Naţati Mamatā Sā Mama Matā II

a. Still one of the *Vāgdevees* (who were ordered through heart by *Śreedevee*, who controls everything and everybody) is dancing on the tip of my tongue, which was holified by the water which was cleaned the holy feet of my worshippable teachers. I look at her as my egoistic form.
b. This verse indicates the modest simplicity of the author. The flow is also so smooth.
c. This can be compared to what was mentioned by *Śree Ādi Śaṇkara* in the beginning of *Subramaŋia Bujanga Stotra*; *Cguḍejā Shadāsyā Hrudi Dyotate Me Mukhānnis Sarante Girachchāpi Chitram*.

5. *Āprāsa*: *Kāmaroopāt Druhiŋasootanadaplāvitāt Āprateeso*
Gāndhārāt Sindhusārdrādraghuvararasaritāt Ā cha Setoravacha: I
Ākedārāt Udeechee: *Tuhinagahanata*: *Santi Vidvatsamājā*:
Ye Ye Tān Esha Yatna: *Sukhayatu Samajān Gachchamatkarttumeeshte* II

a. Let this trial of mine make all the scholars (worshippers), right from Kāmaroopa in the shore of Brahmaputra at the East (Assam) till Gandhāra, which is green by the flow of river Sindu at the West and from *Setu* that was glorified by the holy feet of *Śree Ramachandra* at the South till *Śreeketār* engulfed by ice at the North, happy. Why should we unnecessarily try to please the people other than the worshippers?

b. He plays with the two words *Samājā*: and *Samajā*: The former indicates the group of scholars and the later indicates herb of animals. He indicates that those who are not worshippers are equal to animals.

c. *Śree Bhāskararāya* has mentioned this verse in the introduction of most of his books.

d. These five verses are bowing and explaining the glory. The *Paribhāshā* verses follow.

I. *Tripurām Kulanitdhimeeḍe Aruŋashriyam Kāmarāja Viddhāngeem* I
Triguŋair Devair Ninutāmekāntām Bindugām Mahārambhām II

i. The meaning of this verse can be had in two ways. One relating to *Śreedevee* and the other the method of splitting the names.

ii.

Tripurām	Three types of Puram – three *poopurams* in *Śreechakra* Triangle, three letters (bālā), three groups in *Panchadashaksharee*, three forms of *Kunḍa*linee
Triputee	*Gnana*, *Gnanātru* and *Gneyam* (the knowledge, the object of knowledge and the knower)
She is in all these triad forms.	
Kulanidhim	*Kulam* relates to a caste. *Nidhi* is wealth. *Jānāmeeti Tamevabantamanubatyetat Samastam Jagat* Right from *Paramashiva* till the teacher the *kulam* (caste) is of two types – one by birth and the other by knowledge. *Kulam* – following the ordained actions as per tradition
Aruŋashriyam	one who is red in colour
Kāmarāja Viddhāngeem	One who is physically unified with *Kāmeshwaran*
Trighuŋai Devair Ninutām	One who is worshipped by *Devas* with three qualities (*Brahma*, *Vişhŋu* and *Shiva*)
Ekāntām	One who is alone in secret Important deity

	The *brahmam* without any quality is called *Ekā* or *Mukhyā* or *Kevala* *A + I = E* *Akāra*: - *Shiva*:, *Ikāra*: - Cupid and hence *E* – *Shivakāma* *Kāntām* – consort *Ekāntām* – *Shivakāmasundaree*
Bindugām	One who dwells in the *Bindu*, *Sarvānandamayachakra* at the centre of the *Śreechakra*
Mahārambhām	One from whom this great universe originated

iii. I bow to **Her** who is:

- Of the form of anything and everything indicated by the word triad.
- The wealth of *kulam*, which has many a meaning such as caste, knowledge *triputee*, tradition, base *chakra*, etc.
- Red in colour and physically unified with *Kāmeshwara*.
- Always worshipped by *Brahma*, *Viṣhŋu* and *Shiva*, who predominantly have the three qualities *satva*, *rajas* and *tamas*.
- *Shivakāmasundaree* from whom the entire universe originated.

iv. Second meaning is a guide to split the names. There is a method to indicate the numbers by letters in Samskrit. This was founded by sage *Vararuchi* and it is called *Kaţapayādi*.

क *ka*	ख *kha*	ग *ga*	घ *gha*	ङ *gna*
1	2	3	4	5
च *ca*	छ *cha*	ज *ja*	झ *jha*	ञ *jna*
6	7	8	9	0
ट *ţa*	ठ *ţha*	ड *ḍa*	ढ *ḍha*	ण *ŋa*
1	2	3	4	5
त *ta*	थ *tha*	द *da*	ध *dha*	न *na*
6	7	8	9	0

प *pa*	फ *pha*	ब *ba*	भ *bha*	म *ma*
1	2	3	4	5
य *ya*	र *ra*	ल *la*	व *va*	
1	2	3	4	
श *sha*	ष *sha*	स *sa*	ह *ha*	
5	6	7	8	

Further all the vowels represent number zero.

The numbers corresponding to each of the letters are to be mapped, as per the above table and to be read right to left (in a transposed manner). Also the half letters are not taken into account.

Similarly there is also another method of representing numbers in Samskrit. It is called *Bhoota Sankhya* (Cryptic Method). For example the word *Rishi* will represent the number 7 (since there are seven sages – *saptarishi*). Similar cryptic numbers can be seen then and there we come across them. Still some names do not follow any of these methods. They are split according to some special rules.

Two of the special rules have to be specifically mentioned – each line, that is half of the verse – has 16 letters. The numbers have to be determined as per *Kaţapayādi* or cryptic methods and have to be subtracted from 16 and the remaining numbers have to be determined to the *Paribhāshā* verses. For this letter *Kaţapayādi* rule should not be applied. For instance the 10th verse contains the word *Tanubhedot*. The letter *Ta* in this word indicates a name 6 letters, *nubhe* – a name with 10 letters, *do* – a name with 8 letters and *'t'* also indicates a name with 8 letters. (According to the rules of *Kaţapayādi* half letters like *'t'* are not accounted for. However, as an exception, here it is considered to indicate a name with 8 letters).

The second is – As per the above first special rule, if a number is mapped to a letter, wherever that letter occurs the same number has to be considered – not under *Kaţapayādi* method. For instance, in the 11th verse the letter *mru* is mapped to number 5, as per the first special rule.

Later in verses 12, 14, 16 and 19 also *mru* is mapped only to number 5.

When the letters in the words of these verses and the above said cryptic words, are mapped to letters we get the number of names beginning with a particular letter. *Tripurām* - pu = 1 and *rā* = 2 – when transposed we get 21 – that is the number of names beginning with the letter *tri* is 21. *Kulanidhim – nidhi* is *navanidhi* – that is, it indicates the number 9 - the number of names beginning with the letter *kula* is 9. In the word *Aruŋashriyam, Aruŋa* (means Sun) indicates the number 12 (Suns) – that is the number of names beginning with the letter *shri* is 12. In the word *Kāmarāja, rajā* indicates the number 16 (once upon a time there were 16 emperors) – that is the number of names beginning with the letter *kāma* is 16. In the word *Viddhāngeem, dhā* = 9, *gee* = 3 and hence *dhāngee* indicates the number 39 (after transposing) – that is the number of names beginning with the letter *Vi* is 39. The word *Triguŋai* indicates the number of names beginning with *Guŋa* is 3. *Guŋāteetā, Guŋanidhi*: and *Guŋapriya*. But there is no name as *Guŋapriya*. Instead we have a name as *Gurupriya. Ninutām – nu* = 0, *tā* = 6 and hence the number of names beginning with *Ni* is 60. *Ekāntām* – the number of names beginning with the letter *tā* is only one (*ekā*). *Bindugām – gā* = 3- the number of names beginning with *bindu* is 3. *Mahārambhām – ra* = 2, *bhā* = 4, - the number of names beginning with *mahā* is 42. Thus this verse splits and gives 206 names as:

Beginning with	**Number of names**
Tri	21
Kula	9
Shri	12
Kāma	16
Vi	39
Guŋa	3
Ni	60
Tā	1
Bindu	3
Mahā	42
Total	206

Note: i. We have the name *Gurupriyā* only instead of*Guŋapriya*.

ii. It is not clear why these 206 names are separately mentioned when the below verses explain all the 1000 names.

II. *Lalitā Nāma Sahasre Chalārnasūtrānuyāyina*: I
Paribhāshā Bhāshyante Samkshepāt Koulika Pramodāya II

i. The cryptic meanings based on the *Salākshara Sūtra* of this *Sahasranāma* have been briefly described for the benefit of the worshippers of *Śreevidya*.

III. *Panchāshadeka Ādoou Nāmasu Sārdhadvyacheetisatam* I
Shadaseeti: *Sādhānte Sarve Vimshatisatatrāyam Slokā*: II

i. The first part of the hymn contains 51 verses, the chapter containing the names has 182.5 verses, the last part contains 86.5 names and on the whole there 320 verses.

IV. *Dasabhoo:sārdhanrupālā Adhyushtam Sārdhanavashadadhyushtam* I
Munisuta Hayāmbāshvāmbāshvokti: *Dhyāna Mekena* II

i. The number of verses said by each person has been mentioned in the second half of this verse and the name of the persons are mentioned in the first half of the verse.

The number of verses uttered by	Sage *Agastya*	-	10
	Soota	-	1
	Hayagreeva	-	16.5
	Devee	-	3.5
	Ashva	-	9.5
	Devee	-	6
	Hayagreeva	-	3.5

In addition there is one meditation verse. In practice there are three more meditation verses, but those have not been mentioned in these verses.

V. *Akshusarāchcharavarŋān Tata*: *Samānāntimou Kasayo*: I
Athamadhyānyānstapayo: *Dveteeyamantye Tyajennavamam* II

i. Now it starts to talk about the beginning letters of the names.

Akshu	in the vowels starting from *a*
Charāt	excepting five letters *a*, *ā*, *e*, *ee* and *u*
Charavarŋān	following five letters *oo*, *ru*, *roo*, *lu* and *loo*

Tata:	in the remaining 6 letters *ee, i, o, ou, am* and *a*: the three even letters *i, ou* and *a*:
Kasayo:	among the consonants, in the *ka* and *cha* families
Antyou	the last two letters *gha, gna, jha* and *jna* combined four letters
Ata:	next in the *ta* family
Madhyāyān	excepting the middle letter *da* the remaining four letters
Tapayo:	in the *ta* and *pa* families
Dveteeyam	excepting the second letters *tha* and *pha*
Antye	in the last *ya* and other letters
Navamam	excepting the ninth letter ***ḷa*** (ळ)
Tyajet	not to be considered

ii. Removing the above 19 letters, the entire 1000 names begin with the remaining 32 letters only. The reason for *Vāgdevees* not considering these 19 letters is not known.

iii. This has been mentioned in *Sūta Samhita* as *Dvadrimsat Betabinnā Yā Tām Vandeham Parātparām.*

VI. *Ittham Sishtānushtu Bvarŋārabdheshu Nāmasoo Tu Sankhyā*: I
Arvanata Tridvishvekadvi Chatu: *Kanjapānavaradheerā*: II

VII. *Kim Dhoopa Dvistambhachalabhayamāmse Padevara*: *Sanga*: I
Prakata Gayā Jala Vātee Dhusi Dharme Mā Khakholka Ţeekā Dhee: II

i. The mathematics of the names beginning with these 32 letters is being mentioned here.

The verse	**Beginning letter**	**Number of names**
Arva	*A*	40
Nata	*Ā*	10
Tri	*E*	3 *
Dve	*EE*	2 *
Ishu	*U*	5 *
Eka	*EE*	1 *
Dve	*O*	2 *
Chatu:	*Am*	4 *
Kanja	*Ka*	81
Pāna	*Kha*	1
Vara	*Ga*	24
Dheerā:	*Ca*	29
Kim	*Cha*	1

The verse	Beginning letter	Number of names
Dhoopa	*Ja*	19
Dvi	*Da*	2
Stambha	*Ta*	46
Chala	*Da*	37
Bhaya	*Dha*	14
Māmse	*Na*	75
Pade	*Pa*	81
Vara:	*Ba*	24
Sanga:	*Bha*	37
Prakata	*Ma*	112
Gayā	*Ya*	13
Jala	*Ra*	38
Vātee	*La*	14
Dhusi	*Va*	79
Dharma	*Sha*	59
Mā	*Şha*	5
Khakholka	*Sa*	122
Ţeekā	*Ha*	11
Dhee:	*Ksha*	9
	Total	1000

* The numbers marked as * are explicitly mentioned say using cryptic method. *Ishu* indicates the famous five arrows in the hands of cupid. The other numbers are as per *Kaţapayādi* method of *Vararuchi*.

ii. These 1000 names beginning with 32 letters can be split in one other way also. In *Navāvarŋa* worship, it is imagined that these 8 *Vāgdevees* are dwelling in the seventh hall. In that context the 51 *mātrukā* letters are distributed to all these 8 *Vāgdevees*. It is as below:

Vāgdevee	***Mātrukā* letters**	**The first letter of the names**	**Number of names beginning with the letters of *Vāgdevees***
Vasinee	16 – *A, Ā, E, EE, U, Ū, Ru, Roo, Lu, Loo, Ĕ, I, O, Ou, Am, A*:	8 - *A, Ā, E, EE, U, EE, O, Am,*	68
Kāmeshvaree	5 – *Ka, Kha, Ga, Gha, Gna*	3 - *Ka, Ga, Gha*	106
Moodhinee	5 – *Ca, Cha, Ja, Jha, Jna*	3 - *Ca, Cha, Ja*	48

Vāgdevee	*Mātrukā* letters	The first letter of the names	Number of names beginning with the letters of *Vāgdevees*
Vimalā	5 – *Ta, Tha, Da, Dha, Ṇa*	1 –*Ta*	2
Aruŋā	5 – *Ta, Tha, Da, Dha, Na*	4 - *Ta, Da, Dha, Na*	172
Jayinee	5 – *Pa, Pha, Ba, Bha, Ma*	4 - *Pa, Ba, Bha, Ma*	254
Sarveshvaree	4 – *Ya, Ra, La, Va*	4 – *Ya, Ra, La, Va*	144
Koulinee	6 – *Sha, Şha, Sa, Ha, Ļa, Ksha*	6 – *Sha, Şha, Sa, Ha, Ksha*	206
Total	51	32	1000

Due to the compound of the seed letters, it is apt to map these eight types of names to eight *Vāgdevees*.

VIII. *Ittham Nāmasahasram Sādhakalokopakārakam Vihitam* I
Guŋagaŋasadbhāvāvāsritya Brahmaŋo'mbāyā: II

Thus this *Sahasranāmā* has been told explaining the characters and the forms of existence and non-existence of *Śreedevee*, as a very big help supporting the world of worshippers.

i. In Samskrit language there are presiding deities attached to each of the letters starting from '*A*'. They are 51Devee*s* – *Amrutā, Ākarshiŋee, Indrāŋi* till *Kshamāvati*. The worshippers of these Devee*s* are mentioned in this verse as *Sādhakaloka*. Hence just by pronouncing the letters lot of accomplishments can be achieved. Each name not only describes *Śreedevee*, but also chants the Devee concerned to the beginning letter of that name.
ii. The forms of these 51Devee*s* have been drawn in the roof of the upper hall of the *Harasiddanātāmbikā* temple at Ujjain. Ujjain is one of the 51 *peeţas* mentioned by the name *Pajnchāshatpeetharoopiŋee*.
iii. This verse says that *Śreedevee* is the *Brahmam*. In that, only in the *Saguŋabrahma* state has form and qualities. This indicates those qualities and the forms of existence and non-existence of *Śreedevee*.
iv. In general the words are interpreted on account of 4 reasons viz., character, action, caste and tradition. All the names are interpreted based on these reasons only.
v. It has been mentioned in many a place, that since all the sounds indicate *Śreedevee*, the countless benefit can be reaped by chanting the names individually are in a combined manner as a garland of *mantra*s.

vi. Some names have the power of granting some special results. Those intending on these results can chant them in an ardent manner. For instance, *Annadā*, *Vasudā*, etc.

vii. In the explanation to this *paribhāshā* verse, *Śree Bhāskararāya* has mentioned lot of rare things. All those things have not been dealt with here.

IX. *Mantradyo Jayati Guŋee Navacharaŋastrimshadardhābha*: I
Ekārdhatrāya Deho Bhoomada Hāreeta Shabdapāllecha: II

i. In the forthcoming verses, the letters of each of the names are being mentioned.

ii. This verse prays to the teacher and as well explains the splitting relating to the first 63 names.

iii. *Mantradya*: - the teacher, who is the root cause of all the *mantras*. *Jayati* – shines in an excellent manner.

iv. *Guŋee* – in reality the *Brahmam* is without any qualities, but it is meant here as with attributes since it is in the form of various *mantras*. The statement worshipping the teacher – *Vidyāvatārasamsidyai Sveekrutānekavigraha* may be compared.

v. *Navacharaŋa* – new, novel and reddish-white feet of the teacher. Or if the word *charaŋa* can be taken to mean *chakras*, this can be interpreted as to indicate nine chakras – from *Trilokya Mohanam* till *Sarvānandamaya Chakra*. The teacher is integrated with and nothing different from all these *chakras*.

vi. *Trimshadardhābha*: - half of 30, i.e. 15. It indicates the *Śreevidyā* called as *Panchadashākshari*. The teacher is integrated with and nothing different from this *mantra*.

vii. *Eka*: - the remaining one, i.e. the teacher is the *brahmam*.

viii. *Ardhatrāyadėha*: - the form of *Kunḍalinee* within 3.5 rounds – the teacher has it.

ix. *Bhoomadahāree* – one who removes the ego, which is so big like the earth. Or *Bhoomā* means bliss. He who gives it.

x. *Itashabdapāllecha*: - *bda* means entangled lock of hair - *Shiva* is with that and hence called as *Shabda*. Enabler to reach his feet. *Shabdapālla*: - one who has reached the feet of *Shiva* and has become *Ěshwar*. That is, the teacher is integrated and not different from *Ěshwar*, who can be attained through devotion with *Shiva*.

xi. Now let us see the names indicated by these words:

   a. *Mantradya*: - *Praŋava mantra* (*Om*) is the one to be chant in the beginning of all the *mantras*. Hence *Praŋava* has been indicated by the word *Mantradya*:. Each name of this *Sahasranāma* has to be chant by prefixing and suffixing *Om* to it. It is being described that otherwise the *mantra* will spill over. Each name has to be packed in between two *Oms*.

b. *Guŋee* – *Ga* = 3, *ŋa* = 5 - the first name (*Shreemātā*) has 3 letters and the second (*Shreemahārānjee*) has 5 letters.
In the same manner *Navacharaŋā*: – 9 names as quarter of a verse - that is, 9 names containing 8 letters each.
Trimsadardhābha: - 30 names in the form of half verses – that is, 30 names containing 16 letters each.

Bha: - next name is 4 lettered.
Eka: - one name contains the remaining 12 letters.
Ardhatrāya – three half verse names, that is 3 names containing 16 letters each.
De – one name with 8 letters.
Ho - one name with 8 letters.
Bhoo: - next is one name with 4 letters.
Ma – one name with 5 letters.
Da – one name with 8 letters.
Hā – one name with 8 letters.
Ree – one name with 2 letters.
Ta – one name with 6 letters.
Shabdapād – 7 names with quarter of the verse viz., 8 letters.
Le – one name with 3 letters.
Cha: - one name with 5 letters.

Thus 63 names starting from *Shreemātā* till *Kāmadāyinee* have been accounted here.

Gu	3	*Shreemātā* (1)
Ŋee	5	*Shreemahārānjee*
Navacharaŋā:	9 X 8	*Shreematsimhāsaneshwaree, Chidagnikuŋḍasambhootā, Devakāryasamudyutā, Udyadbhānusahasrābhā, Caturbahusamanvitā, Rāgasvaroopapāshāḍhyā, Krodhākārāngkushojvalā, Manorupekshukodaŋḍā, Panjchatanmātrasāyakā*
Trimsadardhābha :	30 X 16	*Nijārunaprabhāpooramajjadbrahmaŋḍamaŋḍalā, Champakāshokapunnāgasougandhikalasatkachā, Kuruvindamaŋishreneekanatkoteeramaŋḍitā, Ashţameechandra Vibhrājadalikasthala Shobhitā, Mukhachandrakalanngkābhamruganābhivisheshakā, Vadanasmaramāngalyagruhatoranachillikā, Vaktralakshmee Pareevāhachalanmeenābhalochanā,*

		Navachampakapushpābhanāsādaŋḑavirājitā, Tārākāntitiraskāri Nāsābharaŋabhāsurā, Kadambamamjareekluptakarnapooramanoharā, Tāţangkayugaleebhootatapanodupamaŋḑalā, Padmarāgashilādarshaparibhāvikapolabhooh, Navavidrumabimba Shreenyakkāridashanaccadā Shuddhavidyāngkurākāradvijapaktidwayojjwala, Karpooraveetikāmodasamākarshidigantarā, Nijasallāpamādhuryavinirbhartsitakacchapee, Mandasmitaprabhāpooramajjatkāmeshamānasā, Anākalitasādrushyachibukashreevirājitā, Kāmeshabaddhamāngalyasootrashobhitakandharā Kanakāngadakeyoorakamaneeyabhujānvitā, Ratnagraiveyachintākalolamuktāphalānvitā, Kāmeshvarapremaratnamaŋiprathipaŋastanee, Nābhyālavālaromālilatāphalakuchadvayee, Lakshyaromalatādhāratāsamunneyamadhyamā, Stanabhāradalanmadhyapaţţabandhavalitrayā, Aruŋārunakousumbhavastrabhāsvatkateetatee, Ratnakimkinikāramyarashanādāmabhooshitā, Kāmeshanjātasoubhāgyamārdavorudvayānvitā, Mānikyamukuţākārajānudvayavirājitā, Indragopaparikshiptasmaratoonābhajanghikā
Bha:	4	Goodhagulphā
Eka:	1 2	Koormaprushţhajayishnuprapadānvitā
Ardhatrāya	3 X 1 6	Nakhadeedhitisamchannanamajjana Tamoguŋā, Padadvayaprabhājālaparākrutasaroruhā, SinjānamaŋimamjeeramaŋḑitaŚreepadāmbujā
De	8	Marāleemandagamanā
Ho	8	Mahālāvaŋyashevadhi:
Bhoo:	4	Sarvārunā
Ma	5	Anavadyāngee
Da	8	Sarvābharaŋabhooshitā
Hā	8	Shivakāmeshvarāngkasthā
Ree	2	Shivā
Ta	6	Svādheenavallabhā

Shabdapād	7 X 8	*Sumerumadhyasrunggasthā* *Śreemannagaranāyikā* *Chintāmaŋigruhāntasthā* *PanjchaBrahmasanasthitā* *Mahāpadmātaveesamsthā* *Kadambavanavāsinee* *Sudhāsāgaramadhyasthā*
Le	3	*Kāmākshee*
Cha:	5	*Kāmadāyinee* (63)

X. *Ardhachaturvimshati Tanu Bhedodbhava Guŋagaŋo Dashapāt* I
Dambhāvaha Gomedā Bhāveha Chaturguŋa Guŋair Gangā II

The 64 names from 64 till 127 are being dealt with in this verse -

Ardhachaturvimshati	24 x 16	*Devarshigaŋasanghāta Stooyamānātma Vaibhavā* (64) to *Shaktikooţaikatāpannakatyadhobhāgadhāriŋee*
Ta	6	*Moolamantratmikā*
Nubhe	10	*Moolakooţatrayakalebarā*
Do	8	*Kulāmrutaikarasikā*
D	8	*Kulasanketapālinee* (special rule)
Bha	4	*Kulānganā*
Va	4	*Kulāntasthā*
Gu	3	*Koulinee*
Ņa	5	*Kulayoginee*
Ga	3	*Akulā*
Ņo	5	*Samayāntasthā*
Dashapāt	10 x 8	From *Samayācāratatparā* till *Tadillatāsamaruchi:*
Da	8	*Shaţchakroparisamsthitā*
Bhā	4	*Mahāshakti:*
Va	4	*Kunḑalinee*
Ha	8	*Bisatantutaneeyasee*
Go	3	*Bhavānee*
Me	5	*Bhāvanāgamyā*
Dā	8	*Bhavārabyakutārikā*
Bhā	4	*Bhadrapriyā*
Ve	4	*Bhadramoortti:*
Ha	8	*Bhaktasoubhāgyadārinee*

Chatur:	4 x 4	*Bhaktipriyā, Bhaktigamyā, Bhaktivashyā, Bhayāpahā*
Gu	3	*Shāmbhavee*
Ṇā	5	*Shāradārādhyā*
Gu	3	*Sharvānee*
Ṇai:	5	*Sharmadāyinee*
Ga	3	*Shānkaree*
Ngā	3	*Shreekaree* (127)

XI. *Rājā Chaturbalendro Bhootvā Balirāgamāndvdash* I
Guŋa Gaŋa Gouŋyam Gaŋa Gomārge Mārge Mrugeŋa Bhavet II

The 46 names from 128 to 173 are listed below:

Rā	2	*Sādhvee* (128)
Jā	8	*Sharacchandranibhānanā*
Chatur:	4 x 4	*Shātodaree, Shāntimatee, Nirādhārā, Niranjanā*
Ba	3	*Nirlepā*
Le	3	*Nirmalā*
Ndro	2	*Nityā*
Bhoo	4	*Nirākārā*
Tvā	4	*Nirākulā*
Ba	3	*Nirguŋā*
Li	3	*Nishkalā*
Rā	2	*Shāntā*
Ga	3	*Nishkāmā*
Mān	5	*Nirupaplavā*
Dvi	2 x 4	*Nityamuktā, Nirvikārā, Nishprapanjchā, Nirāshrayā*
Dasha	10 x 4	*Nityashuddhā, Nityabuddhā, Niravadyā, Nirantarā, Nishkāraŋā, Nishkalankā, Nirupādhi:, Nireeshvarā*
Gu	3	*Neerāgā*
Ṇa	5	*Rāgamathanee*
Ga	3	*Nirmadā*
Ṇa	5	*Madanāshinee*
Gou	3	*Nishcintā*
Ṇyam	5	*Nirahankārā* (special rule)
Ga	3	*Nirmohā*
Ṇa	5	*Mohanāshinee*
Go	3	*Nirmamā*
Mā	5	*Mamatāhantree*
Rge	3	*Nishpāpā*
Mā	5	*Pāpanāshinee*

Rge	3	*Nishkrodhā*
Mru	5	*Krodhashamanee* (special rule)
Ge	3	*Nirlobhā*
Ṇa	5	*Lobhanāshinee*
Bha	4	*Ni:samshayā*
Vet	4	*Samshayaghnee* (173)

XII. *Guŋa Bhuvi Gomruga Srunge Moolamagā Bhogagouravābhave* I
Sthooŋānga Mahānto Dvirbhava Dooshita Vākchatur Vibhājoshtou II

The 49 names from 174 to 222 are listed below:

Gu	3	*Nirbhavā* (174)
Ṇa	5	*Bhavanāshinee*
Bhu	4	*Nirvikalpā*
Vi	4	*Nirābādhā*
Go	3	*Nirbhedā*
Mru	5	*Bhedanāshinee* (special rule 2)
Ga	3	*Nirnāshā*
Sru	5	*Mrutyumathanee* (special rule)
Nge	3	*Nishkriyā*
Moo	5	*Nishparigrahā*
La	3	*Nistulā*
Ma	5	*Neelachikurā*
Ghā	4	*Nirapāyā*
Bho	4	*Niratyayā*
Ga	3	*Durlabhā*
Gou	3	*Durgamā*
Ra	2	*Durgā*
Vā	4	*Du:hhahantree*
Bha	4	*Sukhapradā*
Ve	4	*Dushţadoorā*
Sthoo	7	*Durāchārashamanee*
Ṇa	5	*Doshavarjitā*
Nga	3	*Sarvanjā*
Ma	5	*Sāndrakaruŋā*
Hā	8	*Samānādhika Varjitā*
Nto	6	*Sarvashaktimayee*
Dvi	5 x 2	*Sarvamangalā, Sadgatipradā*
Bha	4	*Sarveshvaree*
Va	4	*Sarvamayee*
Dhoo	8	*Sarvamantraswroopiŋi*

Shi	6	*Sarvayantrātmikā*
Ta	6	*Sarvatantraroopā*
Vāk	4	*Manonmanee*
Chatur:	4 x 4	*Māheshvaree, Mahādevee, Mahālakshmee, Mruḍapriyā*
Vi	4	*Mahāroopā*
Bhā	4	*Mahāpoojyā*
Jo	8	*Mahāpātakanāshinee,*
Ashţou	4 x 8	*Mahāmāyā, Mahāsatvā, Mahāshakti:, Mahārati:, Mahābhogā, Mahaishvaryā, Mahāveeryā, Mahābalā* (222)

XIII. *Bhuvihi Chatur Dehārdham Chatushpadārdham Bhavedavibhou Pādatrāyaguŋado Dvir Gouŋārho Dvir Vibhāgasharaveera*:

The 40 names from 223 to 262 are listed below:

Bhu	4	*Mahābuddhi*: (223)
Vi	4	*Mahāsiddhi*:
Hi	8	*Mahāyogesvareshvaree*
Chatur	4 x 4	*Mahātantra, Mahāmantra, Mahāyantrā, Mahāsanā*
De	8	*Mahāyāgakramāyādhyā*
Hā	8	*Mahābhairavapoojitā*
Ardham	16	*Maheshvaramahākalpamahātāndavasākshinee*
Chatushpada	4 x 8	*Mahākāmeshamahishi, Mahātripurasundaree, Catushshashţiyupacārādhyā, Catushshashţikalāmayee*
Ardham	16	*Mahācatushshashţikoţiyogineeganasevitā*
Bha	4	*Manuvidyā*
Ve	4	*Candravidyā*
Da	8	*Candramaŋḍalamadhyagā*
Vi	4	*Cāruroopā*
Bhou	4	*Cāruhāsā*
Pādatrāya	3 x 8	*Cārucandrakalādharā, Carācarajagannāthā, Cakrarājaniketanā*
Gu	3	*Pārvatee*
Ŋa	5	*Padmanayanā*
Do	8	*Padmarāgasamaprabhā*
Dvi:	2 x 8	*Panchapretāsanāseenā, Parabrahmasvaroopiŋee*

Gou	3	*Cinmayee*
Ŋā	5	*Paramānandā*
Rho	8	*Vinjānaghanaroopiŋee*
Dvir	2 x 8	*Dhyānadhyātrughyeyaroopā,* *Dharmādharmavivarjitā*
Vi	4	*Vishvaroopā*
Bhā	4	*Jāgarinee*
Ga	3	*Svapantee*
Sha	5	*Taijasātmikā*
Ra	2	*Suptā*
Vee	4	*Pranjātmikā*
Ra:	2	*Turyā* (262)

XIV. *Divi Bhārata Bhuvitādaghamrudujamgamabhovadārtdhadivā* I
Vāk Chaturangridvayardhā Tatphala Moolam Tadeva Vādabalam II

The 40 names from 263 to 302 are listed below:

Di	8	*Sarvāvasthāvivarjitā* (263)
Vi	4	*Srushţikartree*
Bhā	4	*Brahmaroopā*
Ra	2	*Goptree*
Ta	6	*Govindaroopiŋee*
Bhu	4	*Samhārinee*
Vi	4	*Rudraroopā*
Tā	6	*Tirodhānakaree*
Da	3	*Ishvaree*
Gha	4	*Sadāshivā*
Mru	5	*Anugrahadā* (special rule 2)
Du	8	*Panchakrutyaparāyanā*
Jam	8	*Bhānumaŋḑalamadhyasthā*
Ga	3	*Bhairavee*
Ma	5	*Bhagamālinee*
Bho	4	*Padmāsanā*
Va	4	*Bhagavatee*
Dā	8	*Padmanābhasahodaree*
(A)rtdha	16	*Unmeshanimishotpannavipannabhuvanāvalee*
Di	8	*Sahasrasheershavadanā*
Vā	4	*Sahasrākshee*
Vāk	4	*Sahasrapāt*
Chaturangri	4 x 8	*Ābrahmakeeţajananee, Varŋāshramavidhāyinee,* *Nijānjāroopanigamā, Puŋyāpuŋyaphlapradā*

Dvayardhā	2 x 16	*Srutiseemantasindoorikrutapādābjadhoolikā, Sakalāgamasamdohashaktisamputamouktikā*
Tat	6	*Purushārthapradā*
Pha	2	*Poorŋā*
La	3	*Bhoginee*
Moo	5	*Bhuvaneshvaree*
Lam	3	*Ambikā*
Ta	6	*Anādinidhanā*
De	8	*Haribrahmendrasevitā*
Va	4	*Nārāyaŋee*
Vā	4	*Nātharoopā*
Da	8	*Nāmaroopavivarjitā*
Ba	3	*Hreemkāree*
Lam	3	*Hreematee* (302)

XV. *Rājatarekhita Lingaraharattair Dvir Vibhooratou Reta*: I
Hālāmadabhuvirakto Guŋadambhovāji Geerŋam Dvi: II

The 38 names from 303 to 340 are listed below:

Rā	2	*Hrudyā* (303)
Ja	8	*Heyopādeyavarjitā*
Ta	6	*Rājarājārchitā*
Re	2	*Rānjee*
Khi	2	*Ramyā*
Ta	6	*Rājeevalochanā*
Li	3	*Ranjanee*
Ngai	3	*Ramanee*
Ra	2	*Rasyā*
Ha	8	*Ranatkingkinimekhalā*
Ra	2	*Ramā*
Ttair	6	*Rākenduvadanā*
Dvir	2 x 4	*Ratiroopā, Ratipriyā*
Vi	4	*Rakshākaree*
Bhoo	4	*Rākshasaghnee*
Ra	2	*Rāmā*
Tou	6	*Ramanalampaţā*
Re	2	*Kāmyā*
Ta:	6	*Kāmakalāroopā*
Hā	8	*Kadambakusumapriyā*
Lā	3	*Kalyānee*
Ma	5	*Jagateekandā*

Da	8	*Karuŋārasa Sāgarā*
Bhu	4	*Kalāvatee*
Vi	4	*Kalālāpā*
Ra	2	*Kāntā*
Kto	6	*Kādambareepriyā*
Gu	3	*Varadā*
Ŋa	5	*Vāmanayanā*
Da	8	*Vārunee Madavihvalā*
Mbho	4	*Vishvādhikā*
Vā	4	*Vedavedyā*
Ji	8	*Vindhyāchalanivāsinee*
Geer	3	*Vidhātree*
Ŋam	5	*Vedajananee*
Dvi:	2 x 4	*Vişhŋumāyā, Vilāsinee* (340)

XVI. *Mrugajo Dvirbāla: Khe Jeevābham Panchapadārdham* I
Guŋa Bhoovaratejordham RatiguŋaleshoḑahedgaŋamDuritam II

The 38 names from 341 to 378 are listed below:

Mru	5	*Kshetrasvaroopā* (341)
Ga	3	*Kshetreshee*
Jo	8	*Kshetrakshetranjapālinee*
Dvi:	2 x 8	*Kshayavruddhivinirmuktā, Kshetrapālasamarchitā*
Bā	3	*Vijayā*
La:	3	*Vimalā*
Khe	2	*Vandyā*
Jee	8	*Vandārujanavatsalā*
Vā	4	*Vāgvādinee*
Bham	4	*Vāmakeshee*
Panchapada	5 x 8	*Vahnimaŋḑalavāsinee, Bhaktimatkalpalatikā, Pashupāshavimochanee, Samhrutāsheshapāshaŋḑā, Sadāchārapravarttikā*
Ardham	16	*Tāpatrayāgnisantaptasamāhlādanachandrikā*
Gu	3	*Tarunee*
Ŋa	5	*Tāpasārādhyā*
Bhoo	4	*Tanumadhyā*
Va	4	*Tamopahā*
Ra	2	*Chiti:*
Te	6	*Tatpadalakshyārthā*
Jo	8	*Chidekarasaroopiŋee*

Rdham	16	*Svātmānandalavee Bhootabrahmadyānanda Santati*:
Ra	2	*Parā*
Ti	6	*Pratyakchiteeroopā*
Gu	3	*Pashyantee*
Ŋa	5	*Paradevatā*
Le	3	*Madhyamā*
Sho	5	*Vaikhareeroopā*
Da	8	*Bhakta Mānasahamsikā*
He	8	*Kāmeshvaraprāŋanādee*
Dga	3	*Krutanjā*
Ŋam	5	*Kāmapoojitā*
Du	8	*Shrungārarasasampoorŋā*
Ri	2	*Jayā*
Tam	6	*Jālandharasthitā* (378)

XVII. *Dvedve Chedvedve Bhavadohada Bhuvilesha Sheela Jalamohai*: I
Dvyardhachaturbhavagā: *Smo Bhuvi Jalashobhā Bhagola*: *Khe* II
The 44 names from 379 to 422 are listed below:

Dve	2 x 8	*Oḍyānapeethanilayā* (379), *Bindumaŋḍalavāsinee*
Dve	2 x 8	*Rahoyāgakrmārādhyā*, *Rahastarpaŋatarpitā*
Che	6	*Sadya*: *Prasādinee*
Dve	2 x 5	*Vishvasākshinee*, *Sākshivarjitā*
Dve	2 x 8	*Shadanggadevatāyuktā*, *Shāḍguŋyaparipooritā*
Bha	4	*Nityaklinnā*
Va	4	*Nirupamā*
Do	8	*Nirvānasukhadāyinee*
Ha	8	*Nityāshoḍashikāroopā*
Da	8	*Shreekanthārdhashareerinee*
Bhu	4	*Prabhāvatee*
Vi	4	*Prabhāroopā*
Le	3	*Prasiddhā*
Sha	5	*Parameshvaree*
Shee	5	*Moolaprakruti*:
La	3	*Avyaktā*
Ja	8	*Vyaktāvyaktasvaroopiŋee*
La	3	*Vyāpinee*
Mo	5	*Vividhākārā*
Hai:	8	*Vidhyā Vidhyāsvaroopiŋee*
Dvyardha	2 x 16	*Mahākāmeshanayanakumudāhlādakou Mudee*, *Bhaktahārdatamobhedabhānumadbhānusantati*:

Chatur	4 x 4	*Shivadootee, Shivārādhyā, Shivamoortti: Shivamkaree*
Bha	4	*Shivapriyā*
Va	4	*Shivaparā*
Gā:	3	*Shishţeshţā*
Smo	5	*Shishţapoojitā*
Bhu	4	*Aprameyā*
Vi	4	*Svaprakāshā*
Ja	8	*Manovāchāmagocharā*
La	3	*Chichchakti:*
Sho	5	*Chetanāroopā*
Bhā	4	*Jadashakti:*
Bha	4	*Jadātmikā*
Go	3	*Gāyatree*
La:	3	*Vyāhruti:*
Khe	2	*Sandhyā* (422)

XVIII. *Divi Kooţairudite Dve Dvir Dvir Geerŋā Vibhātinadee* I
Chatvāro Rooḍhaphalam Shambhurbhojo Balee Rājā II

The 36 names from 423 to 458 are listed below:

Di	8	*Dvijavrundanishevitā* (423)
Vi	4	*Tatvāsanā*
Koo	1	*Tat*
Tai	1	*Tvam*
Ru	2	*Aye*
Di	8	*Panjchakoshāntarasthitā*
Te	6	*Nisseemamahimā*
Dve	2 x 5	*Nityayouvanā, Madashālinee*
Dvir	2 x 8	*Madaghoorŋitaraktākshee, Madapāţalagaŋdabhoo:*
Dvir	2 x 8	*Chanḍana Drava Digdhānggee, Chāmpeyakusumapriyā*
Gee	3	*Kushalā*
Rŋā	5	*Komalākārā*
Vi	4	*Kurukullā*
Bhā	4	*Kuleshvaree*
Ti	6	*Kulakuŋḍālayā*
Na	10	*Koulamārgatatparasevitā*
Dee	8	*Kumāragananāthāmbā*
Chatvāro	4 x 2	*Tushţi:, Pushţi:, Mati:, Dhruti:*
Roo	2	*Shānti:*

Dha	4	*Svastimatee*
Pha	2	*Kānti*:
Lam	3	*Nandinee*
Sham	5	*Vighnanāshinee*
Bhur	4	*Tejovatee*
Bho	4	*Trinayanā*
Jo	8	*Lolāksheekāmaroopiŋee*
Ba	3	*Mālinee*
Lee	3	*Hamsinee*
Rā	2	*Mātā*
Jā	8	*Malayāchalavāsinee* (458)

XIX. *Galaphapha Shobhāvega*: *Shambhorvede Chaturhoma*: I
Bhoordvistādrājako Modāngaŋa Vāsato Natihrut II
The 35 names from 459 to 493 are listed below:

Ga	3	*Sumukhee* (459)
La	3	*Nalinee*
Pha	2	*Subhroo*:
Pha	3	*Shobhanā* (special rule)
Sho	5	*Suranāyikā*
Bhā	4	*Kālakaŋţhee*
Ve	4	*Kāntimatee*
Ga:	3	*Kshobhiŋee*
Sham	5	*Sookshmaroopiŋee*
Bhor	4	*Vajreshvaree*
Ve	4	*Vāmadevee*
De	8	*Vayo'vasthāvivarjitā*
Chatur	4 x 4	*Siddheshvaree, Siddhavidyā,Siddhamātā, Yashasvinee*
Ho	8	*Vishuddhichakra Nilayā*
Ma:	5	*Araktavarŋā*
Bhoor	4	*Trilochanā*
Dvi	2 x 8	*Khaţvānggādipraharanā, Vadanaikasamanvitā*
Stād	6	*Pāyasānnapriyā*
Rā	2	*Tvaksthā*
Jā	8	*Pashulokabhayangkaree*
Eko	11	*Amrutādimahāshaktisamvrutā*
Mo	5	*Ḍākineeshvaree*
Dā	8	*Anāhatābjanilayā*
Naa	3	*Shyāmābha*
Ŋa	5	*Vadanadvayā*

Vā	4	*Damshţrojvalā*
Sa	7	*Akshamālādidharā*
To	6	*Rudhirasamsthitā*
Na	10	*Kālarātryādishaktyoughavrutā*
Ti	6	*Snigdoudana Priyā*
Hrut	8	*Mahāveerendravaradā* (493)

XX. *Panchapadee*: *Bhāvichatushpadee Dvicharaŋeeva Shambhorvāk* I
Chaturanghree Vashe Panchānghri Bhavedvaikam Chatuspadam *Cha Mama*II

The 39 names from 494 to 532 are listed below:

Panchapadee:	5 x 8	*Rākiŋyambāsvaroopiŋee* (494),*Maŋipoorābjanilayā*, *Vadanatrāyasamyutā*, *Vajrādikāyudhopetā*, *Ḍāmaryādibhirāvrutā*
Bhā	4	*Raktavarŋā*
Vi	4	*Māmsanishţā*
Chatushpadee	4 x 8	*Guḍānnapreetamānasā*, *Samastabhaktasukhadā*, *Lākinyambāsvaroopiŋee*, *Svādhishţānāmbujagatā*
Dvicharaŋee	2 x 8	*Chaturvaktramanoharā*, *Shoolādhyāyudha Sampannā*
Va	4	*Peeţavarŋā*
Sham	5	*Atigarvitā*
Bhor	4	*Medonishthā*
Vāk	4	*Madhupreetā*
Chaturanghree	4 x 8	*Bandhinyādisamanvitā*, *Dadhyannāshakahrudayā*, *Kākineeroopadhārinee*, *Moolādhārāmbujārooḍhā*
Va	4	*Panchavaktrā*
She	5	*Asthisamsthitā*
Panchānghri	5 x 8	*Angkushādipraharanā*, *Varadādinishevitā*, *Mudgoudanāshakachittā*, *Sākinyambāsvaroopiŋee*, *Ānjāchakrabjanilayā*
Bha	4	*Shuklavarŋā*
Ve	4	*Shadānanā*
Dva	4	*Majjāsamsthā*
Ikam	12	*Hamsavateemukhyashaktisamanvitā*
Chatuspadam	4 x 8	*Haridrānnaikarasikā*, *Hākineeroopadhārinee*, *Sahasradalapadmasthā*, *Sarvavarŋopashobhitā*
Cha	6	*Sarvāyudhadharā*
Ma	5	*Shuklasamsthitā*
Ma	5	*Sarvatomukhee* (532)

XXI. *Hedārā: Phalarekhārambha Vivāde Tamomshosti* I
Khedo Dehe Bheeshmo Deve Vātryanghrilinkgapha Le II

The 32 names from 533 to 564 are listed below:

He	8	*Sarvoudanapreetachittā* (533)
Dā	8	*Yākinyambāsvaroopiŋee*
Rā:	2	*Svāhā*
Pha	2	*Svadhā*
La	3	*Amati:*
Re	2	*Medhā*
Khā	2	*Sruti:*
Ra	2	*Smruti:*
Mbha	4	*Anuttamā*
Vi	4	*Puŋyakeertti:*
Vā	4	*Puŋyalabhyā*
De	8	*Puŋyashravanakeerttanā*
Ta	6	*Pulomajārchitā*
Mom	5	*Bandhamochanee*
Sho	5	*Bandhurālakā*
Sti	6	*Vimarsharoopiŋee*
Khe	2	*Vidhyā*
Do	8	*Viyadādijagatprasoo:*
De	8	*Sarvavyādhiprashamanee*
He	8	*Sarvamrutyunivārinee*
Bhee	4	*Agragaŋyā*
Shmo	5	*Achintyaroopā*
De	8	*Kalikalmashanāshinee*
Ve	4	*Kātyāyanee*
Vā	4	*Kālahantree*
Tryanghri	3 x 8	*Kamalāksha Nishevitā, Tāmboolapooritamukhee Dādimeekusumaprabhā*
Li	3	*Mrugākshee*
Nkga	3	*Mohinee*
Pha	2	*Mukhyā*
Le	3	*Mruḑānee* (564)

XXII. *Shambhorbhālema Jjajjeevābheedāchchare Triyanghri:* I
Bhavadrudha Bhaŋḑo Maŋḑo Gouŋārdham Bhooshilāshāḑhe II

The 31 names from 565 to 595 are listed below:

Sham	5	*Mitraroopiŋee* (565)
Bhor	4	*Nityatruptā*
Bhā	4	*Bhaktanidhi:*
Le	3	*Niyantree*
Ma	5	*Nikhilesvaree*
Jja	8	*Maitryādivāsanālabhyā*
Jjee	8	*Mahāpralayasākshinee*
Vā	4	*Parāshakti:*
Bhee	4	*Parānishthā*
Dā	8	*Pranjānaghanaroopiŋee*
Chcha	6	*Mādhveepānālasā*
Re	2	*Mattā*
Triyanghri:	3 x 8	*Mātrukāvarŋaroopiŋee, Mahākailāsanilayā Mrunālamrududorlatā*
Bha	4	*Mahaneeyā*
Va	4	*Dayāmoorti:*
Dru	8	*Mahāsāmrājyashālinee*
Dha	4	*Ātmavidyā*
Bhan	4	*Mahāvidyā*
Do	3	*Shreevidyā*
Ma	5	*Kāmasevitā*
Ndo	8	*Shreeshoḍashākshareevidyā*
Gou	3	*Trikooţā*
Ŋa	5	*Kāmakoţikā*
Ardham	16	*Kaţākshakingkaree Bhootakamalākoţisevitā*
Bhoo	4	*Shira:sthitā*
Shi	5	*Chandranibhā*
Lā	3	*Bhālasthā*
Shā	6	*Indradhanu:Prabhā*
Ḍhe	4	*Hrudayasthā* (595)

XXIII. *Bhedabhuvi Triyanghri Bhuvo Guŋagaŋajārdham Vibhejerdham* I
Bhargo Rogeŋaiko Moolaguror Daŋdamuŋdashilā II

The 35 names from 596 to 630 are listed below:

Bhe	4	*Raviprakhyā* (596)
Da	8	*Trikonāntaradeepikā*
Bhu	4	*Dākshāyanee*
Vi	4	*Daityahantree*

Triyanghri	3 x 8	*Dakshayanjavināshinee, Darāndolitadeerghākshee, Darahāsojjavalanmukhee*
Bhu	4	*Gurumoorti:*
Vo	4	*Guŋanidhi:*
Gu	3	*Gomātā*
Ŋa	5	*Guhajanmabhoo:*
Ga	3	*Deveshee*
Ŋa	5	*Daŋḍaneetisthā*
Ja	8	*Daharākāsharoopiŋee*
Ardham	16	*Pratipanmukhyarākāntatithimaŋḍalapoojitā*
Vi	4	*Kalātmikā*
Bhe	4	*Kalānāthā*
Ja	8	*Kāvyālāpavinodinee*
Ardham	16	*Sachāmararamāvāneesavyadakshiŋasevitā*
Bha	4	*Ādishakti:*
Rgo	3	*Ameyā*
Ro	2	*Atmā*
Ge	3	*Paramā*
Ŋa	5	*Pāvanākruti:*
Iko	11	*Anekakoţibrahmaŋḍajananee*
Moo	5	*Divyavigrahā*
La	3	*Kleemkāree*
Gu	3	*Kevalā*
Ror	2	*Guhyā*
Da	8	*Kaivalyapadadāyinee*
Ŋda	3	*Tripurā*
Mu	5	*Trijagadvandyā*
Ŋda	3	*Trimoortti:*
Shi	5	*Tridasheshvaree*
Lā	3	*Tryaksharee* (630)

XXIV. *Maŋḍiracharatām Vibhava: Shaivo Mārgo Mahān Hito'nuguŋa:* I
Gouŋeeleelārdree Bhāvārdhavibhedā Bhavedeva II

The 35 names from 631 to 665 are listed below:

Ma	5	*Divyagandhāḍhyā* (631)
Ndi	8	*Sindooratilakāñjchitā*
Ra	2	*Umā*
Cha	6	*Shailendratanayā*
Ra	2	*Gouree*

Tām	6	*Gandharvasevitā*
Vi	4	*Vishvagarbhā*
Bha	4	*Svarŋagarbhā*
Va:	4	*Avaradā*
Shai	5	*Vāgadheeshvaree*
Vo	4	*Dhyānagamyā*
Mā	5	*Aparicchedyā*
Rgo	3	*Njānadā*
Ma	5	*Njānavigrahā*
Hān	8	*Sarvavedāntasamvedyā*
Hi	8	*Satyānandasvaroopiŋee*
To	6	*Lopāmudrārchitā*
Anu	10	*LeelākluptaBrahmaŋḑamaŋḑalā*(special rule)
Gu	3	*Adrushyā*
Ŋa	5	*Drushyarahitā*
Gou	3	*Vinjātree*
Ŋee	5	*Vedyavarjitā*
Lee	3	*Yoginee*
Lār	3	*Yogadā*
Dree	2	*Yogyā*
Bhā	4	*Yogānandā*
Vā	4	*Yugamdharā*
Ardha	16	*Ichchāshaktinjānashaktikriyāshaktisvaroopiŋee*
Vi	4	*Sarvādhārā*
Bhe	4	*Supratishţhā*
Dā	8	*Sadasadroopadhārinee*
Bha	4	*Ashţamoortti:*
Ve	4	*Ajājetree*
De	8	*Lokayātrāvidhāyinee*
Va	4	*Ekākinee* (665)

XXV. *Bhoogeerŋābalakhedālambārambhāvibhorvaded Bhāvam* I
Hastee Dvirvaikam Vā Bhajate Vātoolamanda Mrugān II

The 34 names from 666 to 699 are listed below:

Bhoo	4	*Bhoomaroopā* (666)
Geer	3	*Nirdvaitā*
Ŋā	5	*Dvaitavarjitā*
Ba	3	*Annadā*
La	3	*Vasudā*

Khe	2	*Vruddhā*
Dā	8	*Brahmatmaikyasvaroopiŋee*
Lam	3	*Bruhatee*
Bā	3	*Brāhmanee*
Ram	2	*Brāhmee*
Bhā	4	*Brahmanandā*
Vi	4	*Balipriyā*
Bhor	4	*Bhāshāroopā*
Va	4	*Bruhatsenā*
De	8	*Bhāvābhāvavivarjitā*
Dbhā	4	*Sukhārādhyā*
Vam	4	*Shubhakaree*
Ha	8	*Shobhanā Sulabhā Gati*:
Stee	6	*Rājarājeshvaree*
Dvir	2 x 5	*Rājyadāyinee, Rājyavallabhā* (special rule 10 letters as 2 names)
Va	4	*Rājatkrupā*
(*E*)*Kam*	12	*Rājapeethaniveshitanijāshritā*
Vā	4	*Rājyalakshmee*:
Bha	4	*Koshanāthā*
Ja	8	*Chaturangabaleshvaree*
Te	6	*Sāmrājyadāyinee*
Vā	4	*Satyasandhā*
Too	6	*Sāgaramekhalā*
La	3	*Deekshitā*
Ma	5	*Daityashamanee*
Nda	8	*Sarvalokavashankaree*
Mru	5	*Sarvārtthadātree*
Gān	3	*Sāvitree* (699)

XXVI. *Dehaguŋād Bhavaleshād Dvisteroopam Divābhoori* I
Vārigaŋe Bhāvi Guŋāstripada Latābhāva Javavādā: II

The 36 names from 700 to 735 are listed below:

De	8	*Sachchidānandaroopiŋee* (700)
Ha	8	*Deshakālaparichchinnā*
Gu	3	*Sarvagā*
Ŋād	5	*Sarvamohinee*
Bha	4	*Sarasvatee*
Va	4	*Shāstramayee*

Le	3	*Guhāmbā*
Shād	5	*Guhyaroopiŋee*
Dvi	2 x 8	*Sarvopādhivinirmuktā, Sadāshivapativratā*
Ste	6	*Sampradāyeshvaree*
Roo	2	*Sādhu*
Pam	1	*Ĕ*
Di	8	*Gurumaŋḑalaroopiŋee*
Vā	4	*Kulotteernā*
Bhoo	4	*Bhagārādhyā*
Ri	2	*Māyā*
Vā	4	*Madhumatee*
Ri	2	*Mahee*
Ga	3	*Gaŋāmbā*
Ŋe	5	*Guhyakārādhyā*
Bhā	4	*Komalāngee*
Vi	4	*Gurupriyā*
Gu	3	*Svatantra*
Ŋās	5	*Sarvatantreshee*
Tripada	3 x 8	*Dakshiŋāmoortiroopiŋee, Sanakādi Samārādhyā, Shivanjnānapradāyinee*
La	3	*Chitkalā*
Tā	6	*Anandakalikā*
Bhā	5	*Premaroopā*
Va	5	*Priyamkaree*
Ja	8	*Nāmapārāyaŋapreetā*
Va	4	*Nandividyā*
Vā	4	*Naţeshvaree*
Dā:	8	*Mithyājagadadhishţhānā* (735)

XXVII. *Gou:shaive Virate Chaturanghritanurdvichchaturbalam Netu*: I
Dvirme Gangā Mātā Rajachchaturbhāvajalamadād Bhāvai: II

The 43 names from 736 to 778 are listed below:

Gou:	3	*Muktidā* (736)
Shai	5	*Muktiroopiŋee*
Ve	4	*Lāsyapriyā*

Vi	4	*Layakaree*
Ra	2	*Lajjā*
Te	6	*Rambhādi Vanditā*
Chaturanghri	4 x 8	*Bhavadāvasudhāvrushţi:, Pāpāraŋyadavānalā, Dourbhāgyatoolavātoolā, Jarādhvāntaraviprabhā*
Ta	6	*Bhāgyābdhichandrikā*
Nur	10	*Bhaktachittakeki Ghanā Ghanā*
Dvi	2 x 8	*Rogaparvatadambholi:, Mrutyudāruguthārikā*
Chchatur	4 x 4	*Maheshvaree, Mahākālee, Mahāgrāsā, Mahāshanā*
Ba	3	*Aparnā*
Lam	3	*Chaŋḑikā*
Ne	10	*Chaŋḑamuŋḑāsuranishoodinee*
Tu:	6	*Ksharāksharātmikā*
Dvir	2 x 5	*Sarvalokeshee, Vishvadhārinee*
Me	5	*Trivargadhātree*
Ga	3	*Subhagā*
Ngā	3	*Tryambakā*
Mā	5	*Triguŋātmikā*
Tā	6	*Svargāpavargadā*
Ra	2	*Shuddhā*
Ja	8	*Japāpushpa Nibhākruti:*
Chchatur	4 x 4	*Ojovatee, Dyutidharā, Yanjyaroopā, Priyavratā*
Bhā	4	*Durārādhyā*
Va	4	*Durādharshā*
Ja	8	*Pātaleekusumapriyā*
La	3	*Mahatee*
Ma	5	*Merunilayā*
Dā	8	*Mandārakusumapriyā*
Dbhā	4	*Veerārādhyā*
Vai:	4	*Virāḑroopā* (778)

XXVIII. *Guŋabhāve Geerŋe Dvichchaturhru Dām Vibhuguŋe Bhāvānga Makhe* I
Varaguŋa Chaturvibhājām Khala Mada Bhāvāntaranga Khilavaibhavā: II
The 48 names from 779 to 826 are listed below:

Gu	3	*Virajā* (779)
Ŋa	5	*Vishvatomukhee*

Bhā	4	*Pratyagroopā*
Ve	4	*Parākāshā*
Geer	3	*Prāŋadā*
Ŋe	5	*Prāŋaroopiŋee*
Dvi	2 x 8	*Mārtāṇḍa Bhairavārādhyā, Mantrineenyastarājyadhoo:*
Chchatur	4 x 4	*Tripureshee, Jayatsenā, Nistraiguŋyā, Parāparā*
Hru	8	*Satyanjānānandaroopā*
Dām	8	*Sāmarasyaparāyanā*
Vi	4	*Kapardinee*
Bhu	4	*Kalāmālā*
Gu	3	*Kāmadhuk*
Ŋe	5	*Kāmaroopiŋee*
Bhā	4	*Kalānidhi:*
Vā	4	*Kāvyakalā*
Nga	3	*Rasanjā*
Ma	5	*Rasashevadhi:*
Khe	2	*Pushţā*
Va	4	*Purātanā*
Ra	2	*Poojyā*
Gu	3	*Pushkarā*
Ŋa	5	*Pushkarekshanā*
Chatur	4 x 4	*Paramjyoti:, Parandhāma, Paramānu:, Parātparā*
Vi	4	*Pāshahastā*
Bhā	4	*Pāshahantree*
Jām	8	*Paramantravibhedinee*
Kha	2	*Moortā*
La	3	*Amoortā*
Ma	5	*Anityatruptā*
Da	8	*Munimānasa Hamsikā*
Bhā	4	*Satyavratā*
Vā	4	*Satyaroopā*
Nta	6	*Sarvāntaryāminee*
Ra	2	*Satee*
Nga	3	*Brahmaŋee*
Khi	2	*Brahma*
La	3	*Jananee*
Vai	4	*Bahuroopā*
Bha	4	*Budhārchitā*
Vā:	4	*Prasavitree* (826)

XXIX. *Gurugeerŋe Vibhajachaturguŋadango Mruduchaturmatāmshārdham* I
Dvirguŋaguŋitām Likhitām Chatu: Khacharatā Dahedruchim Roshāt II

The 49 names from 827 to 875 are listed below:

Gu	3	*Prachaṇḍā* (827)
Ru	2	*Ānjā*
Geer	3	*Pratishṭhā*
Ŋe	5	*Prakatākruti:*
Vi	4	*Prāneshvaree*
Bha	4	*Prāŋadātree*
Ja	8	*Panjchāshatpeetharoopiŋee*
Chatur	4 x 4	*Vishrungkhalā, Viviktasthā, Veeramātā, Viyatprasoo:*
Gu	3	*Mukundā*
Ŋa	5	*Muktinilayā*
Da	8	*Moolavigraharoopiŋee*
Ngo	3	*Bhāvanjā*
Mru	5	*Bhavarogaghnee*
Du	8	*Bhavachakrapravartinee*
Chatur	4 x 4	*Chanḍa:sārā, Shāstrasārā, Mantrasārā, Talodaree*
Ma	5	*Udārakeerti:*
Tām	6	*Uddhāma Vaibhavā*
Sha	5	*Varŋaroopiŋee*
Ardham	16	*Janma Mrutyajarā Taptajana Vishrāntidāyinee*
Dvir	2 x 8	*Sarvopanishadudghushṭā, Shāntyateetakalātmikā*
Gu	3	*Gambheerā*
Ŋa	5	*Gaganāntasthā*
Gu	3	*Garvitā*
Ŋi	5	*Gānalolupā*
Tām	6	*Kalpanārahitā*
Li	3	*Kāshṭhā*
Likhi: According to this one name with 3 letters and another with 2 letters. But *Kāshṭhā*, with 2 letters comes first and *Akāntā*, the name with 3 letters follows. The reason for the same is not known.		
Khi	2	*Akāntā*
Tām	6	*Kāntārdhavigrahā*
Chatu:	4 x 8	*Kāryakāraŋanirmuktā, Kāmakelitarangitā, Kanatkanakatātangkā, Leelā Vigrahadhārinee*
Kha	2	*Ajā*
Cha	6	*Kshayavinirmuktā*
Ra	2	*Mugdhā*
Tā	6	*Kshipraprasādinee*
Da	8	*Antarmukhasamārādhyā*
He	8	*Bahirmukhasudurlabhā*
Dru	2	*Trayee*
Chim	6	*Trivarganilayā*
Ro	2	*Tristhā*
Shāt	6	*Tripuramālinee* (875)

XXX. *ChaturardhabhavoDevo Vadanvibhe Dam Vibhāga Mārgeŋa* I
Gouŋatarangamati: *Khalu Shambhorvādam Charatryanghri*: II

The 38 names from 876 to 913 are listed below:

Chatur	4 x 4	*Nirāmayā* (876), *Nirālambā*, *Svātmārāmā*, *Sudhāsruti*:
Ardha	16	*Samsāra Pangka Nirmagna Samuddharaŋa Paŋḍitā*
Bha	4	*Yanjayapriyā*
Vo	4	*Yanja Kartree*
De	8	*Yajamānasvaroopiŋee*
Vo	4	*Dharmādhārā*
Va	4	*Dhanādhyakshā*
Dan	8	*Dhanadhānya Vivardhinee*
Vi	4	*Viprapriyā*
Bhe	4	*Vipraroopā*
Dam	8	*Vishvabhramanakārinee*
Vi	4	*Vishvagrāsā*
Bhā	4	*Vidrumābhā*
Ga	3	*Vaişhŋavee*
Mār	5	*Vişhŋuroopiŋee*
Ge	3	*Ayoni*:
Ŋa	5	*Yoninilayā*
Gou	3	*Kooţasthā*
Ŋa	5	*Kularoopiŋee*
Ta	6	*Veeragoshţheepriyā*
Ra	2	*Veerā*
Nga	3	*Naishkarmyā*
Ma	5	*Nātharoopiŋee*
Ti:	6	*Vinjānakalanā*
Kha	2	*Kalyā*
Lu	3	*Vidagdhā*
Sham	5	*Baindavāsanā*
Bhor	4	*Tatvādhikā*
Vā	4	*Tatvamayee*
Dam	8	*Tatvamarthasvaroopiŋee*
Cha	6	*Sāmagānapriyā*
Ra	2	*Somyā(Soumyā)*
Tryanghri:	3 x 8	*Sadāshivakuţumbinee*, *Savyāpasavyamārgasthā*, *Sarvāpadvininārinee* (913)

XXXI. *Khecharatā Dvirbhavadā Dehe Chaikā BhavedDevee* I
*Bhaghaŋe Chaturguŋā Bhoorbhavabhālashatena Gomedā*II
The 37 names from 914 to 950 are listed below:

Khe	2	*Svasthā* (914)
Cha	6	*Svabhāvamadhurā*
Ra	2	*Dheerā*
Tā	6	*Dheerasamarchitā*
Dvir	2 x 8	*Chaitanyārghyasamāradhyā,* *Chaitanyakusumapriyā*
Bha	4	*Sadoditā*
Va	4	*Sadātushţā*
Dā	8	*Tarunāḍityapātalā*
De	8	*DakshiŋāDakshiŋārādhyā*
He	8	*Darasmeramukhāmbujā*
Cha	6	*Koulinee Kevalā*
Ikā	11	*Anarghyakaivalyapadadāyinee*
Bha	4	*Stotrapriyā*
Ve	4	*Stutimatee*
Dde	8	*Srutisamstutavaibhavā*
Vee	4	*Manasvinee*
Bha	4	*Mānavatee*
Gha	3	*Maheshee*
Ŋe	5	*Manggalākruti:*
Chatur	4 x 4	*Vishvamātā, Jagaddhātree, Vishālākshee,* *Virāginee*
Gu	3	*Pragalbhā*
Ŋā	5	*Paramodārā*
Bhoor	4	*Parāmodā*
Bha	4	*Manomayee*
Va	4	*Vyomakeshee*
Bhā	4	*Vimānasthā*
La	3	*Vajrinee*
Sha	5	*Vāmakeshvaree*
Te	6	*Panjchayanjapriyā*
Na	10	*Panjchapretamanjchādhishāyinee*
Go	3	*Panjchamee*
Me	5	*Panjchabhooteshee*
Dā	8	*Panjchasangyopachārinee* (950)

XXXII. *Guŋa Gaŋaravim Khaḍesham Chaturhuntam Chaturdruḍhā Modam* I
Guŋi Hrudi Vibhajubhavad Guruvargam Cha Navacharaŋam Gadamtamiti II

The 50 names from 951 to 1000 are listed below:

Gu	3	*Shāshvatee* (951)
Ŋa	5	*Shāshvataishvaryā*
Ga	3	*Sharmadā*
Ŋa	5	*Shambhumohinee*
Ra	2	*Dharā*
Vim	4	*Dharasutā*
Kha	2	*Dhanyā*
Ge	3	*Dharminee*
Sham	5	*Dharmavardhinee*
Chatur	4 x 4	*Lokāteetā, Guŋāteetā, Sarvāteetā, Shamātmikā*
Ha	8	*Bandhookakusumaprakhyā*
Ra	2	*Bālā*
Ntam	6	*Leelāvinodinee*
Chatur	4 x 4	*Sumangalee, Sukhakaree, Suveshāḍhyā, Suvāsinee*
Dru	8	*Suvāsinyarchanapreetā*
Ḍhā	4	*Āshobhanā*
Mo	5	*Shuddhamānāsā*
In the name *Āshobhanā*, since the letter *Ā* is a hidden one, for the sake of tune, it is treated as a three letter name, *Shuddhamānāsā*, has 5 letters and hence *Dru* is considered as 8 letter name.		
Dam	8	*Bindutarpaŋasantushṭā*
Gu	3	*Poorvajā*
Ŋi	5	*Tripurāmbikā*
Hru	8	*Dashamudrāsamārādhyā*
Di	8	*Tripurāshreevashankaree*
Vi	4	*Njānamudrā*
Bha	4	*Njānagamyā*
Ja	8	*Njānanjeyasvaroopiŋee*
Bha	4	*Yonimudrā*
Vā	4	*Trikhaŋḍeshee*
Dgu	3	*Triguŋā*
Ru	2	*Ambā*
Var	4	*Trikoŋagā*
Gam	3	*Anaghā*
Cha	6	*Adbhutachāritrā*

Navacharaŋam	9 x 8	*Vānjchitārthapradāyinee, Abhyāsātishayanjātā, Shaḍadhvāteetaroopiŋee, Avyājakaruŋāmoorti:, Anjānadhvāntadeepikā, Ābālagopaviditā, Sarvānullangghyashāsanā, Shreechakrarājanilayā, Shreematripurasundaree*
Ga	3	*Shreeshivā*
Dam	8	*Shivashaktyaikyaroopiŋee*
Tam	6	*ŚreeLalitāmbikā* (1000)

i. The letter *Ta* indicates 6 letters. The name *Lalitāmbikā* has only 5 letters and hence *Śree* or *Om* is prefixed to it.

ii. *Iti* – being the last letter of this verse conveys that – thus the 1000 names are completed.

iii. As mentioned earlier, each verse can also be interpreted as a *stotra* praising the God. The first verse was interpreted in two ways - bowing to *Śreedevee* and explaining the number of letters. In the same manner this verse, in addition to the above numbers for the names, is also being meant as a prayer. (*Śree Bhāskararāya* has not given meaning for other verses as a *stotra* and has mentioned three reasons for the same – 1. The book will become a very big volume, 2. any learned person can do it and 3. not much of use)

.

iv. *Guŋagaŋaravim* – equivalent to Sun with a group of characters,
Khagesham - Head of *Devas*
Chaturharantam – remover of four types of sorrows or four types of births
Chaturdrudhā Modam – bestows four types of happiness
Guŋi Hrudi - in the heart with good quality
Iti – in the form of these 1000 names
Gadamtam – clearly communicated
Bhavād – to start with *Paramashiva*
Guruvargam - the lineage of teachers till our teacher
Vibhaja – bow, or meditate upon, or chant.

v. This *Paribhāshā* verse describing the last 50 names, is in such a way that beginning with *Śreenāthātigurutrayeem* and ending with *Vandegurormaŋḍalam* explain the entire hymn itself.

vi. This prayer to the teachers is also mentioned;

Sadāshivasamārambām Bagavad Pādamadyamām I
Admadāchārya Paryantām Vande Guruparampнrām II

vii. It is said that in all these names the meanings of *mahā* statements are hidden. To construe a meaning of a *mahā* statement, it should have a noun and verb. But, these names are only nouns. Hence it needs a verb. Then only the knowledge can be obtained. *Khātyāyana tantra* says; *Astibavanteepara*: *Prathama Purushe Aprayujyamnopyasti*. Following this rule it has to be interpreted that there is the auspicious *Śreemātā* (*Śreemātā Asti*). The other names are also to be considered in the same fashion.

XXXIII. *Śreemaŋisadreemvividhaguḍadarām Deshaichcha Pushţa Nādāpyām* I
Nāmasu Shatakārambhā Na Stobho Nāpi Shabdapunarukti: II

i. This verse indicates the first letter of every 100th name details given in the table below. Further there is absolutely no filler like or meaningless words like *Cha, Vai, Tu, Hi, Eva*, etc. There is also no duplication of names.

1	*Śree*	*Śreemātā*
101	*Maŋi*	*Maŋipoorāntaruditā*
201	*Sad*	*Sadgatipradā*
301	*Hreem*	*Hreemkāree*
401	*Vividha*	*Vividhākārā*
501	*Guḍa*	*Guḍānnapreetamānasā*
601	*Darān*	*Darāndolitadeerghākshee*
701	*Desh*	*Deshakālaparichchinnā*
801	*Pushţa*	*Pushţā*
901	*Nātha*	*Nātharoopiŋee*

ii. Out of these 10 words *Śree* is the first letter of 12 names. However it is apt for the first name *Śreemātā* in this context. Similarly there are 2 names beginning with *Maŋi*, two with *Hree* (301 and 302), but it is only 301 with *Hreem*. Starting with *Da* there are 3 names (601, 602 and 924), there is only one with *Darām*.

iii. The beginning letters of 100th names are mentioned in *Lalitopākyāna* also. However, the 701st, 801st and 901st names differ. This difference could be due to some other way of splitting the verses. *Śree Bhāskararāya*'s commentaries are based on these *Paribhāshā* verses only. He has indicated the other ways of splitting the names as *Suvachan* (good statement).

iv. There is more than one name with the same meanings. They cannot be treated as duplication. There is no duplication of names per se.

XXXIV. *Mativaradākāntā Dāvakāratohena Raktavarŋātou* I
Ākārasya Kvachana Tudapayor Togena Bhetayen Nāma II

i. The duplication is avoided by prefixing *A* to *Mati Varadā*and *Kāntā*, prefixing *Ā* to *Raktavarŋā* and in other places by prefixing suffixing other words/ letters.

ii. *Mati Varadā* and *Kāntā* are seen in two places and hence, in the second time, they are read as *Amati Avaradā*and *Akānta*.

iii. Similarly *Raktavarŋā* is read as *Āraktavarŋā* in the second time.

iv. *Moorttā, Moorttā* and *Anityatruptā* will be read as *Amoorttā* and *Anityatrupta*.

v. The name *Shobhanā* is read *Āshobhanā* in the second place.

vi. The names *Shobhanā Sulabhā Gati:, Koulinee Kevalā* and *Ajājetree* are to be treated as combined words.

XXXV. *Sādhvee Tatvamayeeti Dvedhā Tredhā Budobidyāt* I
Hamsavatee Chānarghyetyardhāntādeka Nāmaiva II

i. The name *Sādhvee* has to be split into two as *Sādhu* and *Ĕ*. Similarly *Tatvamayee* as three *Tat, Tvam* and *Ayee*. Both *Hamsavateemukhyashaktisamanvitā* and *Anargakaivalyapada Dāyinee* are long and single names. There is no need to mention about them for duplication, but for stressing the correct way of splitting they have been mentioned.

ii. In the case of duplicate names, whether the first one or the second one has to be prefixed or suffixed is based on *Salākshara Sūtras*.

XXXVI. *Shaktirnishţā Dhāma Jyoti: Parapoorvakam Dvipadam* I
Shobhana Sulabhā Sutistripadaika Padāni Sheshāŋi II

i. The four names *Shakti:, Nishtā, Dhāma* and *Jyoti:* are of two words each by prefixing *parā* to them. *Parā Shakti:, Parā Nishthā,Param Dhāma* and *Param Jyoti:*. The name *Shobhanā Sulabhā Gati:* is a name with 3 words. All the other names are made of single word.

XXXVII. *Nidhirātmā Dambhoļi: Shavdhiriti Nāma Bumlingam* I
Tatbrahma Dhāma Sādhujyoti: Kleebhe 'Vyayam Svadhāsvāhā II

i. The four *Guŋanidhi:, Ātmā, Rogaparvatadambholi:* and *Mahālāvaŋyashevadhi:* are all masculine names. The five *Tat, Brahma, Parandhāma, Sadhu* and *Pamjyoti* are neutral gender. *Svadhā* and *Svāhā* are genderless. All the other remaining names are feminine gender.

ii. These differences in genders are necessary in using these names while worshipping. For instance the masculine name *Guŋanidhi:* is to be used as *Guŋanidhaye Namahā*and *Ātmā* as *Ātmane Namahā*, etc. They are to be used with masculine case endings. In the same manner no case endings would be used for the genderless *Svadhā* and *Svāhā* names. They are used as they are – *Svadhā Namahā* and *Svāhā Namaha*. If some other meaning is interpreted for these two names they can be considered as feminine and used as *Svadhāyai Namahā* and *Svahāyai Namaha*. Though this is perfectly correct as per grammar, they are against these *Paribhāsha* verses.

XXXVIII. *Āvimshatita*: *Sārdhān Nānāphalasādhanatvokti*: I
Tasya Krmasho Vivruti: *Shatchatvārimshatā Shlokai*: II

i. Henceforth the last part of the hymn is being described. The results or fruits, in general that can be obtained by chanting this hymn are being explained in the first 20.5 verses. Further 46 verses explain the method of chanting this hymn focusing on a particular desire.

ii. *Karma Meemāmsāsāstra* says that a result called *Apoorvam* (rare), not known so far, can be obtained by doing the actions (*karmas*). Whoever does any action expecting any particular desire would get it – that is this *apoorva*. In this manner singing of *Lalitā Sahasranāma* acts like this *apoorva*.

iii. A special result which the actions do not have can be said as the devotion to *Śreedevee*.

XXXIX. *Nāmasraŋāvashyakatokti*: *Sārdhatrayodashshlokai*: I
Upsamhāra: *Sārdhai*: *Panchabhirekena Sootokti*: II

i. The necessity of singing this hymn has been explained in 13.5 verses and the following 5.5 verses explain the last part called *Upasamhāram*. Thus on the whole 85.5 verses were told by Lord *Hayagreeva*. The last one verse was told by sage *Soota*.

ii. The last 5.5 verses beginning with *Iti Tey Kathitam Stotram Rahasyam Kumbha Sambhava* form the closing remarks.

XL. *Iti Paribhāshāmaŋḍalamuditam Narasihma Yajvanā Vidushā* I
Satsampratāyagamakam Shivabhaktānandanāya Shivam II

   i. Thus this *Paribhāshāmaŋḍalam* was written by the great scholar *Narasimha Yajvā* to provide auspicious to the devotees of *Kāmeshwara* and *Kāmeshwaree* and also to join them in a good tradition.

   ii. The word *maŋḍalam* indicates these *Paribhāshā* verses.

   iii. *Vidushā* indicates the greatness of *Śree Narasimhmānanda Nātha*.

   iv. *Shivam* indicates auspiciousness. These verses end with an auspicious word.

Śree Bhāskararāya explained these 40 verses, which described the *Salākshara Sūtras*. He ends his commentaries with the below 5 verses.

1. *Śreevishwāmitravamshya*: *Shivajanaparo Bhāratee Somapheetee*
   Kāshyām Gambheerarāho Pudhamaŋirabhavad Bhāskaras Tasya Soonu: I
   Motachchāyāmitāyām Sharadi Sharadrutāvāshvine Kālayukte
   Shukle Soumye Navamyāmatanuta Lalitānāma Sāhasrabhāshyam II

i. There lived a great scholar by name *Gambheerarāja* in Banaras, who originated in the *Vishwāmitra* race (*gotra*), who involved himself always in the worship of *Shiva*, who was adorned with *Bhāratee* as title and also who performed *Soma* sacrifice. His son called *Bhāskara* wrote the commentary for *Lalitā Sahasranāma* on the ninth day of bright lunar fortnight, during Oct-Nov period of 1728 C.E. If the word *Motachchāyām* is converted into numbers using the *Kaṭapayādi* method we get 1785 (*Vikrama* era based year). We saw that this is the method which was used to describe the numbers in these verses.

ii. This book was written around 280 years back.

2. *Srutismrutinyāyapurāṇasūtra KoshāgamaŚreeguru Sampratāyāt* I
Nishchitya Nimadya Krtāpi Ṭeekā Shotyaiva Sadbhir Mayi Hārdvadbhi: II

i. Following the tradition recommended by *Sruti Smruti Nyāya Purāṇa Sūtra Kosha Āgama* and *Śreeguru* and as a gist of all these, this commentary has been written. Still this is fit for testing and correction by the great scholars who have compassion on me.

ii. This verse shows the humility of *Śree Bhāskararāya*- so simple to that extent that he seeks compassion of the great people for correction of mistakes.

3. *Pramoto Me 'Vashyam Bhavati Matimāndyādalasata*:
Padārthanyāyānāmapi Duravagāhatva Niyamāt I
Param Tvanta: *Santa*: *Sadaya Hradayā Nāmamahimā*
Pyabhoorvastasmānme Na Khalu Khalapapobhayabhayam II

i. There could definitely be some mistakes (in the book) on account of my lack of knowledge, carelessness and since it was difficult to understand the meaning of the words. The elders who notice this have compassion on me (hence they would forgive my mistakes). The greatness of the names is so wonderful and powerful. Hence, I do not have the fear that on account of the mistakes I would get the sin or flaw.

ii. The professed modesty and the confidence on the greatness of the names are seen in this verse.

4. *Amba Tvatpadayo*: *Samarpitamidam Bhāshyam Tvayā Kāritam*
Tvannāmārthavikāsakam Tava Mude Bhooyādatha Tvām Bhajan I
Yonainatparshee Layenna Cha Patedya: *Pustakasyāpi Vā*
Sangrāham Na Karoti Tasya Lalite Mābhood Bhavatyām Mati: II

i. Oh mother! This commentary was made to be written by you through me. This brings out the philosophies in the names and offered back to your feet. Let this please you. Oh *Śree Lalitādevee*! The people who worship and do not read this or consider this book or even do not have a copy of this may not focus on the devotion on you.

ii. Signed – *Tvateeyāpir Vāgpir Tava Janani Vāchām Stutiriyam* (*Soundaryalaharee*).

5. *Nāmaikam Māmanayannāmasaharāmbudhe*: *Param Pāram* I
Jalabindurbhavajaladher Yeshām Te Me Jayanti Guru Charaŋā: II

i. The great feet of my teacher, whose one single name brought me to the other shore of this ocean called *Sahasranāma* and a drop of water from whose feet made me cross this ocean of worldly affairs, shines in a great way.

Note: Two instances are given to understand the quality of *Salākshara Sūtras* – in this context the *sūtras* can be taken as formulae.

i. First one – the formula *Badaŋ* comes after the 108th name. To describe this formula there is another formula viz., *Putoŋ*. According to this *Badaŋ* becomes *Dabada*. That is, the letter *ba* is packed with *da* on both sides. As per third formula *Pheepātprudava*:, if *bru* comes after the letter *pheepā*, they become *da*. On the contrary the letter *da* becomes threefold *phee*, *pā* and *bru*. Based on the other usage *yiyutsā*:, if *e* and *u* are joined it becomes *a*. Or *ā* can be split into *e* and *u*. Now *Pheepātprudava*: becomes 7 letters *pheepru pipapru peepru*.

i.e. *badaŋ* (बडण) – *putoŋ* (पुटाण) – *dabada* (डबड).
da (ड) – *pheepāpru* (फिपापु)
peepru (पीप्रु), *pipu* (पीपु), *proo* (प्रू), *peeproo* (पीप्रू).

In these the consonants indicate the beginning letter of the names and the total number of letters in that name. Again the vowels indicate the number of names.

Through this formula 9 names are accounted.

Letter	Consonant	Vowel
Phee	2 names beginning with *pha*	*ee* = 4 - 109 - *Mahāshakti*: and 110 - *Kunḍalinee*
Proo	1 name beginning with *pa* family.	*roo* = 8 - 111 - *Bisatantutaneeyasee*
Pi	1 name beginning with *pa* family.	*e* = 3 - 112 –*Bhavānee*
Pu	1 name beginning with *pa* family.	*u* = 5- 113 - *Bhāvanāgamyā*

Letter	Consonant	Vowel
Proo	1 name beginning with *pa* family.	*roo* = 8 - 114 - *Bhavāraŋyakuhārikā*
Phee	2 names beginning with *pa* family.	*ee* = 4 - 115 – *Bhadrapriyā* and 116 - *Bhadramoortti*:
Pru	1 name beginning with *pa* family.	*roo* = 8 - 117 - *Bhaktasoubhāgyadārinee*

ii. Second instance: *lroo yā yoo thā too khroo ree droo ki ko ree yroo phee* As mentioned in the previous formula, here also the consonant indicates the number of the name and the vowel indicates the number of letters in that name.

Letter	Consonant	Vowel
lroo –	*la* = 3, 3 names with 8 letters	*roo* = 8, 911 - *Sadāshivakuţumbinee* 912 - *Savyāpasavyamārgasthā* 913 - *Sarvāpadvininārinee*
yā	*ya* = 1	*ā* = 2 – 914 – *Svasthā*
yoo	*ya* = 1	*oo* = 6 – 915 - *Svabhāvamadhurā*
Thā	*tha* = 2	*ā* = 2 - 916 –*Dheerā*
too	*ta* = 1	*oo* = 6 – 917 - *Dheerasamarchitā*
khroo	*kh* = 2	*roo* = 8 918 – *Chaitanyārghyasamārādhyā* 919 - *Chaitanyakusumapriyā*
Ree	*ra* = 2	*ee* = 4 – 920 – *Sadoditā* 921 –*Sadātushţā*
droo	*da* = 3,	*roo* = 8 – 922 – *Tarunāḍityapātalā* 923 – *Dakshiŋā Dakshiŋārādhyā* 924 - *Darasmeramukhāmbujā*
ki	*ka* = 1,	*e* = 3 – 925 – *Koulinee*
ko	*ka* = 1,	*o* = 13 – 926 – *Kevalānarghya kaivalya padadāyinee*
According to *Paribhāsha* verses this name has been split into two		
Ree	*ra* = 2,	*ee* = 4 – 927 – *Stotrapriyā* 928 –*Stutimatee*
Yroo	*ya* = 1,	*roo* = 8 – 929 – *Srutisamstutavaibhavā*
Phee	*pha* = 2	*ee* = 4 – 930 – *Manasvinee* 931 – *Mānavatee*

Thus this verse accounts for 21 names.

iii. Now it would have been very clear to all that what would be the position if there are no *paribhashā* verses.

*****

Śree Lalitā Sahasranāma
पूर्व भागः *Poorva Bhāga*: (Beginning part)

Śree Gurubyo Nama:
Śree Lalitā Mahathripurasundaryai Nama:

Section 1: *Tapinee Kalā*

1. Sage *Agastya* says;

Ashvānāna Mahābuddhe Sarvashāstravishārada **I**
Kathitam Lalitā devyā**:** ***Charitam Paramātbhutam*** **II** 1

2. Sage *Agastya* says to *Śree Hayagreeva*: "Oh horse faced! Oh great intellect and learned in all scriptures! The wonderful and surprising story of *Śree Lalitā Devee* was told by you.

3. These *Lalitā Sahasranāma* (hymns) verses find a place in the *Brahmaṇḍa Purāṇa* in the form of a conversation between *Śree Hayagreeva* and *Agastya*. This (above number 1) is the first verse of that conversation.

Agastya's birth;

There are several stories about *Agastya* in our *purāṇas*. The word *Agastya* means, one who made the mountain stay stable. One story relates to *Śree Agastya* stabilising the *Vindhyā* Mountain, which was going on growing in height. Moreover, it has been stated that *Mitrā* and *Varuṇā*, the two Vedic gods were so bewitched by the beauty of the heavenly damsel *Oorvashi* that their semen spilled and a part of it fell in a pot (*kumbha*) and *Agastya* born out of it. Hence he is variously called as *Kumbhajanma*, *Ghaḍodbhava*, *Kumbhayoni*, *Kalasodbhava*, etc. His height was only that of a thumb, but there was none equal to him in knowledge and power of penance. He was foremost amongst the worshippers of *Śreevidya*. Among the worshippers of *Śreedevee*, 12 are prominently mentioned. They are; *Manu*, Moon, *Kubera*, *Lopamudra*, Cupid, *Agastya*, Fire, Sun, *Indra*, *Skanda*, *Shiva* and *Krodha Bhaṭṭāraka*.

4. *Agastya* addresses *Hayagreeva* as *Ashvānana*. Both words mean horse faced. *Hayagreeva* is Lord *Vişhŋu* himself. The story how he acquired horse face has been mentioned in *Vedas* and *Purāŋas*. This finds a place in the *Madhuvidyā* of *Brahadāraŋya Upanishad* in the *Shukla Yajur Veda*. A sage called *Tatyannātarvaŋa* teaches *Madhuvidyā* to *Indra*. After this *Indra* ordered the sage that he should not teach this to anyone else and if he breaches this condition his head would be chopped off. *Ashwini Devas* requested *Tatyannātarvaŋa* to teach them *Madhuvidya*. The sage told them about the order of *Indra*. *Ashwini Devas* told him that they would replace his human head with that of a horse and he can teach them with the horse's head (*Hayagreeva*). Accordingly, the sage taught them the *Madhuvidya*. Immediately *Indra* cut off his head (horse's head). *Ashwini Devas* replaced the original human head on the sage's body. Thus *Madhuvidyā* was taught by *Hayagreeva*. This *Vidyā* contains the word "*Prāyaţeemuvācha*". The secret is letter '*E*' in this is the *Kāmakalā Beeja* (seed), which is the *praŋavā* of *Śree Vidya*. By this *Vedic* episode, *Hayagreeva* is established as the authority of this *mantra*. Consequently the *Veda* authority for *Śree Vidyā* is also established.

Tāmeekāroksharātdhārām Sārātsārām Parātparām I
Pranamāmi Mahādeveem Paramā Nandaroopiŋeem II

This verse also indicates this *Beeja* letter. However, there seems to be no relationship between the *Hayagreeva* mentioned in the *Vedas* and the *Hayagreeva*, an aspect of *Vişhŋu*, who taught *Śree Lalitā Sahasranāma*.

In the *Purāŋas*, the story of *Hayagreeva* is narrated in the first *Skānḍa* of *Śreedevee Bhāgavatam*. Once upon a time, after accomplishing great tasks like protection of sacrifices, *Śree Vişhŋu* was tired and went to sleep keeping his strung bow as a head rest. At that time, the *Devas* led by *Brahma* had to wake up *Vişhŋu*. They sought the help of *Vamri* (a sought of termite) for this purpose. In return the *Vamris* demanded a share in the sacrificial offerings due to the *Devas*. The *Devas* agreed to this demand and the termite cut the string of the bow. The impact of this was so severe that the bow sprang back with tremendous force and cut off *Vişhŋu's* head and threw it to a long distance. Even after vigorous search, the *Devas* could not find the head. They prayed to *Śreedevee*. She asked them to fetch a horse's head and fix it to the body of *Vişhŋu*. Thus he got the name *Hayagreeva*. Lord *Hayagreevā* was directly taught by *Śreedevee* about all the *mantras* relating to *Śree Vidyā* and he became an authority on all aspects of *Śreevidya*. Both in *Śreevidyā* and *Vaishnavā* traditions, he is considered as the foundation of all knowledge. He is the teacher of *Agastya*. That is why *Agastya* calls him "great intellect" and "expert in all *Sāstras*" and not just by way of respect. In the daily *Sandhyā-vandhanamantra*, in the *Punarmārjanamantra* beginning with *Dadhigrāvnno*, the words *"Jishnor ashvasya Vājina:"*, denotes *Hayagreeva*.

5. "Oh! Expert in all *Sāstras*, great intellectual, *Hayagreeva*! You have told me the wonderful story of *Śree Lalitā Devee*". *Paramadbhuta* also means 'very great', or 'unheard of' or 'incomparable'. The word *Lalitā* is derived from *'Lalānam'*, that is one who is always engaged in playing games, – one who plays with all creatures with motherly affection.

6. ***Poorvam Prādhurbhavo Mātastata: Pattābhishechanam I***
Bhanḍāsuravadhachchaiva Vistarena Tvayodita: II **2**

The story of *Śreedevee*'s appearance earlier, **Her** coronation and **Her** killing of *Bhanḍāsura* was extensively narrated by you. Seven types of strings of events are indicated by the word *'charita'*. *Prāthurbha* means appearance. It does not mean that **She** appeared at a particular time and was non-existent before. **She** had always existed and appeared in a particular form for a specific purpose. *Saptashatee* also says; *Utpanneti Tathā Loke Sā Nityāpyabhidheeyate*.

7. ***Varŋitam Śreepuranchāpi Mahāvibhava Vistaram I***
ŚreematpanchadashākSharyā MahimāVarŋitastathā II **3**

Podā Nyāsādayo Nyāsā Nyāsakhande Sameeritā: I
Antaryāmakrmashchaiva Bahiryāgakrmastathā II **4**

Mahāyāgakramashchāpi Poojākhande Prakeertitā: I
Purashcharaŋakhande Tu JapaLakshaŋameeritam II **5**

Homakhande Tvayā Prokto Homadravyavidhikrama: I
Chakrarājasya Vidhyāyā: Śreedevyā Deshikātmano: II **6**

Rahasyakhande Tādātmyam Parasparamudeeritam I
Stotrakhande Bahuvidhā: Stutaya: Parikeerititā: II **7**

8. *Śreedevee's* residence, *Śreepurā*, was described with all its glory and grandeur and the greatness of *Śree Panchadashākshāree mantra* as well. In the chapter on *Nyāsā* (assignment of the various parts of the body to different deities), the sixteen *Nyāsās* were detailed. In the chapter on *Pooja* (method of worship), *Antaryāgakrama* (mental and internal worshipping method), *Bahiryāgakrama* (external worshipping method) and *Mahāyāgakrama* (a special procedure in *Śree Vidyā* tradition) were all described. In the chapter on *Purashcharaṇa* (the rites to be performed for completion of the process of initiation of a *mantra*) and the procedure for doing a *japa* (chanting of a *mantra*) were explained. In the chapter on *Homa* (sacrificial fire) the procedure to be followed and the materials to be used were detailed. In the chapter called *Rahasya* (secret) *Kāṇḍa* the mutual integrity (non-differentiation) between self, *Śree Chakra*, *Śree Vidyā*, *Śreedevee* and the teacher was explained. In the *Stotra Kāṇḍa* chapter many hymns were stated.

9. In these six verses, whatever has been explained by *Śree Hayagreeva* to *Agastya* has been catalogued;

i. *Śreedevee's residence:* This is called *Śreepuram*. It is *Puram* (city), because it has as its characteristic properties (*Dharma*) both active worldly actions (*Pravrutti*) as well as abstention from actions (*Nivrutti*). It is *Śreepuram* because it is greater than all other cities. It is believed to be situated in three different places. One outside the universe, with twenty five peripheries and extending over many square *yojanās* (a measure of length). The second on top of Mount *Meru*. The third in the midst of the ocean of milk. Each of them has six gardens and nine peripheries. The details of these are listed in the names 55 to 61 of this *Sahasranāma*.

ii. *Śreemad Panchadashākshāree*: This means *Panchadashākshāree mantra* with the *beeja* letter *Śree* prefixed. *Panchadashākshāree* may be either *kādi Vidyā* (the *mantra* beginning with the syllable *ka*) or *hādi Vidyā* (the *mantra* beginning with the syllable *ha*). In some schools it is considered that prefixing the *beeja* letter *Śree* is in accordance with the *vedic* text; *Chatvāra Ĕm Pipratikshemayanta*:. According to other schools consider it as – if *Śree* is prefixed to the fifteen letters, it becomes *Shoḍasākshāree* (sixteen letters). Without giving room for such difference of opinion *Śreemad* should be interpreted to mean great or auspicious and not the *beeja* letter *Śree*.

iii. *Nyāsa Kanḍa*: In the next part called *Nyāsa Kanḍa*, different *nyāsās* are described. *Nyāsā* means assignment of the various parts of the body to different deities. By doing so, the whole body becomes the form of *Śreedevee*. *Shoḍanyāsa* is of two kinds – *laghu* (simple) and *mahā* (great). In the *laghunyāsā*, *Śreedevee* is assigned to different parts of the body in different forms viz., *Gaŋesha*, planets, stars, *Yoginis*, constellations and *Peeṭas*. Similarly in the *mahā* pattern, the six different forms are universe, earth, form, *mantra*, deity and letters – these are the *Mahāshoḍā Nyāsās*. Besides *chakra nyāsā* was also described.

iv. *Pooja Kanḍa*: In the next part called *Pooja Kanḍa*, three types of procedures for worship were mentioned viz., *Antaryāga*, *Bahiryāga* and *Mahāyāga*. *Antaryāga* is the method by which *Śreedevee* is worshipped mentally in the *Ādhārās* without any material. *Bahiryāga* is the method of worship starting from setting up of the materials till the recitation of concluding verses. *Mahāyāga* is the enlarged form of *Bahiryāga* with the addition of eight types of worship (*ashṭaga*).

v. *Homa Kānḍa*: In this chapter, the procedures for conducting sacrificial rites (using fire) and the materials to be used are described.

vi. *Purascharaŋa Kānḍa*: In this chapter, the method of doing meditation/ chanting and the process of completion of initiation and making the *mantras* effective are described. The process of completion of the initiation consists of five steps viz.,

a. After the teacher instructs the disciple about the *mantra*, the disciple should chant the *mantra* as many lakhs (hundred thousand) of times as the number of syllables in the *mantra*.
b. One tenth of the number of times the *mantra* is chant as *homa* (offering in the sacrificial fire).
c. One tenth of the number of times the offerings are made in the *homa* – so many numbers of Brahmins are to be fed.
d. One tenth of the number Brahmins are fed, is the number of times for which the *Tarpaŋa* (presenting liberations of water) is to be offered.
e. One tenth of the number of *Tarpaŋas* made is the number of times for which the *Mārjana* (sprinkling of holy water with the blade of *Kusa* grass).

The *mantra* becomes effective after performing *Purascharaŋa* with the teacher's blessings.

vii. *Rahasyu Kānḍa*: The mutual identify (status of non-differentiation) between self, *Śree Chakra*, *mantra*, *Śree Vidyā*, *Śreedevee* and the teacher is explained.

viii. *Stotra Kāṇḍa*: Many hymns like *Panchamee Stavarājam* are stated.

10. ***Mantriŋeeḍanḍineedevyo: Prokte Nāmasahasrakam* I**
***Na Tu Śreelalitādevyā: Proktam Nāmasaharakam* II** **8**

The *Sahasranāmas* (thousand names) of *Mantriŋee* and *Ḍanḍinee* were told by you, but not that of *Lalitā* yet.

11. Empress *Lalitā Devee* has two ministers – *Mantriŋee* and *Ḍanḍinee*. They are known in the *tantra* texts as *Rājashyāmalā* and *Vārāhee*. The *Sahasranāmas* of these two were told by you, but not that of *Lalitā Devee*. The use of the word *'tu'* indicates that what ought to have been told has not been told.

12. *Mantriŋee* has got another name as *Rajashyāmala*. She has the following sixteen names: *Sangeeta Yoginee, Shyāmā, Shyāmalā, Mantranāyikā, Mantriŋee, Sachivesānee, Pradhāneshee, Sukhapriyā, Veenāvatee, Vainikeecha, Mudriŋee, Priyakapriyā, Neepapriyā, Katampeshee, Kadambavanavāsinee* and *Sadāmada*.

13. *Ḍanḍinee Devee*, also called as *Vārāhi*, is the commander-in-chief of *Rāja Rajeshwaree*. She has twelve other names: *Panchamee, Daŋḍanāthā, Sankeetā, Vārāhee, Pothriŋee, Shivā, Vārttālee, Mahāsenā, Āgnachakreshwaree* and *Arighnee*.

14. These two *Devees* are considered next *Śreedevee* and in the order of worship also they are worshipped after **Her**.

15. Although *Śree Hayagreeva* has told so many things to *Agastya*, the latter through the power of his penance, realised the existence of the most sacred *Sahasranāma* of *Śree Lalitā* and asked *Śree Hayagreeva*, why he has not been taught the same so far.

16. ***Tatra Me Samshayo Jāto Hayagreeva Dayānidhe* I**
***Kim Vā Tvayā Vismrutam Tajgnātvā Vā Samupekshitam* II** **9**
***Mama Vā Yogyatā Nāsti Srotum Nāmasahasrakam* I**
***Kimartham Bhavatā Noktam Tatra Me Kāraŋam Vada* II** **10**

17. Oh *Hayagreevā*! Treasure of kindness! I have a doubt. Have you forgot to teach that *Sahasranāma* to me? Or did you consider that it was not necessary and hence you were careless? Or am I not competent to receive instructions of this *Sahasranāma*? Kindly tell me the reason for not teaching me this *Sahasranāma*.

18. *Agastya* suggests three reasons for not teaching the *Lalitā Sahasranāma* to him. Forgetting is one reason. However, as *Śree Hayagreeva* is all-knowing, this possibility is ruled out and he goes to the next reason – negligence or indifference. For a worthy and great disciple like *Agastya*, this possibility is also ruled out by *Śree Hayagreeva*, who is a treasure-house of kindness. The third reason suggested is his own incompetency to receive the instructions. Just the way the Sun makes the Lotus bed blossom with his rays, the teacher makes his disciple's knowledge blossom and makes him a worthy disciple, by his grace and kindness. Hence the reason of incompetency also does not fit in. Therefore *Agastya* asks *Śree Hayagreeva* himself to tell the reason.

19. *Sootā* said:

According to our *Purāŋas*, all of which were narrated by *Soota* to *Sounaka* and other sages assembled at *Naimisāraŋya* (*Naimisa* forest) at the time of *Satrayāga*. *Brahmāṇḍa Purāŋa* is also one such and hence the statement. "*Sootha* further said":

20. ***Iti Prushto Hayagreevo Muninā Kumbhajanmanā* I**
***Prhrushto Vachanam Prāha Tāpasam Kumbhasambhavam* I 11**

Thus asked by *Agastya*, *Śree Hayagreevā* was pleased and replied. *Śree Hayagreevā* was very happy as *Agastya* asked him about the *Sahasranāma*. It has been mentioned in *Mahābhārata* as follows;

> *Nāprushta*: *Kasyachit Broopiyāt Iti Vedānushāsanam* I
> *Aprushtastasyatat Brooyāt Yasyanechchetparābavam* II

That is, you should not tell anything to a disciple without being asked, but you can tell them to a disciple, who is sincere and interested, even if he is not competent. If a student is qualified and interested, the teacher should teach him, even if it does not occur to the student to ask the question or is not competent to raise the question. In the case of *Agastya*,

Śree Hayagreeva was pleased and is keen to teach him. In this connection, it is worth recalling the story in *Mahābhāratā* about *Vişhŋu Sahasranāma*. *Yudhistira* asked six questions and *Vişhŋu Sahasranāma* was given as a reply by *Bheeshma*.

21. The word *Tāpasam* indicates *Agastya's* competence, which he has acquired by performing various penances and getting rid of all sins and is filled with the desire to acquire knowledge. By calling him *Kumbha-sambhava*, the story of *Agastya's* birth is recalled and another qualification is also indicated that his expertise in *Kumbhakā*, the process of breath control while doing *Pranāyāma*.

22. *Śree Hayagreeva* said:

***Lopāmudrāpate-agastya Sāvadhānamanā*: Shrunu I**
***Nāmnām Sahasram Yannoktam Kāraŋam Tadvadāmi Te* II 12**

Oh husband of *Lopāmudrā*! listen to me attentively. I will tell you the reason why I have not told you the *Sahasranāma* so far.

23. *Agastya's* wife *Lopāmudrā* is one of the twelve most important worshippers of *Śreedevee*. She is considered as a sage, who discovered the *Hādi* version of the *Panchadashāksharee mantra*. *Śreedevee*'s affection towards *Lopāmudrā* is stated in the preface of *Trishatee* also. *Agastya's* competence is increased just because he is the husband of *Lopāmudra*. "You have given three reasons. I shall add a fourth one, please listen".

24. ***Rahasyamiti Matvāham Noktavāmste Na Chānyathā*** I
***Punashcha Pruchchate Bhaktyā Tasmāttatte Vamāmyaham* II 13**

I have not told you as this is very secretive and not for any other reasons. However, since you are asking again and again out of devotion, I shall tell you.

25. ***Brooyāchchishyāya Bhaktāya Rahasyamapi Deshika*: I**
***Bhavatā Na Pradeyam Syādabhaktāya Kadāchana* II 14**
***Na Jhatāya Na Dushtāya Nāvishvāsāya Hahimchit* II 15**

A teacher can teach a devoted student even if it is secret. Therefore, this should never be taught by you to someone, who is not devoted. Nor to a deceitful, wicked or non-believer. The use of the singular word student (*shishyāya*) denotes that the teacher and student should be alone at the time of giving instructions and that no instruction should be given in front of others, even to one's own disciples. The use of the phrase *Shishyāya Bhaktāya* indicates that instruction can be given only to a devoted student. By way of explanation of the term *Abhaktāya, Śree Hayagreeva* adopts the words from *Vedas* like *Satāya, Dushtāya* and *Avisvāsāya.*

Vidyā Ha Vai Brāhmanam Ājagāma, Gopāya Mā Chavatishte Ahamasme I
Assoyakāya Anrujave-yathāya Namābrooyā Veeryavteesyām II

Vidyā (the knowledge of *Vedas*) approached the Brahmin and requested him saying "keep me secret and protect me. I shall be a treasure and can give you anything. Do not give me (do not teach *Vedas*) to any jealous, untruthful or insincere person. Only then only I can keep my potency".

26. ***Śree Mātrubhaktiyuttāya Śreevidyārājavedine* I**
***Upāsakāya Shuddhāya Deyam Nāmasahasrakam* II** **16**

This *Sahasranāma* can be told only to a worshipper of *Śreedevee*, who is properly initiated by a teacher with *Panchadashāksharee mantra*, who is pure and is devoted to *Śreedevee*.

In the previous verse, it was explained as to whom this should not be told. Here the person to whom this can be told is being described. He should be one with unstinted devotion towards *Śreedevee*. He should be a sincere worshipper who should have been initiated by a teacher with the *Panchadashāksharee mantra*. He should be pure without any bad qualities. The need for so many restrictions is explained in the following verses.

27. ***Yāni Nāmasahasrāni Sadhya: Siddhipradāni Vai* I**
***Tantreshu Lalitā Deveeyāsteshu Mukhyamidam Mune* II** **17**

The *tantra sāstras* list the *Sahasranāmas* which give immediate fruits, out of which this *Sahasranāma* of *Lalitā* is the foremost. Oh sage *Agastya*! In the later *phalaśruti* (fruits/ benefits derived by chanting this *Sahasranāma*) part of this hymn, it has been stated that there are one crore *Sahasranāmas* attributed to *Śreedevee*. Ten out of these are very important viz., *Gan, Ga, Syā, La, Kā, Bā, La, Rā, Sa* and *Bha*. These denote *Gangā, Gāyatree, Shyāmalā, Lakshmee, Kālee, Bālā, Lalitā, Rājarājeshwaree, Saraswatee* and *Bhavānee*. The most superior among them is *Lalita*.

28. ***Śreevidyāiva Tu Mantranām Tatra Kādirthathā Parā* I**
***Purāŋām Śreepuramiva Shakteenām Lalitā Yathā* II** **18**
***Śreevidyopāsakānām Cha Yathā Deva*: *Para*: *Shiva*: I**
***Tathā Nāmasahasreshu Parametatprakeertitam* II** **19**

Just as *Śreevidyā* is the prime among all the *mantras, Kādividyā* among other *Śreevidyā mantras, Śreepuram* (*Śreedevee*'s abode) among all cities, *Śree Lalitā Devee* among all *Shaktis, Shiva* among all worshippers of *Śreevidyā*, so is this *Lalitā Sahasranāma* among all *Sahasranāmas*.

29. ***Yathāsya Patanāddhevee Preeyate Lalitāmbikā* I**
***Anyanāmasahasrasya Pādānna Preyate Tathā* I**
***Śreemātu*: *Preeyate Tasmādanisham Keertayedidam* II** **20**

Śreedevee does not get pleased with any other *Sahasranāmā*, as much as **She** does with this one. Therefore this *Sahasranāmā* should always be sung to please **Her**. Two types have been indicated here, namely *paḍanam* (reading) and *keertanam* (singing). *Śreedevee* is pleased either by verbal utterance or meditation. The word *Anisam* should be interpreted to mean "so long as one is alive".

30. ***Bilavapatraishchakrarāje Yorchayellalitāmbikām* I**
***Padmairvā Tulaseepushpairebhirnāmasahasrakai*: II** **21**
***Sadhya*: *Prasādam Kurute Tasya Simhāsaneshvaree* II** **22**

If the *Śree Chakra* is worshipped with this *Sahasranāma* using lotus flower or basil leaves or crataaeva (religiosa) leaves, *Śree Simhāsanesh waree* bestows her grace immediately. The previous verses talk about recitation and the forthcoming ones talk about worshipping and *archana* (bowing with the names). The use of basil leaves or cratāeva (religiosa) leaves is generally prohibited in *Śree Chakra* worship, but *Lalitā Sahasranāma* is an exception.

31. ***Chakradhirājamabhyarchya Japtvā panchadashākshareem* I**
***Japānte Keertayennityamidam Nāmasaharakam* II** **23**

Daily after worshipping *Śree Chakra* and chanting *Panchadashākksharee mantra*, this *Sahasranāmā* should be recited.

32. ***Japapoojādhyashaktaschetpatennāmasahasrakam* I**
***Sāngārchane Sāngajape Yatphalam Tadavāpnuyāt* II** **24**

Even if one is unable to perform chanting of *mantra* (*japa*) or doing *pooja*, full benefits of *pooja*, *ārādhanā* or *japa* can be derived by the recitation of this *Sahasranāma*. Only in case of disability to perform *pooja*, etc., the recitation of *Sahasranāmā* as a substitute is prescribed, not in case of laziness or carelessness. *Poojā* also includes *nyāsa*.

33. ***Upāsane Stuteeranyā*: *Patedabhyudayo Hi Sa*: I**
***idam Nāma Sahasram Tu Keertayennityakarmavat* II** **25**

In the worship of *Śreedevee*, many other prayer verses may also be recited, as a daily ritual. Recital of other prayers increases the benefits of worship. But non-recital will not reduce its merit. The use of the term *Nityakarmavat* indicates that the recital of this *Sahasranāma* is like *Sandhyavandanam*, non-performance of which would be a sin. In the worship of *Śreedevee*, *Śree Chakra Pooja*, *Śreevidyā japa* and recital of *Sahasranāmā* are the three important components. Performance of *archana* (with flowers or vermillion) with this *Sahasranāmā* or *Trishatee* (three hundred names) can be done if time permits and may be dispensed with if there is no time. But the recital of this *Sahasranāmā* verses is mandatory and therefore it is treated as a *Nityakarma* (daily routine).

34. ***Chakrarājārchanam Devyā Japo Nāmnām Cha Keertanam* I**
***Bhaktasya Krutyametāvadanyadabhyudayam Vidu*: II** **26**

Śreedevee's *Śree Chakra Pooja*, *Japa* and recital of this *Sahasranāmā* need to be performed. Others will confer additional benefits.

35. ***Bhaktasyāvashyakamidam Nāmasāhasrakeertanam* I**
***Tatrahetum Pravakshyāmi Shrunu Tvam Kumbhasambhava* II27**

The recital of this *Sahasranāmā* is essential for all devotees. I will tell you the reason Oh *Agastya*!

36. The term *avashyaka* indicates that it is more important than

meditation or *pooja*. Their benefits will also be derived by this recitation. The reasons are elaborated by *Śree Hayagreeva*.

37. ***Purā Śreelalitā Devee Bhaktānām Hitakāmyayā* I**
***Vāgdeveevashineemukhyā*: *Samāhuyetamabraveet* II** **28**

Once upon a time *Śreedevee*, desirous of bestowing grace on her devotees, called *Vasinee* and other *Vāgdevees* and told them as: There are eight *Vāgdevees* viz., *Vasinee, Kāmeshvaree, Moodhinee, Vimalā, Aruŋā, Jayinee, Sarveshvaree* and *Koulinee*. Although *Śreedevee* is devoid of all desires (all desires having been fulfilled), the desire to confer benefits to devotees is still there.

38. ***Vāgdevyā Vashinyādhyā*: *Shrunudvam Vachanam Mama* I**

Oh *Vasinee* and other *Vāgdevees*! Listen to my words. (*Śreedevee* herself explains in the next verse about how they acquired their verbal competence).

39. ***Bhavatyo Matprasādena Prollasadvāgvibhootaya*: I**
***Madbhaktānām Vāgvibhootipradāne Viniyojitā*: II** **29**

All eight of you have acquired this verbal competence with my blessings. You have been nominated by me to bestow the same verbal competence to my devotees. Among *Śreedevee*'s team of servants, *Nakkuli* and *Vāgeesvaree* also possess verbal competence, but they have not been empowered to transmit the same to the devotees.

40. ***Machchakrasya Rahasyagnā Mama Nāmaparāyanā*: I**
***Mama Stotra Vidhānāya Tasmādāgnāpayāmi Va*: II** **30**

In order to emphasise the earlier statement, *Śreedevee* reiterates the reasons for asking to *Vāgdevees* to compose a new verse. "You know the secrets of my *Śree Chakra* and always recite my name with sincerity. Hence I order you to compose a new hymn about me".

41. The details of *Śree Chakra* are stated in different parts of *Veda* like *Aruŋopanishad, Guhyopanishad, Tripuropanishad, Śree Chakropanishad*, etc. *Śreedevee*'s command to *Vāgdevees* is to make these as a subject matter of a string of names for the convenience of devotes.

Moreover it is *Śreedevee*'s desire to make these things known even to those who are not competent to learn *Vedas*. Hence this new hymn.

42. Five reasons have been quoted as to why only the *Vāgdevees* can compose such a great hymn;

43. *Vasinee* and other *Vāgdevees* are masters of word power. Their great word power was obtained due to the blessings of *Śreedevee*. They were nominated by *Śreedevee* to bestow this mastery over their words on **Her** devotees. They were fully conversant with the secrets of *Śree Chakra.*They were always immersed in the names of *Śreedevee,* which themselves are the embodiment of *Śreedevee*'s *mantras*.

44. ***Kurudhvamankitam Stotram Mama Nāmasahasrakai*: I**
***Yena Bhaktai*: *Stutāyā Me Sadhya*: *Preeti*: *Parā Bhavet* II** **31**

Compose a hymn by the recital of which, I will be pleased, consisting of one thousand names, which will be the embodiment of my own self. *Śreedevee*'s commandment to *Vasinees* and others were:

- The hymn you compose should have my name as its insignia.
- It should consist of one thousand names.
- The recital of this hymn by my devotees should give me complete satisfaction.

The last name of this hymn *Lalitāmbikā,* is its insignia. Although there are one thousand names in this hymn itself, *Lalitā* is the greatest of them all and an extraordinary one. Every name individually is beautiful and meaningful and makes both the reciter and the listener happy, because *Śreedevee* herself is immensely pleased by its recital.

45. *Śree Hayagreeva* said; *Śree Hayagreeva* continues after completing *Śreedevee*'s utterances:

***Ityāgyaptāstato Devya*: *Śreedevyā Lalitāmbayā* I**
***Rahasyairnāmabhirdivyaishchakru*: *Stotramanuttamam* II** **32**

So ordered by *Śreedevee,* the *Vāgdevees* composed a great hymn consisting of divine and secret hymns. Since it contains secrets about *Śree Chakra* and inherent meanings of *mantras*, the term *Rahasyair*:

Nāmabhi: was used.

46. ***Rahasyanāmasāhasramiti Tadvisrutam Param* I** **33**

Therefore this hymn became famous as the thousand secret names.

47. ***Tata*: *Kadāchitsadasi Sthitvā Simhāsane-ambikā* I**
***Svasevāvasaram Prādātsarveshām Kumbhasambhava* II** **34**

Oh *Agastya*! Thereafter once *Śreedevee* was sitting on **Her** throne in the hall and gave an opportunity to **Her** devotees to have a sight (*darshan*) of **Her**. Since *Śreedevee* was an empress, **She** sits on the throne and looks after administrative matters and many people came to seek **Her** *darshan* (just see her).

48. ***Sevārthamāgatāstatra Brahmanibrahmakotaya*: I**
***Lakshmeenārāyaŋānām Cha Kotaya*: *Samupāgatā*: I**
***Gowreekoṭisametānām Rudranāmapi Kotaya*: II** **35**

In order to have just a look at *Śreedevee*, crores of *Brahmas* with their consorts *Brahmanis*, *Nārāyaŋās* with *Lakshmees* and *Rudras* with *Gowrees* had visited the hall.

49. *Brahma* – *Vedas*, *Anati* – one who makes them vibrate. *Brahma's* consort *Brahmani* or *Anayati* – *Brahmani* is one who enables *Brahma* to survive (*Saraswatee*). Crores of such *Brahmas* with *Saraswatees*, *Nārāyaŋās* with *Lakshmees* and *Rudras* with *Gowrees* had visited. The purpose of assembling such a large gathering was to spread *Śree Lalitā Sahasranāma* simultaneously in the entire universe.

50. ***Mantriŋeeḍanḍineemukhyā*: *Sevārtham Yāssamāgatā*: I**
***Shakthayo Vividhākārāstāsām Samkhyā Na Vidyāte* II** **36**

Numerous *Shaktis* (*Devees*) assuming various forms like *Mantriŋee* (minister), *Ḍanḍinee* (commander) and others had come to see **Her**. They were countless in number, because the number of universes is countless and the *Shaktis* in each of the universe is too countless.

51. ***Divyoughā Mānavoughāshcha Siddhoughāshcha Samagatā*: I**
***Tatra Śree Lalitā Devee Sarveshām Darshanam Dadou* II** **37**

Hordes of divinities (*divyanghās*) who dwell in heaven, humans who have accumulated good deeds (*Mānavanghās*) and *Yogis* had all assembled there. *Śreedevee* gave *darshan* (opportunity to have a look at **Her**) to all of them. *Divya, Manava* and *Siddha* respectively mean people who dwell in heaven, earth and those who have achieved mystic powers. The word *Ogha* means a horde and also those who have been duly initiated as per tradition. It indicates the lineage of teachers. Under the *Kādi* tradition, *Divya Ongha* refers to the seven *paramagurus* (chief teachers) led by *Paraprakāsānandanātha, Mānava Ongha* refers to the eight *parāpara* teachers led by *Gaganānanda Nāthar* and the *Siddha Ongha* refers to the four teachers led by *Bhogānandanātha*. These teacher traditions and lineages are to be learnt from the appropriate teachers following the prescribed processes.

52. ***Teshu Drushtopavishteshu Sve Sve Sthāne Yathākramam* I**

After having the *darshan* of *Śreedevee*, these crores of devotees occupied their respective seats, which were prescribed like a protocol for seating in government assembly and armed forces hierarchy.

53. ***Tata*: *ŚreeLalitā Devee Kaṭākshakshepachoditā*: II** **38**
***Utthāya Vashineemukhyā Baddhānjaliputāstadā* I**
***Astuvannāmasāhasrai*: *Svakrutailalitāmbikām* II** **39**

There, signaled by a glace from *Śreedevee, Vasinee* and other *Vāgdevees* stood up and sang the hymn (this *sahasranāma*) composed by them with folded hands.

54. ***Srutvā Stavam Prasannābhoollalitā Parameshvaree* I**
***Te Sarve Vismayam Jagmurye Tatra Sadasi Sthitā*: II** **40**

Śree Lalitā Parameshwaree was immensely pleased on hearing the hymn. All those assembled in the hall were awestruck on seeing this.

55. The reasons for happiness and wonder are:

- In this hymn, words, their meanings, phraseology and idioms are all beautifully mixed.
- There is a not a single defect.
- There are no filler words like *cha, vai, tu, hi, eva*, etc.

- There are exactly one thousand names and there is no duplication of a word or a name. In the 927th name, *Storapriyā*, six characteristics of good hymn are described.

All those six characteristics are found in this hymn is a reason for happiness and awe.

56. ***Tata*: *Provācha Lalitā Sadasyāndevatā Gaŋān* I**
***Mamāgnayaiva Vāgdevyashchakru*: *Stotramanuttamam* II** **41**
***Ankitam Nāmabhirdivyairmama Preetividāyakai*: I** **42**

At that time *Śree Lalitā* informed the assembled groups of divinities that the *Vāgdevees* had composed this unequalled hymn without a parallel incorporating **Her** names and giving **Her** full satisfaction, only at **Her** command and hence it is no wonder that they are so.

57. ***Tatpatadhvam Sadā Yooyam Stotram Matpreetivruddhaye* I**
***Pravartayadhvam Bhakteshu Mama Nāmasahasrakam* II** **43**

Therefore you will recite this hymn for my pleasure and spread the same among devotees.

Recital of this *Sahasranāmā* pleases *Śreedevee* and spreading this among devotees is an important part of *Śree Vidyā* tradition and hence it should be a continuous process.

58. ***Idam Nāmasahasram Me Yo Bhakta*: *Padate Sakrut* I**
***Sa Me Priyatamo Gyeyastasmai Kāmān Dadāmyaham* II** **44**

A devotee who recites this *Sahasranāmā* even once becomes my beloved and I will fulfill all his desires. *Prāyatamo* means the most liked. *Sakrut* here means once and *Asakrut* means many times.

59. ***Śreechakre Mām Samabhyarchya Japtvā Panchadashākshareem* I**
***Pashchānnāmasāharam Me Keertayenmama Tushṭaye* II** **45**

After worshipping me in the *Śree Chakra* and meditating *Śree Panchadashāksharee*, this *Sahasranāmā* should be recited for my pleasure. What has been stated earlier that this is like a daily ritual is reiterated here.

60. ***Māmarchayatu Vā Mā Vāvidyām Japatu Vā Na Vā* I**
***Keertayennāmasāhasramidam Matpreetaye Sadā* II** **46**

Even if *Śree Chakra* worship and meditation of *Śreevidyā* is not done, recite this *Sahasranāmā* for my pleasure. This is an elaboration of what was already stated in verses 24 and 25. This recital is not for getting any desire fulfilled, but is a mandatory daily ritual to be performed without any specific desire. By implication, it means that the devotee will achieve salvation by the recital and also will get his desires fulfilled without asking for.

61. ***Matpreetyā Sakalānkāmānllabhate Nātra Samshaya*: I**
***Tasmānnāmasaharam Me Keertayadhvam Sadādarāt* II** **47**

Because of my satisfaction on hearing the recitation of this *Sahasranāmā*, the devotee gets all his wishes fulfilled. There is no doubt about it. Therefore recite this *Sahasranāmā* of mine with sincerity and devotion.

62. *Śree Hayagreeva* said: After stating what *Śreedevee* said above, *Śree Hayagreeva* continues:

***Iti Śreelaliteshāni Shāsti Devānsahānugān* II**

Thus *Śreedevee*, ordered the assembled deities with their entourage. *Lalitā* + *Ěsānee* = *Lalithesānee*. **She** is the empress of the entire universe and hence commands – *Shāsti*. The use of the present tense 'commands' instead of the past tense indicates that **Her** command extends not only to the deities assembled there but also to the future generations.

63. ***Tadāgyayā Tadārabhya BrahamaViṣhŋumahesvarā*: I**
***Shaktayo Mantriŋeemukhyā idam Nāmasaharakam* II** **48**
***Patanti Bhaktyā Satatam Lalitāparidushṭaye* I** **49**

From that time onwards *Brahma, Viṣhŋu, Maheshvara, Mantriŋee* and other deities started reciting this *Sahasranāmā* for the pleasure of *Śree Lalita*. Here again the present tense *patanti* (recite) is being used.

64. ***Tasmādavashyam Bhaktena Keertaneyamidam Mune* II**

Hence, Oh *Agastya*! Every devotee must recite this *Sahasranāma*.

65. ***Āvashyakatve Hetuste Māyā Prokto Muneeshvara* I**
***idāneem Nāmasāhasram Vakshyāmi Shraddhayā Shrunu* II 50**

I have told you the necessity and the reason for reciting this *Sahasranāma*. Now, Oh *Agastya*! I shall recite that *Sahasranāmā* – listen with sincerity.

66. Before starting recitation of this *Sahasranāmā* of great virtue, *Śree Hayagreevā* by way of a preface, narrated the story of its composition and the reason therefore and then proceeds to recite the hymn.

Thus ends the prelude (*poorva bhāga*) in the form of a conversation between sage *Agastya* and *Śree Hayagreeva* forming part of the *Brahmāṇḍa Purāṇa*.

The recital of the *Sahasranāma* should be commenced only after reciting the above prelude.

Since this is a meditation of a *mantra*, if should be done in the traditionally prescribed method. This method or procedure is explained in the following paragraphs.

Thus ends the first *Kalā*, called *Tapinee*.

*****

Section 1A
Śree Lalitā Sahasranāma Japa Vidhānam
(Method of Meditation)

Nyāsa – Assignment of the various parts of the body to different deities and corresponding gesticulations.

1. *Asya Śree Lalitā Sahasranāma Stotra Mālā Mantrasya*
Vasinyādi Vāgdevata Rshaya: I *Anushṭup Chanda*:I
Śree Lalitā Mahā Tripurasundaree Devatā I
Om Im Beejam, *Om Sou*: *Shakti*: *Om Kleem Keelakam*
Śree Lalitā Mahā Tripurasundaree Prasāda Siddhyartte
Sahasranāma Pārāyane Viniyoga:

2. For this great *Lalitā Sahasranāma mantra* (a garland of letters) *Vasinee* and other eight *Vāgdevees* are the sages (the sage who first initiated the *mantra*). The meter is *Anushṭup*. (every verse has 32 syllables). The presiding deity is *Śree Lalitā Mahā Tripurasundaree*.

3. Sages are those who first discovered any *mantra*. Hence before commencing the meditation or recitation of that *mantra*, by way of obeisance to that sage, who gave us that *mantra*, we touch our head with our right hand uttering his name. Next, by way of paying respect to the meter in which the *mantra* is set, we symbolically touch our lips with the right hand – only symbolic because, physical contact with the lips will make the hand impure. Next we touch our heart to pay respect to the presiding deity of the *mantra*.

4. Then the three areas of the *mantra* viz., *beejam*, *shakti* and *keelakam*, are indicated. The *mantra*s include, within self, everything seen in this world like the seeds of a banyan tree. Hence the first part is *beejam* (seed). This seed or the potency contained in the seed is called *shakti* (energy), the second part. The third one *Keelakam* means a nail or peg. It makes the energy of the *mantras* to concentrate in one place instead of unnecessarily getting wasted everywhere. In practice, any *mantra* is split into three – the first one is called *beejam*, the third – *keelakam* and the second *shakti*. The worshipper has to imagine that these three parts are stabilised in those specific organs of the body by touching the corresponding organs. This is called *Beejanyāsam*, *Shaktinyāsam* and *Keelakanyāsam*.

5. For *Lalitā Sahasranāmā*, these three – i.e. *Beeja*, *Shakti* and *Keelaka* are indicated in different methods as explained below;

a. The 15 letters of *Panchadashākssharee mantra* is split into three groups viz., *Vāgbhava*, *Kāmarāja* and *Shakti*. Imagining these three groups as *Beeja*, *Shakti* and *Keelaka* is one method. To protect its secrecy the *mantra* cannot be explicitly mentioned here.
b. The next method is splitting the *mantra* into 5, 6 and 4 letters and using the same explicitly as *Beeja*, *Shakti* and *Keelaka*.
c. Imagining the three letters of *Bālā mantra* as *Beeja*, *Shakti* and *Keelaka* individually.
d. *Śree Bhāskara Rāya* says that the first letters of the three groups' viz., *Ka*, *Ha* and *Sa* of *Panchadashāksharee mantra* can be treated as *Beeja*, *Shakti* and *Keelaka*.

6. Since this is *nyāsam*, any of the above four methods should be followed as initiated by the teacher. There are different ways in which the organs of the body are to be touched;

a. *Beeja* – naval button, *Shakti* – the secret organ and *Keelakam* – the feet.
b. *Beeja* – right shoulder, *Shakti* – left shoulder and *Keelakam* – the secret organ.
c. *Beeja* – the secret organ, *Shakti* – the feet and *Keelakam* – the naval.

Traditionally whatever is taught by the teacher has to be followed.

7. The aim, goal or purpose of the recital follows next. This is called as *viniyoga nyāsa*. By touching all the organs with the right hand. It is believed that *Śreedevee* will accept the recital and will bless the reciter with what is sought for. If any particular wish or requirement is aimed at, that will be fulfilled with her blessings. Thus *viniyoga* is done.

8. Some notably worthy points about what we discussed above;

a. *Vasinee* and other *Vāgdevees* are those who did this hymn. Hence, it was mentioned that they are treated as the sages of this *Sahasranāma* and they are worshipped by touching the head. This is a common rule for chanting of any *mantra*. The concerned sage of the relevant *mantra* has to be thought of. In addition there is a special reason in the case of this *Sahasranāma*. *Śree Ādi Śaṇkara*, in his *Soundaryalaharee* (17th verse) mentions that whenever *Śree Lalitā* is thought of, it should be alongwith *Vasinee* and other *Vāgdevees*;

Savithreebhirvāchām Chashimaŋishilābhangaruchibhir
Vashinyādhyābhistvām Saha Janani Samchintayati Ya: I

b. These eight *Vāgdevees* are worshipped in the eighth hall of *Śree Chakra* called *Sarvarokahara Chakra*; their names are - *Vasinee, Kāmeshvaree, Moodhinee, Vimalā, Aruŋā, Jayinee, Sarveshvaree* and *Koulinee*.

c. These eight *Devees* are being worshipped in one other method also. To worship in the four places alongwith *Bhuvaneshwaree*, the mother of the world - the first four in the triangle and the *bindu* and the second four in the eight corners, internal ten corners and the external ten corners.

d. It was earlier mentioned that the meter of this hymn has to be worshipped as *Anushṭup*. According to *mantrasāstra*,

The *mantra* having one letter is called as –	*Pindam*
Two letters	*Karthree*
Three to ten letters	*Beejam*
Ten to twenty letters	*Mantra*
More than twenty letters	*Mālā mantra*

In this *Sahasranāmā*, each of the verses contains 32 letters – i.e. each quarter verse has 8 letters and this meter is called *Anushṭup*. Hence we call this as *Anushṭup* meter. If the entire *Sahasranāma* is considered, it can be treated as *Mālā mantra*.

***

Karashaḍanganyāsās **(six *nyāsās* in hands)**

9. The *karanyāsam* (*nyāsā* of hands) is being done, to sanctify the hands and the fingers, which do many pure and impure actions and hence are not clean. As mentioned earlier the *mantra* to be chant has to be split into six or three parts. With that respectively, the thumbs, fore-fingers, middle-fingers, ring-fingers, little-fingers and the palm and its back are to be cleaned by touching them with the each part of six parts or twice the three parts of the *mantra*. This is called *karanyāsam*.

***

Nyāsās of Six organs

10. Like *karanyāsā* the *mantra* has to be split into six or three parts. The organs where the *nyāsā* has to be done are heart, head, the hair knot at the back of the head, *kavacha* (shield), eyes and *astra*. The below table details these;

The organ to be touched	The offering *mantra*	The hand to be used	Finger(s) to be used
Heart	*Hrudayāya Nama:*	Right	Ring, middle and fore-fingers
Head	*Sirase Svāhā*	Right	Middle and ring fingers
The hair knot at the back of the head or its place, if it is not there.	*Shikāyai Vashat*	Right	Thumb
Shoulders – both right and left	*Kavachāyahoom*	Both the hands at a time	All the five fingers
Two eyes and the middle of the eye brows	*Netratrayāya Voushat*	Right	Ring, middle and fore-fingers (at a time to be touched)
Left Palm	*Astrāyapaṭ*	Right	Middle and fore-fingers
Around the head from right to left	*Bhoo*: *Bhuva*: *Suva*:	Right	By knuckling middle and fore-fingers.

11. The goal of these *nyāsās*:

Heart – the place where the presiding deity has to be focused. Hence this place has to be sanctified and bowed.
Head – the important place of the body where the intellect originates.
Shikā – when the *Kunḍalinee* energy traverses to and fro *Moolādhāra* till *Sahasrārā*, it dwells in this place.
Kavacha – a shield to keep off the evil energies without the affecting the worshiper.
Eyes – to purify the eyes, which have to identify the deity. (It is assumed that all of us have three eyes – the third one being hidden between the

eye-brows).
Astrāyapaṭ - Like *Kavacha*, to keep off the evil energies around the head – the *vyāhruti mantra Bhoo*: *Bhuva*: *Suva*: is used to bind all the directions.

If this *nyāsā* is done in a concentrated manner before start of the chanting, it is definite that the body of the worshipper itself becomes the form of energy.

***

Meditation Verses

12. *Sindoorārunavigrahām Trinayanām Māŋikya Moulispurat*
***Tārānāyakasekarām Smitamukheem Āpeenavakshoruhām* I**
Panibhyāmalipoorŋaratnachashakam Raktotpalam Vibhrateem
***Soumyām Ratna Gadastta Rakta Charaŋām Dhyāyet Parām Ambikām* II**

13. The meaning of the meditation verse is: I meditate upon *Śreedevee*, who is called as *Parā*:

- One whose form is in crimson colour like *Sindoorā*
- One who has three eyes
- One who wears the shining Moon as a jewel in her crown which is studded with rubies
- One who shines with a smiling face
- One who is with big breasts
- One who has in her one hand a cup studded with precious stones filled with honey (which is being surrounded by bees) and in the other hand a red lotus flower
- One whose red feet are kept on a pot studded with precious stones and
- Who is so sweet to look at

14. The aim of meditation is:

The universal absolute, which does not have any form has to imagined with a form to be kept in mind to facilitate worshipping frequently. *Vichekshena Kruhyate* Since the worshipped deity is imagined in the mind with some identification characters it is called as *Vigraham* (idol).

- The word *Sindoorā* means, the red *kumkum* that ladies wear on the forehead and at starting place of hair in the forehead. The red colour of *Śreedevee* is compared to this. Or since the red is repeated (*sindoora* and *aruŋa*) it can be construed that **Her** form is in dark red.

15. **She** is three eyed. According to our tradition, forms of almost all deities are indicated with three eyes. The reason for this is – the words *deva* or *devata* originate from the root verb *Div*. The meaning of this word is 'to shine'. That is, self-illuminating form. To indicate this, the three shining bodies of the world are compared viz., Sun, Moon and fire – these three form the three eyes.

16. *Tārānāyakan* means the head of all stars viz., the Moon. **She** wears the Moon in her crown in the head.

18. *Smita Mukheem* – one who has a smiling face. This is an important characteristic. *Śreedevee* is an integrated form of all the beauties. There is nothing else more beautiful than **Her**. This is indicated by 48th - *Mahālāvaŋyashevadhi*: and other names also. That is *Śreedevee*'s form is full of beauty. In the same way, **She** is the supreme absolute (*brahmam*) and hence in the form full of bliss. That is the form full of bliss and beauty. How is this possible? Beauty relates to body whereas bliss relates to mind. When the mind is full of bliss, it vents through the face as a smile. The worshipper is shown a little of beauty and bliss. *Śreedevee*'s smile is mentioned in many places in this hymn itself. In *Navāvarŋa Pooja* also, in the 64 offerings - bath, silk attire, jewels, flowers, etc., are offered one by one to *Śreedevee* and the 54th offering is *Ānantollāsa Vilāsa Hāsam Kalpayāmi* – i.e. *Śreedevee* is pleased with our offerings and seated in the lap of *Śree Maheshwara* with an attractive and mild smile in her face, to make us happy.

19. In describing the form of *Śreedevee*, it has been mentioned that **She** has only two hands. In other meditation verses and in the names it has been mentioned that **She** has four hands and the weapons in the hands are also detailed. Why this distinction? In *Śreemad Bhagavad Geeta*, *Śree Krişhŋa* showed his huge form (*Vishvaroopā*) to *Arjuna*. *Arjuna* was scared on seeing this and requested *Krişhŋa* to hide the huge form and be in the normal form;

Kireetinam Katinam Chakrahastam Ichchāmi Tvām Trashṭu Maham Tataiva I
Tenaiva Roopeŋa Chaturbujena Sahasra Bāho Bhavavishva Moorttee II

Accordingly *Śree Krişhŋa* first appeared with four hands. Immediately he becomes two-handed, like an ordinary man (like all of us). *Arjuna* being scared of the huge form, after seeing the four-handed form also requested *Śree Krişhŋa* to show the pleasing human form. That is, instead of un-humanly form, the human form like us is considered to be befitting one for worshipping. This meditation verse indicates *Śreedevee* as pleasing (*soumyām*) - the form which is so sweet for the mind and make us to look at **Her** again when once seen.

20. *Ali* means honey, beetle or alcohol. The precious cup in the hands of *Śreedevee* is filled with honey and hence surrounded by beetles. In some of the secret worships alcohol is also being used. But this method is not recommended. Hence it is apt that we consider the meaning as honey and/ or beetle.

21. In another hand **She** has red Lily or Water Lily or Lotus flower.

22. Since it has been mentioned as *Ratna Ghata* – a pot filled with nine types of wealth (nine gems) and **She** has **Her** feet on it.

23. *Raktacharaŋām* – *Śreedevee*'s feet are red in colour – could be due to the decoration with red cotton paste or *mehandi* or henna.

24. *Parām Ambikām* – The word *parai* means greater than every-thing else – nothing else is greater – *Śreedevee* is such an *Ambika*.

25. As per *Brahmaŋḍa Purāŋa* there is only one meditation verse for this hymn. *Śree Narasimhmanāḍar*, in his *Paribhāshā* verses, mentions as; *Dyānam Ekena*. However three more verses are in vogue.

26. In this single verse there are six words indicating the red colour: *Sindoorāruŋa Vigrahām, Māŋikya Mouli, Ratnachashakam, Raktot palam, Ratna Gaṭastta* and *Rakta Charaŋām*. In the case of *Śreedevee* everything is red. *Pāvanopanishad* says; *Louhitya Metasya Savasya vimarsha:*.

27. Now let us consider the remaining three meditation verses.

Second verse:

***Aruŋām Karuŋātarangitāksheem Dhrutapāshānkushapushpabānachāpām* I**
***Aŋimātibhirāvrutām Mayookhairahamityeva Vibhāvaye Bhavāneem* II**
I meditate upon *Bhavānee* in my mind:

- Who is red in colour
- Who has compassion moving like waves in the eyes
- Who carries *Pasa* (Noose), *Ankusa* (goad), sugarcane bow and flower arrows in hand and
- Who is surrounded by *Aŋimā* and other *shaktis*.

24. Third verse:

Dhyāyeet Padmāsanastthām Vikasitavaḍanām Padmapatrāyatāksheem
***Hemābhām Peetavastrām Karakalitalasaddhemapadmām Varāngeem* I**
Sarvālankārayuktām Satatamabhayadām Bhaktanamrām Bhavāneem
***Śreevidyām Shāntamoorttim Sakalasuranutām Sarvasampatpradātreem*II**

I meditate upon *Śreedevee*:

- Who is seated on a Lotus flower
- Who shines with a bright face
- Who has long eyes like the petals of a Lotus flower
- Whose form is gold in colour
- Who wears yellow silk cloth
- Who has a golden lotus in her hand
- Whose form is so beautiful
- Who always blesses the fearless
- Who blesses by lowering her head to hear the issues of the devotees
- Who is the consort of *Bhavan*
- Who is in the form of *Śreevidyā mantra*
- Whose form is so peaceful
- Who is worshipped by all the *Devas* and
- Who bestows all the wealth

25. Fourth verse:

Sakunkumavilepaŋāmalikachumbikastoorikām
***Samandahasitekshanām Sacharachāpapāshānkushām* I**
Asheshajanamohineemaruŋamālyabhooyāmbarām
***Japākusumabhāsurām Japavidhou Smaredambikām* II**

In thought of my mind, during chanting of *mantra*, upon *Ambikā*:

- Who has applied a gel made of European saffron
- Who is decorated by a musk dot, made from musk deer, on her fore-head
- Who has smiling eyes
- Who carries *Pasa* (Noose), *Ankusa* (goad), bow and arrows in hand
- Who attracts all human being towards her
- Who is adorned with red coloured garland and jewels and
- Whose lustre shines like the hibiscus flower

This fourth verse is found in *Śree Ādi Śaṇkara*'s hymn called *Tripurasundaree Ashṭakam*.

26. Thus the form of *Śreedevee* has to be strongly imagined in the mind during chanting. Before that five offerings have to be made to the form imagined in the mind. These offerings are only imaginative in mind. The 64 offerings and/ or 16 offerings are two types of worship to be done directly. The same is abridged into 5 and done as a sample. Everything used during worship is made with one of the basic five elements. Indicating the same:

- The fragrant sandal is for *Śreedevee* who is in the form earth *tatva*.
- The flower given by ether is for *Śreedevee* who is in the form of ether.
- The fragrant smoke is for *Śreedevee* who is in the form of air.
- The light is for *Śreedevee* who is in the form of fire.
- The food is for *Śreedevee* who is in the form of water.

Śreedevee herself and the things used in her worship are all related to the five basic elements. While (mentally) doing this worship, the *beejas* of the five basic elements viz., *Lam*, *Ham*, *Yam*, *Ram* and *Vam* are to be prefixed.

27. The method of worship and the *nyāsas* mentioned might have given an idea. However, this has to be followed as taught by the teacher.

28. At the end of the chanting the same has to be submitted to *Śreedevee* by keeping her form in mind, after again doing *Karashaḍanganyāsās*, reading the meditation verses and doing the five *pooja* as above. Since the presiding deity is a lady, the submission has to be done in the left hand. We did the prayers to the directions from right to left at the beginning of the chanting. Now it has to be undone from left to right as direction *vimocham*.

29. When *archana* is done with the names mentioned here *Nama*: (I bow) has to be suffixed and the *praŋava mantra* (*Om*) has to be used as a prefix and a suffix as well. For instance the first name has to be sued as *Om Śreemātre Nama*: *Om*.

*****

Section 2: *Tāpinee Kalā*

1. *Śreemātā* - श्रीमाता

i. The supreme mother - When we are in deep trouble, the first word uttered by us involuntarily is *Ma*. Human beings are afflicted by three kinds of *Tapas* (difficulties), which cannot be solved by the mother in her human form. The possession of the power to resolve these difficulties makes **Her** the "Superior Mother". Worshipping **Her**, who has given birth to the whole world, will prevent birth again in this world from the mother's womb. (353rd name can be compared). The best of love is mother's affection. Hence to contemplate and worship **Her** as the mother will give us proximity to Her.

ii. *Śree* means *Lakshmee* (goddess of wealth). Hence *Śreemātā* means *Lakshmee's* mother. *Śree* also means *Saraswathi* (goddess of learning). She is mother of both *Lakshmee* and *Saraswathi*.

iii. *Mā* means 'to measure'. *Śreemātā* therefore means that **She** is capable of measuring wealth. One that measures is superior to the one that is measured. *Ma* also is interpreted to mean one who 'distributes' or 'classifies'. She is the one who classified the *Vedas*. From this angle, *Śreedevee* can also be indicated as *Brahma* and/ or *Vyāsa*. *"Richo Yajumshi Sāmāni Sāhi Srihi Amrtā Sadām"* – when interpreted in the manner this name is masculine.

iv. *Śree* means venom. One who held the venom in her throat (*Māthi*). Lord *Parameshwarā* is called *Srikantā* because he retained the *Hālahāla* venom in his throat. The feminine form which is part of **Him** is also called by this same name.

v. The prefix *Śree* is used to refer respectable men or objects – for instance *Śree Chakra, Śree Vidyā, Śreesailam*, etc. Thus **She** is aptly called as *Śreemātā*, as she is the mother of the whole world. Moreover, the word *Śree* is itself auspicious. Is it not, hence appropriate to commence this series of thousand names with *Śree*?

vi. This hymn of thousand names was first recited by the eight *Vāgdevatā's* led by *Vasinee*. They appeared from the word power of *Śreedevee* herself. They were ordained to perform this holy task of reciting this hymn at her behest. They, in turn, selected and dedicated these thousand names out of millions of powerful names, and, by way of reminiscing the **mother**'s boundless love and compassion bestowed on them, start this series with the name *Śreemātā* (Mother).

vii. Merging the three letters of *Bāla Mantra* to the six consonants *ha, sa, ka, la, ra* and *ta*, we derive a three-part *Mantra*, which is indicated as *Mātha*. This is contained in this name. This secret *Mantra* has to be learnt through an appropriate teacher, in a proper way.

viii. There is a poem (*Shlokā*) called *"Matā Kunḍaliní Kriya Madhumathee"* in the book *"Laghustuthi"* written by a great *Devee Upāsakar, "Laghu Bhattarakar"*. The word *Mātā* mentioned here also has a special cryptic meaning. This name is an indication of that special meaning.

ix. Mother here also indicates that **She** has given birth to the entire universe. It indicates one of the three main functions of the Supreme Being viz. creation. *Vedās* also reflect the same sense in *"Yathoo Vāimanī Bhoothānī Jāyanthee"*.

2. *Śreemahārājnee* - श्रीमहाराज्ञी

(i) The great empress (that is the protector of the whole world); the second of the three functions of the Supreme Being viz. Protection is indicated in this place. The *Vedas* state the same thought as *Yena Jātānee Jeevantee.*

(ii) Three secret syllables of *Śree Vidyā* are hidden in this name. They are to be learnt through an appropriate teacher, in a proper way.

(iii) Any king's wife is called queen. A queen is called as *Rājnee* in Samskrit. The wife of an emperor is Empress – *Śreemahārājnee*. It is not that *Śreedevee* is honoured because **Her** consort is an emperor. **She** on her own carries out the function of governance and hence **She** is *Mahārājnee*.

3. *Śreematsimhāsaneshwaree* - श्रीमत्सिंहासनेश्वरी

(i) **She** controls and rules the world seated on a great grand throne.

(ii) The seat of a king is a throne – *Simhāsana*. The seat of kings is designed as if the ruler is seated on a lion, because the lion is the king of animals. By virtue of **Her** position as a controller and ruler of World Empire, **She** is the lord of *Simhāsan*, symbolises the wealth (*Lakshmee*) of the empire of the Universe and seated in this throne.

(iii) **She** herself rides on a lion and uses it as a seat. It also means that **She** is *Simhavāhinee* – one who rides on a lion. According to *Devee*

Purāŋam, the demon *Mahishan* was killed by *Śreedevee* riding on a lion. **She** thus acquired the names of *Mahishagni* (killer of *Mahishan*) and *Simhāsaneshwaree*.

(iv) The word *Simhā* is derived from the verb *Himsa*. *Simhā* is the corrupted form of *Himsa*. Thus *Himsāsaneshwaree* means, one who has the power to destroy the whole world – the third function of the Supreme Being, viz. to destroy, is indicated here. The *Vedas* refer to this as *Yathprāyanthyapi Samvisanthi*.

(v) The previous name was *Śreemahārājnee* - the empress; it is therefore appropriate that she is seated on a *Simhāsana and* is *called Śreematsimhāsaneshwaree*.

(vi) At the end of the *Devee Navāvarŋa Pooja*, a throne (*Simhāsana*) with five steps is contemplated on the *Bindu*. Five forms of *Śreedevee* are imagined on each of these five steps in the four directions north-west, north-east, south-west and south-east and in the centre. This worship is called *Pancha Panchika*. In the first step are seated the five *Lakshmees viz. Śree Vidyā Lakshmee, Lakshmee-Lakshmee, Mahālakshmee - Lakshmee, Trishakti Lakshmee* and *Sarvasāmrājya Lakshmee*. Since the throne on which *Śreedevee* is seated has these five *Lakshmees*, **She** is referred to as *Śreemat- simhāsaneshwaree*.

(vii) There are also *Mantras* which carry the name *Simhāsana*. These are to be contemplated on the four sides and in the centre of the *Bindu* as described below:

- Three in the East viz. *Bālā, Chaitanya, Bhairavee* and *Sampathpradā Bhairavee*.
- Five in the South viz. *Kāmeshwaree, Rakthanetrā, Shatkūta Bhairavee, Aghora Bhairavee* and *Sampathpradā Bhairavee*.
- Seven in the West viz. *Sanjeevani, Mrithyunjayā, Amruta Sanjeevani Bhairavee, Vajreshwaree, Tripura Bhairavee, Bhayahārini* and *Sampath Pradā Bhairavee*
- Four in the North viz. *Dāmareshwari, Bhayadwamsini Bhairavee, Aghora Bhairavee* and *Sampathpradā Bhairavee*.
- Five in the Centre viz. *Prathama Sundaree, Dwitheeya Sundaree, Tritheeya Sundaree, Chaturtha Sundaree* and *Panchama Sundaree*.

The *Mantras* of these 24 *Devatās* are called *Simhāsana Mantras*. *Śreedevee* is the lord (*Ĕshwari*) of these *Mantras*.

Thus, by the first three names, the three functions of creation, protection and destruction are indicated. *Śreedevee* has the name

Panchakrityaparāyanā (274th name) – one who carries out five functions. The remaining two functions viz. *Thirodhāna* and *Anugrahā* will be dealt with later.

4. *Chidagnikuṇḍasambhootā* - चिदग्निकुण्डसंभूता

(i) One, who emerged from the sacrificial fire of knowledge.

(ii) The word *Chit* means flawless *Brahmam*. It is called *Chidagni* as it is the enemy of the darkness of ignorance. *Śreedevee* emerged from the fire of *Chit that* is knowledge. In other words, *Śreedevee*'s real form emerges from the sacrificial fire of knowledge for the purpose of annihilating ignorance.

(iii) That knowledge as fire is mentioned in several places in Vedic and other spiritual literatures. For instance *Gnānāgni*: *Sarvakarmāni Bhasmasāt kurutee tathā* (*Śreemad Bhagavat Geetā* IV-37).

(iv) The legend of *Bhanḍāsūrā* occurs in the same *Brahmānḍa Pūrānā* where this *Sahasranāma* is also recited. *Indrā* and other *Devās* performed a sacrifice to propitiate *Śreedevee* in order to destroy *Bhanḍāsūrā*, who was harassing them. The sacrificial fire raised by them was called *Chidagnikuṇda*. Once the *Devās* started offering organs of their own bodies in the sacrificial fire, *Śreedevee* emerged from that pit (*Kundā*).The illusory 'I' related to the physical and causal bodies, which are the root cause of self-esteem and arrogance (the false notions of 'I') was thrown into the fire by the *Devās* and *Śreedevee*, who is the real 'I' emerged.

(v) There is one method of worship of *Śreedevee* called *Rahoyāga*. The fire of knowledge, which burns on its own without any fuel, is enhanced by adding the fuel of *Vāsanā*s.

Attributes arising out of previous thoughts and actions and when the fire is aglow, all the good deeds, sins, thoughts, actions and duties are offered therein and the soul assumes the form of pure light, which is *Śreedevee*. (Refer 381st name – *Rahoyāga kramārādyā*). *Antar nirantara nirindana medamānee moohāndhakāra paribandhini samvidagnow* – this is the *Mantra* chant and the special *argya* is poured in the *Samayika* pooja after *Tatvasodanam*. This is the meaning of this name.

5. *Devakāryasamudyatā* - देवकार्यसमुद्यता

(i) One, who came forward to service *Devas*.

(ii) Why should *Śreedevee*, who is of eternal existence incarnate or take a particular form? The purpose is to help the *Devas* achieve their objectives.

Devānām Kāryasidhyartham Āvirbhavati Sā Yadā
Utpanneetitadā Lookee Sā Nithyāpyabhidheeyathee (*Saptashatee*)

The objective of the *Devas* is to annihilate the demons like *Bhanḍāsurā*, *Mahishāsurā*, etc. Although **She** is eternal, **She** takes an incarnation every time to remove the grievances of the *Devas*.

(iii) Demons like *Bhanḍāsurā* are monsters bound by ignorance. Actions arising out of ignorance with selfish goals, take the form of Devils. *Śreedevee* takes different incarnations to release the *Devas* from the bondage of ignorance so that they can carry out their respective divine functions. The $4^{th}$and 5^{th}names describe *Śreedevee*'s *Chit* (*Prakāsa*) form. The description of the *Vimarsa* form follows.

6. *Udyadbhānusahasrābhā* - उद्यद्भानुसहस्राभा

(i) Her lustre is equal to thousands of rising Suns. The word *Sahasram* also means infinite.

(ii) **Her** lustre is equal to infinite (thousands) rays of rising Suns.

(iii) The word *Sahasram* can be attributed to 'Sun' or its 'rays'. In that case **Her** splendor can be equated to countless (thousands) number of rising Suns or countless number of rays of a rising Sun.

(iv) The word *Ābhā* can be interpreted as 'lustre' or 'colour'. *Śreedevee* is famous both for her lustre as well as her Crimson colour. In the morning, the rising Sun graciously reduces his intensity of the heat emanating from his light, just for us to see his cherry coloured rays. Similarly *Śreedevee* is also of Crimson colour. (This colour itself is called *Aruŋa* colour, one of the names of the Sun himself.

(v) Every mood or character has a colour. The colour of kindness or graciousness is Crimson.

(vi) In most of the places the Supreme Being is referred to as a column of light in scriptures:

a. *Na Tatra Sūryo Bhāti Na Chandra Tārakam*
b. *Jyootirmayam* (*Shakti Mahimnā Storam*)
c. *Jyotirmayee* (*Laghustutī*)
d. Many a place in *Bhagavat Geetā*
e. *Vidyutdhāmasamaprabhām* (*Dyāna Shloka of Saptashathee*)

The *Prakasa* and *Vimarsa* forms *Śreedevee* have been described so far. The forthcoming names seek to detail three more forms viz. the *Stūla*, *Sūkshma* and *Param* forms. The *Stūla* form is the one with human physical organs like hands, feet, etc. The *Sūkshma* is in the form of *Mantras*. The *Param* is in the form of *Vāsanās*. The *Stūla* form is taken up first.

7. *Chaturbāhusamanvitā* - चतुर्बाहुसमन्विता

(i) One with four hands.
(ii) *Śreedevee* has four hands – two from each shoulder in front and back. The Four hands only have been indicated in the forms usually contemplated during meditation. Hands come first and foremost whenever we try to concentrate on the form mentioned in the *Dhyāna Slokā* (meditation verse).
(iii) The four *Devees* who are the commandants of *Śreedevee*'s army viz. *Ashwārūdā, Sampatkaree, Mantrinee* and *Vārāhee,* may be deemed to be the four hands of *Śreedevee.*
(iv) The *Mantās* pertaining to the above four *Devees* are indicated by this name.
(v) The *Dhyāna* verse of this *Sahasranāma* mentions only two hands for *Śreedevee*. Preceding part may be referred for the meaning of the *Dhyāna Slokā* (meditation verse).

Mention was made about the four hands and followed by the weapons carried in these four hands.

8. *Rāgasvaroopapāshāḍhyā* - रागस्वरूपपाशाढ्या

(i) One who carries the weapon of desire in the form of a noose.
(ii) A noose is a rope thrown to tie and drag something. *Śreedevee* is holding both the ends of the noose in one hand. It is in the *Stūla* form in her rear left arm. The presiding deity is *Ashwārūda*.
(iii) *Rāgā* and *Anurāgā* are the two features of mind – wish and desire. This is the *Vāsanā* form of the weapon noose. This form has the twin opposite characters viz. love and hatred. *Vāsanā* is the effect of the deeds of previous births of *Jeeva i*n the hands of *Śreedevee* these take the form of Icchā *Shakī* and *Gnāna Shakī*.
(iv) The noose helps us to round up and drag a distant object to oneself. We will be able to do this only if both the ends of the noose are under our control. *Śreedevee* holds both the ends of the noose in her hand. This indicates that "our wishes will get fulfilled automatically by **Her** grace.

9. *Krodhākārāngkushojvalā* - क्रोधाकाराङ्कुशोज्ज्वला

(i) Her lustre is enhanced by holding the goad symbolising anger.

(ii) Goad is a pointed weapon used by a mahout to control an elephant. It has a sharp edge. Elephant is one of the biggest and strongest among all animals. It is extremely difficult to control a rogue elephant. Goad is the only weapon which can control it. In the hands of *Śreedevee* it is in a *Stūla* form.

(iii) Its *Vāsanā* form is anger. If the mind is not able to get what it wants or does not derive the satisfaction expected out of it the mental reaction is anger. It is symbolised by the lustrous goad worn by *Śreedevee*.

(iv) *Krodhākārāngkusham* can be interpreted in two ways – (1) Goad in the form of anger or (2) Anger and *Ākārā* (knowledge). How is *Ākārā* interpreted as knowledge? When we see an object through our eyes, our mind recognises and takes the 'form' (photo print) of that object – that is *Ākāra*. If we see a book, our mind recognises the form of the book and becomes that form (*Ākārā*) itself. Then only we understand that what we see is a book or have the knowledge that it is a book. Recognition of all the objects by the mind taking the form (*Ākārā*) of that object. Hence the word *Ākārā* gives the meaning as knowledge.

(v) Anger is a state of mind arising out of the knowledge of an object. *Śreedevee* adorns the goad that controls anger. Knowledge about an object is destroyed in order to annihilate anger.

(vi) A weapon will act as intended by the person who takes aim. Here these weapons will act as per the wish of *Śreedevee*. For worshippers of *Śreedevee*, **She** will make the 'desire' and 'hatred' act according to the wishes of the devotees and ultimately raise them to **Her** level.

10. *Manoroopekshukodaṇḍā* - मनोरुपेक्षुकोदण्डा

(i) **She** dons a bow made of sugarcane – the physical form of 'mind'.

(ii) *Śreedevee* has in her left forearm a bow made of sugarcane. It's symbolic form is the mind. Its presiding deity is *Mantrinī*.

(iii) The action of the mind executed through the five organs is to take the form of the object seen and realise that "I see the object", "This can give me pleasure", "I desire to get this object", "This gives me sorrow and hence I should avoid it" and the like. This is called *Sankalpa*

At the same time the thought "Is this object suitable for me or not",

"Should I try to get it or not" and the like are called *Vikalpa*. The action of the mind is of these two types. This mind takes the form of sugarcane bow in the hands of *Śreedevee*.

(iv) In general a bow is made up of completely dry bamboo slats and is capable of being bent and unbent. Sugarcane is full of moisture; Sugarcane bow is a weapon, though it is sweet; again it is sweet, though it is a weapon. It shows that *Śreedevee's* mind is full of benignity. Is it not **Her** mind full of sweetness and graciousness?

11. *Panchatanmātrasāyakā* - पञ्चतन्मात्रसायका

(i) One who has five characteristics as arrows.

(ii) In her physical form, *Śreedevee* has five flowers as arrows in her right forearm viz. Lotus, Red Lotus, Red Lily, Red Jasmine and Mango flower. The characteristics of these arrows are the effect they make on the objects attacked by them viz. to induce happiness, to give taste, to enthrall, to dry out and to kill. The presiding deity of these arrows is *Vārāhi* also known as *Daṇḍanātha*.

(iii) The secret form of these arrows is the five self-characteristics (*Tanmātrās*). These characteristics are the unique features of the five elements, which constitute the physical earth.

Elements (*Bhūtās*)	**Self-Characteristics (*Tanmātrās*)**
Space (*Ākāśā*)	Sound (*Shabdā*)
Wind/ Air (*Vāyu*)	Sense of touch (*Sparsha*)
Fire (*Agnī*)	Form/ Colour (*Rūpa*)
Water (*Jala*)	Taste (*Rasa*)
Earth (*Prithvi*)	Odour (*Gandha*)

These characteristics standalone only in the very intricate and atomic state of the elements. The Universe, we perceive is the composite form of these elements and hence each element cannot be perceived separately.

Before the evolution of the universe, from the Absolute (*Mūlaprakritī*), I.*e.* when matter and energy are in a state of indistinguishable union, the elements could be identified by their individual characteristics- space by sound, air by sense of touch and so on. In this state these are called *Tanmātrās*.

(iv) The arrows hit their targets and give their desired effect, as intended by the person who aims them. A sincere devotee targeted by *Śreedevee*'s arrow will experience the good and pleasurable effects of these characteristics. If the devotee is insincere (bad in intention), the arrows also will give only undesirable effects such as agitation or disturbance, maddening or intoxication, etc.

(v) These arrows have three forms in three different states – in the physical (*Stūla*) state, they take the form of flowers; in the secret (*Sūkshma*) state, they are *Mantras*; and in the *Vāsanā* state they take the form of *Para*, a form of sound.

(vi) *Śreedevee* also has weapons - Sugarcane as bow and flowers as arrow, like Cupid (*Manmathā*). Hence S**he** is called as *Lalitā* or *Kāmeshwaree*. As the emotion of love (*Sringāra rasa*) is important to **Her, She** is endowed with beautiful things as weapons.

(vii) The presiding deity of sugarcane bow is *Mantrinī* representing the power of intellect (*Buddhi Shakī*) and the presiding deity of arrows is *Daŋḍanātha* – commander-in-chief representing the physical power. The *Vāg Devees* symbolically emphasise that intellect and power should act in unison.

(viii) *Mantras* of the weapons described are encompassed in these names 8 to 11. These are so secret that they should be learnt through a proper teacher.

12. *Nijāruŋaprabhāpooramajjadbrahmaŋḍamaŋḍalā* -
निजारुणप्रभापूरमज्जद्ब्रह्माण्डमण्डला

(i) One who immerses the zones of galaxy by the flow of her lustre.

(ii) Our Earth, space and the stellar zone constitute one galaxy (*Brahmānḍam*). Universe (*Brahmānḍamaŋḍalam*) consists of millions of such galaxies. *Śreedevee* sinks this entire universe in **Her** red lustre. Again the red lustre alone shines immersing them all.

(iii) The physical form of *Śreedevee*'s red lustre is described in the ensuing names. This description starts from **Her** hair and ends in **Her** feet.

13. *Champakāshokapunnāgasougandhikalasatkachā* -
चम्पकाशोकपुन्नागसौगन्धिकलसत्कचा

(i) One who has beautiful hair studded with Magnolia, Asoka, Rhizophora mucronata (*Punnāga*) and Red Lotus flowers.

(ii) It is *Śreedevee*'s hair bedecked, with flowers, which emerges first out of the sacrificial fire; hence the description of the *Śreedevee*'s physical form commences with the hair.

(iii) The first part of **Her** *mantra* is equated with **Her** face. Hence the description starts with the hair. (for instance85th name –*Śreemad Vāgbhava Kooṭaikaswarūpa Mukapankajā*)

14. *Kuruvindamaŋishreeŋeekanatkoṭeeramaŋḍitā* –
कुरुविन्दमणिश्रेणीकनत्कोटीरमण्डिता

(i) *Kuruvindamaŋi* is the precious stone Ruby. *Śreedevee*'s crown is studded with a string of Rubies.

(ii) Adorning of rubies will result in fulfillment of desires. Attachment will be created to good things; desire, affection, welfare and devotion to *Śree Viṣhŋu* also.

(iii) *Śreedevee*'s crown is of *Koteerā* model. This is a particular design, which does not hide beauty of the hair as well as the flowers adorned. The crowns worn by men will hide the hair and is called *Makuṭā*, *Mukuṭā* or *Kreeṭa*.

(iv) The red rubies match the red lustre of *Śreedevee*'s body.

(v) Meditation of *Śreedevee's* face with the crown will increase the devotion.

15. *Ashṭameechandra Vibhrājadalikasthala Shobhitā* –
अष्टमीचन्द्र विभ्राजदलिकस्थल शोभिता

(i) One whose forehead shines like the Moon on the eighth day of lunar half month.

(ii) Of the fifteen phases of the moon, on the eighth day of bright lunar half month the eighth phase will be seen. Or reduced upto eight phases on the eighth day of the lunar dark half month and moon will be visible as a semicircle. In the emerging form of *Śreedevee* from the sacrificial fire, the crown, hair and flowers come out one after the other and the forehead emerges as an inverted semicircle resembling the eighth day moon, with flawless cool light.

(iii) This can be compared to 46th verse of *Soundaryalaharee* starting with *Lalāṭam Lāvaŋyadvithi Vimalamābhati.*

16. *Mukhachandrakalangkābhamruganābhiviseshakā* –
मुखचन्द्रकलङ्काभमृगनाभिविशेषका

(i) The *bindi* (musk dot) on the forehead of *Śreedevee* resembles the black spot on the surface of the Moon and it further beautifies the face.

(ii) It is a literary tradition to consider the black spot on the moon as a stain on the life of the Moon god. The Moon is sometimes described as *Mrugānka*, as the stain looks like a deer and as *Śasānka* as the stain also looks like a rabbit. When *Śreedevee*'s forehead is described as a semicircular Moon (crescent), there is no stain, but the musk spot beautifies the face.

17. *Vadanasmaramāngalyagruhatoraŋachillikā –* वदनस्मरमाङ्गल्यगृहतोरणचिल्लिका

(i) One whose eyebrows look like festoons in front of Cupid's house which is *Śreedevee's* face.

(ii) The roof at the entrance of the houses will be constructed in a raised manner so that the house is not affected by rain or Sunshine. This is called festoon. *Śreedevee*'s face is so beautiful as to infatuate *Śree Kāmeshwara*. Hence Cupid uses this face as an office for his auspicious activities. The eyebrows look like beautiful festoons in front of this house (office).

18. *Vaktralakshmee Pareevāhachalanmeenābhalochanā –* वक्त्रलक्ष्मी परीवाहचलन्मीनाभलोचना

(i) One whose eyes look like fish swimming in the stream of beauty of *Śreedevee*'s face.

(ii) The beauty of *Śreedevee*'s face undergoes momentary changes and this continuous change looks like a steady and slow stream. The motion of *Śreedevee*'s two eyes is compared to the fast movement of fish in this stream, which increases its beauty.

(iii) Fish are not mammals but lay eggs. It is believed that fish nurse their offspring just by affectionate looks. Similarly, *Śreedevee*'s eyes, which are compared to fish swimming in the stream of beauty uplifts **Her** devotees just by a gracious look. She is therefore called *Meenākshi*, here referred to as *Meenābhalochana*.

19. *Navachampakapushpābhanāsādaŋḍavirājitā –* नवचम्पकपुष्पाभनासादण्डविराजिता

(i) One whose nose is like a fresh *Champaka* flower.

(ii) *Nava* can be interpreted as 'new' or 'partly blossomed'. A partly blossomed *Champaka* bud generates a pleasant aroma.

20. *Tārākāntitiraskāri Nāsābharaŋabhāsurā* -
ताराकान्तितिरस्कारि नासाभरणभासुरा

(i) One whose nose ring challenges the lustre of the stars.
(ii) *Tārā* can also be interpreted to mean the two *Devees* - *Mangalā* and *Suklā* or the *Devatā* - *Tāraka*.
(iii) *Śreedevee*'s nose rings are made of Ruby and Pearl.

21. *Kadambamanjareekluptakarŋapooramanoharā* -
कदम्बमंजरीक्लृप्तकर्णपूरमनोहरा

(i) One who wears a bunch of *Kadamba* flowers in **Her** ears and steals the heart with **Her** beauty.
(ii) Wearing a bunch of flowers in the earlobes increases the beauty. *Kadamba* flower is suitable for such adornment.
(iii) A garden of *Kadamba* trees is situated outside the *Chintamaŋi Graha*, the abode of *Śreedevee*, in *Śreepura*. *Śreedevee* wears the flowers plucked from those trees to adorn **Her** ear.

22. *Tāṭankayugaleebhootatapanodupamaŋḍalā* -
ताटङ्कयुगलीभूततपनोडुपमण्डला

(i) One who wears the Sun and Moon as two large earrings.
(ii) One type of ornament worn by ladies in their ears is called *Tāṭanka* (palm-leaf). The Sun and the Moon take the form of this *Tāṭanka* s to beautify *Śreedevee*'s face.
(iii) The Sun and the Moon have the fortune to become *Śreedevee*'s eyes, earrings and **Her** breasts.
(iv) *Tāṭanka* is considered to be an auspicious ornament for *Sumangalis* (ladies living with their husbands). *Śree Ādi Śaṇkara*, in his *Soundaryalaharee*, describes with awe that *Śree Parameshwarā* could survive, even after consuming the *Halāhala* (poison), only by the power of *Śreedevee*'s *Tāṭankas* (28th verse of *Soundaryalaharee*).

23. *Padmarāgashilādarshaparibhāvikapolabhoo*: -
पद्मरागशिलादर्शपरिभाविकपोलभूः

(i) One whose cheeks are most wonderful than a glass made of *Padmarāgā* (Sapphire).

(ii) *Śreedevee*'s cheeks are smooth and reflect like a mirror. Since it also seems to be red on account of **Her** complexion, the cheeks seem to be superior to a glass made of Sapphire.

24. *Navavidrūmabimba Shreenyakkāridashanacchadā –*
नवविद्रुमबिम्ब श्रीन्यक्कारिदशनच्छदा

(i) One whose (gorgeous) lips challenge the lustre of fresh Corals and the *Bimba* fruit (a fruit of a creeper, which when ripe is Red).

(ii) *Śreedevee*'s lips are Red in colour, by nature. Coral and the *Bimba* fruit are the two usually referred to for comparing lustrous Red objects. *Śreedevee*'s Rosy lips surpass these two objects.

(iii) *Radanacchada* is another version and the meaning is the same.

25. *Shuddhavidyāngkurākāradvijapanktidwayoojjwalā –*
शुद्धविद्याङ्कुराकारद्विजपक्तिद्वयोज्ज्वला

(i) One whose rows of teeth shine like sprouts of *Shuddha Vidya*.

(ii) The word *Dvijā* means twice born. This term is used to describe three different things:

a. **Brahmin** – First birth from the mother and the second when the *Upanayanam* is performed (when the sacred thread is first worn)

b. **Birds** – First birth as egg and the second when the chick comes out of the egg

c. **Tooth** – First as milk teeth and second when the tooth sprouts in place of fallen teeth.

(iii) *Shuddha Vidyā* refers to the superior *Shoḍashāksharī Mantra*. It consists of 16 letters or *beejās*. *Beejās* also mean seeds. The teeth look like the two sprouts from the seeds – the upper and lower rows.

(iv) *Dattātreya Samhitā* and other texts state that *Shuddha Vidyā* is the same as *Śreevidya*. Hence the 16 letters of *Shoḍasī Vidyā* are hidden in this name.

(v) Brahmins learn and propagate *Vedas*. Hence they are called *Vidyānkurās* that is sprout of *Vidya*. *Śreedevee*'s two rows of teeth are compared to two rows of Brahmins, the sprout of *Vidya*.

(vi) In the *Tantra* text 32 types of initiations are mentioned – starting from *Shuddha Vidyā*, *Bālā*, *Dwadasārthā*, *Mātangee* and ending with *Anutthara*.These 32 types form the two rows of teeth of *Śreedevee* –

another interpretation of this name.

(vii) It is indicated only the *Dvijās* (*Brahmins*) purified by these 32 initiations can reach *Śreedevee*'s feet.

(viii) *Śreedevee*'s *Triakshari Mantra* is also called as *Shuddha Vidya*. One becomes eligible for the 32 initiations (*Deekshās*) only after he is inducted into *Triaksharī*. *Shuddha Vidyā* is the base for the two rows of teeth which sprout from *Shuddha Vidya*.

(ix) In the *Paribhāshā Shlokās* in the *Nāma Vibhagā* part of this book, it is stated that the 1000 names begin only with 32 letters out of 51 letters in the Samskrit alphabet, omitting 19 letters. It is also indicated that entire *Sahasranāma Stotrā* is structured on these 32 letters.

26. *Karpooraveeṭikāmodasamākarshidigantarā* – कर्पूटबीटिकामोदसमाकर्षिदिगन्तरा

(i) One who attracts the four directions towards **Her** by the pleasant aroma of the betel (*tāmboola*) emanating from **Her** lotus like mouth, or one who spreads that aroma in all directions.

Veetikā is a small pack (folded inside a betel leaf) with proper mixture of aromatic spices such as camphor, cardamom, cloves, musk, saffron, nutmeg, betel nut, lime, etc. The aroma emanating from *Śreedevee*'s mouth when **She** chews the *Veetikā* spreads in all directions. It is symbolically described as if the directions compete with each other in surrounding *Śreedevee* to have a scent of this aroma. *Dik* refers to the four directions and *Digambarā* is the intervening space between the four directions such as Southeast, Southwest, etc.

(ii) In the latter part of this *Stotrā*, there is another name *Tāmboola Pooritamukhi* (559th name), which describes *Śreedevee* chewing betel leaves.

(iii) The name *Samākarsh**a**digantarā* is also mentioned as *Samākarsh**i**digantarā* in some editions. There is no difference in meaning between these two versions.

(iv) The 14th name in *Śree Lalitā Trishatī*, namely, *Karpooraveeṭi Sourabhya Kallolitakagupthatā* also states the same idea. *Śree Ādi Śaṇkara* in his commentary has stated that the whole world is drenched with this aroma emanating from *Śreedevee*'s mouth and *Śreedevee* is thus *Maharājabhogavathi* (one who enjoys the comforts of an empress).

(v) It is told that there were legendary poets, who were *Upāsakās* of *Śreedevee*, viz. *Kalidāsa* and *Mooka Kavi*, got their excellent capacity to write poems by consuming the juice of *Śreedevee*'s *tāmboola*.

(vi) It is implied that the *Dikpālās* – the regents of the eight cardinal points – encircle *Śreedevee* to offer their prayers.

27. *Nijasallāpamādhuryavinirbhartsitakacchapee* – निजसल्लापमाधुर्यविनिर्भर्त्सितकच्छपी

(i) One whose sweet voice humbles the *Veena* (a string instrument) called *Kacchapi* in the hands of *Śree Saraswathi* (goddess of learning).

(ii) *Kacchapi* is the name of *Śree Saraswathi*'s *Veena*. Normally, in any string instrument like *Veena*, only the musical notes will be heard and not the lyrics of a song. But since *Śree Saraswathi* is the embodiment of sound and music, the musical notes as well as the words in the lyrics are heard from her *Veena*. However, the words would not be explicit, but resemble the utterances of parrot and infants. *Śreedevee*'s voice is so sweet, that it wins over the sweetness of *Śree Saraswathi*'s *Veena*

(iii) There is one verse in *Soundaryalaharee* (66th verse beginning with *Vipanchyā Gāyanthi*). It is stated that when *Śree Saraswathi* played her *Veena* in the presence of *Śreedevee*, **She** admired its sweetness and uttered the word 'awesome'. On hearing this *Śree Saraswathi* was ashamed by the sweetness of *Śreedevee*'s voice which surpassed the sound of her *Veena* and kept it inside its cover.

28. *Mandasmitaprabhāpooramajjatkāmeshamānasā* – मन्दस्मितप्रभापूरमज्जत्कामेशमानसा

(i) One who overwhelms *Śree Kāmeshwara*'s mind in the inundate of **Her** smile.

(ii) *Smita* means smile – without the teeth being visible. Especially *Mandasmita* means a very soft smile.

(iii) *Majjat* means sinking. *Śree Kāmeshwara* does not want to come out of the flood of light that is *Śreedevee*'s smile. At the same time **He** does not want to miss the opportunity of enjoying the beauty of the other parts; hence the use of the expression 'sinking'.

(iv) In *Kāmakalā*, *Kāma* means *bindu*. *Kalā* means Sun, Moon and fire. *Bindu* denotes *ahankāra*. *Kama* and *kala* denote *Kāmakala*. *Kāmeshwara* means both *Rājarājeshwara* and the embodiment of

Kāmakala.

(v) When *Śreedevee* emerged out of the fire of knowledge (*Chidagnikuṇḍa*), before crowning **Her** as empress, the question arose as who can be made as **Her** consort. The only eligible candidate was *Śree Kāmeshwara*. But the *Devas* were perplexed as **His** physical appearance –with knotted locks, covered with an elephant skin or wearing nothing at all, with snakes as jewels and with ash smeared all over the body – was in no way a match to **Her** bewitching beauty. Immediately *Śree Parameshwara* took a beautiful form of *Kāmeshwara*. *Śreedevee* swung a garland declaring that he on whose neck the garland falls would be **Her** consort; it fell on *Śree Kāmeshwara*'s neck and brought forth a smile in *Śreedevee*'s lips. *Śree Kāmeshwara* was drowned in the beauty of **Her** smile. This is narrated in *Śree Lalithopakhyana*.

29. ***Anākalitasādrushyachibukashreevirājitā* – अनाकलितसादृश्यचिबुकश्रीविराजिता**

(i) One who shines by virtue of the incomparable beauty of **Her** chin.

(ii) Even the *Vāgdevatās* (the goddess of words) could not find similes to describe the beauty of **Her** chin.

(iii) *Śree Ādi Śaṇkara* also opines the same, in his *Soundaryalaharee*, as *Kathankāram Bhruma; tavasubukam oupamya rahitam* (67th verse).

(iv) *Chubuka* or *Chibuka* mean the same.

(v) The 85th name *Śreemadvāgbhava Kooṭaika Swarūpa Mukha Pankajā*, states the part of *Śreedevee*'s body above the neck denotes the first part of *Śree Vidyā Panchadashāksharee mantra* viz. *Vāgbhava kooṭa*. The description of this part of the body starts from the 13th name, *Champakāshoka Punnāga Sougandhika Lasatkachā* and ends here.

30. ***Kāmeshabaddhamāngalyasootrashobhitakandharā* – कामेशबद्धमाङ्गल्यसूत्रशोभितकन्धरा**

(i) One whose neck is so beautiful by the auspicious string tied by *Śree Kāmeshwara* at the time of wedding.

(ii) *Śreedevee* is a *Nitya Sumangali*, who is always a *Sumangali*, wearing the *mangala Sūtra*. Although **She** emerged out of *Chidagni Kuṇḍa*, already wearing the *mangala Sūtra*, the *Devās* wanted to see the wedding ceremony of the Holy couple and made **Him** tie the string again on *Śreedevee*.

(iii) *Śree Parameshwara* acquired the name *Kāmāri* after he reduced

Cupid to ashes. Yet on seeing *Śreedevee*, it appears that **He** gave life to Cupid and subjected **Himself** as the aim for the arrows by Cupid so that love would arise in **Him** upon *Śreedevee*, that too through the grace of *Śreedevee*. (84th name – *Haranetrāgni Sandagdha Kāma Sanjīvanoushadhi* may be compared). Hence **He** becomes the lord of Cupid – *Kāmeśan*.

(iv) Induced by His desire to marry *Śreedevee*, *Eshwara* made friendship with Cupid and was worshipped by him as "Thou art my Lord".

(v) This *mangala Sutra* tied by *Kāmesha* showered blessings to the entire world. The first such beneficiary of this shower was *Rathi-Manmatha* (Cupid) couple and that too for the upliftment of the whole world.

31. *Kanakāngadakeyūrakamanīyabhujānvit* - कनकाङ्गदकेयूरकमनीयभुजान्विता

(i) One whose shoulders are adorned by golden shoulder bangles.

(ii) *Angadā* and *Keyūrā* are the two ornaments worn the hands. *Keyūrā* is for beautification whereas *Angadā* acts as a shield for shoulders and arms of warriors. As *Śreedevee* is a queen, **She** wears both the ornaments.

32. *Ratnagraiveyachintākalolamuktāphalānvitā* – रत्नग्रैवेयचिन्ताकलोलमुक्ताफलान्विता

(i) One who wears a necklace with a pendant studded with gemstones and garland of Pearls.

(ii) *Grivā* means neck. *Graiveya* means the pendant in the necklace which adorns the neck and the string of Pearls aligning the necklace.

(iii) The necklace, the pendant and the sting of pearls represent the three types of devotees. Some will be chanting the names of *Śreedevee* (doing *Japa*), but their minds will be wandering somewhere else. Their thoughts of *Śreedevee* stop with the neck. They are *Graiveya Chintākas*, limiting their thought of *Śreedevee* above the neck. They hang and swing from the necklace of *Śreedevee*, hence they are called *Loolās*. For some others, the thoughts and actions will be oscillating between *Śreedevee* and other extraneous thoughts, like a pendant hanging from the necklace. The third type is the *Muktās* – the detached. They have got rid of their extraneous thoughts and action and think of *Śreedevee* only. Thus, this name classifies the devotees into three types.

(iv) The fruits of actions of these three types of devotees are also different. For the *Graiveya Chintāka* and *Loolā* the benefits are few – *Āphala*. For the *Muktās Āphalām* – full benefits. Two meanings are indicated for *Āphalā* – few and full. For those who just utter the names (of *Śreedevee*) without concentration of mind, the benefits are few. For those whose minds oscillate between material things (*Loolās*) the benefits are still less. Those whose mind, word and action act in unison derive full benefits. All the three types of devotees are blessed with the gems like benefits they deserve.

33. *Kāmeshvarapreemaratnamaŋiprathipaŋastanee* –
कामेश्वरप्रेमरत्नमणिप्रथिपणस्तनी

(i) One who offers **Her** breasts as price (or in exchange) for the gem of love of *Śree Kāmeshwara*.

(ii) *Śreedevee* has purchased *Śree Kāmeshwara's* invaluable love for **Her,** with her breasts.

(iii) *Śreedevee* has offered twice the price or price like (two jewels of breasts) for a single jewel of *Śree Kāmeshwara's* love. (Refer - 4th *verse* of *Soundaryalaharee- Phalamapicha Vānchāsamadhikam*)

34. *Nābhyālavālaromālilatāphalakuchadvayee* –
नाभ्यालवालरोमालिलताफलकुचद्वयी

(i) *Śreedevee*'s two breasts are like fruits in a creeper (line of hair) climbing from the trench (the naval).

(ii) The deep naval is like a trench. The narrow line of hair grown upwards from the naval is like a creeper. The two breasts appear as if they are hanging from the creeper (an excellent metaphor).

(iii) 78th *verse* of *Soundaryalaharee* may be referred; *Stanamukula Romāvalilata*.

35. *Lakshyaromalatādhāratāsamunneyamadhyamā*–
लक्ष्यरोमलताधारतासमुन्नेयमध्यमा

(i) One for whom, the existence of a waist base for the climbing creeper of line of hair is to be presumed.

(ii) The creeper of hair line mentioned in the previous name is visible. But the base where the root of the creeper is located is not to be

seen. The existence of a limb as waist is to be presumed.
(iii) As per *Sāmudrika Sāstrā*, the waist of upper classes of women will be so small as to be presumed as non-existent.

36. *Stanabhāradalanmadhyapaṭṭabandhavalitrayā* –
स्तनभारदलन्मध्यपट्टबन्धवलित्रया

(i) One whose three folds in the abdominal area appear to be three bandages worn on the waist to prevent it from breaking due to the weight of the breasts.
(ii) *Sāmudrika Sāstrā* specifies that higher class men and women will have three lines (folds) on their forehead, neck and abdomen. They are signs of extremely good fortune.
(iii) Refer - 80th verse of *Soundaryalaharee – Thridhanaddham Devee thrivalee lavaleevalleebhiriva.*

37. *Aruŋāruŋakousumbhavastrabhāsvatkaṭeetaṭee* –
अरुणारुणकौसुम्भवस्त्रभास्वत्कटीतटी

(i) One whose waist shines with the crimson silk worn on it.
(ii) The dual expression *Aruŋa-Aruŋa* means dark red or Crimson.
(iii) The Red here is like that of *Aruŋa*, the charioteer of the Sun God, who rises before Sun rises.
(iv) *Kausumbha Vastrā* means Red silk cloth. The juice of *Kausumbha* herb is used to dye cloths in Red; hence *Kausumbha Vastra*.
(v) *Śreedevee* has worn *Kausumbha Vastrā* on **Her** waist.
(vi) It appears as though *Aruŋa Vāgdevee*'s name is indirectly stated here.

38. *Ratnakinkiŋikāramyarashanādāmabhooshitā* –
रत्नकिंकिणिकारम्यरशनादामभूषिता

(i) One who wears a girdle string (*Mekalā Sūtra*) lined with tinkling gems.
(ii) The golden girdle string is line with small tinkle bells. The small gems inside the bells make a soft pleasant sound.
(iii) The part of *Śreedevee*'s body below the neck and above the thigh represents the central portion of *Panchadashākksharee Mantra* consisting of six letters. These are indirectly stated from 30th till 38th names.

39. ***Kāmeshagyātasoubhāgyamārdavorudvayānvitā* – कामेशज्ञातसौभाग्यमार्दवोरुद्वयान्विता**

(i) One who has two beautiful and soft thighs known only to *Śree Kāmeshwara*.
(ii) The softness and the smoothness of **Her** thighs are known only to *Śree Kāmeshwara*.
(iii) *Soubhāgyā* here means exquisiteness or beauty.

40. ***Māŋikyamukuṭākārajānudvayavirājitā* - माणिक्यमुकुटाकारजानुद्वयविराजिता**

(i) One whose knees resemble hard, Red caps made of rubies.
(ii) The knees are so Red and seem to be like a hard cap.
(iii) The softness of the thighs mentioned in the previous name is contrasted with the hardness of the knees.
(iv) The reason for hardness of *Śreedevee*'s knees is stated in the 82nd *verse* of *Soundaryalaharee*.
(v) *Mukuṭa* and *Makuṭa* – both have the same meaning.

41. ***Indragopaparikshiptasmaratooŋābhajanghikā* – इन्द्रगोपपरिक्षिप्तस्मरतूणाभजङ्घिका**

(i) One whose shank resembles Cupid's quiver surrounded by fireflies.
(ii) A quiver is a case for carrying arrows, carried by the warriors, with a broad mouth and tapered at the bottom.
(iii) The two shanks of *Śreedevee* are firm and reddish. This resembles Cupid's quiver surrounded by insects sparkling at night. The brightness of the ankles is enhanced by the sparkling insects. The reddish legs are glowing naturally, but as a metaphor this is compared to the fireflies shining in the night.
(iv) *Śreeādi Śaṇkara* says in 83rd verse of *Soundaryalaharee*, that Cupid, who was burnt down by Lord *Shiva* was waiting for an opportunity to seek revenge on **Him** and when **He** was attracted by *Śreedevee*'s beauty, Cupid made *Śreedevee*'s shanks his quiver and **Her** toes his arrows;
Parājethum RudhramdhviguŋaCharagarbhau GIrisute
Nishangou Janghete Vishama Vichikho Badhamakrta

42. ***Gooḍhagulphā* - गूढगुल्फा**

(i) One whose shanks are covered by firm muscles.
(ii) *Gulphā* refers to the calf muscles above the ankles; it means firm and beautiful ankles.

43. *Koormaprushṭhajayishŋuprapadānvitā* - कूर्मपृष्ठजयिष्णुप्रपदान्विता

(i) One whose foot resembles a turtle's back.
(ii) The back of the feet of higher class women would be pyramid like. In the absence of any other suitable comparison, turtle's back (though of an inferior class) is used as a simile.
(iii) The 88th verse of *Soundaryalaharee* also explicitly states that this simile is not the most appropriate one;
Padam Tekeertteenām Prapadam Apadam Devee Vipadām
Ktham Neetam Sadbhi: Katina Khamateekarppara Tulām

44. *Nakhadeedhitisanchannanamajjana Tamoguŋā* – नखदीधितिसंछन्ननमज्जन तमोगुणा

(i) One who removes the darkness of ignorance of those who prostate (*Tamo Guŋa*) before **Her** by the lustre of **Her** toe nails.
(ii) When *Brahma*, *Vişhŋu* and other *Devas* prostate before *Śreedevee*'s feet, the lustre of their crown face the lustre of *Śreedevee*'s toe nails and unable to stand, their brightness go back inside them and remove the darkness of ignorance.
(iii) Or, just by contact, the lustre of the toe nails removes the darkness of ignorance.
(iv) Not only for the *Devas*, but also for all those who worship *Śreedevee*, the same benefit i.e. the removal of ignorance – is obtained.

45. *Padadvayaprabhājālaparākrutasaroruhā* - पदद्वयप्रभाजालपराकृतसरोरुहा

(i) One who won over the lotus flower by the lustre of **Her** two feet.
(ii) Generally, it is a literary tradition to take the lotus flower for comparison with the face, feet and eyes of beautiful men and women. Lustre, softness, beautiful structure and a lovely appearance are the special features of a lotus. In the case of *Śreedevee*'s feet, there is one more special characteristic. Lotus will blossom and shrivel on the same day, whereas *Śreedevee*'s feet remain permanently lustrous and thus they win over lotus.

46. *Sinjānamaŋimanjeeramaŋḍita Śreepadāmbujā* – सिञ्जानमणिमंजीरमण्डित श्रीपदांबुजा

(i) One whose Lotus feet are decorated with anklets with tinkling bells.
(ii) The anklets worn on *Śreedevee*'s feet have bells fixed with gems. They make a sweet and soft jingle while oscillating. They add *Śree* to **Her** lotus feet. (*Śree* is one word which cannot be translated into any other language, to bring forth its entire meaning). Broadly it means "all that is good".
(iii) *Chinjāna* is another expression in some texts. The meaning is the same.

47. *Marāleemandagamanā* - मरालीमन्दगमना

(i) One whose gait is slow and beautiful like a female swan.
(ii) The gait of a swan is always soft and beautiful. The gait of a female swan is all the more graceful. Hence the female swan is compared.
(iii) Everyone stands spell bound by the beauty of *Śreedevee* coming out of the sacrificial fire.
(iv) The same idea is expressed in *Soundaryalaharee* and *Mooka Pancha sati*. The swans in *Śreedevee*'s palace try to learn and copy the gait of *Śreedevee*. The soft sound of *Śreedevee*'s anklets seems to teach lessons to the swans.

Padanyāsa Kridā Parichaya Mivānabdhu Manasa:
Skhalantaste Khelam Bhavanakalahamsā Na Jahati
Athastheeshām Shikshaām Subhagamaŋi Manjīra Raŋita-
Chaladachakshānām Charaŋakamalam Charucharitee
(91st *verse* of *Soundaryalaharee*)

MarālīnāmYāmābhyasanakalanā Moolaguravee
(*Mookapanchashatee – Pādāravinda Shatakam* - 3)

(v) That part of *Śreedevee's* body below the waist represents the *Shaktikūta* of *Śreedevee's mantra* consisting of four syllables.

48. *Mahālāvaŋyashevadhi*: - महालावण्यशेवधि:

(i) **She** is a repository or container of all beauty.
(ii) *Śreedevee*'s divine beauty is unparalleled. **Her** face is described as a container gathering all the beauty. The below 12th verse of *Soundaryalaharee* may also be referred.

Tvadīyam Soundaryam Tuhinagirikanyee Tulayitum
Kaveendrā: *Kalpante Kathamapi Virinchi Prabhrutaya*:

49. *Sarvāruŋā* - सर्वारुणा

(i) **Her** body, garments, jewels, flower and lustre are all Red.
(ii) It was not just because S**he** emerged from the sacrificial fire, but it was natural to **Her**.
(iii) *Lauhityame tasya Sarvasya Vimarsah – Pāvanopanishad* (29) may also be referred.
(iv) This name occurs as the 138th name in *Lalitā Trishatee.* In his commentary, *Śree Ādi Śaņkara* quotes the *Vedic* text *Asau Yastāmroo Aruŋa*:.

50. *Anavadyāngee* - अनवद्याङ्गी

(i) One who has a flawless body structure.
(ii) **Her** flawless body looked at from foot to head or from head to foot bestows bliss on those who are blessed to have a vision.

51. *Sarvābharaŋabhooshitā* - सर्वाभरणभूषिता

(i) One who is adorned with all ornaments.
(ii) The jewels worn by *Śreedevee* (from the *Chooḍamaŋi* worn on the head to the toe ring) are described in the *Kalpa Sūtra, Kālikā Purāŋā*, etc. For one who has a flawless body structure as stated in the previous name, all the jewels try to add to **Her** beauty, but fail in their attempts. On the other hand, the elegance of the jewels is enhanced by their presence on *Śreedevee*'s body. (The list of jewels is given under the 235th name *Chatushshashṭi Upachārādyā*).
(iii) Completely decorated with all the ornaments. It can also be interpreted to mean that *Śreedevee* is the one who endows the status of ornaments on the jewels worn by **Her**.
(iv) The same name occurs as the 140th one in *Lalitā Trishatee as Sarvābharaŋabhooshitā* or *Sarvābhooshaŋabhooshita*.
(v) After describing the physical form of *Śreedevee* from head to foot, the *Sahasranāmā* proceeds to describe *Śreedevee*'s dwelling place.

52. *Shivakāmeshvarāngkasthā* - शिवकामेश्वराङ्कस्था

(i) One who sits on the left lap of **Her** consort *Śree Shivakāmeshwara*.
(ii) *Kāmā* means a beautiful person. *Sivā* means the auspicious one.

Iśwarā is the one who controls (rules over) the actions of others according to his wish. Hence *Shivakāmeśhwara.*

(iii) *Kāmeśhwarā* is one who is capable of taking any form of his choice. It also means that he is more handsome than *Kāmā* (the God of love) – Cupid, hence *Kāmeśhwara.*

(iv) According to *Sruti* (*Vedas*), *Pragnana* is *Kāmeśhwara.*

(v) *Brihadāraŋya Upanishad* (1-4-17) states that the *Eśhwarā* who wished to create the world was called *Kāma.* (*Atmaivedamagra Asiteekaeeva Sookāmayata*)

(vi) The term *Shivakāmeśhwarā* has not been used in the sense *Sādārana Rudra* or *Manmatha*. What is referred to here is the *Icchāshakti* of the Supreme Being.

(vii) *Śreedevee* is *Shivakāmeśhwarī,* as **She** sits on the left lap of *Shiva kāmeśhwara*. All the explanations given above are equally applicable to **Her**.

53. *Shivā* – शिवा

(i) *Shiva* 's consort and hence *Shiva* – inseparable from *Shiva.*

(ii) Embodiment of auspiciousness, bestower of auspiciousness - The *Icchāshakti* of the Supreme Being - Liberation personified.

(iii) Everything ultimately rests with *Śreedevee*. Hence *Shiva.*

(iv) *Parameeśhwarā* has eight forms, viz. Earth, Water, Fire, Wind, Space, Sun, Moon and Jeeva. *Shiva* in the form wind is called *Īsāna*. **His** consort is *Shiva.*

(v) The statement in the *Vedas* – *Yāthee Rudra Sivāthanoo*: may be referred.

54. *Svādheenavallabhā* - स्वाधीनवल्लभा

(i) One who has a loving and amenable consort.

(ii) *Shiva*'s *shakti* (energy) is *Devee*. Energy is a characteristic feature, which cannot exist on its own, but always exists with matter. Thus it means that *Shakti* lives with *Shiva* and is obedient to **Her**. But in fact *Shiva* is controlled by *Shakti* and always seeks **Her** help in all his actions.

(iii) The 1st verse of *Soundaryalaharee* – *"Shiva shakhyā Yuktā Yadibhavati Shakahprabhavitum Nacheedevam Devo Na Kahlu Kusataspaŋḍitumapi"* may be referred.

(iv) In practice, if anybody is idle he is referred as *Shiva nee*.

(v) One by whose grace women got their husbands. *Sukanya* wed *Chyavana, Sachi Devee* wed *Indra* and *Rukmaŋi* wed *Krişhŋa* by worshipping *Śreedevee* and by her blessings.
(vi) Although **She** is independent and not under the control of *Parameeśhwarā*, **She** is his beloved. *Swādhīna* – independent; *Vallabhā* – beloved.
(vii) When *Vāgdevees* started to explain the dwelling of *Śreedevee*, they first talk about the lap of *Shiva* and then continue to describe other dwellings.

55. *Sumerumadhyasrungasthā* - सुमेरुमध्यश्रुङ्गस्था

(i) One who dwells in the central peak of mount *Meru*.
(ii) *Sumeru* is a golden mountain which supports the Earth as its base. There are three peaks located triangularly in the centre of the mountain and there is another fourth and higher peak at the centre of the triangle. The *Śreenagaram* where *Śreedevee* dwells is in this fourth peak. These details are beautifully described in *Lalitā stavarāja* written by sage *Durvāsa*.

56. *Śreemannagaranāyikā* - श्रीमन्नगरनायिका

(i) The head of (*nāyikā*) *Śreenagaram*.
(ii) *Śreenagaram* is always known as *Śreemad Lakshmee Vidyā Nagaram* and *Śreedevee* is its head of state.
(iii) This city (*nagara*) is said to be in two locations; one is as stated in *Lalitāstavarāja*. The other is the centre of *Sudhāsamudrā* as told in *Rudryāmala*.
(iv) *Śreemannagaram* may also be understood to mean *Śree Chakra m* and hence *Śree Chakranāyika*. This has also been stated in *Gouḍapā Sutrās*.

57. *Chintāmaŋigruhāntasthā* - चिन्तामणिगृहान्तस्था

(i) One who dwells in a house constructed of *Chintāmaŋi*.
(ii) *Chintāmaŋi* is a gem stone which bestows all the desires of the mind. *Chintāmaŋigraha* is a palace built with *Chintāmaŋi* gems. **She** dwells in it.
(iii) The syllables in *Śreedevee's mantra* are also capable of bestowing what the mind desires and hence referred to as *Chintāmaŋi*.

Śreedevee dwells in those syllables (*Beejākharās*).

58. *Panchabrahmasanasthitā* - पञ्चब्रह्मासनस्थिता

(i) One who sits on a seat made of five *Brahmams*.

(ii) *Śreedevee* sits, besides *Kāmeśhwarā*, on a seat (cot) whose four legs are *Brahma, Viṣhņu, Rudra* & *Īsāna* and the sitting plank is *Sadāśiva*. When *Parabrahmam* desires to evolve this world, these five *Brahmams* help to materialise this desire by carrying out the five functions of creation (*Srishti*), sustenance (*Sthithi*), destruction (*Samhāra*), screaming from the impacts of material pleasure & displeasure (*Tirodhāna*) and blessings (*Anugraha*) to bring about the changes. These *Brahmams* respectively are the legs on Southeast, Southwest, Northwest and Northeast directions and the sitting plank.

(iii) Since all the five are constantly in meditation, with their eyes closed, contemplating on *Śreedevee*, they are called *Pancha brahmams*. Since all these five emerge from and ultimately converge in the same *Parabrahmam*, they are also referred to as *Brahmams*. Sometimes *Śreedevee* absorbs in herself the energies of these five *Brahmams* like creation, etc. In those situations these five *Brahmams* are called *Panchapretās*. Consequently, *Śreedevee* is referred to as *Panchapretāsanāseenā* (249th name) and *Panchapreta Manjādhisāyini* (947th name).

(iv) The reason for these *Brahmams* being the legs of the cot is their desire to be of faithful service to *Śreedevee* in close proximity.

59. *Mahāpadmāṭaveesamsthā* - महापद्माटवीसंस्था

(i) One who lives in a big Lotus jungle. This jungle is in the centre of *Chintāmaņigraha*.

(ii) One who lives in the *Brahmarandhrā*, below the skull, in a Lotus with thousand (countless) petals.

(iii) *Mahāpadmā* is a superior species of elephants. The forest, inhabited by such elephants is *Gajāranyā*, also known as *Tiruvānaikā* (a temple near Tiruchirappalli, in Tamilnadu). The presiding deity of this temple is *Śree Akilāndeśwarī*).

60. *Kadambavanavāsinee* – कदंबवनवासिनी

(i) One who lives in *Kadamba* woods.

(ii) *Chintāmaŋigraha* is a palace of gems surrounded by a jungle of *Kadamba* trees. *Śreedevee* dwells in this jungle.
(iii) *Śreepura* is surrounded by 25 walls made of metals and gems representing 25 concepts (*Tatvas*). The *Kadamba* jungle is located between the gold and silver walls.
(iv) Madurai (a holy city in Tamilnadu) is also known as *Kadambavana*. *Śreedevee* is the presiding deity here with the name *Meenakshee*.

61. *Sudhāsāgaramadhyasthā* – सुधासागरमध्यस्था

(i) One who lives in the centre of the ocean of nectar.
(ii) The location of this ocean of nectar is given differently in various sources. According to *Rudryāmalā*, the *Chintāmaŋigraha* is located in this ocean.
(iii) The *Vedas* say *Yoovaithām Brahmaŋoovedam Amrithenāvratam Purim* (City surrounded by nectar). *Aruŋa Praśnā* – 27.116.
(iv) The *Bindusthānā* in the *Chandramaŋḍala*, in the Lotus with thousand petals, below our skull is referred to as *Sudhāsindhu* (Ocean of nectar).
(v) According to *Chāndogya Upanishad*, this ocean is located in the city of *Aparājitā*, which can be reached by worshipping a god with attributes (*Saguŋopāsanā*). *Aparājitā* for *Śreedevee* worshippers is like *Kailas* for *Shiva* worshippers and *Śree Vaikuŋtam* for worshippers of *Vishŋu*. There are two tanks in this city called *Āram* and *Nyam*, which are referred to as *Sudhā Sāgara*.
(vi) In the commentary on the *Brahma Sūtra, Anāvrtti*: *Shabdā*: (IV – 4-22), these oceans of nectar are referred to.
(vii) The 8th verse of *Soundaryalaharee*, starting with *Sudha sindhoor madhyā*, also talks of *Sudhā Sagara*.

62. *Kāmākshee* – कामाक्षी

(i) One with beautiful eyes.
(ii) One who has (beloved) *Kāmeshwara* as her eyes.
(iii) One who bestows all desires of **Her** devotees by **Her** eyes.
(iv) One who has *Saraswathi* (*Kā*) and *Lakshmee* (*Mā*) as **Her** eyes.
(v) Kancheepuram is one of the 51 *Shakti Peetams*, where *Śreedevee*'s waist (the place where the waist band, *Kānchi*, is worn) fell. *Brahma* performed a sacrifice in this place seeking the powers of creation. *Śreedevee* was called *Kāmākshee* as she fulfilled *Brahma*'s desires.

(vi) *Kāma* (Cupid) was destroyed by *Paramashiva* 's third eye and restored to life by *Śreedevee*'s vision. Hence *Kāmākshee*.

63. *Kāmadāyinee* – कामदायिनी

(i) One who fulfills Her devotees desires.
(ii) *Dāyini* – one who gives to Her devotees, *Kāma* – *Kāmeshwara*, that is, one who leads Her devotees to *Kāmeshwara* and become one with Him.
(iii) *Kāmada* means *Shiva* - that is one who destroyed Cupid. *Ayini* means auspiciously united. *Kāmadayini* means, one who is auspiciously united with the destroyer of *Kāma*.
(iv) Hereditary property is called *Dāyam*. *Śreedevee* has *Kāma* as *Dāyam*. Her association with *Kāma* is timeless.
(v) 989th name – *Vānchithārthapradiyinee* and *Trishatee* 43rd name – *Īpsithārthapradiyinee* may be referred.
(vi) Names 61, 62 and 63 were separately considered above. Even if read together, it forms a complete sentence i.e. *Sudhā Sāgara Madhyasthā Kāmākshee Kāmadāyinee* - *Kāmākshee*, dwelling in the centre of the ocean of nectar, bestows all that the devotees desire.

64. *Devarshigaṇasanghātastooyamānātmavaibhavā* – देवर्षिगणसंघातस्तूयमानात्मवैभवा

(i) One whom groups of *deva*s and *rishi*s (gods and sages) pray to and celebrate.
(ii) *Vibhu* means omnipresent. *Vaibhava* is omnipresence. *Śreedevee* is omnipresent so that She can bestow Her devotees' desires everywhere and immediately.
(iii) *Sanghātasthooyamāna* means, one whom groups of *devas* and sages pray to. *Sanghāta* also means variously. *Devas* and sages pray to Her in various forms.
(iv) *Sanghāta* also means a kind of hell. *Deva*s and sages pray to *Śreedevee* to get released from this hell.
(v) If interpreted as *Samyak-ghāta* means totally annihilated. The annihilation of *Bhanḍāsura* to be referred to in the next name is indicated here.
(vi) One to whom *Deva*s (*Brahma* and others), sages (*Vasishta* and others), *Devarishis* (*Narada* and others) and *Gaṇas* (*Āditya* and others) pray.

(vii) *Ātma* is the dynamic form of *Śreedevee* – omnipresent, omnipotent, love in all forms (*Sat, chit* and *ānanda* – that is existence, knowledge and bliss). It is in this form to whom groups of devas and sages pray. This *Ātma* is the undivided form of *Śreedevee*. Refer: *Sadānanda* poorŋa: *Svātmaiva Paradevatā Lalitā* (*Bhavanopanishad* – 28). In this name *Śreedevee's* (as *Atma*) omnipresence, omnipotence and boundless energy are indicated.

65. *Bhanḍāsuravadhodyuktashaktisenāsamanvitā* –
भण्डासुटबधोद्युक्तशक्तिसेनासमन्विता

(i) One who is leading an army of *Shaktis* intent on destroying the demon called *Bhanḍa*.

(ii) The objective of *devas* referred to earlier (in name 5) – that is destruction of *Bhanḍasura*, is indicated here. She stands prepared to achieve that objective with an army of *Shaktis* in different forms created by Her.

(iii) One with whom the several form of *Shakti* is an integral part.

(iv) One who has the power or is capable of destroying ego of which *Bhanḍasura* is embodied.

(v) When *Manmatha* (Cupid) was reduced to ashes by the fire of *Shiva*'s third eye, Lord *Gaŋapati* collected the ashes and made a male figure out of them. It came alive, did penance and obtained many boons from *Shiva. Brahma* acclaimed this achievement saying *Bhanḍ, Bhanḍ* (good, good) and hence he got the name *Bhanḍasura*. His cruel (demonist) character was the result of his emergence from the ashes arising out of the fire of anger of *Shiva. Śreedevee* came with the army of *Shaktis* to destroy him.

(vi) *Bhanḍa* was bound by his own ignorance and lived with the thought that sensual pleasures are supreme (*Asushu Mamthee Asura*:). He was ignorant of his *Atmaswarūpa* (soul). It was necessary to destroy his cruel (demonistic) character. What was needed was effort (*Udyama*); when effort was mobilised, the power required to destroy this cruel character would be generated to help him. The power of soul (*atma*), hidden in a state of ignorance, when emerges by a process of knowledge, evolves as various forms of *Shakti*. The real concept (*tatvārtha*) is that, the power of soul, hitherto hidden from *Jeevā* by ignorance, comes out as powerful *Shaktis* when effort is made to achieve self realisation.

(vii) *Gouḍapādu Sūtra*(16) states "*Bhanḍasura Hananārtham Eeka Eeva Aneeka*".

66. *Sampatkareesamāroodhasindhuravrajasevitā* –
सम्पत्करीसमारूढसिन्धुरव्रजसेविता

(i) One who is worshipped by the elephant brigade commanded by *Sampatkaree*.

(ii) *Sampatkaree* is the commander of *Śreedevee's* elephant brigade. *Sindhura* means an elephant. This commander is mounted on an elephant called *Ranakolahala*. She emerged out of the elephant goad in the hands of *Śreedevee* and commanded the elephant brigade of thousands of elephants.

(iii) *Sampatkaree Vidyā* is a powerful *mantra*. It finds a place in the *Swatantra Tantra* and consists of three syllables (*beejāksharās*).

(iv) The mental state which is full of the wealth pleasure is called *Sampatkaree*. This mental state is founded on the objects of senses like sound. These objects are equated with elephants. Hence *Śreedevee* is said to be worshipped by *Sampatkaree* elephant.

(v) The knowledge which enables one to identify the knower, the knowledge and the object of knowledge separately and their correlation is known as *Sampatkari*.

67. *Ashvāroodhādhishtitāshvakotikotibhirāvrutā* –
अश्वारूढाधिष्ठिताश्वकोटिकोटिभिरावृता

(i) One who is surrounded by crores of horses commanded by *Ashvāroodha*.

(ii) The commander of *Śreedevee's* horse brigade is *Ashvāroodhā*, who emerged out of *Śreedevee*'s noose and is mounted always on a horse called *Aparājita*.

(iii) The five sources of knowledge are equated to horses on which is mounted the mind. Hence the mind is *Ashvāroodha and* it is only through the senses (instruments of knowledge and action) that the mind carries out its activities of resolution and implementation. *Śree Devee* is surrounded by horses symbolising senses controlled by the mind. **She** is the master and controller of the senses.

Durga Saptashatee (5.77) may be referred;

Indriyaṇām Adhishṭātri Bhūtānām Chakilishuya
Bhūteshu Satatam Tasyai Vyāptyai Devyai Namo Nama:

(iv) *Ashvāroodhā Devee's Mantra* consists of 13 syllables.

68. *Chakrarājarathāroodhasarvāyudhaparishkrutā* -
चक्रराजरथारूढसर्वायुधपरिष्कृता

(i) One who is mounted on the *Śree Chakra* chariot surrounded by all kinds of weapons.

(ii) *Śree Chakra* is considered as the king of all *Chakras* (*Yantras* of gods) and hence is called *Śree Chakrarāja*. *Śreedevee* is always present in this and this is also the chariot of *Śreedevee*. The nine *āvarŋās* of *Śree Chakra* are the nine tiers of the chariot. The area of *Śree Chakra* is 4 *yojanās* and the height 10 *yojanās*.

(iii) the *Sarvānandamaya Chakra* in the centre of the *Śree Chakra* shines as the flag on the top of the chariot. It is called *Ānandadwaja* (flag of bliss).

(iv) The four weapons of *Śreedevee*, namely, *Pasa* (Noose), *Ankusa* (goad), sugarcane bow and flower arrows mount the chariot before *Śreedevee* enters and take their positions around **Her** seat, assuming the form of *Shaktis*. Similarly all the other weapons also mounted the chariot assuming their respective forms of *Shaktis*. Normally a soldier mounts the chariot carrying all the weapons, but here the weapons assume the forms of *Shaktis* and mount the chariot on their own (that is the meaning of the word *aroodha*).

(v) These weapons are the means for achieving self realisation.

(vi) The *chakrarāja* chariot has the six wheels as the base, or the means for controlling or breaking through the six *chakras* take the form of the weapons (meaning – *Shuddha Vidyā* - *Śreedevee* is adorned by these weapons.

69. *Geyachakrarathāroodhamantriŋeeparisevitā* -
गेयचक्ररथारूढमन्त्रिणीपरिसेविता

(i) One who is worshipped by *Mantrinee Devee*, who rides the *Geya Chakra*.

(ii) *Shyamala* is a *Shakti* created by *Śreedevee* out of her sugarcane bow as an embodiment of mind energy. Her complexion is that of rain-cloud and her knowledge of music is profound. **She** has a Veena in one hand and a parrot in another. **She** is capable of bestowing on her devotees, sweet voice, knowledge of music and power to attract the mind. She has taken charge of administrative functions of *Śreedevee*'s kingdom. (Refer 786th name – *Mantrineeyastha Rajyadhoo*:).

(iii) In *Śreedevee*'s army, *Mantrinee* occupies a position next to **Her**. In statecraft, the king/ queen may have to have consultations on many matters without other's knowledge. This process is known *mantra lochana*. Just as *mantras* are said to be secret, matters in statecraft are also referred to by the same name. One who renders such advice is called *Mantree/ Mantrinee*.

(iv) The name of her chariot is *Geyachakra*. *Geya* means famous. It has seven tiers. When it moves, the sound it makes is like musical notes and that is another reason, why it is called *Geya* (musical) chariot. *Yogini*s occupy the seven tiers of this chariot.

(v) *Geya* – important; *Chakraratha* – Devee mounted on a circular chariot; *āroodha* – one who contemplates on; *Mantrinee* – one who is worshiped by those initiated into the *mantra*.

(vi) The concept, of contemplating *Śreedevee* and self as one and the same, is explained in the *tantrarāja*. This has to be learnt only through a proper teacher.

(vii) *Mantrinee* was once born as the daughter of sage *Matanga* and was thus known as *Mātangee*. Typical of women living in jungles, she wears earrings made of palm leaf and headgear made of wild flowers. The very sound of the Veena in her hands killed her enemies. The parrot in her hand was *Veda* personified. *Dhanur Veda*, which is a part of the *Vedas*, was made into bow (called *Chitrajeeva*) and arrows and given to *Śreedevee*. The Veena and the parrot in the hands of *Shyamala* became the *Shaktis* known as *Yantrini* and *Tantrinee*.

(viii) If the *mantras* are contemplated with controlled mind and clear intellect, they convert the mind into *Śreedevee*'s form. This is *mantra siddhi* (fruition of the power of *mantra*). One who attains that status is *Mantree*.

70. *Kirichakrarathāroodhadaṇḍanāthāpuraskrutā* – किरिचक्ररथारूढदण्डनाथापुरस्कृता

(i) One who is piloted by *Daṇḍanātha* riding the chariot called *Kirichakra*.

(ii) *Kiri* (*kiti*) means a *Varāha* (Boar). *Daṇḍanātha's* chariot is in the shape of a Boar.

(iii) *Daṇḍanātha* is also known as *Vārāhi*. She was created by *Śreedevee* from her five arrows. She is the commander-in-chief of *Śreedevee*'s army. Head of *Daṇḍanātha* army – knight. She carries a weapon called *Dandāyutha* in her hand. She has a very strong physique like a wild boar and hence *Vārāhi*.

(iv) She is shrewd enough to act as per *Śreedevee*'s will and hence known as *Sankeeta*.

(v) *Āgnachakreshwaree* – one who is responsible for carrying our

Śreedevee's orders.

(vi) One who resides in the *Āgna chakra* in the human body.

(vii) The *Kirichakra* has five tiers, which are occupied by *Yoginis*.

(viii) *Kiri* also means the cycle of creation, sustenance and destruction; *Daṇḍanātha* is mounted on the chariot symbolising this cycle. Even then *Daṇḍanatha – Apuraskrita* - one who does not come under the control of *Yama* (Lord of death). The purport of this is that *Yama* will not approach those who concentrate on *Śreedevee* in their mind.

71. *Jwālāmālinikākshiptavahniprākāramadhyagā* – ज्वालामालिनिकाक्षिप्तवह्निप्राकारमध्यगा

(i) One who dwells in the centre of the fort of fire built by *Jwālāmālini*.

(ii) In the *Śree Chakra,* there are fifteen *Nitya Devee*s seated, five each on the three sides of the triangle around the *Bindu*. They are immortal and symbolising the time. They are respectively, *Kāmeshwaree, Bhagamālini, Nityaklinna, Bherundā, Vahnivāsini, Mahāvajreshwari, Shivadūti, Twarita, Kulasundaree, Nithya, Neelapathāka, Vijayā, Sarvamangalā, Jwālāmālini* and *Chitra*. In the centre *Śreedevee* **Herself** occupies the *Bindustāna* as the 16th *Mahānitya*. In the bright half of the lunar month (*Suklapaksha*), they are worshipped starting from *Kāmeshwaree* and ending with *Chitrā* and in the dark half of the lunar month (*Krişhṇapaksha*) starting from *Chitrā* and ending with *Kāmeshwaree*, in the reverse order. *Jwālāmālini* is worshipped on the fourteenth day of bright half and on the second day of the dark half.

(iii) According to *Lalithopākyānā*, in the course of the battle with *Bhanḍāsurā*, in order to protect the army, *Śreedevee* instructed *Jwālāmālini* to build a fort of fire with 100 *yojanas* area and 30 *yojanas* height, in the centre of which **She** staged with **Her** army.

(iv) *Jwālāmālini* represents the five triangles of *Shakti* and *Vahniprākāra* represents the four triangles of *Shiva* (in the form of fire); *Akshipta*– integral, that is all the nine triangles are integrated in the centre of which (*Bindusthana*) is *Śreedevee*.

(v) As mentioned in the previous name, although **She** is the cause of three functions viz. creation, sustenance and destruction, **She** is not affected or does not undergo any change on account these acts. **She** is surrounded by *Jwālamālās* (sparks of fire) and yet remains unaffected.

72. *Bhanḍasainyavadhodyuktashaktivikramaharshitā* – भण्डसैन्यवधोद्युक्तशक्तिविक्रमहर्षिता

(i) One who is pleased with the valour of the *Shaktis*, engaged in destroying *Bhanḍa*'s army.
(ii) *Śreedevee* created an army of *Shaktis* out of her own self to destroy *Bhanḍa*'s army and **She** was pleased when **Her** army achieved that objective.
(iii) *Bhanḍasura* did not realise his self, due to his ignorance. He had created his army out of his own mental aberrations, which was the result of his mental differentiation. To counter this *Śreedevee* herself took various forms of *Shaktis* and destroyed that ignorance. **She** was pleased with the gradual destruction of ignorance and emergence of knowledge.

73. *Nityāparākramāṭopanireekshaŋasamutsukā* – नित्यापराक्रमाटोपनिरीक्षणसमुत्सुका

(i) One who was enthused by the *Nitya Devee*'s celebrating the invasion of the enemy's army.
(ii) *Bhanḍasura* sent his 15 generals to the war. The 15 *Nityas* of *Śreedevee*'s army faced and won over those generals.
(iii) Once in the course of the battle with *Bhanḍasura*, two of his generals *Damanaka* and *Chitragupta* surrounded the *Śree Chakra rāja* chariot and started waging a war by unfair means; at that time the 15 *Thithi Nityas* proved their prowess by destroying them in front of *Śreedevee*, much to **Her** delight.
(iv) Because of their permanence (immortality), the *Atma Shaktis* (the soul) are called *Nityās*. *Parākramātopa* – growing due to inward self realisation. One who is pleased with that. A person attains external bliss when the immortal soul power wins over the demonic forces, which raise their head from time to time within the mind.

74. *Bhanḍaputravadhodyuktabālāvikramananditā* – भण्डपुत्रवधोद्युक्तबालाविक्रमनन्दिता

(i) One who was pleased with the valour of *Bāla*, who ventured to destroy *Bhanḍa*'s sons.
(ii) When *Bhanḍa* saw the destruction of his soldiers, he sent his 30 sons, starting from *Chaturbāhu ending with Upmāya*, etc., to continue the

battle. They were killed by *Bālā Tirupurasundaree, Śree Devee*'s daughter. *Bālā* was a child who was always 9 years old. She wore an armour which emerged our of *Śreedevee*'s armour and fought with *Bhanḍa*'s sons riding a small chariot called *Karniratha*. *Śreedevee* was delighted with *Bālā*'s fighting skills.

(iii) *Śreedevee's mantra* is *Panchadashāksharee*. It consists of three groups of 5, 6 and 4 syllables. These groups are respectively called *Vākbhavam, Kāmarājam* and *Shakti*. The *Bāla mantra* has three syllables viz., *Im, Kleem* and *Sow*:. Each one of these syllables belongs to each one of the above groups. The three groups of *Panchadashākshari* and three syllables of *Bāla mantra* are in no way different in fame or energy. Hence *Bāla mantra* is called as *Laghu Śreevidya*. Before *Śree Vidyā Deeksha* is initiated on any one, *Bāla mantra* is first taught.

(iv) There are three types of sins viz. arrogance, illusion and ignorance. These sins tie the soul to this world (by repeated birth) (names 133 to 135). Each of these sins seen through each of the 10 organs in the body is indicated as 30 sons *Bhanḍa*. *Bala Mantra* destroys these.

75. *Mantriṇyambāvirachitavishangavadhatoshitā* –
मन्त्रिण्यम्बाविरचितविषङ्गवधतोषिता

(i) One who was pleased by the killing of the demon *Vishāngan* by *Mantrinee Devee* (*Shyāmalā*).

(ii) The demon *Bhanḍan* did penance to Lord *Rudra* and got the power to create demons as per his will. Accordingly he created the demon called *Visukran* from his right shoulder and the demon called *Vishangan* from his left shoulder. He treated both of them as his brothers. He appointed *Vishangan* as his minister and *Visukran* as his commander-in-chief. *Shyamala*, the *Mantrini Devee*, killed *Vishangan*. *Śreedevee* was pleased by seeing this.

(iii) *Shangam* means interest. *Vi* means wrongful. Hence *Vishangan* means wrongful attraction. That is, indulging into wrongful acts by the organs. *Mantrini* in the form *Mantra Shakti* of *Śreedevee* destroyed this wrongful attraction.

76. *Vishukraprāṇaharaṇavārāheeveeryananditā* –
विशुक्रप्राणहरणवाराहीवीर्यनंदिता

(i) One who was pleased by the prowess of *Varāhi* while killing the demon *Visukran*.

(ii) *Visukran* was the commander-in-chief of *Bhanḍan*. Varāhi, the commander-in-chief of *Śreedevee* killed him. *Śreedevee* was happy to see this.

(iii) *Vi* – hostile. *Sukram* – light or strength. Hence *Visukran* means one who spends all his energy against the *Atma Shakti*. Or: *Vi* – excess, *Suk* – sorrow, *Ra* – one who brings. That is one who brings excess sorrow. He was killed by *Varāhi*, the *Kriyā Shakti* of *Śreedevee*.

(iv) In *Lalithopakyana*, it is mentioned as *Varāhi* killed *Vishangan* and *Mantrini* killed *Visukran*. However, the version given in *Lalitā Sahasranāma* seems to be appropriate.

(v) *Śreedevee* in the form of *Bala Devee* destroys the three sins and makes the *Atma Tatva* to glow. Be our side in the form of *Mantrini*, helps focus the oscillating mind and soul. In the form of *Daŋḍanātha* make the soul dedicated to Lord *Ěshwara* and gives energy to do all the *karmas* (routines) with determination. It is worth noting that these three names, *mantras*, their meanings and structure, are all easily understandable.

77. *Kāmeshwaramukhālokakalpitaśreegaŋeshvarā* - कामेश्वरमुखालोककल्पितश्रीगणेश्वरा

(i) One who created *Śree Gaŋeshwara* just by looking at the face of *Śree Kāmeshwara*.

(ii) By seeing the destruction of his army, *Bhanḍan* ordered *Visukran* to set the *Vigna yantra*. Made by illusion of demons, this *yantra* was kept in the midst of the army of *Śreedevee*. On account of this, the army of *Śreedevee* was affected by the following eight feelings – laziness, disinterest in fighting, an inferiority complex that we cannot do it, fatigue, feeling sleepy, unconsciousness, lack of motivation like cowards and loss of self-respect. *Mantrinee* complained to *Śreedevee* about this. **She** just made a glimpse at *Śree Kāmeshwara*, who was seated by **Her** side. The two sights merged with smile and affection. Resultantly *Śree Gaŋapathy* emerged with elephant face hugging *Siddha Lakshmee* called *Vallabha*. He had in his ten hands – pomegranate, mace, sugarcane bow, spear, wheel (*chakram*), conch, noose, Lily flower, paddy crops and one of his own tusks. In his eleventh hand, the trunk, he carried a sacred pot (*kalasam*) made of gems.

(iii) There are obstacles like laziness in functioning of the intellect. The yoga energy is the only tool that can enable remove such obstacles and make the mind focus on required things. Śree Gaŋesha is the god who provides such energy. Hence he is treated as provider of clear mind by removing all obstacles. The word *kalpita* indicates the beauty of the *Gaŋesha* incarnation.

(iv) *Kāmeshwara* is the form of *Shiva* without any qualities. Its *mukhāloka* – by reaching that experience, *kalpita* – created, *Śreegaŋeshvarā* – **She** is with that *Eshvarā* alongwith *Puryashṭaka*.

(v) *Puryashṭaka* is the control of the below and reaching the status of *Eshvarā*:

a) Five sense organs
b) Five organs for actions
c) Mind, intellect, egoism and concentration,
d) Five breaths
e) Five basic elements
f) Desires
g) Actions
h) Ignorance.

78. *Mahāgaŋeshanirbhinnavighnayantrapraharshitā* – महागणेशनिर्भिन्नविघ्नयन्त्रप्रहर्षिता

(i) One who rejoiced when *Maha Gaŋesha* destroyed the magical Devices called *Vighnayantra*.

(ii) It is nice to understand the meanings combining the names 77 and 78.

79. *Bhanḍāsurendranirmuktashastrapratyastravarshiŋee* – भण्डासुरेन्द्रनिर्मुक्तशस्त्रप्रत्यस्त्रवर्षिणी

(i) One who directs counter missiles to destroy the armaments of *Bhanḍasuran*.

(ii) The weapons used in the war are of two types –

- Armaments – that are held in the hand like sword, mace, spear, etc. They are used to fight with the nearby enemies.
- Missiles – which are aimed at enemies in a distance.

(iii) *Bhanḍasura* attacks *Śreedevee*, near him, with his armaments. However, *Śreedevee* at the same time counters his attacks with missiles from a distance.

(iv) If anyone thinks that *Śreedevee* is near him or attracted towards him, for him **She** will be in a very long distance. One who longs for **Her,** feeling **Her** at a distance, **She** will emerge very close by. She plays this game for *Bhanḍa*.

(v) The thoughts of God will destroy, from a distance itself, the demonic character of ignorance which attacks the self-character.

80. ***Karāngulinakhotpannanārāyaŋadashākruti*: -**
करांगुलिनखोत्पन्ननारायणदशाकृतिः

(i) One who is alongwith the 10 forms of *Śree Nārāyaŋa* who emerged from the 10 fingers.

(ii) *Bhanḍasuran* created with his missile called *Sarvasurasthram*, the demons *Somakan, Ravanan* and *Hiranyakshan*. They started to fight with *Śreedevee*. In a second, **She** made the ten forms of *Śree Nārāyaŋan* emerge from **Her** 10 finger nails. Each of them fought with each of the demons respectively and killed them.

(iii) The word *Nārāyaŋa* will indicate both *Jeevan* and *Eshwaran*. The word *Dashakruti* means the muscles (*dasha*) of *Jeevan* and the work (*kruti*) of *Ĕshwaran*. This has to be added relevant to the meaning of the word *Nārāyaŋa*. There are five states of the *Jeevā* – awaken (*Jāgrat*), dream (*Swapna*), deep sleep (*Sushupti*), swoon (*Thureeyam*) and transcendental (*Thureeyatheetham*). There are five works of *Nārāyaŋa* - creation (*Srishti*), sustenance (*Sthithi*), destruction (*Samhāra*), screaming from the impacts of material pleasure & displeasure (*Tiroḍhāna*) and blessings (*Anugraha*). **She** does all these through **Her** ten finger nails without any effort.

81. ***Mahāpāshupatāstrāgninirdhagdhāsurasainikā* –**
महापाशुपतास्त्राग्निनिर्धग्धासुरसैनिका

(i) One who burned to death the army of the demons with the fire of the missile called *Mahāpāsupatham*.

(ii) The missile *Pāsupatham* itself is capable of burning the entire world. The presiding God of this is *Paramashiva* called *Pashupathi*. (In *Mahā -bhārata, Arjuna* fought with lord *Paramashiva* and got this missile). *Pashupathi* is a form of all the three *Guŋa*s (characters). The missile *Mahāpāsupatham* is more powerful than *Pāsupatham*. The presiding god of this is *Sadāshivan,* who is beyond the three characters. The army of *Bhanḍan* was burnt by the missile *Mahā pāsupatham*.

(iii) The missile *Mahāpāsupatham* through the astonishment of practice, the *Advaita* grows more and more by. The fire from these missiles burns the army of demons ignorance.

(iv) The difference between *Ĕshwaran* and *Sadāshiva n* is explained in names 271 and 272.

(v) The *mantra* for *Pāsupatham* has 6 letters. The *mantra* for *Mahāpāsupatham* is different from this.

82. *Kāmeshwarāstranirdagdhasabhaŋḍāsurashoonyakā –*
कामेश्वरास्त्रनिर्दग्धसभण्डासुरशून्यका

(i) One who burnt *Bhanḍasura* and his city *Sūnyaka* using the flames from the missile *Kāmeshwara*.

(ii) *Bhanḍasura* built *Sonitha* and *Sūnyaka* exclusively for his capital cities. The missile *Mahā Kāmeshwara* is still powerful than *Mahāpāsupatham*. This missile completely cleared *Bhanḍasura* and his two cities. *Soonyam* means 'Nil'. Typical of the name, the city has become 'Nil'.

(iii) *Sonitha* means blood. The blood is the one which strengthens arrogance in human mind. Because it was as red as blood, it was called *Sonitha. Sunyaka* – zero. It is an illusion that there is something available. In this battle the remainders were *Bhanḍa* and his two cities. They were also made to ashes without even a symptom by *Kāmeshastra*.

(iv) The names so far explained how the *Jeevā* matures to liberation to reach liberation (*moksha*). This name explains that nothing remains – only the *sūnya* remains.

(v) *Kāmeshwara* is the form of *Atma* – self. *Ātmana kāmāya sarvam priyam bhavathi* – that means - likes everything and liked by everything and hence the *Chit Atma* is *Kāmeshwara. Bhanḍasura* has mental differentiation and hence has *Dvaita* in his mind. This mental aberration has been burnt in the *chit* blaze of *Kāmeshwara*. Hence *Jeevā* has merged with *chit-ātma* - self. The balance is only a '**null**' – The form of *Chinmaya*.

83. *Bramopendramahendradidevasamstutavaibhavā –*
ब्रमोपेन्द्रमहेन्द्रदिदेवसंस्तुतवैभवा

(i) One who has the pride of being praised by *Brahma, Viṣhŋu, Indra* and other *Devas*.

(ii) The mother of *Indra* is *Athithi*. *Nārāyaŋa* was born as *Vamana* to *Athithi* and hence becomes younger brother of *Indra*. Hence he attains the name – *Upendra*. (151st name of *Vişhŋu Sahasranāma*, may be referred).

(iii) The festival of inwardly looking and recognising **Her** by *Brahma* and *devas* is called *Vibhutvam* – i.e. *Sarvātmathvam*. One who was praised by recognising the feeling of omnipotence.

(iv) All the names so far explained the purpose and completion of emergence of *Śreedevee* to complete the *deva*'s wishes.

84. ***Haranetrāgnisandagdhakāmasanjeevanoushadhi*: - हरनेत्राग्निसंदग्धकामसंजीवनौषधिः**

(i) One who gave the herb - *Sanjeevi* that revived Cupid's life after he was burnt by flame from the eyes of *Haran*.

(ii) *Sanjeevini* is a herb. It has the capacity to revive a dead person. *Jeevathu* is another name for this.

(iii) It is stated in the story that after killing of *Bhanḍasura*, *Śreedevee* revived the life of Cupid as per the requests of all the *Devas* starting from *Brahma*.

(iv) A child punished by the father goes to the mother for support. In the same fashion, Cupid, who was burnt by the father *Paramashiva,* got back his life from mother *Śreedevee*.

(v) As per the saying *Harourushtegurusthratha Gurouruchenakacchana* – When *Haran* is angry the teacher will support, but when the teacher himself is angry there is no one to support. The word *Guru* instead of teacher, can mean *Śreedevee*. (Refer 603rd name *Guru Moorthy*).

(vi) The word *Hara* means plucking of self-embodiment - guiding to do this – *netha* – i.e. *Avidyā* or cause as ignorance - Since it is pervaded in all places like a fire, it is called as *Haranethragni*. By this ignorance,

- ***Samdakta*** – completely burnt out,
- ***Kāma*** – by the feeling of the soul in form of *Kāmeshwara*
- ***Sam*** – utterly: i.e. by completely destroying all the root cause, ignorance
- ***Jeevā*** – a herb to reach the reality of God

She is the herb to make the ignorant reach the reality of God by destroying all the root causes. It is mentioned that by praying to *Śreedevee* in the form of *Vidhya*, the ignorance is removed, one can reach the actual and real self and the liberation.

(vii) *Haran*, who does the job of destruction is *Virakthar* – does not have interest or feeling in any of the worldly affairs. Hence he burnt Cupid (attachment). *Śreedevee* attracted the same *Haran* towards **Her** and made **Him**, *Ĕshwaran* for Cupid also - *Kāmeshwaran*. The eyes of *Haran* were filled with anger. When *Kāmeshwaran's* sight merged with that of *Kāmeshwaree*, it became the herb to give rebirth to Cupid.

(viii) The *Brahmam*, which got the power from *Haran*, destroyed the whole world. *Ĕshwaran* made this as raw material and merged again with *Brahmam*. Again, *Śreedevee*, by the sight of *Kāmeshwaran* resolved to create the world. **She** became a *Brahmam* called *Sadāshiva n* and started to create the world. **She** is the one who desired to recreate the world (names 264 to 274 may be referred).

(ix) Going ahead the subtle form of *Śreedevee* is described. That is in three forms viz., subtle, subtler and subtlest: *Panchadashee Vidyā swaroopa* – subtlest; *Kāmakalakshararoopa* – subtler: *Kunḍalinee roopa* – subtle. Out of these, first, subtle is explained in the next 3 names.

85. *Śreemadvāgbhavakooṭaikasvaroopamukhapankajā* – श्रीमद्वाग्भवकूटैकस्वरूपमुखपंकजा

(i) One who is the *Vāgbhava* group (having 5 syllables), which is the first group in *Panchadashi*, as **Her** lotus face.

(ii) *Śree Vidyā mantra* has 15 syllables. It is in 3 groups. The first group called *Vāgbhava* has 5 syllables.

(iii) The *Vāgbhava* group has the specialty of providing the knowledge and hence it is prefixed with *Śreemad*.

(iv) *Śreedevee*, when emerged from the sacrificial fire, the first sighted was **Her** face. Most of the organs used by the human mind to go out are all in the face. This group, with 5 syllables, forms the face in *Śreedevee*'s figure, in the form of *mantra*, with the speech as the main one.

86. *Kaŋṭhādha:kaṭiparyantamadhyakooṭasvaroopiŋee* – कण्ठाधःकटिपर्यन्तमध्यकूटस्वरूपिणी

(i) One who shines with *Kāmarāja* group (*Kūta*) as middle region below the neck and upto the waist.

(ii) The second part of *Panchadashi* is called *Madhya Kuta* or *Kāmarāja Koota*. This has six syllables.

(iii) In the figure of *Śreedevee*, in the form *Mantra*, the central portion is below the neck and above the hip. The wishes and desires are expressed through this part of the body. Hence this is in the form *Icchāshakti*.

87. *Shaktikooṭaikatāpannakaṭyadhobhāgadhāriṇee* – शक्तिकूटैकतापन्नकट्यधोभागधारिणी

(i) One who has the part beneath the waist as *Shaktikūta*.
(ii) The third part of *Panchadashi* has four syllables. This constitutes the part beneath the hip of *Śreedevee* in the form of *mantra*. *Kriya Shakti*, the energy for creation, comes out of the lower part of the body. The third part of the *mantra* is also called as *Shaktikūta*. This *kūta* is in the form *Kriya Shakti*.
(iii) In *Panchadashimantra*:
- *Vāgbhava* group is for learning all the areas.
- *Kāmarāja* group in the form of *Icchāshakti* is for getting knowledge – for providing anything sought for.
- The third one *Shaktikūta* provides all energies like creation, etc. This is in the form of *Kriya Shakti*.

(iv) These have been described in detail in the books, *Varivasyā rahasyam*, *Shakti Mahimna Stotram*, etc.

88. *Moolamantratmikā* - मूलमन्त्रात्मिका

(i) One who **Herself** is the *moola mantra*.
(ii) The meaning of the word *mantra* is "protects by repetition or expressing meekness".
(iii) The most important among the *mantras* is *Panchadashakshari*. One who is **Itself**. The philosophy is that there is no difference between the *mantras* and the reigning deities. If anyone differentiates them then he is a sinner.
(iv) The meaning of the word *moola* is 'cause'. *Śreedevee* is the first cause for creation of this world. **She Herself** is in the form of **Her** own *mantra*.
(v) The root cause of the human purpose is *Śreedevee*. One who mediates **Her** *mantra* will be quelled from the disease of birth. She is in the form of *Panchadashakshari*.
(vi) The word *moola* represents *Em – Kāmakala*, which is the primary root of *Panchadashakshari* itself. One who is in this form is *Kāmakalāsvaroopiṇee* (322nd name – *Kāmakalāroopā* may be

referred).

(vii) The inherent meanings of the syllable *Kāmakalā* has to be learnt through a proper teacher.

89. *Moolakooṭatrayakalebarā* - मूलकूटत्रयकलेबरा

(i) One who has **Her** body (in the subtle form) identical to the *moola-mantra* itself with all its three groups or combination of letters.

(ii) One who has the syllables of the three groups respectively 5, 6 and 4 as **Her** body.

(iii) One who has the subtle *Kāmakalā*, which is the root of these, as **Her** body.

(iv) *Kāmakalā* has one *Bindu* at the top, two in the centre and a triangle at the bottom. Similar is **Her** body profile.

90. *Kulāmrutaikarasikā* - कुलामृतैकरसिका

(i) One who revels only in *kulāmrutham* – the nectar flowing from the *Sahasrāra*.

(ii) So far *Śreedevee*'s gross and subtle forms were described. Now the subtle form of energy called *Kunḍalinee* in every human being is being discussed. The *sushumnā nāḍi* runs from the bottom of the butt, till inner part of the skull through the centre of the body along the back bone. In this, the *Kunḍalinee* energy sleeps at the bottom tip, in the form of a snake woven itself in three and half rounds, keeping its head in the centre downwards. If this *Kunḍalinee* energy can be awakened by practicing *Yoga*, it passes through *sushumnā nāḍi* and reaches the inner part of the skull. When this energy bangs with the *Akula Chakra* called *Sahasrārapadmam*, the energy deposited there, melts like butter, seeps, slips down and flows throughout the body as nectar. The nectar thus flows, is called *kulāmrutha*. *Śreedevee* whoops it up in this juice.

(iii) 10th verse of *Soundaryalaharee* reads;

Sudhādhārāsārai: Charaṇaugalantar Vigalitai:
Prapancham Sinchantee Punarapi Rasāmnāyamahasa:
Awapya Svām Bhoomim Bhujaganibha Madhushtavalayam
Svamathmānam Kruthvā Svapishi Kulkunde Kuharini

The shower of nectar, which flows from between two feet, wets all the *nāḍis* in the human body (made of five primary elements). From the Moon, which beams nectar like rays, you return to *Moolādhāram*, your natural dwelling place. You are sleeping there, which has a small hole, as a wound snake.

(iv) We are able to get only a drop of this *kulāmrutham*. On the other hand, a *Yogi* enjoys drenching in the rain of this nectar.

(v) *Moolādhāram* is the place of abode for *Prithvi Tatvam*.
Ku – The earth – One who is enchanted in that *Tatva*
Kulam – The six *kulachakras* which go around

When the complete energy comes out of this, *kulāmrutham* flows. **She** is passionate in spreading this nectar and making the *Yogis* extremely happy. Hence *Kulāmrutaikarasika*.

91. *Kulasanketapālinee* - कुलसङ्केतपालिनी

(i) One who guards the esoteric doctrine of the *Koulas*.

(ii) The energy called *Koula* is kept in a secret place in the body. That energy is sleeping. To awaken the same, raise it upwards and make the *Kulāmrutm* flow along the *nāḍis* of the body, is beyond our knowledge. Why is this energy sleeping without being useful? How to awaken it? How does this awakened *Kunḍalinee* gives various powers (*siddis*)? All these questions have been answered in a cryptic manner in *Tantra* sāstrās. It is explained in a ciphered way so that whoever has the capability can only understand this. The knowledge about *Koula* (*Kunḍalinee*) is also called *Koula*. Its secret language is cryptic. *Kulasanketapālinee* protects it so that the ineligible cannot understand it.

(iii) The cryptic language detailing about *Kunḍalinee* is only known to **Her** and **Her** devotees. Hence *Kulasanketapālinee*.

(iv) *Sāstrās* mention *Āchāram* also as *kulam*. These *Āchārams* are cryptic – secrets. *Śreedevee* protects them.

(v) There are three cryptic ways in the *pooja* (*upāsanā*) of *Śreedevee* – cryptic *chakras*, cryptic *mantras* and cryptic *pooja*.

92. *Kulānganā* - कुलाङ्गना

(i) One who belongs to chaste family (*kula*).

(ii) A lady in a chaste family well protects the pride and secrets of the family. **She** is *kulasthri*. **She** is a *pathivrathai*, born in a chaste family and married to a chaste family.

(iii) A *kulasthri* (*pathivrathai*) is normally not visible to others. Similarly *Śreedevee* hides herself by the veil of *Avidyā* (lack of knowledge).

(iv) *Śreevidyā*, the pooja (*upāsanā*) of *Śreedevee* is a top secret. It has been told that this should not reveal to others in general. Hence the name *Kulāngana*.

Anyāstu Sakalā Vidyā: Prakata Kanika Iva I
Iyamtu Sambavee Vidyā Guptā Kulavaduriva II (*Kulārnavam*)
Veshyaiva Prakatā: Vedadhi Vidyā: I
Sarveshudarsaneshu Gupteyam Vidyā II (*Kalpa Sūtram*)

(v) *Śreevidyā* is protected as a secret. However, for those it was initiated in a proper way and who follow it, it is a known one and not a secret. A *pathivrathai* lady, though will not be seen by others, she moves closely with the near ones.

93. *Kulāntasthā* - कुलान्तस्था

(i) One who resides within *kula*.
(ii) The word *kula* means a tracheotomy in *mathru* (an instrument), *mana* (intellect) and *meya* (the thing which is measured). Out of this **She** is in the form of *mana* – i.e. in the form of an intellect.
(iii) **She** is who can be known through the *kula Tantras*, which explains the method of praying, method of *yogas* and the secrets and things understood from the books explaining all these.
(iv) In all good families, two things would be well known - one the family and the family tree and **She** dwells as *shakti* in such families found in every house, street, village or nations.
(v) The *Shushmnanāḍi* is also known as *kula* and she resides in this. *Kunḍalinee* travels only in this *nāḍi*.

94. *Koulinee* - कौलिनी

(i) The united form of *Shiva* and *Shakti* is called *Koulinee*.
(ii) *Kula* means *Shakti* and *Akula* is *Shiva* and the unity is *Koulam*. **She** is in that form.
(iii) Dualistic – same article split into two and show up and the relationship between the two, which has to be perceived, is the knowledge of *Koula* One who has that knowledge is *Koulinee*
(iv) Independently personifying the *Shiva* Chakras and the *Shakti chakras* independently and identifying *Shiva* and *Shakti* together and at the same individually is called *Koulasariyai*. One who has that is called *Koulinee*.
(v) Feeling the *Kundalinee*, through *yogas*, In the form of *Shiva shakti* in the *Kulachakras* and *Akulachakras* is called *Koulayoga*. One who has

that is called *Koulinee*.

(vi) The *Kulashakti* is always a dynamic one and the *Akula* alias *Shiva - shakti* is a static one. If the unification of *Shiva* and *Shakti* has to happen, then dynamic one has to reach the static one and embrace. This union is called *Koulam*. One who is connected to this is called *Koulinee*.

(vii) One of the *Vāgdevees* (who recited this *Lalitā Sahasranāma*) is also known as *Kowlini*.

(viii) In the external worship of *Śree Chakra* there are three aspects of worship viz. -- the *Upāsaka, Devee* and devotion. This worship method is also known as *Kowlam*. Since **She** is being worshipped in this method is called *Koulinee*.

95. *Kulayoginee* - कुलयोगिनी

(i) **She** is known as *Kulayoginee* connected with *Kula* worship.

(ii) The word Kula has various meaning as explained in previous names. **She** has connection or relationship with each of those meanings and hence *KulaYoginee*.

(iii) **She** is the *Shakti* connected with each of six chakras starting from *Moolādhāram*.

(iv) The conjugation of the *Akula* and *Kula* through yoga is called *Kula-yoga*. She can be reached through this and hence *KulaYoginee*.

(v) It is **She** who paves ways and procedures of contemplating *Śreedevee* in *Śree Chakra* form.

(vi) **She** who blesses the boon to be born in a superior family.

96. *Akulā* - अकुला

(i) *Kula* also means parents, family etc. and *Śreedevee* is beyond all these.

(ii) *Akulā* also means the *Sahasrāra* Lotus at the top of the *Sushumnanāḍi*. **She** resides there.

(iii) *Akulachara* is beyond *kulachara*, which is commonly known as *Samyāchara*. **She** is in the form of *Samyāchara* also.

(iv) *Kula* means the birth place, parents, family tree, etc. Since **She** is beyond birth, **She** has no *kula* and hence *Akula*.

97. *Samayāntasthā* - समयान्तस्था

(i) One who is in the analogous forms of *Shiva* and *Shakti*.

(ii) *Samayā* is commonly explained as offering worship inwardly and jointly to *Shiva* and *Shakti* in the ether of the heart. Outwardly worshipping a *chakra* is called *Kula*. Worshipping a chakra internally through meditation is called *Samaya*. That worship is unanimously accepted by all as the supreme. *Samaya* has been explained in the five books written by *Vashishṭa, Suka, Sanaka, Sanandana* and *Sanatkumara*. **She** dwells in this type of *Samaya*.

(iii) Both and *Shakti* are akin and equal. Hence *Shiva* is called as *Samaya*: and *Shakti* is called as *Samaya*.

This type of analogous is of five types.

Adishtana Samayā – Equal footing in the worship done to *Chakra*, etc.
Anushtana Samayā – Equality in all activities like creation, etc.
Avastana Samayā – Equality in actions like dance, etc.
Nāma Samayā – Equality in names for instance *Shiva–Sivā*
Bhairava – *Bhairavee*
Roopa *Samayā* – Equality in reality like both or crimson colour, etc.

The word *Asthā* means *Swaroopa* – form of the figures.

(iv) The below five similarities in the form of *Shiva* and *Shakti* in the six *chakras* can be perceived as:

Location	Form/ Shape	Activity	Name	Action
Ājna	Luminous	Liberation	*Paran - Parā*	Divine Bliss
Vishuddhi	Colour of *Spatika*	Creation of ether	*Shivan - Sivā*	Removal of darkness
Anāhat	White Colour	Creation of air	*Hamsa – Hamsi*	Spreading the stunts
Maŋipoora	Lightening	Creation of water	*Taditwan – Tadivathi*	Reducing the yearnings
Swādhistāna	Fire	Creation of fire	*Mahān – Mahati*	Burning the world
Moolādhāra	Red	Parents of the world	*Samayan -Samaya.*	Dance

(v) Comprehending and understanding these five similarities and also not finding any disparity between *Shiva* and *Shakti*, worshipping them through medication is the *Samaya* method.

98. *Samayāchāratatparā* - समयाचारतत्परा

(i) One who is interested in *Samayachara*.

(ii) The *samaya* method is an internal worshipping format. Once initiated, with the blessings of the teacher, through *Shatvidaikyanu santhanam* and *Chaturvidaikya Anusanthanam* get *Pavanatartyam* on a *Mahanavami* day and get the *Mahaveda* sacrament (*Samskāram*) done. After all these, the aspirant worships *Śreedevee* in the following method. *Śreedevee*, who is sleeping alone in the *Moolādhāram*, awakes up, dresses **Herself** in **Her** secluded place of *Swadishtanam*, **She** comes out of *maŋipoorakam*, as a gorgeous lady to be seen by everybody. There the aspirant gives **Her,** 47 types of *upachārams* starting from *Pādyam* and ending with *Bhooshaŋa Dhāraŋam*. **She** accepts them all and sits in a chair, made of gems, alongwith her group (*parivāram*). From there **She** moves on to *Anāhatam* and accepts the prayers upto *Tamboola Dhāranam* (chewing of betel leaves). After accepting *Arati* at *Vishuddi*, **She** accepts *Neerājanam* and other *upachārams* at *Ajna*. At the end of all these **She** enters the *Sahasrāra* Lotus. After staying happily alongwith *Shiva* behind a screen, **She** leaves *Shiva* and returns to *Moolādhāra* to hide again. In this way, through imagination, enjoying the game of the grace (*Chitshakti*) is called *Samayacharam*. By alchemy copper becomes gold. In a similar fashion the aspirant becomes *Śreedevee* **Herself** by continuous perception.

(iii) Without any of the tools used in *Bāhya Pooja*, the aspirant imagines the *Śree Chakra* in mind, going forward experience the union of *Shiva* and *Shakti* and through this he also experiences the union of teacher, *mantra, Śreedevee, Śree Chakra* and self. The *chakras* starting from *Moolādhāram* and ending with *Sahasrāram* are imagined as the *Āvaranams*. The *Kunḍalinee* is imagined as *Śree Devee* with the three groups of *Panchadashee*, respectively from **Her** face till bottom. With this imagination he can reach the *Ikyānusanthanam* called *Samaya*. *Śreedevee* is fascinated through this type of *Samayacharam*.

99. *Moolādhāraikanilayā* - मूलाधारैकनिलया

(i) One whose main residence is *Moolādhāram*.

(ii) The backbone of the body is called *Merudhaṇḍam*. The *nāḍi* called *Sushumna* runs inside this. The bottom most part of this is the butt. In the midst of this, the *Linga* stays in a place called *Moolādhāram*. Next the chakra called *Swādhishṭanam*, which resides in the root location of the *Linga*. Third *maṇipoorakam* is at lower abdomen, *Anāhatam* at the chest area, *Vishuddhi* in the neck and *Ajna*, the sixth one, in between two eye brows. Above all these six is the *Sahasrāra Chakra*. Conventionally these are all called as Lotus (*Padmam*). Out of these six, respectively a pair of *chakras* is called as *Kanḍam*. These are called *Agni* (fire), *Soorya* (Sun) and *Chandra* (Moon) *Kanḍas*. Above and below each of the *Kanḍas* there are two knots (*Grantis*).

(iii) Out of these, *Moolādhāra* Lotus has four petals. *Kunḍalinee* always sleeps, keeping it head downwards, in the *bindu* called *Kulakuṇḍam*, in a *karnika* in this *chakra*. Hence it is said as: *Śreedevee*, in the form of *Kunḍalinee*, has *Moolādhāra* as **Her** main dwelling.

(iv) It is called *Moolādhāra*, since it is the base for *Kunḍalinee* and also the root of *Sushumna*.

100. *Brahmagranthivibhedinee* - ब्रह्मग्रन्थिविभेदिनी

(i) One who pierces through the above said *Brahmagranti*.

(ii) As explained in the previous name description, the *Kanḍam* for the first two *chakras* is called *Agni* (fire) *Kanḍam*. This has *Srushṭi* (creation) *chakras* as the dwelling of *Brahma* whose role is the creation.

(iii) In the religion of *Samaya*, these six *chakras* are supposed as *Śree Chakra*. The *Srushṭi chakra* has three *Āvaranas* as *Chaturasram*, *Shoḍasadalam* and *Ashṭadalam*.

(iv) The knot or *Granthi* is a small hole like between two *chakras*. The *Kunḍalinee*, starts from *Moolādhāra* to enter *Swādhishṭana* and again from there to enter *maṇipooraka*, has to pierce and travel through these holes like knots only. The first knot is called *Brahma-Granthi* in the place of *Brahma*. (The verb *Granth* means shortening a long one. A book is called a *Grantham* since a long subject is shortened and given in it. If that is still tightened, it is called *Sūtra* – a stiffened book).

(v) These knots help the *Kunḍalinee* energy with a grip so that it does not fall down when it climbs up and to get momentum to move upwards as well.

(vi) Once the *Brahma Granthi* is drilled and gone forward, the aspirant is released from the smell of creation.

Thus ends the second *Kalā*, called *Tāpinee*.

*****

Section 3: *Dhoomrikā (Dhoomrā) Kalā*

101. *Maŋipoorāntaruditā* -मणिपूरान्तरुदिता

(i) The lotus with ten petals near the belly button is called *maŋipooram*. This is also named as *Sthithi Chakra*, place of *Vişhŋu* and *Soorya Kanḍam*. The *Kunḍalinee* energy pierces the knots (*Brahmagranthi*) in *Moolādhāram* and *Swādhishṭanam* and rises in *maŋipooram*. There **She** accepts 47 *upacharams* from *Padhyam* till offering of jewels (98^{th}name may be referred). (235th name– *Chatu:shashṭyupachārādhyā* talks about 64 *upacharams*). *Śree Devee* is decorated with various gems (*Maŋis*) and hence *Maŋipoorakam*. Since *Śreedevee* rises here **She** gets the name *Maŋipoora-Antar-Udita*.

(ii) As discussed above, imagining that the *Sushumnanāḍi* has relationship between musical sounds and the syllables of *Śree Vidyā* and chanting the *mantra*, is called *nāḍivishuam* (*Varivasya Rahasyam* 1-45, 46).

102. *Vişhŋugranthivibhedinee* - विष्णुग्रन्थिविभेदिनी

(i) The *Kunḍalinee* energy coming out of *Maŋipoorakam*, while reaching *Anāhata Chakra* from *Vishuddi Chakra*, pierces a very narrow path called *Vişhŋu Granthi* (a kind of knot) in between them. **She** conducts the aspirants from the sorrow called *Sthithi*.

103 *Āgyāchakrantarālasthā* - आज्ञाचक्रान्तरालस्था

(i) *Āgyā Chakra* reposes between the two eye brows, in the *Sushumnanāḍi* with two petals. It is the place of the teacher who gives orders (*Āgyā*): Hence *Āgyā Chakra*. On account of practice done so far, the mind is controlled a little (*Ā* also means very little) and knowledge is acquired, this is called *Āgyā Chakra*.

104. *Rudragranthivibhedinee* - रुद्रग्रन्थिविभेदिनी

(i) The knot (small hole) between *Vishuddi* and *Āgya* and again between *Āgya* and *Sahasrāram* are called *Rudra Granthi*. *Śreedevee* pierces this knot and passes through. **She** conducts the aspirant from the ocean of bondage.

Though it was mentioned in the previous name that *Śreedevee* stays in *Āgja chakra*, the *Kunḍalinee* energy can reach the *Āgya chakra* from *Moolādhāra* only after differentiating the *chakras* and piercing through the *Rudra* knot.

(ii) Even in *Śreevidyā mantra* there are four groups – *Agni* (fire), *Soorya* (Sun), *Soma* (God of speech) and *Chandra* (Moon). Between two groups there are knots called *Hreem*. These three knots are respectively called *Brahma, Vişhŋu* and *Rudra Granti*. *Śreedevee* pierces these knots and moves into them. For this reason also *Rudra Granthivibhedinee*.

(iii) Actually, out of the six explanations given in *Thaiteerya Samhita* for the *Panchadashi Mantra*, the *Koulikartham* is described in the six names from 99 – *Moolādhāraikanilayā* till this name – *Rudra granthi vibhedinee*. There itself it is mentioned as:

Moolādhārādikam Chakrashatkam Kulamithi Smruthami
*Granthithrāyam Tatra Devee Chakra Tritaya Garbhitami*I
Pruthvyapya Chakratvitayam Brahma Granthipadoditam I
Vahni Sooryamayam Chakratvayam Tejomayam Mahat II
Vişhŋugranthi Padenoktam Taijasam Sarvasiddhidam I
Rudragranthipadhenoktam Mangalāyatanam Mahath II

This has been described in the *Nityāshoḍashikārnavam, Koulikartham* – 7th *Ullasam*, 17.5 *verses* (from 50.5 to 68). *Śree BhāskaraRāya* also has explained the same in his *Varivasya Rahasyam*, second part, *verses* 30 to 49.

The abundant meaning of *Koulikartham* is *Śreedevee, Mantra, Śree Chakra*, the teacher and the self. The integration of these five is that there is that there is no difference between them.

This has been explained based on the famous *verse*:

Gaŋesagraha Nakshatra Yoginee Rāsi Roopineem I
Deveem Mantramayeem Nowmi Matrukām Peeța Roopiŋeem II

This *verse* followed by 11 *verses* is found in *Tantra Rājam, Nitya Shoḍashikarnavam* and other main *Śākta Tantras*. Since they include the *Śākta* principles they are read also at the end of *Navāvarŋa Pooja*. The *Yoginees* mentioned in this *verse* have been explained later in the names from 475 - *Vishudhichakrajanilayā* to 534 – *Yākinyambaswaroopiŋee*.

105. *Sahasrārāmbujārooḍhā* - सहस्राराम्बुजारूढा

(i) One who stays in a Lotus with 1000 petals below the skull. (**She** was made to reach this place from *Moolādhāra*, crossing all the chakras and piercing through the knots.

(ii) This is the place of *Sadāshiva n.* Out of the 16 phases of the Moon, 15 will be either waxing or waning. Only one is permanent. Hence it is called *Sādā* or *Sādākya* phase. The Lotus in the *Sahasrāram* has this 16th phase. The occupation of *Sadāshiva n* viz. favouring emerges here. (Refer names 272 and 273 also – *Sadāshiva Anugratha*).

(iii) Assuming there are 1000 petals, in the *Mātruka Nyāsam*, renunciation is done for 50 syllables, at the rate of one syllable for 20 petals.

(iv) We can also consider 1000 as infinite or countless. Some school interprets this as *Śreedevee* sitting on the lap of *Kāmeshwara* with infinite number of divine powers.

(v) The 240th name *Chandramaŋḍala Madhyaga* is also to be correlated here.

106. *Sudhāsārābhivarshiŋee* - सुधासाराभिवर्षिणी

(i) *Śreedevee*, seated in the centre of *Sahasrāra* Lotus, pelts the nectar to all the *nāḍis* as rainfall from *Chandra Maŋḍal*. Reaching this nectar flow and enjoying the indescribable bliss is the sole purpose of this *upasana*.

It is mentioned in *Vedas*:

> *Amrutasya Dhārā Bhahudhā Dhohamānami*
> *Charaŋam No Loke Sudhithan Dhadhatu* II

(ii) *Śree Ādi Śaŋkara*, in his *Soundaryalaharee* 10th *Verse* mentions; *Sudhādhārāsārai*: *Charaŋayugalantar Vigalitai*: *Prabancham Sinchantee*.

(iii) It is understood that this name is *Sudhādhārābhivarshinee* by some schools.

107. *Taḍillatāsamaruchi*: - तडिल्लतासमरुचिः

(i) In some schools this name is mentioned as *Taţillatāsamaruchi*. *Śree Bhāskararāya* mentions as *Taḍillatāsamaruchi*. The meaning is one and the same.

(ii) *Śreedevee* glitters like a lightning. *Veda* also mentions this as *Vidyullekeva Bhāsvara*.

108. ***Shaṭchakroparisamsthitā* - षट्चक्रोपरिसंस्थिता**

(i) One who is well settled in the *Sahasrāram* – above *Moolādhāram, Swādhishṭānam, Maŋipoorakam, Anāhatam, Vishuddhi* and *Agna-chakras* – as mentioned earlier.

109. ***Mahāsakti*: - महासक्तिः**

(i) The word *Mahā* has two meaning – festival or splendour. *Āshakti* means immense joy.
(ii) One who is fond of festival (the union of *Shiva* and *Shakti*). This has been clearly explained in the 9th *verse* of *Soundaryalaharee*:
Maheem Moolādhare Kamapi Maŋipoore Hutavaham
Sthitam Svādhishṭāne Hrudhi Marutamākāshamupari I
Manopi Bhrumadye Sakalamapi Bhitvā Kulapatham
Sahasrare Padme Saha Rahasi Patyā Viharase II
(iii) The same description is made by *Śree Ādi Śaŋkara* in his *Chintamaŋi Stavam; Varane Pumsā Sankamya Sankamya Rasam Prasoothe*.
(iv) One who is very much interested in celebrating offering of prayers as a festival.
(v) The word *Mahat* means – so huge expanding to all the directions. **Her** greatness is spread in all directions.
(vi) **Her** unison is spread in all the places and is visible even in an atom.

110. ***Kunḍalinee* - कुन्डलिनी**

(i) One who is in the form of *Kunḍalinee* energy.
(ii) **She** is in the form of a snake coiled in 3.5 rounds.
(iii) The three rounds respectively represent the letters *A, Oo* and *Ma*. The half round is the half scale. That implies *Kunḍalinee* corresponds to *Om* – the *Praŋavamantra*.
(iv) **She** is breathing like the snake sleeping in *Moolādhāra*. The breath of this *Kunḍalinee*, the energy of the soul, is the vital life (*prāŋan*). One can hear the sound of this breath by completely closing the ears. If it is not heard, it is told that death is nearing.
(v) The form of *Kunḍalinee* is explained in detail in the10th *verse* of *Soundarya- laharee;*
Sudhādhārāsāraishcharaŋayugalāntarvigalitai:
Prapancham Sinchantee Punarapi Rasāmnāya Mahasai
Avāpya Sivām Bhoomim Bhujaganibha Madhyushtavalayam

Svamāthmānam Kruthvā Svapishi Kulakuŋde Kuharini II

(vi) The method of awakening the sleeping *Kunḍalinee* energy and taking it to *Brahmarandhram* has been described in the *Yoga Sāstra*. The *Kunḍalinee* energy wakes up, reaches the *Brahmarandhram* and rains the nectar in the *nādis* by – ardent devotion, the results of adoration and the blessings of the teacher in addition to the *Haṭayoga* methods. In the present days for laymen like us, only the first method is best suitable –*Śree Kānchi Kāmakoṭi Paramāchārya* has incanted. (The book *Deivathin Kural*, 6th Volume, Pages 783 to 793). Again the 912th name *Savyāpasavyamārgastha* can be reminded.

(vii) The main theme of the songs sung by *Siddhas* is to awaken the *Kunḍalinee* energy and to bring it to the *Brahmarandhram*. The same is the main object of the famous song "*Ādu Pambe*" and the gestures made during the dance for this song.

(viii) *Chooḍalai Upākhyānam* in *Yoga Vāshitam* advises as to: As the smell in a flower is recognised, the mind called *Puryashṭakam* can also realise the *Kunḍalinee*, which is available inside the self.

(ix) The *Vāgbhava Beeja* is also called as *Kunḍalinee*. Hence it can also be interpreted as **She** is in the form of *Vāgbhava Beeja*.

(x) The 440th name *Kulakuŋḍālayā* can also be referred.

(xi) *Śree Ādi Śaṇkara* in his commentary of *Vişhŋu Sahasranāma* for the 907th name – *Kunḍalee* mentions;

a. *Vişhŋu* is in the form of *Ādi Sesha* – a snake.
b. *Vişhŋu* wears the earrings similar to the Sun's galaxy.
c. *Samkya* and *Yoga* are the two earrings in the form of fish.

(xii) It is told that the entire *Vinayagar Agaval* written by *Aouvaiyar* in Tamil talks about *Kunḍalinee*.

(xiii) It is mentioned in *Mahashoḍa Nyāsam* (*Devatanyāsam*) that **She** was worshipped by thousand crores *Bhairava* lineage.

111. *Bisatantutaneeyasee* - बिसतन्तुतनीयसी

(i) One who is as fine as the fiber of a lotus stalk.

(ii) It is mentioned in the *Veda* also as *Neevārashuka Vatthanvee Peetha Bhasvastyanoopamā* – (*Purusha Sooktam*).

(iii) Starting from 90th name (*Kulāmrutaikarasikā*) till now the subtle *Kunḍalinee* form of *Śreedevee* as was described. These have been very clearly explained in *Vāmakeshwara Tantra*.

Bhujangākāra Roopena Moolādhāram Samasrithā ----
---- *Sā Cha Avasthā Parā Geyā Saiva Nirvruthi Kāraŋam*

(iv) *Śree Lakshmeedharar* interprets *Ima Nugam Bhuvanā Sėshwatema*, 27th chapter of *Aruŋa Prasnam* as the form of *Śree Chakra*. *Śree Bhāskara Rāya* also seconds it in his commentary. He also quotes the name *Aruŋopanisht Geetha* in *Shyāmala Sahasranamam*. The gist of the meaning "in the form of *Śree Chakra* " is;

All the *Devas*, including *Indra*, advise us all to follow the *Śree Chakra Vidyā* and pray to *Śreedevee* to bless with all the wealth and rain the nectar in all our 72000 pulses. Bless us with the liberation to the body, soul and universe. Let us permanently focus on the form of *Śreedevee*.

The 360 rays rising from *Śreedevee* formed bodies in the form of 360 days. Mother - The knowledge about you should not leave me. Those who adore *Bharathi* – i.e. *Saraswatee* – *Śree Vidyā* – don't sleep. They wake up early in the morning, Illuminate the fire in the *Swādhistanam*; meditate *Shiva* with *Śreedevee* in the *Sahasrāra*. Derive happiness from the nectar that flows from the lotus feet of *Shiva*. Wearing the best attire in the young age by adoring *Śreedevee* become the best among the born. A valiant, who has control over the organs and who mentally adore the devatas only can reach this stage.

Worship *Śreedevee* in the *Śree Chakra* with eight *chakras* and nine holes. Those who are unlucky cannot reach the immortal *Śree Vidyā* city, the place where the earth *tatwa* dissolutes (*Moolādhāram*) and the corresponding deity is *Kumari*. She rises from sleep at *Moolādhāram* and gigantically shouts in a louder voice. She, as a young girl, reaches *Vişhŋu Granthi* and screams to pierce it (only *Yogis* can hear this sound). Third, as a *pativratha*, reaches *Śree Kāmeshwara* in *Brahmarandhram*. **She** multiplies the nectar there. All these are possible by the fire in the *Swādhistānam*. Thus speak the *Brusni* sages among themselves.

One other interpretation is – the *Kunḍalinee* when started from *Moolādhāram* makes sound like a child and hence *Kumari* – a small girl.

(v) *Śree BhāskaraRāya* quotes from *Sanatkumar Tantram*, *Sukasamhitai* and *Vashishṭa Tantram* that the same meaning has been explained. In the *phalaśruti* (result/ effect) part of *Lalitā Trishatee* also;

Achruta Sa Srutasasscha Yajvānoo Yepyayajvana: I

Swaryantho Napeshante Indrmagnim Chayevidu: II
Sikatā Iva Samyanthi Rasmibhi: *Samoodeeritā*: I
Asmāllokādamushmācchetyāha Chāraŋyaka Sruthi: II

Śree Chidānanda Nāthar explains the meaning of the above as:
If it is taken that the following people also have rights to do *Śree Chakra Vidyā pooja*;

- One whose mind is filled with sins and dirt
- One with immaculate interest
- One who has wealth, knowledge, ability and the right to do sacrificial rites
- One who absolutely does not have the right to do sacrificial rites then it is inferred that everybody has the right.

Those who adore *Śree Vidyā* do not even care the enjoyment of heaven, on account of their non-differentiating capability.

Those who worship:
- The deities of the directions starting from *Indra*,
- Other *devas*
- The philosophies (*tatwas*) starting from the Earth and ending with *Sadāshiva* thinking that they are disintegrated

Treating them higher than *Śreedevee*, they become minute than sand, would be bound by the noose of *Yama* and suffer the sorrows both in this life and post life – says *Aruŋasruti*.

112. ***Bhavānee*** - भवानी

(i) The word *Bhava* has three meanings – Lord *Mahadeva*, the human life cycle and Cupid. **She** gives life (*Ānayathee*) to all these three and hence *Bhavānee*.
(ii) Since Lord *Paramashiva* creates all the living things his name is *Bhava*. His consort is *Bhavānee*.
(iii) Out of the eight forms of Lord *Paramashiva,* the form of water is called *Bhava*. His consort is *Bhavānee*. One who gives life to the living form of water is *Bhavānee*. (*Tayonmruḍa Jeevase* – *Śree Rudra* verse has to be reminded).
(iv) The name of *Śreedevee* in *Sthaneshwara Shetra* is *Bhavānee*.
(v) In the 22nd verse of *Soundaryulaharee*, assuming two usages for the word *Bhavānee* the grace of *Śreedevee* is explained. The word

Bhavānee is used as an exclamation and as a predicate.
A devotee thinks to address *Śreedevee* as Bhavanee! and ask **Her** – why can't you pass your graceful sight on the slave like me? In this regard the devotee just starts with the two words "*Bhavanee* You" – Instantly *Śreedevee* takes the request as "I have to become you". **She** provides the salvation, which is rare even for the *Devas* including *Brahma* also. Thus goes the verse:

Bhavani Tvam Dāse Mayi Vitara Drushtim Sakaruṇām
Iti Sthothum Vanchan Kathayati Bhavāni Tvamiti Ya: I
Tadaiva Tvam Tasmai Dishasi Nijasāsyujya Padaveem
Mukunḍa Brahmendrasputa Makuta Neerājitapadām II

(vi) *Mahashoḍanyāsam* (*Prapanchanyāsam*) says that **She** is in the form destruction of the Universe.

113. *Bhāvanāgamyā* - भावनागम्या

(i) One who can be realised through devoted mediation.
(ii) Thus the five forms viz. physical, gross, subtle, subtler and subtlest, of *Śreedevee* were described and now the ideas to reach them are being mentioned.
(iii) The method of adoration through meditation is explained in *Pavanopanishad*. *Śree Bhāskararāya* himself has written a method to use this.
(iv) The 870th name – *Antharmukhasamārādhyā* can be referred.
(v) As per the saying *Yadbhāvam Tadbhavati* – we become that whichever was incessantly thought of. A worm becoming a grub is being taken as an instance in this regard.
(vi) Meditation is of two types –One is about the word and the other is about the meaning. Relating to the word - is the one – To worship the words i.e. sounds, (it has to be taken as holi religious words or sounds) as taught by the teacher and as per his wish. In his book *Meemamsa Vāda Koutoohalam*, *Śree Bāskara Rāya* writes that he has described it only by the wish of Lord *Ĕshwara*.
(vii) *Śree Bhāskararāya* says that he has described (in the above said *Meemamsa Vāda Koutoohalam*) that the meditation relating to meaning (meditation tending towards action *Pravrttiroopa*)and the sensuous form are co-related.
(viii) Two opposite meanings can be given – **She** is unreachable by all these by splitting *Bhava* + *Agamyā* or **She** is reachable by splitting as *Bhāvan*

+ *Āgamya.*

(ix) It can also be interpreted as meditation with word is *Saguŋa Upāsanā* (meditation imagining some form). In due course when it becomes meditation with meaning, it becomes *Nirguŋa Upāsanā* (meditation on the formless and attribute-less).

(x) In addition, by interpreting the word *Bhavanā* as attaining salvation through religious rites (*karma mārga*), the meaning is conveyed as before by splitting as *Agamyā* or *Āgamya*. Another meaning is that **She** is not attainable through religious rites (*karma mārga*); One other meaning is **She** is attainable by untainted mind got through religious rites (*karma mārga*).

(xi) Or – (*Bhāvanā*) Meditation is of three types. It is mentioned in the *Koorma Purāŋā* as;

Brāhmi, Maheshwaree Chaiva Tataivākshara Bhavanāi
Tisrastu Bhāvanā Rudra Vartante Satatam Dvijā: II

I.e. *Brahmi, Maheshvaree* and *Akshara* type of meditations are always with Lord *Rudra*.

(xii) In yet other place:

Trividhām Bhāvanām Procyamānām Nibodhame I
Eta Madvishyā Tatra Dweteeyāvyaktasamsrayā II
Antya Tu Saguŋā Brahmi Vigjyeyā Triguŋātridhā II

This was taught by *Śree Bhagavān* to *Indradyumnan* during his *Matsya* (fish) incarnation. *Śree Baskara Rāya* opines that since this has been clearly explained by *Appayya Deekshitar* in his *Ratna Traya Pareekshā*, it can be referred there itself.

Śreemathkoormena Yātyāsramaratavishayā Bhāvanoktā Triteeyā
Divya Sthānapradatree Saguŋavishayinee Sankarālambhanā Sā I
Ye Tvanyee Bhāvanee Te Sarasijanayaneenā Dishaktyā Sayukte
Prāpinyou Te Tu Tasyā: *Kramika Balayute Boutikam Sankhyamāpte* II

Śree Appayya Deekshitar in his *Ratna Trāya Parikshā* has himself given the meaning for the above verse quoting proofs from *Koorma Purāŋa*;

- **First** – The formless meditation is possible only for those who adore *Śreedevee* on a daily basis. He explains this based on the preaching of the sage *Swetashvatara* and keeping the *Upanishad* saying in mind.
- **Second** – Meditating the chit energy of Lord *Parameshwara*.
- **Third** – *Saguŋa Upāsana* - meditation imagining some form or other.

(xiii) Or - there are three states of meditation namely *sakala* (with form), *sakala-nishkala* (full manifestation) and *niskulu* (formless and undifferentiated). It has been described in *Nityāshoḍasikārnavam*, after explaining the meaning of *Śree Chakra Pooja* – One who has the capability to feel Macrocosm (*Brahmānḍam*) and Microcosm (*Pindāndam*) as an integrated one can only imagine the three *chakras* in the body.

114. *Bhavāraŋyakuṭhārikā* - भवारण्यकुठारिका

(i) One who is like an axe for clearing the jungle of trans migratory existence (the ocean of *Samsāra*).

(ii) The forest is dense with trees which grow again and again. Similarly this life cycle (*Samsāra* Ocean) also, makes repeated birth again and again on account of cravings on various external objects in this world. The forest will be destroyed only when all the trees are cut. In the same way only if the desires on the worldly matters are destructed the *Samsāra* forest will be shattered. She is mentioned to be the axe to cut the trees.

(iii) It has to be understood that once we get the knowledge of *Śreedevee* the bonding to this world will be cut.

115. *Bhadrapriyā* - भद्रप्रिया

(i) One who is fond of everything auspicious.

(ii) **She** is too fond of offering all the auspicious things to **Her** devotees.

(iii) A kind of species in elephants is called *Bhadram*. **She** has affection to that species of elephants.

116. *Bhadramoorti*:– भद्रमूर्त्तिः

(i) One who has an auspicious form.

(ii) *Brahma Tanmangalam Vidu*: - *Brahmam* is the only one that is auspicious, says *Vişhŋu Purāŋa*.

(iii) In the initial part of *Vişhŋu Sahasranāma*, it is mentioned as *Mangalanām cha mangalam*. *Śree Ādi Śaŋkara*, in his commentary – *Mangalam* means felicity, its tool and to instruct the same; something above auspicious and hence *Mangalanām cha mangalam*.

(iv) 200th name *Sarvamangala* and 932nd name *Mangalakruti*: can be referred.

117. *Bhaktasoubhāgyadāyinee* – भक्तसौभाग्यदायिनी

(i) One who grants all round advancement to **Her** devotees.

(ii) In the *Agni Purāṇa* the word *Bhaga* has been given various meanings like – wealth, desire, praising stories, vigor, preparation, illumination, pride, etc. Since **She** holds all these, **She** has a name *Subhagā* (name 761). **Her** nature is prosperity (*Soubhāgyam*).

(iii) Also exemplary and fortune are other meanings. The one, who contemplates all these, is *Soubhāgyam*. One who grants prosperity (*Soubhāgyam*) to **Her** devotees.

(iv) Again, as per *Agni Purāṇam*, since these eight things are used in auspicious occasions – Sugar Cane, Peepul tree, sprouted cumin, coriander, cow's milk (including its variations as curd, butter, ghee, etc)., things that are in yellow colour, flowers and salt, these are called *Soubhāgyashṭakam* (eight auspicious things). It can also be understood as **She** offers all these to **Her** devotees.

(v) *Śree Ādi Śaṇkara*, in his commentary to *Viṣhṇu Sahasranāma*, for the 559th name *Bhagavān*, he quotes the verse with the meaning below and says that one who has all these is called *Bhagavān*:
Bhaga means complete wealth, charity, glory, richness, relinquishment and liberation from all the bondage. It is appropriate to mean that **She** provides all these to the devotees.

From name 109-*Mahāshakti*:, nine names were explained by the *Salākshara Sūtra Banḍaṇ*. This has been described in detail in the part about *Paribhāsha* verses.

118. *Bhaktipriyā* - भक्तिप्रिया

(i) One who fond of devotion. *Śreedevee* loves the adoration with devotion.

(ii) Worship is of two kinds, primary (*mukhya*) and secondary (*gauna*); primary devotion is a particular mental modification called 'longing' direction towards *Eshvara*. This type of mental status is called *Anurāga* – says *Sanḍilya Sūtra* – *Sā Prānuraktireeshvare*.

(iii) It is as below in *Nāradha Bhakti Sūtra*; It (worship) is the sincere affection on lord. (These are the symptoms for this – without pride and selfishness, there is no room for any other thought in the mind and the status of completely forgotten self). That is worship;

- Upon reaching which the man gets the nectar form, becomes accomplished, becoming immortal and a contended person.
- Upon reaching which the man does not have desires, does not regret, does not have aversion, (by having affection on external

objects) long the happiness and does not have interest.

- Upon realising it, he feels as if he has consumed alcohol, becomes somatic and feels pleased on his own self.

(iv) *Śree Ādi Śaṇkara* in his *Shivānandalaharee* (verse 61) explains the characteristics of devotion;

Ankolam Nijabeeja Santatirāyaskāntopalam Soochikā
Sadhvee Naijavibhum Latā Kshitiruham Sindhu Saridvallabham I
Prāpnoteeha YathātathāPashupatee: Pādhāravindhadhvyam
Chetovruttiroopeetya Tishtati Sada Sā Bhāktirityuchyate II

The below noted are naturally attracted and reaches the other one. In the same way, if mind can reach the lord that is devotion:

- Seeds of *Azhinchil* (Alangium decapitalum) tree to the parent tree
- A needle to a magnet.
- A loyal wife to her husband.
- A climber to a tree/ stick.
- A river to the ocean.

(v) *Śree Ādi Śaṇkara* in his *Viveka Chooḍāmaṇi* (verses 32, 33);

Moksha Kāraṇa Sāmagriyam Bhaktireva Gareeyasee I
Svasvaroopānusandānam Bhaktiretyabhidheeyate I
Svātma Tatvānusandhānam Bhaktirityapare Jagu: II

Devotion is the most important tool to instill knowledge, which is a media to attain liberation. To contemplate the form of *Brahmam* in the self, in an uninterrupted manner, is called devotion. It is mentioned in some schools that realisation of identifying the individual soul with *Brahmam* is called devotion. (There is a subtle difference in these two. It is explained that the latter one is a little inferior since, it shows the difference (between the soul and the universal absolute) every now and then.

(vi) The secondary devotion is in the form of services to Lord. This originates from the root word *bhaj*. This has been treated differently in different books - Eight types in *Garuḍa Purāṇā*, Nine types in *Viṣhṇu Bhāgavatam* and ten types in *Brahannāradeeyam*. The famous verse in *Viṣhṇu Bhāgavatam* goes;

Sravaṇam Keerthanam Vishno: *Smaranam Padasevanam* I
Archanam Vandanam Dhasyam Sakyam Āthmaṇiveedhanam II

In *Śreemad Bhagavat Geeta* also it is seen in various places as a testimony of the Lord's interest in devotion;

Madbhaktā Yānthi Māmapi (7.23)
Patram Pushpam Phalam Toyam Yo Me Bhaktyā Prāyacchat II
Tadaham Bhatyupahrutamasnāme Prāyatātmana: II (9.26)
Ye Bhajanti Tu Mām Bhaktyā Mayi Te Teshu Cāpyaham II (9.29)

119. *Bhaktigamyā* - भक्तिगम्या

(i) Three interpretations can be made for this name. By true devotion **She** will be present, can be attained and can be recognised.

(ii) In the *Veda*:

Parānchikhāni Vyatrunat Swayambhoo:
Tasmat Parānpashyati Nāntarātman I
KasChiddheera: *Pratyagātmānamaikshadavruita Chakshu*:
Amrutatvamichchan II

The self-existent (*Swayambhoo*:) constraints the senses. They turn to external objects; therefore man sees the external objects, not the internal self; but the wise, with eye averted and desirous of immortality, behold the inner self.

(iii) The *Veda* also says, the *Yogins* see the eternal Lord. In the *Yoga Sūtra*, *Rāja Marthānda* interprets *Pranidhāna* (in *Ĕshwara pranidhā nātvā*) as devotion.

(iv) In the *Brahma Sūtra* also (III-2-24) *Api Samprādhane Pratyakshānumānabhyām* (In the state of the entire universe being receded and the soul is in the form, which cannot ordinarily be perceived, can be comprehended by the *Yogis* through devotion/ meditation. To be seen like this, to focus on the soul etc., are evidenced through *Vedas* (*Śree Ādi Śaṇkara*'s commentaries). Even in the unperceivable nature, the *Brahmam* can be comprehended through devotion.

(v) In *Śreemad Bhagavat Geeta* also it has been stressed that it can be reached only through devotion (11 – 54):

Bhaktyā Tvananyayā Shakya Ahamevam Vidhorjuna I
Gyātum Drashṭum Cha Tatvena Praveshtum Cha Parantapa II

The word *Praveshtum* here means liberation in the form of *Brahmam*. Hence in this name we can mean *Gamyā* as "**She** can be reached".

(vi) In *Chandokya Upanishad* (II 23.2) – *Brahmasamasttho Amrutatvameti* – One who stays in the *Brahmam* is immortal. In this context the word 'stays' means devotion.

(vii) It is the apt meaning for the word 'stay', since it has been mentioned in *Sānḍilya Sūtra* as *Tatsamsttasyām Rutatvopadesat* (I – 4) and in *Brahma Sūtra* as *Tannishtasya Brahmopadesat* (I – 1 – 7).

(viii) In *Nityā Tantra* also, after describing the nature of devotion, it is mentioned that all the worldly substances can be obtained through this. There itself it is mentioned that the people who are without devotion would suffer both in this world and the celestial worlds.

(ix) Or – devotion also a meaning of characteristic features. (*Śree*

Bhāskara Rāya quotes this as used in *Jaimini Sūtra*). In this regard, it can be interpreted as, even though **She** is actually invisible, **Her** form can be recognised through **Her** characteristic features. The words truth and knowledge mean divine bliss. But they explain only the characteristic features and not the actual form. (*Yato Vache Nivarthanthe* – cannot be explained). Hence the 72nd name in *Trishatee – Lakshaŋagamya*.

(x) For the 192nd name in *Trishatee – Labdhabhaktisulabhā - Śree Ādi Śaṇkara* has given two interpretations:
   a. **She** can be easily identified by those knowledgeable people who have realised *Brahmam* through devotion.
   b. **She** will be present to those who have ardent devotion on **Her** without any thought of anything else.

120. *Bhaktivashyā* - भक्तिवश्या

(i) One who can be won through true devotion – *Parādeenai*.

(ii) The statement "God will yield to devotion" has ample proof through the story of: *Kaŋŋappa Nāyanar, Druva, Gajendra Moksha, Prahlāda, Sabari Moksha* and *Kuchela Upākyana*.

(iii) *Śree Ādi Śaṇkara* in his *Shivanandalaharee* (verse 63) mentions about *Kaŋŋappa Nāyanar*:
Mārgāvartita Pādukā Pashupate: *Angasya Koorchchāyate*
Gandooshamboo Nishechanam Puraripo: *Divyābhishekāyate* I
Kinchit Bhakshitamāmseshu Kabalam Navyopahārāyate II
Bhakti: *Kim Na Karootyaho Vanacharo Bhaktāvatamsāyate* II

(iv) Without devotion, also with an inimical mind Cupid aimed an arrow of flowers on *Parameshwara* and was burnt into ashes by **him**.

(v) The below verse lists down that God will bless those who has true devotion, without even minding the ills in him:
Vyāthasya Ācharaŋam Dhruvasyachavaya: *Vidyā Gajendrasyakā*
Gājāti: *Vidurasya Yādavapate*: *Ugrasya Kim Pourusham*
Gupjāyā: *Kāmeeyaroopam Adhikamkim Tatsudamno Dhanam*
Bhaktyā Tushyati Kevalam Natu Kunai: *Bhaktipria*: *Kesava*:

(vi) It can be reminded of the guarantee given by *Śreemad Bhagavat Geeta* (9 – 31) viz. *Namĕ Bhakta*: *Pranasyati*. Again Lord *Śree Krişhŋa* says:
Ananyāsh Chintayanto Mām Ye Janā: *Paryupasate* I
Tesham Nityabhiyuktānām Yogakshemam Vahāmyaham II (9– 23)
Yo Mām Pashyati Sarvathra Sarvamca Mayi Pashyatee I

Tasyāham Na Pranashyāmi Sa Ca Me Na Pranashyati II (6 – 30)

For the 192nd name in *Trishatee – Labdhabhaktisulabhā - Śree Ādi Śaṇkara's* commentary may be referred. In brief this was given at the end of the previous name.

121 *Bhayāpahā* - भयापहा

(i) One who dispels all fears.

(ii) Drives away all the fears from water and earth. Hence *Bhayāpaha*.

(iii) *Veda* says *Ānandam Brahmaŋo Vidwan Na Bhibheti Kutaschana* – One who has reached eternal bliss knows no fear.

(iv) In the *Vāyu Purāŋa* also it is mentioned that when frightened the very thought of *Śreedevee* alleviates all fears.

Aranye Prantare Vāpi Jale Vāpi Sthalapivā I
Vyāghra Kumbheera Chorebhyo Bhayastāne Visheshata: II
Ādhishvapi Cha Sarveshu Devee Nāmāni Keertayet: II

(v) The same has also been mentioned in the 12th chapter of *Saptashatee*;

Yuddheshu Charitam Yanme Dushṭadaitya Nibarhanam I
Tasminchrute Vairikrutam Bhayam Pumsām Najāyate II
Aranye Prantare Vāpi Davāgniparivārita: I
Dasyubhirvā Vruta: *Soonye Gruheeto Vāpi Satrubhi*: II
Simhavyāghrānuyāto Va Vane Va Vanahstibhi: I
Rāgnā Kruddhena Chāk Gyapto Vadhyo Bandhagatopivā II
Āghoornito Vā Vātena Sthita: *Pote Maharnave* I
Patatsu Chāpi Shastreshu Sangrāme Bhrushadarune II

Sarvābhādhāsu Ghorāsu Vedanābhyarditopi Vā I
Smaran Mamtaccharitam Naro Muchyeta Sankatāt II
Mama Prabhāvāt Simhādyā Dasyavo Vairinastathā I
Doorādeva Palāyante Smratascharitam Mama II

(vi) *Śree Doorvāsa* in his *Shakti Mahimnā Stotram* (55th verse) mentions this as "*Praseeda Paradevate Mama Hrudi Prabhutam Bhayam Vidhayarāya*".

(vii) *Śree Ādi Śaṇkara* in his *Shivānandalaharee* (4th verse) mentions as;

Twadanya: *Pānibhyā Mabhayavarado Daivatagaŋa*: I
Tvameka Naivāsi Prakatita Varābheetyabhinayā II
Bhayāt Trātum Phalamapi Ca Vānchāsamadhikam I
Sharanye Lokānām Tava Hi Caranāveva Nipunou II

(viii) *Veda* says "*Tveeteeyādhvai Bhayam*" (*Brahdāraŋyaka Upanishad*

1.4.2) – there is nothing else other than *Śreedevee* and hence no fear; i.e. *Śreedevee* blesses the knowledge of *Brahmam* that all is one and there is no second.

(ix) From *Śree Ādi Śaṇkara's* commentary for *Viṣhŋu Sahasranāma*

a. 935th name – *Bhayāpaha*: -– One who relieves the fear of cycle of birth and death.

b. 834th name – *Bhayanāshana*: - **He** destroys the fear for those who do follow the convention of caste and *ashramas*.

(x) *Parāsarā* mentions in *Viṣhŋu Purāŋam* (3.8.9);

Varŋasramāchāravatā Purushena Para: *Pumān* I
Viṣhŋurārādhyate Panthā Nānyas Tattoshakāraka: II

In *Śreemad Rāmāyana* –

Sakrudeva Prapannaya Tavāsmeetica Yāchate I
Abhayam Sarva Bhootebhyo Datamyetatvratam Mama II

Again in *Durgā Saptashatee* (Chapter XI) –

Saranāgata Deenārttaparitrāna Parāyane I
Sarvasyārttihare Devee Nārāyaŋi Namostute II

122 *Shāmbhavee* – शाम्भवी

(i) Consort of *Shambu*. (In his commentary to *Viṣhŋu Sahasranāma* for 38th name –*Śree Ādi Śaṇkara* says – One who gives comfort to the devotees is *Shambu*).

(ii) Mother of devotees of Lord *Shiva*. The below verses from *Soundarya-laharee* can be reminded;

Shareerardham Shambhoraparamapi Shanke Hrutamabhoot (23)
Shareeram Tvam Shambho: (34)
Shivāyuvathi Bhāvena Bibhrushe (35)
Shivam Seve Deveemapi Shiva samāna Vyvasitām
(37)

(iii) *Shāmbavee Devee* is mentioned in *Śree Vidyāratna Sūtra*s of *Śree Gowḍapādar*. This has been described in detail in the commentary as; Nobleness of mind (*Satva Guŋa* form), white in colour, consort of *Rudra*, creator of *uttarāmnāya mantra*s in the form of *Sāma Veda*, etc.

(iv) During festival days like *Navarāthri*, during *Navāvarŋa Pooja* and at the end of *Chaŋḍi Homa*, worship is done on *Sumangali* (auspicious ladies with husband), young girls (*kanyā*) and young boys (*brahma-chari*). 971st name *Suvāsinarchana Preetā* can be referred.

Worship is done on a girl child of 8 years old, who is called naming as *Shāmbhavee*. Worshipping girls (*kanyā*) is described in detail in the 26th chapter, third *Skanda* of *Devee Bhāgavatam*. Worship is done on girl children of ages 2 to 10. The name and the results of worshipping of each age of girls are explained here.
The list goes:

Age	Name	Results of *pooja*
2	*Kumāri*	Removal of sorrows and poverty, destruction of enemies, enhancement of wealth and strength, long life
3	*Trimurthy*	Long life, enhancement of wealth and grains, long lineage of the family
4	*Kalyāni*	Education, Success, Statehood, Welfare
5	*Rohinee*	Free from diseases
6	*Kālikā*	Free from enemies
7	*Chaṇḍikā*	Prosperity and wealth
8	*Shambavee*	Attracted by the rulers, removal of sorrows and poverty, success in wars.
9	*Durgā*	Free from cruel enemies, success in all vehement deeds and goodness in other world also.
10	*Subhadrā*	To get all that is wanted

The verse to be used while worshipping *Shāmbhavee*;

Akāraṇānāt Samutpatthiryanmayai: Parikeertitā I
Yasyāstām Sukhadām Deveem Shambhaveem Poojayāmyaham II

Similarly different verses are available for different names of the girls. Different verses are used to worship the girl at the end of *Chaṇḍi Homa*. The verse to worship *Shāmbhavee* here is;

Sadānandakareem Shantām Sarvadeva Namaskrutām I
Sarvabhootātmikām Lakshmeem Shāmbhaveem Poojayāmyaham II

It has to be understood that *Shāmbhavee* is described here.

(v) There is a symbol by name *Shāmbhavee* in *Yoga Sāstra*. That is Seeing outwardly the void without even twinkling the eyes and seeing the innerself. **She** is in the form of this symbol.

Anthar Lakshyam Bahirdrushti: Nimeshonmesha Varjitā I
Eshā Sā Shāmbhavee Mudrā Sarvatantreshu Gopitā II

(vi) Or – The teacher teaches the *mantras* to the student after initiation. Initiation has been explained in *Paramānanda Tantra* and *Kulārnava* as;

Deeyate Shiva Sāyujyam Sheeyate Pashabandhanami
Ato Deeksheti kathitā........

Initiation is given in many a type. Three main types are explained in *Parasurāmakalpa Sūtra* (22);

Dheekshās Tisra: *Shāktee Shāmbhavee Mantree Chet* II
Tatra Shaktee Shakti Pravechanāt Shāmbhavee
Charaŋa Vinyāsāt Mantree Mantropatishtyā
Sarvāscha Kuryāt Māntri

In this commentary, *Shāmbhavee* initiation is described such that the teacher imagines the *Kāmeshwaree* and *Kāmeshwara* in the form of *Rakta-sukla* feet, on the student's head.

(vii) In *Mahāshoḍā Nyāsa* (*Prapancha Nyāsa*), it has been said that **She** is in the form of day time.

(viii) It can also be taken as *Shāmbhavee Vidyā* as mentioned in *Bahuvruchopanishad*.

(ix) It can also be taken as pellucid as explained in 14th verse of *Soundaryalaharee*.

(x) It can also be taken as *Shuddagnānatā Shāmbhavee Vidyā* in *Rashmimālā*, which is being by devotees during their daily meditation. *Parāshāmbhava* and *Parāshāmbhavee mantra*s in *Uttarāmnāyamantra* can also be referred.

123 *Shāradārādhyā* – शारदाराध्या

(i) One who eligible to be adored by *Shārada*. *Shāradā* means *Saraswatee* (consort of Lord *Brahma*) or *Vāg Devee*s beginning from *Vasinee*.

(ii) **She** is fit to be worshipped during autumn season. The period from mid-April to mid-June is called spring season (*Vasantha Rutu*). The period from mid-October to mid-December is called autumn season (*Sharat Rutu*). The nine days (*Navarātri*) worship of *Śreedevee* during these two seasons is called *Vasantha Navarātri* and *Sharada Navarāthri*. These two are most apt for adoring *Śreedevee*. *Rudrayāmalam* suggests worshiping *Rakta Danḍika* during *Vasantha Navarāthri*. The devotees know that this season is a period of *Rāma Navami* and *Rakta Dandika* is *Sita* herself. In addition, *Śreedevee*'s main *devatas* are *Mantrinee* (*Shyāmalā*) and *Ḍanḍinee* (*Mahā-vārāhee*). They are to be specially adored during mid-January to mid-February and mid-July mid-August periods respectively.

This reminds the verse in *Saptashatee* (12th Chapter) – *Sharatkāle*

Mahāpoojā Kriyate Yā Cha Vārshakee.

(iii) *Shārada* means *Vishāradas* – that is learned people. In particular those who have attained the abode called *Sāleenam*. **She** is fit to be adored by these.

(iv) By splitting the name as *Shārada + Ārādhyā*, it can be meant as – One who has the name as *Shārada* and worthy of worshiping. The *Prapancha Nyāsa* in *Mahā Shoḍānyāsā* describes *Shāradā* as *Avasthā chatushṭaya roopā* - four states viz. awaken (*Jāgrath*), dream (*Swapna*), deep sleep (*Sushupti*) and swoon (*Thureeyam*).

The below verse in *Kālikā Purāŋā* says that **She** was awakened by *Devas* during autumn season.

Shratkāle Purā Yasmānnavamyām Botidhāsurai: I
Shāradā Sā Samākhyātā Peeṭe Loke Chanāmata: II

The monastery (*Peeṭa*) is also called as *Shārada*. The *Shāradā* monastery at *Sringeri* in *Karnataka* state of India is very famous.

(v) As per the dictionary called *Anekārtta Dwani Manjari* – *'A'* implies *Vişhŋu* and *'Ā'* implies *Brahma*. It has to be taken that **She** was adored by both.

124 *Sharvāŋee* – शर्वाणी

(i) Consort of Lord *Paramashiva.*

(ii) One of the eight forms of Lord *Paramashiva* is earth. His consort is *Sukesee*. Their son is *Angārakā* (Mars). It can be seen:

In *Linga Purāŋā*

Charācharānām Bhootānām Dhātā Vishva mbharātmakai
Sarva Ityucyate Deva: *Sarva Sastrāntha Pāragai*: I
Vishva mbharātmanstasya Sarvasya Parameshtinai
Sukesee Kathyate Patnee tanujongāraka: *Smrutai* I

In *Vāyu Purāŋā*

Sarvasya Yā Truteeyā tu nāma Bhoomitanu: *Smrutā* I
Patnee Tasya Sukeseeti Putraschangārako Mata: II

(iii) *Śree Ādi Śaŋkara* in his commentary of *Vişhŋu Sahasranāma* for the 26th name – *Sharva*: writes that he destroys all the living beings during the great dissolution of the universe (*Pralaya* period). In this it can be taken as the consort of *Sharva*.

(iv) In *Mahāshoḍā Nyāsa* (*Prabancha Nyāsa*), it has been said that **She** is in the form of zodiac sign.

125 *Sharmadāyinee* – शर्मदायिनी

(i) Bestower of happiness.
(ii) It is said as *Sharma Gyata Sukānicha* in *Agni Purāŋam*. Here the word *Sharma* implies happiness. **She** is in the habit/ practice/ nature of giving happiness. Hence *Sharmadāyinee*.
(iii) In the *Devee Bhāgavatam* also it is mentioned; *Sukham Dadāti Bhaktebhyastenaishā sharmadāyinee*. These are also to be referred – 192nd name *Sukapradā*, 953rd name *Sharmadā* and 968th name *Sukakaree*.

126 *Shānkaree* –शान्करी

(i) Consort of Lord *Shankara*.
(ii) *Sham* (bliss): Who gives this is Lord *Shankara*.
(iii) Or *Sham* (propitious-ness). One who has this in his hands is Lord *Shankara*. His form of energy is *Shānkaree*.
(iv) In *Kālikā Purāŋā*:

Pratisargādimadhyāntamaham Shambhum Nirākulam I
Stree Roopenānuyāsyāmi Prāpya Dakshādaham Tanum II
Tatastu Vişhŋumāyām Mām Yoganidrām Jaganmayeem I
Shānkareeti Stuvishyanti Rudraneeti Divougasa: II

(v) In the first chapter of *Saptashatee* it is mentioned that *Brahma* praised *Yoga Nidrā* and again in the last chapter it is cited that *Devas* praised *Vişhŋu Māya*.
(vi) In *Mahāshoḍā Nyāsa* (*Prapancha Nyāsa*), it has been said that **She** is in the form of night time.

127 *Śreekaree* - श्रीकरी

(i) One who gives prosperity.
(ii) For the word *Śree* many a meaning can be taken as; prosperity, wealth, goddess *Lakshmee*, auspiciousness, splendour, exultation, beauty, lustre, etc.
(iii) In *Vişhŋu Sahasranāma* we have a name *Śreekara*: (611th name). *Śree Ādi Śaņkara* interprets this as – one who gives affluence to the devotees.

The feminine of *Śreekara*: is *Śreekaree*.

Since *Śreedevee* and Lord *Vişhŋu* are inseparable the name *Śreekaree* is apt for *Śreedevee*.

Similarly these names can also be referred – *Govindaroopiŋee* (267), *Nārāyaŋee* (298), *Mukundā* (838), *Vaishŋavee* (892) and *Vişhŋuroopiŋee*

(893).

The ardent devotees of *Śreedevee* do *sankalpa* (declaration of intention to do a *pooja*) describe the time, besides describing usual five elements time as per the normal almanac (star of the day [*nakshatra*], day [*vāra*] and *thithi* [counting from previous new or full moon day], *yoga* and *karaŋa*), also adopt *Deveemāna Ashṭānga* method (during any *sankalpa* it is a custom to describe the place, the time and the intention). Eight elements of time as per *Śreedevee*'s measurements are as follows;

1. *Tatva Yuga*
2. *Tatva Varsha* (year – total 36 years)
3. *Kalā Māsa* (months – total 16 months)
4. *Tatva Dina* (day – total 36 days)
5. *Dina Nitya* (total 15)
6. *Thithi Nitya* (total 15)
7. *Vāsara* (total 9)
8. *Udhaya Ghatika* (total six)

In Samskrit the numbers are represented by letters through *Kaṭapayādi* method (as explained in the introductory part). In this, if the first letters of the day and the *Udhaya Katikā* are the same, it is called a *Parvādayor Śreekaree*. The specialty of these *parvā* days has been explained in the 19th *Ullasā* of *Paramānanda Tantra*. *Śree Maheshwarānanda Nāthar* in his commentary for *Rudra Māyālam* shows the 5 similarities.

The names *Vimalā* (347th) and *Mohinee* (562nd) also explain about *Parvā* days. (In the 732nd name *Nāmapārāyaŋa Preetā* also, the details about *Ashṭānga* can be seen).

128 *Sādhvee* – साध्वी

(i) One who is paragon of virtue (the names – 709 *Sadāshiva pathivrathā* and 820 *Sathee* can also be referred).

(ii) The pride of loyalty to her consort by *Śreedevee* is specially mentioned. When *Daksha*, father of *Śreedevee* (in one of **Her** incarnations) despised **Her** consort, Lord *Shiva*, **She** could not tolerate it and left **Her** body. She took another incarnation as daughter of *Himavān*, did penance and got Lord *Parameshwara's* hand. This is a famous story known to all. There are other places too where *Śreedevee* did penance and married Lord *Parameshwara* (for instance Mylapore in Chennai, India).

(iii) In *Devee Bāgavata* it is mentioned as – *Sādhveetyananya Sāmānya*

Pātivratyena Keeyase.

It is specifically mentioned that *Śreedevee* did not marry anybody else anytime (any of the incarnations also). It is the practice of poets to call as *Lakshmeepathi* - who has wealth and *Vākpathi*- the learned one, etc. Hence, *Lakshmee* and *Saraswatee* may not qualify to be called as *pathivratha*. *Śree Ādi Śaṇkara*, in his *Soundaryalaharee* 96th verse describes that since *Śreedevee* has never had a consort other than Lord *Parameshwara*, **Her** *pāthivrathya* is much special than anybody else's.

Kalathram Vaidhāthram Katikati Bhajante Na Kavaya:
Sriyo Devyā: *Ko Vā Na Bhavati Pati*: *Kairapi Dhanai*: I
Mahādevam Hitvā Tava Sati Sateenā Macharame
Kuchābhyā Māsanga: *Kuravaka-taro-rapyasulabha*: II

129 *Sharacchandranibhānanā* – शरच्चन्द्रनिभानना

(i) One whose face shines like the autumnal moon, gives pleasure to those who see **Her**.

130 *Shātodaree* - शातोदरी

(i) One who has a slender waist.
(ii) Daughter of *Himavān* (king of mount *Himalayās*) with hundreds of caves.
(iii) *Shātam* means slim. **She** has that type of waist. It is mentioned in the *Sāmudrikā Sāstrā* (explaining the body shapes) that ladies who have slim waists are beautiful. 847th name *Talodaree* may be referred.

It is mentioned in the *Gnanārnava Tantra* (16th section) of pooja method as defined by Śree Chitānanda Nāthar (one of the teachers in the teacher lineage of the authors of the original book in Tamil which is translated here), in the verse to deify *Śreedevee*; *Alakshyamathyamām Nimnanābhim Cātodareem Parām*. Similarly in *Śree Deekshitar*'s *Āvaran* (shelter) *Keertanās* (songs in classical music) the names *Sākambari* and *Sātodari* are used at the beginning and at the end.

131. *Shāntimatee* - शान्तिमती

(i) One who has controlled mind.
(ii) One who does not have any vehemence on devotees.
(iii) The below names can be referred – 141 *Shantā*, 447 *Shānti* and 963 *Shamātmika*.

132. ***Nirādhārā* - निराधारा**

(i) One who starts rises from *Moolādhāra*.
(ii) One who has no support other than **Herself**, (since **She** herself is the support for all).
(iii) This indicates the *Nirādhāra* (without any support like image, etc). pooja. From this name upto 187th name (*Niratyayā*), *Śreedevee*'s *Nirguŋa* (without any qualities) form and the results of meditating the same has been explained.
(iv) *Ādhāra* can be taken as *Moolādhārā* from where **She** rises upwards.
(v) *Tatrāpi Sā Nirādhārā Yuyudhe Tenachantikā* (*Durgā Saptashatee* – 10-23). When *Śreedevee* was fighting with *Sumbhāsuran*, **She** was standing in the sky without any support.
(vi) *Sabhagava*: *Kasmin Pratishtita Iti Sve Mahimna Iti Hovāca* (*Chāndokya Upanishad* VII-24-1). It is replied for the question "Where is that *Brahmam* stationed?" as; it is conspicuous without any support other than self.

There are two kinds of worshipping *Śreedevee* as external (*Bāhyam*) and internal (*Āntaram*). And again the external has two divisions, *Vedic* and *Tantric*. The internal method is also of two kinds with support (*Sādhāra*) and without support (*Nirādhāra*).

The *Sādhāra* worship is to worship mental images in the form of *mantras* as taught by a teacher.

The *Nirādhāra* worship is by pure intellect – focusing the mind on *Śreedevee*'s image obtained by knowledge. In reality, pure intellect means nothing else, but the supreme *Śreedevee*. Hence for the destruction of *samsāra*, one should worship the *Śreedevee*, the very self, the witness, free from the glamour of the maŋifold universe. By one's own direct experience of *Maheshwaree* as the self, **She** should be worshipped with much reverence, this is the worship which leads to salvation.
As an evidence for this, the verses in the 5th chapter – *Māhātmya Kāṇḍa* of *Sootha Samhitai* can be considered.

133. ***Niranjanā* - निरन्जना**

(i) One who is free from any stain.
(ii) *Anjana* means black collegium used for eyes. Though it is used for

beautification, still it is a stain. In this context *Anjana* implies ignorance or illusion. The knowledge disappears due to ignorance (owing to its quality of darkness in mind). It has to be construed that *Śreedevee* has no relevance to ignorance or illusion.

(iii) There are three kinds of ignorant souls (*Pashus*):

a. The *Vijnanākevala*, he who sees the self in the non-self and has arrogance as the only impurity;

b. The *Pralayakevala*, he who has the impurity of *karma*, which is unperceivable and which gives him new births; he also has the impurity mentioned in 'a' above.

c. The *sakala*, he who has the impurity of the illusion (*māyā*). He has the idea of duality in all matters. He also has the impurities mentioned in 'b' above.

Śree BhāskaraRāya himself explains all these, in his *Sethu Bandam* (explanation to VI-27 in *Nityāshotasikārnava*). There he has also mentions to refer his explanation to 354th name *Pashupacha vimochanee*.

(iv) *Śreedevee* has no impurities of *sakala* and hence *Niranjana*.

Swetasvatara Upanishad (VI-19) indicates *Brahmam* as *"Niravatyam Niranjanam"*.

(v) One who is - *Ni* (more) – *Ranjanam* (happiness/ delight)

134. *Nirlepā* - निर्लेपा

(i) One who is free from affectations (on account of results of actions [*karma*]).

(ii) The form of *Śreedevee* is knowledge. Hence she does not have any connection to the actions.

In *Śreemad Bhagavat Geeta* (IV-14)also we read *"Namām Karmāni Limpanti"*

When one get to the knowledge of *Brahmam* i.e. *Śreedevee* – he is free from impurities. This is also mentioned in *Lipyate Na Sa Papena Padmapatramivāmbasa*. (V-10) Further it is mentioned in *Yagna Vaibhava Kāṇḍa* of *Sootha Samhita* as;

Karmabhi: Sakalarapi Lipyate Brahmavpravarsya Na Sarvathai
Padma Patramivātbhirago Parabrahmavitpravarasyatu Vaibhavami I

(iii) *Śreedevee* is free from the impurity called *Pralayakevala*.

(iv) By meditating *Śreedevee* one becomes free from impurities of actions.

135. *Nirmalā* - निर्मला

(i) One who is free from all impurities.
(ii) **She** does not have the impurity of arrogance. Hence **She** does not have the impurity called *Vijnanākevala*.
(iii) **She** is free from the impurity of *Tamo* character.
(iv) **She** does not have the impurity of uneducation. Liberation is the aim of the soul. Through this name and *Nityamuktā* (147th name) the liberated form of the soul is indicated.
(v) By meditating this name one can be free from the impurity of arrogance.
(vi) The 347th name *Vimalā* can be referred.

136. *Nityā* - नित्या

(i) One who is eternal. Same intention has been indicated later in 951st name *Shaswatee*. We read *Avināāshi Vā Areyamātmā* (IV-5-14) in *Brahdāraŋya Upanishad*.
(ii) This soul is eternal. Hence the argument of *Kshanigavigyāna* that the world vanishes every second is not valid.
(iii) Fifteen *tithi Nityā Devees* are being mentioned in the method of worshipping *Śreevidya*. *Śreedevee* herself is the 16th*Mahā Nitya*. The names of these 15 *Nityā Devees* have been mentioned in *Tantra Sāstrās*. The era of these *Nityā Devees* is mentioned in *Vedas* as *Darsā* and *Drushta*. This name indicates that *Śreedevee* is beyond any era. The details of these can be got in 391st name *Nityāshoḍasikāroopā* and 610th name *Pratipanmukyarākānta Tithi Maŋḍala Poojita*.
(iv) Some of the names of *Nityā Devees* have been mentioned in this *Sahasranāma*;

SL. # of the Name	Phase of waxing moon	Phase of waning moon	Name of *Nityā Devee*
71	14	2	*Jwālāmālini*
136	10	6	*Nityā* (the current name)
200	13	3	*Sarvamangalā*
277	2	14	*Bhagamālinee*
346	10	6	*Vijayā*
352	5	11	*Vahnivāsinee* (*Vahnimaŋḍalavāsinee*)
388	3	13	*Nityaklinnā*

SL. # of the Name	Phase of waxing moon	Phase of waning moon	Name of *Nityā Devee*
405	7	9	*Shivadootee*
468	6	10	*Vajreshvaree*

(v) Earlier in 73rd name it was mentioned that *Śreedevee* was delighted seeing the 15 *Nityā Devees* staging the war with the 15 knights of *Bhanḍasura*. This has the name of a *Nityā Devee* as foremost.

(vi) The meditation *mantras* and *poojas* of these 15 *Nityā Devees* have been described in *Tantra Rāja Tantra*. Depending on the expected results (*Kāmya phalan*) the meditation will vary. By meditating *Nityā* one can be free from ruins.

137. *Nirākārā* - निराकारा

(i) One who is not limited to and by any form. There is some specialty in everything we see. The various forms of *Śreedevee* seen by us are illusions. **Her** real form is formless. The sense of this name is; since **She** is omnipresent there is no form relating to characters.

(ii) With this the *Madyamikās*theory/ philosophy of science is nullified here.

138. *Nirākulā* - निराकुला

(i) One who is never agitated.

(ii) Even though **She** has connection with ignorance **She** is never agitated.

(iii) **She** is in a distance from those who are agitated in their mind. i.e. **She** cannot be reached by those type of people. This implies that **She** can be reached only by those who has unambiguous knowledge.

(iv) *Ākula* is a vacoom state. **She** is not like this and is omnipresent. With this the vacoom argument of profounder is nullified.

(v) 178th name – *Nirābādhā* can be referred.

139. *Nirguŋā* - निर्गुणा

(i) One who is beyond the three characters - *Guŋas*.

(ii) The opinion of the *tarka* (logic) school is rejected here.

(iii) In *Swetāsvatara Upanishad* (VI-11) we read *Sākshee Chetā Kevalo Nirguŋasca* – Witness, the philosopher, one who is uncontaminated and who is free from characters. This has been explained in *Matsya* and *Padma puranās*. The traits of *Devas* are their identities; characters are related to bodies. Since *Śreedevee* is in the form of *Chit*, **She** has no characters neither identity.

Yaduktam Ca Māyā Devee Lakshaŋair Varjitetica I
Srunu Tasyāpi Vākyasya Samyagartham Vicharaŋāt II
Lakshaŋam Deva Kotyanka: Sareeraikāsrayo Kuna: I
Iyam tu Nirguŋā Devee Naiva Lakshayitum Kshamā II

(iv) *Śreeādi Śaṇkara* also in his commentary for *Viṣhŋu Sahasranāmā* – 840th name *Nirguŋa*: quotes the same verse from *Vedas* and gives the same meaning.

140. *Nishkalā* - निष्कला

(i) One who is partless (organless) unitary whole.
(ii) This declines the school of thought that *Brahmam* has organs.
(iii) In *Brahma Sūtra – Amsha Athikaran* – II-3-43;

Amsho Nānā Vyapadesāt Anyathā Api
Dasha Kitavādhitvam Atheeyate Eke

It is mentioned as since some differences are located the human soul is a part of universal absolute (*param porul* or *Brahmam*). In *Śreemad Bhagavat Geeta* also it is seen as *Mamaivamsho Jeevaloke* – the eternal soul in this world is a part of **Myself**. In reality the form of soul is nothing different from *Eshwar*. However, on account of delimitations caused by ignorance during worldly actions, some differences are interpreted between the soul and *Eshwar*. This is not true. A small fire of spark is part of the whole fire. Similarly the soul is part of *Eshwar*. Again by the delimitation of pot, the ether is seen as *Akāsam* and *Guḍākāsam*. Similarly, by the delimitations of the mind, the form of *Eshwar* is split into soul and *Eshwar*. Like many a Moon is seen reflecting in various water vessels, the soul is also seen as many, since the minds are many. With the knowledge of *Brahmam* once the ignorance is removed the delimiters also get removed and hence the soul is not seen separately. *Śree Ādi Śaṇkara* has also concluded that *Brahma* form only will be visible.

(iv) The same meaning is stressed in this name. Or meditating *Brahmam* without any characters is *Nishkala*. He has evidenced it through the below verse of *Vighnāna Bhairava Battarakar*;

Dhyānam Ya Nishkalā Chinta Nirādhārā Nirāsrayā I
Na Tu Dhyānam Shareerasya Mukha Stādhikalpanā II

141. *Shāntā* - शान्ता

(i) One who is tranquil.

(ii) The verses *Nishkalam Nishkriyam Shāntam* can be read from *Svetāsvatara Upanishad* (VI-19). (Without organs, actionless, soothful, ...). **She** is *Shantimatee* (131st name), *Shānti* (447th name) and *Shamātmikā* (963rd name).

(iii) Or, it can also be understoodas; it is the letter to which the letter *'Sha'* follows.In the order of Samskrit alphabets, the letter previous to *'Sha'*is *'Va'*. This is considered as the seed of nectar (*Amruta Beejam*). Hence **She** is in the form of seed of nectar.

(iv) Or, this can be taken as *Āshānta*. The prefix *'Ā'* is understood. *Āsha* means directions. That implies **She** is spread in all directions. This nullifies the theory of *Digambaras* that universal absolute is limited.

142. *Nishkāmā* – निष्कामा

(i) One who is without any desires.

(ii) As per the *Veda* verses; *Satyakāmā Satya Sankalpā*; this nullifies the school - the wish and thought of the Universal Absolute is eternal.

Avāptākhila Kāmāyāstrushnā Kim Vishayā Bhavet – the verses can be read in *Devee Bhāgavatam*; once all the desires are fulfilled there is nothing to wish.

It can be read in *Brahadāraŋya Upanishad* (II-3-6); *Nethi, Nethi* – No no. There itself it can be read; *Poorŋamada*: *Poorŋamidam*. Other verses from *Veda* about the characters are all about delimiters.

143. *Nirupaplavā* – निरुपप्लवा

(i) One who is free from destructions.

(ii) *Upaplavam* means destruction. **She** is free from this.

(iii) The same meaning is conveyed in 180th name *Nirnāsha*.

(iv) Or, if it is split as *Nir, Upa, Plava* – it can understood as **She** creates the nectar shower in the body. 106th name *Sudhāsārābhivarshinee* and 111th name *Bisatantutaneeyasee* can be referred.

(v) The verse from *Aruŋopanishad* - *"Āplavasva Praplavasva Āndeebhavajamāmuhoo"* can be referred. The gist of this verse about *Śreedevee* has been explained in 111th name.

144. *Nityamuktā* - नित्यमुक्ता

(i) One who is ever free from worldly bonds.
(ii) Since **Her** devotees are bonded to this world, **She** has got this name.
(iii) **She** is in the form of liberation, typically as per the character of *Nityamuktās*.

145. *Nirvikārā* –निर्विकारा

(i) One who is not subject to any change.
(ii) The soul and nature are the two origin-less truths accepted in *Sānkhya Siddantha*. Out of these the soul is intellect. It is different from body, organs and mind. It lives as witness to the changes in the world and but does not change itself.

Nature is the root for the world. This is origin-less, eternal matter and ever changing. This has the three characters goodness (*satva*), passion (*rajas*) and ignorance (*tamas*).

The world is created by the unison of the soul and the earth. *Buddhi* (intellect) is the next direct evolute from *mahat* (intelligence) followed by *ahankara* (ego). This is followed by sense organs, organs for actions, mind, five basic elements and five primary elements. As per the *Sankhya* Philosophy (enumeration or analysis of the Universe) there are 24 principles of creation, starting from nature. The soul is the 25thone.

These philosophies are divided into four parts – that are:

1. Only causes.
2. Only effects.
3. Causes for some and effects for some other.
4. Neither as cause nor as an effect.

Out of these the basic entity (*Moola Prakruti*), also the foremost one, is always a cause. These are described in *Sankhya Tatva Kārikai* and its commentary *Sankhya Tatva Koumudee*. In *Sankhya Tatva Kārikai*, it is very clear that the basic entity is a cause.

Moolaprakrutiravikrutir Mahadādyā: *Prakrutivikrutaya*: *Sapta* I
Shoḍashakastu Vikāro Naprakrutirnavikruti: *Purusha*: II

Śree Ādi Śaṇkara, in his commentaries for the *Brahma Sūtra* also mentions about this.

The seven - Intelligence, ego and 5 basic elements are both cause and effects. Five sense organs, 5 organs of action, mind and 5 primary elements are effects. The soul is with neither cause nor effect.

(iii) **She** has been described in this name as not subject to 23 types of changes.

(iv) As per *Śree Vidyā Sāstrā*, *Śreedevee* **Herself** is the universal absolute. Hence the *Sankhya* philosophers do not accept that nature (either primary or unmanifest) is matter. However, they accept these 25 principles, with a little Deviation in the meaning of soul. In *Śree Vidyā* 11 more principles are added totaling to 36 as in *Saiva* philosophy of Kashmer.

146. *Nishprapajnchā* – निष्प्रपञ्चा

(i) One who is beyond all the controls.

(ii) The word *Prapanchā* has three meanings; to unite (*Sanchaya*:), to extend (*vistāra*:) and to expand (*pratārana*:).

(iii) Since **She** is complete in **Herself** and omnipresent, **She** is beyond all these three controls of universe.

(iv) One thing expanding to many is *Prapancha*. Contraction and expansion are the characters of changing things. The worldly character is not seen in *Śreedevee*, who is unchanging.

(v) Or, it can be understood as; **She** from whom the universe starting from the earth, manifested – since *Mānḍukya* Upanishad (7th verse) says *Prapanchopashamam Shiva madhvaitam Chaturtam Manyante*.

147. *Nirāshrayā* - निराश्रया

(i) One who is not dependent on anything or anyone.

(ii) Everything depends on **Her**; but S**he** does not depend on anything.

(iii) With this Sarvarkar's philosophy is ruled out.

(iv) In the 8th chapter of *Chāndogya Upanishad*, it is described as *Virochanan* misunderstood the advice of *Prajāpathi* as the body is *Brahmam*.

(v) 132nd name *Nirādhārā* can be compared.

148. *Nityashuddhā* - नित्यशुद्धा

(i) One who is eternally pure.

(ii) **She** is beyond any impurity in all the three times (tenses); hence this name.

(iii) *Veda* says; *Asparshascha Mahān Shuci*: - **She** does not touch anything, elder to all and always pure.
(iv) Another verse of *Veda* says; *Atyanta Malino Deho Dehee Chātyanta Nirmala*: - The body is untidy, but the person inside is clean.

149. *Nityabuddhā* - नित्यबुद्धा

(i) One who is always knowledgeable and wise.
(ii) **She** is in the form of *Chit* and hence always knowledgeable.
(iii) *Brahdāraŋyaka Upanishad* (IV-3-30); *Na Hi Vigyāturvigyāter Viparilo Povidyāte* – The knowledge is inseparable from the wise.
(iv) Or, the two *devatas* worshipped in Jain religion are *Śreedevee* herself. It is told in 148th and 149thnames that, with **Her** blessings the two Jains, *Suddhar* and *Bhuddar*, attained eternity.
(v) In *Navāvarŋa pooja*, after *māya chakra pooja*, it is the practice to worship **Her** as the goddess of 6 religions; Buddhism/ Jain religion, *Vaidheeka* religion worshipping *Gayatri*, *Saiva* religion worshipping *Shiva*, *Soura* religion worshipping *Sun*, *Vaishnava* religion worshipping *Vişhŋu* and *Śākta* religion worshipping *Shakti*.

150. *Niravadyā* - निरवद्या

(i) One who is flawless/ blemishless.
(ii) *Avadyā* means not to be revealed; that means flaw or deficiency. These types of flaws are induced only due to ignorance. *Śreedevee*, who is in the form of knowledge, is beyond all these defaces.
(iii) *Veda* says "*Niravadyam Niranjanam*" (*Swetāsvatara Upanishad* VI.19) – defectless and pure.
(iv) Or, *Avadyā* is the name of one of the hells. *Koorma Purāŋa* says that one who is always (day and night) in the thought of *Śreedevee* does not go to the hell called *Avadya*.

Tasmādaharnisham Deveem Samsmaretpurushoyad II
Na Yātyavadhyam Narakam Samksheeŋāsheshapātaka: II

Linga Purāŋā says;

Māyāntāschaiva Ghorādyā Ashțavimsati Kotaya: I
Narakāŋāmavadhyānām Pashyante Tāsoo Pāpina: II
Anāsharitā Bhavānĕshwam Shankaram Neelalohitam II

One who does not worship the consort of *Śreedevee*, who has blue neck, will be burnt in the hells called *Gorā* onwards till *Māya*.
The devotees of *Śreedevee* are protected and liberated from these hells.

Hence *Niravadya.*

(v) *Kurai Onrum Illada Seergovinda –Thiruppavai* by *Anḍāl* can be compared.

151. *Nirantarā* - निरन्तरा

(i) One who is without any division (gaps).
(ii) The word *Antarā* has many a meaning like – gap, extent, end, attire, death and difference.
(iii) *Taitreeya Upanishad* advises (II-7-1); *"Ya Ethasminnudaramantaram Kurute Thatasya Bhayam Bhavati"* - One gets scared if he sees even an iota of difference.
(iv) By this name, the thought of the school, which sees three types of differences (*Sahāteeya, Vijāteeya* and *Svagata*) in *Brahmam*, is nullified.

152. *Nishkāraŋā* –निष्कारणा

(i) One who is without cause.
(ii) *Śreedevee* **Herself** is the root cause of everything. Hence **She** has no cause for **Herself**.
(iii) In *Swetāshvatara Upanishad* (VI-9) it is mentioned as; *"Sakāraŋam Karanādhipādhipo Na Chāsya Kashchijjanitā Na Chādhipa:"* – **He** is the cause and chief of heads of all the causes. Nobody created **Him**. **He** does not have a chief or head.
(iv) Or, five things are used in the *Navāvarŋa Pooja*. The first one is honey, which gives pleasure. (The actual meanings of these 5 things have been explained elsewhere). In the terminology for this method, this has three meanings as; cause, source and root.
(v) When *Śreedevee* is installed in *Śree Chakra* the verse read is; *"Mahāpadma Vanāntasthe Kāraŋānandavigrahe"*. **She** is complete of this causal thing and hence **She** is associated with the pleasure caused by this.

153. *Nishkalankā* – निष्कलंका

(i) One who is not connected with any stain (the result of sin).
(ii) Sin cannot near *Śreedevee* and hence *Nishkalanka*.
(iii) *Íshāvāsya Upanishad* (8th verse) reads as; *Shuddamapāpavidtam* – pure and untouched by sins.

154. *Nirupādhi*: – निरुपाधिः

(i) One who has no limitations.
(ii) *Upa* – near; *Ādhi* – gives (one's own characters). When a hibiscus flower is brought near a *Linga* idol made of crystal, the idol looks like red. This is an instance for limitation.
(iii) Similarly the ignorance creating differentiation in the mind is also limitation.
(iv) *Śreedevee* is in the form of pure *Chaitanya*. Hence **She** does not have any limitations due to ignorance. Hence *Nirupādhi*.
(v) Or, *Upādhi* is of two types – complete and partly. **She** does not have both these limitations. 708th name *Sarvopādhivinirmuktā* can be referred.

155. *Nireeshvarā* – निरीश्वरा

(i) One who has no superior or protector.
(ii) **She** is the head of everything. Hence there is no superior to **Her**.
(iii) *Meemamsā* and *Sānkhyā* are two philosophies. *Sānkhyā* has further sub philosophies as with-*Ĕshwar* and without. The former is non-dual (*Advaitam*) and the latter is atheism. **She** belongs to both.

156. *Neerāgā* - नीरागा

(i) One who has no desires.
(ii) This is again repeated in 937th name *Virāginee*.
(iii) From this name onwards till 187th name *Niratyayā*, it proceeds to reject the theory that, the differences in the four types of mind viz. mind, intellect, volition and ego belong to the self (soul). Further to teach that renunciation is the means of overcoming the six impediments; desire, wrath, covetousness, bewilderment, pride and envy.
(iv) One, who (by mistake) believes that these enemies are the characters of the soul, travels in the way shown by them and get destroyed. But, they never go along with the soul. One, who understands that these are the actions of the mind, controls them or to turn aside or to be unrelated with them, gets pride.
(v) Because **She** has obtained all her desires, **She** is *Neerāgā*
(vi) *Shāndilya Sūtra* mentions as; *Dvesha Pratipakshā Bhāvādrasa Shabdācca Rāga* – since without hatred and since it is mentioned as

essence (fervent longing is called *Rāgā*). Since, *Śreedevee* is beyond all these and **She** has no object for longing and hence **She** is *Neerāga*.

(vii) *Neera* - water and *Aga* – immobile, mountain. *Śreedevee* is in both these forms and hence *Neerāga*.

157. *Rāgamathanee* –रागमथनी

(i) One who churns and completely removes all the desires (longings of **Her** devotees - *Rāgās*) and gives zeal to them.

(ii) During churning, all other similar things in that object come out; then they can be separated easily – as butter is taken from curd. It has to be taken as; **She** churns the mind of the devotees and takes out all the serious desires.

(iii) It is mentioned in *Yoga Sūtra* (II-3) as; *Rāgadveshāpiniveshā*: *Kleshā*: *Rāgā* as mentioned in this name is - Desire, aversion and ardent attachment.

158. *Nirmadā* – निर्मदा

(i) One who is without pride.

(ii) Pride is – to think that one has something which is not with others or has succeeded in doing something which others could not and propagate the same.

(iii) When *Śreedevee* is not seen by others the question of pride does not arise.

(iv) 508th name is *Atigarvita*. When contemplating the *Brahmam*, *Veda* mentions contradicting characters. Smaller than the smallest, bigger than the biggest – *Anoraneeyān Mahato Maheeyān*. Hence there is no controversy between this name – without pride and 508th name with high pride.

159. *Madanāshinee* –मदनाशिनी

(i) One who destroys all pride.

(ii) By splitting as; *Madanam* (the flower of thorn apple) + *Ashnāti* (one who eats it) – it is interpreted as – One who is interested in eating the flower of thorn apple.

(iii) The flower of thorn apple is very much liked by Lord *Parameshwara*. It is said that he wears it in his head. Also, it is said that it is used to make gold (alchemy).

(iv) It is apt that the flower of thorn apple is liked by *Śreedevee* also since it is liked by *Parameshwara*. (It has to be considered that there is no difference between them and they are one and the same).

(v) It also implies that – like an ordinary metal is being converted to gold, an ordinary devotee is taken to a great position.

(vi) *Maheshastvām Dhatte Shirasi Rasarājasya Jayinee/ Vishitdhis Tvat Sangat Kanakmayam Ett Tribhuvanam.*

(vii) It is also interpreted as - *Madana* means acute anxiety; **She** removes it (eats it out).

160. *Nishchintā* - निश्चिन्ता

(i) One who is free from all anxieties.

(ii) In general - *Chintā* means recollection of earlier thoughts; in particular recollection of painful topics is *Chintā* or anxiety.

(iii) *Chintā Chitāsamānoyā Chintā Vai Bindunādhikā Chitā Dahati Nirjeevam Chintā Dahati Jeevitam* - Anxiety should be known as (resembling) a funeral pile, the only difference is that additional 'n' sound (additional dot when written in Samskrit) in *chintā*, but as the pile (*chitā*) burns the corpse, so anxiety burns the living man.

(iv) According to the dictionary called *Vishva, chintā* means get cheated, to cheat, deceit, gambling, fraud and delusion. In this sense also **She** does not have any delusion and hence *Nishcinta*.

161. *Nirahankārā* – निरहंकारा

(i) One who is without any ego.

(ii) Ego is of three kinds; *Vaikhareeka*, *Taijasa* and *Bhutādi*, according to *satva*, *rajas* and *tamas* characters, respectively. 397th name *Moolaprakruti* can be referred.

(iii) Earlier in 139th name – *Nirguṇā*, it was mentioned that **She** is beyond the three characters viz. *satva*, *rajas* and *tamas*. Accordingly **She** does not have the ego relating to those characters also. Hence *Nirahankāra*.

162. *Nirmohā* – निर्मोहा

(i) One who is free from bewilderment (fascination or perplexity).

(ii) Bewilderment is indication of confusion of thought or distraction of the mind. It infers the wavering of mind or illusioning one to the other. **She** is beyond all these.

163. *Mohanāshinee* – मोहनाशिनी

(i) One who dispels all illusions.
(ii) By imparting the idea of unity to her devotees **She** destroys bewilderment.
(iii) The *Veda – Íshāvāsya Upanishad* 7th verse; "*Tatra Ko Moha*: *Ka*: *Shoka Ekatvamanu Pashyata*:" - to him, who perceives unity, what bewilderment and what sorrow can there be?

164. *Nirmamā* - निर्ममा

(i) One who has no self-conceit.
(ii) Self-interest necessarily implies separating things as "this is mine". Since **She** is everything there is no room for such a thought and hence no question of conceit.

165. *Mamatāhantree* –ममताहन्त्री

(i) One who destroys the above said self-conceit.
(ii) We could relate this to the request of *Vaisya* in the 13th chapter of *Durga Saptashatee*. It has to be noted that *Vaisyā* has a special adjective here as *Prāgya*: - *Sopi Vasyas Tato Gnanam Vavre Nivinamānasa*: *Mametyahamiti Prāgya*: *Sanka Vishyuti Kārakam*.

166. *Nishpāpā* – निष्पापा

(i) One who is without any sin.
(ii) Any sin or virtue is created only deeds -primarily due to desires on actions. Earlier it was explained in 156th name *Neerāgā* that **She** is without any desires. No actions for **Her**. Resultantly no sin or virtue also.
(iii) In *Śreemad Bhagavat Geeta* (IV-14) we see as:

Na Mām Karmāni Limpanti Na Me Karmaphale Spruha.

167. *Pāpanāshinee* – पापनाशिनी

(i) One who destroys the sins of devotees.

(ii) By the repetition of **Her** *mantra*, etc., **She** destroys the sins of devotees.

(iii) In *Veda* (*Chāndogya Upanishad* IV-24-3) it is mentioned as; *Yateshikā Toolamagnou Pradooyataiva Mevāsya Papmana*: *Pradooyante* - Like the point of a reed in the fire, all the sins are burnt up.

(iv) In the *Vashisṭa Smruti*;

Vidyā Tapobhyām Samyaktam Brāhmanam Japa Naityakam I
Sadāpi Pāpa Karmānameno Na Pradhiyujyate II
Jāpinām Hominām Chaiva Dhyāyinām Teerthavāsinām I
Na Samvasanti Pāpāni Ye Cha Snātā: *Shirovratai*: II

If a person is always devoted to learning, penance and continually repeating *mantras*, even if he is always committing sinful actions, he is not afflicted thereby. Sin never touches those who repeat the *mantras* or offer oblations, or meditate, or make pilgrimages, or who perform *sirovrata* (the rite of carrying the fire on the head).

(v) The *Padma Purāŋa*, in its *Pushara Kanda* says - The mass of sins though as great as mount Meru is instantly destroyed by worshipping *Kātyāyanee*. He, who is devoted to Goddess *Durgā*, is not stained even by committing heinous crimes, in the manner as the lotus leaf is not affected by water;

Meru Parvata Matropi Rashi: *Pāpasya Karmaŋa*: I
Kātyāyaneem Samāsādya Nashyati Kshaŋamātrata: II
Durgārchanaroto Nityam Mahāpātaka Sambhavai: I
Doshair Na Lipyate Veera Padmapatramivāmbhasā II

(vi) In *Devee Bhāgavatam* also same effect is spoken:

Chitvā Bhitvā Ca Bhootāni Hatvā Sarvamidam Jagat I
Pranamya Shirasā Deveem Na Sa Pāpair Vilipyate II
Sarvāvastāgato Vāpi Yuktovā Sarvapatakai: I
Durgām Drushitvā Nara: *Poota*: *Prayāti Paramam Padam* II

(vii) Again in *Brahmāŋḍa Purāŋā*;

Varŋāsrama Viheenānām Papishtānām Nrunāmap II
Yadroopa Dhyāna Matrena Dushkrutam Sukrutāyate II

The sinful actions of those who are devoid of *Varŋa* and *Ashrama* and the wretched also, by mere meditation on *Devee*, become virtuous. These names are worth referring here: 555 – *Kalikalmasha Nāshinee*, 743 – *Pāpāraŋyadavānalā* and 860 – *Akānta*.

It is mentioned in the *Phalaśruti* (results/ effects) part of this *Sahasranāma* itself as;

Rahasya Nāmasāhasre Nāmaikamapi Ya: *Patet* I

Tasya Pāpāni Nashyanti Mahāntyapi Na Samshaya: II
Nityakarmananushtānāt Nishiddha Karanātap II
Yatpāpam Jāyate Pumsām Tatsarva Nashyati Drutam II
Bahoonātra Kimuktena Sharunutvam Kalaseesoota I
Atraika Nāmno Yā Shakti: *Pātakānām Nivartne* II
Tannivartyamagham Kartum Nālam Lokās Chatudasha II
Yastyaktavā Nāmsahasram Pāpahānima Bheepsat II
Sa Hi Sheeta Nivrutyartham Himashailam Nishevate II

(viii) *Śree Ādi Śaņkara* in his commentary of *Vişhŋu Sahasranāmaa* for the 924th name – *Dushkrutihā* says – **He** destroys the bad act of sin or one who does sinful acts.

992nd name – *Pāpanāshana*: - **he** destroys the sins in bunches, of those people, who sing hymns in praise of **him**, or worship **him** or meditate upon **him** or just remember **him.**

(ix) *Śree Ādi Śaņkara* for his commentary of *Vişhŋu Sahasranāma* for the 992ndname, he quotes from *Vrittashātāpa*;

Pakshopavāsādyatpāpam Purushasya Pranashyati I
Prānāyāmshatenavai Tatpāpam Nashyate Nrunām II
Prānāyāma Sahasrena Yatpāpam Nashyate Nrunām I
Kshanamatreŋa Tatpāpam Harerdhyānāt Pranashyati II

(x) *Śree Ādi Śaņkara's* commentary for the 31st name of *Lalitā Trishatee* – *Ena*: *Kooţa Vināshinee* and 112th name – *Hatyāti Pāpashamanee*, can be referred.

168. *Nishkrodhā* – निष्क्रोधा

(i) One who is without anger.
(ii) **She** has no hatred on anyone; **She** does not get angry also.
(iii) In *Śreemad Bhagavat Geeta* (IX-29) we read; *Na Me Dveshyosti Napriya*:
(iv) To protect the devotees, Lord destroys the wicked. Still **He** does not get angry with the wicked people. The below verses from *Durgā Saptashatee* (2nd story, 4th chapter) clearly mentions; destruction of wicked and looking with anger are done at them with sympathy on them, just to correct and liberate them.

Eebhirhatairjagadupaiti Sukam Tathate
Kurvantu Nāma Narakāya Chirāya Pāpami
Sangrāmamrutyumadhigamya Divam Prayāntu
Matveti Noonamahitānvinihamsi Deve II
Drushtvaiva Kim Na Bhavateeprakaroti

Bhasmasarvāsurānarishuyat Prahinodhi Shastrami
Lokān Prayānturipavopihishastra
Pootā Ittam Matirbhavati Teshva Hiteshu Sadhvee II
Turvrutta Vruttashamanam TavaDevee Sheelam
Roopam Tataitdavichintyamatulya Manyai: I
Veeryam Cha Hantru HrutaDeveevaparākramānām
Vairishvapi Prakatitaiva Dayātvayetthami I
Kenopamā Bhavatu Tesya Parākramasya
Roopam Cha Shatrbhyakāryatihārikutrai
Chitte Krupā Samaranishturatā Ca Drushtā
Tvayyeva Deveevarate Bhuvanatratepi II

169. *Krodhashamanee* – क्रोधशमनी

(i) One who destroys the tendency to get angry.
(ii) Every human has six internal enemies – lust, anger, stinginess, libidinous, recklessness and amusement. **She** suppresses the anger of the devotees and destroys the lust in them.
(iii) Sage *Āpastambā* explains the cruelty of the anger as;

Krodha Yukto Yadyajati Yajjuhoti Yadarsati I
Sa Tasya Harate Sarvamāmkumbho Yathodakam II

He, who sacrifices, offer obligations, or worships with anger, is deprived of all benefits therefrom like water in a vessel of unbaked clay.
(iv) In *Śreemad Bhagavat Geeta* (II-62/63) and again in III-37 the result of anger is explained;

Dhyāyato Vishayānpumsa: *Sangasteshupajāyate* I
Sangāt Samjāyate Kāma: *Kāmātkrodhobhijayate* II
Krodhadbhavati Sammoha: *Sammohātsmrutivibhrama*: I
Smrutibhramshāddhināsho Buddhināshatpranashyati II
Kāma Esha Krodha Esha Rajokunasamudbhava: I
Mahāshano Mahāpāpmā Viddhy Enamiha Vairinam II

(v) In *Arkala* verses read as part of *Durgā Saptashatee* also, the below verse is prayed for 18 times; *Roopam Dehi Jayam Dehi Yasho Dehi Dvisho Jahi* – Here *Dvisho Jahi* means, to destroy the enemies lust and anger.

170. *Nirlobhā* – निर्लोभा

(i) One who is free from any greed.
(ii) Because **She** is exceedingly liberal.

171. *Lobhanāshinee* – लोभनाशिनी

(i) One who destroys greed.
(ii) Since, greed destroys all other good qualities, it is important that it has to be destroyed first. *Śreedevee* destroys the greed in the minds of the devotees.

172. *Nissamshayā* – निःसंशया

(i) One who is without doubt.

173. *Samshayaghnee* – संशयघ्नी

(i) One who destroys doubt.
(ii) It is easy to combine these two names and read. *Śreedevee* is in the form of a teacher – 603rd name *Gurumuoorthi*: can be referred. A devotee has to enhance an integrated thought process with him, the *mantras*, the goddess, the *yantra* relating to the concerned goddess and the teacher. This is called five types of Integrated *Anusanthānam*. *Veda* (*Muŋḍaka Upanishad*- I-2-12) says *Srotriyam Brahmaŋishṭam*.
(iii) In *Tantra Rāja Tantra* also (I-18);

Asamshaya: *Samshayaccinnarapekshogururmata*:
Asamshayastatvapodhe Tacchaktipratipādanāt I
Nairapakshyamavictecchāgurutvamhitavātinā II

(iv) A teacher himself should be beyond having doubts. He needs to completely teach the philosophies and clear all the doubts of the students. He should not be expecting wealth and even should not even have interest in it.
(v) Since *Śreedevee* is in the form of a teacher, **She** has all those qualities. She does not have doubts and she clears all the doubts.
(vi) *Muŋḍaka Upanishad* (II-2-8) says; *"Bhidyate Hrudayagranthi*: *Chdyante Sarva Samshayā"* - all doubts are removed.

174. *Nirbhavā* – निर्भवा

(i) One who is without origin.
(ii) In *Śreemad Bhagavat Geeta* (XIII-12) *"Anātdimati Parabhrahmā"* - The Supreme *Brahmam* is without origin. 136th name *Nityā* and 866th

name *Ajā* can be referred.

175. *Bhavanāshinee* – भवनाशिनी

(i) One who destroys worldly bondage.

(ii) The *Shakti rahasya* says, "In the ninth day of the bright lunar half month, according to the rule, as to him who anoints *Chaṇḍikā* with ghee, hear the result of that action; he is raised out of the ocean of *samsārā* and shines in the *Durgālokā*, together with the preceding ten and also succeeding ten generations;

Navamyām Shuklapakshaetu Vidhivacchaṇḍikam Nrupa I
Grutena Snāpatedhyastu Tasya Puṇya Phalam Srunu II
Dashapoorvān Dashaparānātmānam Ca Visheshata: I
Bhavārnavāt Samuddhrutya Durgā Loke Maheeyate II

The *Koorma Purāṇa* also speaks the same effect as;

Saishātātree Vdhātree Cha Paramānandamicchatām |
Samsāra Tāpāgnikilānnihanteeshvara Samgjyā II

Similarly in *Devee Bhāgavatam*;

Aham Vai Matparān Bhaktān Ishvaram Yogamā Shritān I
Samsāra Sagarādasmāduddharām Yachirenatu II

(iii) Or, according to the *Brhajjābāla Upanishad* (No 26) *Bhavanāshinee* is the name of a river. *Śree Bhāskara Rāya* says **She** is in the form of this river. (At present this *Upanishad* is not available).

176. *Nirvikalpā* – निर्विकल्पा

(i) One who is without the notion of covering by mere words without the corresponding objects.

(ii) The *Yogasutrā* (I.9) says; *Shabda Matrānupātee Vastu Vastu Shoonyo Vikalpa*:. *Vikalpa* (fancy) is a notion conveyed by mere words, but of which there is no object corresponding to reality. For instance: horns of rabbit, horns of horse, etc. That, which is not real, which is created in the mind. This name advises that – *Śreedevee* is in the form of unconditioned eternal knowledge.

(iii) Or, *Nirvikalpā*, in the last mental modification, (last stage of meditation), there are no specific distinctions (*vikalpa*).

(iv) Or *vi* - opposed; *kalpa* - theory. There is no theory opposed to *Śreedevee* because everything is inseparable from her, i.e. *Śreedevee* is devoid of all separateness. The *Brahma Sūtra*(III–2-14) says, *Aroopavat Eva Hi Tatpradhānatvāt* - For Brahmam is merely devoid of form, on account of this being the main purport of Scripture".

(v) The very meaning of *Veda* is to explain that the *Brahmam* has no characters like form, etc.

(vi) Everything is integrated with *Śreedevee* and hence there is no object separate from **Her**.

177. *Nirābādhā* – निराबाधा

(i) One who has undisturbed mind.

(ii) The mind is disturbed by (mis) seeing the shell as silver. This disturbance is removed once the illusion vanishes. There is no object other than *Śreedevee*. Hence **She** does not have any such disturbance in mind.

178. *Nirbhedā* – निर्भेदा

(i) One who is without any difference.

(ii) **She** does not have anything, which will create a difference in mind. Hence *Nirbheda*.

(iii) The *Koorma Purāņā* says;

Tvam Hi Yā Paramāshakti: *Anantā Parameshtinee* I
Sarvabhedavinirmuktā Sarva Bhedavinashinee II

In the same book in yet another place;

Shakti Shaktimatorbhedam Vadantyapara Mardhata: I
Abhedam Chānupashyanti Yoginas Tatva Chintakā: II

Thou art the supreme *Shakti*, infinite, supreme ruler, devoid of all differences and the destroyer of all differences.

Some ignorant people say that, there is a difference between *Shakti* and the possessors of it (*Shiva*), but those *Yogins* who meditate on reality recognize non-separateness.

179. *Bhedanāshinee* – भेदनाशिनी

(i) One who destroys the feeling of difference.

(ii) **She** causes the destruction of the feeling of difference, by creating the knowledge of philosophy (*tatva*).

180. *Nirnāshā* – निर्नाशा

(i) One who is eternal/ imperishable/ endless.
(ii) *Nāsha*– end, destruction. **She** is without this.
(iii) The *Veda* (*Taitiriyopanishad* III) says; *Satyam Gnanam Anantam Brahma–Brahmam* is Truth, Knowledge and Infinity.

181. *Mrutyumathanee* –मृत्युमथनी

(i) One who saves the devotees from death.
(ii) Like Lord *Parameshwara* saved **his** devotee *Mārkaŋḍeya* from *Yamā*, *Śreedevee* also saves her devotees from death.
(iii) Death is for the body and not for the soul. **She** makes her devotees realise this philosophy. Like the curd is churned to get butter, **She** churns the fear of death and creates the knowledge of philosophy and removes the fear.
(iv) The *Traipuro Upanishad* (No 82) says;

Ata Kasmāduchyate Māmrutādityamrutatvam
Prāpnoteetyakshyatvam Prāpnoti Svayam Rudro Bhavat I

From mortality he obtains immortality, he attains imperishable state; attains the eternal existence; and he himself becomes *Rudra*.
(v) The devotee becomes **Herself** by imagination and hence indestructible.

182. *Nishkriyā* – निष्क्रिया

(i) One who is without any action to do.
(ii) Actions are of two types - ordained and prohibited. **She** is with neither type of actions.
(iii) In *Chāndogya Upanishad* VIII-12-1); *"Ashareeram Vāva Santam Na Priyāpriye Sprushata:"* - Only who has no body is unaffected by likes and dislikes.
(iv) Or without doing anything and without any actions, **She** becomes the actor.
(v) For instance as told in *Vishnu Purāŋā*; just as a fragrant object, by its very presence distracts the mind, so does Lord *Parameshwara* in the creation of the universe.

Yathā Sannidhi Mātrena Gandha: *Kshobhāya Jāyate* I
Manaso Nopakartrutvāttathasou Parameshwara: II

183. *Nishparigrahā* – निष्परिग्रहा

(i) One who does not acquire or accept anything as gifts.

(ii) According to the dictionary called *Medinee*, *parigraha* means attendants, wife, gifts and root. She is none of these. *Śreedevee* creates the whole universe, protects and destroys it. **She** does not get anything as gift. Hence *Nishparigraha*.

(iii) **She** does not have any origin and hence also *Nishparigraha*.

184. *Nistulā* – निस्तुला

(i) One who is incomparable/ unequal/ peerless.

(ii) There is nothing to compare with **Her** and hence *Nistula*. We cannot weigh **Her** comparing with anything else. *Hetu Drushtānta Varjitam*- without cause or comparison (*Tripura Upanishad* 82).

(iii) This reminds verses 26-27 of 110th chapter in *Yuddha Kāṇḍa* of *Śreemad Rāmāyana*;

Gaganam Gaganākāram Sāgara: *Sāgaropama* I
Rāmarāvanayoryuddham Rāmarāvayoriva II

(iv) 389th name *Niroopamā* can be referred.

185. *Neelachikurā* – नीलचिकुरा

(i) One who has shining and beautiful black (blue) hair. (*Vāgdevees* were explaining the formless *Śreedevee* by these names. In the midst the black hair could have been seen as a lightning and hence this name suddenly).

186. *Nirapāyā* – निरपाया

(i) One who is imperishable. Means of danger being completely destroyed.

187. *Niratyayā* – निरत्यया

(i) One who is without transgression.

(ii) As per *Vishva* dictionary, *atyaya* means transgression, punishment, obstruction, fault and emaciation.

(iii) *Śreedevee* has created many a limit to all those who do the three jobs (creation, protection and destruction) and for this universe. **She** seems to be bound by those limits and cannot cross those limits. **She** sets an example to others by not crossing the limits set by **Her**.

188. *Durlabhā* – दुर्लभा

(i) One who is difficult to attain (even to *Yogins*).The text now sets forth **Her** qualified form (*saguṇa*).

189. *Durgamā* – दुर्गमा

(i) One who is hard to approach.
(ii) It is not easy for the Yogins also to approach her by doing achievements. Hence *Durgama*. Her devotion method has to be followed with concentration and control like walking on the edge of a knife.
(iii) Or, if it is split as *Adurgamā*;
  a. One meaning is – one who is easily approachable.
  b. The other meaning is – one who killed the demon called *Durgaman*.

190. *Durgā* – दुर्गा

(i) One who is with the name *Durga*.
(ii) As mentioned in the previous name **She** is *Durgā* since she killed the demon called *Durgaman*. In *Devee Saptashatee* (11th chapter) and in the *Lakshmee Tantra* of the *Pāncharātra*;

Tatraiva Cha Vadhishyāmi Durgamakhyam Mahāsuram I
Bheemā Deveeti Vikhyātam Tan Me Nām Bhavishyati II

I am going to kill the demon named *Durgaman*, hence my name shall be *Bheema*.

(iii) The same is mentioned in *Kāsi Kanḍa* also. Or this is the goddess who resides in the place called *Sannati* on the bank of the river, *Bheemarathi*.
(iv) Or, *Durga* protected *Indra* and other *devas* from the mental fear and war, from *Subalan* and others.
(v) Or, as per *Devee Bhāgavatam*, *Durgā* is, as solicited by king *Subāhu*, established herself under this name at *Benaras*.
(vi) Or, 122nd name *Shambhavee* can be referred - a nine-year old girl is called *Durga*.

According to *Devee Bhāgavatam* (III-26) the meditation verse for this girl is:

Durgāt Trāyati Bhaktam Yā Sadā Durgārti Nāshinee I
Durgjeya Sarva Devānām Tām Durgām Poojayāmyaham II

(vii) The verse read for a 9 year girl during *Kanyā Pooja* in *Chaṇḍi Homam* is;

Durgame Dustare Kārye Bhavatu: Khavināshineem I
Poojayāmi Sā Bhaktyā Durgām Dirgārti Nashineem II

(viii) It is read in *Durgā Sooktam* as; *Durgām Deveem Sharanamaham Prapadye.*

(ix) In *Prapancha Nyāsa* of *Mahāshoḍa Nyāsa*, **She** is said to be in the form of *Kāshṭha*.

191. *Dukkhahantree* –दुःखहन्त्री

(i) One who is the destroyer of sorrows.
(ii) She removes the sorrow, pain caused by wordly affairs.
(iii) The *Goutama sutrā* (I-22) says; *Tadatyarta Vomoko Pavarka*: - Salvation is the complete release from that pain.
(iv) In *Veda* also; "*Dukkhenātyanta Vimuktas Charati*" - He lives completely free from pain.

192. *Sukhapradā* – सुखप्रदा

(i) One who bestows happiness.
(ii) It is not enough if sorrow is removed, happiness is also needed. This name indicates that **She** is the giver of happiness. Depending on the individual mind set, the happiness is provided in this world or in the next world or in both.
(iii) In *Veda – Taitireeya Upanishad* (II-7); "*Rasa: Hyevāyam Labdhvānandee Bhavati*" - only after obtaining the essence does one become blissful.
(iv) This has been explained in detail in the *Padma Purāṇa, Pushkara Kāṇḍa*, last six chapters:

Yatrāsti Bhogo Na Ca Tatra Moksha: Yatrāsti Moksho Na Ca Tatra Bhoga: I
Sundaree Sādhaka Pungavānām Bhogashca Mokshashca Karastha Eva II

When there is enjoyment there is no liberation or vice versa. It is mentioned that the ardent devotees of *Śreedevee* get both.

The names 125 – *Sharmadāyinee*, 953 – *Sharmadā* and 968 – *Shukhakaree* also explain the same effect.

193. *Dushṭadoorā* – दुष्टदूरा

(i) One who is unattainable by wicked people.
(ii) For the faulty people **She** is at a distance and hence not reachable.
(iii) In *Devee Bhāgavatam* also it is mentioned as; **She** is unreachable for those who argue illogically/ sophistically;
"Nabhajanti Kudarkagya Deveem Vishveshvareem Shivām".

194. *Durāchārashamanee* – दुराचारशमनी

(i) One who puts an end to evil customs.
(ii) Evil customs are contrary to the scriptures.
(iii) Later in the results/ effects part of this *Sahasranāma* it is said as; **She** quickly destroys all the sins of men committed by neglecting the daily rites and observing the prohibited ones.

195. *Doshavarjitā* – दोषवर्जिता

(i) One who is free from all faults.
(ii) A fault is something which spoils the mind, talking and acting in a way, which reflects the feelings of longings and aversion. Since **She** is free from longings and aversion, **She** is faultless.

196. *Sarvagnā* – सर्वज्ञा

(i) One who is omniscient.
(ii) *Muṇḍako Upanishad* (I-1-9) says; *"Ya: Sarvagna: Sarva Vid"* – one who perceives all and knows all.
(iii) In *Devee Purāṇam* it is said as; *Sarvagna Sarva Vetrutvāt* – As **she** knows everything **she** is called omniscient.

197. *Sāndrakaruṇā* – सान्द्रकरुणा

(i) One who shows intense compassion.

198. *Samānādhikavarjitā* – समानाधिकवर्जिता

(i) One who neither has equal nor a superior.
(ii) We read in *Svetāswatara Upanishad* (VI-8); *Na Taṭ Samas Capyadhikaṣ Ca Drushyate* - No one is seen equal or superior tohim.

199. *Sarvashaktimayee* – सर्वशक्तिमयी

(i) One who has all the divine powers (omnipotent).

(ii) By the saying; *Ulagam Brahmamayam*, it can be perceived as there is no difference between the world and the *Brahmam*. The article *Maya* indicates in-differentiation. Similarly this name indicates *Śreedevee* is not different from the *shakties* called *Pālai* and *Pakalai*.

(iii) In *Bahuvrushopanishad* also it is mentioned that *Śreedevee* is called by various names as in the below verse;

Saishā Shoḍasee Śreevidyā Pancathashaksharee
Śree Mahātripurasundaree Bālāmbiketi Bagaleti Vā
Mātangeeti Svayamvarakalyāneeti Bhuvaneshwareeti
Camuŋḍati Candeti Vārāheeti Tiraskariŋeeti
Rājamātangeeti Vāsukashyāmaleti Vā Laghu Syāmaleti
Vā Ashvārooḍheti Vā Pratyankirā Dhoomavatee
Savitree Gāyatree Sarasvatee Brahmananda Kaleti

(iv) Or, **She** is in the form of energy *Samooha*. The energies of all the *Devas* are felicities of *Śreedevee* only and only with **Her** blessings *Devas* have acquired the energies.

(v) *Sarva* may mean infinite.

200. *Sarvamangalā* – सर्वमंगला

(i) One who is the source of all that is auspicious. **She** is the root of all those.

(ii) *Devee Purāŋā* says;

Sarvāni Hrudayasthāni Mangalāni Shubhānica I
Eepsitāni Dadātheeti Tena Sā Sarvamangala II
Shobhanāni Ca Sreshtāni Yā Devee Dadate Hare I
Bhaktanamartiharanee Teneyam Sarvamangala II

(iii) Or, *Sarvamangala* is a *Thiti Nityā Devee*. Hence it can be inferred that this name indicates the *Pranavā* (in the *mantra* of *Sarva mangalā*) sound (*Om*).

(iv) It is mentioned as *Thiti Roopa* in *Prapancha Nyāsa* of *Mahā Shoḍā Nyāsa*.

(v) The 124th name of *Lalitā Trishatee* – *Sarvamangalā* – *Śreedevee* is the *Chit* energy nothing different from *Brahmam*. **She** gives all good fortune to those who satisfy **Her** through meditation, praising through songs and worshipping through *poojas* (even if they are stupid).

(vi) This can be compared with *Mangalānām Mangalam* in *Vişhŋu Sahasranāma*, first part.

Thus ends the third *Kalā*, called *Dhoomrika*.

*****

Section 4: *Mareechi Kalā*

201. *Sadgatipradā* - सद्गतिप्रदा

(i) One who leads along the path of salvation.
(ii) The word *sadgati* means all stages from heaven to *moksha* as per our wish. **She** who gives various stages of liberation as per eligibility.
(iii) *Gati* – goal. Heaven and *moksha* are attainable goals by two ways. *Śreedevee* guides to reach the goals easily.
(iv) *Gati* – wisdom; *Śreedevee* gives good knowledge.
(v) *Gati* – way to reach; *Śreedevee* enlightens good path.
(vi) *Sat*– eternal absolute. *Śreedevee* provides the path to reach it (path to knowledge).
(vii) *Satgati* means the path followed by good people. *Śreedevee* enables us to reach the good place.
(viii) *Sat* – **She** is the *Sat*. *Gati* – the goal to reach is also **Herself**. I.e. **She** is the path and the goal.
(ix) *Śree Ādi Śaṇkara*, in his commentary for *Lalitā Trishatee* 229th name *Sadgatidāyinee*, says – **She** destroys the ignorance and gives self-illuminating bliss.
(x) *Śree Ādi Śaṇkara*, in his commentary for *Vişhŋu Sahasranāma, 699*th name *Sadgati*: says;
   a. **She** who can be reached by those who understands that the *Brahmam* is the truth.
   b. **She** has elegant, best *Gati* – knowledge.

If we take the previous meaning it can be taken as **She** gives herself (*Brahmam* itself).

202. *Sarveshvaree* - सर्वेश्वरी

(i) One who is the mistress of the whole universe.
(ii) Because She leads all into the right path, **She** is *Sarveshvaree*.
(iii) There is no place where the control of *Śreedevee* is obstructed. Hence **She** is the *Eshvaree* of all.
(iv) One among the eight *Vāgdevees*.

203. *Sarvamayee* - सर्वमयी

(i) One who is omnipresent and omnipotent.
(ii) **She** is in the form of all things.

(iii) This universe has within it, thirty-six *tatvas* – the universal absolute and the incarnations.
   a. This universe that is 24 self *tatvās* (*Āthma tatvās*) or static *tatvās* (*jada tatvās*);
      i. Five basic elements,
      ii. Five self-characteristics (*Tanmātrās*) – subtle mediums of the sensations,
      iii. Five sense organs,
      iv. Five organs for actions,
      v. Ego, mind, intellect, nature
   b. Seven *vidyā* (or *māyā*) *tatvās* - the soul, the system that controls it to make it a slave for *Shiva,* fate, smell, art, education and ignorance.
   c. Five *Shiva tatvās* viz.;
      i. The knowledge of *Suddha Vidyā* which clearly explains that *Parabrahmam* and the world are one and the same.
      ii. *Eshwar* disintegrated from *Brahmam* and showing himself as this world.
      iii. *Sadashivā* who got the knowledge that this world and its root cause is self.
      iv. *Shakti* (which seems to be disintegrated from *Brahmam* to create this world).
      v. *Shiva,* who has that *Shakti* inside himself.

Worshipping *Śreedevee* in the form of above 36 *tatvās* is called *tatvātva*. This is one of the six methods to reach **Her**.

204. *Sarvamantrasvaroopiṇee* - सर्वमन्त्रस्वरूपिणी

(i) One who is in the form (very essence) of all *mantras*.
(ii) It is said that there are seven crores (70 millions) of *mantras*. **She** is in the form of all these *mantras*. Or **Her** form itself is these *mantras*.
(iii) **She** is in the form of *mantras* in the method of worshipping called *Mantratva*, one of the six *tatvās*

205. *Sarvayantrātmikā* - सर्वयन्त्रात्मिका

(i) One who is in the form of all the *yantras*.
(ii) *Yantras* are in the form lines which have in themselves, the concerned presiding deities.

206. *Sarvatantraroopā* - सर्वतन्त्ररूपा

(i) One who is the spirit of all *Tantras* in her form.

(ii) Since all the *Tantras* indicate *Śreedevee* **Herself** and prove **Her**, **She** is in the form of all *Tantras*.

Bahudāpyāgamair Bhinnā: Panthāna: Siddhihetavai
Tvayyeva Nipatantyete Srotasvinya Ivārnave II

(iii) The literature *Kāmikā* describes each of *Tantras* to the organs of **Her** body:

1	*Kāmikā*	–	the lotus feet
2	*Yogaja*	–	ankles
3 & 4	*Kāranā* and *Prastā*	–	the right and left toes
5	*Ajita*	–	the knees
6	*Deepta*	–	the thighs
7	*Amsumat*	–	back
8	*Suprabheda*	–	navel
9	*Vijaya*	–	stomach
10	*Nisvāsa*	–	heart
11	*Svāyambhuva*	–	the bosom
12	*Anala*	–	the three eyes
13	*Virāgama*	–	throat
14	*Ruru*	–	ears
15	*Makuta*	–	crown
16	*Vipulā* (*Vimalā?*)	–	arms
17	*Candrajnāna*	–	chest
18	*Bimba*	–	face
19	*Prodgitā*	–	tongue
20	*Lalitā*	–	cheeks
21	*Siddha*	–	forehead
22	*Samtāna*	–	earrings
23	*Kirana*	–	jewels
24	*Vātula*	–	garments

Thus **She** has all the *agamās* or *Tantras* in her body.

(There are some differences between what is said above and what is told in *Shiva Āgamās*. Four of the *Saiva Agamās* are not mentioned here; *Sarvokta, Parameshwara, Chintya* and *Sookshma*. Again the *Āgama* called *Prasrut* as mentioned above does find a place in *Shiva Āgamā* as *Sahasra*).

207. *Manonmanee* - मनोन्मनी

(i) One who is in the form of *Manonmaṇi* – transcendent consciousness.

(ii) There are nine places from *Agnā chakra* (in the centre between the eyebrows), till the *Brahmarandhra*; *Bindu, Rothinee, Nātha, Nāthanta, Shakti, Vyāpinee, Samanā, Unmanee* or *Manonmanee* and *Mahābindu*. This *Mahābindu*, also called as *indu* or half-moon, is the *Sahasrāram*. The eighth one in this viz. *Unmanee* is in the form of minute energy. This is called *Manonmanee*. The characteristic of *Manonmanee* is;

Yāshakti: *Kāraṇatvena Tatoortvam Chonmaneesmrtā* I
Natrakālatalāmānam Natatvam Nachdevatā II
Sunirvānam Param Suddam Rudravattram Tatvashyate I
Shiva Shaktiritikyātā Nivikalpā Niranjanā II

(iii) It is said that in the *Hreemkārā*, above the *Bindu* there are eight divisions – one is subtler than the other. The *beeja 'M'* is in the form of eight small ellipses. (299th name *Nātharoopā* can be referred). *Śreedevee* is in the form of that *Unmanee*.

(iv) As per the *Veda* saying *Vāmadevāya Namo*, the forms of *Shiva* are; *Vāmadevar, Jyeshtar, Sreshtar, Rudrar, Kālar, Kalavikaraṇar, Balar, Balavikaraṇar, Balapramatanar, Sarvabhootadamanar and Manonmanar*. Out of these, the consort of *Manonmanar* is *Manonmanee*.

(v) As per *Yoga Sāstrā*, when the mind is in a controlled state, free from attachment to objects, fixed on the mind it attains the state of *Unmaṇi*. *Mana* – mind, *Unmana* – in a state of longing. *Tirupuropanishad* says;

Nirastavishayāsankkam Sanniruddham Manohrudi I
Yatāyātyunmaneebhāvam Tadātadparamampadam II

(vi) Again *Manonmanee* is a kind of *Mudrā*, its characteristics are described thus; By this process the eyes neither close nor open, by which breath is neither inhaled nor exhaled and the mind is a blank neither speculating nor doubting, meditating the form of *Śreedevee*.

Netre Yayonmeshaṇimeshamukte Vāyuryayā Varjita Recapoora: I
Manachcha Sankalpa Vikalpa Soonyam Manonmanee Sā Mayi Sannidhattām II

(vii) As per *Brahannāradeeyam*, the hidden state of mind is called *Unmaṇi*:

Dyānadhyādhrudhyeya Pāvo Yatanachyati: *Nirparam* I
Tatonmanatvam Bhavati Gnānāmruta Nishevanāt II

(viii) In the process of meditation of *Śreedevee*, meditator and the object of meditation are entirely destroyed, then *Unmanee* state arises;

consequently he enjoys the ambrosia of wisdom.

208. *Māheshvaree* - माहेश्वरी

(i) One who is the consort of Lord *Maheshvara* (*Paramashivā*).
(ii) The three gods *Brahma, Vişhŋu* and *Rudra* do three main functions of creation, protection and destruction. *Maheshvara* is above these three and is transcending the three characteristics (*Guŋas- Rajas, Tamas* and *Satva*) in equal proposition. His *Shakti* form is *Maheshvaree*.
(iii) As per below verse of *Veda, Maheshvara* is devoid of the three *guŋās* (*nirguŋa*) and his consort of *Maheshvaree;*

Yovedādhou Svara: *Prokto Vedāntecapratishtita*: I
Tasya Prakruti Leenasya Ya: *Para*: *Sa Maheshvara*: II

(iv) The word *Maheshvara* means – one who is the head of all the *Bhoota Gaŋas* or by all the great practicing celebacies. His consort is *Maheshvaree. Linga Purāŋā* says;

Tamasā Kālardrākyo Rajasā Kanakāŋța Ja: I
Satvena Sarvako Vişhŋu: *Nairguŋyena Maheshwara*: II

209. *Mahādevee* - महादेवी

(i) *Mahatee* means one who has immense and immeasurably big body. *Shiva Purāŋā* says;

Bruhadasya Sareeram Yat Aprameyam Pramāŋata: I
Dhatur Mahetipoojāyām Mahādeveetata: *Smrutā* II

(ii) *Shiva* in his eighth form, namely that of the moon is known as *Mahādevā*; his consort is *Rohini* or *Mahādevee*.
(iii) *Mahādevee* is the presiding deity at the *Sāligrāma Chakrateertha* on the banks *Gandakee* river in Nepal.
(iv) **She** has got entire energy of all *devas*. **She** is the greatest of all the *Devees*. Hence *Mahādevee*.

210. *Mahālakshmee* - महालक्ष्मी

(i) One who is in the form of a great giant (*Mahatee*) *Lakshmee*.
(ii) **She** is in the form *Mahālakshmee*, the consort of *Mahā Vişhŋu*.
(iii) As per *Padma Purāŋa, Mahālakshmee* is the presiding deity at the *Karaveera* in Kolhapur.
(iv) In *Durga Saptashatee*, it is mentioned that *Śreedevee* took the form

of *Mahālakshmee* with 18 hands to kill *Mahishāsura*.

(v) There is a story (in *Mairālatantram*) that *Mahālakshmee*, an element of *Śreedevee* killed the demon called *Mahālan*;

Mahālanāmakam Daityam Sayati Kshapayateeticha I
Mahālasā Mahālakshmee Ritikhyātimāgatā II

(vi) In many places, it has been mentioned that *Śreedevee* has the name *Mahālakshmee*;

Tasyānga MaŋḍalārooḍhāShaktir Maheshvareeparā I
Mahālakshmeeritikhyātā Shyāmāsarvamanoharee II
(*Shiva Purāŋam*)

Shriyam Lakshmeem Ambigām Aoupalāngam
(*Āyushya Sooktam*)

(vii) As per the saying – *Trayodashe Mahālakshmee* - a girl of thirteen years of age is called *Mahālakshmee*. She is fit to be worshipped on the thirteenth day from full or new moon day (*Tirayodashi thithi*).

211. *Mruḍapriyā* - मृडप्रिया

(i) One who is the consort of *Shiva* by name *Mruḍa*.

(ii) Lord *Shiva,* while doing the three main tasks as creation, protection and destruction, takes the names *Bhava*, *Mruḍa* and *Hara*. When he is in *Mruḍa* form, his character is predominantly *Satva*. **She** is the consort of that *Mruḍa*. *Shiva Mahimnā Stavam* says; *Jana Sukrute Satvotritou Mruḍāya Namonama*:- I bow down to *Mruḍa* who predominates in *Sāttvika* nature for the sake of conferring happiness on men.

(iii) The word *Mruḍa* means – protecting this world by stroking mildly to provide happiness. Because of this protecting energy **She** is *Mruḍapriya*.

212. *Mahāroopā* - महारूपा

(i) One who is in great magnificent form.

(ii) Supreme *Brahmam* has four forms; *Purusha*, the manifested (*vyakta* - five gross elements) and unmanifested (*avyakta* - *Pradhāna*) and lastly time. These four are the root cause for creation, protection, destruction and core values (*moolatatvā*). She is the root cause for all these and hence greater than these.

(iii) A part of the supreme *Brahmam* that emerged in the beginning of all creations is called unmanifestation. That is, it is in an unrecognizable form. It is in a state to be formed as this world. Again at the end of this cosmos, the universe in the individual state turns into the root matter (*moola porul*) and reaches the form of unmanisfestation. When the unidentified form of manifestation is turned into unmanifested form it is called *Mahat*. **She** is in the form of this *Mahat* and hence *Mahāroopa*.

(iv) *Brahma, Viṣhŋu* and *Shiva,* who do the three main tasks of creation, protection and destruction, are the great gods (*mahān*). Since She does these three tasks by taking those forms She is called Mahāroopa. Similarly **She** is also in the form of other Yogis and *siddhas* and hence *Mahāroopa*.

213. *Mahāpoojyā* - महापूज्या

(i) One who is most worshippable.

(ii) **She** is worshipped even by *Brahma, Viṣhŋu* and *Rudra*, who themselves are worshipful.

(iii) Greater than the great people and hence *Mahatee*. Since **She** is worshipped by *Brahma, Viṣhŋu* and *Shiva,* **She** is *Poojya*. Hence as *Mahatee* and *Poojyā*, **She** is *Mahāpoojya*.

(iv) It has been mentioned in *Padma Purāŋa* and *Devee Bhāgavatam* as; each of the *devas* worship *Śreedevee* in different forms and/ or *yantras* – out of these *Agni, Sukra* and *Soorya* worship *Śreedevee* in an idol form made of ruby;

Shiva Brahma Viṣhŋu Kubera Vishvedeva Vāyu Vasu Varuŋa
Agni Sukra Soma Soorya Graha Rākshasa Pisācha
Mātru Gaŋāti Pedhena Tattatpoojaneeya Devee Moortti Bedho
Mantre Chailendra Neela Svarŋa Roubhya Pittala Kāmasya
Spatika Mānikya Muktāpala Pravāla Vaidoorya Trpuseesa Vajya Loha

(v) The *Brahmānḍa Purāŋa* says that the expiation for all the sins, knowingly or unknowingly done, is just remembering the lotus feet of *Śreedevee*. Hence *Mahāpoojya*.

214. *Mahāpātakanāshinee* - महापातकनाशिनी

(i) One who destroys great sins like *brahmahathi* (killing of a *brahmin*).

(ii) There are five great sins (*mahāpāthakās*) – *brahmahathi*, looting, drinking alcohol, liking of elder's wife and being supportive to those who do these four sins.

(iii) Expiation for all these sins has been described in various *Santhi* books. One such expiation for these sins and completely destroying the very thought of those sins also, is remembering upon the lotus feet of *Śreedevee*. The thought would tempt to do the sins again and again. Hence worshipping *Śreedevee* would completely destroy this thought and generate the thought of good deeds.

(iv) It has been mentioned in the results/ effects part of this book – if one has chant at least one name out of these 1000 names so much sins are destroyed that nobody could have committed as many sins as in all the 14 worlds;

Atraika Nāmno Yāshakti: *Pātakānām Nivarttane* I
Tannivartyam Agham Karttum Nālam Lokā: *Chaturdasha* II

215. *Mahāmāyā* - महामाया

(i) **She** is in the form of great illusion (*Mahāmāyāroopiŋee*), (since **She** creates lust to all *devas* starting from *Brahma*).

(ii) *Durgā Saptashatee* says;

Gnānināmapi Chetāmsi Devee Bhagavateehisā I
Balādākrushya Mohāya Mahāmāyā Prāyacchati II

(iii) The name of the *Shakti* seed letter *Hreem* is *Māyā* or *Shakti*. The complete energy of *Śreedevee* is hidden in this. This *Hreem* seed is a knot like for all the three *kooṭās* of *Panchadashāksharee mantra*. **She** is in the form of that *Hreem* seed letter as *Mahāmāya*.

(iv) This seed letter *Hreem* has four splits as - *'H'* + *'R'* + *'E'* + *'M'* – it is similar to - a tree's all the parts (organs) are subtly hidden within a seed. Hence *Mahāmāya*.

(v) The *Kālikā Purāŋā* says; **She** who always makes him devoid of knowledge, the being who possessed knowledge (of his real nature) whilst in the womb, compelled him to take birth by means of the wings of delivery and leads him by reason of the *samskāra* of previous births to desire of food etc.; thence into confusion, egotism, doubt, subsequently leading him again and again to undergo (the stages of) anger, distress and greediness and then leads him into (sensual) desire causing anxiety day in and day out, producing sometimes pleasures and sometimes pain, is called the *Mahāmāyā* (great illusion).

(vi) According to one lexicon *māyā* means compassion; hence *Mahāmāyā* means full of compassion.

216. *Mahāsatvā* - महासत्वा

(i) One who is the supreme reality – full of *Satva* character.
(ii) *Satva* means - character, strength and state of existence. *Śreedevee* has great character or great strength or great existence.
(iii) *Satva* also means mind. *Śreedevee* has such a broad mind so that **She** does not distinguish any soul from *Brahma* onwards till a worm.
(iv) *Satvam* – seat or the state of sitting. I.e. the character and strength to show case the individuality of anything. **She** is in both these forms in all things.

217. *Mahāshakti*: - महाशक्तिः

(i) One who has boundless energy.
(ii) **She** has so much energy to administer the entire universe.
(iii) *Shakti* means strength. Even in that sense *Śreedevee*'s strength and the weapons are so great to be called as *Mahāshakti*.
(iv) When compared to 109th name *Mahāshakti* – the difference in ***Sa*** and ***Sha*** has to be noted. With that difference it has to be taken as not repetitive.

218. *Mahārati*: - महारतिः

(i) One who has boundless delight.
(ii) The word *Rati* means affection. That is – *Rati* means - mind getting enjoyment and delight on anything. A person getting *Rati* on an object is due to the mind or the object? If this is researched, it can be concluded that it is only due to the mind of the enjoying person and not the object. The reason is the affection in the self. This self-affection is *Śreedevee* herself in the form of *jeevātma*. On account of ignorance we search the affection outside without understanding that it is self in the form of affection. The person with this know-ledge gets self-satisfaction within himself. *Śreedevee* is in that form of *Rati*.
(iii) *Rati* – beautiful lady -wife of Cupid – most beautiful lady. *Śreedevee* is more beautiful than *Rati* and hence *Mahārati*.
(iv) *Mahārati* - the consort of *Mahākāma*.

219. *Mahābhogā* - महाभोगा

(i) One who is a great enjoyer.
(ii) *Bhogā* – the feeling of enjoying the happiness. Any wealth giving this feeling is *Bhoga*. **She** has the unlimited means to the wealth and

enjoying that feeling without any obstruction. Hence *Mahābhoga*.

(iii) *Abhogā* means extension. **She** is boundlessly extended in the form of this universe and hence *Mahābhoga*.

220. *Mahaishvaryā* - महैश्वर्या

(i) One who possess supreme sovereignty.

(ii) *Ishvarya* – the state of being an *Eshvaree* – the ability and energy to rule others as per will and pleasure. **She** has this capacity and hence *Mahaishvarya*.

(iii) The individual parts of *Ishvaryā* are called divine manifestations. An individual's personality, the incomparable beauty of a lady, the ignorance of a child, odour of a flower, etc., are all manifestations of *Eshvar*. These individual characters felt as part of *Eshvar*, without relating to the base where it originated, is called manifestation. *Śreedevee* is an integral part of all these – hence *Mahaishvaryā* (*Śreemad Bhagavat Geeta* – *Vibhooti Yoga* – chapter X).

221. *Mahāveeryā* - महावीर्या

(i) One who is supreme in valour.

(ii) The word *veeryā* means - semen, might, glory and strength. *Śreedevee* has all these in a great way.

222. *Mahābalā* - महाबला

(i) One who has great might.

(ii) The word *balā* means - army, strength, fragrance, taste, form, soul, etc. *Śreedevee* has all these abundantly.

(iii) The word *balā also* means a crow. Great *Yogins* like *Bhusundā* worshipped *Śreedevee* in the form a crow and got great strengths. Hence *Mahābala*. This has been addressed in *Yogavāsistha*. We are twenty-one crows, brothers, sons of *Chaṇḍa*; by us, together with our sisters, the great *Śreedevee* was worshipped for a long time, after finishing her contemplation *Śreedevee* **Herself** wishing to bless us favoured us; thus we were liberated;

Bhrātara: Chanḍatanayā: Vāyasā Ekavimsati I
Bhrātrubhi: Sahahamseebhi: Brāmhee Daguvulee Tatha II
Chiramārādhitā Asmābhi: Samādhiviramesati I
Prasadaparayākāle Bhagavatyā Tata: Svayam I

Tataivānugraheetāsmo Yena Muktāvayam Sthitā: II

223. *Mahābuddhi*: - महाबुद्धिः

(i) One who has great wisdom.
(ii) Intellect is, understanding the inner consciousness. **She** has got the wisdom to understand everything at a micro level. Which, when known, the whole universe is known or, from whom one obtains the highest intelligence. **She** is such an intellect form.
(iii) By worshipping which *Devee* one can get great acumen, that *Devee* is *Mahābuddhi*:.

224. *Mahāsiddhi*: - महासिद्धिः

(i) Attainments (*siddhis*) are of eight types as detailed below;

Aṇimā	Reducing one's body to the size of an atom and roaming around without being seen by others.
Mahimā	Expanding one's body to an infinitely large size
Garimā	Becoming infinitely heavy
Laghimā	Becoming almost weightless
Prāpti	Having unrestricted access to all places.
Prākāmva	Getting all desires without any restriction.
Lesitvā	Control of all movable or immovable things.
Vasitvā	The power to subjugate all.

In addition to the above there are various other *siddhis* like, creating passions like erotic and heroic as per one's wish, not becoming slaves of happiness, sorrow, chillness, heat, desires, aversion, etc. **She** is in the form of all these *siddhis* and also gives it.

225. *Mahāyogeshvareshvaree* - महायोगेश्वरेश्वरी

(i) One who is worshipped by all spiritual adepts – who is *Eshvaree* of all *Yogesvaras*.
(ii) *Mahāyogas* are the best in yoga methods. The experts in this are called *Mahāyogeesvaras*. **She** is the head of all those.
(iii) Integrating those that are differentiated is called *Yoga*. What is differentiated from us is the *Eshvara's* quality. The tool to integrate is *Yoga*. *Yogees* are those who got this *Eshvara's* quality through this.

The experts among those are called *Mahāyogees*. **She** provides the *Eshvara's* quality to *Mahāyogees*.

226. *Mahātantra* - महातन्त्रा

(i) One who is the greatest *Tantra*, which conveys the method of worshipping **Herself**.
(ii) The methods of worshipping and the books which explain them are called *Tantras*. They are *Kulārnavā, Jnānārnavā* and others. Since each of these is all great by itself, **She** is *Mahātantra*.
(iii) When compared to other *Tantras, Swatantra*, explains the method of worshipping *Śreedevee* exclusively. It is a *Mahātantra*. Since **She** is worshipped with *Mahatantra* method, **She** is also *Mahātantra*.
(iv) Lord *Parameshwarā* showed 64 *Tantras*. These are about various reigning deities giving various results. *Śreedevee* asked *Parameshwarā* to tell **Her** a *Tantra* which is greater than all these, which is complete and independent of itself. Then **he** explained a *Mahātantra* called *Swatantra*. This has been mentioned in *Soundaryalaharee*.
(v) This *Swatantra* book is also called as *Rāja Tantra*.

227. *Mahāmantra* - महामन्त्रा

(i) One who has *mantras* about **Her**.
(ii) There is infinite number of *mantras* used for worshipping. Lot many like *Bālā, Bagalā, Kali, Annapoorŋā*, etc., are used to worship *Śreedevee*. Among these the greatest one is *Panchadashākssharee Mahāmantra* called as *Śree Vidya*. Since **She** is worshipped with this *mantra* **She** is also called as *Mahāmantra*.

228. *Mahāyantrā* - महायन्त्रा

(i) One who has lot many great *yantras*, which are used to worship **Her**.
(ii) A *yantra* is a drawing with lines, circles, shapes like lotus petals, etc. A *yantra* will have straight line drawn length and breadth wise in the form of rectangles or triangles with intersection points of two or three lines.
(iii) *Yantras* are two dimensional figures with length and breadth. If the third dimension height is also added, then it is called *Meru*. *Śree chakra* made in three dimension one layer above the other with the

centre *Bindu* at the top then it is a *Meru*. In this if the bottom layers are two dimensional and above half are one top of the other then it is called *Ardha* (half) *Meru*.

(iv) The great of all the *yantras* are *Śree Chakra, Pooja Chakra, Padma Chakra, Amrutakata Yantra, Meru Siddhavajrāyantra, Lingā*, etc. Since **She** is in the form of all these – **She** is *Mahāyantra*.

229. *Mahāsanā* - महासना

(i) One who is seated in a great seat.
(ii) The thirty-six *tatvās* beginning with the earth, created by **Her** is her seat.
(iii) The *Devee Bhāgavatha Purāŋā* says; *Eshā Bhagavate Sarva Tatvānyāsritya Tishtati* - The divine one remains dwelling in all *tatvās*.
(iv) The 36 *tatvās* – individually, a combination or all put together are seat of *Śreedevee*.
(v) **She** has the heart of great people as **Her** seat and hence *Mahāsana*.
(vi) **She** is seated in great seats like *Panchabrahmāsanā, Chakrarājaratā* and *Simhāsanā* and hence *Mahāsana*.

230. *Mahāyāgakramārādhyā* - महायागक्रमाराध्या

(i) One who is the worshipped by the method of *Mahāyāga*.
(ii) *Mahāyāga* is the worship of *Śreedevee* alongwith sixty-four *Yoginees*. This gives quicker results than other methods.
(iii) *Bhāvanopanishad* explains the method of worshipping this body imagining it as *Śreedevee* with the organs and inner consciousness as *Yoginees*. Those who had practiced this and got accomplished by *Shiva Yogins* alone. She is being worshipped by this method. This has been explained in detail in the in the commentary for *Bhāvano-panisad*.
(iv) The word *kramā* means – energy, arrangement, movement and shaking. If it is considered as *Yāgakramā* – **She** is worshipped by a powerful method called *Mahāyāga*.

231. *Mahābhairavapoojitā* - महाभैटबपूजिता

(i) One who is worshipped by *Mahābhairava*.
(ii) Each letter in the word *bhairavā* has a significance; *bha* - creation (*bharaŋa* – to fill), *ra* - protection (*ramaŋa*) and *va* - destruction

(*vamana*); indicates all the three tasks. Hence this indicates Lord *Paramashiva,* the accomplisher of creation, preservation and destruction (of the universe) and hence *Mahābhairava. Padma Purāṇā* says that he worshiped *Śreedevee.*

Shambhu: *Poojayate Deveem Mantra Shaktimayeem Shubhām* I
Akshamālām Kredhrutvā Nyāsenaiva Bhavotbhava: II

(iii) In the beginning of this *Sahasranāmā*, we read that Lord *Mahābhairavā*, by a great sacrifice (by *Mahāyāgākramā*) caused *Śreedevee* to become manifest from alter of the fire of consciousness (*Chidagnikuṇḍa*). Hence *Mahābhairavapoojita.*

(iv) The word *Bhairavā* means – *Bheeroonām Samooha*: - a group of panicky ladies. **She** was worshipped by them.

232. *Maheshvaramahākalpamahātānḍavasākshiṇee –* महेश्वरमहाकल्पमहाताण्डवसाक्षिणी

(i) One who is the witness to the great awesome destructive cosmic dance of Lord *Maheshvarā* at the end of creative cycle.

(ii) *Mahākalpa* means the great dissolution (*pralayā*) of this universe; destruction means – the entire universe sub-merged with Lord himself. This is the fourth task of *Śreedevee* called *Thirodana*. Lord *Maheshvara* was pleased by sub-merging within him all that was created. On account of this he gives a visual treat in the form of a dance called *Mahātāndava*. At this time *Śreedevee* was the only witness remaining to this dance. **She** is the only witness right before creation till complete destruction.

(iii) This has been described in *Panchadashistava* (8-11) says as - your form alone is excellent, having the noose, elephant hook, bow of sugarcane and the arrow of flowers and witnessing the dance of the axe-bearing *Parabhairavā* started at the time of his drawing the universe;

Kalpopa Samharana Kalpita Tāndavasya
Devasya Khanda Parasho: *Parabhairavasya* I
Pashānkuchaikshava Sharāsana Pushpabānai:
Sa Sakshinee Vijayate Tavamooritrekā II

(iv) The dance by men is called *tāndavā* and that of women is *lāsya*. It has been mentioned that when *Maheshvara* did the *Tāndavā, Śreedevee* also did the *Lāsya*. When both are dancing, at the request of *Śreedevee*, both started the fifth task called *Anugrahā* by re-creating the entire universe with most compassion. *Ambāstavā* and 41st verse of *Soundaryalaharee* can be read here;

Kalpopa Samharana Kelishu Paŋḍitāni
Chanḍāni Khanda Parachorabhitāndavani I
Āloknena Tava Komalitāni Māta:
Lāsyātmanā Parinanti Jagatvibhootyai II

(*Ambāstavā*)

Tavādhāre Moole Saha Samayayā Lāsyaparayā
Navātmāna Manye Navarasa Mahātāndava Natam I
Ubhābhyā Bhetābhyā Mudaya Vidhi Muddhishya Dayayā
Sanāthābhyām Jagye Janakjananeemat Jagadidam II

(*Soundaryalaharee*)

233. *Mahākāmeshamahishee* - महाकामेशमहिषी

(i) One who is the consort of *Mahākāmeshvara*.
(ii) In the 2nd name **She** was called as *Sreemahārājnee*, since **She** is the great empress of *Mahākāmesvara*.

234. *Mahātripurasundaree* - महात्रिपुरसुन्दरी

(i) One who is the great *Tripurasundaree* – the divine beauty known by that name.
(ii) **She** takes all the three forms as – one who knows, the intellect which knows and the knowing object. Depending on the person and the object the intellect can be differentiated as small and large. However, the divine knowledge, which is the base and the root cause of all the knowledge (*Mahātripurā*). **She** is in the form of *Mahātripurā* and does not undergo any changes/ transformation by becoming the knower or the known (*Māthru* or *Meyā*). In addition **She** is also the divine beauty. Hence *Mahātripurasundaree*.
(iii) **Her** beauty is so great that it cannot be seen in any of the three worlds.

235. *Chatu:shashṭiyupacārādhyā* – चतुःषष्टियुपचाराढ्या

(i) One who is being adored by sixty-four offerings/services/ ingredients.
(ii) Ordinarily there are two methods in any worship – with five or sixteen *upachārās* (services). *Gandha* (sandal), *pushpa* (flower), *dhoopa* (smoke with freshening odour), *deepa* (light) and

naivedyam (offering of food) are the five offerings. In addition a little more expanded services (offerings) is sixteen – *Dhyānā* (meditation), *Āvāhanā* (imagining the god's form on the image), *āsana* (seat), *pādyam* (washing of feet), *arghyam* (freshening), *āchamaneeyam* (offering of water to drink), *snāneeyam* (bathing), *vastram* (cloths), *gandha – kumkum, pushpa, dhupa, deepa, naivedyam, Neerājanam* (camphor light), *Pradhakshinam* (going around) and *Namaskaram* (bowing). The same is still expanded as 64 offerings in worshipping *Śreedevee*. Those who have facilities have to do all the 64 services with the concerned offerings. Those who could not can do it with flower and rice. Last five have to be done by self-doing it.

(iii) The 64 offerings are listed below;

1.	*Pādhyam*	Water to wash the feet – includes *argyam* and *āchamaneeyam* also.
2.	*Ābharaŋa Avaropaŋam*	Removal of ornaments
3.	*Suganthi Taila Abhyantham*	Applying fragrant oil
4.	*Manjanasalā Pravesam*	Entering the bath room
5.	*Manjanasalāmaŋipeetopavechan am*	Taking the seating made of gems in the bath room.
6.	*Divyasnāneeya Udvarddhanam*	Applying the fragrant powders.
7.	*Ushnodhakasnānam*	Bathing in hot water
8.	*Kanak Kalachachutasakala Theerthābhishekam*	Bathing in auspicious water brought in golden pots.
9.	*Dyouna Vastra Parimarjanam*	Drying off with dry clothes.
10.	*Aruŋatukoolaparidanam*	Wearing of red silk dress
11.	*Aruŋakuchottareeyam*	Wearing of red tops
12.	*Ālepa Manḑapa Pravesham*	Entering the room for fragrance.
13.	*Ālepa Manḑapa Maŋipeetopavechanam*	Taking the seating made of gems in the fragrant room.
14.	*Sandanākaru Kumkuma Mrugamata Karpoora Kasthoori Korochanāthi Divyaganda Sarvānkeena Vilepanam*	Applying all the fragrances like Sandal, eaglewood, European saffron, *javvadu*, *kasturi*, cow-bezoar, etc.
15.	*Kesapārasyakālākarutoopam*	Applying eaglewood smoke to hair
16.	*Mallika, Mālatee, Jāteechampaka, Ashoka, Chatapatra, Pooka, Kuhalee, Punnaga, Kalhāramukya Sarvartum Kusumamālā Samarpanam*	To offer a garland made of Jasmine, Lotus, flower of petal nut, Ashoka Red Lotus, Red Lily and Red Jasmine flowers.

17.	*Bhooshaṇa Manḍapa Prevesam*	To enter the room to wear ornaments.
18.	*Bhooshaṇa Manadapa maṇipeetopavechanam*	Taking the seating made of gems in the ornaments room.
19.	*Navamaṇi Makutam*	Wearing the crown made of nine gems.
20.	*Chandrakalasam*	Wearing a crescent like on the forehead.
21.	*Seemantasintooram*	To apply *kumkum* on the forehead at the start of parting of the hair.
22.	*Tilakaratnam*	Wearing a dot on the forehead.
23.	*Kālānchanam*	To apply collyrium to the eyes.
24.	*Vāleeyugalam*	To wear ear drops
25.	*Maṇikunḍalayugalam*	To wear earrings made of gems.
26.	*Nasābharaṇam*	To wear nose rings.
27.	*Adarayāvakam*	To apply lipstick.
28.	*Pratama Bhooshaṇam*	To wear the *mangala Sūtra* – auspicious ornament.
29.	*Kanaka Chintakam*	To wear golden necklace.
30.	*Patakam*	To wear pendants.
31.	*Mahāpatakam*	To wear large pendants.
32.	*Muktāvali*	To wear chain of pearls.
33.	*Ekāvali*	To wear a chain of 27 pearls.
34.	*Channaveeram*	To wear an ornament in both sides of the body like a *yagyopaveeta*
35.	*Keyoorakala Catushtyam*	Bangles that are worn in the four shoulders.
36.	*Valaiyāvali*	A series of bangles.
37.	*Uoormikāvali*	A series of finger rings.
38.	*Kānchitāma*	Wearing a Girdle around the waist.
39.	*Katisootram*	Wearing a thread around the waist in the lower abdomen.
40.	*Soubhāgyābharaṇam*	A golden ornament in the form of a leaf of a fig tree worn in a thread (39 above).
41.	*Pādakatakam*	To ear bangles in the ankle.
42.	*Ratnanoopuram*	To wear ankle rings made of precious gems.
43.	*Pādāmkuleeyakam*	To wear rings in the toes.
44.	*Pāsam*	To have the noose in the top right hand.
45.	*Ankusam*	To have a goad in the top left hand.

46.	*Pundrekshu Shabam*	To have a bow made of sugarcane in the bottom left hand.
47.	*Pushpabānam*	To have an arrow made of flowers in the bottom left hand.
48.	*Śreeman Maŋikya Patuke*	To wear a pair of shining footwear made of red rubies.
49.	*Sva Samāna Veshāpi: Āvaranadevatāpi: Sahamahāchakratirohanam*	To take seat on the *Mahāchakrapeeța* alongwith other deities wearing equal ornaments.
50.	*Kāmeshvarākkaparyanka Upavechanam*	To sit on the lap of *Kāmeshvara.*
51.	*Amrutāsavachashakam*	A cup filled with nectar.
52.	*Āchamaneeyam*	Water to goggle.
53.	*Karpooraveetikā*	Petal leaves with cardamom, bay leaf, bitter orange peel, dehydrated orange flakes, cloves, dried papaya - ripe, coconut - copra, rice - sona masoori, cooking banana slices, white pepper and turmeric powder
54.	*Ānantollāsahāsam*	Laughing to show the delight.
55.	*Mangalārtikam*	Auspicious *ārti*
56.	*Chatram*	Umbrella
57.	*Chāmaram*	Fan
58.	*Darpanam*	Mirror
59.	*Tālavruttam*	Percussion instruments
60.	*Gandam*	Sandal
61.	*Pushpam*	Flowers
62.	*Doopam*	Smoke with freshening odour
63.	*Deepam*	Light
64.	*Neivedyam*	Offering of food

Upachārān Allape Pushpādyair Manasā Smareth I
Gandhapushpa Dhoopa Deepa Neiveyānyat Maheshwaree I
Gandhādi Panchkāva Poojā Vyarttaiva Sarvadā II

It is a usual practice to do last five offering directly with the concerned objects and remaining by imagination. It would be great to do, out of the remaining also - whatever is possible, with the concerned items. It is a difference worth noting that the petal leaves are offered before the food (*neivedyam*).

(iv) *Śree Ādi Śaņkara*, in his *Chatushshashțiupchāra Pooja Storam* has well explained the order starting from *Śreedevee Supraņātam* (waking up verses).

(v) In other *Tantras*, in addition to the above 64, eight more (offerings) are mentioned;

i. Wearing the flowers offered to *Śreedevee*, after dedication.
ii. Making religious endowments
iii. Worshipping the teacher
iv. Worshipping the devotees
v. Worshipping the religious books – *mantra sāstra* books
vi. Doing *homa* through sacrificial fires
vii. Consuming the water, which has washed the feet of god
viii. Performing the full ceremony called *Prānāgnihotra*

All these seventy-two are explained in *Varivasyā rahasya* in the *pooja* chapter by *Bhāskara Rāya*.

(vi) It has been described here by *Bhāskara Rāya* that the weapons of *Śreedevee* – noose and goad in the top hands and the sugarcane bow and flower arrow in the bottom hands. This has been reversed in *Dakshiṇā Moorthy Samhita*. It has to be followed however one has been taught by the teacher.

(vii) Making the offerings by imagination or if the concerned item is not available, using flower or rice instead is permitted.

(viii) Rice means – not the simple white rice – but made yellow or red by adding turmeric or *kumkum*. Also it should be complete and not broken at the ends.

Shvetākshadair Napoojāsyāt Tripurā Parameshvaree I
Kashmerair Vā Haridrairvā (*Kumkumarivāpi*) *Rakta Chanḍana Pankakai*: I
Rajnjitān Chalijān Shuddhān Akandān Arpayetbudha: II

236. *Chatu:shashṭikalāmayee* – चतु:षष्टिकलामयी

(i) One who embodies the sixty four forms of arts.

(ii) **She** has all the arts in **Her** form.

(iii) It has been mentioned that there are sixty four arts. But there are differences in views while listing down the 64 arts.

(iv) The below list is as given by *Bhāskara Rāya*;

1. The knowledge of the scripts of eighteen languages – Samskrit, Prakrut, Udeechi, Mahārashtree, Magatee, Mishramāgatee, Chakāpeeri, Avanti, Drāvedee, Otriyā, Pāchādyā, Prāchyā, Bāhveekā, Rantikā, Dākshinādyā, Paichachee, Āvantee and Chourasenee.
2. Writing these scripts.
3. The power of writing and reading these languages quickly.
4. Drawing
5. Knowledge of different languages

6. Composing verses in them
7. The art of repeating what is heard.
8. Gambling
9. 9 to 12 – Knowledge of the four *Vedas – Rig, Yajur, Sāma* and *Atharva*
13. 13 to 16 – Knowledge of the four auxiliary *Vedas – Gāndharvā, Ayur Veda, Danur Veda* and *Artha Sāstra*.
17. 17 to 22 – Knowledge of six *sāstrās – Nyāsa, Vaiseshikā, Sānkhyā, Yoga, Meemamsā* and *Vedāntha*.
23. Knowledge of six *vedāngās – Shikshā, Vyākaranā, Chandas, Nruktā, Jyothishā* and *Kalpa*.
29. Knowledge of *Tantra Purāŋā* and *Smrutee*
30. Knowledge of poetry, rhetoric and drama
31. 31 to 36 Knowledge of pacifying, controlling, attracting, enmity, ruining by magical practices and killing
37. 37 to 43 The art of opposing the effects of motion, water, sight, fire, weapons, speech and semen
44. The art of making scriptures
45. 45 to 48 Art of training elephants, horses, chariots and men
49. The knowledge of divination by bodily marks (*sāmudrikā*)
50. Art of boxing
51. Art of cooking
52. Art of removing venom
53. Art of playing string instruments
54. Art of playing wind instruments like flute
55. Art of playing percussion instruments
56. Art of playing heavy instruments made of bronze.
57. Creating illusion (*Indrajāla*)
58. Art of dancing
59. Art of singing
60. The art of alchemy
61. Knowledge of testing gems
62. Thieving
63. Knowledge of the pulse
64. Art of disappearance

(v) *Kalā* also means *Tantra*. It has been mentioned in *Soundaryalaharee* that there are 64 *Tantras*. *Śreedevee* has all these as **Her** form.

237. *Mahācatu:shashṭikoṭiyogineegaŋasevitā* – महाचतुःषष्टिकोटियोगिनीगनसेविता

(i) One who is worshipped by a host of 64 crores of *Yoginees*.

(ii) There are 8 *Prakata Yoginees* as *Matrukā Devees*, in the middle layer of *Chatusrā* (*Noopurā*) of *Śree Chakra*. They are; *Brahmee*,

Māheshwaree, Koumāree, Vaişhŋavee, Vārāhee, Māhendree, Chāmuŋḍā and *Mahālakshme*. Each of these has 8 *Yoginees* as allied *Devees*. Each of these 8 Yoginees has one crore as retinue. Hence 8 x 8 = 64 crores *Yoginees*. Hence *Śreedevee* is called as being served by these *Yoginees*. *Mahācatushshashţikoţi Yogineegaŋasevita*.

(iii) The word *Mahā* means nine. *Mahācatushshashţikoţi* means 9 x 64 = 576 crores of *Devees*. In every *Āvaraŋachakra* of *Śree Chakra* there are 64 crores of *Yoginees*. Hence in all the 9 *Āvarŋas* there are 576 *Yoginees*. *Śreedevee* is being worshipped by all these *Yoginees*.

238. *Manuvidyā* - मनुविद्या

(i) One who is in the form *Vidyā* adored by *Manu*.

(ii) It is being told that earlier *Śree Vidyā* was adored by twelve devotees; *Manu, Chandra* (Moon), *Kubera, Lopāmudrā, Agasthyā, Manmatha* (Cupid), *Agni* (fire), *Soorya* (Sun), *Indra, Skanda, Shiva* and *Doorvāsa*. Each of them, by the skills of penance, felt a type of *mantra* and worshipped. *Manu* is the top most among them. *Śreedevee* is in the form of *Śree Vidyā Mantra* formed by him.

(iii) *Śree Vidyā* worshipped by these 12 devotees has been mentioned in 13 names – 239, 297, 305, 359, 375, 406, 558, 586, 647, 715, 720, 733 and 785.

239. *Chandravidyā* - चन्द्रविद्या

(i) One who is in the form of *Śree Vidyā* worshipped by *Chandrā* (Moon).

(ii) *Chandrā* (Moon) is the second in the 12 people mentioned in the earlier name. That *Vidyā* is being mentioned here.

240. *Chandramaŋḍalamadhyagā* - चन्द्रमन्डलमध्यगा

(i) One who is residing in the centre of the Moon's disc.

(ii) It has been mentioned that the full moon is present in the *Sahasrāra Kamala* in the head. **She** is residing in the centre of that moon.

(iii) It can also be interpreted as - *Śreedevee* woken up from the *Moolādhāra* breaks through the six *chakras* and reaches the Lord *Parameshwara* in the *Sahasrāra Kamala*, called *Chandra maŋḍala*.

(iv) If one contemplates *Śreedevee* in the Moon's disc in the sky on a full Moon day and worships **Her** by chanting this *Sahasranāmā*, he gets long life devoid of all diseases – says verses 21 to 23 of the *phalaśruti* (results) part. This method is also named as *Āyushkara Prayoga*.

(v) In the *Shiva Purāṇā* it has been mentioned as - *Shiva* resides in the head of fire and *Śreedevee* resides in the centre of the Moon's disc.

Aham Agni Shiro Nishta: Tvam Soma Shirasi Stitā I
Agni Shomātmakam Vishvam Āvābhyām Samdhishṭitam II

(vi) The inherent meaning is that the Moon's disc is the *Śree Chakra* itself.

(vii) It has been mentioned in the *Tantra Sāstrās* that the worshippers of *Śreedevee* have to do *Śree Vidyā Sandhyāvandhanā* in every session and at mid-night, after the routine and normal *Sandhyāvandhana*. *Śreedevee* has to be meditated as **She** is the in the Moon's disc during the *Śree Vidyā Sandhyāvandhanā* done at the evening.

241. *Chāruroopā* - चारुरूपा

(i) One whose form is exquisite.

(ii) **She** has such a beautiful form as mentioned in the names *Tripurasundaree, Lalitā* and *Sundaree.*

242. *Chāruhāsā* - चारुहासा

(i) One who has a charming smile.

(ii) It has been mentioned by some - The Moon is thy sweet smile - This saying means there is a certain stage of consciousness (*prabodhā*) which gives the highest bliss and which should be known from a teacher alone.

243. *Chārucandrakalādharā* - चारुचन्द्रकलाधरा

(i) One who is wearing a comely crescent moon in **Her** crown.

(ii) The word *Chāru* means neither waxing nor waning, *Chandrakalā*, is the everlasting. In that sense, **She** is the basis for the *Chandrakala*.

(iii) This name is interpreted based on a story told in *Devee Bhāgavatham* (3rd chapter). A king of Kāsi had a daughter by name *Sashikalā* or *Chandrakala*. In her dream *Śreedevee* appeared and told her to marry a prince by name *Sudarsana* who was **Her** devotee. Accordingly they got married and lived happily for a long time. *Śreedevee* was the cause of the happiness of the princess, *Chandrakala*.

244. ***Charācharajagannāthā* - चराचरजगन्नाथा**

(i) One who is the ruler of the world full of animate and inanimate things.
(ii) This world is dynamic a one. Similarly it has a character of in animation also. **She** is the head of both the forms.

245. ***Chakrarājaniketanā* - चक्रराजनिकेतना**

(i) One who is abiding in the *Śree Chakra* itself.
(ii) *Śree Chakra* is called *Chakra Rāja* (king of all chakras), since it has all the nine *chakras* beginning with *Trailokyamohana* till *Sarvānanda-mayā* in it. **She** dwells in it alongwith all her attendants.

246. ***Pārvatee* - पार्वती**

(i) The daughter of Mount *Himavān*, the king of all mountains (*Parvata Rāja*). Also called as *Shailendrathanayā* (634th name).

247. ***Padmanayanā* - पद्मनयना**

(i) One whose eyes are like lotus.

248. ***Padmarāgasamaprabhā* - पद्मरागसमप्रभा**
(i) One who shines like ruby.
(ii) *Padma* - lotus – **Her** lustre is comparable to the red colour of lotus.

249. ***Panchapretāsanāseenā* - पन्चप्रेतासनासीना**

(i) One who has her seat formed of five corpses.
(ii) The five forms of *Shiva* as *Brahma*, *Viṣhŋu*, *Rudra*, *Esānā* and *Sadāshivā* appeared from *Brahmam*. They, as per the order of *Śreedevee*, do the 5 tasks respectively of creation, protection, destruction, *thirodhānā* and *anugraha*. During the destruction of the universe (*mahāpralayā*) they are relieved from their respective duties and merge with *Śreedevee*. That is, *Sadāshiva* becomes the sitting plank and the four others become the four legs of the seat. Since they deprived of their power, they are called as corpses. *Pra* + *Ita* – the one that has started from the place of dwelling to other

place.

(iii) The above five have respective *Shaktis* such as *Vāmā, Gyeshtā, Roudhree*, etc. Since they are deprived of their *Shaktis*, they are individually incapable of action and hence corpses.

(iv) *Paramashivā*, who is the sitting plank, is the 25th *tatva* above all. When *Shakti* unites with him it becomes the 26th *Sādākya tatva*. This is the *Sāmarasya* form of *Shakti* and *Paramashiva*. They are an integrated form without any difference.

(v) This can be compared with 947th name - *Panchapreta Manchadhisāyinee*.

250. *Panchabrahmasvaroopiŋee* - पञ्चब्रह्मस्वरूपिणी

(i) One who has the five *Brahmams* as her form.

(ii) *Brahma, Vişhŋu, Rudra, Esānā* and *Paramashivā*, mentioned in the previous name, are also called as five *Brahmams*. **She** is in the form of these five, who form **Her** seat.

(iii) The five faces of Lord *Parameshwarā - Esāna, Tatpurusha, Aghora, Vāmadeva* and *Sadyojāta* are also called as five *Brahmams*. **She** is in the form of these five.

(iv) The soul, nature, intellect, ego and mind are all forms of *Brahmam*. **She** is in these five forms also.

(v) The *Garuḍa Purāŋā* says that *Vişhŋu* has five forms namely, *Nārāyaŋā, Vāsudeva, Pradyumna, Aniruddha* and *Sankarshana*. **She** is in these five forms also.

(vi) One other philosophy is that *Śreedevee* is in the form of anything, which has five elements.

251. *Chinmayee* - चिन्मयी

(i) One who is in the form of *chit* (pure consciousness itself).

(ii) *Chit* – knowledge. **She** is in the form of knowledge itself. That is, pure knowledge without the distinction of the knower, the known and the intellect.

252. *Paramānandā* - परमानन्दा

(i) One who is the Supreme Bliss.

(ii) The complete contended form. Hence *Paramānanda*. Nothing greater or bigger than this.

253. *Vigyānaghanaroopiṇee* - विर्ज्ञानघनरूपिणी

(i) One who is wisdom personified.
(ii) She is the essence of consciousness.
(iii) The soul (*Vigyānā* reflecting in intellect) is in the form of self. Remaining in *Vijnana* is explained as mass or aggregate of souls. *Śreedevee* is in that form. *Hiraṇyagarbha* is the synthesis of the aggregate of the souls. **She** is in his form.

254. *Dhyānadhyātrudhyeyaroopā* - ध्यानध्यातृध्येयरूपा

(i) One who is in all the three forms - meditation, the meditator and the objector meditation.
(ii) Meditation implies the understanding of the mind. That is, understanding *Śreedevee*, imagined by the mind and merging in that form is called meditation. This is also a threesome like knowledge. *Śreedevee* is in the form of this threesome.

255. *Dharmādharmavivarjitā* - धर्माधर्मविवर्जिता

(i) One who is devoid of both virtue and vices.
(ii) The word *Dharma* has lot of meanings. In general it indicates virtues. The opposite *Adharma* indicates vices. In this context *dharma* cannot be taken only as virtues. Because something good for one person or in one state could be bad for other person or in other state. The ultimate decision here is only *veda*. These are rules or laws to conduct the human in virtue path. These will never bind *Śreedevee*. **She** only created all these rules.
(iii) *Dharma* indicates a sort of limit or restrains. That is, the controls for the caste, religion and other *āshramās* respectively are called *dharma*. If these are broken, it is *adharma*. In this context also, **She** is not bound by these distinctions. Hence *Śreedevee* is beyond *dharma* and *adharma*.
(iv) *Dharma* is a quality or character. For instance to be hot is a character, hence *dharma*. One who has a character is called *dharmee*. If the fire loses its character of heat then it is *adharma* (In *Rāmāyana*, Sita requests [not orders] fire to be cool with *Hanumān – sheeto bhava hanumata*: - hence it was cool).. If one loses its character it is *adharma*. *Śreedevee* is not bound by any character and hence **She** does not have *dharma* or *adharma*.

(v) *Dharma* also means bondage. The soul is bound by various bondages like husband, wife, son, friend, etc. Each relationship is cramming the soul with different bondages. Being without these bondages or getting relieved of them is called liberation, hence it is *adharma*. *Śreedevee* is beyond bondages or relief from them.

(vi) *Dharma* is a quality or character. A *dharmee* is with this. Hence **She** can be called also as *adharmee*. *Śreedevee* is without any quality or attachment to it.

(vii) *Dharma* indicates that letter of *Shakti* and *adharma* that of *Shiva.* In the letters of *Panchadashākksharee mantra* the three *'K'*s and two *'HA'*s indicate *Shiva* letters. The letters *'A'*, *'E'* and three *'L'*s indicate *Shakti* letters. The three *'HREEM'*s are that of united *Shakti* and *Shiva*. This is indicated in the results part of *Lalitā Trishatee*. The same has also been mentioned by *Śree BhāskaraRāya* in his *Varivasyā rahasyam*. The word *Vivarjitā* means to grow. The inherent meaning is that because of the letters in the form *Shiva* and *Shakti* the *Panchadashākksharee* is completely grown.

256. *Vishvaroopā* - विश्वरूपा

(i) One who is in the form of the world or *Vishvan*. Since *Śreedevee* (*Brahmam*) thought "I will take various forms", this world was formed. Hence *Śreedevee* is in the form of this world itself.

(ii) The soul is also called as *Pashu*. *Sva* means dog, the lowest kind of form, comparable to that of a dog. Since the soul worships *Śreedevee* it is released from *svaroopa*. The *roopā* becomes *vikatham*, *Śreedevee* is called as *Vishvaroopa*.

(iii) In the order of creation, i.e. in the formation of all the *tatvās* from nature (*prakrutee*) till universe (*prithivee*), it has been mentioned that all the subtle *tatvās* one above the other merges with nature. The creation, from the *Brahmam* the first manifestation is darkness (*tamas*), the next is that of intellect called *mahat*, then that of the soul threefold egotism (*ahamkārā*), followed by the five subtle elements beginning with sound; among these are the five energies of knowledge and the five energies of action, in these energies the former five individually generate the five senses and collectively the *antahkkaraṇa*. The latter five generate individually the five organs of action and collectively the *prānās*. The sound and the others four subtle forces generate the five gross elements. This is an established doctrine. There the *chaitanya* manifested through the gross, subtle and causal vehicles respectively termed, *Vishva*, *Taijasā* and *Prāgnā*; these manifested ones (three groups of vehicles) respectively are turned *Vaisvānara*, *Hiraŋyagarbha* and *Eshvara*. Among this *Vishvā* is in awaken (*Jāgrath*) state, *Taijasā* in the dream (*Swapna*) state and *Prāgnā* in the deep sleep *state* (*Sushupti*). In *Vedantha* the three states are awaken, dream and deep sleep; *Vishva*, *Taijasā* and *Prāgnā* in those states as forms of soul and creation, protection and destruction as the three tasks; are only accepted. In *Tantra sāstrās* two more states swoon (*Thureeyam*) and transcendental (*Thureeyātheetham*); material pleasure & displeasure (*Tiroḍhāna*) and blessings (*Anugraha*) are two more tasks. Since in the deep sleep state the soul does not completely merge with *Brahmam*, two more states as material pleasure and displeasure and blessings are added. During deep sleep the soul is with the causal body and in the swoon state the soul takes the subtle body, it mixes completely with *Brahmam* in the transcendental state. Each of these states is being mentioned as names of *Śreedevee* above.

(iv) Each night of the fifteen days of bright half of lunar month has a different name as; 1. *Darsa* 2. *Drshtā*, 3. *Darsathā* 4. *Vishvaroopā*. 5. *Sudarsanā*; 6. *Apyāyamānā*, 7. *Pyāyamānā*, 8. *Apyāyā* 9. *Soonrtā*. 10.*Irā*, 11. *Apooryamānā* 12. *Pooryamānā* 13. *Poorāyantee* 14. *Poorŋā* and 15. *Pourŋamāsi*. Out of these **She** is in the form of 14th day.

(v) These 15 days are the 15 letters in the *Panchadashee*. Out of these **She** is in the form of the 4th letter *'La'*.

(vi) The day time of dark half of lunar month is 15. They start from the last seed till first one. Out of these the 5th day's *Nityā* is *Vishvaroopam* and the corresponding letter is *'LA'*. Thus **She** is the in the form of day time during dark half and night time during bright half of lunar month.

(vii) *Śree Ādi Śaṇkara* in his commentary of *Vişhŋu Sahasranāma* for the 717th name – *Vishvamoorthi*: – He is this world and its form since everything is himself. First name *Vishvā* can also be compared– this has been interpreted elaborately. Some of the main points are;

1. Since he is the cause for this world called *Vishvam*, *Brahmam* is called *Vishvam*.
2. This *Vishvam* is not something different from *Paramapurusha*. Hence *Brahmam* is called as *Vishvam*.
3. Since it pierces in, *Brahmam* is called as *Vishvam*.
4. The word *Vishvam* indicates *'Om'*.

257. *Jāgariṇee* - जागरिणी

(i) One who is in waking state of the soul.
(ii) *Jāgram* means to awake. *Jāgariṇee* – the soul being in conscious state. Her name at this state is *Vishvaroopa*. This *Vishvaroopā* is the state of the soul in the conscious state. Hence **She** is *Jāgariṇee*.

258. *Svapantee* - स्वपन्ती

(i) One who is in the dreaming state of the body fond of soul in a subtle form.

259. *Taijasātmikā* - तैजसात्मिका

(i) *Śreedevee* is in the state of dream wherein the name of the soul is *Taijasan*.
(ii) *Taijasā* is called *Hiranygarbha* in the collective form of the souls. **She** is in that form.

260. *Suptā* - सुप्ता

(i) *Śreedevee* is in the state of sleep of the soul.

261. *Pragyātmikā* - प्रज्ञात्मिका

(i) The soul fond of the body, when in deep sleep state is called *Prāgyan*. She is in that form.
(ii) In the deep sleep state, there are three different experiences. Knowing nothing (*Agnānam* - ignorant), *Ahamtā* – the thought that I am different and happy (*Sukhā*) – To say after getting up - I had a good sleep, I do not know anything. In this state he gets the name *Prāgyan*. This form is also *Śreedevee*. The same in a collective form of all the souls is called *Eshwara*. **She** is in that form also.

262. *Turyā* - तुर्या

(i) One who is the soul in the fourth state (state of ecstasy).
(ii) *Shuddhavidyā* philosophy is to clearly understand the three states

awaken, dream and deep sleep and distinguish the differences between the souls in each of these states *Vishva*, *Taijasā* and *Prājna*. Such an understanding state is called the fourth state or *Tureeya*. Hence *Śreedevee* also acquires that name.

(iii) The bliss obtained in the fourth state makes the enjoyer feels that this is the true state and other three are not. The soul which has reached this state still has the other states, based on the worldly trends. But, still he would not be affected by those.

(iv) The state mentioned in *Vedas* - *Shiva matvaitam Chaturttam Manyante* is called *Tureeya*.

(v) The *Tripura Siddhānta* says, as **she** presented herself to *Turiyānandanātha* (a certain teacher) *Śreedevee* is known by the name *Tureeya*.

Tureeyānanda Nathasya Prasannatvādh Varānane I
Turyeti Nāma Vikyātam Tasya Devyānirantaram II

(vi) It is mentioned in *Soundaryalaharee* as; as the *Sadāshiva* form is above *Brahma*, *Vişhŋu* and *Rudra* – the fourth form *Mahāmāyā* is above the three forms *Saraswathee*, *Lakshmee* and *Pārvathee*.

263. *Sarvāvasthāvivarjitā* - सर्वावस्थाविवर्जिता

(i) One who is devoid of all states.

(ii) It was mentioned that in addition to the three states, the fourth state is called swoon (*Thureeyam*). Beyond this state is transcen-dental (*Thureeyatheetham*). It is not called as a state. This is transcendental – beyond the fourth state. Since by crossing all the four states the soul merges with the Supreme being, *Śreedevee*, there is no state for it. Further in this state there is nothing like individual or collective forms.

(iii) This state – even if this is not correct – because this is not a state – this is not the fifth one – this is unexplainable. Beyond comprehension by the mind and speech. To be understood only by experience. *Bhāskararāya*'s *Varivasyā Rahasyam* states;

Ānandaikaghanastvamya Dvāchāmapi I
Nagocharon Roonām Tuyādheedhāvasthā II

264. *Srushţikartree* - सृष्टिकर्त्री

(i) One who does the task of creation.

(ii) Creation is the function of *Eshvarā* when the rajas quality predominates. To distinguish the forms like *Brahma* from supreme-being is an illusion (*Māyā*).

265. *Brahmaroopā* - ब्रह्मरूपा

(i) One who is in the form of *Brahma*.
(ii) *Brahma*, who takes care of the creation task, is the distinguished form of *Śreedevee* created by illusion (*Māyā*).

266. *Goptree* - गोप्त्री

(i) One who does the task of protector.
(ii) *Śreedevee* takes up the protection function to sustain the created universe – when **Her** *satva* quality predominates.

267. *Govindaroopiṇee* - गोविन्दरूपिणी

(i) One who is the in the form of *Govinda* that is, *Viṣhṇu*.
(ii) The protector of the universe *Viṣhṇu*, who predominantly has *Satva* character, is also *Śreedevee* only.
(iii) *Go* – speech. *Govinda* - who can be understood by it (speech). The supreme being is beyond reach by speech. Since *Govinda* has taken the protection task, once he hears the crying of the soul, he immediately appears to him.
(iv) *Go* – earth. Once the creation of the universe is complete the earth, on account of overweight it became unstable and started to submerge in the water. *Viṣhṇu* bore it. Also when *Hiranyāksha*, the demon, seized the earth *Viṣhṇu* only protected it from him. Hence among all the names of *Viṣhṇu*, the name *Govinda* stresses the task of protection. *Śreedevee* herself is in the form of *Govinda*.
(v) *Śree Ādi Śaṇkara* in his commentary of *Viṣhṇu Sahasranāma* mentions for the 187th name – *Govinda*;
  1. Since he bore and takes out the earth that is being destructed, he is *Govinda*.
  2. Head of cows.
  3. One who makes speech to him. 539th name *Govinda*:
  4. One who can be reached through languages (*Gobhi:*)
  5. One who understands the souls through the statements of *Vedānta*.

268. *Samhāriņee* - संहारिणी

(i) One who is does the task of destruction (*Samhārā*).
(ii) Destruction of the universe by reducing into atoms is the third task. This is the function of *Śreedevee* in the form *Esvarā* when the *tamas* quality predominates. Hence **She** is *Samhāriņee*.

269. *Rudraroopā* - रुद्ररूपा

(i) One who is the in the form of *Rudra*.
(ii) The form of *Śreedevee* when the *tamas* quality dominates is called *Rudra*. This destroys the world. *Rudra*, who drives away sorrow; because of the *samsārā* cycle. *Rujam* – sorrow. *Drāvayati* – removes. *Rotayati* means to make other cry. The separation on account of destruction makes others cry. Hence *Rudran*.
(iii) Sun is also called as *Rudra*. During great dissolution Sun rises and burns the entire world. On account of this torridly rains and world submerges in the waters.
(iv) To start with he originated from the forehead of Brahma. He wept loudly and fearfully; because he wept, he is called the weeper(*Rudra*).

270. *Tirodhānakaree* - तिरोधानकरी

(i) One who is the cause of the disappearance of all.
(ii) *Tirodhāna*, complete destruction, that is, the absorption of even the atoms into finer atoms and integrating ego, intelligence and intellect and integrating that with the nature – in the order in which the universe originated. *Śreedevee* does this in this form.
(iii) *Tiraskariņee* is the name of one of associates of *Śreedevee*. **She** is in that form. *Tiraskariņee* – One who hides her form for those who do not have devotion.

271. *Eeshvaree* - ईश्वरी

(i) One who is in the form of *Ěshwar*.
(ii) One who does the fourth task called *Tirodhāna* is *Ěshwar*, completely in the form *satva* quality. *Śreedevee* is in this form.
(iii) The quality of *Eshvara* is Lordship, activity, independence, conscious ness, etc. Since *Śreedevee* is with all these qualities, **She** is called

Ĕshwari.

(iv) *Śree Ādi Śaņkara* in his commentary of *Vişhŋu Sahasranāma* for the 36th name – *Ĕshwara*: mentions; one who has all the wealth without being affected by any type of sorrows (natural rule).

272. *Sadāshivā* - सदाशिवा

(i) One who is in the form of *Sadāshiva.*
(ii) *Sadā* – always. *Shivā* – in auspicious form.
(iii) *Śreedevee,* taking the form of *Sadāshivā* does the fifth task called *Anugraha.*

273. *Anugrahadā* - अनुग्रहदा

(i) One who confers blessings.
(ii) As described earlier, to re-create the *Tirodhāna* world, after complete annihilation, the universe again assumes the form of the primordial atoms and the process is called *Anugraha*. This is the function of *Śreedevee* in the form of *Paramashiva.*
(iii) *Tirodhāna* and *Anugraha*, means respectively bondage and release. In this meaning *Eshwara* and *Paramashivā* who are respectively the external and the internal manifestations, are the causes of bondage and release. *Śreedevee* in those forms gets two names.
(iv) The state of *Eshwarā*, who does *Tirodhāna*, has powers to function within some prescribed laws. *Eshwarā* does the functions which are externally seen by all – *Bahirunmesha Lakshaŋan.*
(v) *Sadāshiva n* shows so much compassion on the souls, so that they do not suffer a lot. His quality is not known to others, but he has so much empathy. Hence his function is not known to others, *Antarunmesha Lakshaŋan*. Both these are forms of *Śreedevee* only.

274. *Panchakrutyaparāyaŋā* - पन्चकृत्यपरायणा

(i) One who is devoted to the five functions mentioned earlier.
(ii) **She** has much interest and involvement in all the five tasks.
(iii) It can also be interpreted that all the five functions depend on **Her**.
(iv) The five functions viz. creation, protection, destruction, annihila- tion and causing their appearance of the universe are that of *Brahma, Vişhŋu, Rudra, Eshwara* and *Paramashiva.* These five are different forms or *Shaktis* of that of *Śreedevee* only.

(v) The officials of these five functions carry out their tasks with the permission of *Śreedevee* only. It is **Her** order to make them do these functions. *Soundaryalaharee* says that She issues those orders just by twinkling her eye-brows for a micro second;

Jagatsoote Dhātā Hari Ravati Rudra: Kshapayat I
Tiraskurvannetatsvamapivapureecha: Stakayat II
Sadāpoorva: Sarvam Tadidam Anugrun Hāticha Shiva :
Tavāgyām Ālambaya Kshanachalitayo: Bhroolatikayo: II

275. *Bhānumaṇḍalamadhyasthā* - भानुमन्डलमध्यस्था

(i) One who is in the midst of the solar orbit.
(ii) It is a method of worshipping *Śreedevee* meditating upon **Her** in the Sun's disc.

Soorya Maṇḍala Madyasththām Deveem Tripurasundareem I
Pāsānguchadhanurbānān Tārāyanteem Sivām Bhaje II

(iii) It is said that the golden man seen within the Sun etc., is the supreme Lord *Parameshwarā*; *Ya Esho Antarāditye Hiranmaya: Purusho Rudtāte*. This name indicates that *Śreedevee* is in that form.
(iv) It is also described that *Bhānumaṇḍala* is the *Anāhatachakra*. *Śreedevee* is in the form of *Kunḍalinee* there.

276. *Bhairavee* - भैटबी

(i) The consort of *Bhairava*.
(ii) Since *Bhairavā* does the three functions, he is in terrific form. **She** is his energy.
(iii) It is a natural quality of ladies to get scared. *Bheeru* – woman. All women taken collectively are called *Bhairavam*. Since **She** is in that form, *Bhairavee*.
(iv) In the eighth *Āvarana Devatā Tripurāmbā Chakresvaree mantra*, in the middle division, when *'R'* is eliminated, it is known as *Bhairavee mantra*. *Śreedevee* is in that form.
(v) A girl of twelve years old is worshipped in the name of *Bhairavee*.

277. *Bhagamālinee* - भगमालिनी

(i) One who is in the form of *Bhagamālinee*.
(ii) The word *Bhaga* has various meanings – beauty, desire, detachment, discrimination, dispassion, effort, excellence, fame, glory, liberation,

lordliness, magnanimity, power, prosperity, omniscience, righteousness, supremacy, Sun, trying, wisdom, womb, worldly concerns, etc. *Śreedevee* is possessor of all these qualities and hence *Bhagamālinee*.

(iii) Conventionally it is the practice, to call those who have the male emblem (*Lingā*) are the manifestation of *Shiva* ; and those having the female emblem (*Bhagā*) are the manifestation of *Śreedevee*.

(iv) The *thithi Nityā Devee* pertaining to the second day of bright lunar half month and the 14th day of dark lunar half month is *Bhagamālinee*.

(v) One among the three in the eighth *Āvarana Devatās*.

278. *Padmāsanā* - पद्मासना

(i) One who has lotus flower as **Her** seat.

(ii) *Brahma*, *Saraswathee* and *Lakshmee* have the lotus flower as their seats. *Śreedevee* is in the all these three forms and hence *Padmāsana*.

(iii) The lotus flower has the nature (*prakruti*) as leaves, the categories (*vikruti*) as filaments and knowledge as the stalk. *Śreedevee* has such a flower as **Her** seat.

(iv) *Padmāsanā* is a sitting of posture as per *yoga sāstra*. **She** is in that form.

(v) **She** distributes the wealth (*Padmā* or *Lakshmee*) to her devotees.

Asoubhāgyam Datte Parama Sukhbhogāspadamayam
Vichitram Tatgeham Bhavati Prutu Kārtasvābrootam I
Nivishta: *Palyankesa Kalayati Kāntārataranam*
Prasadam Kopam Vā Janani Bhavateeyatra Kurute II

(By splitting the words in this verse, one can feel the blessings and anger of *Śreedevee* and the corresponding results).

(vi) *Padma* - the demon *Soorapadma* - the slayer of that demon.

(vii) *Padma* - the *bindu*. **She** is seated on this.

279. *Bhagavatee* - भगवती

(i) One who is with prosperity i.e. the power of *Ĕshwara*.

(ii) The meanings of the word *Bhaga* was detailed in previous names. *Śreedevee* has all those qualities without any shortage.

(iii) As **She** knows the origin and dissolution, the going and coming of beings, knowledge and ignorance, **She** is called *Bhagavatee*.

(iv) *Śree Ādi Śaṇkara* in his commentary of *Viṣhŋu Sahasranāma* for the 558th name – *Bhagavān* – *Bhaga* means complete wealth, charity, fame, liberation, etc. He has all these and hence *Bhagavān*; or he knows everything about the living beings like birth, death, destruction, movement, knowledge, ignorance, etc., hence *Bhagavān*.

280. *Padmanābhasahodaree* - पद्मनाभसहोदरी

(i) One who is a sister of *Viṣhŋu* (*Padmanābhā*).

(ii) *Viṣhŋu* created Lotus from his naval button and hence *Padmanabhan*. As per *Mārkaŋḑeya Purāŋā*, *Śreedevee* created three pairs of twins as per **Her** desire. The three pairs of brother-sisters are *Brahma* & *Lakshmee* in gold colour, *Viṣhŋu* & *Śreedevee* in blue colour and *Shiva* & *Saraswathi* in white colour. Their colours respectively indicate the three qualities (*Guŋas*). As per this Hindu mythology *Viṣhŋu* and *Śreedevee* are siblings.

(iii) Similarly *Brahma Purāŋā*, in the *Purusottamakshetra Mahātmya* says, *Pārvati*, who was born from the womb of *Menakā*, wife of *Himavān* in a former birth, in the next birth is born as *Subhadrā*, sister of *Śree Kriṣhŋa* in the womb of *Devaki*.

(iv) Again we read *Kātyāyaneeti Yā Jātā Kamsa Shatros Sahodaree*.

(v) In another place, *Śreedevee* alongwith **Her** brother *Śree Viṣhŋu* appeared to *Brahma*, the grandsire of all the worlds, who once performed a severe penance in the sacred Kānchi. A special interpretation – *Śree BhāskaraRāya* has explained in many a place that each letter of this *Sahasranāmā* is a root letter of a *mantra*. Accordingly the three names *Padmāsanā*, *Bhagavatee* and *Padmanabha Sahodaree* explain the five letters of the *Vāgbhava* (first) division of *Panchadashee mantra*. This is the inherent meaning.

281. *Unmeshanimishotpannavipannabhuvanāvalee*– उन्मेषनिमिषोत्पन्नविपन्नभुवनावली

(i) One who makes this world arise and disappear with the opening and shutting of **Her** eyes.

(ii) Is it correct to say opening and closing of eyes relating to *Śreedevee*, since *Devas* do not blink their eyes? *Śreedevee* cannot be treated as belonging one race called *Devas*. Hence, the expression "opening and shutting" refer to the influence of the destiny of beings.

(iii) The expression also means, **She** does the task of creation with so much ease, just by blinking **Her** eyes.

(iv) *Śree Ādi Śaṇkara*, in his *Soundaryalaharee* (55th verse),describes the same meaning with different interpretation as; if *Śreedevee* closes **Her** eyes the entire world will be destroyed and hence **She** never closes **Her** eyes –

Nimeshonmeshabhyām Pralayamudhayam Yāti Jagati
Tavetyāhoossantodharaŋidhara Rājanyatanaye I
Tvatunbheshājjātam Jagadidamshesham Pralayata:
Paritrātum Sanke Parihruta Nimeshāstavadrcha: II

282. *Sahasrasheershavadanā* - सहस्रशीर्षवदना

(i) One who has countless heads and other organs.

(ii) The word *Sahasra* means infinite or countless.

(iii) It is opt to remind ourselves the *Vishwaroopa Darshanam* (cosmic form) of Lord *Krişhŋa* in *Śreemad Bhagavat Geeta* (XIII – 13);

Sarvata: *Pānipādam Tatsarvatokshidhiromukham* I
Sarvata: *Srutimlloke Sarvamāvrutya Tishtati* II

283. *Sahasrākshee* - सहस्राक्षी

(i) One who has countless eyes.

(ii) The same meaning is conveyed for the 226th name – *Saharāksha*: in *Vişhŋu Sahasranāma*.

284. *Sahasrapāt* - सहस्रपात

(i) One who has countless feet.

(ii) The same meaning is said for the 227th name – *Sahasrapāth* in *Vişhŋu Sahasranāma*. From 281st to this name, the second and third divisions of *Panchadashee mantra* are established.

285. *Ābrahmakeeţajananee* - आब्रह्मकीटजननी

(i) One who is the mother of all from *Brahma* onwards till a worm.

(ii) *Brahma*, was the first one to be created by *Śreedevee* in the form of creation. He created the other beings. *Keeţa* - the small insect eater of spider's web – a micro worm; **She** gave birth to all these beings.

(iii) It is indicated as, though there is a huge difference between a worm and *Brahma*, as a mother **She** has equal affection with all.

286. ***Varŋāshramavidhāyinee*** **- वर्णाश्रमविधायिनी**

(i) One who established the social divisions and castes.

(ii) After creating all from *Brahma* to worms, **She** created the *Vedas*, which are her own commands, in order to lead the created beings into the right path. The *Vedas* are divided into two parts, the *Karma Kānḍa* and *Gnana Kānḍa* ; as according to the rule, the *Devas* and lower animals have no share in the *Karma Kānḍa,* the (divine) mother established righteousness (*dharma*) through *karma Kānḍa* after dividing human beings into four castes and four orders.

(iii) These details are explained in *Koorma Purāŋa*; *Devee*, the life of the universe having heard his words, remembering her husband (*Shiva*) answered her father with a smile. Oh Lord of Mountains, hear from me this doctrine, which is supreme, secret, known to *Eshvara* only, practiced by *Brahmavādins* alone... describing the means of attaining... by meditation, *Karma Yoga*, devotion and wisdom, Oh Lord of Mountains, this is to be attained by these means, not by crores of other actions (*karmās*); thus concluding again she says in order to describe Karma Yoga...*Karmā* is ordained by *Sruti*s and Smrutis according to castes and orders; always perform this action associated with the knowledge of the Self, for the sake of liberation. Devotion arises from righteousness (*dharma*), by devotion, the supreme is attained.

Srutismrutyuktam Samyak Karma Varŋāsra Mātmakam I
Adyātma Gnana Sahitam Muktaye Satatam Kuru II
Darmātsanjāyate Bhakti: *Bhaktyāsangyāyate Param* I
Srutismrutibhyām Utitodharmo Yāgyadiko Mata: II
Nānyatogyāyatedharma: *Vedatdharmohi Nippapou* I
Tasmān Mumukshurdharmārttam Matroopam Vedamashrayet II
Madāgyaiva Guptyarttam Vedānām Bagavānaja: I
Brahmaŋateen Sasarjatasvesvekarmanyayojayat II

287. ***Nijāgyāroopanigamā*** **- निजार्ज्ञारूपनिगमा**

(i) One who has the *Vedas* as the expressions of **Her** commands.

(ii) *Veda* statements command human beings with the do's and don'ts in this life what set forth the object to be attained, the means and the practical directions. These commands limit the social divisions and castes. These *Vedas* originated from *Śreedevee*.

(iii) The same meaning is said in *Koorma Purāŋā* as; the ancient and supreme energy called *Vedas*, which are my commandments, are manifested at the beginning of creation in the form of *Rig Yajus* and *Sāman*;

Mamaivākgyā Parāshakti: *Veda Samgyā Purādanee* I
Rigyajussāma Roopena Sargadou Sampravarttate II

288. *Puŋyāpuŋyaphalapradā* – पुण्यापुण्यफलप्रदा

(i) One who is the dispenser of fruits of righteous as well as evil actions (sins).

(ii) As mentioned in the previous name, *Śreedevee* decides the fruits of the good and bad results arising from ordained and prohibited actions respectively.

(iii) It is mentioned as *Puŋya* (righteous) and *Apuŋya* (unrighteous) and not as *Puŋya* (righteous) and *Pāpa* (sins). Unrighteous is something looking like righteous. It is quiet natural to do the unrighteous deeds thinking as righteous on account of ignorance or ego. *Śreedevee* directly confers the results of righteous and unrighteous actions.

289. *Srutiseemantasindoorikrutapādābjadhoolikā* – श्रुतिसीमन्तसिन्दूरीकृतपादाब्जधूलिका

(i) One who has the dust of **Her** lotus feet forming the vermilion mark on the parting of the hair on the head of the *Vedas*, personified as ladies.

(ii) This is a great metaphor. The ladies in the form of *Vedas* bow to the feet of *Śreedevee*. Thus the dust in the feet of *Śreedevee* sticks to the head of the ladies (*Vedas*). *Śreedevee*'s feet are decorated with red cotton paste (*mehandi* or henna) and hence the dust is also red in colour. This red colour sticks to the parting of the hair and the meeting point of the forehead and the parting of the hair becomes red.

(iii) It is a must for the auspicious ladies to wear *kumkum* at the forehead (start of the parting of the hair). That is the reason they are called *Seemunthinee*. The word *Sruti* (*Vedas*) is also of feminine gender. Hence this metaphor is very apt.

(iv) *Upanishads* are treated as the head of *Vedas*. These are *Gnana Kānḍa*, which teaches the *Brahmam*. The earlier names *Varŋā-shramavidhāyinee*, *Nijāgyāroopanigamā* and *Puŋyāpuŋya-phlapradā* relate the *karma Kānḍa.* This name relates to *Gnana Kānḍa*. Hence to indicate the *Brahmam*, *Upanishads* are considered.

(v) Even the *Upanishads* are unable to explain the real *Brahmam*, by direct assertions or by complete definition. It is described as this is not, this is not, etc. Hence the word dust is used. The dust in the lotus feet of *Śreedevee* means that the *Vedas* are unable to explain the real form of Devee by direct assertions, by complete definition, describe **Her** by the method of negation, like one ashamed and afraid, standing afar, describing inadequately, that (description also) creates no clear idea as to "this or that". By the word dust, it is described here the iota of knowledge about *Brahmam*, one can get by adoring *Śreedevee*.

(vi) The grandeur of the dust in the feet of *Śreedevee* has been specially mentioned in 2nd verse starting with *Thaneeyāmsampāmsum* in *Soundaryalaharee*.

290. ***Sakalāgamasandohashaktisampuṭamouktikā* – सकलागमसंदोहशुक्तिसंपुटमौक्तिका**

(i) One who has the pearl (composing nose stud) enclosed in a shell (composed) of the collected scriptures and all *Vedas*.

(ii) The sacred doctrines and scriptures, originated from *Vedas*, are indicated as a shell. The pearl in that shell is compared to the nose stud of *Śreedevee*.

(iii) *Vedas* themselves could not describe *Brahmam* completely, then the sacred doctrines also cannot describe. Hence by comparing it to the nose stud of *Śreedevee*, it has been explained in a hidden way.

(iv) It is also apt to interpret that *Śreedevee* herself is the pearl in the shell.

(v) By the previous name it is indicated by the word *Veda* (*Sruti*) that **She** is to be worshipped by the first three castes viz. Brahmins (who learn and teach *Vedas*), *Kshatriya* (kings) and *Vysya* (business people). This name indicates (since it is mentioned as *Sakalāgama*) that **She** can be worshipped by all. *Rudrayāmalam* says - The abode indicated by the *Vedas* is also indicated by other scriptures; hence all *Brāhmanās*, *Kshatriyās*, *Vaisyās* and *Sudras* are fit to worship;

Yatvedairgamyate Stānam Tat Tantrairapi Gamyate I

Brahma Kshatriya Vit Sudrāstena Sarvedikārina: II

(vi) The beauty of the pearl is clearly visible even within the shell. In the same way, the philosophy of *Śreedevee* is clearly indicated by the sacred doctrines.

291. *Purushārthapradā* - पुरुषार्थप्रदा

(i) One who bestows fourfold values of human desire.

(ii) The four objects of human desire are religious virtue, wealth, bliss and liberation. These are called *Purushārathās*. A human being can get all these four only by the blessings of *Śreedevee*.

(iii) The worship of the unconditioned *Brahmam* and the results thereof is with the blessings of *Śreedevee*'s alone.

292. *Poorŋā* - पूर्णा

(i) One who is the all-encompassing whole.

(ii) **She** is free from the limitation of time, place and circumstance. Hence *Śreedevee*, in the form of *Brahmam*, is fully omnipresent in everything and everywhere.

(iii) *Poorŋā* means the fifth, tenth and fifteenth *Nityā* deities. The fourteenth bright night is also called *Poorŋa*.

(iv) *Poorŋā* is also the name of a sacred river.

293. *Bhoginee* - भोगिनी

(i) One who is the enjoyer.

(ii) *Bhogā* means bliss. **She** enjoys it. **She** is the bliss and the enjoyer as well. *Veda* says *Annam Cha Brahma Aham Cha Brahma*.

(iii) The word *Bhogā* means the body of a snake. *Śreedevee* is in the form *Kunḍalinee* in energy in the human body as a female snake.

(iv) *Bhoginee* is the name of a female serpent (*Nāgakanyā*).

294. *Bhuvaneshvaree* - भुवनेश्वरी

(i) One who is the sovereign ruler of the universe comprising of fourteen worlds.

(ii) There are seven worlds beneath this earth viz., *Athalam*, *Vitalam*, *Sutalam*, *Talātalam*, *Mahātalam*, *Rasātalam* and *Patālam*. There are six worlds above the earth viz., *Bhuvarloka, Suvarloka, Mahālokā, Janolokā, Tapo Lokā* and *Sathya Loka*. These 13 alongwith earth are the 14 worlds. **She** steers these 14 worlds as per **Her** wish.

(iii) The word *Bhuvanā* has many meanings – earth, heaven, water, etc. **She** is the head of all these.

(iv) The *Māyābeeja, Hreem* is called *Bhuvaneshvaree beeja*. **She** is the presiding deity of this. The letter *'Ha'* indicates the sky, *'R'* indicates fire and *'E'* indicates water. Since **She** only created all these and originated this world, **She** is called *Bhvanesharee*.

(v) The word *Hreem*, has many meanings like *Hrullekā Beeja, Lajjā Beeja, Chintāmaṇi Beeja*, etc.

(vi) There are three divisions viz., *Divya, Sidda* and *Mānvaugha* in the lineage of teachers. In this, in the *Mānvaugha* division there was a teacher by name *Bhuvanānandanātha*. As per *Tripurasiddhānta*, since **She** appeared before and blessed him, **She** got the name *Bhuvaneshvaree*.

Bhuvanānanda Nāthasya Prasannatvāt Maheshvaree I
Bhuvaneshvareetivikhyātā Shambhavee Bhuvaneshvaree II

295. *Ambikā* - अंबिका

(i) One who is a great mother.

(ii) *Amma, Ambha* and *Ambikā* are the words used to call a mother with affection. Since *Śreedevee* is the mother of this entire universe, **She** is *Ambika*.

(iii) The word *Ambikā* means *Jaganmātā* (mother of the world), *Bhāratee* (the goddess of speech) and earth; also, *Ambikā* – form of *Rudran* - the aggregate of three *shaktis* – *Icchā* (desire), *gnāna* (knowledge) and *kriyā* (action). *Śreedevee* is in these forms.

(iv) *Ambikā* means night or sleep. *Śreedevee* in the form of night and sleep, as a mother hugs with affection and gives compulsory rest and peace. Only because of this rest and sleep, *Viṣhṇu* took the incarnation as *Hayagreevā* and through him we got this *Sahasranāma*. It can be compared to *Devee Mahātmyā* verse –

Yā Devee Sarva Bhooteshu Nidrā Roopena Samsthita.

296. *Anādinidhanā* - अनादिनिधना

(i) One who exists without a beginning or an end.

(ii) The Supreme Being has neither a beginning nor an end. On the other hand, the human being begins in the middle and ends in the middle. This name indicates a difference between humans and *Śreedevee*. This difference itself helps to deduce **Her**. I am with beginning and end, *Śreedevee* should be without these two.

(iii) The word *Nidhanā* indicates destruction. Anything that obstructs worshipping *Śreedevee* is called *Nidhana*. According to the systems of Vararuchi's *Kaṭapayādi* method of number notation, the word *Ādi* means eighty, (*da* = 8 and *na* or *a* = 0); hence she whose worship delivers a man from the eighty causes of death. These eighty are divided into two as 52 *Pāsa* and 28 *Vadha*.

(iv) The above *Vadha*, which is of three kinds; *ashakti*, *Tushṭi* and *siddhi* is the first obstacle to perfection. *Ashakti* is inability of the senses to receive their respective objects, defects caused by blindness, deafness, etc.; they are eleven because there are eleven senses – five sense organs, five organs for actions and mind.

(v) *Tushṭi* (elation) is a misleading form of happiness. An illusion that a man thinks – I am liberated by the absorption of mind, when he is far off from it (liberation is the final destination of worship).

(vi) This is nine fold; 1. *Prakruti* – nature is a matter. When the mind is attached to this, it is impossible to come out. This is called *Prakruti* elation. 2. The second is - when a man thinks that he has succeeded on merely wearing the robes of an ascetic, etc. This is called *upādāna* elation. 3. The third is when one says, what is the use of painful actions like meditation? Success will come with time; this is called *kāla* elation. 4. The fourth one is when one says, success will come by the intervention of *Śreedevee*; this is called *bhāgyā* (luck elation). 5-9. Trying to reach **Her** thorough the five sense organs and a kind of elation arises when after observing the disadvantages attached to the gratification of objectives senses, he ceases their pursuit. This is called *Indreeya Thushti* (organic elation). Thus are the nine elations.

(vii) In the same way there are eight kinds of *siddhis*. In the beginning of worship, the devotee gets some powers automatically; 1. *Ooha* (intuition) means understanding the meanings without being taught, by intuition. 2. *Shabda* (hearing), understanding the meaning by accidentally hearing the words. 3. *Adhyayana* (study), understanding the real meaning from the teaching of a teacher and thinking over it. 4.By having friendship with those who has understood *Śreedevee*'s philosophy. This is *Suhruda*. 5. *Sushrusha* is to get an opportunity to serve the teacher, ascetics and the learned. 6 to 8. The other three siddhis are the reverse of the three kinds of misery, concerning himself, concerning *Devas* and concerning the elements (*adhyātma, adhibhoota* and *ādhidaivata*). By gaining good friends, he attains *arthasiddhi*. Thus there are twenty-eight kinds of obstructions for the adoration of *Śreedevee*. Since **She** ensures that the devotees are not affected by these, **She** is *Anādinidhana*.

(viii) A *pāsa* is the one which creates obstruction in thought process and make the yoga impossible to get. There are fifty-two *pāsas*, arising from the knot of ignorance. These have been described in *Linga Purāŋa*.

297. *Haribrahmendrasevitā* - हरिब्रह्मेन्द्रसेविता

(i) One who is adored by *Hari, Brahma* and *Indra*.

(ii) In the *Śreecakra* (*nagara*), the *Chintāmaŋigraha* is the dwelling place of *Śreedevee*. Around this, between the seventeenth and the eighteenth walls, is the seat of *Vişhŋu*; between the sixteenth and the seventeenth, is of *Brahma*; between the fourteenth and the fifteenth, is of *Indra* and other *digpālas*. They all always meditate upon *Śreedevee*.

(iii) There is an opinion that though they are *Hari, Brahma, Indrā* and others, since they adore *Śreedevee*, **Her** devotees need not worship them. The same is opined by *Śree Ādi Śaṇkara*, in his *Sivānanda-lahar*ee about lord *Shiva* ;

Sahasram Vartante Jagativibudhā: *Kshudraphaladā*
Namanye Svapne Vā Tatanusaranam Tatkrutaphalam I
Haribrahādeenāmapi Nikata Bhājām Asulabham
Chiramyāche Sambho Shiva tavapadām Bhojabhajanam II

298. *Nārāyaŋee* - नारायणी

(i) One who is called as *Nārāyaŋee*.

(ii) The word *Nara* indicates *Brahmam*. The water is called *nāram*, because it emanated from *Nara* (*Brahmam*). Since *Vişhŋu* has water as abode (*ayana*), he is named *Nārāyaŋa*. *Nārāyaŋee* is related to him, i.e. his sister. It can also be taken as the word *Nārāyaŋā* indicates *Shiva*. In that case *Nārāyaŋee* is *Shiva*'s consort.

(iii) There is no difference between *Nārāyaŋa* and *Śreedevee*. In the form *Artthānaree*, *Śreedevee* is left half. In the form of *Śaṇkara nārāyaŋa*, *Nārāyaŋā* is the left half. Hence they both are one and the same.

(iv) *Naran* means the soul. The last abode of the souls is *Ayana*. Hence

Nārāyaŋa also indicates *Shiva.* **She** is the consort of *Shiva.*

(v) *Śree Ādi Śaņkara*, in his *Soundaryalaharee*, has mentioned that only by the blessings of *Śreedevee, Vişhŋu* took the incarnation as *Mohinee*, to distribute the nectar – *Haristvāmārādhya* (5th verse).

(vi) In this *Sahasranāma* itself the names *Govinda Roopiŋee, Mukundā* and *Vişhŋu Roopinee* indicate that there is no difference between *Vişhŋu* and *Śreedevee*.

(vii) According to the *Padma Purāŋā, Nārāyaŋee* is the name of the goddess worshipped in the sacred place of Supārsva; *Nārāyaŋee Supārsve Tu Trikooţe Padtasundaree.*

(viii) The *Nārāyaŋee stuti* in *Saptashatee* can be compared.

(ix) From the commentaries of *Śree Ādi Śaņkara* for *Vişhŋu Sahasranāma* for the 245th name *Nārāyaŋa*:

1. *Nara*: - soul; the sky and other things of action, originated from it, are called *Nārāyaŋee*. For those things of action, he is the cause and hence *Nārāyaŋee*. For him those are the dwelling places (*ayanā*) and hence *Nārāyaŋa*:
   Yachcha Kinchitjjagat Sarvam Drushyate Shrooyatepivā I
   Anthar Bahishcha Tat Sarvam Vyāpya Nārāyaŋa: *Stita*: II
   Narājjātāni Tatvāni Nārāneeti Tato Vitu: I
   Tānyeva Chāyanam Tasya Tena Nārāyaŋa: *Smruta*: II
2. *Nārānām* - During the great dissolution he is the place of refuge and hence *Nārāyaŋa*: - *Brahmavaivartta Purāŋā* says; *Yat Prāyantyapisamcishanti, Narānāmayanam Yasmāt Tasmān Nārāyaŋa*: *Smruta*:
3. One who has water as his dwelling –
   Āpo Nārā Iti Proktāpo Vai Narasoonava: I
   Tā Yatasyāyanam Poorvam Tasmānnārāyaŋa: *Smruta*: II

299. *Nādaroopā* - नादरूपा

(i) One who is in the form of sound.

(ii) There are four stages in the formation of sound viz.,

1. *Para* which finds manifestation only in *Prāna,*
2. *Pashyanti* which finds manifestation in the mind,
3. *Madhyama* which finds manifestation in the organs and
4. *Vaikharee* which finds manifestation in articulate expression.

All these four are found as names of *Śreedevee* in this *Sahasranāma*. The last stage *Vaikharee* is the form which we hear as sound. There are nine notes (*nadās*) between the third stage *Madhyama* and the fourth

Vaikharee; Avikrutam, Soonyam, Sparsam, Nātham, Dvani, Bindu, Shakti, Beejam and *Aksharam*. These are Samskrit letters *A, Ka, Cha, Ta, Tha, Pa, ya, Sha* and *La*. As a cause *nātham* is spread in all these. That *nātham* is *Śreedevee* herself.

(iii) In this sound, in the *beeja* like *Hreem*, the last half letter '*M*' sounds in an extended way. There are eight notes (*varŋas*) above the *bindu* of the syllable *hreem*, etc., such as *ardhacandra, rodhinee, nātha, nādānta, shakti, vyāpikā, samanā* and *unmaŋi*. Each of these will have different light forms and colours. These are clearly explained in *Varivasyā Rahasyā* by *Śree Bhāskara Rāya*. This name says that *Śreedevee* is in the form of third one *Nātha* in these eight. *Nātham* is in the form of suture with the luminosity like the red precious stone Zircon (Padparadscha – *Pushparāgā*).

300. *Nāmaroopavivarjitā* - नामरूपविवर्जिता

(i) One who has neither name nor form.

(ii) Everything in this world is identified only by name and form. She is without both. She cannot be indicated by name or form.

(iii) Everything created in this universe has identification in five forms viz. existence (*Asti*), knowledge (*Pāti*), bliss (affection – *priyam*), name (*nāmam*) and form (*roopam*). The first three indicate the relationship of Chit with this world as a matter. They are called *Chitgranthi*. The latter two, name and form are illusory and they are called *Achitgranthi*.

(iv) The details are:

1. *Asti* – existence – one who exists. The essence of *Brahmam* reflects in the feeling that 'I exist' (self). Thus all actions take place.
2. *Pāti* - knowledge – that could be understood by the knowledge. The chit part of *Brahmam* is 'I'. Only because every object reflects on this, it is understood by the mind.
3. *Priyam* - bliss – affection. Every living being has affection on self just because of the activities of this world. All the activities happen only because of the love on the things where the human being has affection.

   These three are permanent and route for activities.
4. *Nāmam* – name. It is not only the name given to us by others, it is also the feeling that "I am a man", "This is a horse", etc. This is in general applicable to all perceivable matters.

5. *Roopam* – form. Individual person or thing by form. The form is important for all activities.

She does not have name and form.

(v) Only the *Brahmam* is beyond name and form. Hence *Śreedevee* is the *Brahmam*.

Thus ends the fourth *Kalā* called *Marichi*.

*****

Section 5: *Jvālinee Kalā*

301. ***Hreemkāree* - ह्रींकारी**

(i) One who is in the form of *Hreem beeja* letters.

(ii) *Hree* means modesty, shyness and bashfulness. One who does this is *Hreemkāree*. In *Saptashatee*, it is mentioned that we bow to *Śreedevee*, who is in the form of bashfulness in all the souls;

Yā Devee Sarvabhooteshu Lajjāroopena Samsthitā I
Namastasyai Namastasyai Namastasyai Namo Nama: II

(iii) In *Swatantra Tantra* it is mentioned as; since *Śreedevee* takes care of creation, protection and destruction tasks, **She** is called as *Hreemkāree*. The letters in the corresponding verse here is wantonly in a dispersed manner. As per the hints to rearrange them the verse is as below;

Vyomnā Prkāshamānatvam Grasamānamagninā I
Tayorvimarsha Egāro Bindunā Tanniphālanam II

(iv) *Hreem* itself is one of the names of *Śreedevee* – 99th name in *Lalitā Trishatee* also. *Śree Ādi Śaṇkara*, in his commentary mentions – all energies are attributes of *Śreedevee*. By disconnecting them we get **Her** liberated form. **She** is seen as a complete liberated goddess.

(v) This is the *Māyābeeja-a*lso called as *Bhuvaneshvaree beeja*.

(vi) This *beeja* is in the *Panchadashee mantra* at the end of every division. The letters *'Ka'* and *'Ha'* in the *Panchadashee mantra* correspond to *Shiva*. The letters *'A'*, *'E'*, *'La'* and *'Sa'*, correspond to *Shakti*. In *Trishatee* itself, it is mentioned as *Hreem Upayātmakam*.

(vii) *Om* in general is called as *Praŋavam*. *Hreem* is called as *Śākta Praŋavam*.

(viii) *Lalitā Trishatee* has 300 names corresponding 20 names for each of the letters in *Panchadashee mantra*. It has 60 names corresponding to *Hreem*. The detailed meanings can be seen in the commentary of *Śree Ādi Śaṇkara*. We read in *Purusha Sookta* as

Hreeshcha Te Lakshmeescha Patnyou.

302. ***Hreematee*- ह्रीमती**

(i) One who has shyness.

(ii) *Vedas* indicate *Śreedevee* as shyness, mind, satisfaction, interest and cherish; *Lajjāmatee Tushṭirishtā Cha Pushṭa.*

(iii) Those who belong to good family race, those who have good education, those who have good character and those who move with good people, will feel ashamed to do awful actions. That is, the shame prevents them to do such acts. *Śreedevee* is in the form of shame. In *Saptashatee* (IV-5), *Śreedevee* is worshipped as;

Yā Śree: *Svayam Sookrutinām Bhavaneshvalakshmee*:
Pāpātmanām Krutadhiyām Hrdayeshu Buddhi: I
Shraddhā Satām Kulajanaprabhavasya Lajjā
Tām Tvām Natā: *Sma Paripālaya Devee Vishvam* II

Again in 5th chapter **She** is worshipped as;

Yā Devee Sarvabhooteshu Lajjaroopena Samsthitā I
Namstasyai Namstasyai Namstasyai Namonama: II

(iv) The 79th name *Lajjadhyā* and 195th name *Lajjapada Samāradhyā* in *Trishatee* can be referred.

303. *Hrudyā* - हृद्या

(i) One who abides in the heart.
(ii) **She** lives in the heart of ascetics/ devotees.
(iii) It can also be interpreted that **She** is delightful or pleasant to the mind.

304. *Heyopādeyavarjitā* - हेयोपादेयवर्जिता

(i) One who has nothing to regret or accept.
(ii) Because the scriptures, which describe injunction and prohibition are confined to the ignorant ones. Since *Śreedevee* is in a form of knowledge, **She** has no relationship to these.
(iii) *Geyam* – to abstain since people do not have interest. *Upādeyam* – to accept since people are interested. *Śreedevee* has no interest or disinterest or aversion. Hence **She** does not have anything to accept or reject or regret. Hence *Heyopādeyavarjita*.

305. *Rājarājārchitā* - राजराजार्चिता

(i) One who was adored by *Rājarāja*.
(ii) *Rājarāja* indicates 12 – presiding deities of various *mantras*, starting from Manu, Moon, etc. This name is due to worshipping of *Śreedevee* by them.
(iii) It can also be interpreted that **She** is in the form of different *Śree*

Vidyā types taught by them.

(iv) It is described in *Lalitā Stavaratnam* by sage *Śree Durvāsar* - The *Chintāmaŋigraha*, In the *Śree Chakra* (*nagara* - city), is the dwelling place of *Śreedevee*. Here in between 14th and 15th walls, *Kuberā* is seated with his associates like *Maŋibhadrā* and adore **Her**. Thus **She** was worshipped by *Kubera*.

306. *Rājnee* - राज्ञी

(i) One who is a queen.

(ii) *Śreedevee* is the empress of *Rājarājeshvara* (*Mahākāmeshvara*). Hence **She** is *Rājnee*.

307. *Ramyā* - रम्या

(i) One who the most beautiful.

308. *Rājeevalochanā* - राजीवलोचना

(i) One whose eyes are like deer, fish and red lotus flower.

(ii) The word *Rājeeva* means deer, fish and red lotus flower. Her eyes are compared to all these. 561st name *Mrugākshee* can be referred. 103rd name *Harinekshanā* in *Trishatee* may also be referred.

(iii) The word *Rājeeva* also means one who is dependent on king. Since **She** sights, with affection and blessings, the devotees of **Her** consort *Rājarājesvara*, **She** is *Rājeevalochana*.

309. *Ranjanee* - रञ्जनी

(i) One who delights her devotees.

(ii) **She** delights her devotees by providing bliss in this world and liberation in the other world.

(iii) *Ranjayatee* means to make red. It has been mentioned in more than one place that the colour of *Śreedevee* is red. For instance, the *dhyāna* verse may be referred – by her presence, the rosy-tinted *Devee* colours the pure *Paramashiva* as the red flower colours the crystal. *Śree Ādi Śaŋkara*, in his *Soundaryalaharee*, 92nd verse, describes the same sense;

Gatāste Manchatvam Drhina Hari Rudresvara Bhruta:

Shiva : *Svaccha Cchāyā Ghatita Kapata Pranchadapata*: I
Tvateeyānām Bhāsām Pratiphalana Rāgārunatayā
Shareeree Srungaro Rasa Iva Drushām Dogdhi Kutukam II

(iv) **She** is mentioned as the consort of *Prajāpati*, in *Mahāshoḍa Nyāsam* (*Moorthynyāsam*).

310. *Ramaṇee* - रमणी

(i) One who rejoices – simply moves with the devotees.
(ii) On account of her greatness and pride, the devotees with fear, amazement and admiration, may not come close to **Her.** By making herself simple, **She** moves closely with the devotees.
(iii) In *Śreemad Bhagavat Geeta* (XI – 14) also, *Krişhṇa* described *Arjuna*, who was seeing the cosmic form, as; *Vismayāvishto Hrushtaromā*:. *Arjuna* describes himself as; *Bhayena Cha Pravyathitam Mano Me* (XI – 45). Thus *Śreedevee* makes the devotees move closely without any fear.
(iv) The *Veda* (*Chāndokya Upanishad* VIII–12-3) says, laughing, playing and rejoicing.

311. *Rasyā* - रस्या

(i) One who is to be tasted of the essence (of bliss of realization of self).
(ii) The feeling that follows the continuous experience that the mind gets is called essence (*rasa*). If it is tasteful it is *rasa* else it is *virasa*.
(iii) The universal absolute is called *rasa* by the *Vedas* – (*Taitireeya Upanishad* II.6.1) - *Raso Vai Sa*: - He is alone the essence. Thus **She** is to be experienced as essence. We squeeze the fruits, take out the juice and enjoy it. Likewise from the gross physical, the subtle is taken out as essence and enjoyed. In the same way **She** is to be enjoyed.

312. *Raṇatkinkiṇimekhalā* - रणत्किङ्किणिमेखला

(i) One who wears a girdle with tinkling bells.
(ii) *Śree Ādi Śaṇkara*, in his *Soundaryalaharee* (7th verse), describes the same sense; *Kvanatkāncheedāma*.

313. *Ramā* - रमा

(i) One who is in the form of *Lakshmee*.
(ii) The *Soota Samhitā* (IV-47-66) says, **She** appears like a dancer in the form of *Laksmee*, *Sarasvatee*, etc.
(iii) In *Saptashatee* also (IV-5), **She** is worshipped as; *Yā Śree*: *Svayam Sukrutinām Bhavaneshu*.
(iv) The fourth vowel '*Ĕ*' of Samskrit letters is indicated by this name. This is the third letter in *Panchadashee mantra*. Related to this 315th name *Ratiroopā* can be referred.
(v) In *Mahāshoḍa Nyāsam* (*Prapanchanyāsam*), **She** is indicated as in the form of a river.

314. *Rākenduvadanā* - राकेन्दुवदना

(i) One who has face like a full moon.
(ii) We get happiness to see again and again an ocean, an elephant and the moon. We never get tired. **She** has such a face.
(iii) By referring as moon, it is described as circle and crescent.

315. *Ratiroopā* - रतिरूपा

(i) One who is in the form of *Rati* (Cupid's consort).
(ii) *Rati* is the external interest and involvement on anything. Unless it is achieved people do not get peace. *Rati* is the consort of Cupid. Cupid's goal is the person who has wish. *Rati* helps Cupid by creating love and interest on things. *Śreedevee*'s energy only comes out in the form *Rati* and hence *Ratiroopa*.
(iii) Or. In the previous two names the letter '*E*' (*bindu* and *anusvāram*) were cryptically indicated. When these two integrate the *Kāmakala* letter '*Em*' is created. It is a known fact that Cupid creates the erotic feeling and hence his consort is identified as *Kāmakalā* and hence this meaning.

316. *Ratipriyā* - रतिप्रिया

(i) One who is beloved of *Rati*, the wife of Cupid.
(ii) *Rati* means copulation and erotic art. For instance, in *Rāmāyana*, *Dasaratha*, after fixing up the crowning of *Rāmā* as prince, went to the palace of *Kaikeyee*. This has been mentioned as *ratyartham* by *Vālmeekee*.
(iii) *Soundaryalaharee* (9th verse), says that the *Kunḍalinee* energy has

united happily with the consort at *Sahasrāram*; *Sahasrāre Padme Saha Rahasi Patyā Viharase*.

317. *Rakshākaree* - रक्षाकरी

(i) The protector.
(ii) One who does the task of guarding and protecting. 266th name *Goptree* may be referred.
(iii) *Rakshā* means the holy ashes taken from the sacrificial fire. The various articles ablated in the sacrificial fire become ashes. In this fashion, *Śreedevee* burns everything and makes them into ash, i.e. **She** does the task of destruction. **She** does both the tasks of protection and destruction.

318. *Rākshasaghnee* - राक्षसघ्नी

(i) Slayer of demons.
(ii) Verse (IV-8) in *Śreemad Bhagavat Geeta* may be referred; *Paritrānāya Sadhoonām Vināshāya Cha Dushkrutām*.
(iii) *Saptashatee* verse (XI-55) also can be compared; *Ithdam Yadā Yadā Bādā Dānavotthā Bhavishyati*.
(iv) 599th name *Daityahantree* can also be referred.

319. *Rāmā* - रामा

(i) A woman.
(ii) In *Linga Purāṇā*, it has been mentioned that all the masculine words are *Sankarā* and all the feminine words are *Śreedevee*. The same is narrated as *Hari* and *Lakshmee* in *Viṣhṇu Purāṇa*.
(iii) *Bruhat Parāsara Smruti* says; Just as women get pleased or displeased, so are the *devas* are pleased or displeased. If they are pleased the family grows, if they are displeased the family is spoilt. *Saptashatee* (XI-6) says; *Vidyā*: *Samastā*: *Tava Devee Bhadā*: *Striya*: *Samastā*: *Sakalā Jagatsoo*.
(iv) Since, *Yogins* delight in meditating and adoring *Śreedevee* (try with delight), **She** is called *Rāma*. (*ram* = to delight, *rāmā* = woman).

320. *Ramaṇalampaṭā* - रमणलम्पटा

(i) One who is devoted to her husband.
(ii) **She** is interested in uniting with her consort *Kāmeshvarā* in *Sahasrāram*.
(iii) This indicates that, every woman is interested in her husband, only because she is part of *Śreedevee*.
(iv) *Ramanā* - enjoyment, play; *Lampata* - devoted.

321. *Kāmyā* - काम्या

(i) One who is most liked (by the learned).
(ii) Those who desire liberation desire, to obtain **Her** by knowledge. Hence *Kāmya*.
(iii) *Kāmyā* is the deity of the twelfth night of the dark fortnight of the lunar month. *Taitreeya Brāhmaṇam – Kātakam* says; As per *Śree Vidyā* practice, the 12th day of the dark fortnight and 4th day of bright fortnight (of the lunar month) have same presiding deity. This deity is called *Bherunda*. But as per *Veda* the presiding deity of 4th night of bright fortnight is *Vishvaroopā* and the presiding deity of 12th night of dark of fortnight is *Kāmya*. 256th name *Vishvaroopā*, 329th name *Kānthā* and 391st name *Nityāshoḍāshikāroopā* can be referred.

The names of the presiding deities, for the days and nights of bright and dark fortnights are differently mentioned in *Vedas* and *Śree Vidyā* practice. The relationship between these is described by *Lakshmeedarar* in his commentary for the 32nd verse of *Soundaryalaharee*.

322. *Kāmakalāroopā* - कामकलारूपा

(i) One who is in the form of *Kāmakala*.
(ii) The mention of *Kāmakā* in 88th name *Moolamantrātmikā* and 89th name *Moolakooṭatrakalebarā*, can be recollected.
(iii) It has been mentioned earlier that there are three *bindus* (one above and two in the sides) and the *hārdakalā*, in a triangle form at the bottom. This is described by the letter *'Em'*. It is very clear from *tantra sāstras* that this indicates the union of *Shiva* and *Shakti*. The first *bindu* is called *kāmā* and the *hārdakalā* is called as *kala*. According to the rule of *Pratyāhāra* of Samskrit, *Kāmakāla* includes all the four.
(iv) The real nature of that *Kāmakalā* is set forth in the book called *Kāmakalā Vilāsa*. Also in the *tantra* books like *Sāradā Tilakam*, *Prapanchasāram*, etc. The 19th verse of *Soundaryalaharee* starting with *Mukham Bindum Krutvā* also describes the same. This has not

been explained further, since it has to be understood through a proper teacher.

(v) *Śreedevee* has the names as *Kāmā* and *Kalā* and hence *Kāmakala*. (There is a *Kāmāgyā Peeṭa* at Gauhati in Assam. The *Kālikā Purāṇa* explains *Śreedevee* came to this place for the sake of desire and hence *Kāmāgyā*). There is a letter in Tamil language called *'Āyuda'* letter in the form of three vertices as a triangle (ஃ). It can be noted that three *bindus* are in this form.

323. *Kadambakusumapriyā* - कदम्बकुसुमप्रिया

(i) One who is fond of *kadamba* flowers.

(ii) We earlier read in 60th name as *Kadambavanavāsinee*. Only since **She** is fond of *kadamba* trees, a *kadamba* jungle has been set up outside her *Chintāmaṇigraha* house.

(iii) This indicates the goddess *Meenākshee*, who is blessing the devotees at Madurai. The 11th name in *Trishatee* is *Kadamba Kusumapriya*. The note given by *Śree Sir Subramaṇia* Iyer while translating, *Śree Ādi Śaṇkara*'s, commentary of this name is; *Kadamba* tree is one of the *Kalpaka* trees (*deva* tree). Inner-self is a group of Satva quality of five elements. Similarly *Kalpaka* tree is a common name for five types of trees viz., *Santānam, Harisantānam, Mantāram, Pārijātam* and *Kadambam*. The five parts of inner self is mind, intellect, volition, ego and heart. Mind is the *satva* part of wind. Intellect is the *satva* part of fire. Similarly, volition – water, ego – earth and heart or combined inner-self *satva* part of ether. Hence *kadamba* is mind; one who resides in the forest of mind is called *Kadambavanavāsā* (10th name in *Trishatee*) or *Kadamba- vanavāsinee* (60th name). *Kadambakusumā* is the expansion of the mind. Knowledge and expansion are inseparable forms. There is no knowledge without expansion and vice versa. Hence for *Śreedevee*, who is in the integrated form of knowledge on subjects and *tatvās*, is very much of fond of *kadamba* flower in the form of expansion of mind.

324. *Kalyāṇee* - कल्याणी

(i) One who is in an auspicious form.

(ii) *Śreedevee* is the complete auspicious.

(iii) *Kalyā* - good words, *ana* - to utter. *Kalyām* + *Anatee* = one who always utters good words.

(iv) According to the *Padma Purāŋā* - in the Malaya Mountain, **She** is worshipped as *Kalyānee*.

(v) The 2nd name in *Śree Lalitā Trishatee* is *Kalyānee*. *Śree Ādi Śaņkara*'s, commentary of this name is; auspiciousness is happiness. This happiness in worldly activities, as per *Veda* (*Taitireeya*, etc)., is health and youth – that is, happiness enjoyed by this body right from general human till four-faced *Brahma*. These are all atom sized drops from the complete bliss. *Śreedevee* is the complete bliss. As per *Veda* saying – *Vignānamānandam Brahma* – **She** is the complete bliss in the form of *Brahmam*, without any blemish.

325. *Jagateekandā* - जगतीकन्दा

(i) One who is the root cause of this universe.

(ii) The word *Kandā* has lot of meanings like to fill, root of the plants, cloud, etc. The root of the plants supports the entire plant. It provides the required strength. Same way **She** supports and provides strength to this whole world.

(iii) This can be compared verse to XV-1 of *Śreemad Bhagavat Geeta*, which talks about the imperishable *Ashvattha* tree with its root above and branches below;

Oordhvamoolamadha:shākham Ashvattham Prāhuravyayami
Chandamsi Yasya Parnāni Yastam Veda Sa Vedaviti I

326. *Karuŋārasa Sāgarā* - करुणारस सागरा

(i) One who is the ocean of compassion as water.

(ii) *Śreedevee* is like an ocean with compassion as water and hence this name. I.e., her compassion is bigger than an ocean. Later in 992nd name *Avyāja Karuŋamoorthi:*, it is going to be explained that – *Śreedevee* is with so much compassion on **her** devotees without any gambling, dispute, deceit, partiality or expectation.

(iii) In the meditation verse of this *Sahasranāmā* also it has been mentioned as; *Aruŋām Karuŋā Tarangidākshim* – stressing *Karuŋā*, the compassion.

(iv) In *Trishatee* also the compassion of *Śreedevee* is described in various names like, 9th name *Karuŋāmruta Sāgarā*, 151st name *Kaţākshasyandi Karuŋā* and 153rd name *Kārunya Vigraha*. *Śree Ādi Śaņkara*'s, commentary of these names;

9th name *Karuŋāmruta Sāgarā*; **She** is the like the ocean of nectar in the form of liberation originated by compassion. Ocean does not move from its place, but gives life to the entire world by vaporising its water as clouds and raining in all places based on the temperature. Similarly as per *Veda* sayings – *Brahma Veda Brahmaiva Bhavati* and *Brahmavidāpnoti Param* – **She** is in the form of ocean of nectar of liberation. As told by Lord *Krişhŋa* himself; *Labhadesa Tata*: *Kāmān Mayaiva Vihitān Hitān* – **She** provides the strength to all corresponding to the results of the adorations and obligatory duties done by each of the officials. Hence, **She** is compared to ocean.

Or, **She** has the duty to protect the devotees surrendered to **Her**– that is compassion. Here also **She** is like an ocean. Or, with compassion, **She** took the form of *Bhāgirathee* (river Ganges) and liberated the kings of *Sāgarā* (*Sāgar* – ocean) race, arranged them to reach the *Brahma* world and made them highly pride. Hence again **She** was compared to ocean.
151st name *Kaţākshasyandi Karuŋā*; the thought, the deities, great in all respects, get to protect the indigence in all respects, is called compassion. It is a form of invisible viscera. The taste of sugarcane juice can only be experienced. Similar is the essence of this compassion also - it can be identified through smiling, sweet discussions, benign look of eyes and happy facial expression. Just like the sweet essence was compared to sugarcane juice, this compassion is also compared to liquid. *Syandi Karuŋā* = flood like flowing compassion, *Katākshā* – one who is with the benign look; this means that **She** is with the compassion flooding through **Her** benign eyes.

153rd name *Kārunya Vigrahā*; earlier described as compassion is the beneficence; i.e. the form of inner self. **She** has compassion only as her body (idol). The body is important to give the required boons to the devotees – hence it has been indicated as - mind form, a dimension of the inner-self, benign look, smiling words, etc., the body form can be deliberated through these words – compassion is the body of *Śreedevee*. A body has necessarily be formed for the imagine prone *Brahmam*, whose qualities are; the goal is aiming to create the universe, not bound by any actions, full of awareness bliss, mother's thought aiming only to bless the devotees, etc. Without such a body form the devotees cannot meditate upon. The devotion with body form is the basis for devotion without form. That is the reason identification for each of the gods – like

Indra has the *Vajram* in hand, etc. This has been explained in the self-proven *Vedas* as – there is no harm in mapping a body form to gods.

Again in the commentary to *Kenopanishad – Bahushobhamānā Mumām Haimalateem*; *Śreedevee* with jewels made of gold, daughter of *Himavān*, dazzling, etc. Hence the brightness itself is the body of *Śreedevee*. Hence forming of such a body has been approved to help, the learned and self-illuminating gods like *Agni* (fire), *Vāyu* (air), *Indra* and so on, can meditate upon. Hence there is no place for the preaching of atheists.

327. *Kalāvatee* - कलावती

(i) One who is the embodiment of the 64 arts.
(ii) The 64 arts have been described in 236th name *Chatush shashṭi kalāmayee*.

328. *Kalālāpā* - कलालापा

(i) One who has arts as **Her** conversation.
(ii) Everything *Śreedevee* talks is an art.
(iii) According to the *Amarakosha* dictionary (V 86), *kala* means sweet sounding; *Ālāpa* means speech. Hence one who has sweet speech is *Kalālāpa*.
(iv) *Kam - Brahmam*. *Lālā* means saliva; *Āpa* - attainment. We experience the natural secretion of saliva just by thinking of a tasty food. The attainment of the *Brahmam* becomes, through **Her** grace, as natural as easy flow of saliva and leads along the path of salvation.

329. *Kāntā* - कान्ता

(i) One who is beautiful.
(ii) Since **She** is effulgent, **She** is looks like the Ultimate beauty. The lustre is the beauty and brightness of the body. The 449th name *Kānthi* and 465th name *Kānthimathee* can be referred.

Later 860th name *Akāntā* can also be referred – it has to be understood as destructor of *Akam* - sorrow or sin.

(iii) *Kam – Brahmam. Anta* - final. Unconditioned *Brahmam* is her final form. This is the last philosophy of *Śreedevee*'s form without any quality (*nirguṇā*). To start as a teacher, followed by *saguṇā* form and *nirguṇā* form is made perceived by **Her**.

(iv) The presiding deity of the eleventh night of the dark fortnight of the lunar month is called *Kānta*. **She** is in that form. **She** is in the form of all the presiding deities of all the days and nights and hence this is very apt. Corresponding 321st name *Kāmyā* can be referred.

330. *Kādambareepriyā* - कादम्बरीप्रिया

(i) One who is fond of mead.
(ii) In the *Navāvarŋa Pooja* there are five *articles* starting with the letter *'Ma' – Madhu, Māmsam, Mangai, Meen* and *Mudra* (alcohol, meat, girl, fish and signet). In the mead is also one of the five. These are consumed as propitious of *Śreedevee* after offerings to **Her**. It is read in *Tripurā Upanishad*, by offering Mead, fish, flesh and cooked cereals in the triangle representing the great *Devatā*, the lucky devotee, recovering his self, attains perfection;

Parirutam Jashamādyam Palam Cha Bhaktāni Yonee: Suparishkrutāni II
Nivedayandevatāyai Mahatyai Svātmeekrutya Sukrutee Siddhimeti II

Those who are not restricted to consume (for instance *Kshatriyās*) only can use it. *Brahmins* cannot definitely use it. They can only use its representatives. Even then they can use it by keeping the corresponding philosophies (*tatvās*) in mind. The corresponding commentaries of *Tripuropanishad* by *Śree Appaiya Deekshitar* can be referred. He advises that these are only for reading and not for adhering, for instance *Ashvamedha Yāga*. The philosophies of these five articles were also are discussed. *Śreedevee* is fond of high quality mead. At this juncture the following names can be referred;

98 – *Samayāchāratatparā*	333 – *Vāruneemadavihvalā*
441 – *Koulamārgatatparasevitā*	510 - *Madhupreetā*
575 – *Mādhveepānālasā*	717 – *Madhumatee*
912 – *Savyāpasavya Mārgasthā*	923 – *Dakshiŋā Dakshiŋārādhyā*

In *Saptashatee* also, in the 3rd chapter, it is mentioned that *Śreedevee* consumed mead. It has been described that **She** consumed alcohol to bring the *Rajo* quality to the forefront and not to have mercy on the demons.

Tata: Kruddhā Jaganmātā Chaŋḍikā Pānamuttamam I
Pabou Puna:punashchaiva Jahāsārunalochanā II

331. *Varadā* - वरदा

(i) One who bestows boons.

(ii) She grants boons to *Brahma, Vişhŋu* and other devotees. Śree BhāskaraRāya explains what is told by *Nārada* in *Matsya* and *Padma Purāŋās* –*Śreedevee*'s uplifted hand ever confers boons. She will give boons to all *Devas, daityas* and ascetics. It has to be understood that the words *Nārada* indicate that the hand is the instrument of giving, here the hand of *Śreedevee*, is said to confer boons. In reality, the expression means simply to fulfill the desire of the *Devas*; not having the emblem of granting boons.

(iii) *Śree Ādi Śaņkara* says in his commentary to *Soundaryalaharee* 4th verse; without even the emblem of boons in hands, *Śreedevee* provides the boons more than expected to the devotees;

Tvadanya: Pānibhyā-mabhayavarado Daivatagaŋa:
Tvamekā Naivāsi Prakatita Varābheetyabhinayā I
Bhayāt Trātum Dātum Phalamapi Cha Vānchāsamadhikam
Sharanye Lokānām Tava Hi Charaŋāveva Nipunou II

(iv) *Devee Purāŋa* also says; **She** fulfills the desires of the *Devas* who seek boons. From the root *'Vr'* to choose, **She** is called *Varadā*, conferrer of boons, i.e. giver of the things chosen.

(v) In the *Varāha Puranā* also in the chapter on the *Vetrāsuravadha*, *Śreedevee* is always to be worshipped, by concentration on the ninth day of the lunar fortnight; **She** will certainly become the giver of boons to all worlds.

(vi) *Śree Ādi Śaņkara* in his commentary of *Vişhŋu Sahasranāma* for the 330th name – *Varada*: mentions;

a. He gives the boons desired by the devotees in their minds.

b. He becomes the doer of sacrificial fire and gives the boons i.e. the cow as a price. *Gourvai Vara*: is the *Veda* saying quoted for this.

332. *Vāmanayanā* - वामनयना

(i) One who has beautiful/ graceful eyes.

(ii) *Vāmam* – beauty, *Nayanam* – eyes or proof. Hence it can be taken as – one who has beautiful eyes or beautiful proofs. Instead of proof it can also be taken as method of understanding, or order.

(iii) *Vāma* - left handed. **She** leads the devotees who follow the left handed path.

(iv) It has been mentioned in *Chāndogya Upanishad* IV-15 2 & 3 as, *Vāma* is the fruits of action. In this context **She** makes the devotees to reap the fruits of their actions. 288th name *Puŋyāpuŋya Phalapradā* can be referred.

(v) *Śree Ādi Śaṇkara* in his commentary of *Lalitā Trishatee* for the 20th name explains – corresponding to the actions, the results will be reaped later. The reason for the same is un-seeable or rareness – argues the atheists (followers of *poorva meemāmsa*). But this is not true. Un-seeable is so micro or atom level matter that it does not have the capacity to provide fruits. The fruit for every action is definite. It has to be accepted that one who gives the fruit for the actions should be superior to the doer of the action - as *Veda* says; *Karmādhyaksha*: and *Mayaivi Vihitān* – *Śreedevee* is the one who provides the fruits based on the actions.

(vi) *Vāmanayana* – left eye. As per *Mātrukā Nyāsam* the *beeja* for this is *'Em'*. Since this is a *Kāmakalabeejam*, it can be considered that this name indicates *Kāmakala*.

333. *Vāruṇee Madavihvalā* - वारुणी मदविह्वला

(i) One who is perturbed by the intoxicating liquor (the wine of spiritual bliss).

(ii) *Vārunee* – a type of liquor obtained from the date fruit. It is called as *Vārunee*, because the god *Varuṇa* is very fond of it. The expression means forgetting external objects and simply enjoying. 878th name *Svātmārāmā* can be compared.

(iii) As per *Taitreeya Upanishad* the *Brahma Vidyā* taught by *Varuṇa* to *Bruhu* is called *Varuṇee*.

(iv) It can be split as *Vārunimat* + *Avihvala*. Belonging to the regions of *Varuṇa*, i.e., *Ādishesha*, (the son-in-law of *Varuṇa*) the thousand-hooded snake that supports this earth, because he dwells in that region; *Avihvalā* not perturbed or fatigued, i.e., by **Her** grace *Ādishesha* is not fatigued, in supporting the universe.

(v) The *Vishnu Purāṇa* says; in the *Varuṇa* regions he (*Ādishesha*) worships *Śreedevee* with his own glorious body or with the liquor called *Vārunee* – says 2nd verse of *Soundaryalaharee*.

Taneeyamsam Pāmsum Tava Charaṇa Pankeruha Bhavam
Virinchi: *Sanchinvan Virachayati Lokā Navikalam* I
Vahatyenam Shouri: *Kathamapi Sahasrena Shirasām*
Hara: *Samkshudyainam Bhajati Bhasitoddhoolana Vidhim* II

(vi) *Varuṇee* is a *nāḍi* which has *Vāyu* (air) as the deity in the body. One who has conquered it through *yoga* is called *Vāruniman*. *Śreedevee* reduces *avihvālam* (weary, tired and exhaustion) for the devotees and hence this name.

334. *Vishvādhikā* - विश्वाधिका

(i) One who transcends the whole world.
(ii) **She** is above the 36 *tatvās* starting from earth till *Shiva. Veda* says – *Vishvādhiko Rudro Maharshi*: and *Pādosya Vishvābhootāni*. Since **She** is the united form of *Shiva -Shakti* and in the form of *Sādakya Tatva*, **She** is *Vishvādhika*.
(iii) *Śreedevee* is in the swoon (*tureeya*) state, still further in transcend dental (*Thureeyatheetham*) state beyond awaken, dream and deep sleep states (*Vishva, Taijasā* and *Prāgnā*). Names from 256 *Vishva-roopa* till 263 *Sarvāvasthāvivarjitā* can be referred.

335. *Vedavedyā* - वेदवेद्या

(i) One who can be known through the *Vedas*.
(ii) **She** can be realized through *Rig, Yajus, Sāma* and *Atharva Vedas*. In *Śreemad Bhagavat Geeta* (XV – 15) also Lord *Śree Krişhŋa* himself says; *Vedaiccha Sarvairahameva Vedhya*: - I am verily that which has to be known by all the *Vedas*.
(iii) In *Śree Nagara*, the dwelling place of *Śreedevee*, the four *Vedas* are the four entrances. Only by passing through these entrances one can reach *Śreedevee*. Hence *Vedavedya*.

The same is mentioned in *Veda – Taitreeya Brāhmana – Ruchām Prāchee Mahatee Diguchyate Dakshiŋāmāhur Yajushāmapārām Atharvanām Angirasām Prateechee Sāmnāmudeechee Mahatee Tiguchyate*. The Great quarter, the east, is said to be of the *Rig*; the endless southern quarter, they say, is that of the *Yajus*; the west of the *Atharvan*; and the great northern quarter is that of *Sāman*.

(iv) In the centre of the *Śree Chakra,* in the *Bindu*, we worship *Āmnāya* (*Veda*) deities. They are the four goddesses, who are the deities of the four *Vedas*, namely *Shuddha vidyā, Saubhāgyā Vidyā, Lopāmudrā Vidyā* and *Turiyāmbā Vidya*. The heads of *Samaya Vidyā* are *Unmodinee, Bodinee, Kunchikā* and *Kālika*. Since **She** is recognized by these *Vidyās, Śreedevee* is *Vedavedya*.

336. *Vindhyāchalanivāsinee* - विन्ध्याचलनिवासिनी

(i) One who resides in the Vindhya mountains.
(ii) In *Saptashatee* (XI Chapter) and *Pāncharātra Lakshmee Tantra, Śreedevee* incarnated during *Vaivasvata Manvantara*, in the house of

Nandagopa to destroy *Shumba* and *Nishumba* demons.

Nandakhopagruhe Jātā Yashodāgarbhasambhavā I
Tatasthou Nāshayishyāmi Vindhyāchala Nivāsinee II

337. *Vidhātree* - विधात्री

(i) One who supports this universe.
(ii) Since **She** supports and nourishes the universe, **She** is *Vidhātree*. Hence the same is conveyed in 935th name *Jagatdhātree*.
(iii) *Vidhātā* means *Brahma*. His consort is *Vidhātree*.
(iv) *Vi* - much, *Dhātri* - myrobalan, because **She** is fond of myrobalans, **She** is *Vidhātree*.
(v) *Dhātree* – mother, who bears the baby in her womb and releases at the appropriate time. A great mother is *Vidhātree*. 1 – *Śreemātā*, 457 – *Mātā*, 823 – *Jananee*, 826 – *Prasavitree* and 985 – *Ambā* may also be referred.

338. *Vedajananee* - वेदजननी

(i) One who created the *Vedas*.
(ii) It has been mentioned in many a place in *Vedas* that they originated from *Brahmam*; *Yasya Nisvasitam Vedā:, Asya Mahato Bhootasya Nisvashitametadrugvedo Yajurveda, Rucha: Sāmāni Jagjire*, etc.
(iii) The *Devee Purāŋā* says; because, there arose from the *Kunḍalinee*, which is triangular in form, the vowels and consonants; hence **She** is the mother of all the *Vedas* and hence *Vedajananee*. 386th name *Shadangadevatā Yuktā* may be referred.

339. *Vişhŋumāyā* - विष्णुमाया

(i) One who is *Vişhŋu Māyā Shakti*.
(ii) *Vişhŋu* is all-pervading, unlimited by place, time, *Brahmam*, in the form of inner self in all souls, etc. *Vişhŋu Sahasranāma* 2nd name – *Vişhŋu*: - *Śree Ādi Śaņkara*'s commentary can be compared. **She** is the *Māyā* of Universal Absolute. The *Shakti*, which limits this Absolute is illusion.
(iii) *Śreemad Bhagavat Geeta* (VII – 14); *Daiveehyeshā Guŋamayee Mama Māyā Duratyayā* - says, this is my divine illusion, consisting of *Guŋas* is hard to surmount. In *Saptashatee* also we read as;

Yādevee Sarvabhooteshu Vişhŋu Mayeti Shabtitā I
Namastasyai Namastasyai Namastasyai Namo Nama: I I

(iv) The *Kālikā Purāŋā* also says *Vişhŋumāyā* is that which differentiates, everything, into manifested and un-manifested according to the *tamas, rajas* and *satva* qualities. 399th name *Vyaktāvyakta Svaroopiŋee* can be referred.

340. *Vilāsinee* - विलासिनी

(i) One who is playful – showing the same thing in different forms.
(ii) Illusion (*Māyā*) is of two types – hiding the existing one (*Āvaranam*) and showing the same things in different forms (*Vikshepam*), i.e. showing the unrealistic form as a real one.
(iii) *Vilāsam* means pastime, play, erotic actions, etc. **She** possesses all these.
(iv) As per the saying *Nityā Vilāsinee Dogtiree* – **She** is in the form of a *Peeṭashakti*.
(v) Again as per the saying *Vabayorabhetāt* (as there is no difference between the syllable *vi* and *bi*), this name can also be had as *Bilāsinee*. *Bilā* is the cavity at the top of the *Brahmarandhra* (in *Sahasrāra*). *Svachcha Tantra* says that this is the route for liberation and the energy called *Brahmaŋee* is blocking this route. *Śreedevee* - at **Her** pleasure - either opens the way to self-realization, or closes it to the same for the devotees.
(vi) *Vilā* is a place in *Kāmakottam* in *Kāncheepuram*. **She** dwells in this place.

341. *Kshetrasvaroopā* - क्षेत्रस्वरूपा

(i) One whose body is matter – body of all beings.
(ii) *Kshetram* is the field ready for cultivation through the acts of removing the weeds, ploughing, watering, etc. Similarly, if a place is made ready through the rules of *mantra, tantra* and *yantras*, or naturally ready for nearing godliness is called *Kshetram* – for instance Kancheepuram, Banaras, Kāmaroopa, etc. **She** is in the form of those *Kshetras*.
(iii) Thirty-six categories (*tatvas*) from earth to *Shiva,* form her body. That is why *Parameshwara* is called as *Kshetragnan*.
(iv) *Śreemad Bhagavat Geeta* (chapter XIII) describes the relationship between *Kshetra* and *Kshetragnan*.

342. ***Kshetreshee* - क्षेत्रेशी**

(i) One who is the ruler of matter or the consort of *Kshetresha* (*Shiva*).

(ii) There is absolutely no difference between *Śreedevee* and *Parameshwara*. It can be reminded that *Tripuro Upanishad's* saying that ;

Bhaga: *Shaktir Bhagavānkām Esha Ubhā Dātārāv Soubhagānām*
Samprdhānou Samasatvou Samotayo: *Sama Shaktirajarā Vishvayoni*:

343. ***Kshetrakshetragnapālinee* - क्षेत्रक्षेत्रज्ञपालिनी**

(i) One who is the protector of matter and the knower of matter.

(ii) *Kshetram* is the body and *Kshetragnar* is the soul. **She** protects both. *Śreemad Bhagavat Geeta* (chapter XIII) may be referred.

(iii) *Linga Purāŋā* says that 24 *tatvas* are *kshetras* and the *purush*, who enjoys it is the *kshetragnan*. *Vāyu Purāŋa* says unmanifestation is *Kshetra* and *Brahma* is the *kshetragnar*. *Brahma Purāŋa* says, body is *kshetram* and one who follows *yoga* only can understand it and he is the *kshetragnan*. *Śreedevee* only takes the form of all these *kshetras* and *kshetragnas*.

344. ***Kshayavruddhivinirmuktā* - क्षयवृद्धिविनिर्मुक्ता**

(i) One who is free from decay and growth.

(ii) Growth and decay belong to *kshetra*. Though **She** is related to *kshetra* (as discussed in the earlier 3 names – in the form of *kshetra*, ruler of *kshetra* and protector of *kshetra* and *kshetragnan*), **She** is free from decay and growth. *Śreemad Bhagavat Geeta* (II – 23) also confirms this statement - weapons do not cleave the soul;

Nainam Chintayanti Shastrāni Naninam Dahati Pāvaka: I
Na Chainam Kledayantyāpo Na Shoshayati Māruta: II

(iii) **She** is free from these two which are the result of actions and **She** is not connected with actions. *Brahadāraŋyaka Upanishad* IV-4-22 says, this is the eternal glory of the knower of *Brahmam*. He neither increases by action nor decreases. Neither becomes more by good actions nor less by bad ones; *Sa*: *Na Sādhunā Karmana Bhooyānno Evāsādhunā Kaneeyānee*. Again in the next verse it is advised as; *"Esha Nityo Mahimā Brahmaŋasya Nakarimanā Vardhate No Kaneeyān"*.

345. *Kshetrapālasamarchitā* - क्षेत्रपालसमर्चिता

(i) One who well adored by *Kshetrapāla*.

(ii) As per *Linga* and other *Purāŋas*, *Kāli* was created by *Shiva* to slay the demon, *Dārukāsura*. Even after killing him the fire of her wrath was not appeased. Seeing the confusion of the world, *Shiva* in order to dispel her anger assumed the form of a crying infant. She suckled the child who drank up the fire of her anger with milk. This child is called *Kshetrapāla*, incarnation of *Shiva.* **She** was prayed by this *Kshetrapāla*.

(iii) In the results part of this *Sahasranāma*, it is mentioned that *Kshetrapāla* kills anyone who snatches the wealth of those who pray this *Sahasranāma*. This way, *Kshetrapāla* protects the devotees. **She** was worshipped by that *Kshetrapāla*.

(iv) The literal meaning is - *Kshetra* is the precinct of the sacrificial ceremony and *pāla* - the protector. *Kshetrapāla* protects the sacrificial ceremonies. **She** was worshipped by that *Kshetrapāla*.

(v) *Kshetra* is the body. The protectors in this body are fire, air, Sun, etc. **She** is worshipped by them.

346. *Vijayā* - विजया

(i) One who is called by the name *Vijaya*.

(ii) One who is ever with special victories.

(iii) The consort of *Sudarsana Chakra* of *Vişhŋu* is *Vijayalakshmee*.

(iv) **She** is the conceptual form. The differentiated feeling of '**I**'.

(v) According to the *Devee Purāŋa*, *Vijayan* is the *Shiva* form in Kashmir, which is one of the sixty-eight sacred places. Since **She** is in that form, **She** is called as *Vijaya*.

(vi) Again as per *Devee Purāŋa*, after conquering the king of demons named *Padman*, **She** is known in the three worlds by the epithet *Vijaya* (ever victorious) and *Aparājitā* (unconquerable).

(vii) In *Silpa Sāstra* (sculpture science) a type of building is called *Vijayam*. **She** is in that form of and hence *Vijaya*.

(viii) According to the *Cintāmaŋi*, *Vijaya* is an auspicious hour - in the month of *Āshvin*, in the tenth day of the bright fortnight, when the stars appear, that time is known as *Vijaya*, giving success to all undertakings started during this time. In the *Ratnakosa*, we read, the time, just after the twilight (*Sandhyā*) when the stars begin to shine, is called *Vijaya* favourable to all undertakings. The eleventh *muhoortha* (eight hours and forty-eight minutes after midday) is named *Vijaya*. A journey should be begun at the time by all who desire success. *Śreedevee* is in this time form.

(ix) **She** is in the form of *Tithi Nitya*.

(x) **She** is the *'Im' beeja* in the above *Tithi Nityā mantra*. This is called as *Vāgbhava Beeja*. The first letters of the three *Vedas A, E* and *U,* when merged as per the rules of grammar it becomes 'I'. When *bindu* is added, it becomes *'Im' beeja*. Hence it can be interpreted as **She** is in the form of the *Vedas*.

(xi) In *Mahāshoḍanyāsa* (*Devata Nyāsa*), we read as **She** was worshipped by thousand crores *Gandharva* race.

(xii) In *Devee Upanishad* **She** is indicated as;

Tāpāhariŋeem Deveem Bhuktimuktipradāyeeneem I
Anantām Vijayām Sootthām Sharanyām Shiva dām Shivām II

347. *Vimalā* - विमला

(i) One who is unsullied.

(ii) *Mala* (impurity) belongs to *avidyā* (ignorance). *Śreedevee* is the full form of knowledge. **She** is without ignorance and impurity. 135th name *Nirmalā* may be referred.

(iii) According to the *Padma Purāŋa,* when taking count of auspicious water bodies in *Purushotama Kshetra* (present day *PooriJagannath*), *Vimalā* is the *Shakti Peeṭa* deity.

(iv) The *Vishva karmasāstra* (sculpture science) enumerates the names/ characters of big houses as;

Dhruvam Dhānyam Jayam Kāntam Vipulam Vijayam Tathā I
Sumukham Vimalam Nandam Nidhanam Cha Manoramam II

(v) Worshippers of *Śreedevee* during *Sankalpa*, while describing the time in the *Ashṭānga* method, if the letters of the month and the *Udaya ghatikā* are the same then it is a *Parvā* day or *Vimala*. (Similar to what was described in 127th name). The specialty of such *Parvā* days is mentioned in *Paramānanda Tantra*, 19th *Ullāsam*. The five chapters from *Rudrayāmalam* are explained here.

348. *Vandyā* - वन्द्या

(i) One who is adorable. It is explained in the next name that the unlimited affection shown to Her devotees makes Her eligible to get this status.

349. *Vandārujanavatsalā* - वन्दारुजनवत्सला

(i) One who is fond of **Her** worshippers. *Śreedevee* loves **Her** devotees as **Her** children. **She** blesses the devotees considering them as **Her** own children and guarding them with love.

350. *Vāgvādinee* - वाग्वादिनी

(i) One who is the speaker of the world and who has the power that prompts to speak words.
(ii) *Vāgdevatā* – a form of *Saraswathee*.
(iii) *Vāgvādinee* is a deity; the organ deity *Rājashyāmalā* (also called as *Rāja Mātangi*), a minister of *Śreedevee*.
(iv) *Vāgvādinee* is a deity specified in *Uttarāmnāyam*. The *Tripura Siddhānta* says; as **She** always abides in the form of speech on the tongue of all **Her** devotees, **She** is known in the world as *Vāgvādinee*.
(v) It is also mentioned in the *Laghustava* of *Kālidāsā* as (V-15); Since thou art the origin of all worlds, thou art known in the world as *Vāgvādinee*.

351. *Vāmakeshee* – वामकेशी

(i) One who has beautiful hair.
(ii) *Vāmaka* - men and Is*a* - Lord, i.e. *Vāmakesha*. His consort is *Vāmakeshee*.
(iii) According to the *Devee Purāŋa*, *Vāmakesha* is the deity of *Jata*, one of the sixty-eight sacred places of *Shiva* and his consort *Vāmakeshi*.
(iv) *Vāmakesha* is one of the 28 *tantras* promulgated by *Shiva*; as **She** is treated in that work, **She** is *Vāmakeshi*. 945th name *Vāmakeshvaree* may be referred.

352. *Vahnimaŋḍalavāsinee* - वह्निमण्डलवासिनी

(i) One who resides in the circle of fire.
(ii) *Agnimaŋḍala*, is that in the *Moolādhāra*, or that in the supreme ether *Paramākāsa*.
(iii) *Vahni* means fire or number three. Hence three *maŋḍalās* (fire, Sun

and Moon), thus **She** resides in the three circles. These are respectively in *Moolādhāra, Anāhata* and *Sahasrāra*.

(iv) The three circles indicate the three groups in *Panchadashee mantra*.

(v) It can also be taken as *Vahnivāsini* indicates one of the *Thithi Nityās*.

353. *Bhaktimatkalpalatikā* - भक्तिमत्कल्पलतिका

(i) One who helps the devotees like the *Kalpaka* climber.

(ii) The *Kalpaka* climber will give whatever is asked for, to those who sit under it. In the same way *Śreedevee* bestows to **Her** devotees, whatever they ask for. (It is convention to indicate *Kalpaka* as a tree if masculine and as a climber is feminine).

(iii) *Kalpa* indicates something short – not having the complete devotion. That means those who have a little diminutive devotion, are called *Bhaktimat Kalpās*. *Lata* means climber. Its tendency is climbing. *Śreedevee* makes the *Bhaktimat Kalpās* to climb as a climber and reach **Her**. Even if they have a little devotion, **She** spreads it and conjoins with **Her**. It has to be taken as – even if people have a little devotion or even if they do not know the correct methods of worshipping – *Śreedevee* teaches them the complete method of worshipping and makes them a complete devotee, during their lifetime. It has been mentioned in *Shakti Rahasyā* as;

Akramenārdhabhaktayā Vā Bhavānyā: Krutamarsanam I
Janmāntare Krama Prāptyai Poorŋabhaktyai Cha Kalpate II

(iv) *Latikā* – musk deer climber. This has a very good odour – mind soothing. *Śreedevee* is like mind soothing musk deer climber for **Her** devotees.

354. *Pashupāshavimochanee* - पशुपाशविमोचनी

(i) One who releases the ignorant from bondage.

(ii) *Pashu* (literal meaning is cattle) are those who are devoid of the conviction of non-separation (*abhedajnāna*). The *Brahādāraŋya Upanishad* (I-4-10) says, now, he who worships another deity, thinking the deity is one and himself another individual, he does not know. He is like a *pashu*. Here the word *yo'nyām* (yah - one and *anyam* – another) means the triangular *Śree Chakra*; *"Yo'nyām Devatāmupāste'nyo'sā Vanyo'hama Smeeti Na Sa Veda Yathā Pashu:"*. In *Taitreeya Upanishad* it is mentioned as; in the golden three-petalled bud three (syllabled *mantra*, i.e. of *Śreedevee*) is established.

(iii) *Pa* - thirst, *Asa* - hunger. Hence *Pasa* indicate these two. These two - hunger and thirst are due to five types of afflictions (bondages or bindings). These afflictions themselves are bindings only; hence on the whole there are seven bondages. *Śreedevee* releases the ignorant, who get satisfied from these bondings (*vi* - completely, *mocini* – releases). The ignorant people are called *pashus* because they possess the desire of eating and drinking only. We read in the *Veda*; pashus understand only hunger and thirst; they do not speak of the known *Brahmam*; they do not see the known, they do not know the future, nor this nor the other world;

Athetaresham Pashoonāmashanāpipāse Evābignānam Na Vighnanatam Vadanti Na Vighnanām Pashyanti Na Vidu: Shvastanam Na Lokālokou.

She releases such *pashus* from the bondings.

Note: *Pashu, Pāsam* and *Pathi* have been explained in the 88th and 89th chapters of *Upadesa Kāṇḍa, Shiva rahasya Kāṇḍa, Śaṇkara Samhita* in *Skānḍam, Śree Anantharāma Deekshatar*'s edition may be referred.

(iv) The five types of afflictions referred to are;

(1) Nescience, ignorance or *Avidyā* – the absence of discrimination between the self and the not-self.

(2) Egoism or *Asmitā* – thinking the body, mind and organs as 'I', on account of ignorance and thinking that I am in that form (for instance eyes) - assumption of that body, etc., which are not-self as self.

(3) Strong desire for worldly things or *rāgā* due to *Asmitā* – having interest on the things, which are perceived by the organs and self-involvement in it. Desire is the craving for flowers, scents, etc., which are the means of bodily enjoyment.

(4) Anger, hatred or *Dwesham* on account of *rāgā*; when the interest is affected or if one does not get the things of interest, it results in anger and consequent hatred. Even if the interested things are got, but not the expected results, frustration is created. This is *dwesham* (created on account of *rāgā*).

(5) Ardent attachment is not renouncing a thing even though one knows it is no beneficial. The *dwesha* discussed above is temporary; however the affect in the mind on account of it is a long standing one. Even if the person knows that this is not good or not a suggested one, he cannot leave it. This is *Abhinivesam*.

These are explained in detail in the *Yoga Sūtra*, (III.3-9). But in *Devee Bhāgavatam* these are explained under different names. This is explained

in *Linga Purāŋa* also under different names. Again each of these has many sub- divisions.
The list goes;

Affliction	Alternate name in *Linga Purāŋā*	Number of sub-divisions
Nescience	*Tamas*	8
Egoism (*asmitā*)	Bewilderment (*moha*)	8
Desire (*rāgā*)	Great bewilderment (*mahāmoha*)	10
Hatred (*dwesham*)	*Tāmisram*	8 (18 as per some schools)
Ardent Attachment (*apinivesam*)	*Andatāmisram*	18
	Total	52
	If *Tāmisram* is considered as 18 then the total	62

As per *Kulārnava Tantra*, there are eight afflictions. They are; *kruņā*, *shankā*, fear, shyness, *jugupsā*, race, fame and caste. These eight and the above 52 (or 62 as the case may be) are created by compiling the sub-divisions in various forms. By the fear that the size of the explanation will be uncontrollable, *Śree Bhāskararāya* has not explained further sub-divisions of each of these eight.

According to *Kaṭapayādi* method *Pāsha* indicates the number 51. But he says that this has to be taken as 52. As an evidence for this, he shows the learned men like *Harsha Deekshitar*'s commentaries for the 1st verse of a *tantra* book called *Shārada Tilakam*. Here *panchāshat* (50) is considered as 51. Again he himself, interprets in 833rd name *Panchāshat Peeṭaroopiŋee* – here also *panchāshat* is considered as 51. He also indicates the afflictions are 52 in *Shiva Rahasya*.

The base line is that **She** releases the devotees from all the afflictions discussed above – whether 51 or 52 or 62, etc. This is the commentary of *Pourānikās* (one who discourses *Purāŋās*) – says *Śree BhāskaraRāya*.

(v) The afflictions are of three types; atom, differentiation and action. Ignorance is atom – two types viz. absence of self-esteem in the intellectual soul and self-esteem in the non-souls like body. Both are due to the impurity called ego.

Since they seem to be within controlled limits they are called atoms. The statement from *Soura Samhita* is quoted - since within some control they are atom and since impure it is a dirt.

One thing split into many is the difference. The root cause is illusion (to be added as a sixth one to the above five). All these six is one compilation. The *tatvas* from 7th to 36th is another compilation. Both these compilations are called illusory impurity (*māyāmalam*).

Actions are two types ordained and prohibited – a sort of feeling created in the body not recognised by the organs. This also of two types good and bad and called as action-impurity.

The later discussed items have the characters of the previous ones also. These have been explained in *Pratyabhigna Sāstra* and *Shiva Sūtra*.

Those bound by these three afflictions can be taken as seven types (three bound by one each, two bound by two each and one bound by all the three). However, since there are two impurities within action-impurity and atom is a sub-set of differentiation, we have to take that those bound by afflictions as three types only.
Those bound by one affliction is called *Shuddhā*:, by two *Misrā*: and by three *Ashuddhā*:.
These names are explained in the book called *Nityāhrudam*. In *Svachchanda Tantra*, the names are respectively *Vijnanākevala*, *Pralayakevala* and *Sakala*.
In each of these types there are sub-types viz., the impurities completely combusted and not combusted. From the impurities completely combusted type, 118 *siddhas* have been originated. With the complete blessings of Lord *Shiva*, they have got full knowledge of all the *mantras*. They are indicated as below;

Shata Rudras	-	100
Shata Maṇḍalis	-	8
Krodha Battarakās	-	8
Veereshwar	-	1
Shree Kanḍar	-	1

Total	-	118

Among the *Sakalās*, those impurities are not completely combusted - Lord *Parameshwara* ensure rebirth in this world. In each of the births they enjoy the fruits of their actions and combust the impurities. *Parameshwara* makes this happen through proper teachers and that is the reason, repeated births are given.

It has already been mentioned that those bound by atom and action afflictions are called *Pralayakevala*. Out of these, those impurities that are completely combusted become the heads of worlds. Others take birth in high races, enjoy the fruits of actions, combust the impurities and merge with *Parameshwara* **Himself**.

Those bound by a single affliction called atom are called *Vijnanākevalas*. Among them, those impurities, which are completely combusted become the heads of knowledge. Others become the presiding deities of seven crores of *mantras*. These *mantra*s should not be treated as materialistic sounds. They have intellects.

Proportionate to the combustions of impurities, there are infinite sub-divisions in the afflictions. The births and levels taken by those are all for combustion of impurities and getting liberation.

It is a natural question that can be derived that, if liberating the people is the duty of *Parameshwara*, what is the role of *Śreedevee* here? Without the liberating energy of *Śreedevee, Shiva* cannot do anything. As evidence to this, Śree Bhāskara*rāya* quotes the verses from old books, *Pratyabhigna Sāstra* and *Shiva Sūtra*.

It can also be taken as *Shiva* and *Shakti* are one and the same – inseparable and hence *Śreedevee* does all these.
Thus *Śreedevee* releases the devotees from the above afflictions depending on the impurities.

(vi) *Pashu* means full – without any balance. In *Vedas* in the statement; "*Lodham Nayanti Pashumanyamānā*:" - this has been interpreted as indeclinable word with complete as its meaning. *Pāshās* – **She** releases from the noose of *Varuṇa*.

(vii) *Pāsa* - dice, *vi* - much, *mochini* - throwing the dice on the board. She conquered Lord *Parameshwara* in the game of dice. 374th name *Krutagnā* may also be referred.

(viii) *Pashupa* – protector of cattle, *Parameshwara*. *Āsha* – those who are interested in reaching Lord *Shiva.* **She** completely releases those people.

(ix) From *Brahma* to the most inert everything has the character of *Pashu* (animal). The tool that binds them is ignorance. The various methods of these are called *Pāshās*. **She** releases them through devotion to Lord *Shiva.*

(x) The names 133rd - *Niranjanā*, 134th – *Nirlepā* and 135th – *Nirmala* may be referred.

(xi) Also, it can be remembered – in *tatva sodhana* - to examine the impurities ego, illusion and action respectively the physical, subtle and causal bodies are examined.

Note: In the *Saiva Siddanta* religion followed in Tamilnadu, *Pashu, Pathi* and *Pāsham* are the basic principles. These are explained in Samskrit also. In particular *Śree Appaiya Deekshitar* has written *Shivarkamaṇi Deepikā* based on the commentaries of *Śree Kanḍa*. His *Ratnatrāya Pareekshā* can be taken as stirred version of the commentary of *Śree Kanḍa*. Śree Bhāskararāya has quoted this book as reference in many a place. But it is a surprise that he has not quoted *Saiva Siddanta* anywhere.

355. *Samhrutāsheshapāshaṇḍā* - सम्हृताषेशपाशण्डा

(i) One who is the destroyer of all heretics, those who are averse to spiritual values.

(ii) The *Linga Purāṇa* describes the nature of the heretics thus; observers of vows not enjoined in the *Vedas* and those who are excluded from the ceremonies enjoined by *Sruti* and *Smrutis* are called heretics, they are not to mingle with or even be spoken with by the twice-born (*Brahmins*).

(iii) The *Brahma Vaivarta Purāṇa* also; *Purāṇas, Nyāya, Mimāmsā, Dharma Sāstras,* six *Vedāngas* (i.e. the supplements *Sikshā* to *Jyotisha*), the four *Vedas*, which are the source of knowledge, these fourteen are the seat of righteousness (*dharmasthāna*). Taking these fourteen – these are the true, what is beyond these imagined by men is called heresy (*pāshaṇḍā*). **She** destroys all these *pāshaṇḍās*.

(iv) In some schools it is written as *Pākhanda*, it gives the same meaning. *Pa - Vedas* and *khanda* - cutting off. **She** destroys all those *pākhandās* also.

356. *Sadāchārapravarttikā* - सदाचारप्रवर्त्तिका

(i) One who inspires into right action.

(ii) Because **She** destroys the wicked (as discussed above), **She** incites men to right actions.

(iii) *Sat* – great - **She** routes the men into great actions. *Sat* – great/ auspicious men. Their actions are *Sadāchāras*.

(iv) The actions of *Sat* - **She** gives the inclination to observe the precepts enjoined in the *Karma Kāṇḍa* in *Vedas* and the *Advaita Brahmam* in the *Jnāna Kāṇḍa,*through the means laid down in the *Purāŋas*. It is said in the *Koorma Purāŋa* by *Devee* herself; the eighteen *Purāŋas*, were promulgated by *Vyasa*, by the command of *Brahmam*; in them righteousness (*dharma*) is established. The other supplementary *upa-purāŋas* were promulgated by his disciples. In every era (*yuga*) he (*Vyāsa*) the knower of the science of righteousness, is the promulgator of all *Purāŋas*, etc. *Siksha*, *Kalpa*, *Grammar*, *Nirukta*, *Chandas* and *Jyotisha* and logic etc., are the source of knowledge. The righteousness (*dharma*), is not to be found elsewhere. Thus the supreme *dharma*, which has come down from the grandsire, *Manu*, *Vyāsa* and others, is established till the dissolution of the universe. Thus said *Śreedevee*.

357. *Tāpatrayāgnisantaptasamāhlādanachandrikā*– तापत्रयाग्निसन्तप्तसमाह्लादनचन्द्रिका

(i) One who gives, like a Moon, soothing for those who suffer from the three types of distress of fire.

(ii) The sufferings are of three types viz., *ādhyātmikam*, *ādhi-daivikam* and *ādhi-bhoutikam*.

- *Ādhyātmikam* - disturbances stemming from the self – fully relating to body and 5 sense organs, 5 organs of actions, mind, intellect, ego and volition.
- *Ādhi-bhoutikam* - disturbances that come from the world – five basic elements relating to the above organs.
- *Ādhi-daivikam* - mental disturbances that come from God – beyond the control of human beings, like flood, etc.

The above three are the characters of the life cycle. This name indicates that **She** makes the soul, suffering from the above disturbances, happy (by removing the sufferings) through her Moon like compassion.

358. *Taruŋee* - तरुणी

(i) One who is ever young.
(ii) *Śreedevee* does not have growth or reduction. 344th name *Kshayavruddhivinirmuktā* may also be referred.
(iii) *Śreedevee* does not have a beginning or an end. 296th name *Anādinidhanā* may be referred. If there is a beginning there will be growth. If there is an end, there would be reduction also. *Śreedevee* does not have all these.
(iv) **She** is eternal - present in all the three times. 136th name – *Nitya*. She is encompassing whole. 292nd name – *Poorŋa*. The same sense is communicated in 430th name *Nityayouna*.
(v) The sense conveyed by *Brahadāraŋyaka Upanishad* (IV-4-25); *ajarom'mruta*: is reflected here - *Brahmam* has neither ageing nor death.

359. *Tāpasārādhyā* - तापसाराध्या

(i) One who is worshipped by ascetics.
(ii) Or, *tāpa* - *samsāra* (the father of misery), *sāra* - essence (a deep), *Adhyā* - meditation, i.e. *Śreedevee*, who is the root cause of this *samsāra* life cycle, is the essential object of meditation.

360. *Tanumadhyā* - तनुमध्या

(i) One who has a slender waist.
(ii) Earlier in 35th name – *Lakshyaromalatādhāratā samunneya madhyamā* the hip portion of *Śreedevee* was described.
(iii) *Tanumadhyā* is the deity worshipped in the country of Kānchi; for it is said, may *Śreedevee, Tanumadhyā*, the consort of *Bilvesvara* residing on the bank of the *Nivā* (river), protect me.

Mām Bātu Nivāyā: *Dheere Nivasantee* I
BilveshvarakāntāDevee Tanumadhyā II

(iv) *Tanumadhyā* is the name of certain metre. With 6 letters for each word it has 24 letters. The above verse is in that metre. The metre of the *Gāyatree Mantra* (*chandas*) also has 24 letters. The *Śreemad Bhagavat Geeta* (X-35) verse; *Gāyatree Chandasamaham* also can be remembered. (The *Pingala sūtra*, says, if there is one *tagaŋa* and *yagaŋa* in each foot it is called *Tanumadhya*).

361. *Tamopahā* - तमोपहा

(i) One who is the remover of darkness.
(ii) Remover of the darkness called ignorance from the devotees.
(iii) The *Íshāvāsya* Upanishad (9th verse) says, they who worship ignorance enter blind darkness; *"Andham Tama: Pravishanti Y'vidyā mupāsate"*.
(iv) In the last part (*uttara bhagā*) of *Lalitā Trishatee* (79th and 80th verses) we read as;

Andham Tama: pravishanti Ye'vidyāmupāsate
Iti Srutirapāhaitānavidyopāsakān Puna: I
Vidyānyopāsakāneva Nindatyārunekeesruti: II

362. *Chiti*: - चितिः

(i) One who is in the form knowledge.
(ii) In the book called *Pratyabhigyā Hrudayā*, it is mentioned as - Chit is independent and the cause of the establishment of the universe; *Chiti: Svatantra Vishvasidti Hetu*:
(iii) We read in the *Mahāvāsishtha*, that *Śreedevee* is called *Chit*, because **She** is the life of those who desire life; *"Saisha Chitiriti Proktā Jeevanāt Jeevitaishinām"*.
(iv) In *Saptashatee* (V chapter) it is mentioned that *Chit* means the intellect form of the soul;

Chiti Roopena Yā Krutsnam Etat Vyāpya Sthitā Jagat
Namastasyai Namastasyai Namastasyai Namo Nama:

363. *Tatpadalakshyārthā* - तत्पदलक्ष्यार्था

(i) One who is the connotation of the word *Tat* in the *Mahāvākya*.
(ii) In the *Mahāvākyā Tatvamasi* – the word *Tat* means – the various forms of *Brahmam* doing the tasks of the world like creation, etc. The ideal meaning of this word is that the same *Brahmam* in an idle form without any task to do. These two are one and the same. Thus She is in the form of *Brahmam* indicated by the ideal meaning.
(iii) 425th name *Tat* may also be referred.

364. *Chidekarasaroopiṇee* - चिदेकरसरूपिणी

(i) One who is completely in the form of knowledge.
(ii) Even the unconditioned *Brahmam* has the attributes of bliss, etc. Hence how does the previous name fit in? To answer this question

this name is given. The attributes bliss, consciousness, intellect, etc. are inseparable from **Her**. Though **She** appears to be in different forms, intellect and conscious form of hers is full of knowledge. It has to be considered that knowledge is the only essence or the main essence. This is explained in the *Panchapādikā* by *Padmapādā-chārya* - Bliss, the perception of the objects and the eternity are attributes which although inseparable from consciousness appear as different.

(iii) The unconditioned *Brahmam* is not the real nature of *Ishvara* (the conditioned one), because both are different, hence the relation between the two just described above is not possible. To remove this doubt this name is introduced. **She** is ever non-separated from the *Chit*. The relation of these two is possible as they are one and the same. Though they appear different by attributes, yet they are actually one and the same.

365. *Svātmānandalavee Bhootabrahmadyānanda Santati*: -
स्वात्मानन्दलवीभूतब्रह्माद्यानन्दसन्ततिः

(i) The totality of the bliss of *Brahma* and others, is but a minute portion of **Her** own bliss.

(ii) The three gods who do the tasks of creation, protection and destruction and *Indra* and other *devas* also enjoy the bliss. But this is only a drop in the ocean, in comparison with the bliss of *Śreedevee*. That is, the bliss of *Śreedevee* is multiple times greater than others. *Taitireeya Upanishad* (II-8) says, other beings live on a mere part of this bliss; *"Ethasyaiva Ānandasya Anyāni Bhootāni Mātrām Upajeevanti"*.

(iii) Again in the same *Veda* we read a table starting from the bliss of human till bliss of *Brahmam*. Until *Prajāpati* though the bliss increases in grades, but it is still limited. It is the bliss of *Brahmam*, which is unlimited and immeasurable. Hence it is not proper and fit for human aspiration.

(iv) To confirm that the meaning of the word *tat* (in previous name) indicates the unconditioned *Brahmam*, this name is explained. In order to agree with authorities (scriptures), which establish the meaning of them by (the rule) of beginning, etc., (*upākrama*, etc). as the knowledge as the means of *Purushārthas*.

(v) *Lava*, according to the *Visvā* dictionary, means, particle and sports.

366. *Parā* - परा

(i) One who is in the form sound called *Para*, the transcendent word.

(ii) The power of expression depends upon the correspondence of the words and their meanings. Hence, as the unconditioned *Brahmam* also is included in the sound (*Shabdabrahmam*), *Brahmam* indirectly (*Lakshaŋa*) indicates (as the *Vedāntins* say) by the words existence, etc. Because the words which are the physical forms of speech (*Vaikharee*) only express or identify the physical form of *Brahmam* (the *Virāt*) and do not correspond to the pure unconditioned *Brahmam*, the speech is divided into four forms; *Parā*, *Pashyantee*, *Madyamā* and *Vaikharee*.

(iii) To clearly understand these it is necessary to mention some background information. Earlier in the names 256 to 274 (*Vishvaroopā* onwards till *Panchakrutya-parāyanā*), the creation of this universe was explained from one dimension. Now other perspective follows.

(iv) During great dissolution (*Pralaya*) when the actions (*karmas*) of beings about to be manifested are not yet ripe, the *Brahmam*, bound by illusion (*māyā*) and by those actions (*karmābhinnamāyā* literal meaning being illusion itself in the form of actions) is called *ghanibhoota* (the congealed one). When, in course of time, the actions begin to ripen and the former state of unripeness disappears, that state is called *vichikrisā* (longing for action). At the moment of ripeness, when the modification of illusion appears, *Brahmam*, endowed with illusion in the form of ripened actions, is called *avyakta* (unmanifested). Hence creation is attributed in the *Smrutis* to the avyakta; Oh best of twice-born, from that is sprung the *avyakta* with the three qualities. That *avyakta*, as it is the sprouting root of the universe, is termed as the *kāraŋabindu* (the causal dot). The *Prapanchasāra* says, that Intelligence, the congealed one, desirous of action, attains the state of *kāraŋabindu*. From this *kāraŋabindu* proceeds in order the *kāryabindu* (effective dot). From the latter *nada* (sound); thence the *beeja* (the seed); thus the three came into being. These three are also called by the words the supreme, subtle (*sookshma*) and physical (*sthoola*). In their nature they partake respectively intelligence (*chit*), combined-intelligence (*achit*) and non-intelligence (*Chidachit*). Hence the *Rahasyāgama* says, that *bindu* (the causal dot) in the course of time it sprouts and become three. Its three divisions are gross, subtle and supreme. These are called, *bindu*, *nada* and *beeja*. These four, including the *kāraŋa-bindu* in their divine aspect (*ādhidaivata*) are *avyakta*, Ishvara, *Hirānyagarbha* and *Virāt*. They are called by various names and forms in the *Sāstras*. They are;

Form (*Swaroopa*)	**Effective Dot (*Kāryabindu*)**	**Sound (*Nātha*)**	**Seed (*Beeja*)**	**Causal Dot (*Kāraŋabindu*)**
Ādhidaivata	*Eshwara* *Vāmā* *Icchā Shakti*	*Hiraŋyagarbha* *Jyeshtā* *Gnana Shakti*	*Virāt* *Roudhree* *Kriyā Shakti*	*Avyakta* *Brahmam* *Shāntā* *Amibikā*
Ādhibhoutikam	*Kāmaroopa Peeṭa*	*Poorŋagiri Peeṭa*	*Jālantara Peeṭa*	*Oḍyāna Peeṭa*

(v) In the bodily aspect (*adhyātma*) the *Kāraŋabindu* resides in the *Moolādhāra* and is known by the words *shakti* or *pinda* (mono-syllable *mantra*), *Kunḍalinee*, etc. This has been mentioned in *Kalidāsā's Laghustava* (V-1) by the following words about the *Kunḍalinee*; there is a *shakti* called *Kunḍalinee*, having known her who is ever engaged in the work of the creation of the universe, a man never again enters his mother's womb as a child (i.e. he has no *samsāra*). Similarly mentioned in other books also.

Shakti: *Kundalaneeti Vishvajanana Vyāpāra Baddhodhyamām* I
Gnātvettham Punarnavishanti Jananeegarbhe'rbhagatvam II

(vi) This is the *kāraŋa bindu* in its non-differentiated condition. When it sprouts in order to create the three, namely *kāryabindu*, etc., then the unmanifested sound called *Shabdabrahmam* (*Brahmam*) arises from it.

Bindos Tasmāt Bhityamānātavyaktātmā Ravo I
Sarava: *Sruti Sambannai*: *Shabdabrahmeti Geeyate* II

(vii) It is also said as, from this differentiation of that bindu comes the unmanifested sound, that sound is termed as *Shabdabrahmam* by those learned in sound. This sound, since it is one with the *Kāraŋabindu* and is therefore all-pervading, yet first appears in the *Moolādhāra* of persons by the power of air acted upon by the effort of manifestation. It is said, in the *Moolādhara* in the body the air first appears, that air acted upon by the effort of a person desiring to speak, produces the all-pervading *Shabdabrahmam*". That *Shabda-brahmam*, which is in the *kāraŋabindu*, when it is manifested remaining motionless (*nishpanḍa*).

Dehe'pi Moolādhāresmin Samudeti Sameerana: I
Vivakshoricchayotthena Prāyatnena Susamskrta: II

(viii) Though the *kāraŋabindu* originated as *shabdabrahmam*, it remains motionless in its own place *Moolādhāra* and hence is called *parā* speech.

(ix) The same *Shabdabrahmam*, produced by the same air proceeding as far as the navel, joined with the reasoning intellect mind (*Manas*), possessing the nature of the manifested *Kāryabindu* with simple motion (*sāmānyaspanda*) is named *pashyanti* speech. Next the same *Shabdabrahmam*, produced by the same air proceeding as far as the heart, joined with the determining (understanding *Buddhi*), in the manifested sound, endowed with special motion (*visheshaspanda*) is called *madhyamā* speech. Next the same (*Shabdabrahmam*), produced by the same air, proceeding as far as the mouth, developed in the throat, etc., in the form of articulation, capable of being heard by the ears of other's possessing the nature of the manifested *beeja*, with the universal motion (*spashṭatara*) is called *vaikharee* speech.

Moolādhāre Para Proktā Pashyantee Nabhisam Stitā I
Madyamā Bhuddhi Samyuktā Ashṭasthāneshu Vaikharee II

It is also explained by *Śreemad Acārya* in his *Prapancha Sāram* (II-43) that sound which first arises in the *Moolādhāra* is called *Parā*, next the *pashyanti*; next when it goes as far as the heart and is joined to the understanding *Buddhi* it is called *madhyamā*; and the full manifestation is *vaikharee*. Thus, articulated sound is produced by air;

Moolādhārāt Prathama Mudito yashcha Bhāva: *Parākhya*:
Pashchāt Pashyantyatha Hrudayago Bhuddhiyun Madyamāgya:
Vyakte Vakharyata Rurudishorasya Janto: *Shushumnā*
Pandhas Tasmādbhavati Pavane PreritāVarŋa Samgnā

(x) The same idea is mentioned in *Nityā Tantra* also, the *parā* form arises in the *Moolādhāra* produced by air; the same air rising upwards, manifested in the *Svādhistāna*, attains the *pashyanti* state. The same slowly rising upwards and manifested in the *Anāhata*, united with the understanding is termed *madhyama*. Again rising upwards appearing in the *Vishuddhi* and comes out from the throat is *vaikharee*. Thus, though there are four kinds of speech gross minded men who do not understand the first three, think *vaikharee* alone to be the speech. The *Veda* says; hence men think *Vaikharee* alone to be speech which is imperfect. That is to say imperfect by not possessing the first three forms; *Tasmāt Yatvācho' Nāptam Tam Manushyā Upajeevanti*.

Another *Veda* statement also (*Rig Veda* I-164-45) says; four are the definite grades of the speech; those Brahmins who are wise know them; three are deposited in secret and motionless; men speak the fourth grade speech;

Chatvāri Vāg Parimitā Padani Tāni Vidur Brāmhanā Ye Maneeshina: I
Guhā Treeni Nihitā Nengayanti Tureeyam Vācho Manushyā Vadanti II

(xi) It was earlier explained (363rd name *Tatpadalakshyārthā*), that *Śreedevee* is in the form of *Tat* in the *Mahāvākyā – Tatvamasee*. From this 363rd to 371st names it has been described that *Śreedevee* only is in the all the four grades of speech.

(xii) The *Tripurasiddhānta* explains the word *parā* in different ways. As **She** is pleased with *Parānandanātha* (a teacher) **She** is called *Para*. As **She** is celebrated in the work called *Parānanda*, **She** is *Parā* and as **She** is the supreme source of grace, **She** is *Para*.

367. *Pratyakchiteeroopā* - प्रत्यक्चितीरूपा

(i) One who is in the form of inner consciousness.

(ii) The quality and character of the organs are to move out - i.e. *Parāk*. But on the other hand, *Parā* grade of great form of sound can be recognised only by the inwardly looking mind. Inward looking is called *Pratyak*. A high level of attempt is needed for this. Thus with a high level of attempt and inward looks the mind recognises the *Parā* knowledge in the form of *Brahmam* and without any distinction from matter, energy and character. (It can be reminded that earlier in the 362nd name *Chiti*, it was explained that *Śreedevee* is in the form of knowledge). Thus *Śreedevee* is in the form of *Pratyak* or *Chiti* – great knowledge.

(iii) Those who have an idea of Samskrit grammar can appreciate the explanation of *Śree BhāskaraRāya*. It has been given below for them;

(*Pratikoolam Svātmābhimukhamanchateeti Prateechee Sācha Chitee Cha Pratyakchitee Avyaktasangnam Brahma Saiva Roopam Yasyāstathā* I *Chinote*: *Ktijantat "Krudikārāt" Iti Deep* II)

368. *Pashyantee* - पश्यन्ती

(i) One who is in the form of *Pashyantee* – speech in the inaudible stage.

(ii) Earlier in 366th name *Parā*, the four stages of the speech were discussed and it was seen that the name of the second stage is *Pashyantee*. **She** is in that form.

(iii) The *Soubhāgya sudhodaya* says, as **She** sees all and **She** sees all in **Herself** and **She** is called *Pashyantee*. Since **She** rises (*Utteernā*) above the path of action, **She** is also called *Utteerna*. 714th name *Kulottheernā* also may be referred.

369. *Paradevatā* - परदेवता

(i) One who is the object of Supreme devotion.
(ii) It has to be taken as **She** is worshipped as the supreme deity and the ultimate Godhead to be meditated upon.

370. *Madhyamā* - मध्यमा

(i) One who is in the form of *Madhyamā*– speech in the middle stage of its external expressions.
(ii) This is neither like *pashyanti*, stopping immediately after rising, nor like *vaikharee* with articulation fully developed, it is called *Madhyamā* - intermediate stage between the two;

Pashyanteeva na Kevalam Utteernā Nāpi Vakhareeva Bhahi: I
Sphutatara NikhilāvayavāVāgroopā Madhyamā Tayorasmāt II

371. *Vaikhareeroopā* - वैखरीरूपा

(i) One who is in the form of *vaikharee* – the uttered audible speech.
(ii) The great hard form of letters – sound from the neck - *vaikharee*. The scattered sound, in the form of air, becomes dense by hitting against the walls of the narrow passage, the form of words (sound) and gets the name called *Vaikharee*.
(iii) According to the *Saubhāgya Sudhodaya, vai* - certainly (in a clearly understandable format that this is that), *kha* – sky (the cavity of the ear); *rāti* - to enter. Hence *Vaikharee*.
(iv) According to the *Yogasāstras*, **She** is called *vaikharee* because **She** was produced by the air called *vikhara* (the air bringing the sound from heart via throat is called

vikaran; Prānena Vikharākyena Preritā Vaikharee puna:

372. *Bhaktamānasahamsikā* - भक्तमानसहंसिका

(i) One who is in the form of a swan in the lake like minds of the devotees.

(ii) The creator, Brahma created a lake, by his mind. It is in the top of mount *Kailāsh*. Its water is so pure. The swans, which always like purity, live there in an infinite number. It has been described that wherever they travel, during rainy season return to this lake.

It has been said in this name as – imaging the pure minds of the devotees to this lake (since it was created by mind, it is called *Mānasa Sarovar* (*Manas* – mind, *Sarovar* – lake) and *Śreedevee* compared to the swans living there.

(iii) The same sense is conveyed in the 38th verse of Soundaryalaharee also;

Samunmeelat Samvitkamala Makarandaika Rasikam
Bhaje Hamsadvandvam Kimapi Mahatām, Mānasacharam I
Yadālāpā Dshtādasha Guŋita Vidhyāparinati:
Yadādatte Doshād Guŋa Makhila Madbhya: *Paya Iva* II

(iv) **She** is invisible for others, that is those other than devotees, mount, *ka* is suffixed and mentioned as *Hamsika*.

(v) 816th name *Munimānasa Hamsikā* may also be referred.

373. *Kāmeshvaraprāŋanāḍee* - कामेश्वरप्राणनाडी

(i) One who is very life of **Her** consort *Kāmeshvara*.

(ii) During the complete destruction of the universe (during the *pralayā* period), *devas* will also be destroyed, even if they have earlier consumed the nectar. But on the other hand *Parameshwara*, who has consumed the most tyrant venom, is not destroyed – due to the grandeur of the earrings of *Śreedevee*. The idea that **She** is the *jeeva nāḍi* (soul pulse) of *Parameshwara* has been conveyed in the 28th verse of *Soundaryalaharee*;

Sudhāmabhyāsvādhya Pratibhaya Jarāmurtyu Hariŋeem
Vipadhyante Vishve Veidhi Shatamakhādhyā Divishada: I
Karālam Yat Kshvelam Kabalitavata: *Kālakalanā*
Na Shambhostanmoolam Tava Janani Thātanka Mahimā II

(iii) The same sense is communicated in *Śree Rudram* also; "*Ya Te Rudra Shivā Tanoo*: *Shivā Vishvā Ha Bheshajee Shiva Rudrasya Bheshajee Tayā No Mruḍa Jeevase*".

374. *Krutagyā* - कृतज्ञा

(i) One who knows all that is done.

(ii) **She** knows all the actions done by those who live in this world. The Sun, the moon, the god of death (*yama*), time and the five elements, these nine are the witnesses of good and bad actions. Only *Śreedevee* is in all these nine forms.

(iii) *Kruta* – done (good) actions, *Gnā* – knowledge (gives as a reward). **She** does this with gratitude.

(iv) *Kruta* (*vat*) – **She** possess already available (self-acquired) knowledge.

(v) It is told that in *Kruta Yuga*, the golden age, the righteousness was perfectly established; knowledge also was perfect. Later as time passes by it gets reduced in the next *yugas* (eras). However, **She** has perfect knowledge (as the golden age had).

(vi) According to the science of dice there are four *yugas* which are called *Kruta, Tretā, Dvāpara* and *Kali* and numbered respectively four, three, two and one; but they count then, six, three and one, respectively; because in the higher number the lower ones are included. *Chāndogya Upanishad* (IV-3-8) says, now these five and other five, make ten, that represents the *Kruta* cast. The meaning is like the *Kruta* cast, **Her** knowledge is all pervading and all embracing;

Te Vā Ete Panchānye Panchānye Dasha Sandas Tat Krutam.

(vii) *Chāndogya Upanishad* (IV-1-4) says, as in the game of dice all the lower casts belong to him who has conquered with the *kruta* cast. The meaning is like the *Kruta* case her knowledge is all pervading and all embracing. Hence *Krutagyā; Krutāya Vijitāyāta Re'yā: Samyanti.*

(viii) **She** knows the *kruta* cast as explained above. This expression is that **She** always conquers when **She** casts the dice with *Shiva.*

(ix) *Śree Ādi Śaṇkara* in his commentary of *Viṣhŋu Sahasranāma* for the 82nd name – *Krutagna*: – he who knows the sins and virtues of the living beings.

375. *Kāmapoojitā* - कामपूजिता

(i) One who was adored by Cupid.

(ii) *Taitireeya Āraŋyaga* says; *Putro Nirrutyā Vaideha Achetā Yashcha Chetana: Sa Tam Maŋimavindat* - The learned has interpreted this statement as - Cupid, son of *Mahālakshmee*, is without a body, but has attained great knowledge (*Maŋiyai, Panchadashee Vidyā*, etc).

(iii) Cupid is one among the 12 great worshippers of *Śreedevee*. This has been mentioned in the names 238th – *Manuvidyā*, 239th – *Chandravidyā* and 305th – *Rajarajārchita*.

(iv) *Śree Ādi Śaṇkara* also conveys this message, in his commentary of 5th and 6th verses of *Soundaryalaharee*.

Smaro'pi Tvām Natvā Ratinayana Lehayena Vapushā I
Muneenāmapyanta: Prabhavati He Mohāya Mahatām II
Dhanu: Poushpam Mourvee Madhukaramayee Pancha Vishekhā:
Vasanta: Sāmanto Malayamarudāyodhana Ratha: I
Tathāpyeka: Sarvam Himagirisute Kāmapikrupām
Apāngātte Labdhvā Jagadida Manango Vijayate II

(v) Cupid is also called as *Kāman*. *Kāman* worshipped *Śreedevee* in *Kāncheepuram*. Hence we see the names *Kāmakottam*, *Kāmakoṭi* and *Kāmapeeṭam*. These names and the name of *Śreedevee* as *Kāmākshee* – having blessed sight on *Kāman*, indicate the greatness of the worship of *Kāman* on *Śreedevee*.

(vi) Among the *Peeṭas* of *Śreedevee* the four important ones are *Kāmagiri Peeṭam*, *Poorŋagiri Peeṭam*, *Jālandhara Peeṭam* and *Oḍyāna Peeṭam*. *Kāmagiri Peeṭam* is talked about in this name and the remaining discussed in the later names.

(vii) Considering our body as a *kshetra*, it has to be construed that all the four *peeṭams* are within the body;

- *Kāma Peeṭam* – *Moolādhāram* – the place of *Parā* speech.
- *Poorŋagiri Peeṭam* – *Maŋipoorakam* – the place of *Pashyanti* speech.
- *Jālandhara Peeṭam* – *Anāhatam* – the place of *Madyamā* speech.
- *Oḍyāna Peeṭam* – *Vishuddhi* – the place of *Vaikharee* speech.

(viii) Cupid aimed the arrow of flowers on *Shiva,* to unite *Shiva* and *Śreedevee* for the birth of *Kumaran*. In this process he lost his body. By dedicating his body, he united *Śreedevee* with *Shiva.* As a gratitude for the same, **She** accepts his worship and provides him all the greatness. Like him, **She** also holds the bow made of sugarcane and arrows made of flowers. It is very apt that this message follows up the name *Krutagja*.

(ix) 586th name *Kāmasevitā* may also be referred.

376. *Shrungārarasasampoorŋā* - श्रृंगाटटससम्पूर्णा

(i) One who is filled with the essence of love.

(ii) In the previous name, reference was made to *Kāmagiri Peeṭam*. *Jālandhara* and *Oḍyāna* centres (*peeṭas*) will be referred in 378th and 379th names. In this name with the word *Poorŋa*, *Poorŋagiri Peeṭa* is referred.

(iii) It is said that *Poorŋagiri Peeṭa* resides in *Maŋipooraka* of the body. It may be remembered that it is the place of *Kāryabindu* and *Pashyanti* sound.

(iv) It is important to note that in all special forms of *Śreedevee* the form of *Lalitāmbikā* form has the *Sringarā* (erotic) emotion as the main one. This is further discussed in the last name *Lalitāmbika*.

(v) The letter *'A'* originated first and the other letters are all its varied forms. Again the sweet taste originated first and the other five are formed from it. Similarly *Sringāra* is the first emotion to origin and the other eight originated from it. That is, the other eight are the effects of *Sringāra* emotion. Hence it can be construed that, when **She** is full of the first emotion viz., *Sringāra*, **She** is full of the other eight also.

(vi) 51st verse of Soundaryalaharee and its commentary may be referred– here it is mentioned as *Śreedevee* gestures all the emotions one at a time excepting the tranquility emotion (which **She** always gestures);

Shive Srungārārdrā Taditarajane Kutsanaparā
Saroshā Gangāyām GIrishcharite Vismayavatee I
Harāhibhyo Beetā Sarasiruha Soubhāgya Jananee
Sakheshu Smerā Te Mayi Janani Drushti: *Sakaruṇā* II

(vii) *Srunga* - horn. Since animals have two horns each, this word cryptically indicates the number two. Similarly, since tastes are six in variety the word taste indicates the number six. (Such a type of indicating numbers in Samskrit is called *Bhoota Sankhya* or cryptic method). Both these words put together indicate 2 x 6 = 12. The letter 'A' means petal of a flower. Hence the word *Srungāra* indicates *Anāhata chakra*, which has 12 petals. *Sam* – frequently and *Poorṇa* – remains. Combining all these it can interpreted that **She** frequently remains in the *Anāhata chakra*. 595th name *Hrudayasthā* may also be referred.

(viii) *Srunga* – main or chief, *Arara* - covering, that is to say the *Avidyā* (ignorance), which veils, *Sa* with *Sampoorṇa*, *Brahmam* (literal meaning perfect).

(ix) The synopsis and the summary of the meaning of this name is that - **She** is both the conditioned and unconditioned *Brahmam*.

377. *Jayā* - जया

(i) One who is with the name *Jaya*.

(ii) According to the *Padma Purāṇa*, *Jayā* is the deity worshipped in the *Varāha* Mountain.

(iii) *Jayā* - victory. **She** is in that form. 346th name *Vijaya* may also be referred.

(iv) In the *Shilpasāstra* (science of sculpture), mention is made about a house by name *Jaya*. **She** is in that form. Relating to this, 346 – *Vijaya* and 347 – *Vimalā* may be referred.

(v) In *Mahāshoḍanyāsa* (*Prabancha Nyāsa*), we read as **She** was worshipped by thousand crore *Apsara* ladies race; *Sahasrakotyapsara*: *Kula Sevita*.

(vi) *Śree Ādi Śaṇkara* in his commentary of *Vişhŋu Sahasranāma* for the 509th name – *Jaya*: – one who is victorious of all the living beings.

(vii) It can be taken that this name, in a hidden manner, indicates *Jayini*, one of the eight *Vāgdevees*.

378. *Jālandharasthitā* - जालन्धरस्थिता

(i) One who dwells in *Jālandara* centre (*Peeṭa*).

(ii) According to *Padma Purāŋa*, **She** is called as *Vişhŋumukhee* in the *Jālantaramkshetra* (place).

(iii) **She** dwells in the *Anāhata Chakra* in the body. Hence **She** takes the sound form of *Nātha* in *Shabdabrahmam*; further **She** is the *Madhyamā* sound stage.

379. *Oḍyāŋapeeṭhanilayā* - ओड्याणपीठनिलया

(i) One who abides in the centre called *Oḍyāna*. Hence **She** takes the sound form of *Beeja* in *Shabdabrahmam*; further **She** is the *Vaikharee* stage of sound.

380. *Bindumaŋḍalavāsinee* - बिन्दुमन्डलवासिनी

(i) One who dwells in the *bindu* centre.

(ii) **She** resides in *Bindu Maŋḍala*, which is the innermost point (ninth *āvarana*) in *Śree Chakra*, representing *Sarvānandamaya Chakram*. The *Shiva Chakra* circle is the *Bindu Maŋḍalam*.

(iii) According some schools, in the body, *Bindu Maŋḍala* is the *Sahasrāra Chakra*. **She** dwells there.

381. *Rahoyāgakrmārādhyā* – रहोयागक्रमाराध्या

(i) One who is to be worshipped through secret rites.

(ii) In the *Bāhya Pooja* (*Navāvarŋa Pooja*), a series of preliminary activities are done like – offering prayers to the teacher, entering the *pooja* room, offerings to the seat, *nyāsās* (mental appropriation), establishing the vessels, etc. Before *Āvāhanā* of *Śreedevee* (deifying *Devee's* form on the image), the worshipper has to remove all blemishes of self. The concerned method is *Rahoyāgam*. This has to be done in a secret manner. This does not mean that it has to be done in a secret place. Lonely, without the knowledge of others, has to be imagined within self. At this juncture ceremonial fire rites have to be done. These have eight pourings in the fire. This *homa* (ceremonial fire) is virtually done in the mind. At *Moolādhārā*, the never subsiding fire i.e. *Kunḍalinee* energy, as thin as the head of a hair, is glowing. It glows itself, no other support is needed. We add our impurities to it and make it glow further. This is the *agni* (fire) centre in the *chitagni* centre. The eight things that separate us from *Śreedevee* are; the good & bad deeds, virtues & sins caused by those deeds, to resolute and irresolute to do those deeds and righteousness and unrighteousness arising out of those. Only when these are removed the integrated form with *Śreedevee* can be created. Hence these eight are to be offered in the *Chidagni* fire in *Kunḍalinee* and imagine that they have become ashes and think that all our impurities have been destroyed. Once all these, which control the soul, are destroyed, the soul automatically merges with the Supreme Being.

(iii) The sage *Āpasthambar* lists down those who will not get liberation – those who focus only on *Shabda Sāstra* (*vyākaraŋa* [grammar] *sāstra*), interested in mind blowing house, etc., having great interest in food, cloth, etc. and those who have bondage in the worldly affairs. He also lists down those who will get liberation – lonely manner, with stubborn will power, disinterest in those actions, which gives satisfaction, those with interest in *Adyāthma yoga* and who always avoid harm/ violence to all beings. Even in this manner only secret worship will give results.

(iv) All the *tantra sāstras* unanimously confirm that *Śree Vidyā* has to be kept in a very secret manner;

Veshyā Iva Prakatā Vedādividyā: *Sarveshu*
Darshneshu Gupteyam Vidyā II (*Parasurāma Kalpasūtra*)
Yadi Pravichet Mitho Charitvā Pravichet (*Aruŋōpanishad*)
Anta: *Shaktā*: *Bahi*: *Shaivā*: *Sabhayām Vaishnavā Matā*: I
Nānāmoorttidharā: *Koulā*: *Vicharaŋti Maheetale* II
(*Shyāmā Rahasyam*)

382. *Rahastarpaŋatarpitā* - रहस्तर्पणतर्पिता

(i) One who is gratified by secret oblations.
(ii) *Devatas* gets satisfied only if the complete meaning of the *mantras* is understood. This is called *tarpaŋam*. As mentioned in the previous name worshipping alone without the knowledge of others is called *rahasya tarpaŋam*. **She** gets satisfied by such worshipping.
(iii) The method of destroying the virtue, etc., in the fire, as discussed in the previous name, are explained in *pooja paddathis* (traditions of worshipping).

First;

Antar Nirantara Nirindhanam Edhamāne Mohāndhakāra Paripanthine I
Samvidagnou Kasmimshachit Adbhuta Mareechi Vikāsa Bhoomou II

I offer all the thirty-six *tatvas* starting from *Prithvee* till *Shiva* in the *samvitagni* (*gnanāgni*) – I sacrifice the universe from earth to *Shiva* in the fire of *samvit*, ever burning without any fuel and ever increasing, dispelling the darkness of illusion, the centre from which emanates eternal beautiful rays.

Second;

Prakāshāmarsha Hastābhyām Avalambyonmanee Srusami
Dharmādharmakalāsneham Poorŋa Vahnou Juhomyahami I

Holding in both hands, representing brightness and darkness (*prakāsa* and *vimarsa*) the sacrificial ladle of *unmaŋi* (a *Yogic* state), pouring out the ghee of righteousness and unrighteousness and the senses (*kalās*) in the fire of consciousness, I sacrifice. This verse is not available in some of the *pooja* methods.

Third;

Ārdram Jvalati Jyotirahasmi, Jyotir Jvalati Bramhāhamasmi, So'hamasmi Bramhāhamasmi, Ahamasmi Bramhāhamasmi, Ahamevāham Mām Juhomi Svāhā –

Even the wet objects (the virtue etc., which was offered into fire, which was an obstruction to recognise the self being, being wet they have inimical character to fire) glow well in the fire. I am like splendor. Splendor glows. I am like *Brahmam*. I am *Brahmam* and I myself is the *Brahmam*. So far considered '**I**', self has been offered in the fire.

383. *Sadya: Prasādinee* - सद्यः प्रसादिनी

(i) One who immediately bestows **Her** grace.
(ii) Made pleased by the secret method and *Raha:Tarpaŋam*, as

explained in the previous two names, *Śreedevee* right away bestows **Her** blessings to the devotees.

(iii) In the same fashion, *Paramashiva* also gets pleased early – *Āshutoshi*. This has been mentioned in the 88th chapter, *Uttarārttam*, tenth *skandam* of *Śreemad Bhāgavatam*.

(iv) *Śree Ādi Śaṇkara* in his commentary of *Viṣhŋu Sahasranāma* for the 905th name – *Swasti Dakshiŋa*: mentions three meanings; one among them is "**He** has the capability to bestow fortunes early".

384. *Vishvasākshiŋee* - विश्वसाक्षिणी

(i) One who is the witness of everything.

(ii) *Śreedevee* sees the entire world. **She** sees the entire world as **Her** own form.

385. *Sākshivarjitā* - साक्षिवर्जिता

(i) One who has no witness for **Herself**.

(ii) Since **She** is the witness to everything, **She** has no witness.

(iii) **She** was there before this universe originated and **She** will continue to be there even after the universe is destroyed. **She** has no beginning or end. Hence **She** is the witness to everything, there is no witness to **Her**.

(iv) In the 232nd name *Maheshwara Mahākalpa Mahātāndava Sākshinee*, it was mentioned that **She** was a witness to the great awesome destructive cosmic dance of Lord *Maheshvarā* during great dissolution (*pralaya* period).

(v) If one can understand that *Shiva* and *Shakti* are one and the same, as a role they seem to be different, then it is very clear that only *Śreedevee* is present during great dissolution period also.

386. *Shaḍangadevatāyuktā* - षडङ्गदेवतायुक्ता

(i) One who is accompanied by the deities of six limbs.

(ii) There are six limbs for the *mantra* form of *Śreedevee* (in general for all deities' *mantras*). It is the practice to mentally appropriate those deities in our body, while chanting the *mantras*. If the *mantra* is chanted without such appropriation, the fruit of the *mantra* cannot be obtained. If one after having taken good bath, decorating self with all the jewels, etc., but comes out without a dress – how much burlesque he may be undergo in public – it is similar to this. These six *angas* (limbs) are respectively heart, head, tuft of hair, armour (shoulders), eyes and weapons (assuming defense weapons around the head). During *Navāvarŋa pooja*, the *maŋḍalas* are drawn to keep the vessels and *shading archana* is done for the *maŋḍalas* and the vessels. Again at the stage of *Layānga pooja*, in the *bindu* in *sarvānandamaya chakra* at the ninth *āvarŋa*, *archana* is done for all the six *anga* deities.

(iii) The quality of *Eshwara* has six parameters (*angas*) viz., omniscience, contentment, wisdom without any origin, independence (to conduct everything as per self-wish), unfading power and endless. The deity with all these six angas is *Mahaehswara*. **She** is united with him.

(iv) *Veda* also has six parameters (*angas*) viz., knowledge of phonetics, lexicography prosody, grammar, astronomy and ceremonial (*kalpa*). These are respectively considered as nose, mouth, legs, ears, eyes and hands of the mother *Veda*. Hence *Veda* is with *Shadangas*. Since *Śreedevee* **Herself** is the mother *Veda* (338th name *Vedajanani* may be referred), **She** is *Shadangadevatāyuktā* - surrounded by the deities of these six *angas*.

387. *Shāḍguŋyaparipooritā* - षाड्गुण्यपरिपूरिता

(i) One who possess the six good qualities.

(ii) According to the *Kāmandakaneeti sāstra* (ethical code) the six characters a king should have are; peace, co-operation with other kings, war, marching with the armies, encamped, arranging his forces and allies. *Śreedevee* is a great empress (2nd name *Sremahārājnee*, 306th name *Rāgjee* and 684th name *Rāja-rajeshwaree*). **She** completely has all the above 6 characters.

(iii) The *Purāŋas* give out the following six as great characters; Prosperity, righteousness, fame, wealth, wisdom and dispassion. **She** is filled with these characters.

388. *Nityaklinnā* - नित्यक्लिन्ना

(i) One who is ever compassionate.

(ii) *Klinnā* means wet. **Her** heart is always wet due to the compassion over the devotees. 326th name *Karuŋārasasāgarā* may be referred.

(iii) In *Devee Mahātmya*, 4th chapter we read as;

Durgesmrutā Harasi Bheetimasheshajanto:

Svasthai Smrutā Matimateeva Shubhām Dadāsi I
Dāridriyadu:khabhayahāriṇikātvadanyā
Sarvopakārakaranāya Sadārdrachittā II

(iv) *Nityaklinnā* is the deity of the third day of the lunar fortnight. This deity has been described in the *Garuḍa Purāṇa* as giving happiness and salvation. In *Tantrarāja Tantra* also it is mentioned as; *Nityaklinnā matho Vakshye Tripurām Bhuktimuktidhām.*

(v) In the *mantras* of *thiti Nityas*, the word *klinnā* is specially mentioned in *Kāmeshwaree, Bagamālinee, Nityaklinna* and *Mahāvajreshvaree.* In the *Navāvarṇa pooja* also, while offering the special *argyās*, *Śreedevee* is addressed as *Klinna Roopine* or *Klinne* and the eternity and liberation are sought for. The same request is made in *Pancha panchikā pooja* and *Sudhāsukāmadughāmba Mantra* also.

389. *Niroopamā* - निरूपमा

(i) One who is peerless or without any comparable person.

(ii) Simile can be made with equal or peer objects only. There is no one equal to *Śreedevee*. Hence **She** has no comparison.

(iii) *Swetāvāsya Upanishad* (IV-19) advises as; *Na Tasya Pratimā Asti* – No one is equal to him. In Tamil Literature it is mentioned as; *Oppārum Mikkārum Illai* – No one equal to or above is available.

(iv) 184th name *Nistulā* may be refereed.

390. *Nirvāṇasukhadāyinee* - निर्वाणसुखदायिनी

(i) One who confers the bliss of *nirvāna*.

(ii) *Vāna* (or *bāna*) means body; In *Sruti* (*Prasna Upanishad* II-2) *Vedāntins* say; *Etad Bānamavashṭambhya* - Holding this bow (body) and in the word *Geervāna* by *Mimāmsakas* this word has been used in the same sense as body. Also in *Amarakosa*, for the word *Bāna* two meanings, body and bow, are given. Hence nirvāna means without body. That is the meaning of this name is - **She** offers bliss indescribable by words to **Her** devotees.

(iii) In the *Koorma Purāṇa* - *Śreedevee* says to *Himavan*; if you neglect me, Oh king of mountains, you cannot attain the pure rest of the supreme *nirvāna*, therefore seek refuge in me;

Mām Anādrutya Paramaṃ Nirvānam Amalam Padam I
Prapyate Nahi Shailendra Tato mām Sharanam Vraja II

(iv) The verses V-24/25 of *Śreemad Bhagavat Geeta* may be referred;

Yo'nta: Sukho'ntarārāmastathāntajyortireva Ya: I
Sa Yogi Brahmaŋirvānam Brhmabhooto'dhigachchati II
Labhante Brahmaŋirvānamrudhaya: Ksheenakalmashā: I
Chinnadvaidhā Yatātmāna: Sarvabhootahite Ratā: II

He whose happiness is within, whose delight is within, whose illumination is within only, that Yogi becomes *Brahmam* and gains the beatitude of *Brahmam*.

With sins destroyed, doubts removed, minds disciplined, being delighted in the welfare of all beings, the sages attain the beatitude of *Brahmam*.

391. *Nityāshoḍashikāroopā* - नित्याषोडशिकारूपा

(i) We have presiding deities for the 15 days from first to full moon day. They are all the limbs of *Śreedevee*. *Śreedevee* herself is the sixteenth *nityā* – i.e. *Mahānitya*. **She** is also called as *Sādākya Kala*. The description, method of *pooja*, *mantra*, *yantra*, etc., are described in detail in *Tantrarāja Tantra*.

(ii) The 15 *thities* and names accordingly *Śākta* practice are;

***Śākta Veda* Practice**	**Bright lunar fortnight**		**Dark lunar fortnight**	
	Days	**Nights**	**Days**	**Nights**
Kāmeshwaree	*Samgnanam*	*Darshā*	*Prastutam*	*Sudhā*
Bagamālinee	*Vgnanam*	*Drushtā*	*Vishtutam*	*Sunvatee*
Nityaklinna	*Pragnanam*	*Darshatā*	*Samstutam*	*Prasootā*
Perundā	*Jānat*	*Vishvaroopā*	*Kalyānam*	*Sooyamānā*
Vahnivāsinee	*Abhinānat*	*Sudarshanā*	*Vishvaroopa m*	*Abhishooyamā nā*
Mahāvajreshwar ee	*Sankalpamāna m*	*Āpyāyamān ā*	*Sookram*	*Bheetee*
Shivadootee	*Prakalpamāna m*	*Pyāyamānā*	*Amrutam*	*Prabhā*
Dwaritā	*Upakalpamāna m*	*Āpyāyā*	*Teshavee*	*Shambā*
Kulasundaree	*Upakluptam*	*Sunrutā*	*Teha:*	*Trupti*
Nityā	*Kluptam*	*Irā*	*Samittam*	*Tarpayantee*
Neelapadākā	*Sreya:*	*Āpooryamā nā*	*Aruŋam*	*Kāntā*
Vijayā	*Vaseeya:*	*Pooryamān ā*	*Bānumat*	*Kāmyā*
Sarvamangalā	*Āyat*	*Poorāyante e*	*Mareechima t*	*Kāmajātā*
Jvālāmālinee	*Sambootam*	*Poorŋā*	*Abitapat*	*Āyushmatee*
Chitrā	*Bootam*	*Pourŋamāse*	*Tapasvat*	*Kāmadukā*

(iii) We are aware that the bright lunar fortnight has been divided in three parts viz. 5, 6 and 4. This indicates the 3 *kandās* in the *Pancha-dashee mantra*.

(iv) These *thiti nityās* are worshipped from *Kāmeshwaree* to *Chitra* during bright lunar fortnight and from *Chitra* to *Kāmeshwaree* during dark lunar fortnight.

(v) These *thiti Nityā Devees* indicate that *Śreedevee* is in the form of era. *Pāvano Upanishad* advises as; *Panchatashatithiroopeṇa Kālasya Parināmvalokanam*.

(vi) It is also told that these are created by visualisation of five primary elements.

(vii) These indicate each of the letters in *Panchadashee mantra*.

(viii) During the bright lunar fortnight the Moon grows by absorbing the rays of the Sun. During dark lunar fortnight the brightness of the Moon decreases step by step. The *tithi nityās* are in this form.

(ix) 136th name *Nityā*, 256 – *Vishvaroopā*, 321 – *Kāmyā*, 329 – *Kāntā* and 610- *Pratipan Mukyākānta Tithimaṇḍala Poojitā* may be referred. To know more in detail about *Tithi Nityās*, *Tantra Rāja Tantra* and the commentary of *Śree Lakshmeedhara* for the 32nd verse of *Soundaryalaharee* may be referred.

392. *Shreekanṭhārdhashareeriṇee* - श्रीकण्ठार्धशरीरिणी

(i) One who has a body constituting one half of *Shiva*.

(ii) The word *Shree* has venom as a meaning. Since Lord *Paramashiva* venom in his neck, he got the name as *Shreekantan* (*kantam* – neck). **She** has *Paramashiva* as **Her** half body or **She** has in-differentiable half body with *Paramashiva*.

(iii) The 23rd verse of *Soundaryalaharee* also conveys the same sense;

Tvayā Hrutvā Vāmam Vapuraparitruptena Manasā
Shareerardham Shambhoraparamapi Shanke Hrutamabhoot I
Yadetat Tvadroopam Sakalamarunābham Trinayanam
Kuchābhyāmānamram Kutilashashichooḍālamakutam II

(iv) *Brahadāraṇya Upansihad* (verses I-3, 1-4) explains the universal absolute (*Parabrahmam*) becoming two as husband and wife; starting from *Ātmaivedamagra Āseet* till *Sa Imamevātmānam Dvetā'bhātayat Tata*:.

(v) It is mentioned in the *Vāyu Purāṇa* as; Lord *Paramashiva* 's body is white in colour whereas his neck is black (on account venom). Similarly *Śreedevee*'s body is partly in the form of *Gowree*, which is white in colour and partly in the form of *Kālee*, which is black in colour. *Saptashatee* (V chapter) also says that *Ambikā* form came out of *Gowree* form and *Kālee* form.

Tasyām Vinirgatāyām Tu Krshnā'bhootsā'pi Pārvatee I
Kāliketi Samākhyātā Himāchalakrutāsrayā II

(vi) According to *Mātrukā Kosa*, the word *Shreekanta* indicates the letter *'A'*. *Sruti* also says that the letter *'A'* is all the words and it merges with the consonants to form various words; *"Akārovai Sarvā Vak Saishā Sparshosh Mapir Vyāgyamānā Bahvee Nānāroopā Bhavati"*.

Its meaning goes – First pronounced *'A'* is the in the *Parā* stage of sound. Later it moves to the stage *Vaikharee*. Since *Śreedevee* is in the form of sound and since the letter *'A'*, called *Shreekantā*, is half of all the letters, **She** got the name *Shreekantārdhashareeriŋee*. Hence it is mentioned in *Soota Samhitā* (I-4-9) as;

Vākudbhootā Parāshaktiryā Chidroopā Parābhidhā I
Vande Tāmaŋisham Bhaktyā Shreekantārdha Shareeriŋeem II

(vii) This verse can also be interpreted as – *Śreedevee* having half body, filled up the remaining half body with that of *Shreekantan*. Here itself it is mentioned as; *"Ichchā Samgnā Cha Yā Shakti: Paripoorŋā Shivodara"*.

(viii) As per *Saiva Sāstras*, in *Mātrukā Nyāsam* (appropriation), half body is filled with various *shaktis* like *Poorŋodri*, etc. and other half being filled with *Shiva Mātrukās* like *Shreekantan*, etc. This name indicates the same.

(ix) When the letter *'A'* is written in Samskrit, half form equal to *Kāma kalā* is got. Hence it can also be interpreted as that **She** has got a body nothing different from *Kāma Kala*.

(x) The 52nd name in *Trishatee* is *Eshvarārtānka Shareera*. This has been interpreted as – **Her** body is in the form of *Ānanda*. The letter *'Ha'* in Samskrit indicates *Eshwar*. **She** is that half body of *Eshwar* i.e., It has been interpreted as that **She** is in the form of the letter *'E'* in Samskrit as *Shakti Beeja*. The letter *'HA'* can also be written as ':' (*visarga*). In some schools it is mentioned that **She** is half of it (*Anusvāram*).

393. *Prabhāvatee* - प्रभावती

(i) One who is endowed with the power of effulgence (luminescence).

(ii) *Prabhā*, the surrounding *Āvarana devatās*, namely *Aŋimā*, etc., because there is a saying, *Śreedevee* is surrounded by *aŋimā* and other luminaries. They originated as radiating light from the body of

Śreedevee. In the *dyānā* (meditation) verse of this *Sahasranāma* also we read as; *Aŋimādibhirāvrutām Mayookhai*:. In the 30th verse of *Soundaryalaharee* also it has been mentioned as;

Svadehod-bhootābhir Ghruŋibhiraŋimādyābhirabhito.

394. *Prabhāroopā* - प्रभारूपा

(i) One who is in the form of *Prabhā* (*Aŋimā*, etc). brightness.

(ii) Learned Jains, *Haribhadra* and others, record in their works *Dharmasangrahinee*, etc., the rays are the qualities, they are not substratum; among these even, the quality of brightness is not the substratum. There is no difference between the character and the person having that character, *Śreedevee* can be considered as *Prabhāroopa*.

(iii) Similarly we read in *Chāndokya Upanishad* (III-14-2) as; *Manomaya*: *Prāŋa Shareerobhāroopa*: - mind itself, brightness itself.

(iv) **She** is in the form of *chandas* (metre) called *Prabha*. (*Mandākinee* is also another name for **Her**).

(v) The name of the seventh night of dark lunar fortnight is called *Prabha*.

395. *Prasiddhā* - प्रसिद्धा

(i) One who is celebrated by all.

(ii) *Śreedevee* is known by all in the shape of 'I' or *'aham'*. **She** is that 'I' known by all and hence *Prasiddha*. The *Devee Bhāgavatam* says, that all men recognise *Śreedevee* under the form of 'I'; *"Tām Ahampratyayavyājāt Sarve Jānanti Jantava:"*. The first verse of the same book also says, we meditate upon the primeval *vidyā* in the form of the universal *chaitanya*; *"Sarva Chaitanya Roopām Tām Ādyām Vidyām Cha Dheemahi"*.

396. *Parameshvaree* - परमेश्वरी

(i) One who is the Sovereign Supreme.

(ii) **She** is the *Ĕshwari*, the *shakti* of the universal absolute.

(iii) In *Mahāshoḍanyāsa* (*Prabancha Nyāsa*), it has been mentioned that **She** is in the form of seasons.

(iv) *Śree Adi Śuŋkara* in his commentary of *Vişhŋu Sahasranāma* for the 377th name – *Parameshwara*: – he is *Parameshwara*: since he has great wealth and supreme ruling power.

397. ***Moolaprakruti*****: - मूलप्रकृतिः**

(i) One who is the in the form of *prakruti* (nature), which is the primary cause of everything in the universe.

(ii) For *Śreevidyā*, which is the root *mantra*, has two causal letters *prakāsa 'A'* and *vimarsa 'Ha'*. **She** is in the form those two root letters.

(iii) *Prakruti* is the one without any changes/modifications. If it undergoes changes it is called *Vikruti*. That prakruti, which does not undergo any modifications, is called as *Moola Prakruti* by those who follow *Sankhya* religion. She is in the form of that famous *Moola Prakruti*.

(iv) According to the *Mrugendra Samhita*, the *Kuṇḍalinee* is called *Moolaprakruti* with its seven productions (*mahat*, etc).. Since *Śreedevee* is in the form of *Kuṇḍalinee* (110th name), **She** is *Moolaprakruti*.

Mahadādi Saptaka Roopa Sushumnā Veshtitā I
Kuṇḍalinyeva Ashṭaprakrutiroopā Moolaprakrutiruchyate II

(v) From earth to ether, each is the prakruti (origin) of the succeeding one; i.e. earth from water, water from fire (*Agnorāpa*:), fire from air (*Vāyoragni*:) and air from ether (*Ākāshāt Vāyu*:) originated. At last for the ether *Brahmam* is the origin; as per the *Taitireeya Upanishad* (II-1) statement; *Ātmana Ākāsha*: *Sambhoota*: - from the self-arose ether. That *Brahmam* has no *prakruti* (origin). Hence he is the root (*moola*), the first cause or *Moolaprakruti*.

(vi) The world being created from the *moolaprakruti* in the form *vikruti* is called *srushṭi* (creation). That *vikruti* form merging with the *moolaprakruti* is called *pralaya* (dissolution). Hence creation, in the middle *layam* for some time and dissolution and again creation is in a cyclic form.

(vii) Amongst the actions (*karma*), which are to become ripe in a certain time, those that ripen are exhausted by fruition, the others which are not ripe and have not come, consequently, to fruition, a new creation for their sake being useless, a *prāktruta* (temporary) *pralaya* (dissolution) takes place. At this stage they are not destroyed. They return fresh as if they were kept in a refrigerator.

(viii) This ignorance (*avidyā*) is called as *avyaktā* (un-manifested) or illusion (*māyā*).

(ix) Such *layā*, is not similar to the complete destruction like liberation. During meditation, the feelings of the organs are under control. Similarly the feelings of the *māyā* also are not visible during dissolution. They seem to be un-illuminated.

(x) Then *māyā*, consuming entire world, is absorbed into the independent *Paramashiva*, who is without attributes; it (*māyā*) abides thus, till the ripening of the remaining actions. The modification of *māyā* in the form of desire for creation arises in *Paramashiva* for the sake of bestowing the fruit on those whose unripe actions are absorbed in *māyā*; when their actions become ripe in course of time, that state of *māyā* is variously named by the words sight, desire, thought, desire of action, etc., by *Vedas* (*Ekshana, Kāma, Tapas* and *Vichikeershā*).

The *AItreya Upanishad* (I-1) says, he thought, let me create the worlds;

Sa Eshata Lokānnu Srujai.

The *Chāndokya Upanishad* (VI-2-3) says, if I thought, let me become many; *"Tataikshata Bhahusyām Prarajāyeya"*.

The *Taitireeya Upanishad* says, let it become many;

So'kāmayata Bhahusyām Prarajāyeya.

The *Muṇḍaka Upanishad* (I-1-8) says - by penance *Brahmam* is increased; *"Tapasā Cheeyate Brahma"*.

This manifestation of *māyā*, characterised by objective distinctions, is the first creation, the creation of darkness (*tāmasa sarga*), void of consciousness. The *Rig Veda* (X-129) beginning with "there was no being, in that time, nor, was no being - in the beginning darkness was hidden by intelligence," also confirms the above; *"Nāsadāseenno Sadāseet, Tama Āseetatamasā Goolahamadre"*.

(xi) The *Prādānika Rahasya* of *Saptashatee* also conveys the same sense.

(xii) The statements like *"Avyakta* originated from it" in *Vedas* confirm the same thought.

(xiii) From this creation called *tāmasa*, in which the three qualities (*Guṇas*) were differentiated, arose the creation of partially manifested, *mahat*. This is the second creation. It is said, "from *avyakta* comes the category of *mahat* in which are distinctly manifested the three *Guṇas*; so also from *mahat ahamkāra* (egoism)". From that (creation of *mahat*) arises the third, the creation of *ahamkāra* in which the three *Guṇas* are manifested objectively. It is said, "From *mahat* arose the three-fold egoism, namely *vaikārika* (pure), *taijasa* (passionate) and *tāmasa* (dark), which last is the origin of the elements". Here, as "*tāmasa* is the origin of the elements," it follows that the rest of the creation belong to *satva* and *rajas*.

From that *tāmasa* egoism which is called the origin of the elements, arose, with the aid of the *rajas*, creation of the five subtle elements (*tanmātras*). This is the fourth creation.

From the pure egoism called *vaikārika*, with the aid of rajas, arose the creation of the aggregate of eleven senses. This is the fifth creation.

From the *rajas* egoism, the deities, *Dik*, *Vāta*, *Arka*, *Prachetas* and *Ashvini Devas* who are the deities of the above two (fourth and fifth creations). This is the sixth creation. The *Samkhyā Karikai* says (25th verse) says; from the pure egoism arose the eleven *sāttvika* creation (senses); from the *bhootādi* (*tāmasa* egoism) the subtle elements and from *rajas* egoism (the deities presiding over both);

Sāttvika Ekādashaka: *Pravartate Vakkirutādahankārāt* I
Bhootādes Tamasadas Tanmātram Taijasādubhayam II

(xiv) But in the *Saiva* school it is said, from pure egoism comes mind, from passionate egoism, the ten senses; thus there is a difference. For the *Saivas* say, it (*mahat*) becomes threefold by differentiation of *satva*, *rajas* and *tamas*; that is called by names *vaikārika*, *taijasa* and *bhootadi*; from *taijasa* mind comes, from *vaikārika* senses and from *bhootadi* the subtle elements. Thus are the creations from that *mahat*;

*Sātvika Rājasa Tāmasa Bhedhena Sa Jāyate Punasredhā*I
Sa Cha Taijasa Vaikārikabhootādika Nāmabhi: *Samullashati* II
Taijasatas Tatra Mano Vaikārikato Bhavanti Sākshāni I
Bhootādes Tanmātrānyeshām Sargo'yametasmāt II

(xv) These six creations are *prākruta* (belong to *prakruti*). The *vaikruta* (belonging to products, *mahat*, etc). creation, comprises trees, etc., whose life-current tends upwards; animals, whose life current is horizontal; and *bootha*, *preta* (corpse), etc., whose life-current tends downwards. These *prākruta* and *vaikruta* creations, taken together are called the *koumāra* creation.

(xvi) *Śreemad Bhāgavata Purāṇa* (III *Skanda*, 10th chapter) says, the first is the creation of *mahat*, therein the inequality of the *Guṇas* arises. The second is egoism therein arise object (*dravya*), knowledge (*jnāna*) and action (*kriyā*). The third is the creation of the elements. Therein arise the subtle elements, having the energies of *dravya*. The fourth is the creation of the senses, which consists of knowledge and action. The fifth is the *vaikhārika*, the creation of the *Devas*, which consists of mind. The sixth is the creation of *tamas* which is the creation of the all-pervading *māyā*, devoid of knowledge. These six are called *prākrta* creations. Hear from me the *vaikruta* creation, etc.

Ādyastu Mahata: *Sargo Kunavaishamyamātmana*: I
Dveteeyastavahamo Yatra Dravyagnanakriyodaya: II
Bhootasarigastruteeyastu Tanmātro Dravya Shaktimān I
Chaturtha Indriya: *Sargo Yastu Gnanakriyātmaka*: II
Vaikāriko Devasarga: *Panchamo Yanmayam Mana*: I
Shashṭastu Tamasa: *Sargo Yastvabhuddhikruta*: *Prabho* II
Shadime Prākrtā: *Sargā Vakrutānapi Me Srunu* II

(xvii) Here the creation of *tamas* called *avyakta*, is the sixth in the order, but according to its meaning, it should be taken as first. In these creations beginning with the *avyakta* creation, the previous one is the origin of succeeding ones. *Brahmam* alone is the origin of the *avyakta*. Hence, as he is the root of all creations and as he has no root, he is the root-matter (*moolaprakruti*). Hence *Kaṭopanishad* (III-10-11) says, beyond the senses there are the objects. Beyond the *mahat*, the *avyakta*, beyond *avyakta* there is the person. Beyond the person, there is nothing. This is the goal and the Supreme abode.

(xviii) Thus the names 397 to 401 the order of creation is explained in 5 names. *Prakruti* is the root cause of everything. This has no cause. *Prakruti-vikruti* (it may look like *prakruti* for one and *vikruti* for others), *Vikruti* (the *mahā bootas* originated from *tanmātrā*), the organs, mind, etc. – there is no cause for all these. *Śreedevee* only is all the cause and results of the nature's *tatvas* in these three stages – that is what is advised by these 5 names. In this name it is said as the root cause or *moolaprakruti*. This is a combined form of I*chchā Shakti*, *Kriyā Shakti*, *Gnana Shakti*, *Kunḍalinee*, *Parā* and *Mātruka*. 110th name – *Kunḍalinee*, 145 – *Nirvikārā*, 256 *Vishvaroopa*, 366 – *Parā*, 577 – *Mātrukā Varŋaroopiŋee* and 658 – *Icchā Shakti Kriyā Shakti Gnana Shakti Swaroopiŋee*, may be referred.

(xix) Another interpretation for this name is – Based on the *Kaṭapayādi* method of number system, *ma* is five (the five subtle elements) and *la* is three, (i.e. *avyakta*, *mahat* and *ahamkāra*). Therefore *moola* is eight *prakruti* causes for creation. The *Samāsa Sūtra* (the abridged version of this is assumed as *Sānkhya Sūtra*) says, there are eight *prakrutis*; *Ashṭouprakrutaya*:.

(xx) For reference; in the 826th name – *Prasavitree*, it is mentioned that there are five different names for a mother. All those five names can be found in this *Sahasranāma*.

398. ***Avyaktā* - अव्यक्ता**

(i) One who is not visibly seen – is in an un-manifested state.

(ii) As discussed above, when the Brahmam (*Vichikeershā*) feels to create, the form taken by it on account of *māyā* (illusion) is called *Avyaktam*. According to the Samkhya School, it is expressed by the words, *Prakruti* (matter), *pradhāna* (foundation) and *avyakta*. 145th name *Nirvikārā* may be referred.

(iii) It is said in the *Samkhyasaptami* that is the *avyakta* which is subtle, without characteristics, inanimate, without beginning or end, capable of production, without parts, one and universal;

Sookshmam Alingam Achetanam Anāḍinidanam Tathā Prasavadharmi I
Niravayavam Ekameva Hi Sādhāranam Etat Avyaktam II

(iv) *Viroopaksha Panchasikhā* also says, *Pradhāna*, say the wise, is the *avyakta*, which is without beginning or middle, beyond *mahat* and permanent. It is the collective form of the three qualities;

Anāḍimadhyam Mahata: *Param Dhruvam*
Pradhānam Avyaktam Ushanti Shoorāya: II

(v) The *Samkhya Sūtra* (VI-39) says, *Satva* and the rest are not qualities of that *Brahmam*, because they are the qualities of that *avyakta*;

Sattvādeenāmetaddharmatvam Tadroopatvāt

Thus the *Prakruti* called *Avyakta* is explained here.

(vi) By the word *Avyakta* the *Brahmam* is indicated. In *Brahma Sūtra* (III-2-23) it is said, that *Brahmam* is *avyakta* for the scriptures say so;

Tadavyaktamāha Hi.

(vii) *Śree Ādi Śaṇkara* explains this with the following *Veda* statements – *Muŋḍaka Upanishad* (III-1-8), He is not to be felt by the eyes, nor by the speech, nor by the other senses, nor by penance, nor by actions; "*Nachakshushā Gruhyate Nāpi Vāchā Nanyaidevais Tapasā Karmanā Va*". Further this has been evidenced through *Brahāraŋya Upanishad* (III-9-26), *Muŋḍaka Upanishad* (II-1-6) and *Taitreeya Upansihad* (II-7-1).

(viii) Again *Śree Ādi Śaṇkara* quotes the *Śreemad Bhagavat Geeta* (verse II-25) also - this *ātman* is said to be unmanifested, unthinkable and immutable. Therefore, knowing it as such you should not grieve;

Avyakto'yamachintyo'yam Avikāryo'yamuchyate I
Tasmādevam Viditvainam Nanushochitumarhasi II

(ix) The *Linga Purāŋa* says that *avyakta* means *Viṣhŋu*. The names of *Viṣhŋu*, who is ever capable of creation, are *Pradhāna, Avyaya, Yoni* [origin), *Avyakta, Prakruti* and *Tamas*. This name stresses that

Śreedevee is in the form of *Vişhŋu;*

Pradhānamavyayam Yoni: Avyaktam Prakrutis Tama: I

Vishnoretāni Nāmāni Nityam Prabhava Dharmina: II

(x) *Śree Ādi Śaņkara* in his commentary of *Vişhŋu Sahasranāma* for the 305th name – *Vyaktaroopa*: - his gross form as universe can be clearly perceived. (It need not be mentioned that this is opposite to the meaning of *Avyakta*).

399. *Vyaktāvyaktasvaroopiŋee* - व्यक्ताव्यक्तस्वरूपिणी

(i) One who is in a manifest as well as un-manifest state.

(ii) To start with *Vyakta*, the category *mahat*, is called so because it was first manifested and also from its greatness. This name can be split as *Vyakta* + *Āvyakta*. Since *Vyakta*, manifested, i.e., egoism the product of the above, *Āvyakta*. Thus **She** is in the form of *Mahat* and *Ego*.

(iii) In some schools, this name is taken as two names *Vyaktā* and *Avyaktasvaroopiŋee* and they take name *Brahmajanani* (822 and 823) as a single one. (*Śree Bhāskara Rāya* says, if 822 and 823 are taken as two names, 819 *Sarvāntaryāminee* has to be treated as two names. But as per *Paribhāsha* verse this is a single name). According to this view, *vyakta* is the supreme egoism, for supreme egoism is in the form of *Tripurasundaree*, because **She** is manifested in the category of egoism. Or, **She** is in the form of both manifested and un-manifested. That is, **She** is and is not subjected to the modifications of the elements.

(iv) The *Linga Purāŋa* says, *Vyakta* is called *sat* (existence), as it is the second modification of the elements; *avyakta* is called *asat* because it is devoid of that modification;

Bhootabhāva Vikārena Dviteeyena Sat Uchyate I

Vyaktam Tena Viheenatvāt Avyaktam Asat Ityapi II

(v) *Vyakta* is perishable and *avyakta* is imperishable. **She** has both the characters. The *Matsya Purāŋa* says; *"Uktam Aksharamavyaktam Vyaktam Ksharam Utāhrutam"*.

(vi) *Vyakta* is individual and *avyakta* is collective form. This has been mentioned in the *Narasimha Purāŋa* as, the *avyakta* is known as collective and *vyakta*, Oh lord of ascetics, is individual; *"Samshtim Viduravyaktam Vyaktam Vyashţim Muneeshvarā:"* I

(vii) According to the *Brahmāņḍa Purāŋa*, the wise say the twenty three categories are meant by the word *vyakta* and by the word *avyakta*, the supreme nature;

Trayovimshati Tatvāni Vyakta Shabdena Surāya: I
Vadantyavyakta Shabdena Prakrutim Cha Parām Tathā II

(viii) By splitting this name in three different ways - *vyakta, avyakta* and *vyaktāvyakta*; thus there are three kinds of *lingas* (of *Shiva*). **She** is in all the forms. The three kinds of *lingas* are described in the *Brahma Vaivarta Purāṇa* - there are three *lingas*, namely *Svayambhuva* (self-originating), *Bānalinga* (got from a certain river) and *Sailalinga* (made of stone); these are respectively called *Vyakta, Avyakta* and *Vyaktāvyakta. Vyakta,* they say, gives salvation, the *Avyakta* gives worldly happiness and *Vyaktāvyakta* gives both happiness and salvation. The *Bānalinga* is said to be that which outweighs even two or three *tulas* (a measure of weight). The rest are called *Saila* (mere stone) by the learned;

Svāyampuvam Bāṇalingam Shailalingamiti Tridhā I
Keertitam Vyaktamavyaktam Vyaktāvyaktamitikramāt II
Vyaktam Bhuktipradam Muktipradamavyaktamuchyate I
Bhuktimukti Pradam Lingam Vyaktāvyaktam Prachkshate II
Dvitristulām Samārooḍham Vruddhimeti Na Heeyate I
Tat Bhānalingamuditam Shesham Sailam Vidurbudhā: II

(ix) **She** is manifested (*avyakta*) in those whose deeds are ripened; and not manifested (*avyakta*) in those who are bound by the noose of *Māya*. The *Shaktirahasya* says when it describes the descent of the *Shakti* into man - how do you say that the supreme *Shakti,* which is all-pervading descends, the descent is from above downwards; only that which has form and is not all-pervading can descend? True, **She** is all pervading, eternal, co-exist with *Shiva* ; yet **She** is hidden in those who are bound by the noose of impurity, action, etc. and manifested in them whose sins are burnt out, in this way **She** is said to descend;

Vyāpinee Paramā Shakti: *Patitetychyate kadam* I
Urdhvāt Adho Gati: *Pāto Murtasyā Sarvagasyacha* II
Satyam Sā Vyāpinee Niytā Sahajā Shiva vatstithā I
Kimtviyam Malakarmādhi Pāshabaddheshu Samvrutā II
Pakvadosheshu Suvyaktā Patitatyupacharyate I

400. *Vyāpinee* - व्यापिनी

(i) One who is all pervading.
(ii) As per discussed earlier, in the 397th name *Moolaprakruti,* **She** is called all-pervading, because **She** assumes the forms of the three

creations of the threefold egoism. Hence She is *Vyāpinee*.

(iii) In *Devee Upanishad* we read as;

Ekaiva Sarvatra Vartate, Tasmāduchyate Ekā I
Ekaiva Vishvaroopiŋee, Tasmāduchyate Naikā II

(iv) *Saptashatee* (XI-5) says;

Tvayaikayā Pooritamambayatat Kā Te Stuti: *Stavyaparā'parokti*: II

(v) 282nd name – *Sahasrasheershavadanā*, 283 – *Sahasrākshee* and 284 – *Saharapād* may be referred.

Thus ends the fifth *Kalā* called *Jvālinee*.

*****

Section 6: Ruchi *Kalā*

401. *Vividhākārā* - विविधाकारा

(i) One who has multi forms.

(ii) In 397th name *Moola Prakruti,* different forms of creation viz., *Prākruta, Vaikhareeka* and *Koumāra* were explained. **She** is in those forms.

(iii) The order of creation of the universe was explained so far.

(iv) We read in *Saptashatee* (XI chapter) also as; *"Roopairanekair Bahadhātma Moortheem Krutvā'mbike Tatprakaroti Kānyā"* II

(v) 824th name *Bahuroopa* may also be referred.

402. *Vidyāvidyāsvaroopiņee* - विद्याऽविद्यास्वरूपिणी

(i) One who is in the form of both knowledge and ignorance.

(ii) *Vidyā* (knowledge) means self realisation. In this context *Avidyā* does not exactly mean ignorance, but the knowledge in the form of the last modification (of duality, i.e., just before realisation). These two are mentioned as forms of *Śreedevee* here. *Vidyā* and *Avidyā* are explained in the *Isāvasya Upanishad* (11th verse) ; one who simultaneously knows both knowledge and ignorance having crossed over the death by ignorance attains immortality by knowledge; *Avidyāyā Mrutyum Teertvā Vidyāyā'mrutatvam Asnute.*

(iii) The *Bruhan Nāradeeya Purāņa* also says, the supreme *Shakti* of *Vișhņu,* capable of absorbing the universe, in the form of existence and non-existence, is sung by *vidyā* and *avidyā;*

Tasya Shakti: Parā Vishnor Jagatkārya Parikshamā I
Bhāvābhāvasvaroopā Sā Vidyā'vidyetigeeyate II

(iv) In *Devee Bhāgavatam* also, **She** being *Brahmam* **Herself** is very difficult to attain and is in the form of *vidyā* and *avidyā;*

Brahmaiva Sātidushprāpā Vidyāvidyā Svaroopiņe

In another place, "Oh king, know, that *vidyā* and *avidyā* are two forms of *Śreedevee*; by one men is freed, by the other they are bound;

Vidyāvidyeti Devyā Dve Roope Jāneehi Pārthiva I
Ekayā Muchyate Janturanyayā Badyate Puna: II

(v) *Vidyā*, the knowledge in the form of the last modification of duality or of the false knowledge (*karmavrutti*). *Avidyā*, confused knowledge of separateness; i.e., the knowledge of wrongly recognising one to the other. *Sva*, the knowledge belonging to supreme *Brahmam*;

because according to one lexicography, *sva* means - relations and self; *roopa* - these three are **Her** forms.

(vi) *Linga Purāŋa* says *Shiva* has three forms, *Bhrānti, Vidyā* and *Para*. The knowledge of different objects is called *Bharānti* (confused) by the learned. Knowledge in the form of self, is called *vidya*. Knowledge concerning *Brahmam* without ambiguity is called *parā* (supreme):

Brāntir Vidyā Param Cheti Shiva svaroopamidam Trāyam I
Artheshu Bhinnaroopeshu Vighnanam Brāntiruchyate II
Ātmākāreŋa Samvittirbudhair Vidyeti Kadyate I
Vikalpa Rahitam Tatvam Paramityabhiteeyate II

403. *Mahākāmeshanayanakumudāhlādakoumudee* – महाकामेशनयनकुमुदाह्लादकौमुदी

(i) One who gladdens the eyes of *Mahākāmeshwara* as the moon gladdens the lilies in water.

(ii) *Mahākāmeshwara* indicates one who is *mahān* (great) as well as *Kāmeshwar*. *Kāmeshwaree* is one of the names of *Śreedevee*. *Kāmeshwarar* is one of the names of *Paramashiva*.

(iii) One who is *Mahākāman* (*kāmam* means amorousness) as well as *Eshwar* is *Mahākāmeshar*.

(iv) *Mahakāmeshar* looks at *Śreedevee* and due to the consequential happiness, his eyes gladden. *Śreedevee* is described as a Moon to gladden his eyes. *Kumudam* means flowers Lily, *Kairavam, Rakta Pankajam* and Red Lotus. *Koumudam* is the name for the full moon day of the month *Kārthikai*. *Yādava* dictionary says;

Kumudam Kairave Raktapankaje Kumuda: *Kapou* I
Koumuda: *Kārtike Māsi Chandrikāyām Cha Koumudee* II

(v) *Ku* – lower, *muda* = happiness; *kumuda* means the happiness gained due to welfare of worldly affairs. Since the sorrow also comes alongwith that it is mentioned as lower one. *Kumuda* also means – one who needs mercy. In the *Shasvata* dictionary we read as; *Krupane Kumude Kumude*. In the dictionary called *Vishvam* it is mentioned as; "*Syātkumuda Krupane'nyavat*".

(vi) That is, **She** gives liberation (*Āhlādam*) by taking along (*nayana*), to those who pray to *Mahākāmeshar*, who involve in the worldly affairs/happiness and who need mercy. In other words, the meaning of this name is, **She** is like the moon, which gives cool light to liberate them, has compassion on those who have interest in the worldly affairs and takes them along to *Shiva*.

(vii) That is, this name has two meanings –

1. Like the Moon gladdening the flowers like eyes of *Mahākāmesha*.

2. Like the Moon which gives liberated bliss to those who have interest in the worldly affairs and takes them along to *Shiva*.

404. *Bhaktahārdatamobhedabhānumadbhānusantati*: - भक्तहार्दतमोभेदभानुमद्भानुसन्तति:

(i) One who is like the bunch of Sun's rays, dispelling the darkness of ignorance in the minds of the devotees.

(ii) *Banu* – rays. *Banumān* – Sun. The ignorance in the minds of the devotees is the darkness. **She** removes it and hence compared to Sun.

405. *Shivadootee* - शिवदूती

(i) One who has *Shiva* as herald.

(ii) It is a famous story in *Devee Mahātmyam* (8th chapter) that – when *Śreedevee* was ready to wage the war with *Shumba* and *Nishumba*, **She** had consideration on them and wanted to give a chance for them to give refuge, **She** sent *Paramashiva* himself as her messenger;

Sā Chāha Dhoomra Jatilameeshānamaparājitā I
Dootastvam Gaccha Bhagavān Pārshvam Shumbhanishumbhayo: II

(iii) In *Padma Purāṇa* (*Pushkara Kāṇḍa*), it has been mentioned that the name of the deity in the holy waters called *Pushkaram* is *Shiva-dootee*.

406. *Shivārādhyā* - शिवाराध्या

(i) One who is fit to be worshipped by *Shiva*.

(ii) It is mentioned in *Brahmāṇḍa Purāṇa* that *Shiva* himself worshipped *Śreedevee*. By meditating **Her** and on account of the strength of yoga, **He** became the head of all *Siddhis* (*Eshwaran*) and *Ardha Nāreeshwaran*;

Shivopi Yām Samārādhya Dhyānayoga Phalenacha I
Ĕshwara: *Sarvasiddheenāmardhanāreeshvar' Bhavat* II

(iii) **She** is in the form of four groups worshipped by *Shiva*.

407. *Shivamoortti*: - शिवमूर्त्तिः

(i) One who has *Shiva* himself as **Her** form.

(ii) The non-differentiation between *Shiva* and *Shakti* is discussed here. *Sruti* says, one *Rudra* hidden in all beings, he is with *Māyā*, with and without organs. He is *Śreedevee* herself and is not separated from **Her**. By knowing this, one attains immortality.

Eko Rudra: *Sarvabhooteshu Goodha*: *Māyārudra*: *Sakalo Nishkalashcha* I
*Sa Eva Devee Na Cha Tadvibhinnā Hyetat Gnātvaivāmrutatvam Vrajanti*II

(iii) The same sense is conveyed in names 665 – *Ekākinee*, 725 – *Dakshiṇāmoortiroopiṇee* and 861 – *Kāntārdhavigraha*.

(iv) **She** has an auspicious form.

(v) *Shiva* - beneficent, *Moorti* - form; or *Shiva* - salvation, *Moorti* - form. Because salvation is the realization of the very self. The *Soura Samhitā* (XIV chapter) says - now I shall explain concisely to you the nature of salvation. Hence the supreme salvation is the realization of the Self, those who were bound by *avidyā*, are freed by *vidya*.

Tasmādātma Svaroopaiva Parā Muktira Vidyāyā I
Pratibaddhā Vishuddhasya Vidyāyā Vyāgyate'naghe II

(vi) In *Śree Rudram* also;

Yāte Rudra Shivā Tanooraghorā'pāpakāshinee I
Tayā Nastanuvā Shantamayā Girishantābhichākasheehi II

Again *Śree Rudram* (X *Anuvāham*) we read;

Yā Te Rudra Shivā Tanoo: *Shivā Vishvāhabheshajee* I
Shivā Rudrasya Bheshajee Tayā No Mruḍa Jeevase II

In *Śree Mahābhārata* also, it is mentioned that *Paramashiva* has one crude body and another auspicious giving body. Learned people say that those two bodies alone split into hundreds of various other forms.

Śree Anantharāma Deekshitar's book on *Śree Rudram* says;

Dvee Tanoo Tasya Devasya Vedagnnā Brāhmanā Vidu: I
Ghorā Chānyā Shivā Chānyā Te Chaiva Shatadhā Puna: II

(vii) 736th name – *Muktidā*, 737 – *Mukti Roopinee* and 839 – *Mukti Nilayā* may be referred.

408. *Shivamkaree* - शिवंकरी

(i) One who dispenses happiness/ auspiciousness.

(ii) *Shiva* means auspicious or *kalyānam*. **She** does this.

(iii) **She** makes her devotees happy by removing the noose of *avidyā* and leads them to *Brahmam*, which is to be attained by liberated souls.

(iv) *Vasinee* and other Devees pray *Śreedevee* by the name *Agnāna*

Dhvānta Deepikā (993rd name) also.

409. *Shivapriyā* - शिवप्रिया

(i) One who is the beloved of *Shiva.*
(ii) Or **She** has *Shiva* as **Her** lover.

410. *Shivaparā* - शिवपरा

(i) One who is above Lord *Shiva.*
(ii) Since *Shiva* is owner of *Śreedevee*, **She** is considered above him.
(iii) *Śree Ādi Śaṇkara*, in his *Soundaryalaharee*, (1st verse) mentions as; *Shiva*: *Shaktiyā Yukto...*
(iv) **She** has only *Shiva* above **Her**.
(v) **She** guides *Shiva* to **Her** devotees.

411. *Shishṭeshṭā* - शिष्टेष्टा

(i) One who is dear to the righteous people.
(ii) **She** likes virtuous people.
(iii) **She** is liked by upright people.
(iv) **She** likes the actions destined in *Vedas*.
(v) The character of a righteous person is; origins from faithful actions. *Viṣhŋu* is the head of qualities; ("*Āchāraprabhavo Dharmo Dharmasya Prabhurachyuta*:" - Verse 17 of the closing remarks for *Viṣhŋu Sahasranāma*).
(vi) In *Vashishṭa Sūtra* explains *Shistās* (virtuous people) as who have control of organs, speech and the body, who have hereditarily adopted *Vedas* and *Vedāngas* and who have their goals in accordance with *Vedas*. These people are to be known as upright people;

Na Pānipādachapalo Na Netrachapalo Bhavet I
Na Cha Vāgangachapala Iti Shishṭasya Gochara: II
Pāramparyāgato Yeshām Veda: *Saparibrumhana*: I
Te Shishtā Brāhmanā Gyeyā: *Sruti Pratyaksha Hetava*: II

(vii) **She** is worshiped as per the prescribed actions. God has to be adored as per the prescribed actions to the individual *Āshram* and race/ religion, not by mere flowers, sandal, etc.;

Svasvavarŋāshrama Dharmai: *Samyag Bhagavadarpitai*: I
Yatpoojanam Na Tadgandha Mālyādeenām Samarpanai: II

(viii) *Śree Ādi Śaṇkara* in his commentary of *Viṣhŋu Sahasranāma* for the

317th name – *Shishṭeshṭa*: mentions;

I. He is liked by the knowledgeable people (*Shishṭa*).
II. He likes the knowledgeable people (*Shishṭa*) (*Śreemad Bhagavat Geeta* verse VII-17 is quoted here).
III. He is adored by *Shishṭa*.

412. *Shishṭapoojitā* - शिष्टपूजिता

(i) One who is worshipped by the great people.
(ii) The characters of great people were explained in the previous name.
(iii) **She** is adored by the wise people.
(iv) Those wise people, who are blessed by **Her** are respected everywhere.
(v) In *Saptashatee* (IV chapter) also the same sense is conveyed;

Te Sammatā Janapadeshu Dhanāni Teshām
Teshām Yashamsi Na Cha Seedati Dharmavarga: I
(in some books it is mentioned as *Banduvarga*:)
Dhanyāsta Eva Nibhrutātmajaprutyatārā:
Yeshām Sadhā'bhyudahyadā Bhavatee Prasannā II

413. *Aprameyā* - अप्रमेया

(i) One who is immeasurable.
(ii) *Prameya* means **She** is measurable. This is not possible and hence *Aprameya*.
(iii) The letter *'A'* indicates *Brahma, Vişhŋu*, etc. **She** is to be known, or measured by them only.
(iv) *Ap* – water. *Aprameyā* abiding in water. In *Sruti* (*Rātri Sūktam* and *Devee Upanishad*) also we read as; "my origin is in the water of the ocean"; *Mama Yonirapsvanta*: *Samudre*.
(v) *Śree Ādi Śaŋkara* in his commentary of *Vişhŋu Sahasranāma* for the 46th name – *Aprameyā* mentions;

Since He does not have the qualities like sound, etc., he cannot be practically recognised by organs; not even by inferences, because there are no symbols relating to him; cannot be frozen through comparisons, because there are no comparisons, since he himself is undefined. He cannot be recognised by signification also. If he is not there then what will happen to the auxiliaries/supporting evidences. He cannot be recognised by the proof of negation also. He cannot be recognised by form, as witness to a non-form and proof of *sāstras*. There is no surprise for the knowledge understood by proof, then how he is understood by *sāstras* – he is the witness for all the proofs and he is in the form of explanation for all these. There is no room for further proof. Still since it is a great thing, by removing the false matters, which are not of the universal absolute (*tat*), the *Sāstra* becomes the evidence. Thus since he is the in the form of witness, he is *Aprameya*:. The below is the translation from *Kāmakoṭi Gochastānam* – from *Śree Ādi Śaṇkara's* commentaries;

Shabdādi Rāhitatvānna Pranyakshagamya: I
Nāpyanumānagamya: *Tadvayāpta Lingābhāvān* I
Nāpyanumānasiddhi: *Nirbhāgatvena Sādrushyābhāvāt* I
Nāpyarthāpatthigrāhya: *Tadvinānuprapadyamāna Syāsambhavāti*
Nāpyabhavagochara: *Bhāvaroopatvāt, Abhāvabhāvāt Yadyevam,*
Shāstrayonitvam Katham? *Uchyate Pramānāḍisākshitchena*
Prakāshasvaroopasya Pramānāvishayatve'pi
Adhyastātadroopanivartakatvaina Shāstrapramāŋakatvamiti
Aprameya: *Sākshiroopatvāt* II

414. *Svaprakāshā* - स्वप्रकाशा

(i) One who is self-luminous.
(ii) **She** has luminary powers, which is nothing different from **Her**. With her luster only the other objects get light. There is no object luminating **Her**. **She** is self-luminous and self splendour;
(iii) *Brahadāraŋya Upanishad* (IV-3-9) says, here this person becomes self-luminous; *Atrāyam Purusha*: *Svayam Jyoti*:

Na Tatra Sooryo Bhāti Na Chandra Tārakam
Nemāvidyutobhāntikuto'yamagni: *Tameva Bhāntamanubhāti Sarvam*
Tasya Bhāsā Sarvamidam Vibhāti II

(iv) *Su* - much, *ap* - water, *prakāsha* – manifested. Hence this can also be interpreted as **She** shines much brighter in water.

415. *Manovāchāmagocharā* - मनोवाचामगोचरा

(i) One who is beyond the range of mind and speech.
(ii) That is, **She** is not comprehendible by mind and speech. *Sruti* also (*Taitreeya Upanishad* II-9-1) says, from whence speech and mind turn away unable to reach; *"Yato Vācho Nivartante Aprāpya Manasā Saha"*.
(iii) In *Viṣhŋu Purāŋa*, *Prahlāda* says, "I bow down to the supreme *Eshvaree* who transcends speech and mind and who can be grasped

by the wisdom of the wise alone";

Yāteetagocharā Vāchām Manasām Chāvisheshanā I
Gnanignanaparichchedyā Vande Tāmeesvareem Parām II

(iv) **She** is in whom is not to be found any object of thought or speech.

(v) By mentioning mind and speech, all the eleven organs and Parā, etc., speeches are indicated.

(vi) These have their own ways of understanding the objects. Only if the objects to be understood are within some limits, these organs can recognise them. But whatever *Śreedevee* has are all limitless/ boundless/ infinite. Hence **She** does not have anything, which mind and other organs can recognise – *Manovāchāmagochara.*

(vii) When read with the previous name (in the verse), *'A'* is to be prefixed to the name, then it can be split as *Amano + Vāchāma + Gochara.* That is **She** is beyond the reach of those whose mind and speech are immature; Alternatively **She** can be reached only by those whose mind and speech are mature.

(viii) *Kaṭopanishad* (IV-11) says, by mind alone it should be perceived, etc.? This contradiction is removed in the *Bhāmati* by adding "immature and mature or not purified and purified" respectively to the word 'mind'.

416. *Cichchakti*: - चिच्छक्तिः

(i) One who is in the form of energy called *Chit.*

(ii) *Chitshakti*, the power of removing ignorance and is also termed *chaitanya*. Since *Śreedevee* is in the form of knowledge **She** got this name.

(iii) According to the *Svetāsvatara Upanishad* (V-1) - in imperishable and infinite highest universal absolute (*Parabrahmam*), wherein the two, *vidyā* and *avidyā* are hidden, one is imperishable and the other is perishable, **She** who rules these two is different from either;

Dve Akshare Brahmapare Anante Vidyāvidye Nihite Yatra Gooḍhe I
Ksharam Tvavidyā Hyamrutam Tu Vidyā Vidyāvidyā Ěsshate Yastu Sonya: II

(iv) In *Devee Bhāgavatam* (V chapter) – Oh king, in all beings, there is *shakti* with all its powers, any being devoid of that *shakti* becomes like a corpse. That *Chit-Shakti* is in allbeings that is her form;

Vartate Sarvabhooteshu Shakti: *Sarvātmanā Nrupa* I
Shavavachchaktiheenastu Prānee Bhavati Sarvadhā II
Chitshakti: *Sarvabhooteshu Roopam Tasyāsta Deva Hi* II

(v) *Chit*, according to the *Yāskar*, who wrote the grammar for the language of *Veda*, means comparison; *Chitiyutmāyām*. The same is written by *Pāŋini* (VIII-2-101) in his grammar book on languages, as; *Chititi Chopamārde Prayujyamāne*. This method is to describe one unknown object by comparing it with a known object. The knowledge of comparison is *Śreedevee* herself.

(vi) In *Saptashatee* (V chapter) we read as;

Chitiroopena Yā Krutsnam Etad Vyāpya Stitājagat I
Namastasyai Namastasyai Namastasyai Namo Nama: II

417. *Chetanāroopā* - चेतनारूपा

(i) One who is in the form of consciousness (*chaitanya*).

(ii) The *chetana* energy in all the beings is *Śreedevee* only. In *Saptashatee* this has been prayed as – *Chetana* means inner sense. Only because of this, we can recognise the objects shown by eye, ear and mind. Only through the action of this we can recognise the availability of this. Not by any other means;

Yādevee Sarvabhooteshu Chetanetya Bhideeyate I
Namastasyai Namastasyai Namastasyai Namo Nama: II

(iii) In *Kenopanishad* (First *Kaṇḍa*) says; *"Srotrasya Srotram Manaso Mano"*.

(iv) *Samkshepa Sāreerakam* says, the pure *chit shakti* of the supreme Lord is called *chaitanya*; *"Chitshakti: Parameshvarasya Vimalā Chaitanya-mevochyate"*.

(v) In the *Gouḍapāda's Śree Vidyā Śree Vidyā Ratna Sūtra* (3) also it is mentioned that, *Shakti* is *chaitanya* itself; *Chaitanya Swaroopā Shakti*:

(vi) The first verse *Devee Bhāgavatam* itself says, we meditate upon that primeval *Vidyā*, which is in the form of *chaitanya* of all and which guides our senses; *"Sarvachaitanya Roopām Tām Ādyām Vidyām Cha Deemahi Bhddhim Yā Na: Prachodayāt"*.

(vii) In the *Taitreeya Upanishad*, (II-8-1) – The letter *'SA'* is in the form of *Chitshakti* only - thus the holy *Śree Sankarāraŋyar* explains it in his commentary called *Vidyāratna*.

418. *Jaḍashakti*: - जडशक्तिः

(i) One who manifests as the mechanical forces of the inanimate creation.

(ii) A certain modification of *māyā*, which is correlative to the power which creates the animate world and simply denotes the creative energy.

(iii) The *Viṣhŋu Purāŋa* says, the energies of all beings are not to be grasped by our intellects. The creative energies of *Brahmam* are a hundred times more difficult to grasp; they are in him as heat is in fire. The *Brahmam* is only the instrumental cause of the creation of the world. The creative energies are the material cause. Except the instrumental cause, the creative energies depend on nothing. An object becomes itself by its own energy;

Shakaya: *Sarvabhāvānām Achintya Gnāna Gocharā*: I
Shatasho Brahmaŋas Tāstu Sargādyā Bhāvashaktaya: II
Bhavanti Tapasām Shreshta Pāvakasya Yathoshnatā I
Nimittamātramevāsou Srujyānām Sargakarmaŋi II
Pradhāna Kāraneebhootā Yato Vai Srujya Shaktaya: I
Nimittamātram Muktvaikam Nanyadkin Chida Pekshate II
Neeyate Tapasām Shreshta Svashaktyā Vastu Vastutām II

419. *Jaḍātmikā* - जडात्मिका

(i) One who is the innermost essence of all mechanical forces.

(ii) It has been mentioned above that this static universe is the specialty of cosmic manifestation.

420. *Gāyatree* - गायत्री

(i) One who is in the form of *Gāyatree*.

(ii) *Veda* says "*Gāyatreem Chandasām Mātā*" – *Gāyatree mantra* is the mother of all *mantras*. The *Gāyatree* meter has 24 characters. In *Śreemad Bhagavat Geeta* (X-35) Lord *Śree Kriṣhŋa* says; *Gāyatree Chandasāmaham*. In *Koorma Purāŋa* also the same is conveyed as; *Gāyatree Chandasāmasi*.

(iii) According to *Padma Purāŋa*, *Gāyatree* is a daughter of a shepherd (*Gopakanyā*), a junior wife of *Brahma*. Once when *Brahma* was performing a sacrificial fire (*Yāga*), he called his wife *Sāvithree*. She told that *Lakshmee* and others are yet to come and that she would come with them. With this *Brahma* got wild and brought a daughter of a shepherd from *Shakti* (*gopakanyā*) and told *Viṣhŋu* that they would go quickly to the *yāga* and there is a *Devee* called *Gāyatree* there. *Viṣhŋu* also said "She is given by me to you: you marry her as per the *Gāndarvā* method". *Brahma* did so. (For the word *Gopakanyā*

– *Go* has several meanings. One of them is *Veda*. Those who guard *Veda* are *Gopar*).

(iv) *Gāyatree* protects those who recite her *mantra*. *Gāyatree kalpa* says; "*Gāyantam Trāyate Yasmāt Gāyatree Tena Gadyate*".

Other reasons – *Devee Purāṇa* says; *Gāyanāt Gamanatvāpi Gāyatree Tridashārchitā* – *Devas* worship *Gāyatree* by singing and nearing her. *Chāndogya Upanishad* (3-12-1) says; *Gāyatree Cha Trāyate Cha* – singing and protection. *Mahā Vāshista Rāmāyana* says; *Gāyatree Gāyanātmatvāt* – Since **She** is in the form of songs, **She** is called *Gāyatree*.

(v) *Padma Purāṇa* says that *Śreedevee* is in the form of *Gāyatree* - "Especially after taking bath in the holy *pushkara*, my *mantra* has to be recited. I dwell in the eight letters (eight letters in every group). I am always omnipresent;

Visheshāt Pushkare Snātvā Japen Mām Veda Mātaram I
Ashṭṭākshara Sthitā Chāham Jagadvyāptam Maya Dvidam II

(vi) Ordinarily recited *Gayatree mantra* has 3 groups and the complete *Gāyatree mantra* has four. It is told that *Brahma* absolved the first three groups as a capsule form of *Rig*, *Yajur* and *Sāma Vedas*. The fourth one is a gist of *Atharva Veda*. It is said that since this is a very special one, to know it, we need to have *Upanayana* again. It is told that *Śree Bhāskara Rāya* also had *Upanayana* again and learnt *Atharva Veda*.

(vii) It is well known that *Śreemad Rāmāyana* includes *Gāyatree mantra* and the 24 verses are read as *Gāyatree Rāmāyana*.

(viii) *Tripura Tāpinee Upanishad* advises that *Panchadashee mantra* has the meaning of *Gayatree mantra* in every group. This has also been explained in *Nityā Shoshikārnavam*. *Śree Bhāskara Rāya* also in his *Varivasya Rahasya* explains this.

(ix) In *Mahāshoḍanyāsa* (*Prapancha Nyāsa*), it has been mentioned that **She** is in the form of three *Guṇas*.

421. *Vyāhruti*: - व्याहृतिः

(i) One who is in the form of *Vyāhrutis* (invocations).

(ii) Some special *mantras* are called *Vyāhrutis*. Before creating this world *Brahma* chanted the *Praṇava mantra 'Om'*, by joining the first letters of three *Vedas* (*'A'*, *'U'* and *'M'*). Then he chanted *'Bhoo:'*, *'Bhuva*: and *'Suva:'* and then created the world. It expanded to chant the words *'Maha:'*, *'Jana:'*, *'Tapa:'* and *'Satyam'* and expanded as seven worlds. Hence the *Praṇava* the names of these seven worlds are called *Vyāhrutis*. **She** is in this form.

(iii) According to *Vāyu Purāŋa*, **She** is in the form of *Vyāharanam* that is pronunciation – you were addressed by me and hence you approached me. Hence you are the *Vyāhruti*;

Māyābhivyāhrutam Yasmāt Tvam Chaiva Samupastitā I
Tene Vyāhrutirityevam Nāma Te Sddhimeshyati II

(iv) It can be said that this and the next two names respectively indicate awaken (*Jāgrath*), dream (*Swapna*) and deep sleep (*Sushupti*) states. 423rd name *Dwijavrundanishevitā* may be referred.

422. *Sandhyā* - सन्ध्या

(i) One who is in the form of *Sandhyā Devee* (deity of twilight).

(ii) *Sandhyā* means sound meditation. **She** is worshipped with the idea of the non-separation of ourselves.

(iii) *Sandhyā* means junction (time of night and day) or meditation. The meeting of day and night occurs both in the morning and in the evening. Similarly the junction occurs at the noon and midnight also. These junctions (morning, noon and evening), the *Brahmins* (*dwijas*, those to whom the *Upanayana* has been done) worship with the integrated thought and that of *chaitanya*, which is in the Sun. That kind of worship is the real meaning of *Sandhya*. In that way worshipped *Gāyatree* and *Brahmam* are one and the same. It is told that *Śreedevee* is in the form of *Gāyatree* and the *Brahmam* are one the same. The below verses in this connection may be referred;

Sandhyeti Sooryagam Brahma Sandhyānāt Avibhāgata: I
Brahmadyai: *Sakalair Bhootais Tadamshai*: *Sacchidātmana*: II
Tasya Dāso'hamasmeeti So'hamasmeeti Yā Mati: I
Bhavedupāsakasyeti Hyevam Vedavidovidu: II - *Mahābhāratam*
Na Bhinnām Pratipadyeta Gāyatreem Brahmaŋā Saha I
Sāhamasmeetyupāseeta Vidhinā Yena Kenachit II (*Vyāsa*)
Brahmadyākāra Bhetena Yā Bhinnā Karma Sākshinee I
Bhāshvateeshvara Shakti: *Sā Sandhyetyabhihitā Budhai*: II
(*Bharadvāja Smruti*)
Gāyatree Sashirās Tureeya Sahitā Sandhyā Mayeetyagamairāgyātā
Tripure Tvameva Mahatām Sharmapradā Karmanām (*Lagustuti*)

Mādava says "hence this word indicates the *Devee* to be worshipped during the junction of day and night".

Note: As per *Tantra Sāstras* during *Sandhyā* period, *arghyā* has to be given aiming the mainly worshipped deities. It has been lined that this *arghyā* has to be given after the *Vedic Sandhyavandanam*. In this fashion, *Śreevidyopāsakās*, who have been invocated with *Pancha- dashee mantra* (something above *Shoḍashee mantras* also) give *Arghyā* in the all the four *Sandhyas*. This type of giving *Arghya* is called *Śree Vidyā Sandhyāvandanam* according to *Śākta Tantra Sāstra*.

(iv) This *Sandhyā* is the mind-born daughter of *Brahma*. This story follows; once when *Brahma* was meditating, a beautiful girl originated. Thus formed girl was called as *Sandhya*. She did a very malicious penance and by giving up her body, became *Aruŋdati*, wife of sage *Vashishta*. The below verses in *purāŋas* are seen. The *Kalikā Purāŋa* says "Born from his mind, beautiful in form, having beautiful limbs, named *Sandhyā*, she is the victorious deity of the twilight. Because she was born to *Brahma*, while he was engaged in meditation, she is known as *Sandhya*";

Tadā Tan Manaso Jātā Chāruroopā Varānganā I
Nāmnā Sandhyeti Vikhyātā Sāyam Sandhyā Jayantikā II
Brahmaŋo Dhyāyato Yasmātsamyagyātā Varānganā I
Ata: *Sandhyeti Loke'sminnasyā*: *Khyātir Bhavishyati* II

Bhagavatee Purāŋam says;

Yā Sā Sandhyā Brahmasutā Manojātā Purā'bhavat I
Tapastaptvā Tanum Tyaktvā Saiva Bhootā Hyarundhatee II

(v) In *Renukā Purāŋa*, it is said that, three pulses viz. *Idā, Pingala* and *Susumna* are integrated in the body. Similarly *Sandhya* is an integrated form of three *Devees Mahākālee, Mahālakshmee* and *Ekavirā*;

Idaikāsya Mahākālee Mahālakshmeestu Pingalā I
Ekaveerā Shushumneyamevam Sandhyā Trayātmikā II

(vi) According to *Dhaumya* a one year old girl is called *Sandhya*. *Śreedevee* is in that form also.

(vii) The three names *Vyāhruti*:, *Sandhyā* and *Dvija Brunda Nishevitā* respectively indicate awaken, dream and deep-sleep states. The further explanation on this can be seen in the next name.

423. *Dvijavrundanishevitā* - द्विजवृन्दनिषेविता

(i) One who is well worshipped by the groups of twice born.

(ii) She has been well meditated by all the twice born - *Brāhmins, Kshatriyas* and *Vysyas*. (One birth from the mother and the other during the *Upanayanam* to understand *Gāyatree mantra*).

(iii) **She** is so worshipped because she is *Sandhya*. The *Renuka Purāṇa* says – this *Sandhyā* is to be worshipped by *Devas*, the twice-born and by great souls, in sitting down, in lying down, in moving about, in eating and she is *Renukā* herself;

Sandhyaika Sarvadā Devair Dvijair Vandyā Mahātmabhi: I
Āsane Shayane Yāne Bhojane Renukaiva Hi II

A *Brahmin* who does not worship *Sandhyā*, is no more a *Brahmin*. He is unfit to do any other religious actions. *Sāstra* says, even if he does any actions, it will be fruitless. The importance of worshipping *Gayatree* has been described in detail in *Devee Bhāgavatam* (11th *Skanda*).

(iv) It can be said that the three names (421, 422 and 423) *Vyāhruti*:, *Sandhyā* and *Dvija Brunda Nishevitā* respectively indicate awaken, dreamanddeep sleep states. *Vyāhrti* is the operation of speech and indicates the waking state. *Sandhyā*, because it is between the other two, indicates the dreaming state, since the *Veda Sūtra* (III-2-1) says, "In the intermediate place there is a creation, for the scriptures say so". And it means the dreaming state. *Dvija* also means birds and hence the *jivas*, by all these three states **She** is worshipped (*sevitā*) by realising union (*ni*) with her. The sleeping state; as birds fatigued with flight, fold their wings and enter their nests, so that tired *jivas* quitting the waking and dreaming states, are absorbed in the supreme *Brahmam*. The *Brahadaranya Upanishad* (IV-3-19) says, "just as in this sky a hawk or an eagle after a long flight closing its wings goes to its nest, so does this person rush to that goal, where by sleeping he neither desires, nor dreams". Thus these three names indicate that **She** is worshipped in all the three states.

Tadyathā'sminnāgāshe Shyenā Vā Suparno Vā I
Viparipatya Srānta: *Samhatya Pakshou Samlayāyaiva* II
Dhriyata Evamevāyam Purusha Etasmā Antāyadhāvati Yatra Supto
Na Kanchana Kāmam Kāmyate Na Kanchana Svapnam Pashyati II

(v) *Chāndokya Upanishad* (VI-8-1) also, "Oh child, there he becomes seized of *Brahmam*"; *Sadā Samya Tadā Sampanno Bhavati*

(vi) The four names 420, 421, 422 and 423 were discussed individually. When all these four names are merged a complete sentence is formed get; *"Gāyatree Vyāhruti*: *Sandhyā Dvijavrundanishevitā"* – *Śreedevee* in the form of *Gāyatree*, is worshipped or chanted by *Brahmins* through *Vyahruti mantra Bhoo*:-*Bhuva*:-*Suva*:, during *Sandhyā* times.

424. *Tatvāsanā* - तत्वासना

(i) One who has a seat constituted by the Cosmic Elements (36 *tatvas*).

(ii) *Sankhyas* say that there are 24 *tatvas* from *Moolaprakruti* till earth. One religion says there are 96 *tatvas*. Thus the number varies in different schools. The details can be seen in *Śreemad Bhāgavatam* (11th *skantam*, 22nd chapter).

Saiva Sāstras and *Śākta Sāstras* unanimously accept that there are 36 *tatvas* from *Shiva* till *Prithvee*. **She** has these 36 *tatvas* as her *yoga* seat.

(iii) One other meaning is that **She** pushes out the *tatvas*, i.e. **She** is beyond all these *tatvas*. For the 906th name *Tatvādhikā* it has been interpreted that **She** continues even when these *tatvas* are destroyed.

425. *Tat* - तत्

(i) One who is in the form *Tat*.

(ii) The word *tat* signifies the revolution of mind, as *Śreedevee* revolves in the *Buddhis* of all the souls **She** is signified by the word *tat*.

(iii) *Śree Ādi Śaṇkara* in his commentary of *Viṣhŋu Sahasranāma* for the 730th to 733rd names – *Yat Tat Padamanuttamam* has mentioned the same sense.

(iv) In usage of *nāmāvali* this name appears as *Tasmai Nama*:

426. *Tvam* - त्वम्

(i) Thou.

(ii) In the 36 *tatvas* mentioned above, the *Shiva tatva* is called *Parā Samvit*. This is the Supreme Being without any quality or blemish. Even though it is without any dispositions, with energy for creation. Hence, the *Shiva Tatva* without any dispositions and the *Shakti Tatva*, the cause of the dispositions on account of creation, are one and the same in the *Parā Samvit*. Hence when *Śreedevee* is in the form of *Parabrahmam*, **She** is referred to as *Prkāsha Vimarsha Sāmarasya Roopinee*. *Kāmeshwaree* is in the form of brightness. This form of knowledge is integrated with *Aham* (I-self), *idam* (this), *Etat* (these) and *Tat* (that).

(iii) This form is described in the 24th name *Trishatee*, *Etattadityanir-Deshya*.

(iv) In *Pāvanopanishad* we read as;

Nirupādhikā Samvideva Kāmeshvara: *Sadānandapoorŋa*: *Svātmaiva*
Paradevatā Lalitā Louhityametasya Sarvasya Vimarsha: II

(v) *Vasinee Devees* explained the confident form of self in the previous name and the experimental form in this name.
(vi) Since it is said as *Tatvamayee* later in 907th name, these 425, 426 and 427th names are split into *Tat, Tvam* and *Ayee*.
(vii) In usage of *nāmāvali* this name appears as *Tubyam Nama*:

427. *Ayee* - अयी

(i) One who is referred as *Ayee*.
(ii) The word *Ayee* is normally used to address mother or sister with affection. *Śreedevee* is the mother of the entire universe. Hence it is more apt to call her as *Ayee*. It can be remembered that the verse starts as "*Ayigiri Nandinee*" in the *Mahishāsura Mardhinee Stora,* which is famous in Tamilnadu.
(iii) The word *Aya*: means good luck. Since in that form **She** is called *Ayee*.
(iv) In usage of *nāmāvali* this name appears as *Tasyai Nama*:

428. *Panchakoshāntarasthitā* - पञ्चकोशान्तरस्थिता

(i) One who dwells amidst the five *kosas* (psychological sheaths of the personality).
(ii) In the *Navāvarŋa Pooja*, after the ninth *Āvarŋa* above the *bindu, Pancha Panchikā Pooja* is done imagining that there are five thrones. These five *Panchikās* respectively are; five *Lakshmees*, five sheaths, five *kalpalatas*, five *kāmadenus* and five gems. The names of five sheaths are; *Śree Vidyā, Paramjyothi, Parānishkalā Shāmbavee, Ajapā* and *Mātruka*. These details are available in the book called *Gnānārnava Tantra*. 3rd name *Śreematsimhāsaneshwaree*.
(iii) *Śree Vidyā* sheath is worshipped in the *bindu*. The other four are worshipped outside differentiating the individual and the combined ones. Since *Śree Vidyā* sheath is worshipped in the *Bindu*, amidst these four, this name to *Śreedevee*.
(iv) The impressions/ results of these five *Panchikā pooja* has been explained in detail in the book called *Saparyā Patthati Vāsanai* by *Śree Chidānanda Nāthar*. He says, "Though this has not been found in the *Vāsanā Sāstras*, completely depending on the help of the feet of the teacher, I have made an attempt to explain this". Gist of his explanation follows;

Bindu chakra is distinguishable union (*savikalpa samādhi*). Five thrones over it, means normal state on the distinguishable union. It has to be imagined that till integrated union there are five different positions. These positions are;

A. *Sāmyam* – impartial – The sufferings of the soul are the subtle *Tripudi* form merged in the broad sufferings of *Brahmam*. The black water of Yamuna river and the white water of Ganges river mix in the *Triveni* junction, but still maintain their own individuality (colour) for some distance. Similar is the impartial union (*sāmya samādhi*). The first *Panchikā* viz. *Lakshmee panchikā* indicates this.

B. *Layam* – dissolution – when self (*aham*) merges with the absolute being (*Brahmam*) and subtly maintains the individual form, it is dissolution union (*Laya Samādhi*). The second *Panchikā* viz. sheath *panchikā* indicates this.

C. *Vināsham* – perishable – The destruction of the sufferings of the universe in the form of universal development is called perishable union. The abolition (*nivruti*) is of two types as *laya* (dissolution) form and *nāsa* (destruction) form. The *laya* form is in deep sleep state and the *nāsa* form is in swoon state. Thus it is made clear - in the dissolution union (previous one) the *laya* form of the sufferings of the universe and now in the perishable union its destruction. The third *Panchikā* viz. *kalpalatāpanchikā* indicates this.

D. *Adyanta bhāvam* – boundless condition – In addition to the natural affluences whatever is understood individually as knowledge of self (*Jeevabotham*), knowledge of *Brahmam* (*Brahmabotham*) and perfect wisdom (*Akanḍabotham*) are all due to the thought of differentiation only and not due to the states.

The boundless condition (*Adyantabhāvam*) is that understanding of non-availability of these differences in all the three periods (tenses). The fourth *Panchikā* viz. *kāmadenu* (*kāmadukā*) *panchikā* indicates this.

E. *Ikkiyam* – merger – Some *sāstras* mention this as *Ateetotitam*. This state is something above than thinking "beyond recognition". Hence this is *Anāmākyai* (nameless) and *Achintyam* (unthinkable). This cannot be indicated as this or that. The *tatva* form of this *panchikā* is denoted by the fifth one called *Ratnāmba* (gems).

Śree Chidānanda Nada himself says that the five sheaths can be named as below;

First	-	*Āntra Drushyānuvitta Samādhi*
Second	-	*Āntra Shaptānuvitta Samādhi*
Third	-	*Bāhya Drushyānuvitta Samādhi*
Fourth	-	*Bāhya Shaptānuvitta Samādhi*
Fifth	-	*Bāhya Nirvikalpa Samādhi*

(v) It has been told that there are five sheaths in our body; *Annamaya* (food), *Prāŋamaya* (*prānic* or energy), *Manomaya* (mental), *Vignanamaya* (intellectual) and *Ānandamaya* (bliss). Each of these is covered in the previous one. Hence this name is given to *Śreedevee*, since **She** is in the integral form with *Brahmam* as *Ānandamaya* sheath. This meaning is given based on interpretation by some schools for the *Taitireeya Upanishad* verse (2-5); *Anyontara Ānandamaya*:

(vi) However, *Śree Ādi Śaṇkara* has quoted that it is not correct to say that *Ānandamaya* sheath is the universal absolute (*Brahmam*) and these two are different. Based on this philosophy, it has been told that *Ānandamaya* sheath is in the form of *Chit Shakti*, which is the luminous form of *Brahmam*. (*Ānandamaya karaŋam* and *Samānādhikaraŋam* of *Śree Ādi Śaṇkara*'s commentary for *Brahma Sūtra* may be referred). The same method is explained in *Śreekanda Bhāshyam* and the books explaining it. Based on this opinion, this name has to be taken as, **She** is in the midst of the five sheaths. That is, *Brahmam* is beyond *Ānandamaya* sheath, but completing it, being witness to all actions and in the form of truth and knowledge.

(vii) In the *Brahma Geeta* (*Sootha Samhitā* III-45, 46) also;

Tathānandamaya Shchāpi Bramhanānyena Sakshinā I
Sarvottarena Sampoorŋo Brahma Nānyena Kenachit II
Yathidam Brahma Pucchākhyam Satya-Gnana-Dvayātmakam
Sarasa: *Sarvadā Sākshāt-nānyathā Surapugavā*: II

(viii) Sage *Durvāsā* (*Kroda Pattārakar*) also mentions that *Śreedevee* is in the form of the supreme being;

Anna-prāŋa-mana: *Prabodha Paramānandai*: *Shira*: *Pakshayuk*
Puchchātmaprakaṭair Mahopanishadhām Vakyai: *Prasiddheekruta*: I
Koshai: *Panchabhirebhireva Bhavateemetat Praveenāmiti*
Jyoti: *Prajvaladu Jvalātma Chapalām Yo Veda Sa Bramhavit* II

429. *Nisseemamahimā* - निस्सीममहिमा

(i) One whose glory is boundless.

(ii) *Seemā* – boundary. *Nisseemā* – boundless. **Her** pride and glory are boundless.

(iii) In many a book it has been printed as *Nisseema Mahimne Nama*:. *Śree Bhāskara Rāya* allows *Nisseema Mahimāyai Nama*: also.

430. *Nityayouvanā* - नित्ययौवना

(i) One who is eternally young.
(ii) **She** is juvenile and youthful without any growth or deterioration.
(iii) 136 – *Nityā*, 344 – *Kshyavruddhi Vinirmuktā*, 358 – *Tarunee* and 470 – *Vayovastā Vivarjitā* may be referred.
(iv) 272nd name – *Labdha Youvanashālinee* in *Trishatee* can also be referred.

431. *Madashālinee* - मदशालिनी

(i) One who is inebriated with bliss.
(ii) *Mada* – without interest in any other things, focusing only on bliss and the mind submerged in it. **She** shines in this stage with rapture.

432. *Madaghoorŋitaraktākshee* - मदघूर्णितरक्ताक्षी

(i) One whose eyes are rotating owing to the exuberance of bliss.
(ii) *Ghoorŋanam* means diverting from outside matters or circulating. As discussed in the previous name, on account of bliss, naturally reddish eyes are further red-tinged and are rotating without interest in outside matters.

433. *Madapāṭalagaŋḍabhoo*: - मदपाटलगण्डभूः

(i) One whose cheeks are rosy on account of rapture.
(ii) As discussed earlier, *Śreedevee*'s cheeks are rosy or whitish red on account of the mind being full of bliss. *Pātala* – rosy or colour of trumpet flower.
(iii) *Mada* also means alcohol. By drinking it her cheeks are reddish.
(iv) *Mada* also indicates musk deer. **Her** cheeks are painted with the figures of trumpet flower by musk deer.
(v) *Ganḍa* includes all cheeks, dot on the forehead, etc. Hence **Her** *Ganḍa* areas are painted with the figures of trumpet flower by musk deer.

434. *Chanḍanadravadigdhāngee* (*ngā*) - चन्दनद्रवदिग्धाङ्गी (ङ्गा)

(i) One whose body smeared with scent of sandal paste.
(ii) 740th name in *Viṣhŋu Sahasranāma* – *Chandanāngadee* – He is decorated with a bracelet which gives happiness.

435. *Chāmpeyakusumapriyā* - चाम्पेयकुसुमप्रिया

(i) One who is fond of the fragrant *Champaka* (Magnolia) flower. In some schools it is mentioned as *Punnaka* (Rhizophora mucronata) flower.
(ii) It can be reminded that in the 13th name it was mentioned that – *Champakāshoka Punnāga sougandhikalasatkachā* - **She** has these flowers studded in her hair.
(iii) In the *Āvarŋa Pooja*, one of the 64 offerings is submitting flower garlands. At that time these *Champaka* and *Punnaka* garlands are mentioned; *Mallika Punnāka Kalhāra Mukya Sarvartu Kusuma Mālā*: *Kalpayāmi Nama*:

436. *Kushalā* - कुशला

(i) One who is skillful.
(ii) **She** is skilled in activities like creation, etc.
(iii) *Kusham* – water, *lāti* – accepts. Hence *Kushala*.
(iv) *Śree Bhāskararāya* takes the meanings from the Vishva dictionary as; *Ku* – lowered/ backward, *Shala*: - Moon. When compared to the lustre of *Śreedevee*, the Moon's lustre takes a beating. That is **Her** lustre is above that of Moon's.

437. *Komalākārā* - कोमलाकारा

(i) One who has a soft form.
(ii) **Her** form is tender/ delicate and beautiful.

438. *Kurukullā* - कुरुकुल्ला

(i) One who has the form of the deity called *Kurukulla*.
(ii) In the city of *Śree*, between the halls *Ahamkārā* (egoism) and *chit* (consciousness) there is a well called *Vimarsham*. The presiding deity of this well is *Kurukulla Devee*.
(iii) **She** has been described in the book called *Lalitā Stavaratna* by *Śree*

Durvasar;

Kuruvindatarani Nilayām Kulāchala Spardhi Kuchanaman Madhyamām I
Kunkuma Vilipta Gātreem Kurukullām Manasi Kurmahe Satatam II

(iv) **She** has also been described in the 22nd chapter of *Tantra Rāja Tantra* (verse 11-12).

(v) In *Pāvanopanishad* we read as; *Vārāhee Pitruroopā Kurukullā Balidevatā Māta*. The meaning of this verse has to be read from the commentary given by *Śree Bhāskara Rāya* himself for this *Upanishad* and also from the usage methods.

439. *Kuleshvaree* - कुलेश्वरी

(i) One who is the ruler of the triad.

(ii) *Kula* is the triad, namely the measurer, the measurement and the thing measured.

(iii) 90th name *Kulāmrutaika Rasikā* may also be referred.

440. *Kulakuṇḍālayā* - कुलकुण्डालया

(i) One who is abiding in the *Kulakuṇḍa*.

(ii) *Kulakuṇḍa* is the *bindu*, which is in the centre of the pericarp of the *Moolādhāra*. It is like the small cavity in the centre of the pericarp of the lotus. This *bindu* is also called as place of *Shiva, Kulakuṇḍa, Akula Chakra* and *Akula Sahasrāra*. **She** has this as **Her** dwelling place. *Kunḍalinee* energy always sleeps here by placing its head in the above said cavity, winding three and half times around this *bindu*. *Śree Ādi Śaṇkara*, in his *Soundaryalaharee* (10th verse) describes, "After reaching your own place assuming the form of a coiled serpent you sleep in the cavity of the *Kulakuṇḍa*";

Avāpya Svām Bhoomim Bhujaganibha Madhyushtavalayam I
Svamātmānam Krutvā Svapidhi Kulakuṇde Kuharini II

(iii) *Ālayam* – completely reaching place like *Sushupti*. As mentioned above it is the place for the *Kunḍalinee* energy and the dwelling place for *Śreedevee*.

(iv) 110th name *Kunḍalinee* has to be read alongwith this.

441. *Koulamārgatatparasevitā* - कौलमार्गतत्परसेविता

(i) One who is worshipped by those, devoted to the *Koula* tradition.

(ii) *Mārga*, the path handed down by family tradition. One has to worship only following those methods. We read that only using those tradition *Śreedevee* is worshipped with sandal paste, offerings, etc.;

Yasya Yasya Hi Yā Devee Kulamāgena Samsthitā
Tena Tena Cha Sā Poojyā Baligandhānulepanai: II
Naivedyair Vividhaishchaiva Poojayet Kulamārgeta:

In worshipping *Śree Vidyā*, there are three different modes viz., *Samaya, Koula* and *Mishra*. The *Samhitas* of *Sukar, Vasishtar, Sanakar, Sanandanar* and *Sanathkumarar* (jointly called as *Supākāma Panchakam*) follow the *Vaideeka* tradition. This is *Samaya* tradition to be followed by *Vaideekas*. The *Misra* tradition has been described in the eight *Tantras*, viz., *Candrakalā, Jyotssnāvati, Kalāniti, Kulārnava, Kuleshwaree, Bhuvaneshwaree, Bārhaspatyam* and *Durvasa*. It is called mixed because it partakes of both the *Samaya* and *Koula* modes. Everyone is eligible for to use method. Aiming at the *dwijas* (*Brahmins, Kshatriyas* and *Vysyas*) the rightist method (*Savya* or *Pradakshiṇa* method) has been suggested. And the leftist (*Apradakshiṇa* or *Apasavya*) method has been suggested for the *Soodras*. Relating to this, the names 98 – *Samayāchāratatparā* and 912 – *Savyapasavya mārgastha* can be referred. The rightist method has been differently interpreted there.

(iii) The *Koula* mode is described through 64 *tantras*. This has very subtle *tatvas*. In this method fish, flesh and ladies are practically used. Those who are involved in these by nature are being differentiated little by little, in the interest of bringing them up, these are allowed in *poojas*. *Koula* method *tantras* say, however, these have to be cleaned up through tough methods being using them in *poojas* to offer to *Śreedevee*. Those *tantras* themselves say that this is equivalent to walking on the edge of a sword. If the worshipper does not have the mind to offer to *Śreedevee*, he goes down to the bottom most state. Hence this is equivalent to walking on the edge of a sword, embracing the neck of a tiger and wearing a snake;

Krupāna Dhārā Gamanāt Vyāghra Kandāvalambanāt I
Bhujanga Dhāranān Noonam Ashakyam Kulavardhanam II

Those who follow this method should have special qualities like control over the organs. Others cannot. Those who do not have these qualities and those who have wavering mind will reap ill effects only.

The detailed description and differences between these three methods can be read in the commentary of *Śree Lakshmeedhara* for *Soundarya-laharee*.

442. *Kumāragaṇanāthāmbā* - कुमारगणनाथाम्बा

(i) One who is the mother of *Kumara* and *Gaŋapati*.
(ii) i.e. Mother of *Kumara* and *Gaŋapati*.
(iii) Since *Muruga* more handsome than Cupid, he is called *Kumara*; *"Kutsito Māra: Yena"*.
(iv) **She** controls the heads of renounceable obsession groups. The root word *'Abi'* means to control.
(v) *Kumara* is the presiding deity of egoism. As per *Vārāha Purāŋa* – *Viṣhŋu* (also called as *Shiva*) is the *purush*. The lotus figure *Uma* (also called as *Lakshmee*) is unmanifested (*Avyakta*). Ego is created by the union of these two. This is called *Guha* or *Senapathi* (knight). **She** controls those who have ego.

Purusho Viṣhŋurityukta: Shivo Vā Nāmata: I
Avyaktam Tu Umādevee Shrrevā Padma Nibhekshanā II
Tatsamyogādahankāra: Sa Cha Senāpatir Guha: II

443. *Tushṭi:* - तुष्टिः

(i) One who has the form of contentment.
(ii) There are seven names, viz.; contentment, nourishment, wisdom, might, tranquility, benevolence and beauty. It is proceeded to praise *Śreedevee* under these names and treating her as these forms. Whosoever has got these qualities, it can be concluded that they have got the complete and special blessings of *Śreedevee*.
(iii) In *Saptashatee* also we read as;

Tvam Śree Tvame Eshvaree Tvam Hree: Tvam Buddir Bodhalakshnā I
Lajjā Pushṭistathā Tushṭistvam Shānti: Kshāntireva Cha II

Again *Yā Devee Sarvabhooteshu Tushṭiroopena Samsthitā* I
Namstasyai Namstasyai Namstasyai Namonama: II

There itself **She** has been described as peace and lustre.

(iv) In *Devee Bhāgavata* (III *Skanda*) also the same meaning is conveyed, "That Mother, as is well-known, is in all beings in the form of understanding, fame, firmness, prosperity, energy, faith, intelligence and memory";

Bhuddhi: Keerttir Dhrutir Lakshmee: Shakti: Shraddhā Mati: Smruti: I
Sarveshām Prāninām Sā'mbhā Pratyaksham Tannidarshanam II

(v) According to *Padma Purāŋa*, *Tushṭi* is the deity in the *Vasreshvara*, *Pushṭi* is the deity in the *Devatāru* forest and *Druti* is the deity in the *Pindāraka Kshetra*.
(vi) *Śree Bhāskara Rāya* shows a verse from the *Mallari Māhatmya* as an example, which explains *Paramashiva* in the same way;

Yodeva: *Sarvabhooteshu Dosharoopena Samsthita*: I
Namstasyai Namstasyai Namstasyai Namonama: II

Śree Ādi Śaṇkara in his commentary of *Viṣhŋu Sahasranāma* mentions for the; *"Paramānandaika Roopatvāt Tushṭi*: *Sarva Sampoorŋatvāt Pushṭa*:". 391st name *Tushṭa*: - he is in a single unmixed form of *Brahmānandam*. 392nd name *Pushṭa*: - he is omnipresent.

(vii) *Śree Bāskara Rāya* in his book called *Guptavatee Bhāshya* (commentary to *Saptashatee*) says that in *Saptashatee* after the names *Tushṭi* and *Lakshmee*, respectively the names *Tushṭi* and *Druti* names occur. (These names are not there in the *Gātyāyanee Tantra* followed by him). In the commentary for *Saptashatee*, called *Shantanavee* also the names *Tushṭi* and *Druti* are indicated and explained. It can be noted that these two names are mentioned in the *Chanḍi Āvarŋa Pooja* also.

444. *Pushṭi*: - पुष्टिः

(i) One who is complete.
(ii) That is, **Her** form is full of thriving-ness, nourishment, plenty and body full (complete in all aspects of organs and constituent parts of the body). This has to be read in conjunction with the previous name.

445. *Mati*: - मतिः

(i) One who is in the form of wisdom and intellect.
(ii) This has to be read in conjunction with the descriptions for the name 443.
(iii) *Mati* is explained in the *Vāyu Purāŋa* thus, "*Purusha* bears the measuring (rod), understands division and thinks himself composed of parts, hence he is known as *Mati*";

Bibharti Mānam Manute Vibhāgam Manyate Pi Cha I
Purusho Bhoga Sambaddhas Tena Chā'soumati: *Smrutā* II

(iv) The *Soota Samhitā* (VIII-89) says, *Mati* is the form of *Śreedevee* - "Let us adore that *Shiva* who is worshipped by *Viṣhŋu* and others, who is the bestower of bliss, who is known as *Mati* derived from experience, supreme, who knows the *Vedas*, beneficent";

Yānubhootiruditā Mati: *Parā Vedamāna Niratāshubhāvahā* I
Tāmateeva Sukhadām Vayam Shivām Keshavadi Janusevita Numa: II

(v) Later explained 537th name – *Amati*: - hangs over the letter '*A*'. Hence it has been explained by splitting *Svadhā* + *Amati*: (536th and 537th).

446. *Dhruti*: - ध्रुतिः

(i) One who is fortitude.
(ii) The word *Dhruti* indicates – boldness, firmness and permanence.
(iii) This can be read in conjunction with the explanations given for the 443rd name.

447. *Shānti*: - शान्तिः

(i) One who is in the form of tranquility.
(ii) *Shānti* indicates that, which gives control and the resultant peace of mind status. Release of organs from the interest on worldly affairs is called *Shānti*.
(iii) This can be read with conjunction to the details given in 443rd name.
(iv) During *Navāvarŋa Pooja*, after establishing special *argya*, *kalas* (parts) relating to Fire god, Sun, Moon, *Brahma*, *Vişhŋu*, *Rudra*, *Ěshwara* and *Sadāshiva* are chanted. In that the *kalas* relating to *Sadāshiva* are 16 in number. The fourth one is *Shānti kala*. *Shānti*, a certain *Kalā* (part) belonging to *Vāyu* (air god). The *Saivāgama* says, "That which gives peace to a man (struggling with) the flood of impurity, illusion and change (of *Karma*), that *Kalā* is called *Shānti*. That is the abode which is the seat of dominion.

Malamāyā Vikārougha Shānti: *Pumsa*: *Punaryaya* I
Sākalā Shāntirityuktā Sādhikārāspadam Padam II

(v) The *Parāsara Bruhat Samhita* says, "Beyond the fifteen finger's breadth from the end of the nose where the soul is purified, is the sixteenth part, that *Kalā* is called *Shānti*";

Starting from -

Dasa Panchāngula Vyāptam Nāsikāyā Bahi: *Stitam* I
Jeevo Yatra Visheedhyata Sā Kalā Shoḍaseesmrutā II

till - *Sā Cha Shānti*: *Prakeertita*.

448. *Svastimatee* - स्वस्तिमती

(i) One who is in the form of eternal truth.
(ii) One who is in the form of benediction.
(iii) *Sushţu* – properly or beautifully. *Sattha* – existence/ the state of existence. One who has this is called *Svastimatee*. (The learned frequently use the phrase *Asti Bhāti Priyam* – the same *Asti* is used here. The word *Sattha* is used in the same sense as in the phrase *Sat*

Chit Ānandam.

(iv) Since it is immortal, in the spiritual parlance it is used as *Sattha*. (The learned speak of *Satthā* in three different ways – *Pratibhāsika* [relating to fate], *Vyāvahārika* [relating to worldly business] and *Pāramartika* [spiritual knowledge]). Explaining all these here may not be possible and are to be learned from *Vedānta* books.

(v) Names 136 – *Nityā*, 180 – *Nirnāshā* and 443 – *Tushṭi*: may be referred.

(vi) According to *Yāska* – *Svasti* means immortality; *Svasteetyavināshi Nāma.*

(vii) *Svasti*, according to the *Ratna* dictionary, means - benediction, benevolence, sinless, holy and auspiciousness.

(viii) A verse should have 6 characters. This name has the character *Āshirvādā* (blessings). 927th name *Storapriyā* may be referred.

449. *Kānti*: - कान्तिः

(i) One who is in the form of effulgence.

(ii) The body which attracts others is called luminous or refulgent.

(iii) *Veda* says Sun, Moon, etc., are luminous only because of the effulgence of the Supreme Being.

Na Tatra Sooryo Bhāti Na Chandra Tārakam Nema Vidyuto Bhānti
Kuto'yamagni: Tameva Bhāntamanubhāti Sarvam Tasya Bhāsā
Sarvamidam Vibhāti II

(iv) *Kānti* indicates the *Icchāshakti.*

(v) The same sense in conveyed in 465th name *Kāntimatee.*

(vi) 329th name *Kāntā* also may be referred.

(vii) This need to be read in conjunction with the explanations given for 443rd name *Tushṭi*:.

450. *Nandinee* - नन्दिनी

(i) Daughter of *Nandagopa.*

(ii) It has been mentioned in *Śreemad Bhāgavatam* (X *Skanda*) that *Śreedevee* was (*Mahāmāyā*) born as daughter of *Nandagopa.*

(iii) Since **She** bestows delight **She** is *Nandinee.*

(iv) *Nandinee,* a certain cow born in the family of the celestial cow *Kāmadhenu*. It has been indicated in *Raghuvamsa* by *Kalidāsā* that *Nandinee* did services to the emperor *Dileepa* and got a baby.

(v) In the form of river Ganges.

451. *Vighnanāshinee* - विघ्ननाशिनी

(i) One who removes all obstacles.

(ii) **She** has the ability of removing all the obstacles in the *Śree Vidyā Upāsana*. She is in the form of *Mahāgaŋapati*, who destroys all the obstacles. Hence, it is a practice to worship *Gaŋapati* in all activities. In *Parasurāma Kalpa*, it has been mentioned that even in *Śree Vidyā Upāsanā*, it is a practice to worship *Mahāgaŋapati* in the beginning.

(iii) 854th name *Gambheerā* also may be referred in this regard.

452. *Tejovatee* - तेजोवती

(i) One who has splendor.

(ii) *Tejas* – lustre. *Brhadāraŋyaka Upanishad* (III-8-11) says, the *Brahmam* is the support of the sun and other luminaries; *"Etasmin Khalvakshare Gārgi Sooryāchandramasou Vidhrtou Tishtara:"*.

453. *Trinayanā* - त्रिनयना

(i) One who is endowed with three eyes.

(ii) It is told that the Moon, Sun and the fire god are the three eyes of *Śreedevee*. (These are the names of other three *bindus* split from *Mahābindu*). 762nd name *Triambikā* may also be referred. This is also told as the form of *Kāmakala*. It can be referred that the Tamil alphabet ஃ is in this form.

(iii) Since the word *Voushat* has a cryptic name as *Trinayanā*, *Śreedevee* is in that form – this name indicates.

(iv) *Nayanam* – to take along. The cause of our knowledge about an article or anything is called proof. It can be called as *Nayanas*, which takes our mind along and creates the knowledge of something. As per *Sāndilya Sūtra* (99), such proofs are three in number like the eyes of *Rudra*; i.e. *Shabdam* (or word), *Anumānam* (assumption) and *Prathyaksham* (evidence). Since hearing is a route for retention of what is heard, for assumption – memorising and for evidence – proving, are all indicated. As a proof of all these explanations *Śree Bhāskara Rāya* quotes some statements from various books;

Pratyaksham Chānumānam Cha Shāstram Vividhāgamam I
Trāyam Suviditam Kāryam Dharma Soodtimabheepsatā II

Manusmruti

Trividham Pramāṇam - *Sānkya Samāna Sūtra*
Pratyakshānumānāgamā: - *Pramānāni YogaSūtra*

Since **She** is recognisable with these three types of proofs, **She** is *Trinayana.*

(v) In worshipping *Śreedevee* there are three methods viz., *Dakshiṇa, Uttara* and *Brahma*. The names; 441 – *Koulamārga Tatpara Sevitā*, 912 – *Savyāpasavya Mārgasthā* and 923 – *Dakshiṇā Dakshiṇārādhyā* may be referred.

Depending on their abilities/ qualities, **She** takes **Her** devotees in these three methods and hence *Trinayana.*

(vi) *Devee Purāṇa* says;

Dakshiṇam Chottaram Lokam Tathā Brahmayanam Param I
Nayam Sanmārgam Vargam Cha Netree Trinayanā Matā II

(vii) Quoting a grammar note, the author says that there is no letter *'Na'* in this name;

Kshubhrāderākrutigaṇatvātsamgnāshabdatve'pi Ṇatvābhāva: II

454. *Lolāksheekāmaroopiṇee* - लोलाक्षीकामरूपिणी

(i) One who is in the form of the affection in women.

(ii) **Her** love does not end up with *Shiva.* To indicate that it spreads to all it is given as love in women. The interpretation reads;

Shiva- kāmaṇirāsāya Lolākshee Sambandhitvam Kāma Visheshanami I

Śree R. A. Sastry's translation goes; "To show **Her** love is not limited to *Shiva,* **She** is so called".

(iii) 320th name *Ramanalampaṭā* may also be referred.

(iv) **She** is in the form of *Yogeshvaree*, who is the deity of desire. (The *Svayamvara Kalyānee mantra* may be reminded).

(v) The *Varāha Purāṇa* says, desire, anger, greed, passion, bewilderment, envy, calumny and scorn, thus there are eight mothers. Their names respectively are; *Yogesvari, Māhesvaree, Vaisnavee, Brahmānee, Kalyānee, Indree, Yamadaṇḍa* and *Varāhee.* (The famous names of eight mothers are; *Brahmee, Māheshvaree, Koumāree, Vaiṣhṇavee, Vārāhee, Indree, Chāmuṇḍā* and *Mahālakshmee*.

(vi) In some schools this name is split into two names *Lolākshee* and *Kāmaroopiṇee*. In that case some other two names have to be taken as one. Which are those two names? It is not known.

455. *Mālinee* - मालिनी

(i) One who is wearing garlands.
(ii) *Mālinee* is the name of the presiding deity of fifty-one letters in Samskrit.
(iii) In *Pancha Panchikā Pooja*, worship is done by *Kushāmbha mantra* also. 428th name *Pancha Koshāntarasthita* may be referred.
(iv) In *Āmnāya Pooja* also worship is done by a *mantra* called, *Mālinee Mantra Rājam*.
(v) *Mālinee* is a companion of *Śreedevee*, mentioned in the *Vāmana Purāṇa*, in the section on the marriage ceremony of *Pārvatee*; The *Mālinee* clasped the foot of *Hara*. *Hara* said "whatever you ask I will give, release my foot". *Mālinee*, then replied to *Shiva,* "Oh *Shiva,* bestow your prosperity on my friend, then you will be released". Then *Shiva* said, "I have already given, release me, etc".

Tato Harānghrir Mālinyā Gruheeto Dāyakāraṇāt I
Kim Yāchase Dadāmyesha Munchasveti Harobhraveet II
Malinee Shankaram Prāha Matsakhyai Dehi Shankara I
Soubhāgyam Nijagotreeyam Tato Mokshamavāpsyasi II
Atho'vācha Mahadevo Dattam Mālinee Munchamām II

(vi) *Mālinee* is a certain meter. Its character is 15 letters –
Na Na Ma Ya Ya.
(vii) According to the *Vishva* dictionary, *Mālinee* means, a certain meter, a woman of the florist caste, the city of Champā, Gouree and river Ganga.
(viii) *Mālinee*, according to *Dhaumya*, is a girl of seven years of age.

456. *Hamsinee* - हंसिनी

(i) One who is alongwith swans.
(ii) Swan birds are famous for their beauty in walking. It is the practice of poets to compare the gait of great ladies to that of swan birds. (Great gentlemen's gait is compared to that of elephants or lions). *Śree Ādi Śaṇkara*, in his *Soundaryalaharee*, (91stverse beginning with "*Padanyāsa Kreedā*") describes that the swans are inspired by *Śreedevee*'s gait beauty and go behind **Her**.
(iii) A type of *sanyāsins* called *Paramahamsā* is indifferent to **Her** (i.e. those great *sanyāsins* are always meditating upon **Her**), **She** is called as *Hamsinee*.
(iv) The exhale and inhale of breath together is called *Hamsa Mantra* or *Ajapā Mantra*. This is a *mantra* about *Śreedevee* and hence **She** is *Hamsinee*.

457. *Mātā* - माता

(i) One who is the form of a mother.
(ii) Since *Śreedevee* is the mother of this entire universe, **She** is *Māta*.
(iii) *Śreedevee* is in the form of a mother. All the *mantras* originated from **Her** and hence the name *Mātā*: *"Skānḍam – Mantranām Matrubhoota Cha Matrukā Parameshwaree; Devee Upanishad – Mantrānām Matrukā Devee Shabdānām Gnanaroopiŋee"*.
(iv) The presiding deity of the tenth day of bright lunar fortnight and sixth day of dark lunar fortnight is called *Nitya*. The *nāmapārāyaŋa* says that the cryptic name for her *mantra* is called *Māta*.
(v) *Padma Purāŋa* says that the deity of *Kāyāvarohana Kshetra* is called as *Māta*.
(vi) As per *Vishva* dictionary, the *Lakshmee Beeja* is called as *Māta*.
(vii) The very first name *Śreemātā*, 337th name *Vidhātree*, 823rd name *Jananee*, 934th name *Vishva Mātā* and 985th name *Ambā* may be referred.
(viii) Born in *Śree Appayya Deekshitar*'s race and a great blessed and learned person called *Śree Neelakaŋṭa Deekshitar* in his book called *Neelakaŋṭa Vijaya* (II *Āshvāsam* 20th verse) says that - The left part of *Ĕshwar* in the form of a lady, sometimes seen as male having *Kamalā* as his consort and wearing the *Koustuba* gem in his heart. What is the difference in this? Same supreme being. In one sense mother of universe (*Jaganmātā*) and in another sense the *Trivikrama* form measuring all the three worlds. In this context the poet uses the word *Mātā* in a dual sense indicating *Śreedevee* and *Mahāviṣhŋu*, reminding the oneness to us;

Yadetadvāmāngam Ghanajaghanakeshastanabharam
Kadhāchittach Chambhor Bhavati Kamalākoustubhadharam I
Jaganmātaryevam Yadapacharitam Tanmaghavatā
Jaganmātā Deva: Prabhavati Sa Eva Kshapayitum II

458. *Malayāchalavāsinee* - मलयाचलवासिनी

(i) One who is residing in the Malaya mountain (*Malayāchalam*).
(ii) This deity is described in the *Sābarachintāmaŋi* as the famous *Malayālaya Bhagavatee*. (*Malayā* mountain is in Kerala and hence it is told as *Malayālayā Bhagavatee* or *Malayālaya Bhagavatee*).

459. *Sumukhee* - सुमुखी

(i) One who has a lovely face.
(ii) **She** has a beautiful and splendid face. It is told that with wisdom, the lustre of the face is enhanced. In many a place the *Veda* says, "One who knows this (*Brahmam*), his face shines"; *Chāndogya Upanishad* (IV-14-2) – *Shobhatesya Mukhamya Evam Veda*; "Oh dear child, your face shines like that of a sage (*brahmavit*)"; *Brahmavidiva Te Soumya Mukhamābhāti*.
(iii) The name of one of the *Anga* (organ) *mantras* of *Shoḍasee mantra* is *Sumukhee*.
(iv) It has been described in 347th name *Vimalā* that *Vishvakarma*, the architect of *Devas*, has indicated various building types, in the scripture *sāstra*. *Sumukham* is one such type.
(v) The first in the sixteen great names of Lord *Gaŋesha* is *Sumukha*:. This appears in *Gaŋesh Sahasranāmā* also. The *shakti* of *Sumukha*: is *Sumukhee*.
(vi) *Sumukhee* is a type of meter in music. As per *Vruddha Ratnāvali* of *Venkatesar*, its character is - *Na Ja Ja La Ga*. But, as per *Vruddha Maŋimālā* of *Baingānādu Gachchapee Gaŋapati Sastrigal*, its character is of 10 letters – *Sa Sa Ja*.
(vii) *Śree Ādi Śaṇkara* in his commentary of *Viṣhŋu Sahasranāma* for the 456th name – *Sumukha*: mentions as;
   a. One who has a handsome face. The verse from *Viṣhŋu Purāŋa* has been quoted – *Prasanna Vadanam Chāru Padmapadrāya Dekshanam*.
   b. He teaches all the knowledge (*vidyās*) and hence *Sumukha*: The *Swetashvatara Upanishad* (6-18) verse starting with *"Yo Brahmanam"* has been quoted.

460. *Nalinee*- नलिनी

(i) One who is like a Lotus flower.
(ii) **Her** hands, feet, face, eyes and other limbs are like a lotus flower and hence *Śreedevee* **Herself** is entirely described as lotus flower.
(iii) *Nalinee* is one of the names for river Ganges. **She** is in that form.
(iv) *Nala*, a king, as he was identified with *Śreedevee* by devotion, **She** is called *Nalinee*.

461. *Subhroo*: - सुभ्रूः

(i) One who has beautiful eye brows.

(ii) *Śree Ādi Śaṇkara*, in his *Soundaryalaharee*, (47th verse beginning with "*Bhruvou Bhughne*") describes the beauty of the eye brows of *Śreedevee*.
(iii) Earlier in 17th name *Vadanasmara Māngalya Gruhatorana Chillikā*, the beauty of *Śreedevee*'s eye brows were described.
(iv) Within the time taken for *Śreedevee*'s eye brows to bend up and come down, many four *yugas* would have completed. While detailing the period by *Ashṭānga* method it has been mentioned as; "*Oordhva Bhroo Vibhrame*".

462. *Shobhanā* - शोभना

(i) One who is all radiant with beauty.
(ii) It can be noted that – 683rd name *Shobanā Sulabhā Gati*: has to be split into three words – again the 972nd name *Āshobhanā* has to be split and understood.

463. *Suranāyikā* - सुरनायिका

(i) One who is the leader of the *Devas*.
(ii) *Tripuropanishad* says - (**She** is) the supreme power of the *Devas*; *Adhishṭāyaināmajarā Purānee Mahattarā Mahimā Devatānām*.

464. *Kālakaŋṭhee* - कालकण्ठी

(i) One who is the consort of *Kāla Kanḍar*.
(ii) Lord *Parameshwara*, when he swallowed the venom, it stayed in his neck and hence his throat is coloured in black. Hence he is called *Neelakaŋṭar* or *Kālakaŋṭar*. The consort of that *Kālakaŋṭar*. *Vāyu purāŋa* says, "In the presence of a multitude of *Devas*, *Pishāchas*, serpents and demons, the virulent poison became transfixed in the throat; hence I am called *Kālakaŋṭar*".

Pashyatām Devasanghānām Pishāchoraga Rakshasām I
Dhrutam Kante Visham Ghoram Kālakaŋṭas Tatosmyaham II

(iii) According to the *Devee Purāŋa*, among the sixty-eight sacred places, *Kālanjara* is a place where *Kalakaŋṭā* is worshipped; *Kālanjare Kālakaŋṭa*:. The presiding *Devee* in that place is mentioned here in this name.
(iv) *Kalu* - a soft low sound, *kanta* - throat, i.e. a soft low sound proceeds from her throat and hence *Kālakaŋṭee*. The sweetness of *Śreedevee*'s

voice has been explained in 27th name – *Nijasallāpa Madhurya Vinirbhartsita Kachchapee*.

(v) There is a story in the *Linga Purāŋa* that in order to destroy the demon *Dārukā*, "*Shiva* created *Kāli, Kapardinee* and *Kālakaŋṭee*"; *Sasarja Kāleem Kāmāri*: *Kālakaŋṭeem Kapardineem*.

465. *Kānthimatee* - कान्तिमती

(i) One who is radiant/ resplendent.
(ii) Earlier in 449th name *Kāntee*, this was explained.

466. *Kshobhiŋee* - क्षोभिणी

(i) One who is causing emotion/ or one who agitates.
(ii) Before the start of creation, when the Supreme Being was alone, the illusion (*Māyā*) created an excitement in him and thus this universe was created. That excitement was created by *Śreedevee*. The *Viṣhŋu Purāŋa* says, "The Lord *Viṣhŋu* entering the *Prakruti* and *Purusha*, by his own will excite at the time of creation".;

Prakrutim Purusham Chaiva Pravishayātmechchayā Hari: I
Kshobayāmāsa Bhagavān Sarga Kāle Vyāpāshrita: II

(iii) The *Varāha Purāŋa* says, "*Vaishnavee* (the consort of *Viṣhŋu*) once went to the *Mandāra* mountain to perform penance; after she had performed penance for a long time she became excited (by passion); from that excitement young women of fair appearance, with blue curling hair, with lips as red as the *Bimba* fruit, lotus-eyed, with body like the red lotus wearing an anklet, beautiful, when the mind of *Śreedevee* was agitated, hundreds and millions of such women arose with different faces";

Yā Mantram Gatādevee Tapastaptum Tu Vaiṣhŋavee I
Tasyās Tapantyā: *Kālena Mahata*: *Kshubhitam Mana*: II
Tasmāt Kshobhāt Samuttasthu: *Kumārya*: *Soumyadarshanā* I
Neela Kunchita Keshāntā Bimboshtya: *Padmalochanā*: II
Indeevarasamā Dāma Noopurādhyā: *Suvarchasa*: I
Evam Vidhā Sthriyo Devya: *Kshobhite Manasidrutam* II
Uttasthu: *Shatasāhasrā*: *Koṭisho Vividhānanā*: II

467. *Sookshmaroopiŋee* - सूक्ष्मरूपिणी

(i) One who has a very subtle, not to be easily be recognised, form.

(ii) *Kaivalyopanishad* (16) says – it is subtler than the subtle and eternal; *Sookshmāt Sookshmataram Nityam*. *Kaṭopanishad* (II-20) says – it is subtler than an atom; *Anoraneeyān*.

(iii) The sacrificial fire done in the fire at *Kunḍalinee*, in the midst of *Mooladhāram*, is subtle. It is called *Rahoyāgam*. This indicates, in the *Navāvarŋa Pooja*, after establishing the vessels through *mantras*, offering special *argyās*, offering prayers to teacher, the following are offered as oblations in the fire of *Kunḍalinee*; virtues, sins, decisions, indecisions, justice, injustice, actions and inactions. This *homa* (sacrificial fire) is explained in *Tantra Rāja Tantra* in verses starting from *Nityā Nityodite* ending with *Evam Dvādshadhā Homamaksharai*: *Syādudheeritai*:. **She** is in the form of that *homa*.

(iv) *Śreedevee*'s gross, subtle and subtler forms were discussed in 6th name *Udyadhbānu Sahasrābhā* and 11th name *Panchatanmātra Sāyaka*. Here the subtle form is described.

(v) *Śree Ādi Śaṇkara* in his commentary of *Vişhŋu Sahasranāma* for the 457th name – *Sookshma*: mentions as; the ether and all are material causes. Since there is no material cause like sound, etc., he is subtle. *Muŋḍakopanishad* (I-1-6) says; *"Sarvagatam Susookshmam"*.

468. *Vajreshvaree* - वज्रेश्वरी

(i) One who is in the form of the deity called *Vajreshvaree*.

(ii) The presiding deity of the sixth day of bright lunar fortnight and tenth day of dark lunar fortnight is called *Vajreshvaree*.

(iii) The deity of the *Jālandhara Peeṭa* is called *Vajreshvaree*.

(iv) *Pāvano Upanishad* says that three *Devees* viz., *Kāmeshwaree, Vajreshvaree* and *Bhagamālinee* are worshipped in the eighth *Āvaranam*; *Kāmeshvaree Vajreshvaree Bhagamālineyontas Trikoŋagā Devya*:

(v) The *Śree Chakra* has twelve walls, all built of diamonds; in the centre of the eleventh, there is a river called *Vajramayee* and she is its deity. Sage *Durvāsa* in his *Lalitāstavarathan*, (44 and 45) says, "There let the ever flowing river called *Vajra*, be everlasting, filled with the sound of the sweet notes of the swans gliding on the beautiful waves; on the pleasant bank of that river *Vajreshee* flourishes decked with diamond ornaments praised by *Devas* headed by *Indra*, the hurler of the thunder-bolt";

Tatru Sadā Pravahanti Tatinee Vajrāpbhidhā Chiram Jeeyāt I
Chatolormi Jāta Nrutyat Kalahamsee Kula Kalakvanita Pushṭā II

Rodhasi Tasyā Ruchire Vajreshee Jayati Vajra Bhooshādyā I
Vajra Pradāna Toshita Vajrimukha Tridasha Vinutachāritrā II

(vi) The *Brahmāṇḍa Purāṇa* says, when *Indra* performed penance in the water, "From that water *Śreedevee* arose and gave I*ndra* the weapon called *Vajra*".

469. *Vāmadevee* - वामदेवी

(i) The consort of *Vāmadeva*.
(ii) There are five forms viz., *Eesana, Tatpurusha, Agora, Vāmadeva* and *Sadyojāta* of *Shiva.* In that **She** is the consort of *Vāmadeva*.
(iii) In *Shiva Purāṇa, Shiva* has been described; "Of beautiful appearance, red as the red paste (*kunkuma*), the north face of the Lord called *Vāma* is firmly established";

Kumkumakshoḍa Sankāsham Vāmāgyam Vanaveshdrut I
Vaktramuttaram Ĕshwasya Pratistāyām Pratishtitam II

(iv) *Vāma* - to be worshipped, *deva* - the deity. The *Aitreya Sruti* says, "The *Devas* addressed him; he indeed is to be worshipped by all of us, hence he is called *Vāmadeva*";

Tam Devā Abruvan Ayam Vai Na: *Sarveshām Vāma It*
Tasmādvāmadeva:

(v) *Vāma* – the left side, *Deva* - he shines, i.e. *Ardhanāreeshvara* (half body is *Shiva* and the other half is *Devee*) is called *Vāmadeva*.
(vi) *Vāma* – fair; beautiful *Devee*.
(vii) *Vāma* - the fruits of actions, Devee, the presiding deity of them. *Vāma* - those devoted to the left-hand path (*Vāmāchārā*). **She** is their goddess. (In worshipping *Śreedevee* there are two types; viz. *Vāma* method and *Dakshiṇa* method). This has been explained in detail in 912th name – *Savyapasavya Mārgasthā* and 923rd name – *Dakshiṇā Dakshiṇārādhya*. There itself, *Śree Bhāskara Rāya* advises that *Vāmā* method is not suitable to us.
(viii) The *Devee Purāṇa* says, *Vāma* means opposite or inverted; as *Śreedevee* gives bliss through that path **She** is called *Vāmadevee*.

Vāmam Viruddharoopam Tu Vipareetam Cha Geeyate I
Vāmena Sukhadā Devee Vāma Devee Tata: *Smrutā* II

470. *Vayovasthāvivarjitā* - वयोऽवस्थाविवर्जिता

(i) One who is devoid of old age and other changes.
(ii) **She** is exempt from the states of life - childhood, boyhood, youth etc.;

because **She** is eternal.

(iii) 136th name *Nityā*, 344 – *Kshayavruddhi Vinirmuktā*, 358 – *Tarunee* and 430 – *Nitya Youvanā* may be referred.

471. *Siddheshvaree* - सिद्धेश्वरी

(i) One who is the goddess of *Siddhas* or spiritual adepts.

(ii) **She** is the queen of *siddhas* like *Gorakshānandar, Matsyendra nāthar* and others.

(iii) Those who got the *siddhis* like *Aŋimā, Mahimā*, etc., through adoration are called *Siddhas*. Hence the controls of nature do not apply to them. For instance – water will not wet them, fire will not burn them, wind cannot move them and they can be omnipresent like ether. But the primary goal of worship is not to win over these basic elements. The aim is to experience the oneness with the God by using those *Siddhis*, control the mind and do penance. These are tools to help doing penance. Those who do not use such powers for doing penance, but use it for worldly affairs will not develop self-knowledge. They would repeatedly be bound by the cycle of birth. It is apt to call those who use the *Siddhis* for attaining the self-knowledge as *Siddhas*. **She** is the queen of such *Siddhas*.

(iv) In the *Guru Maŋḍala Pooja*, it is usual to worship three different races of teachers like *Divyoukas, Sidhoukas* and *Mānavoukas*. It is the practice to worship these three teacher groups out of the *Sarvasiddhiprada Chakra*, (central triangle) by imagining three lines. It is mentioned in the *Poorva Bhāga* (first section) of this *Sahasranāma*, that these three groups seated in their respective places in *Śreedevee*'s assembly and heard *Vāgdevees* chanting this *Sahasranāma*.

(v) There is also a deity of this name at Banaras.

472. *Siddhavidyā* - सिद्धविद्या

(i) One whose *mantra* (*Śree Vidyā*) is always fruitful.

(ii) *Mantra* is that which protects those who chant it. If the deity of the *mantra* is a male it is called *mantra*, if it is a female it is called *Vidya*.

(iii) Only after verifying whether the *mantra* (or the *Vidyā*) will give the fruit for self, one has to accept that *mantra* from a teacher as advise. There are four methods of such verification.

a. *Siddham* – chanting for a particular number of times. Give results by doing *Purascharaŋam* (The four sacrificial fire, food, *tarpaŋa* and *mārjanā* together are called *Purascharaŋam*).

b. *Susiddham* – Give results even if chanted for lesser number of times than the prescribed one. (It can be thought that in the previous births this *mantra* was chanted and for some reason did not give full results and is in credit for this person and hence gives fruits early in this birth).

c. *Susādhyam* – Against the above, the person is in debt to the *mantra* in the previous births, since he might have mis-used it and hence it gives results in this birth only if chant for more number of times than the prescribed one.

d. *Ari* – One who makes enmity with the presiding deity of the *mantra* by misbehaving with the deity, the *mantra* will not give its fruits. On the contrary, it will try to destroy him and his family.

(iv) To identify which method a *mantra* belongs to, a diagram called *Siddhāri Koshtam* is used.

(v) For some *mantras*, *Siddhāri Koshtam* need not be used. Such *mantras* give result to all and at all times. One such *mantra* is *Śreedevee's Panchadashākshare Vidyā*. **She** is in the form of *Siddha Vidyā* and offer fruits of chanting.

473. *Siddhamātā* - सिद्धमाता

(i) One who is the mother and guard of *Siddhas* (aspirants).

474. *Yashasvinee* - यशस्विनी

(i) One who is most renowned.

(ii) *Mahā Nārāyaŋa Upanishad* (1-10) says; *Tasya Nāma Mahādyasha*:. In the 511th name - *Bandhinyādi Samanvitā* the names of the Devees around *Kākinee Yogini* will be explained. One among them is *Yashasvinee*.

(iii) The *Yoginee* forms of *Śreedevee*; in the next 60 names (475 to 534) *Śreedevee* is worshipped under *Yoginee Nyāsa* (*Nyāsa* – mental appropriation) method. As a background to understand this, we need to know some details.

Nyāsa is something established, to make the energy of the *devata* in our body and mind, i.e. imagining in that way. In this fashion the idea that self itself in the form of *devata*, is formed. That is the purpose for which

Nyāsa is done.

Every *mantra* has corresponding sage, meter, *nyāsam* and *dhyānam* (meditation verse). *Nyāsa* is done, in general dividing the *mantra* into six parts (or divided into three parts and used twice) and on fingers, heart, head, tuft of hair, armour (shoulders), eyes and weapons (assuming defense weapons around the head). The *japa* (chanting) done without *nyāsa* or counting is not considered as *japa* at all. In addition, some other special types of *nyāsās* are also done. It is understood from the first part (*poorva bāga*) of this *Sahasranāma* that those *nyāsās* were advised by *Hayagreeva* to *Agasthya* in the *Nyāsā Kānḍa*. According to *Śree Vidyā* method, the oneness with the *devatas* happens in five ways viz., *Śree Chakra, Śree Vidyā* (*mantra*), *Śreedevee*, one's own teacher and self – it has to be assumed that all these five become one.

Shaḍa Nyāsa (six types) is one of the special *nyāsās*, as per the *Śree Vidyā* method. This also is of two types. One is *laghu* (brief) *Shoḍā Nyāsa*. This has six sub-types viz., *Gaŋesha Nyāsa, Graha* (planets) *Nyāsa, Nakshatra* (star) *Nyāsa, Yoginee Nyāsa, Rāsi Nyāsa* and *Peeṭa Nyāsa*. Only those who have been invocated with *Panchadasheemantra* can do this.

Second is *Mahāshoḍa Nyāsa*. This also has six sub-types viz., *Prapancha* (universe), *Bhuvana* (world), *Moorthy* (form), *Mantra, Devata* and mothers. Only those who have been invocated with *Shoḍasee mantra* can do this, with the permission of the teacher.

In this *Sahasranāmā, Vasinee Devees* worship *Śreedevee* as per *Yoginee Nyāsā* method as explained in names from 475 to 534. *Peeṭa nyāsā* method is explained in 833rd name – *Panchāshat Peeṭaroopiŋee*.

Laghu Shoḍā Nyāsā has to be done as indicated in various *Śākta Tantras*. *Śree Bhāskararāya* himself has explained this in his *Varivasya Rahasya, Sethu Bandam* (the explanation for *Nityāshoḍashikārnava*).

Gaŋesha Graha Nakshatra Yoginee Rashi Roopineem I
Deveem Peeṭamayeem Vande Mātrukām Sundareem Parām II

These *nyāsās* have to done in alongwith the 51 letters in Samskrit language.

It has to be imagined that the forms of *Gaŋesha*, etc., are all *Śreedevee*'s only. It has been explained in *Tantra Sāstras*, to touch different constituent parts of the body for each of the *nyāsās*. These are to be learnt from a proper teacher.

Gaŋesha	-	51
Graha (planets)	-	9
Nakshatra (star)	-	27
Yoginee	-	7
Rāsi (Aries to Pisces)	-	12
Peeṭa(*Shakti Peeṭa*, etc).	-	51
Total	-	157

Yoginee Nyāsa is done in all the six *chakras* from *Moolādhāra* till *Agna* and in *Sahasrāra* Lotus. There are seven *Yoginees* viz., *Dāginee, Rāginee, Lāginee, Kāginee, Sāginee, Hāginee* and *Yāginee*. It is usually mentioned as *Daralakasahaya* by combining the first letters of these names.

They are presiding deities for each of the *chakras*. Also they are the deities in-charge of skin, blood, flesh, fat, bone, marrow and semen.

Meditation verses are available for each of them. Their dwelling place, form and weapons are also mentioned. Supporting deities are also available.

List of *Yoginee* forms of *Śreedevee*.

Name		Name of the *Yoginee*	*Chakra*	Form	Colour	No. of faces	Weapons	Character	Supporting Deities - (First Name)	Body Part	Rice - interested	Petals	Letters
From	To												
475	484	*Ḍāginee*	*Vishuddhi*	Three eyes	Reddish White	1	Club	*	*Amrutā*	Skin	*Pāyāsānnam*	16	Vowels
485	494	*Rāginee*	*Anāhata*	Fangs	White	2	*AkshaMālā*	@	*Kālarātree*	Blood	Rice with ghee	12	*Ka* to *Da*
495	503	*Lāginee*	*Maŋipooraka*	Explained in Dyāna verses	Red	3	Thunderbolt	#	*Dāmaree*	Flesh	Rice mixed with jaggery	10	*Da* to *Ba*
504	513	*Kāginee*	*Svādishṭāna*		Yellow	4	Trident	$	*Bandinee*	Fat	Curd rice	6	*Ba* to *La*
514	520	*Sāginee*	*Moolādhāra*		-	5	Goad	-	*Varadā*	Bone	Rice with green gram dhal	4	*Va* to *Sa*
521	527	*Hāginee*	*Agna*		White	6	-	-	*Hamsavatee*	Marrow	Yellow rice	2	*Ha* to *Ksha*
528	534	*Yāgi*	*Sahasrāra*		Mixed	All dir	All		-	Semen	All type	10	All

		ne e				ecti ons					s of rice	0 0	

* - Creator of fear for the souls who do not have the knowledge of oneness
@ - Giver of boon for the brave
# - Giver of happiness to all devotees
$ - Pride and interested in alcohol
Note: wherever '-' is mentioned, the details are not available in the *Sahasranāma*.

These details are listed as mentioned in this *Sahasranāma*. It would be convenient to read the below names with the help of this list.
While discussing the *chakras*, it is usual to start from *Moolādhāram*. However, it is the practice to list down the parts of the body as above. In that sense, the names of the *Yoginees* are listed. i.e. It has started from *Vishuddhi*. Also, it is in the ascending order of number of faces of *Yoginees*.

All these *Yoginees* are different forms of *Śreedevee* only. By fixing them, who have *yoga* energy, in the concerned parts of the body, one can control all the five basic elements.

With this *nyāsā*, *Śreedevee* is experienced in an integrated form. 653rd name – *Yoginee* and 655th name – *Yogyā* – **She** herself is the *Yoginees*.

A small note about the body parts:-
The essence of the food intake is converted into the energy. That without essence passes away as stools. That milky essence is further cooked by heating inside the body and a major chunk is turned into skin. Further heated up it becomes blood. The gist of blood is flesh. The gist of flesh is fat. Its gist is bone, further marrow and then the root semen.

In *Pāvanopanishad* also seven constituent parts of the body only are mentioned. *Kāmikāma* says, by adding *Prāŋan* (breath) and *Jeeva* (soul) it is counted as nine. The tenth is *Parameshwaree* herself. There itself it is mentioned that the five viz., skin, blood, flesh, fat and bone are *Shiva* related corners and the four viz., marrow, semen, breath and soul are *Shakti* related corners. *Sāstrās* say that these nine corners are *Śree Chakra* itself. And the body itself is the *Śree Chakra*. 11th verse in *Soundaryalaharee* may be referred.

475. *Vishuddhichakra Nilayā* - विशुद्धिचक्रनिलया

(i) One who abodes in the *Vishuddhi Chakra*.
(ii) This *chakra* is in the cavity of the throat. In this *chakra*, the soul gets purified by looking at the *Brahmam*, in the form of a swan. Hence this is called as *Vishuddhi Chakra*. **Her** abode is in the pericarp of the sixteen-petalled lotus.

476. *Āraktavarŋā* - आरक्तवर्णा

(i) One who is rosy/ crimson coloured.
(ii) **Her** colour is like that of a trumpet flower.
(iii) The letter *'Ā'* is prefixed to this name. Later 499th name has to be read as *Raktavarŋa*.

477. *Trilochanā* - त्रिलोचना

(i) One who has three eyes.
(ii) It has to be reminded that though 453rd name has the same meaning, some other explanations were also provided there.
(iii) 762nd name *Tryambikā* also calls *Śreedevee* as three-eyed.

478. *Khaṭvāngādipraharaŋā* - खट्वाङ्गादिप्रहरणा

(i) One who is armed with a club, etc.
(ii) *Khaṭvānga* is a club with a human skull at its end. *Khaṭvā* – cot. Hence it can be taken as **She** has the leg of a cot as a weapon.

479. *Vadanaikasamanvitā* - वदनैकसमन्विता

(i) One who is with a single face.
(ii) **She** has one face which explains the ether *tatva*.

480. *Pāyasānnapriyā* - पायसान्नप्रिया

(i) One who loves rice mixed with *pāyasā* (milk pudding).
(ii) *Pāyasam* is made by cooking rice in cow's milk.
(iii) *Pāyasānnam* (also called as *Paramānnam*). This is a healthy food and helps the growth of body parts.

481. *Tvaksthā* - त्वक्स्था

(i) One who is the deity of organ of touch.

482. *Pashulokabhayangkaree* - पशुलोकभयङ्करी

(i) One who is frightful to the ignorant.
(ii) *Pashus* are those devoid of the knowledge of non- duality.
(iii) In the 133rd name *Niranjanā*, the word *pashu* was explained. 354th name *Pashupāshavimochinee* may also be referred.

483. *Amrutādimahāshaktisamvrutā* - अमृतादिमहाशक्तिसंवृता

(i) One who is surrounded by 16 *Shaktis* starting from *Amruta*.
(ii) Counting as each for one petal and one for one letter there are 16 *Shaktis* around *Śreedevee*. They are; *Amrutā, Ākarshinee, Indrānee, Esānee, Umā, Oordvakeshee, Ruddhitā, Rookārā, Lukārā, Lookārā, Ekapadā, Ishvaryātmikā, Omkārā, Oushadee, Amibikā* and *Akshara*.

484. *Ḍākineeshvaree* - डाकिनीश्वरी

(i) One who is having the name of *Ḍākineeshvaree*.
(ii) One who possesses the nine attributes discussed above.

485. *Anāhatābjanilayā* - अनाहताब्जनिलया

(i) One who abides in the *Anāhata* Lotus.
(ii) This is in the heart with twelve-petalled lotus. This is the place of air.

486. *Shyāmābhā* - श्यामाभा

(i) One who is shining with dark (mixed with green) complexion. It is the colour of clouds.
(ii) A girl with 16 years of age is called *Shyāma*. **She** is in that form. (It can be noted that at the end of *Mahā Shoḍanyāsa* the verse starting with "*Amrutārna Madhyastam*" the statement *Shoḍasha Vārshikam* is mentioned).

487. *Vadanadvayā* - वदनद्वया

(i) One who has two faces.
(ii) To explain the two *tatvas* – ether and air – **She** has two faces.

488. *Dhamshṭrojvalā* - दंष्ट्रोज्वला

(i) One who has shining tusks/ fangs.

489. *Akshamālādidharā* - अक्षमालादिधरा

(i) One who wears a rosary etc.
(ii) The garland made of Samskrit letters (numbering 51) starting from *'A'* ending with *'Ksha'* is called *Akshamāla*. This is useful for counting while chanting *mantras*.
(iii) In the *dhyāna* (meditation) verse of *Śreedevee*, it has mentioned that **She** wears *Aksham, Shoolam, Kabālam* and *Damaroo*. *Aksham* is the wheel of a chariot. It can also be interpreted as that **She** has the *chakra* weapon in that model. 998th name of *Vişhŋu Sahasranāma* – *Rathāngapānee* may be compared.

490. *Rudhirasamsthitā* - रुधिरसंस्थिता

(i) One who is the presiding deity of the blood part of the body.

491. *Kālarātryādishaktyoughavrutā* - कालरात्र्यादिशक्त्यौघवृता

(i) One who is surrounded by *Kālarāthree* and other *Shakti Devees*.
(ii) It has been mentioned in *Varāha Purāŋa* about a *Shakti Devee* called *Kālarāthree*. She is the destruction energy originated from *Tamo* character of *Rudra*. It is mentioned that she did penance at *Neelagiri* to complete a vow.
(iii) As a pre-announcement of one's death, he/ she will get a dream in the night previous to death. That night is called *Kālarāthree*.
(iv) In *Brahmastuti* of *Saptashatee* (first chapter) it has been mentioned that *Kālarāthree* is the dissolution at the end of *kalpa* and *Moharāthree* is the great destruction. **She** is in that form; *Kālarāthrir Mahārāthrir Moharātrshcha Dāruna*.
(v) In the *Kavachā* read as part of *Saptashatee*, it has been mentioned that *Kālarāthree* is the seventh one of the nine names of *Durga*.
(vi) In some schools it has been mentioned that in *Rāmayanā*,

Kālarāthree only took the incarnation as *Sitā* to kill *Rāvana*.

(vii) In *Laghu Shoḍanyāsa*, the names of 12 *Devees* are mentioned as; *Kālarāthree, Khantitā, Gāyatree, Ghantākarshinee, Gnārnā, Chanḍā, Chāyā, Jayā, Jangāriŋee, Gnanaroopa, Dangahastā* and *Dankāriŋee*.

(viii) It can be also be taken as – **She** is in the form of *Kālarathree* mentioned in the *Devata Nyāsā* of *Mahāshoḍanyāsa*.

492. *Snigdhoudana Priyā* – स्निग्धौदन प्रिया

(i) One who fond of rice mixed with ghee.

(ii) This food is very good for enrichment of blood. This gives energy to the blood to create flesh out of it. **She** is fond of it.

493. *Mahāveerendravaradā* - महावीरेन्द्रवरदा

(i) One who grants boons to the chiefs of warriors.

(ii) *Vi* - many, *Ira*, - excited or intoxicated; the meaning is that the *veeras* are the trained orators gifted with eloquence. She grants boons to their leaders.

(iii) *Mahaveera* - a kind of vessel used in *the* Soma sacrifice, as explained in *Sruti*; *Mahāveeram Tu Vibādhamrujeshwam*. The meaning is the *mahāveeras* are those who are continually drinking the nectar of *Brahmam* or *Indras*, those who know *Brahmam*. *idam*, those who directly realise *Brahmam*, which is the Self, the witness of all, saying "I am He". *Srutis* say, "He perceived, hence he is called *Indra*"; *idamadarshamidamadharshamiti Tasmādindro Nāma*.

(iv) *Veeras* are those who are beyond the distinction of *Aham* and *idam*, who are valiant and who are *Svātmā Rāmas* (those who do not know Self and not blessed). **She** gives boon to the great and leader like among them.

Ahami Pralayam Kurvannidama: *Prati Yogina*: I
Parākramam Paro Bhunkte Svātmānamashivāpaham II

(v) The *Shiva Sūtra* (I-11) says, "He is *veeresa*, who enjoys in the threefold way". That is, *Veerendras* are those who realise the fourth state (*tureeya*) in the other three states also (awaken, deep sleep and swoon); *Tritayābhoktā Veeresha*:. This is based on the *Kshemarāja's Vimarsanee*.

(vi) The commentator *Varadarāja* interprets the *Sūtra* thus, "*Veeras*, senses causing the miseries of separateness, extending within and without and Isa is the lord of the senses";

Veeresha Iti Veerānām Bhedavyasana Kārinām I
Antar Bhahir Visaratāmindriyānām Dheeshvara: II

(vii) *Mahāveera* is the name for *Prahlāda*. The *Devee Bhāgavatam* (book IV) says that *Indra* and *Prahlāda* praised *Devee* after their fight which lasted a hundred divine years and **She** granted them boons.

494. *Rākiŋyambāsvaroopiŋee* - राकिण्यम्बास्वरूपिणी

(i) One who is in the form of the *Rākinee Yoginee*.

495. *Maŋipoorābjanilayā* - मणिपूराब्जनिलया

(i) One who resides in the lotus called *Maŋipoora*.
(ii) It is in the belly button with 10 petals.

496. *Vadanatrāyasamyutā* - वदनत्रयसम्युता

(i) One who has three faces.
(ii) The abdomen is the place of water. Hence **She** has three faces To explain the three *tatvas* – ether air and water.

497. *Vajrādikāyudhopetā* - वज्रादिकायुधोपेता

(i) One who is armed with the thunderbolt and other weapons.
(ii) In the *dhyāna* (meditation) verse of *Śreedevee*, it has mentioned that **She** has in her four hands thunderbolt, *Shakti*, *Daŋḍam* and *Abhayam*.

498. *Ḍāmaryādibhirāvrutā* - डामर्यादिभिरावृता

(i) One who is surrounded by *Dāmaree* and others.
(ii) The names of 10 *Devees* are; *Dāmaree*, *Dhankāriŋee*, *Nārnā*, *Tāmasee*, *Sthānvee*, *Dhākshāyanee*, *Dhātree*, *Nāree*, *Pārvatee* and *Phatkāriŋee*.

499. *Raktavarŋā* - रक्तवर्णा

(i) One who is red/ blood coloured.

500. *Mamsanishṭā* - मांस्सनिष्ठा

(i) One who is fond of flesh/ meat.

Thus ends the sixth *Kalā* called *Ruchi*.

*****

Section 7: *Sushumnā Kalā*

501. *Guḍānnapreetamānasā* - गुडान्नप्रीतमानसा

(i) One who gets satisfied with the rice cooked with jaggery.

502. *Samastabhaktasukhadā* – समस्तभक्तसुखदा

(i) One who bestows happiness to all the devotees.

503. *Lākinyambāsvaroopiŋee* – लाकिन्यम्बास्वरूपिणी

(i) One who is in the form of *Lākinee Devee*.

504. *Svādhishṭānāmbujagatā* – स्वाधिष्ठानाम्बुजगता

(i) One who abides in the *Svādhishṭāna chakra* (in the lower abdomen of the body).

505. *Chaturvaktramanoharā* – चतुर्वक्त्रमनोहरा

(i) One who is fascinating with **Her** four faces.
(ii) *Svādhishṭāna* is the place of water. Hence starting from ether until water the four primary elements represent the four faces of *Śreedevee*. This is explained in the book by *Śree Radhakrişhŋa Sāstrigal*. The 14th verse of *Soundaryalaharee* can also be referred, which states *Svādhishṭāna* as the place of fire and *Maŋipooraka* as the place of water.

506. *Shoolādyāyudha Sampannā* – शूलाद्यायुधसंपन्ना

(i) One who has weapons like trident (trident, noose, skull and goad are the weapons of *Śreedevee*).

507. *Peetavarŋā* – पीतवर्णा

(i) One who is yellow in hue (golden in colour).
(ii) The word *Hiranyavarŋām* in *Śree Sooktam* can be reminded. *Peeṭa* also means Saffron flower. Hence it can also be taken as that

Śreedevee is rosy in colour like the Saffron flower. The reddish/ rosy colour of *Śreedevee* has been described in many a place;

Example 1; *Sindoorāruna Vigrahām* in the *dhyāna* verse of this *Sahasranāma*.

Example 2; *Louhityametasya Sarvasya Vimarsha*: in *Pāvanopanishad*.

508. *Atigarvitā* – अतिगर्विता

(i) One who is very proud/ dignified.
(ii) **She** is proud because **She** is so beautiful.
(iii) In *Saptashatee* (V chapter – *Doota Samvādam*), we read *Śreedevee*'s own words that **She** has pride; *"Yo Me Darpam Vyapohati"*.
(iv) In the 158th name (*Nirmadā*), we read that **She** does not have pride. It is the character of *Brahmam* as subtler than an atom, bigger than the biggest, etc., – *"Anoraneeyān Mahato Maheeyān"*. Hence there are no contradictions in such names.

509. *Medonishṭhā* – मेदोनिष्ठा

(i) One who is residing in/ presiding over the fatty tissues of the body.
(ii) Since **She** is the presiding deity for these tissues, **She** was mentioned as pride in the previous name.

510. *Madhupreetā* – मधुप्रीता

(i) One who gets satisfied (fond of) with mead.
(ii) *Madhu* also indicates honey.
(iii) *Sruti* also says, "One who presents an oblation with *madhu*, pleases the great Devee";

Yan Madhunā Juhoti Mahateemeva Taddevatām Preenāti.

511. *Bandhinyādisamanvitā* – बन्धिन्यादिसमन्विता

(i) One who is surrounded by *Bandhinee* and others.
(ii) These are the six deities from *Bandhinee, Bhadrakālee, Mahāmāyā, Yashasvinee, Raktā* and *Lamboshtee*.

512. *Dadhyannāshakahrudayā* – दध्यन्नासक्तहृदया

(i) One who is fond of curd rice.

513. *Kākineeroopadhāriṇee* – काकिनीरूपधारिणी

(i) One who is in the form of *Kākinee Devee*.

514. *Moolādhārāmbujārooḍhā* – मूलाधाराम्बुजारूढा

(i) One who dwells in *Moolādhāra* Lotus.
(ii) *Moolādhāra* is the lower abdomen in the body. **She** resides in the Lotus in that place.

515. *Panchavaktrā* – पन्चवक्त्रा

(i) One who exhibits five faces.
(ii) *Moolādhāra* is the place of earth *tatva*. Hence **She** has five faces indicating the five primary elements ether till earth.

516. *Asthisamsthitā* - अस्थिसंस्थिता

(i) One who presides over the bones of living beings.

517. *Ankushādipraharaṇā* - अङ्कुशादिप्रहरणा

(i) One who is armed with goad and other weapons. (**She** has goad, Lotus, book and knowledge sign [of hands – *mudra*] in her hands).

518. *Varadādinishevitā* – वरदादिनिषेविता

(i) One who is attended by *Varadā* and other *Shaktis*. Their names are *Varadā*, *Śree*, *Shaṇḍā* and *Sarasvathee*.

519. *Mudgoudanāshakachittā* – मुद्गौदनासक्तचित्ता

(i) One who is fond of rice mixed with green gram pulse.
(ii) Such a food item is called *Pongal* – *Śree Bhāskararāya* explains the recipe for preparation of *Pongal*.

520. *Sākinyambāsvaroopiṇee* – साकिन्यम्बास्वरूपिणी

(i) One who is in the form of *Sākinee*.
(ii) In the *dhyāna* verse of this *Sahasranāma* it has been mentioned as **She** is in the colour of smoke (*Dhoomrābhām*). It is also mentioned as; *Madhumadamuditām* – **She** is much pleased under the influence of alcohol.

521. *Āgnāchakrabjanilayā* – आज्ञचक्राब्जनिलया

(i) One who resides in the *Āgnā chakra* Lotus – in between the eye brows.

522. *Shuklavarŋā* – शुक्लवर्णा

(i) One who is white in complexion.

523. *Shaḍānanā* – षडानना

(i) One who has six faces.
(ii) *Āgnā chakra* is the place of the mind. To exhibit the energy of the five primary elements and that of mind, **She** has six faces. To show that it is the controlling chief of all the five *chakras* from *Vishudhi* till *Moolādhāra*, **She** has six faces.

524. *Majjāsamsthā* – मज्जासंस्था

(i) One who is the presiding deity of bone marrows.

525. *Hamsavateemukhyashaktisamanvitā* – हंसवतीमुख्यशक्तिसमन्विता

(i) One who is surrounded by *Hamsavatee* and other *Shaktis*. Their names are *Hamsavatee* and *Kshamāvatee*.

526. *Haridrānnaikarasikā* – हरिद्रान्नैकरसिका

(i) One who is fond of yellow or rice mixed with turmeric.

527. *Hākineeroopadhāriŋee* – हाकिनीरूपधारिणी

(i) One who is in the form of *Hākinee*.

(ii) In the *dhyāna* verse of this *Sahasranāma* it was mentioned that **She** has knowledge sign, *Udukkai* (a kind of goat-skin drum), garland of letters (Samskrit alphabets) and skull in her hands and provides all the happiness to **Her** devotees.

528. *Sahasradalapadmasthā* – सहस्रदलपद्मस्था

(i) One who dwells in the *Sahasrāra* Lotus (*Brahmarandram*).

529. *Sarvavarŋopashobhitā* – सर्ववर्णोपशोभिता

(i) One who shines with all colours.
(ii) **She** is with Black, Green, Red, Yellow and the colour of trumpet flower.
(iii) *Sarva* - all, *Varŋa* – Samskrit alphabets (the fifty-one letters from *A* to *Ksha*), that is the fifty *shaktis* from *Amruta* to *Kshamāvati*; **She** shines with these letters and the corresponding presiding deities. Counting these fifty letters backwards and forwards we obtain a hundred *shaktis*, each of these reside in ten petals.
(iv) According to *Vararuchi's Kaṭapayādi* method the word *'Upa'* indicates the number ten. I.e. it is apt that each deity residing in ten petals – mentioned above.
(v) Based on this method some repeat in the *Yogininyāsa*, ten times each of those *shaktis* to make up a thousand.

530. *Sarvāyudhadharā* – सर्वायुधधरा

(i) One who is armed with all weapons.
(ii) In *Sruti* also (*Śree Rudram*) we read as;

Sahasrāni Sahasradhā Bāhvos Tava Hetava:

(iii) *Viṣhŋu Sahasranāmā* 759th name *Sarvashastrabhrutāvarā* and 1000th name *Sarvapraharanāyudha*: may be referred.

531. *Shuklasamsthitā* – शुक्लसंस्थिता

(i) One who is the presiding deity of semen.
(ii) According to the *Bhavishyottara Purāŋa*, *Shukla* is the name of a kind of meditation at the time of sexual enjoyment. It can also be taken as that **She** is in that form.

532. *Sarvatomukhee* – सर्वतोमुखी

(i) One who has faces in all round directions.
(ii) In *Śreemad Bhagavat Geeta* (XIII-13) it is mentioned as; *Sarvatokshishiromukham* - Everywhere eyes, heads and mouths.
(iii) In *Sruti* (*Purusha Sooktam*) also it is mentioned as;

Sahasra Sheershā: *Purusha*: *Sahasrāksha*: *Sahasrapād*

533. *Sarvoudanapreetachittā* – सर्वौदनप्रीतचित्ता

(i) One who gets pleased with all kinds of rice.
(ii) As mentioned earlier, right from *Pāyasa* rice till Yellow rice and other rice, **She** gets pleased with all kinds of rice.

534. *Yākinyambāsvaroopiṇee* – याकिन्यम्बास्वरूपिणी

(i) One who appears in the form of *Yākinee*.
(ii) In the meditation verse of this *Sahasranāma* it was mentioned that it is the quality of *Śreedevee* to admire *Paramashiva* ; *Parashiva-rasikām*.
(iii) Thus having described *Śreedevee* under the forms of *Yoginees*, it is proceeded to describe **Her** with other forms/ qualities. This has been given as a list.

535. *Svāhā* – स्वाहा

(i) One who is in the form of *Svāhā*, the sacred exclamation with which oblations are made in sacrificial fire for gods.

536. *Svadhā* – स्वधा

(i) One who is in the form of *Svadha*.
(ii) The words *Svāhā* and *Svadhā* are used when oblations are offered to gods in the sacrificial fire. *Devee Bhāgavatam* (IX-43-7) says – the word *Svāhā* is uttered when the sacrificial fire is about gods and the word *Svadhā* is used when it is about pitrus (predecessors in the family race);

Svāhādevee Havirdāne Prshastā Sarvakarmasu I
Pitru Dāne Svadhā Shastā Dakshiṇā Sarvato Varā II

(iii) It is also to be construed that **She** is in the form of *Devees* in these names (*Svāhā* and *Svadhā*). *Saptashatee* (chapter 4-9) says - by uttering your name all the host of gods, Oh *Devee*, is satisfied in all sacrifices, for thou art *Svāhā* and thou art named *Svadhā*, the word which gives satisfaction to the host of *pitrus*;

Yasyā: *Samastasuratā Samudeeraŋena*
Truptim Prayāti Sakaleshu Makheshu Devee I
Svāhāsi Vai Pitrugaŋasiya Cha Truptihetu
Ruchchāyase Tvamata Eva Janai: *Svadhā Cha* II

(iv) The *Mārkaŋḍeya Purāŋa* says - there are seven words which are used in the *Homa* (sacrificial fire), in the oblation and in the cooking. By repeating (or uttering) your name only, Oh *Devee*, the merit of repeating these names are obtained by *Brahmavādins*;

Somasamsthā Havi: *Samstha*: *Bāgasamsthāshcha Sapta Yā*: I
Tāstvaduchchāranād Devee Kriyante Brahmavādibhi: II

While interpreting this, it has to be uttered as *Svāhā Namahā* and *Svadhā Namaha*.

(v) Hence *Śreedevee* is said to be in the form of *Svāhā* and *Svadhā* (combining the previous name also).

(vi) The *Linga Purāŋa* says – the consort of *Shiva* in the form of fire is said to be *Svāha*. The divine six-faced one (*Skanda*) is called by the learned, the son;

Svāhā Vahnyātmanastasya Proktā Pashupate: *Priyā* I
Shanmukho Bhagavān Devo Budhai: *Putra Udhāhruta*: II

The same message is confirmed in the *Vāyu Purāŋa* also;

Nāmnā Pashupater Yā Tu Tanuragnir Dvijai: *Smrutā* I
Tasya Patnee Smrutā Svāhā Skandashchāpi Suta: *Smruta*: II

According to the *Padma Purāŋa*, *Svadhā* is the presiding deity of the city of *Māhesvarapuram*.

(vii) *Shushṭu* - well, *Am* – *Viṣhŋu* or self, *Dadhāti* - nourishes or protect. Hence *Svadha*.

(viii) While considering these meanings it has to be uttered as *Svāhāyai Namaha* and *Svadhāyai Namaha*.

(ix) *Śree Bhāskararāya* explains some more meanings also;

a. According to the *Taitireeya Sruti* - your own (*sva*) speech (*Āhā*) - means one's own speech.
b. The *Sāmaveda Brāhmanam* and the *Yāskara's Nirukta* also explain *Svāha* thus; *Su* - well, *Āhā* speech, or *Sva* - Self, *Āhā* -, to speak.
c. *Su* - good, *Āhā* - to be given as an oblation.

d. *Sva* - one's own people, *Āhā* - to recognise – i.e. **She** recognises the people as her own self.
e. *Su* - well, *A* - *Brahma, Ha* - to go – i.e. to take along to *Brahma*.

(x) In *Devee Bhāgavatam* (9th *Skandam* 43rd & 44th chapters) *Śreedevee*'s episodes and the verses are explained.

537. *Amati*: - अमतिः

(i) One who is in the form of ignorance.
(ii) *Mati*: - knowledge. Its opposite is *Amati*:.
(iii) *A* – small, *Mati*: - knowledge. i.e. to be expanded knowledge.
(iv) While interpreting *Shukla Yajur Veda, Durgāchārya* has given meaning of this word as self-soul science.
(v) It is said that in the order of creation, unmanifested, manifested and egoism *tatvas* were created from *Moolaprakruti* (root nature). Intellect *tatva* is hidden in these and is in the stage of invisible individual entity. I.e. it indicates unmanifestation.

538. *Medhā* – मेधा

(i) One who is in the form of special knowledge.
(ii) After the above said *Amati*:, the next creation was intelligence (*Medhā*). **She** is in this form also.
(iii) *Agni Purāṇa* says *Medhā* is remembrance; *Dheerdhāranāvatee Medha*.
(iv) *Śreedevee* in the form of *Medhā* has been explained in *Saptashatee* in two places - "Oh *Devee*, thou art intelligence, thou art the essence of all the scriptures"; and "Devee who resides in all beings in the form of intelligence";

Medhāsi Devee Viditākhila Shāstra Sārā I
Yā Devee Sarvabhooteshu Medhāroopena Samsthitā I

(v) We worship *Śreedevee* through *Medhā Sookta* also.
(vi) According to the *Padma Purāṇa*, the deity called *Medhā* is in Kashmir.

539. *Sruti*: - श्रुतिः

(i) One who is in the form of *Vedas*.

540. *Smruti*: - स्मृतिः

(i) One who is in the form of *Smrutis*.

(ii) *Sruti* - hearing and *Smruti* – recollection – **She** is in the form of knowledge obtained through both these.

(iii) It has been mentioned in many a place that the *Vedas* and the *Smrutis* of Manu etc., are but **Her** form. For instance in *Saptashatee* (4th chapter);

Shabdātmikā Suvimalaigyajushām Nidānam
Udgeetaramya Pada Pātavatām Cha Sāmnām I
Devee Trayee Bhagavatee Bhava Bhāvanāya
Vārttāsi Sarvajagatām Paramārtihantree II

(iv) The *Koorma Purāŋa*, says, "*Rig, Yajus, Sāma* and *Atharva* are the inherent form of *Brahmam*, thus is the eternal *Shakti*";

Rucho Yajoomshi Sāmāni Tataivātharvanāni Cha I
Brahmaŋa: *Sahajam Roopam Nityaishā Shaktiravyayā* II

(v) The *Vāyu Purāŋa* says, "As **She** recollects all actions, present, past and future, **She** is called *Smruti*";

Vartamānānyateetāni Tathaivānāgatānyapi I
Smrate Sarvakāryāni Tenāsou Smrutiruchyate II

(vi) The *Devee Purāŋa* also conveys the same message - "**She** is the *Smruti* because **She** recollects"; *Smruti*: *Samsmaranād Devee.*

(vii) *Saptashatee* (chapter V) says;

"Yā Devee Sarvabhooteshu Smrutiroopena Samsthitā I"

541. ***Anuttamā* – अनुत्तमा**

(i) One who has none superior.

(ii) *Svetāshvatara Upanishad* (VI-8) says; *"Na Tatsamashchābh Yadhikashcha Drushyate"*.

(iii) In *Śreemad Bhagavat Geeta* (XI-43) also conveys the same message - Nothing is to be found equal or superior to him; *"Na Tavatsamostyabhyadhika*: *Kuto'nya*:"

(iv) The *Devee Bhāgavatam* (book III) - people never say that a man devoid of strength, nor do they say that he is deprived of *Rudra* or of *Viṣhŋu*, but they always say, "deprived of *Shakti* (energy)";

Rudraheenam Viṣhŋuheenam Na Vadanti Janās Tathā I
Shaktiheenam Yathā Sarve Pravdanti Narādhamam II

(v) It can be split as; *Na Nutta* - not depending, *Mā* - intelligence or dominion. i.e. whose intelligence or dominion is not derived from others, because there is none superior to **Her**.

542. *Puŋyakeertti*: - पुण्यकीर्त्तिः

(i) One who is famed for virtue/ righteousness/ holiness.
(ii) Just thinking and communicating the fame of *Śreedevee* will give virtue.
(iii) **She** has the reputation of giving virtue to **Her** devotees.
Note: Good deeds are said to be virtues. The enjoyment of fruits of good deeds (either in this birth or in other births, including living in the heaven) is also called as virtues.
(iv) *Śree Ādi Śaņkara* also conveys the same message, in his commentary of *Vişhŋu Sahasranāma* for the 688th name – *Puŋyakeertti*:.

543. *Puŋyalabhyā* – पुण्यलभ्या

(i) One who can be attained only through virtues/ righteousness.
(ii) *Puŋya*, good actions performed in previous births – only through this **Her** blessings can be attained.
(iii) The *Devee Bhāgavatam* says, "Only those ever righteous ascetics, who are devoted to wisdom, see; but the men of desire see not the holy and beneficent *Devee*";

Pashyanti Puŋya Punjā Ye Ye Vedāntas Tapasvina: I
Rāgiŋo Naiva Pashyanti Deveem Bhagavateem Shivām II

(iv) *Śree Ādi Śaņkara* also conveys the same message, in his commentary to 1st verse of *Soundaryalaharee*;

Atasvāmārādhyām Hariharavirinchādibhirapi I
Pranantum Stotum Vā Kathamakrutapuŋya: *Prabhavati* II

544. *Puŋyashravaŋakeerttanā* – पुण्यश्रवणकीर्त्तना

(i) It is a virtue to hear about **Her** and to praise **Her.**
(ii) Merely hearing *Śreedevee*'s stories and singing of **Her** greatness are meritorious.
(iii) Hearing *Śreedevee*'s stories and singing of **Her** greatness are must duties of human beings – ordained actions.
(iv) *Śree Ādi Śaņkara* also conveys the same message, in his commentary of *Vişhŋu Sahasranāma* for the 922nd name – *Puŋyashravanakeertana*.

545. *Pulomajārchitā* – पुलोमजार्चिता

(i) One who is worshipped by *Pulomajā*, consort of *Indra* and daughter of *Pulomar*.

(ii) This story occurs in *Devee Bhāgavatam* (Book VI); *Indra* married *Sasee Devee*, daughter of *Puloman*, after killing him. When it was necessitated that he has to hide and live (due to curse of *Gowtama* when he misbehaved with *Ahalyā*), *Nahusha* was ruling the heaven. He insisted *Sasee Devee* (wife of *Indra*) to become his wife. *Saseedevee* came out of this situation by worshipping with powerful *mantra* of *Śreedevee* obtained from the teacher (*Brhaspati*) and worshipped earnestly *Tripurasundaree*, by oblations of foods, flowers etc. *Indra* also was removed from the curse of *Gautamā* and restored to rule the heaven. It is said that his happened at *Seerkali* near *Māyavaram* in *Tamilnadu*;

Ityuktā Sā Tadā Tena Shakrapatnee Sumānasā I
Jagrāha Mantram Vidhivadguror Devyā: *Susādhanam* II
Vidyām Prāpya Gurordevee Deveem Tripurasundareem I
Samyagārādhayāmāsa Balipushpārchanai: *Shubhai*: II

546. *Bandhamochanee* – बन्धमोचनी

(i) One who liberates from bondages.

(ii) *Bandha*, bonds of ignorance or bondage with the worldly affairs.

(iii) *Bandha* also means being imprisoned. *Śreedevee* saves from all these. In *Saptashatee* (12th chapter - the boons of *Śreedevee*), we read;

Rāgnā Krudto Chakgnapto Vadhyo Bandhagato'pi Vā
Smaran Mamtachcharitam Naro Muchyeta Sankatāt I

The same sense is conveyed by *Appaiya Deekshitar* in his book called *Durga Chandra Kalāstuti*, treated as the gist of *Saptashatee*. He says;

Bandhe Vadhe Mahati Mrutyubhaye Prasanne
Vittakshaye Cha Vividhe Cha Mahopatāpe I
Yatpada Poojanamiha Pratikāramāhu:
Sa Me Samasta Jananee Sharanam Bhavānee II

(iv) In the *Harivamsa* (based on which in the above *Durga Chandra Kalāstuti* also), *Aniruddha*, who was imprisoned by the demon *Bānāsura*, prays to *Śreedevee*, "Oh *Shankharee*, thou art praised by these and other names by me; by thy grace, let me be soon freed from prison. Oh large-eyed one, behold, I take refuge in thy feet. You are to liberate me from every bond. *Durga*, the powerful one, thus praised, set free the brave *Aniruddha*, who was confined in the town of *Bāna*;

Bāŋāsura Prahita Pannaga Bandha Moksha:
Tadbāhudarpa Dalanāt Ushayā Cha Yoga: I
Prādyumninā Dhrutam Alabhyata Yat Prasādāt
Sā Me Shivā Sakalamayashubham Kshiŋotu II

(v) Thus in *Devee Bhāgavatam* also (book VI) it is mentioned as, "Once a princess named *Ekāvali* was imprisoned by a demon called *Kālaketu* and was freed by *Śreedevee* who was worshipped by *Yasovati*, the friend of the princess".

547. *Bandhurālakā* (*Barbarālakā*) – बन्धुरालका (बर्बरालका)

(i) This name is mentioned in both the above ways by different schools. But the second is in vogue.
(ii) One whose top forehead hair is curly, black and short like waves.

548. *Vimarsharoopiŋee* – विमर्शरूपिणी

(i) One who is In the *Vimarsa* form.
(ii) According to *Śree Vidyā* philosophy, the form of unison of *Shiva* and *Shakti* is the *Parabrahmam*. Here there is no distinction between *Shiva* and *Shakti*. *Śreedevee* in this form without distinction with *Shiva* is called as *Prakāsha Vimarsha Sāmarasya Roopinee*. The same sense is conveyed 999th name *Shiva Shaktyaikya Roopinee* also. *Shiva,* in the *Prakasā* aspect, is in the form of pure consciousness (*chaitanya*). This universe is formed, when *Śreedevee*, in the form of *Shakti*, creates a vibration in that pure *chaitanya*. Though *Shiva* has the capacity of creating that vibration himself, *Śreedevee* in that form is called *Vimarsa* form. That is the reason pure conscious *Shiva* is said to be like crystal and *Śreedevee* is said to be in red colour.
(iii) *Parabrahmam* is in the form of *Prakāsā*, the pure luminosity and unrecognisable by all. *Shakti* makes it recognisable to all, by creating a vibration in it. Thus far unrecognised *Parabrahmam* is able to be identified through motion, quality and actions. **She** is the energy through which the Parabrahmam can be identified. The same sense is reflected in 727th name *Shiva grana Pradhāyinee*.
(iv) The *Saubhāgyasudhodaya* says, She is the *Shakti* that produces the animate and inanimate universe, the same also destroys it;

Svābhāvikee Sphurattā Vimarsha Roopasya Vidyāte Shakti: I
Saiva Charācharamakhilam Janayati Jagadetadapi Cha Samharati II

(v) Thus *Śreedevee* in the form of *Vimarsa* is described in this name. As per *Śree Vidyā* practice, *Kāmeshwara* is considered to be in *Prakāsa* form and *Kāmeshwaree* in *Vimarsa* form.

(vi) *Vimarsa* means words, i.e. speech. The *Mātrkāviveka* says, "Without *Vimarsa* (speech) how is thought (*Prakāsa*) manifested? Without thought to be spoken of, how can there be speech? Therefore thought is required for the existence of speech and thought, even when there is self-consciousness (for its own existence) requires speech";

Vāchakena Vimarshena Vinā Kim Vā Prakāshyate I
Vāchyenāpi Prakāshena Vinā Kim Vā Vimrushyate II
Tasmādvimarsho Visphoortaou Prakāsam Samapekshate I
Prakāshashchātmano Gnāne Vimarsham Samapekshate II

The gist of this is mentioned in *Raghuvamsa* by *Kālidāsa;*

Vāgartthāviva Sampruktou Vāgartha Pratipattaye I
Jagata: *Pitarou Vande Pārvatee Parameshwarou* II

(vii) The statements from *Pāvanopanishad* can also be reminded;

Nirupādhika Samvideva Kāmeshvara: *Sadānanda Poorṇa*: I
Svātmaiva Paradevatā Lalitā Louhityametasya Sarvasya Vimarsha: II

549. *Vidyā* – विद्या

(i) **She** is the *vidyā* which confers salvation.

(ii) *Saptashatee* (4th chapter) says - The holy supreme *Devee* is *vidyā*; *"Vidyāsi Sā Bhagavatee Paramā Hi Devee"*. First chapter says; *"Sā Vidyā Paramā Mukter Hetu Bhootā Sanātanee"*.

(iii) The *Gouḍapāda* says in his *Śree Vidyā Ratna Sūtra*, **She** herself is *vidyā*; *"Chaitanya Svaroopā Shakti*: I *Saiva Vidyā* II"

(iv) *Vidyā*, a certain kind of art, which is in the light (*tejas*) and its nature are described in the *Saiva Tantra* - "By the discrimination of the products of *māyā*, one recognises the state of wisdom, that supreme art is known as *Vidyā*, consisting of knowledge and action";

Māyākārya Vivekena Vetti Vidyāpadam Yayā I
Sā Kalā Paramā Gneyā Vidyā Gnāna Kriyātmikā II

550. *Viyadādijagatprasoo*: - वियदादिजगत्प्रसूः

(i) One who is the mother of the universe consisting of ether, etc.

(ii) In the *Taitireeya Upanishad* (II-2) it has been mentioned as, Ether arose from Supreme Being, air from ether, fire from air, water from fire and the earth from water. These are primary elements for creation of this dynamic universe.

(iii) *Vyeti Iti* – to be at a distance – the ether is visible as so close, but when we go near it seems to be still farther. I.e. it cannot be perceived. Similar to it is the supreme being. It would seem to be perceived and get a feeling that it has been understood. At the same time it would seem to be at a faraway distance. This status is with ether, the first origin from supreme being and hence it is called as *Viyat*. *Śreedevee* was the first to originate this. Hence **She** is called *Jagāmba*.

(iv) *Prasoo*: - One who delivered. **She** delivered ether, etc.

(v) 837th name *Viyat Prasoo*: may also be referred.

551. *Sarvavyādhiprashamanee* – सर्वव्याधिप्रशमनी

(i) One who cures/ alleviates all illness/ diseases.

(ii) The same message is conveyed in 876th name – *Nirāmaya*.

552. *Sarvamrutyunivāriṇee* – सर्वमृत्युनिवारिणी

(i) One who dispels all forms of deaths.

(ii) Since it is mentioned as all forms of deaths – untimely death and death due to old age; untimely death is due to accident or fatal disease. **She** refrains from all these.

(iii) Anybody born in this world should definitely face the death. Depending on the actions during the life time, the further births are decided. The results or fruits of the actions are called *Mrutyus*. **She** saves from these Mrutyus by making one realise the self-form and reach the nectar stage. *Srutis* also advise the same; *Svetasvatara Upanishad* (IV-15) - knowing **Him** thus, he tears up the nooses of death; *"Gnātvā Devam Mrutyu Mukāt Pramuchyate* II"
Kaṭopanishad (III-15) says - he is freed from the power of death; *"Tamevam Gnātvā Mrutyu Pāshānsha Chinatti* II"

(iv) The same is mentioned in the results of this *Sahasranāma* also.

553. *Agragaṇyā* – अग्रगण्या

(i) One who is to be reckoned as first.

(ii) Since **She** is the root cause for the entire universe, **She** has to be treated as first.

(iii) **She** is the head of *Marut* and other groups and hence this name.

554. *Achintyaroopā* – अचिन्त्यरूपा

(i) One who is of unthinkable form or inaccessible to mind.
(ii) Because **She** is free from connection with the qualities, **Her** nature is unthinkable. 139th name *Nirguŋā* and 415th name *Mano vāchāmagocharā* may be referred.

555. *Kalikalmashanāshinee* – कलिकल्मषनाशिनी

(i) One who is destroyer of sin/ transgression of *Kali*.
(ii) The *Kali* age (*yuga*) will be full of dire thoughts and deeds. Consequently sins will be predominant in the *Kali* age. These are described in detail in *Devee Bhāgavatam*. Chanting *Śreedevee*'s name is the only way out to ward off this.
(iii) The *Koorma Purāŋa* says - water is able to quench the fire, the presence of the sun to dispel darkness and the repetition of the names of *Śreedevee* to destroy the multitude of sins in the *Kali* age;

Shamāyālam Jalam Vahnes Tamaso Bhāskarodaya: I
Shāntyai Kaleraghelaghasya Devee Nāmānu Keertanam II

(iv) The *Brahmānḍa Purāŋa* says - the remembrance of the feet of *Supreme Shakti* is said to be the highest expiation for sins consciously or unconsciously committed;

Krutasyākhila Pāpasya Gnānato'gnānato'pi Vā I
Prāyashchittam param Proktam Parāshakte: *Padasmrti*: II

(v) In *Saptashatee* (12th chapter) it is said as; *"Srutam Harati Pāpāni"*.
(vi) 167th name *Pāpanāshinee,* 743rd – *Pāpāraŋya Davānalā* and 860 – *Akāntā* and again the below names in *Trishatee* may be referred; 31st – *Ena*:*Kooṭa Vināshinee* and 112th – *Hatyādi Pāpashamanee*.

556. *Kātyāyanee* – कात्यायनी

(i) One who is the daughter of a sage named *Katar*.
(ii) The *Vāmana Purāŋa* says - this is the name of the deity in the collective form of the brightness (*tejas*) of all the *Devas*. (This can be compared to what is mentioned in *Saptashatee* that all the brightness of all the *Devas* combined to form *Mahālakshmee* – *Mahishāsura Mardinee*).

Tata: *Samasta Devānām Tejo Rāshi Samudbavām*

Tachchāpi Tejo Varamuttamam Mahannāmnā Prutivyāmabhavat Prasiddham I
Kātyāyaneetyeva Tadā Babhou Sā Nāmnā Cha Tenaiva Jagatprsiddhā II

(iii) According to the *Kālikā Purāŋa*, this is the deity at *Oḍyāna Peeṭa;*

Kātyāyanee Choddiyāne Kāmāgyā Kāmaroopake I
Poorneshvaree Poorŋagirou Chanḍee Jālandharesmrutā II

She is *Kātyāyanee* in *Oḍyāna Peeṭa, Kāmagyā* in *Kāmaroopa, Poorŋeshwaree* in *Poorŋagiri* and followers of *Chanḍi* in *Jālandara Peeṭa.*

(iv) According to *Devee Purāŋa, Kam – Brahmam, Shiras* – stone. Since *Śreedevee* supports the whole world and is omnipresent there, **She** gets this name as *Kātyāyanee.*

Kam Brahma Kam Shira: Proktamashsāram Cha Kam Madam I
Dhāranādvāsanād Vāpi Tena Kātyāyanee Matā II

(v) Elders say that the name *Kātyāyanee* only evolved as *Kāttāyee* in villages. (Similarly they say that the name *Pechāyee* in villages indicates *Saraswatee*).

(vi) *Gopika* ladies worshipped *Kātyāyanee* during *Mārgaseersha* month and got *Krişhŋa* as their husband.

(vii) In the *Kavacha* (shield) read as part of *Saptashatee*, it has been mentioned that the sixth, out of the nine names of *Durga*, is *Kātyāyanee*. 584th name *Mahāvidyā* may also be referred.

557. *Kālahantree* – कालहन्त्री

(i) One who is the destroyer of time (*Mrutyu*).

(ii) *Sruti* (*Svetasvatara Upanishad* VI-2) says, omniscient, time of time, possessed of all qualities, all knowing – *Brahmam* is the *Kāla* (death) for *Yama* (god of death) himself; "*Gna*: *Kālakālo Guŋee Sarva Vidyā*:"

558. *Kamalāksha Nishevitā* – कमलाक्ष निषेविता

(i) One who is specially worshipped by (lotus eyed) *Mahāvişhŋu.*

(ii) The *Padma Purāŋa* says, *Vişhŋu* ever worships the sapphire *Devee,* hence he attained his own state;

Indra Neelamayeem Deveem Vişhŋurarchayate Sadā I
Vişhŋutvam Prāptavāms Tena.. II

(iii) A story may be reminded – once *Mahāvişhŋu* was worshipping *Parameshwara* with Lotus flowers. One flower was in short – he plucked his eyes and continued the worship. Since there is no difference between *Shakti* and *Shiva,* it can be treated as that he did this worship to *Śreedevee* also.

559. *Tāmboolapooritamukhee* – ताम्बूलपूरितमुखी

(i) One whose mouth is full of betel leaves.
(ii) The specialty of *Śreedevee* chewing betel leaves was described in 26th name – *Karpooraveetikāmoda Samākarshi Digantara.*
(iii) *Śree Ādi Śaṇkara*, while interpreting the 14th name of *Trishatee* – "*Karpoora Veeti Sourabhya Kallolita Kakuptatā*" – specially indicates as *Mahārāja Bogavatee.*
(iv) It is told that legendary poets, like *Kalidāsa*, *Kālamegha* and others, got their excellent capacity to write poems by consuming the juice of *Śreedevee*'s *tāmboola* (betel leaves).

560. *Dāḍimeekusumaprabhā* – दाडिमीकुसुमप्रभा

(i) One who has lustre like that of the hue of pomegranate flower. There are two varieties of pomegranate – one will flower and also bear fruits and the other will only flower, but does not bear fruits. The *Dādima* is of second kind of pomegranate tree which bears no fruit but only flowers. The flowers of these will be brilliantly red.

561. *Mrugākshee* – मृगाक्षी

(i) One who is deer eyed.
(ii) The eyes of the deers will not be static at one place – it wavers all the sides. This is to escape, in times of danger. Like that of the deers, the eyes of the high society ladies also will be wavering. This adds to their beauty. Since **She** belongs to the highest class, *Śreedevee*'s eyes also wavers like this. One other reason is also apt– **She** wants the sympathy and compassion of her sight to fall on all her devotees on all sides and hence her eyes are wavering.
(iii) 103rd name of *Trishatee* – *Harinekshanā* may be referred.

562. *Mohinee* – मोहिनी

(i) One who is bewitching/ enchanting.
(ii) *Lagu Nāradeeya Purāŋa* says, **She** makes the entire universe to libidinous with **Her** charming beauty and hence **She** is called as *Mohinee*;

Yasmādidam Jagat Sarvam Tvayā Sundaree Mohitam I

Mohineetyeva Te Nāma Svaguṇottham Bhavishyati II

(iii) It can also be considered as – while churning the milky ocean, *Mahāviṣhṇu* took the incarnation as *Mohinee* by meditating upon *Śreedevee*. 5th verse of *Soundaryalaharee* may be referred in this regard;

Haristvāmārādhya Pranatajanasoubhāgya Jananeem I
Purā Nāree bhootvā Puraripumapi Kshobhamanayat II

Again, *Śreedevee* took this form. The first one was the form of nature on account of meditating power of *Brahma*. This has been described in *Brahmāṇḍa Purāṇa*. It has also been mentioned there that *Viṣhṇu* took the *Mohinee* form by meditating upon *Śreedevee*.

(iv) The ardent devotees of *Śreedevee*, do *sankalpa* (declaration of intention to do a *pooja*) describe the time, with eight parts called *Ashṭānga* method. In Samskrit the numbers are represented by letters through *Kaṭapayādi* method. In this, if the first letters of the day and the year are the same, it is called a *Parvā* day *or Mohinee*. It can be taken as that **She** is in the form of this *Parvā* day.

(v) The name of the presiding deity in the temple of *Nivāsapura* at the banks of river *Pravarā*, is *Mohinee*.

563. *Mukhyā* – मुख्या

(i) One who is the first or the prime.

(ii) When a child is born the first organ that comes out is the face (*Mukha*). Hence anything that is first is called *Mukhya*.

(iii) **She** is the first among all the things that originated. **She** is the main among all the *devatās*. *Taitireeya Upanishad* (III-10-6) says – I am the first born of truth or I am the first born out of truth;

Ahamasmi Prathama Jā Rutasya.

564. *Mruḍānee* – मृडानी

(i) One who is the consort of *Mruḍa* (*Paramashiva*).

(ii) The word *Mruḍa*, as a verb, indicates giving happiness. Since he gives happiness to all *Paramashiva* is called as *Mruḍa*. His consort.

(iii) It can be considered as *Mruḍānee*, indicated in the form of *Paksha* in the *Mahāshoḍanyāsa* (*Prapancha Nyāsa*).

565. *Mitraroopiṇee* – मित्ररूपिणी

(i) One who is in the form of Sun or friend.
(ii) One of the twelve names of Sun is *Mitra*. Hence **She** is in the form of Sun, illuminating and helping all the beings.
(iii) In *Śree Vidyā Tantra*, fire indicates *Shiva* and Moon indicates *Śreedevee*. Sun indicates the unified form of both. Hence this name indicates the unified form of *Śreedevee*.
(iv) *Mitra* also means friend. **She** is like a friend. The self-form is the friend and hence **She** is the self here.

566. *Nityatruptā* – नित्यतृप्ता

(i) One who is eternally content.
(ii) **She** is complete in all respects. She does not need anything. Hence **She** is always contented.
(iii) **She** is contented with the permanent and eternal form of bliss.
(iv) It may be noted that the 815th name has been split as *Anitya Trupta*.

567. *Bhaktanidhi*: - भक्तनिधिः

(i) One who is a treasure for devotees.
(ii) **She** offers whatever is asked for by the devotees. 989th name *Vānghitārtha Pradāyinee* may be referred.
(iii) The 4th verse of *Soundaryalaharee* says that **She** gives more than what is asked for by the devotees; *Vānchāsamadhikam*.
(iv) This name has to be used as *Bhakta Nidhaye Namaha*.

568. *Niyantree* – नियन्त्री

(i) Since **She** designates the entire universe, **She** is the guide and controller of it.

569. *Nikhileshvaree* – निखिलेश्वरी

(i) One who is the ruler of all.
(ii) Since **She** controls the universe, **She** is the ruler of it.

570. *Maitryādivāsanālabhyā* – मैत्र्यादिवासनालभ्या

(i) One who is to be attained by the dispositions of cheerfulness, etc.

(ii) The *yoga* books teach us to remove the bad dispositions and inculcate the good ones in our mind. Being envious about those who are happy, making fun or not having compassion for those who are suffering, being happy at other's sufferings and overlooking or not mindful of the sinful are some of the examples of bad tendencies. Removing all these dispositions and having friendship with those who are happy, having compassion for those who are suffering and possibly reducing sufferings of others are good tendencies.

(iii) *Śreemad Bhāgavatam* says - the good dispositions are of four types- friendship with those who are happy without being envious (*maitree* or friendship), compassion for those who are suffering (*karuŋā*), gladness to see the righteous (*muditā*) and overlooking or not mindful of the sinful (*upekshā*).

(iv) These four tendencies (*vāsanās*) contribute to clarity of mind and purify it. *Yoga Sūtra* says;

Matree, Karuŋā Muditopakshānām Sukhadu:kha Puŋyāpuŋya
Vishayānām Bhāvanātasha Chitta Prasadanam

(v) The *Māghar* (IV-55) says, they, whose minds are purified by friendship, etc., removing their sorrow and who obtain here (in this body) the seed of *Yoga* and attaining glory by discriminating *Purusha* from matter and who remaining in the state of *samādhi* (the highest state of meditation), desire to transcend even that state;

Maitriyādi Chitata Parikarma Vido Vidhāya
Klesha prahānamiha Labdha Saveeja Yoga: I
Khyātim Cha Satva Purushānyatayādhigamya
Vānchanti Tāmapi Samādhibruto Niroddhum II

(vi) It is easy for those, who have such tendencies, to reach *Śreedevee*.

571. *Mahāpralayasākshiŋee* – महाप्रलयसाक्षिणी

(i) One who is the witness of the great dissolution.

(ii) As the entire universe perish at the time of the great dissolution. *Brahma* and *Viṣhŋu* also merge with *Śreedevee*. However, *Shiva* does not perish just because of the pride of your earrings only, says *Śree Ādi Śaṇkara*, in his *Soundaryalaharee* 26th verse; *Virinchi*: *Panchatvam Vrajati*...

(iii) The same message is conveyed in a book called *Kuru Kala*. *Śreedevee* is the only *Suvāsinee* and others are not;

Surendra Rudra Padmajāchyutādayo'pi Ye Mruter
Vashmvadā Na Tatstriya: *Suvāsinee Padasprusha*: I

Maheshvarasya Mrutyu Ghasmarasya Sākshinee Tu Ya
Sumangaleeriyam Vadhoorimām Sameta Pashyate II

(iv) A witness is that person who does not participate in the action, is not affected by the fruit of it and completes seeing the action. She is such a witness to the great dissolution.

(v) 232nd name *Maheshvara Mahākalpa Mahātāndava Sākshinee* and 385th name *Sākshivargitā* may be referred.

572. *Parāshakti*: - पराशक्तिः

(i) One who is the Supreme energy/ power.

(ii) Among the elementary substances in the body, skin, blood, flesh, fat and bone were derived from energy (*Shakti*). Marrow, semen, breath and vitality (soul) derived from *Shiva* (this was explained earlier also). The tenth one is called *Parāshakti*. This has been explained in the *Kāmikāgama*;

Tvagasrunmāmsa Medo'sthi Dhātava: *Shakti Moolakā*: I
Majjā Sukla Prāŋajeeva Dhātava: *Shiva Moolakā*: II
Navadhā Turāyam Deho Navayonesamudbhava: I
Dashamee Dhātu Rekaiva Parāshaktiriteeritā II

(iii) *Parāshakti* can also be interpreted as very great energy. (*Parā – Utkrushṭa* – very great). The principle of *Sāktās* is that just by unison with *Shakti, Shiva* attains enormous greatness. In the first verse of *Soundaryalaharee* (*Shiva*: *Shaktyāyukto*.) and other books stress the same principle.

(iv) *Sruti* also (*Svetāswara Upanishad* IV-8) says, His supreme *Shakti* is known in different form; "*Parāsya Shaktir Vivdhaiva Shrooyate*".

(v) The *Linga Purāŋa*, says, whatever energy is attributed to any substance is *Śreedevee* and the ruler of all energized substance is the great *Shiva*. Those substances, which possess energy are the manifestation of *Shiva*. The wise recognize the energies in substance to be *Śreedevee*.

Yasya Yasya Patārtthasya Yāyāshaktirudā Hrutā I
Sā Sā Vishveshvaree Devee Sa Sa Sarvo Maheshvara: II
Shaktimanta: *Padārtthā Ye Te Vai Sarva Vibhootaya*: I
Patārttha Shaktyo Yāyās Tāstā Gowreem Vidur Budhā II

(vi) The *Shakti* form of the *mantra* called *Para*.

(vii) In practice this is used as *Parāyai Shakyai Namaha* or *Parāshaktyai Namaha*.

573. *Parānishṭhā* – परानिष्ठा

(i) One who is the end of speech, action and thought.
(ii) A certain kind of knowledge - this alone is the goal of all desires and all worlds. It has been mentioned in the *Bhagavad Geeta* (IV-33) also as - Oh *Pārtha*, all kinds of actions end in knowledge; *"Sarvam Karmākhilam Pārtha Gnāne Parisamāpyate"*.
(iii) That kind of knowledge is described in the *Soota Samhita* (*Soota Geeta* V-50-54) - Convinced by logic/ argument/ instructions derived from the scriptures and from teachers, that he is himself the witness of all, his mind becomes fixed, knowing the whole which appears different from Self as his own Self, again fully convinced by his own experience that he himself is the pure, non-dual *Brahmam*; merging that conviction in his own pure consciousness which is unchangeable and non-dual; knowing that even that merging is of the nature of thought, he should remain as the absolute. This ascetic is indeed the best of those who know *Brahmam*; this is the highest end result of scriptural teachings and of experience. This is the self realisation also;

Shāstrāchāryopadeshena Tarkai: *Shāstrānusāribhi*: I
Sarvasakshitāyātmānam Samyannishchitya Susthira: II
Svātmamano'nyatayā Bhātam Samstama Visheshata: I
Svātmamātratayā Bhddhvā Puna: *Svātmanamadvayam* II
Shuddham Brahmeti Nishchitya Svayam Svānubhootenacha I
*Nishchayam Cha Svachinmātre Vilāpyā Vikriye'dvaye*II
Vilāpanam Cha Chidroopam Bhddhvā Kevalaroopata: I
Svayam Tishtedayam Sākshād Brahma Vidvaro Muni: II
Edrusheeyam Parā Nishtā Sroutee Svānubhavātmikā II

(iv) In practice this is to be used as *Paranishṭāyai Namaha*. In some books it is mentioned as *Parāyai Nishṭāyai Namaha*.

574. *Pragnānaghanaroopiṇee* – प्रज्ञानघनरूपिणी

(i) One who is in the form pure, concentrated and great knowledge.
(ii) *Pra* - superior, i.e. different from the mental modifications, *Gnāna* – the eternal wisdom, *Ghana* - concentrated, i.e. not contaminated by ignorance. The *Brhadāraṇya Upanishad* (IV-5-13) says - just as taste of a quantity of salt is neither inside nor outside but everywhere, this Self is neither within nor without, but is full and concentrated knowledge". **She** is the solidified form of Supreme wisdom. **She** is the state of consciousness in which nothing is experienced except Self;

Sa Yathā Saindhavaghano'antaro'bhāhya: Krutsno Rasaghana Yevaivam Vā Areyamātmā'nantro bāhya: Krutsnonta: Prajnāna Ghana:

575. *Mādhveepānālasā* – माध्वीपानालसा

(i) One who is languid by drinking alcohol.
(ii) The alcoholic drink mixed with grapes and honey is called *mādhvee*. Having consumed it **She** is lethargic.
(iii) In many a place it has been mentioned *Śreedevee* drinks alcohol – 333rd name – *Varuŋeemadavihvalā*, 432 – *Madaghoorŋita Raktākshee*, 510 – *Madhupreetā* and 717 – *Madhumatee*.
(iv) In *Saptashatee* it has been mentioned as - when *Śreedevee* originated from the brightness of all the *Devās*, they offered gifts to **Her**. At that time *Kuberā* gave **Her** a drinking vessel filled with alcohol;

Dadāvasoonyam Surayā Pānapatram Dhanādhipa: I

Again in third chapter;

Tata: Kruddhā Jaganmātā Chanḍikā Pānamuttamam I
Babou Puna: Puna: Chaiva Jahāsārunalochanā II

Again - *Garja Garja Kshanam Moodha Madhuyāvatpibāmyaham* II

(v) In the *Navāvarŋa Pooja* a special *argyā* is used. This is also mentioned as alcohol. One of the 64 offerings is a vessel filled with alcohol – *Amruta Āsava Chashakam*.
(vi) In all these places *Madhu* (alcohol) indicates supreme bliss. Since it is a quality of the Supreme Being, it has to be taken as **She** is engulfed in the Supreme self-bliss.

576. *Mattā* – मत्ता

(i) One who is unconscious.
(ii) As mentioned in the previous name, She is unconscious due to alcohol in the state of languid/ lethargic.
(iii) *Mat* indicates self. The thought of self indicates ego. In the 7th verse of *Soundaryalaharee*, it has been mentioned that She is in the ego form of *Paramashiva*; *Purastādāstām Na: Puramathiturāho Purushikā* II

577. *Mātrukāvarŋaroopiŋee* – मातृकावर्णरूपिणी

(i) One who is in the form of all the letters of Samskrit.
(ii) That is, She is in the form of all the 51 Samskrit letters. Since the

letters give colour to the words, they are called as *Varŋams*. (Sometimes it is also said as *Arnam*). *Devee Upanishad* says; "*Mantranām Mātrukā Devee*".

(iii) It is said that all these 51 letters have colours. In the *Yoginee Nyāsa*, the letters in each of the *chakra* has colours. According to *Sanatkumara Samhita*;

Chakra	**Samskrit Letters**	**Colour**
Vishuddhi	*A* to *A:*	Smoke
Anāhatam	*Ka* to *Tha*	Reddish Rose (*Sindoora*)
Maŋipoorakam	*Da* to *Pha*	White like Jasmine
Svādishṭānam	*Ba* to *La*	Red
Moolādhāram	*Va* to *Sa*	Gold
Ajnā	*Ha* to *Ksha*	Lightning

(iv) Different *tantras* mention these colours differently. One *tantra* says:

A to *A:*	White like a crystal
Ka to *Ma*	Coral like red
Nine letters from *Ya*	Yellow
Ksha	Colour of Sun (Red mixed with White)

Some other *tantra* attribute white colour to all the letters. *Matrukā Viveka* maps one colour to each of the letters.

(v) Thus **She** is in the form of *Shakti* presenting the individuality of the letters.

(vi) *Soota Samhitā* (*Yagna Vaibhava Kāṇḍa* IV-4-2-22) says that **She** has been established (described or given form) by the letters. *Parashambu* has two divisions as *Shiva* and *Shakti*. Similarly *Matrukā Devee* also has two divisions viz. *Shiva Vāchā* (through the names like *Śreekanda* and others) and in another form called as *Shakti Vāchā* (through the names *Poornodaree*, etc.). This splits letters into masculine and feminine. Some letters are neutral also.

(vii) It can also be said as that **She** is in the form of *Akshamālā* (garland of letters). The garland of letters was described in the 489th name – *Akshamālādidhara*. The letters *A* to *Ksha* can be used to count the chanting of names. Though *Śreedevee* is in the form of *Shabda Brahmam* (sound), She is of still further ahead form.

(viii) She creates the *Mātrukā* colours. *Soubāgya Sudodaya* explains the method of creation of colours through unison of *Icchā Shakti* with the excellent form of *Shiva* (*Janayitree* – mother).

(ix) In the sixth chapter of *Mātrukā Viveka*, it has been described in detail that the *Mātrukā* colours are the same as *Śreechakra*. Hence in *Sanandana Samhita* says to imagine the integrated form of the letters and the *Śreechakra* is called *Kailāsa Prastāram*. **She** is in that form.

(x) In some schools this name is treated as two names – *Mātrukā* and *Avarŋaroopiŋee* and some other two names are combined. The mother of *Skanda* is called *Mātrukā* and hence it is also valid.

(xi) *Śreechakra* is imagined in three ways viz., *Meru Prastāram, Kailasa Prastāram* and *Bhoo Prastāram*. The integration of *Titi Nityā* and *Śreechakram* is *Meru Prastāram*. The integration of *Vasinee Devatās* and *Śreechakram* is *Bhoo Prastāram* and the integration of *Mātrukās* (letters) and *Śreechakram* is *Kailāsa Prastāram*.

578. *Mahākailāsanilayā* – महाकैलासनिलया

(i) One who resides in the great *Kailāsa*.

(ii) *Shiva* and other *Purāŋas* mention that *Mahākailāsa* is a place much beyond the *Kailāsa*, the abiding place of *Paramashiva.*

   a. It can be noted that *Vāgdevees* have used the word *Mahā* when indicating very great thought, things and *Devatas*. For instance:

Number	Name
48	*Mahālāvaŋyashevadhi*:
59	*Mahāpadmātaveesamsthā*
78	*Mahāgaŋeshanirbhinnavighnayantrapraharshitā*
81	*Mahāpāshupatāstrāgninirdhagdhāsurasainikā*
109	*Mahāshakti*:
209	*Mahādevee*
210	*Mahālakshmee*
212	*Mahāroopā*
213	*Mahāpoojyā*
214	*Mahāpātakanāshinee*
215	*Mahāmāyā*
216	*Mahāsatvā*
217	*Mahāshakti*:
218	*Mahārati*:
219	*Mahabhogā*
220	*Mahaishvaryā*

Number	Name
221	*Mahāveeryā*
222	*Mahābalā*
223	*Mahābuddhi:*
224	*Mahāsiddhi:*
225	*Mahāyogesvareshvaree*
226	*Mahātantra*
227	*Mahāmantra*
228	*Mahāyantrā*
229	*Mahāsanā*
230	*Mahāyāgakramārādhyā*
231	*Mahābhairavapoojitā*
232	*Maheshvaramahākalpamahātāndavasākshinee*
233	*Mahākāmeshamahishee*
234	*Mahātripurasundaree*
237	*Mahācatushshashṭikoṭiyogineegaŋasevitā*
493	*Mahāveerendravaradā*
571	*Mahāpralayasākshinee*
582	*Mahāsāmrājyashālinee*
584	*Mahāvidyā*
750	*Maheshvaree*
751	*Mahākālee*
753	*Mahāshanā*

b. Since he was there even before the creation of this universe, he is *Kilāsa*: (*Āseet Kila*), his dwelling place is *Kailāsa*.

Note: This is written based on the 12th verse of *Chitkakan Chandrikā* of *Śree Kālidasa* and its interpretations; "*Ya*: *Kilāsa Sa Kilāsa Eshvara*:"

Interpretation –

Ya: *Eshvaro Jagatsargāt Prāg Eko'dviteeya Eva Āsa Āseet Kila* I
Tathā Cha Kilāsasyāyam Nivāsa: *Kailāsa Iti Loke Kailāsapadaprasiddhi*: II

(iii) It can also be construed – as mentioned in the previous name it indicates the integrated form of *Kailāsa Prastāram*. In the sense that this is something much above the two integrations viz., with *Vasinee* and other *Devees* and with *Nityā Devees* and hence the word *Mahā* is used here.

(iv) *Kailāsa* is the *Sahasrāra* which is in the *Brahmarandhra*. The *Tripurāsāra* says - this is called *Kailāsa*, the *Kula* and the seat of *Akula*, where the lord of the lords, *Shiva* in the form of *bindu* resides; "*Etat Kailāsa Samgnam Padamakalapadam Binduroopee Svaroopee Yatrāste Deva Deva...*".

579. *Mruŋālamrududorlatā* – मृणालमृदुदोर्लता

(i) One whose arms are smooth and slender like a pair of Lotus stalks.
(ii) It can be reminded that earlier in 111th name – *Bisatantu Taneeyasee*, **She** was described as fine as the fiber of a lotus stalk. In the 130th name – *Shātodaree*, **She** was mentioned as having a slender waist

580. *Mahaneeyā* – महनीया

(i) One who is the embodiment of worship by all.
(ii) 213th name *Mahāpoojya* may be referred.
(iii) In *Viṣhŋu Sahasranāma* – 679th name *Stavya*: (adored by all) and 873rd name *Arha*: (Worth of worshipping with the offerings like welcoming, seat, water, etc). may also be referred.

581. *Dayāmoorti*: - दयामूर्तिः

(i) One who is the personification of mercy/ compassion.
(ii) Earlier in 326th name – *Karuŋārasasāgarā* also, this sense was conveyed. Further 197th name – *Sāndrakaruŋā* and 992nd name *Avyājakaruŋāmoorthi* may be referred. In the *dhyāna* verse of this *Sahasranāma* also we read as *Karuŋātarangitākshee*. The meditation verse of *Trishatee* also says *Atishayakarnām*.
(iii) In *Trishatee*, 9th name – *Karuŋāmrutasāgarā* and 151st name – *Kārunyavigrahā* may be referred. For the second one, *Śree Ādi Śaṇkara*'s commentary is (based on the translation of *Śree Chitānanda Nāthar*) – the thought of very great people to have mercy on the people in distress is called *Karuŋā* (compassion); *"Yadyapi Deeneshu Paripālyanābuddhideivānām Mahatām Karuŋetyuchyate"*.
(iv) The famous *Śree Śreedara Venkatesar* also called as *Ayāvāl* has written an epic of poems called *Dayā Shatakam* about compassion. This book has been written metamorphosing the compassion of *Shiva* as another *Devee*. It would be apt to consider the 11th verse of this book here;

Nānyo Madastyagatiko'gatikastava Shiva m
Shambhor Daye'ghapishunā Mayi Shashva Dāste I
Sarvagnatā Vidadhāti Tava Durlabham Māṃ
Sajjasva Mā Janani Bhoorapade Tu Ni:svā II

The joint wife of *Shiva, Sarvagnatai* was jealous of the other wife *Dayā* (compassion). *Dayā Devee* creates assets for her by protecting those who are in dire need; but *Sarvagnatai* goes to *Shiva* and tells him secretly that "those people are sinners and do not qualify for such a protection and still *Dayā* protects her". Thus she tries to make *Shiva* forsake them. If *Sarvagnatai* becomes stronger there will be no one to support *Dayā*; Hence the poet cautions *Dayā* as "Beware! *Sarvagnatai* is trying to single you out – don't allow". The actual meaning of this is that– if the bad deeds of a person are highlighted, then he is not fit to have compassion. I.e., the knowledge of bad actions and the compassion do not go together. The quality of compassion is to forgive the sins and protect. The good deeds done by them will protect the good people, whereas the bad people have to be protected only by compassion.

(v) *Śree Parāsara Battar* also describes compassion in detail in his book called *Kshamā Shoḍasee*. In the first verse itself, he says – **She** ensures the safety of the world herself, setting aside the independence of *Shiva.*

(vi) *Śree Vedanta Desikar* also in his book called *DayaShatakam* (verse 51-14) mentions about the compassion of *Śree Venkatachalapathi* as below;

Atikrupaŋo'pi Janturadhigamya Daye Bhavateem
Ashidiladharmasetu Padaveem Ruchiramāchirāt I
Amita Mahormijālamatilangya Bhavāmbu Nidhim
Bhavati Vrushāchalesha Padapattana Nityadhanee II
Krupana Janakalpalatikām Krutāparādhasya Nishkriyāmādhyām I
Vrushgirināthadaye Tvām Vidanti Samsāratāriŋeem Vibudhā: II

582. *Mahāsāmrājyashālinee* – महासाम्राज्यशालिनी

(i) One who has a vast empire.

(ii) A *Samrāt* is the one who controls many a petty kings. A *Mahāsamrāt* is one who controls many a *Samrāt*. This name is very much apt, in the sense that She is not different from *Parameshwarā* and **She** is the empress of the dominion of *Mahākailāsa*.

583. *Ātmavidyā* – आत्मविद्या

(i) One who is the doctrine to help understand the self.

(ii) This is the *Vidyā* (a *mantra* whose presiding deity is a female, is called *Vidyā*), which advises the form of *Brahmam*. 727th name – *Shivagnāna Svaroopiŋee* says that **She** bestows the knowledge of *Brahmam*. The story of explaining the knowledge of *Brahmam* to

Indra has been described in *Kenopanishad*.

(iii) In some schools it is meant that **She** is in the form of *Tureeya* (fourth) *Gāyatree*.

(iv) It also means that it is the *Ātmavidyā* (self-knowledge) with eight letters. This is used when bowing to teachers, during *Śree Vidyā Sandhyavandana* and at the end of *Mahāshoḍanyāsa*; *"Om Hreem Hamsa: Soham Svāha"*.

584. *Mahāvidyā* – महाविद्या

(i) One who is the great doctrine.

(ii) Since the above said *Ātmavidyā* is the great *Vidyā* (since it teaches the *Brahmam*) it is called as *Mahāvidyā* in this name.

(iii) **She** is in the form of *Mahatee* – the great (774th name). Since **She** removes all sorrows, **She** gets the greatness.

(iv) *Navadurgā Vidyā* (in some books it is mentioned as *Vanadurgā Vidyā*) is called *Mahāvidya*. **She** is in that form. The names of *Navadurgā* have been mentioned in the *Kavachā* read as part of *Saptashatee*. They are; *Shailaputree, Brahmachāriṇee, Chandra-ghantā, Kooshmāndā, Skantamātā, Kātyāyanee, Kālaratree, Mahāgowree and Siddhidhātree*.

(v) It is also mentioned as *Chanḍi Navāksharee Vidyā* in one of the books.

585. *Śree Vidyā* – श्रीविद्या

(i) One who is in the form of *Panchadashee Vidya*.

(ii) *Vidyā* is of four types. They are respectively;

a. *Yagna Vidyā* – about actions
b. *Mahā Vidyā* – devotion to deities
c. *Guhya Vidyā* – secret science of *mantras*
d. *Atma Vidyā* – the science of *Brahmam*

The word *Vidyā* has these meanings. **She** is in all these forms. The *Viṣhṇu Purāṇa* says, "Oh fair one, the sacrificial science, exalted science, secret science and spiritual science. Oh *Devee*, thou art all these, the bestower of salvation; also thou art logic, *Trayee*, *Vārtā*, trade and justice";

Yagna Vidyā Mahā Vidyā Guhya Vidyā Cha Shobhane I
Atma Vidyā Cha Devee Tvam Vimukti Phaladayinee II
Ānveekshikee Trayee Vārtā Daṇḍaneetistvameva Cha II

(iii) *Tripuradāyinee Upanishad* says that each group of *Panchadashee Mantra* explains the meaning of *Gāyatree mantra*.

(iv) Six meanings have been given in *Nityāshoḍasikārnavam*.
(v) *Śree Bhāskara Rāya* gives 15 meanings in his book called *Varivasya Rahasyam*.
(vi) In recent times, a great devotee *Śree Veerarāgava Sastree* in Kerala has given some more meanings. The preface of this book says that these names were read to the 33rd *Peeṭadhipati* of Sringeri Mutt, *Śree Abhinava Nrusimha Bhāratee Swāmi* and has nodded the same.
(vii) It is appropriate to call this as *Śree Vidyā,* since it gives exemplary meanings with very few letters. It can be noted that the results/ fruits part of *Trishatee* says – the path of salvation is *Śree Vidyā* only. No doubt in it; "*Mokshaika Hetu Vidyā Sā Śreevidyaiva Na Samshaya*:".

586. *Kāmasevitā* – कामसेविता

(i) One who was adored by *Kāma* (cupid).
(ii) *Kāmā* is *Mahākāmeshvar*. **She** was worshipped by him.

It has been mentioned in *mantra sāstras* that *Mahākāmeshwar* and *Kāmeshwaree* had both mutually taken the role of teacher and student at different times and have given advises mutually. It is very clear from the *Poorva* part that they both have said the *Trishatee mantra*.

(iii) *Kāma* indicates the bodiless god of love. *Kādi Vidyā* is one other form of *Panchadashee Vidya*. *Kāma* is the presiding sage of this *Vidya*. This is very clear from the verse starting with; "*Manush Chandra*: *Kubherashcha Lopāmudrā Cha Manmatha*: II". Here *Sevitā* means a garland of precious gems.
(iv) The *Aruŋopanishad* (*Taitireeya Āraŋyam* I-11) says, the bodiless son of *Lakshmee*, though without mind, has animation. He got a jewel (*Śree Vidyā*). He, though without fingers, worshipped (folding his hands). Though without neck, he adorned himself with a necklace. Though without tongue, he tasted it. Without knowing that taste one should enter the city. When one enters, he should enter after performing secret rites. Secret rites i.e., the knowledge of the essential equality of *Shiva* with *Devee*. The meaning is that worship performed without the knowledge of the essential equality of *Shiva* with *Devee* cannot be effective. This is the vow of *Manmatha*. *Śree Lakshmeedhara* has given this commentary for the verse;

Janko Ha Vaideha: I *Aho Rātrais Samājagāma* II
Putro Nirutyā Vaideha: I *Achetā Yashcha Chetana*: II

Śree Bhāskararāya also conveys the same sense. 32nd verse of *Soundaryalaharee* starting with *Shiva shakti*: may also be referred.

(v) In the *Panchadashee mantra,* if the repeated letters are removed, nine letters remain. *Tripurā Rahasya* says that *Mahālakshmee* advised Cupid, 108 names, at the rate 12 per letter (9 x 12).

(vi) Cupid worshipping *Śreedevee* and reaching her has been explained in 84th name *Haranetrāgnisamdagdhakāmasamjeevanoushadhi:*. This has been mentioned in 145th name of *Trishatee – Kāmasanjeevinee* also. It can be reminded that in 375thname – *Kāmapoojitā* – it was explained that *Śreedevee* also has a bow made of sugarcane and arrows made of flowers, like Cupid.

(vii) Fifth verse of *Soundaryalaharee* explains that Cupid worshipped *Śreedevee* and got her blessings;

Smaro'pi Tvām Natvā Ratinayana Lehayena Vapushā
Muneenāmapyanta: Prabhavati Hi Mohāya Mahatām II

Again the 6th verse of *Soundaryalaharee* explains that the reason for the success of Cupid is the benign look and the blessings of *Śreedevee* only;

Dhanu: Poushpam Mourvee Madhukaramayee Pancha Vishikhā:
Vasanta: Sāmanto Malayamarudāyodhanaratha: I
Tathāpyeka: Sarvam Himagirisute kāmapi Krupām
Apāngātte Labdhvā Jagadidamanango Vijayate II

587. *Shreeshoḍashākshareevidyā* – श्रीषोडशाक्षरीविद्या

(i) One who is in the form of *mantra* with 16 letters.

(ii) By suffixing one seed at the end of the *Panchadashee mantra,* we get the *Vidyā* with 16 letters. (According to the rule since the *mantra*s are to be learnt through appropriate teachers, they have not been detailed here).

(iii) By prefixing eight letters to *Panchadashee mantra,* by adding a descent of five letters at the end, counting each of the letters separately and by considering each group of *Panchadashee mantra* as a letter, the *Mahāshoḍasee mantra* of 16 letters can be got. *Śree Gowḍapāda*'s *Sūtra* says that the *Mahāshoḍasee mantra* is of 28 letters. There, instead of counting each group as a letter, each letter is considered and hence 28 letters.

(iv) *Mahāshoḍasee mantra* itself has got different versions. Those are indicated by this name.

(v) The names 583 – *Ātmavidyā*, 584 – *Mahāvidyā*, 585 – *Śree Vidyā and* this name respectively indicate;

   a. *Karmavidyā* teaching the action methods.

   b. *Vishvaroopavidyā* teaching the *Virāt* form (*mahat*) taken to show the *Brahmam* as this world – the *Vishvaroopa* view in the 11th chapter of *Śreemad Bhagavad Geeta* may be referred.

c. Instructing the *mantra* form of *Śreedevee*.
d. Some schools say that this is the *Brahmavidyā* instructing the *Parabrahma* form of *Śreedevee*.

588. *Trikooṭā* – त्रिकूटा

(i) One who has groups of letters (*kooṭās*) in threes.
- In *Praŋava* (*Om*) there are three groups *A*, *U* and *Ma*.
- Three Gods doing the main three tasks of creation, protection and destruction.
- Worlds are three viz. *Bhoo*:, *Bhuva*: and *Suva*:.
- Three states of soul – awaken (*Jāgrath*), dream (*Swapna*) and deep sleep (*Sushupti*).
- Three forms of body viz., physical, subtle and causal.
- Three qualities – *Satva*, *Rajas* and *Tamas*.
- Three tenses – past, present and future.
- Three *Kanḍas* of *mantras* – fire, Sun and Moon.
- Three *Shaktis* viz. *Icchā*, *Gnāna* and *Kriya*.

The same sense is mentioned as *Vāgbhava Kooṭa*, *Kāmarāja Kooṭa* and *Shakti Kooṭa*. 85th, 86th and 87th names – *Śreemad Vāgbhava-Kooṭaikasvaroopamukhapamkajā*, *Kanthādhakatiparyanta Madhya Kooṭa Svaroopiŋee* and *Shaktikooṭaika Tāpannakatyadho Bhāgadhāriŋee*.

Thus **She** is in the form of all that are in groups of three. 626th name *Tripurā* may also be referred.

589. *Kāmakoṭikā* – कामकोटिका

(i) One who is in the form of *Kāmakoṭi*.
(ii) Since the supreme being is in the form unified form of *Shiva* and *Shakti*, *Śreedevee* is called as *Kāmakoṭika*.
(iii) **She** is the *Kāmakoṭi Peeṭa* at *Kāmakoṭṭam* in *Kāncheepuram*.
(iv) **She** is the limit (*koṭi*) of the third wish called *Kāmam* - i.e. **She** is in the form of salvation.
(v) 259th name in *Trishatee* – *Kāmakoṭi Nilayā* may be referred. *Śree Ādi Śaŋkara* has interpreted this as residing in *Śree Chakra*.

590. *Kaṭākshakingkaree Bhootakamalākoṭisevitā* – कटाक्षकिङ्करी भूतकमलाकोटिसेविता

(i) One who at a mere glance makes crores of *Lakshmees* (goddesses) wait upon to attend and worship.
(ii) If the glance of *Lakshmee* falls on a person for a micro second, he will become a millionaire. In that case, if crores of *Lakshmees* attend to *Śreedevee*, it is evident that **Her** greatness cannot even be imagined by us.
(iii) If the benign look of *Śreedevee* falls on one person, crores of *Lakshmees* will attend to him. Indirectly this says that he would get all the wealth in this world.
(iv) The greatness of *Śreedevee*'s benign look is described with poetic taste in *Mookha Panchasatee* (*Kaṭāksha Shatakam*).

591. *Shira:sthitā* – शिरःस्थिता

(i) One who resides in the head.
(ii) In the *Brahmarandhra*, wherein **She** resides assuming the form of a teacher.
(iii) **She** is in the form of the last *mahābindu* in the sound *'M'* in the seed *'Hreem'*. This has to be learnt through a teacher.

592. *Chandranibhā* – चन्द्रनिभा

(i) One who has Moon-like lustre.
(ii) There is a Moon in the lower part of the *Brahmarandhra* that is the third division of the *Panchadashee Vidya*. Hence this name to *Śreedevee*.
(iii) 240th name *Chandramaṇḍalamadhyagā* may also be referred.

593. *Bhālasthā* – भालस्था

(i) One who resides in the forehead.
(ii) **She** resides in the *Agnāchakra* in the forehead in the form of the *bindu* of the syllable *hreem*.

594. *Indradhanu:prabhā* – इन्द्रधनुःप्रभा

(i) One who has brightness like that of a rainbow.
(ii) *Indradhanus* (bow of *Indra*) indicates rainbow.
(iii) The *Nityāshoḍashikārnava* (*Yoginihrdaya* I-28) says, the *Ardhamātra* (i.e. the dot or *bindu* of *Om* or *Hreem*) is in the forehead in the form of a light; above that there is the *ardhachandra* (crescent) in the same form (i.e. of light) and it is a quarter of that - i.e. one *mātrā* consists of 256 *lavas*; 128 in *ardhamātrā* and 64 in *ardhachanrda*);

Deepākāro'rrdha Mātrashcha Lalate Vrutta Ishyate I
Ardhachandrastathākāra: *Pādamātras Tadoordhvata*: II

Śree Bhāskararāya also in his *Varivasyā Rahasya* (I-22) repeats this;

Madhye Phālam Bindur Deepa Ivābhāti Vartulākāra: I
Tadupari Gato'rdhachandro'nvartha: *Kāntyā Tathā'krutyā* II

595. *Hrudayasthā* – हृदयस्था

(i) One who resides in the heart.
(ii) **She** is to be meditated keeping **Her** form in the heart.
(iii) The *Kalpa Sūtra* says he who knows the heart of the Lord finds happiness at every step; "*Prabhuhrudaya Gnātu*: *Padepade Sukhāni Bhavanti*". Here heart means the *Parābeeja* and **She** resides there.
(iv) The *Upanishad* in the name of *Paramesvarahrudaya* is called as *Hrudaya* (heart). Since *Śreedevee* is contemplated there eternally, **She** is called as *Hrudayastha*.
(v) *Hrudaya*, the seed of the universe, because it is the seed of all. The *Anuttarātrimsikā Sāstra* says just as a great Banyan tree is contained potentially in a tiny seed, so the animate and inanimate universe resides as a seed in the heart;

Yathā Nyagrodha Beejastha: *Shaktiroopo Mahādruma*: I
Tahā Hrudaya Beejastham Jagadetachcharācharam II

596. *Raviprakhyā* – रविप्रख्या

(i) One who has brightness like the Sun.
(ii) In the heart there is a solar disc that is the second division of the *Panchadashee mantra*. Hence *Śreedevee* is called as *Raviprakhya*.
(iii) The *Āryā Shatakam* (verse 50) of *Mookha Panchashatee* indicates the same message;

Madhye Hrudayam Madhye Nitilam Madhye Shiro'pi Vāstavyām I
Chanḍakara Chakra Kārmuka Chandra Samābhām Namāmi Kāmāksheem II

597. *Trikoṇāntaradeepikā*- त्रिकोणान्तरदीपिका

(i) One who is like a light within a triangle.

(ii) There is a triangle in the pericarp of the *Moolādhāra*, in that there is a disc of fire that is the first division of the *Panchadashee mantra*. Hence She is called as *Trikonāntaradeepika*.

(iii) The *Tantrarāja Tantra* (XXX-51,52) says, in the centre of the eternally manifested *Moolādhāra* of all beings, there is a fire; similarly in the heart, there is the Sun. In the head below the *Brahmarandhra*, there is the moon. Thus, the first, the ancient *mantra* is threefold;

Nityā Nityodite Moolādhāramadye'sti Pāvaka: I
Sarveshām Prāninām Tadvad Hrdaye Cha Prabhākara: II
Moordhani Brahmarandhrādha: *Chandramāshcha Vyavasthita*: I
Tat Trayātmakāmeva Syāt Ādyā Nityā Trikhandakam II

(iv) In the previous name it was mentioned that **She** is as bright as Sun. Here the Sun illuminating the world is being explained. When the Sun circumambulates the eight-angled *Meru* mountain, he illuminates only three angles at a time, for when the Sun is at zenith in the city of I*ndra*, it is sunset and sunrise in the cities of *Soma* and of *Yama* respectively. The *Viṣhṇu Purāṇa* says, when the sun (at midday) passes over either of the cities of the gods, his light extends to three cities and two intermediate points; when situated in an intermediate point, he illuminates two of the cities and three intermediate points. The meaning is that **She** illuminates the three cities which are in the triangular form, at a time.

598. *Dākshāyaṇee* – दाक्षायणी

(i) One who is daughter of *Daksha*.

(ii) According to the *Vishva* dictionary, *Dākshyāni* means, the wife of *Shiva, Rohini* and constellations (they are also daughters of *Dakshā prajāpati*); It is evidenced through – "*Dākshāyanee Tvaparnāyām Rohinyām Tārakāsucha*".

(iii) *Dākshyāna* means a certain sacrifice repeating the performance of the *darsha* and *poorṇamāsa* sacrifices. **She** is in that form.

599. *Daityahantree* – दैत्यहन्त्री

(i) One who is the slayer of demons *Bhanḍāsura* and others. 318th name *Rākshasagnee* may also be referred.

600. *Dakshayagnavināshinee* – दक्षयज्ञविनाशिनी

(i) One who destroyed the sacrifice of *Daksha.*

(ii) There were two *Dakshas*, one is known as *Daksha Prajāpati* and the other was a human king, an incarnation of the former.

(iii) On account of ego, he did not respect and did not give the due offerings to *Shiva.* Hence **She** destroyed the sacrificial fire. Though actually it was destroyed by *Shiva* and his groups, *Śreedevee* was the instrument for the destruction and hence it is mentioned that **She** destroyed it.

(iv) *Shiva* destroyed the sacrificial fire done by the other *Dakshā* also. This has been mentioned in *Brahmānḍa Purāŋa* and *Vāyu Purāŋa.*

Thus ends the seventh *Kalā* called *Sushumna.*

*****

Section 8: *Bogatā Kalā*

601. *Darāndolitadeerghākshee* - दरान्दोलितदीर्घाक्षी

(i) One who has wavering wide eyes extending upto her ears.
(ii) *Darā* means a little/ slightly. The eyes of *Śreedevee* slightly waver on all sides.
(iii) The eyes of *Śreedevee* are extended upto her ears. As per the characters declared in physiognomy the eyes extending upto the ears are the best.
(iv) *Dara* also means fear. The eyes of *Śreedevee* remove the fears. I.e. just by the sight of the long eyes of *Śreedevee* the fear is removed.
(v) Since **She** wants her compassionate benign look to fall on all the devotees, **She** has long eyes and **Her** retina waves here and there.
(vi) The mention of long and wavering eyes can be compared with the names; 18th–*Vaktralakshmee - pareevāhachalanmeenābhalochanā*, 454th– *Lolāksheekāmaroopinee* and 936th– *Vishālākshee*.
(vii) The verses described the eyes in *Soundaryalaharee* and *Mookha Panchashati Kaṭāksha Shatakam*) may also be referred.

602. *Darahāsojvalanmukhee* - दरहासोज्वलन्मुखी

(i) One whose face shines with smile.
(ii) *Darā* means little and hence *Darahāsa* means smile. The physical form of *Śreedevee* is beautiful in many ways as described in many a name. In the same way, **She** is ecstatic with a smiling face as a sign of **Her** inner bliss. The beauty and the state of bliss are together indicated by the smile. The *dhyāna* verse also says *Smitamukheem*. The last offering out of the 64 is *Ānandollāsa Hāsa Vilāsam Kalpayāmi*.
(iii) The smile not only adds beauty, but also welcomes and makes it interesting to those who want to reach **Her**. The same message is conveyed in 924th name *Darasmera Mukhāmbuja*. This can also be compared with the 60th name in *Trishatee – Eshatsmitānana*.
(iv) *Dara* also means fear. Hence *Darahāsa* can be considered as loud and scary laughter. During war times with demons, the loud and scary laughter of *Śreedevee* has been mentioned in many places. **Her** face is lit with this laughter.

603. *Gurumoorti*: - गुरुमूर्तिः

(i) One who assumes the form of a teacher.
(ii) The confirmed opinion of the *mantra sāstras* is - the teacher, the *mantra* and the deity are all one and the same and should not be distinguished. Adding *Śreechakra* also with these three, the devotee should realise that these are not different from the self.
(iii) It has been mentioned in *Varivasya Rahasya* as;

Ittam Mātā Vidyā Chakram Svaguru: *Svayam Cheti* I
Panchānāmapibhetābhāvo Mantrasya Koulikārttho'yam II

(iv) *Aruŋagirināda* also sings about Lord Muruga as *"Guruvāi Varuvāi Arulvāi Guhane"*. *Śreedevee* **Herself** reaches the devotee in the form of a teacher and gives him invocation of *mantra*.
(v) *Gu* means darkness of ignorance and *Ru* removes that. Hence the word *Guru* itself means removing of the darkness of ignorance.
(vi) The letter *Gu* is an existence (*Sat* letter) and *Ru* is knowledge (of *Brahmam*) and because one is with the knowledge of *Brahmam*, he is called *guru*.
(vii) *Śree Ādi Śaņkara* in his commentary of *Vișhŋu Sahasranāma* for the 209th name – *Guru*: mentions - **He** is called *Guru* since **he**; (i) invocates/ advises all *Vidyās* or (ii) gave birth to all living beings (as a father).

604. *Guŋanidhi*: - गुणनिधिः

(i) One who is the treasure house of qualities.
(ii) The *Sānkhya* doctrine says that though the qualities are specifically three viz. *satva, rajas* and *tamas,* they have endless modifications. **She** is the treasure house of all such qualities.
(iii) *Guŋa* means aggregate (*Vyoohas*). Like nine *nidhies,* these *vyoohas* also are nine in number. *Parameshwara* is of the form of these nine aggregates of qualities. They are; *Kālavyooha* (time), *Kulavyooha* (family race), *Nāmavyooha* (name), *Gnānavyooha* (knowledge), *Chittavyooha* (mind), *Nadavyooha* (*Nātha*), *Binduvyooha* (*Bindu*), *Kalpavyooha* (*Kalpa*) and *Jeevavyooha* (soul). Since **She** is of these forms **She** is called as *Guŋanidhi*. The details of these are given in the commentary of *Lakshmeedhara* for the 36th verse starting as *Tavāgnā Chakrastham* in *Soundaryalaharee*.
(iv) The word *Guŋa* also means rope. The rope called *Vairikā,* which tied the ship during the *pralaya*; *Nidhi,* the deity to whom it was tied. The following story occurs in the *Matsya* and *Kālika Purāŋas* thus; at the time of dissolution all seeds and sages entered the boat at the

command of *Manu*, who was directed by the Lord *Viṣhŋu* and the boat was tied to the horn of the fish-incarnation. That rope became firm when *Śreedevee* held it. "Make a great rope of hides to be called *Vatrikā*, nine *Yojanas* long and three cubits broad. *Śreedevee* who is the protector of the universe, the great *Māyā*, the mother of the world, the world itself, will make that rope firm so that it will not give away".

605. *Gomātā* - गोमाता

(i) One who is in the form of *Kāmadhenu* (the divine cow), the mother of all cows or greatest of all cows.
(ii) According to *Anekārthadhvanimanjari* and *Vishva* dictionaries, the word *Gow* has many a meaning like speech, rays, heaven, etc. **She** is the root form of all these.

606. *Guhajanmabhoo*: - गुहजन्मभूः

(i) One who is the mother of *Guhā* (Lord *Murugā*).
(ii) **She** is the mother of *Guha*, (Lord *Subrahmaŋya*) and hence *Guhajanmabhoo*:.
(iii) The root word *Guhoo* means to cover. The *jeevas* veiled by ignorance are called *Guhās*. Just as sparks come from the hot iron so do the souls have come out from the Self. Hence **She** is called as *Guhajanmabhoo*:.

607. *Deveshee* -देवेशी

(i) One who is the head of all divine forces like *Brahma, Viṣhŋu, Shiva* and others.

608. *Daŋḍaneetisthā* - दण्डनीतिस्था

(i) One who administers justice by punishing the culprits.
(ii) *Daŋḍaneeti* is the *sāstra* which describes the crimes and the corresponding punishments for the criminals. The *Devee Purāŋa* says, because **She** leads to certainty men who wander into good and bad ways by restraining and by soothing them, **She** is called *Daŋḍaneetistha*;

Nayānayagatān Lokān Avikalpe Niyojanāt I
Daŋḍanāt Damanād Vāpi Daŋḍaneetiriti Smrutā II

609. *Daharākāsharoopiŋee* - दहराकाशरूपिणी

(i) One who is the subtle ether in the cave called heart.
(ii) There is a subtle hidden cave in the heart of every soul. **She** dwells there in the form of ether.
(iii) *Ākāsha* means sky, ether, vacuum, place, etc. There is subtle ether in the heart of every human being. This is worshipped as *Parabrahmam* or *Śreedevee*.
(iv) *Brahma Sūtra* says, the small ether is *Brahmam*; *Dahara Uttarebhya*:. The *Chāndogya Upanishad* (VIII-1-1) says, there is in this city of *Brahmam* the small lotus house and in it that small ether that should be sought for. Hence the ether of the heart is said to be *Brahmam*;
Atha Yadasmin Brahma Puredhaharam Pundareekam Vechma
Dhaharo'sminnandarākāsa: *Tasminyadantasdanveshtavyam*.

This is also called as *Taharavidya*.

(v) The same is advised by *Śree Appayya Deekshitar* in his book called *Ratnatrāya Pareekshai*;
Vedagnā Dharmametam Pravitatamakhilādhāramākāshamāhoo
Kinchānandam Manovāgavishayamadhikam Dharmino Varŋayanti I
Sattāsphoortti: *Sukancha Tryamapi Jagatām Sangirante*
Tadamsham Prānākāshādyupāstee: *Katichidapi Tadālambanāste Vadanti* II

610. *Pratipanmukhyarākāntatithimaŋḍalapoojitā* – प्रतिपन्मुख्यराकान्ततिथिमण्डलपूजिता

(i) One who is worshipped on the group of fifteen days from the *Pratama* (the first day) to the full Moon.
(ii) *Pratipat* means *Pratama*, the first day. *Rākā* means full Moon. She is being worshipped in all these fifteen days. The mode of worshipping on each day has been described in *Tantra Sāstras*.
(iii) There are names given in *Vedas* for each of the fifteen days of the bright lunar fortnight viz.; *Darshā*, *Drushtā*, *Darshadā*, *Vishvaroopā*, *Sudarshanā*, *Apyāyamānā*, *Āpooryamāna*, *Poorāyantee*, *Poorŋā* and *Pourŋamasee*. Above all these there is a *kalā* called *Sādā* in the galaxy of Moon (*Chandramaŋḍala*). All these sixteen are called *Tithimaŋḍala*.
(iv) For each of the day there is *Tithi Nitya* (deity) and the sixteenth

Mahanityā described in the methods of *Shakti* worship. They are (for the bright lunar fortnight); *Kāmeshvaree, Bhagamālinee, Nityaglinnā, Bherundā, Vahnivāsinee, Vajreshvaree, Shivadootee, Tvaritā, Kulasundaree, Nityā, Neelapatākā, Vijayā, Sarvamangala, Jvālāmālinee* and *Chitra*. The 16th is *Lalitā Mahānitya*. They dwell in the *Bindu* and the surrounding triangles in *Śreechakra* - five for each line of the triangle and the *Mahānityā* in the *Bindu*. 391st name *Nityāshoḍashikā* may be referred.

(v) *Tithinityā Yajanam* is an important part of *Śree Vidyā Pooja*.

(vi) It has been mentioned in *Varāha Purāŋa* that *Agni* (fire) and other gods are the presiding deities for all these *Tithies*.

611. ***Kalātmikā* - कलात्मिका**

(i) One who is in the form of art.

(ii) The word *kalā* indicates various *kalās* viz.

kalās of fire	-	10
kalās of Sun	-	12
kalās of Moon	-	16

These 38 *kalās* are *Tejomaŋḍala kalās*. There are *kalās* relating to *Brahma* and other *Devas* also;

kalās of *Brahma*	-	10
kalās of *Viṣhŋu*	-	10
kalās of *Rudra*	-	10
kalās of *Ĕshwar*	-	4
kalās of *Sadāshiva*	-	16

These 50 *kalās* are *Brahma-maŋḍala kalās*.

There is some other set of well-known sixty-four *kalās* is also in vogue with the human beings. These were explained in 236th name *Chatushshashṭikalāmayee*. All these *kalās* are forms of *Śreedevee* only.

(iii) Each of the four states awakens(*Jāgrath*), dream(*Swapna*), deep sleep (*Sushupti*) and swoon (*Thureeyam*) are related to different *kalās*. They are;

Awaken (*Jāgrath*) - Rising, waking, thought and the continuous mental action.

Dream (*Swapna*) - Desire, confusion, anxiety and recollection of sense objects

Deep sleep (*Sushupti*) - Faintness, oblivion, Insensibility and sleep abounding with darkness

Swoon (*Thureeyam*) - dispassion, desire of salvation, the mind purified by concentrated meditation and determination of reality and unreality.

Thus it totals to 16 *kalās*. Out of these the *kalās* pertaining to awaken state relate to *Shakti*. The *kalās* pertaining to dream state relate to *Shiva -Shakti*. The *kalās* pertaining to deep sleep state relate to *Shiva.*

(iv) In the *Dooteeyāgaprakaraṇa*, sixteen *kāmakalās* are described. In the *Antaradooti Prakaraṇa*, sixteen *kalās* are attributed to the *Śreevidya*. Also some more, such as the *Kalās* of *Bindu, ardhachandra, rodhini*, etc., are described. The real form of *kalās* in all these types is *Śreedevee.*

612. ***Kalānāthā*** **- कलानाथा**

(i) She is the head of all the *kalās* described above. All these *kalās* are conspicuous only by **Her**.

(ii) Moon is called as head of *kalās* or *kalānāthan*. Since the *Śreechakra* itself is in the form of *Chandramaṇḍala* (Moon's galaxy), the name *Kalānāthā* for *Śreedevee* is very apt.

613. ***Kāvyālāpavinodinee*** **– काव्यालापविनोदिनी**

(i) One who gets delighted with poetical speech, dialogue, description, etc.

(ii) The books written by poets are called *kāvyās*. Eighteen characteristics have been declared for a *kāvya*. It is told that the story of *Rama* written by sage *Vālmiki* is the oldest *kāvya*. **She** gets very much pleased specially by such *kāvyās*.

(iii) The characters of a *kāvyā* has been described as; "*Vākyam Rasātmakam Kāvyam* and *Ramaneeyartthapratipādaka*: *Shabda*: *Kāvyam*". Accordingly **She** enjoys *kāvyās* and its characters like the flavour of the descriptions, rhetoric speech, figures of speech, etc.

(iv) A devotee who worships *Śreedevee* methodically gets the capability of writing *kāvyās*. For instance, *Kālidāsa, Mookha* and others. Same sense is conveyed by *Śree Ādi Śaṇkara*, in his *Soundaryalaharee*, 17th verse and 1st verse mention as;

Savitreebhirvāchām Chashimaṇishilābhangaruchibhir
Vachinyādyābhistvām Saha Janani Sanchintayati Ya: I
Sa Kartā Kāvyānām Bhavati Mahatām Bhangiruchibhir
Vachobhirvāg Devee Vadana Kamalāmoda Madhurai: II

(v) 798th name *Kāvyakalā* and 242nd name of *Trishatee – Kāvyalola* may also be referred.

614. ***Sachāmararamāvāŋeesavyadakshiŋasevitā* - सचामटटमावाणीसव्यदक्षिणसेविता**

(i) One who is attended on either side by *Lakshmee* and *Saraswatee* holding *chāmaras* (hand fans).
(ii) It has been mentioned that *Lakshmee* and *Saraswatee* serve *Śreedevee* on both the sides. A devotee of *Śreedevee* also becomes merged with *Śreedevee*. Hence this indicates that *Laskhmee* and *Saraswatee* bless/ serve the devotees of *Śreedevee* also.
(iii) In *Soundaryalaharee*, (99th verse) also we read; "*Saraswatyā Lakshmyā Vidhihari Sapatno Viharate*".
(iv) In general *Savya* means right side. Since right side has been mentioned by the word *Dakshiŋa*, the word *Savya* has been taken as left side.
(v) In *Soundaryalaharee*, (47th verse) also the same meaning is considered; "*Dhanurmanye Savyetarakagruheetam Ratipate*:".
(vi) Same sense is conveyed in *Trishatee* – 63rd name *Lakshmee Vānee Nishevitā* and 104th name *Lagna Chāmarhasta Śree Shāradāpariveejita*.

615. ***Ādishakti*: - आदिशक्तिः**

(i) One who is the primordial power.
(ii) She does the three main tasks of creation, protection and destruction of the entire universe and pervades everything in the form of root cause energy (*shakti*).

616. ***Ameyā* - अमेया**

(i) One who has immeasurable form and greatness.
(ii) Since her form is immeasurable, **She** is *Ameya*. i.e. there is no way to measure **Her**.
(iii) The *Linga Purāŋa* says, heaven, *pātāla*, the end of the world in these eight coverings of the *Brahmāŋḍa*, all that can be measured, is in the form of *Uma* and the measurer is the great Lord *Shiva* ;

Svargapātala Lokānta Brahmānda Vanāshtake I
Meyam Sarvam Umāroopam Mātā Devomaheshvara: II

617. ***Atmā* - आत्मा**

(i) One who is in the form of *Ātman* or *Jeeva* (soul).
(ii) This name indicates *Jeevātmā* and the next name indicates *Paramātma*.
(iii) The word *Ātmā* has several meanings - body, mind, *Brahmam*, nature, firmness and intelligence. Since *Śreedevee* is in these forms this name is very much apt for **Her**.
(iv) *Ātmā* word can be taken to mean *Paramātmā* (the Supreme Being).
(v) The *Ātmā* indicates body. Hence all bodices of embodied souls are the forms of *Śreedevee* only.

618. ***Paramā* - परमा**

(i) One who is the great in all things and all ways.
(ii) **She** who limits and shows us the immeasurable *Brahmam*.
(iii) The word *Parama* means "at a distance". i.e. **She** is at a distance for those who do not have devotion.
(iv) According to *Viṣhŋu Purāŋa*, the supreme being has four forms viz., Male, Twice Born, Time and *Param*. **She** is in the fourth form *Param*.
(v) For the previous name, if we consider *Jeevātma* as a meaning, this name is *Paramātma*. In this sense the usage in *archana* is *Paramātmane Namaha*.

619. ***Pāvanākruti*: - पावनाकृतिः**

(i) One whose body is holy and sanctifying both in form and character.
(ii) The very thought of *Śreedevee* washes away all sins and makes one the purest.
(iii) *Pāvana* – of pure form.
(iv) *Kruti* also means actions. i.e. who does holy actions – of pure form and actions.
(v) The names 542nd - *Puŋyakeertti*: and 544th – *Puŋyashravana keerttanā* also convey the same message as holy.

620. ***Anekakoṭibrahmaŋḍajananee* - अनेककोटिब्रह्माण्डजननी**

(i) One who delivered many crores of worlds.
(ii) *Virāt*, *Hiraŋyagarbha* and *Ĕshwara* are the three forms of *Brahmam*

created crores of worlds. **She** is a mother for them also.

(iii) *Brahmānḍa*, results from combination of the five gross elements, consisting of sixteen modifications. *Virāt* is the individuality of this. *Svarāt* is the individuality of the unmanifested, which is the cause of these two. *Samrāt* is the root cause of all these.

(iv) 49th name in *Trishatee* – *Ekshanashrushtāndakoṭi* may also be referred.

621. ***Divyavigrahā*** **- दिव्यविग्रहा**

(i) One who has a very gorgeous/ divine form.

(ii) *Divya* - ether, *Vigraha* – war/ quarrel. The *Mārkaŋḍeya Purāŋa* says, even in the ether without support, *Chanḍikā* fought with the demon *Subāsura*.

Utpatya Pragruhyochchair Deveem Gagaŋamāsithita:
Tatrāpi Sānirādhārā Yuyudhe Tena Chanḍikā
Niyuddham Khetadā Daityach Chanḍikā Cha Parasparam II

622. ***Kleemkāree*** **- क्लींकारी**

(i) One who is the personification of the letter *Kleem*, which is the *Kāmarāja* seed (*beeja*).

(ii) The letter *Kleem* is *Kāmarāja* or *Manmatha* (Cupid) *beejam* (seed).

(iii) *Kleemkara* means *Shiva kāma* or *Kāmeshwara*. **She** is the consort of him or *Kāmeshwaree*.

(iv) The *Kāmarāja Beeja* is the combined form of *Icchā Shakti* (wish) and *Vashya* (attraction) *Shakti*.

(v) As mentioned in the final part of *Trishatee, Ka* indicates *Shiva* and *La* indicates *Shakti*. *Em* indicates *Kāmakala*. Hence this name indicates the unison of *Shiva* and *Shakti*.

623. ***Kevalā*** **- केवला**

(i) One who is the absolute, devoid of all attributes.

(ii) In practice, nowadays, the *kevala* is used to indicate the least or low level. But its actual important meaning is very great, individual and not mingled with any other attribute or righteousness.

(iii) **She** is *Ekākinee* (single) as **She** is devoid of any attributes. The only remaining sense of non-duality philosophy is *Kevala*.

(iv) *Kevalā*, a kind of knowledge described in a *Shiva Sūtra* (III-35) - that which is freed from that is the absolute "*kevalā; Tadvimuktistu-*

kevalee".

(v) With reference to the *Kleembeeja*, mentioned in the previous name, when the *ka* and *la* are eliminated from the *kleem*, the remaining is *kevala*. This is called *Kāmakalābeeja*. This has to be learnt through a teacher.

(vi) One who worships the *beeja Kleemkāree* obtains the world, attainable by unconditioned knowledge alone. The meaning is, the three objects *dharma* (righteousness), *Artha* (money) and *Mokshā* (salvation). The *kāmakala* (i.e. *Im*) enables the worshipper to reach the *tureeya* state. This is the state of *Kevala* or *Kaivalyam*.

624. *Guhyā* - गुह्या

(i) One who is most secretive both in form and meanings.

(ii) *Guhyā* means one who dwells in a cave, i.e. heart.

(iii) **She** is secretive and dwelling in our heart. Hence **She** can be identified only by inward search.

(iv) The word *Guhyā* can be considered to mean *Jeevātma* (soul), *Paramātmā* (supreme) and the union of both. The presiding deity who can bestow these results is called *Guhya*.

(v) This can be compared with 707th name – *Guhayaroopiŋee*.

(vi) *Śree Ādi Śaṇkara* in his commentary of *Viṣhŋu Sahasranāma* for the 542nd name – *Guhya*:– one who can be understood by the secret *Upanishads* or one who dwells in the secret cavity viz., heart. 545th name – *Gupta*: - **He** is beyond speech and mind.

(vii) *Kaṭopanishad* (I-2-12) says; "*Esha Sarveshu Bhooteshu Kooṭātmā na prakāshate*".

625. *Kaivalyapadadāyinee* - कैवल्यपददायिनी

(i) One who is the bestower of the solitary abode i.e. non-dual salvation.

(ii) This state has been described by *Śree Appayya Deekshitar* in his book called *Ratnatrya Parikshā* as the form of *Brahmam*. **She** offers that state to the devotees.

(iii) There are five kinds of salvation, namely *sālokya, sāroopya, sāmeepya, sāyujya* and *kaivalya*. The *Sālokya* is remaining with the god in the same world. *Sāroopya* is receiving the same form with the god. *Sāyujya* is becoming one with the deity. *Sāmeepya* is remaining near the deity. *Kaivalya*, the state of singleness without attributes. That is the fifth state of consciousness, understanding of self. She bestows all these four *padas* and the *kaivalya* state.

(iv) Instead of imagining the form of gods in idols or *yantras*, understanding the form as different from self but still imagining it on the self and by worshipping the same, one can get *Sāroopya*. This is also called as *Sārshtita*. Here the god is imagined with some attributes that are not with oneself, one can get the nearness of the form (*roopasāmeepyam*) only. *Sāyujya* is worshipping as himself the deity with attributes and he becomes one with the deity. *Sāmeepya* is attained by those celibates who perform the duties as ordained to their states in life. The *Taitireeya Upanishad* says - those who are peaceful, learned, who live on alms, in the forest performing penance and having faith, without passion, proceed through the Sun to the place of the immortal person, the eternal self;

Etāsā Meva Devatānām Sāyujyam, Sārshtitām Samana Lokatā Māpnoti.

The fourth *pāda* is described in *Muŋḍaka Upanishad* (I-2-II) as;

Tapa: *Sratte Ye Hyubhavasantyaranye*
Shāntā Vidvāmso Paikshasaryām Charaŋta: I
Sooryatvārena Te Virajā: *Prayānti*
Yatrāmruta: *Sa Purushohyavyayātmā* II

(v) The above said four pertain to actions and the corresponding results and hence temporary. Hence they are called *padas* (abode).

(vi) The fifth one, *Kaivalya*, pertains to the result of knowledge and offers the eternal bliss. Thus says *Taitreeya Sruti*.

(vii) The *Yoga Sūtra* (IV-33) says, *Kaivalya* is the establishment in its own nature of the energy of consciousness;

Kaivalyam Svaroopa Pratishtāvā Chitshakti.

(viii) The same message is in brief conveyed in *Shakti Rahasya* as – a mortal who worships by ceremonies, by images, by mind, by identification, by knowing the Self, attains *kaivalya*;

Ātma Budhyā Prateekena Mātrubudyāpyaham Dhiyā I
Karmanāpi Bhajan Martyā Kaivalya Padamachnute II

(ix) The above four names *Kleemkāree*, *Kevala*, *Guhyā* and *Kaivalya Padadāyinee* together form a single line (half verse). When their meanings are read together we get an interesting explanation; **She**, who is in the form of *Kāmarāja Beeja*, endows salvation if the *Kleem Beeja* is worshipped in a secret manner, after removing *Ka* and *La*.

(x) 926th name *Anarghya Kaivalya Padadāyinee* may also be referred.

626. *Tripurā* - त्रिपुरा

(i) One who is elder to the three Gods viz., *Brahma, Viṣhŋu* and *Rudra.*
(ii) **She** takes three forms as *Brahma, Viṣhŋu* and *Rudra* to do the three tasks viz., creation, protection and destruction. Hence **She** is elder or senior to these three gods; *Moorttitrāyasyāpi Purātanatvāt Tatambikāyās tripuretināma.*
(iii) There are three *Devas*, three *Vedas*, three fires, three energies, three notes (*svaras*), three worlds, three abodes, (or according to another reading, three cities), three sacred lakes, three castes, etc. Whatever in the world is threefold, such as the three objects of human desire, all these, are **Her** form. Hence **She** is beyond and older than all these.
(iv) The *Tripurārnava* says, *Tripurā*, means the three *nāḍis* viz., *Sushumnā, Pingalā* and *idā*; and *Manas, Buddhi* and *Chitta*; as *Śreedevee* dwells in all these **She** is called *Tripurā*;

Nādeetryam Tutripurā Sushumnāpingalāidā I
Manobhuddhistada Chittam Puratrāyamudāhrutam II
Tatra Tatra Vasatyeshā Tasmāttu Tripurā Matā

(v) The same is conveyed in *Kālikā Purāŋa* also as, your sphere is triangular, because everything is threefold you are called *tripurā*;

Trikoŋam Maŋḍalam Chāsyā: *Bhoopuram Cha trirekhām* I
Mantro'bhitryakshare Prokta: *Tathā roopatryam Puna*: II
TrividhāKunḍalee Shakti: *Tridevānām Cha Srushtaye* I
Sarvamtrāyam Trāyam Yasmāttasmāttu Tripurāmatā II

(vi) *Śree Bhāskararāya* has written a book called *Sethu Bandam*, as commentary for *Nityā Shoḍashikārnava*. In this book (IV-4 to IV-16) in the verses starting from *Tripurā Paramāshakti* till the verse ending with *Tripurā Kyātimākatā*, more details about this can be found.

627. *Trijagadvandyā* - त्रिजगद्वन्द्या

(i) One who is worshipped by all the three worlds.
(ii) One who is worshipped in all the three worlds.

628. *Trimoortti*: - त्रिमूर्त्तिः

(i) One who is in the form of the three gods' viz., *Brahma, Viṣhŋu* and *Rudra.*
(ii) One who is in the form of three elderly spinsters.
(iii) *Śreedevee* having the three qualities – *Satva, Rajas* and *Tamas*, has three forms with *Rakta, Shukla* and *Misra* as three feet. This is meditated upon in the *guru manadala*.

(iv) **She** is three-fold forms – *Brahma, Viṣhŋu* and *Rudra – Vāma, Jeshtā* and *Roudhree – Ichā, Gnāna* and *Kriya.*
(v) Earlier, *Brahma, Viṣhŋu* and *Rudra,* subtly sighted each other and a stunning girl originated. The three gods asked her, "Who are you?" She said, "I am the form of your three energies. Reflecting upon the character of the three, She was of three colours viz., black, white and red. Hence **She** is called as *Trimoortti.*
(vi) Only this girl form split into three as *Brāhmee, Vaiṣhŋavee* and *Roudhree* and respectively did penance in three mountains called white, red and black. This story has been described in *Varāha Purāŋa.*
(vii) *Gouḍapāda Sūtra* mentions this type of three forms according to three qualities as; *Shambhavee Vidyā Shyāma.*
(viii) *Devee Bhāgavatam* also mentions the same as;

Shāmbhavee Shuklaroopā Cha Śree Vidyā Rakta Roopikā I
Shyāmalā Shyāmroopā Syāt Ityetā Guŋashaktaya: II

629. ***Tridasheshvaree* - त्रिदशेश्वरी**

(i) One who is the head of all the *Devas.*
(ii) Each human being has four stages in the life as childhood, youth, adult and old age. But the *Devas* always have only the third stage and hence they are called *Tridashā*: **She** is head of them.
(iii) The word *Tridasha* can be taken as 3 x 10 = 30. By adding three, *Devas* becomes 33 viz., *Vashus* – 8, *Ādityas* – 12, *Rudras* – 11, *Vishve Devas* – 2 – Total 33. Each of these has one crore followers as a group. Hence totally it is called 33 crores of *Devas.*
(iv) The three states awaken, dream and sleep – individually and collectively have *Śreedevee* as head.

630. ***Tryaksharee* - त्र्यक्षरी**

(i) One who is in the form of three letters.
(ii) *Bālāmantra* has three letters. *Panchadashee mantra* also has three groups viz., *Vāgbhava, Kāmarāja* and *Shakti.*
(iii) *Vāmakeshwara Tantra* says;

Vāgeeshwaree Gnānashakti: *Vāgbhave Moksharoopiŋee* I
Kāmarāje Kriyā Shakti: *Kāmeshee Kāmaroopiŋee* II
Shakti Beeje Parashakti: *Icchaiva Shiva Roopiŋee* I
Evam Devee Triyaksharee Tu Mahatripurasundaree II

(iv) *Gouḍapāda Sūtra* mentions that *Panchadashee* is mentioned as

Triyaksharee, Shuddha Vidyā and *Kumāree.*

(v) According to the *Veda* statements, this name can be taken to mean heart or truth; *Tat Etat Tryaksharam Hrudayam* and *Tat Etat Trāyaksharam Satyam.*

(vi) There are six types of *mantra*s of *Śreedevee*. Those end with the letters *Ā* and *Ĕ*. These are considered as the integration of *Yugakshara* (letter of one era), *Māsākshara* (letter of a month) and *Nityākshara* (letter of a day). These three letters are called *Tryaksharee*. This has been mentioned in *Lagustuti* as;

Āĕ Pallavitai: *Parasparayudai*: *Dvitrikramādyaksharai*:
Kādyai: *Kshāntagatai*: *Svarātibhiradakshāntai*: *Tai*: *Sasvarai*: I
Nāmāni Tripure Bhavanti Khalu Yānyatyanta Guhyāni Te
Tebhyo Bhairavapatni Vimshati Sahasrebhya: *Parebhyo Nama*: II

(vii) *Nāthapārāyaŋa, Katikā Pārāyanā, Tatva Pārāyanā, Nāma Pārāyanā, Nityā Pārāyanā* and *Mantra Pārāyanā* are called six *Pārāyanās.*

(viii) 732nd name *Nāmapārāyaŋapreetā* may be referred.

631. *Divyagandhāḍhyā* - दिव्यगन्धाढ्या

(i) One who is full of divine fragrance.

(ii) *Divya* means anything in the upper world. i.e. **She** is full of aroma of divine sandal, flowers like *Kadamba, Parijātā,* etc.

(iii) *Divya* means the things pertaining to *Devatas*. **She** is full of smell of sandal, saffron flower, *kastoori,* etc., that are fragrant in this world also.

(iv) The meaning of this name is also mentioned in *Vedas* as; *Gantatvārām Durādharshām.*

(v) *Śreedevee* is surrounded by *Devas*. In addition **She** is with the kings of this world and their fragrances.

(vi) According to *Yoga* statement – *Samyamāttivyam,* the ears and its relevant element viz., ether, with the profound practice, the devotee gets divine hearing powers. In the same way, *Śreedevee,* through all the elements by practicing *Yoga,* etc., gives divine powers like divine smelling power, etc.

632. *Sindooratilakānchitā* - सिन्दूरतिलकाञ्चिता

(i) One who is adorned with a vermillion mark on the forehead.

(ii) *Sindooram* means red *Kumkum, korochan,* etc.

(iii) The word *Tilakā* means the hair falling on the forehead. Her form is so beautiful with *Sindooram* and *Tilaka*. *Vishva* dictionary says;

Tilakam Chitrake Prāhoo Lalāte Tilakālake.

(iv) It is the practice that *Sumangali* ladies (ladies living with their husbands) to wear red *kumkum* on the starting place of the hair in the forehead.

(v) *Sindoora Tilakā* means female elephant. *Anjitā* means one who is worshipped. Or, **She** is worshipped by ladies called *Hastinees*, whose walk is comparable to that of female elephants.

(vi) Accordingly *Śreemad Bhāgavatam*, *Gopikā* ladies and *Rukmaŋi* also worshipped *Śreedevee* to marry *Śree Krișhŋa*.

633. ***Umā* - उमा**

(i) One who has the great name *Uma*.

(ii) *Śreedevee* was born as daughter to *Himavan* and his wife *Mena* and had the name *Pārvatee*. **She** started to do ardent penance at the age of 5 aiming to marry *Parameshwara*. Hence *Mena* became anxious and wanted to prevent *Pārvatee* from doing penance. I.e. **She** called *Pārvatee* as *'U'* and said *Mā* (not to do penance). Hence the name *Uma*.

(iii) The letter *'U'* relates to *Shiva, Mā* means *Lakshmee* (auspicious). Hence Umā means the auspiciousness of *Shiva.*

(iv) **She** limits (*Mā*) *Shiva* (*'U'*).

(v) The word *Umā* has several meanings *Umā, Adasee, Haimavatee, Haridra, Keerthi* and *Kāntishu*. **She** is all these forms;

Yā Devee Sarvabhooteshu Kāntiroopena Samsthita.

(vi) The *Soota Samhita* (IV-1-20) says, "I adore the supreme experience which destroys the noose of earthly existence, which purifies even *Sadāshiva,* called *Umā*, which produces the bright state and manifests in many kinds of worlds;

Umabhitām Uttama Chittavruttim Namāmi Nānā Vidhaloka Vaibhavām.

(vii) In *Linga Purāŋa, Shiva* says to *Śreedevee* - In my *Praŋava* there are letters *A-U-M* (UMA) in the form of *Vișhŋu, Shiva* and *Brahma*. These letters are in the order in the *Praŋava,* with the three notes (*mātrās*) and with the highest pluta;

Ukāram Cha Makāram Cha Akāram Cha Krameritam
Tvadeeyam Praŋavam Vitdhitrimātram Plutamuttamam.

The *Mahāvāshista* says - Uma is so called because it contains the essence of the *Praŋava*; "*Omkāra Sāra Shaktitvāt Umetiparikeerttitā*"

(viii) In the heart of all beings, whether asleep or awake there is a cavity whence arises the sound being produced without contrast, which is *Shabdabrahmam*, the *Praŋava*, without the letters *'A'*, etc. The cavity is *Shiva and* in his head there is an *Indukalā* (crescent), which is the form of *bindu*.

(ix) According to the *Shiva Sūtra* (I-13) *Uma* means the *Iccha Shakti* of *Yoginis*. "The young *Umā* is called the *Iccha Shakti*".

(x) As per the statement; *Uma Devee Vinayake* - *Umā* is the deity worshipped at the *Vināyaka Peeṭa* and again based on *Umā Sindhuvane* - at the *Sindhuvana*.

(xi) *Umāshatvārshikee Matā* - a girl of six years old is called *Uma*.

(xii) *Kenopanishad* says *Uma* invocated *Brahmam* to *Indra*.

634. ***Shailendratanayā* - शैलेन्द्रतनया**

(i) One who is daughter of the king of mountains.

(ii) *Himavan* is the king of mountains. Being his daughter **She** is called as *Pārvatee*, *Haimavatee* and *Girija*.

(iii) Mountain is a static object. **She** is full of consciousness (*chaitanya*). To give credit to the static objects also, **She** originated the consciousness from it.

(iv) In *Kenopanishad* **She** has been described as; *"Bahushopamānām Umām Haimavateem"*.

635. ***Gowree* - गौरी**

(i) One who is of fair complexion.

(ii) Yellowish white colour is called as *Gowra*: i.e of gold colour.

(iii) *Devee Purāŋa* says, when *Śreedevee* incarnated as daughter of *Himavān*, her complexion was as white as conch, or Moon or jasmine flower. Hence **She** was called as *Gowree*; *Chankhakunḍandu Varŋā Chetyato Gowreeti Sā Smruta*.

(iv) The consort of *Varuŋa* (god of water) is also called as *Gowree*. A girl 10 years of age is also called *Gowree*. Since *Śreedevee* is of these forms, **She** is called as *Gowree*.

(v) According to *Padma Purāŋa* the presiding deity of *Kānyagupta Peeṭa* is called as *Gowree*; *Kānya Kuje Tadā Gowree*.

(vi) The *Uttamacharitram* of *Saptashatee* says that *Mahāsaraswatee*, who destroyed the demons *Shumba* and *Nishumba*, originated from *Śreedevee*'s body.

636. ***Gandharvasevitā* - गन्धर्वसेविता**

(i) One who is worshipped by *Visuvāvasu* and other *Gandharvās*, who are celestial musicians.
(ii) Almost the verses about all the gods mention that they were praised by the songs of two *Gandharvās* called *Hāhā* and *Hoohoo*. This implies that the songs of *Gandharvās* are an important part of every *pooja*; the name in *Trishatee* as *Hāhā Hoohoo Mukhasttya* may be referred here.
(iii) The word *Gandharva* also means horse. The head of horse wing of *Śreedevee*'s army is *Ashvāroo*ḍ*ha*. *Śreedevee* was worshipped by her.
(iv) The songs of *devas* are called *Gandharvam*. **She** was served with such songs.

637. ***Vishvagarbhā* - विश्वगर्भा**

(i) One whose womb contains the universe.
(ii) The corpulent visible universe is called *Vishvam*. **She** contains this universe in her womb.

638. ***Svarŋagarbhā* - स्वर्णगर्भा**

(i) One who is in the form of *Hiraŋyagarbha*.
(ii) One who contained gold in her womb. For the word *Suvarŋa* – *Su* + *Varŋa* – excellent letter (alphabet). i.e. **She** has *mantras* with holy *beejams* in her womb.
(iii) **She** gives holiness to the *Mātrukās* (*beejāksharas*). I.e. since **She** has them in **Her** *mantras* they become *Suvarnas* (holy or excellent) and contained in **Her** womb.
(iv) *Hiraŋyagarbhā* is interested in the group of subtle bodies. This group shines like gold. Hence he was called as *Hiraŋyagarbha*. The same is called as *Svarŋagarbhā* also.

639. ***Avaradā* - अवरदा**

(i) One who defeated the demons.
(ii) *Avara* means dishonest people, one who does cruel and low class. **She** punishes and controls them.
(iii) If it is split as *Ava* + *Radā*, it will mean – one who has shining teeth.

(iv) The single word *Svarŋagarbhāvaradā* has been split into two names and described as *Svarŋagarbhā + Avarada*. If it is taken as *Svarŋagarbhā + Varadā*, it would mean as one who bestows boons. Since the name *Varadā* (331st) is already there, this name has been taken as *Avarada*.

640. *Vāgadheeshvaree* - वागधीश्वरी

(i) One who is the head of speech.
(ii) **She** is the head of the eight *Vasinee* and other *Vāg Devees*. That is the reason, they wrote this *Sahasranāma*, by **Her** order.
(iii) **She** has *Vāgvādinee*, who is the head of speech and letters, as her part. Hence *Vāgadheeshvaree*.
(iv) *Śree Ādi Śaṇkara* says, in his 100th verse of *Soundaryalaharee* that all types of letters, words and speeches belong to *Śreedevee* only;
Tvadeeyābhir Vākbhis Tava Janani Vāchām Stutiriyam.

641. *Dhyānagamyā* - ध्यानगम्या

(i) One who can be attained by meditation.
(ii) Meditation is to keep the mind stuck to one place. When we try to keep *Śreedevee*'s form in mind and focus the thoughts on her, other thoughts would distract the mind. Bringing back again and again this wavering mind back to the thoughts of *Śreedevee* is called *Dhārana*. Settling this and focusing on **Her** is called meditation. She can be attained only by meditation.
(iii) The *Svetāsvatara Upanishad* (1-3) also says the same message as, the sages devoted to meditation, saw the *shakti* of the divine Self-hidden by its own qualities; *Te Dhyānayogānugatā Apashyan Devātmashaktim Svaguŋai Nigoodhām*.
(iv) If this name is read in conjunction with the previous name it will mean, by talking about *Śreedevee*, we get attracted and get interested in her. Hence **She** can be focused by meditation.
(v) 119th and 120th names *Bhaktigamyā* and *Bhaktivashyā* may be compared.

642. *Aparicchedyā* - अपरिच्छेद्या

(i) One who is indivisible by anything.
(ii) Space, time and thought neither limit nor divide **Her**. **She** is always

omnipresent.

(iii) But still, **She** is controllable through meditation and worship.

643. *Gnānadā* - ज्ञानदा

(i) One who bestows knowledge.

(ii) Knowledge is of two types. As discussed in the previous name, attaining the complete form of *Śreedevee*, who is not limited by anything. The second is – thinking this un-soul body and universe as soul – this is actually ignorance. *Śreedevee* only gives both these.

(iii) *Gnānadā* – bestower of knowledge. *Agnānadā* – who cuts off/ removes ignorance.

(iv) *Śree Bhāskararāya* explains by combining two of the *Shiva Sūtras* viz. *Gnānam Banda* and *Gnānam Annam*. These are not further dwelled here.

644. *Gnānavigrahā* - ज्ञानविग्रहा

(i) One who whose form is knowledge.

(ii) The three - the knower, the knowledge and the object of knowledge – is called *Tripudee*. **She** is of the form hiding all these and only remaining is the knowledge/ supreme bliss.

(iii) *Vigraha* means expand. With the blessings of *Śreedevee* the knowledge expands further and knowledge only will remain at the end. Our little knowledge expands and become the supreme one.

645. *Sarvavedāntasamvedyā* - सर्ववेदान्तसंवेद्या

(i) One who is known through all the *Upanishads*.

(ii) Upanishads are the last part of *Vedas* and indicate the form/ philosophy of *Brahmam*. Since that form is *Śreedevee*, **She** is known through *Upanishads*.

(iii) *Brahma Sūtra* also says; *Sāstrayonitvāt*.

(iv) *Śreemad Bhagavad Geeta* (XV-15) also says; *Vedaishcha Sarvairahameva Vedya*:.

(v) The *Varāha Purāņa* says - This *Śreedevee* is explained as the threefold energy and set forth as the end of logic. **She** is the energy of wisdom, set forth in all the *Vedāntas*.

646. *Satyānandasvaroopiŋee* - सत्यानन्दस्वरूपिणी

(i) One who is Supreme knowledge and bliss.
(ii) The word *Sat* means eternal or indestructible. Bliss is pure happiness - form of *Brahmam*. That *Brahmam* is *Śreedevee*.
(iii) The form of *Brahmam* is called as *Satchitānandam* indicated as three *Sat* + *Chit* + *Ānandam*. Among this *Chit* is knowledge. Earlier described by 644th name – *Gnānavigraha*. The remaining two *Satyam* and *Ānandam* are indicated by this name.
(iv) In some schools this name is considered as two names viz. *Satyā* and *Ānandasvaroopiŋee*. In that case 616th and 617th names *Ameyā* and *Ātmā* are merged as a single name *Ameyatma*.
(v) As per the *Veda* statement; *Stiti Prāŋasteetyannamayam Ityasāvāditya*: - the word *Satyā* indicates *Prāŋam* (breath), *Annam* (food) and *Ādityam* (Sun).
(vi) It also means as **She** has a liking over *Sat*. I.e. **She** is in the form of *Satyabama*.

647. *Lopāmudrārchitā* - लोपामुद्रार्चिता

(i) One who was worshipped by *Lopāmudra*.
(ii) *Lopāmudrā* is the wife of sage *Agasthya*. She is called as *Lopā*, since she does not have interest on the forms which are ironically indicated by names.
(iii) *Lopāmudrā* is one of the greatest devotees of *Śreedevee*. She is the founder of *Hādi Vidyā mantra*, which is another version of *Śreevidya*. In *Trishatee*, *Śreedevee* herself has indicated her as an important devotee; "*Patnyasya Lopā Mudrākhyā Mām Upāste Atibhaktita:*".
(iv) *Tripurasiddānta* says that there is no difference between the *mantra*, the sage who found the *mantra* and the presiding deity. Accordingly *Śreedevee* got this name. It can also be meant as **She** is prayed as *Lopāmudrā* herself.
(v) **She** is worshipped with *Hādividyā* also called as *Lopāmudrā Vidya*.

648. *Leelākluptabrahmaŋḍamaŋḍalā* – लीलाक्लुप्तब्रह्माण्डमण्डला

(i) One for whom the creation of many a universe is just a game.
(ii) That means, She does the task of creation effortlessly and without any fatigue.
(iii) 281st name *Unmesha Nimishotpanna Vipannabhuvanāvalee* also

indicates the same sense.

(iv) By the word *Kluptam* the value system in creation is indicated. Every living being and things follow some system in the universe, indicated by the word *Kluptam*. The precision and the quality of the creation task are mentioned here.

649. *Adrushyā* - अदृश्या

(i) One who is invisible.

(ii) Not to be perceived by eyes and other senses or organs.

(iii) *Drushyā* means one who is seen. It is not to be felt by mere sight, but to be recognised/ understood. Hence not perceived by any senses.

(iv) The *Brahādāraŋya Upanishad* (III-4-2) says, "You do not see the seer of sight". The *Devee Bhāgavatam* (book III) says, "Your unqualified form is not an object of visual perception. *Shakti* is without quality, difficult or approach. The Supreme Person also is without qualities".

650. *Drushyarahitā* - दृश्यरहिता

(i) One who is without any object of seeing.

(ii) **She** cannot be perceived, since **She** does not have any attributes that are felt by human senses through objects, qualities, actions, forms and organs.

(iii) Without any attributes, **She** can only be seen by the intellect.

651. *Vignātree* - विज्ञात्री

(i) One who has special intelligence.

(ii) Her form cannot be perceived.

(iii) **She** is within every soul and makes him scientifically knowledgeable.

(iv) The *Brhādāraŋya Upanishad* (II-4-14) says, "O, how is the knower to be known?" - **She** is the power behind all knowledge as *Chit Shakti*, but distinct from the object of knowledge.

652. *Vedyavarjitā* - वेद्यवर्जिता

(i) One who has nothing more to know.

(ii) Being omniscient, **She** does not have anything more to know.

(iii) *Nityā Shoḍasikārnavam* says, since **She** is the supreme knowledge, there is no one to know her;

Atyāpi Yasyā Jānanti Na Manāgapi Devatā: I
Keyam Susmāt Kva Keneti Saroopāroopa Bhāvanam II

653. ***Yoginee* - योगिनी**

(i) One who has a *Yoga* form.
(ii) *Yoga* means union (based on the root *Yuj*). Hence **She** is called as *Yoginee*.

654. ***Yogadā* - योगदा**

(i) One who bestows *Yoga* to votaries.

655. ***Yogyā* - योग्या**

(i) One who can be reached through *Yoga*.
(ii) The *yoga* bestowed by **Her** is the route to reach **Her**.
(iii) *Yoga* is the assumption of union. Since **She** is in that form and since **She** bestows that to the devotees, **She** is in the form known by the same. This has been described by the three names (653 to 655) *Yoginee*, *Yogadā* and *Yogya*.
(iv) *Yoga* has four parts – *mantra, laya, hata* and *rāja*. *Rājayoga* has three parts – *Sānkya, Tāraka* and *Amanska*. These details are to be learnt from *Yoga sāstra*.
(v) Similarly in Astronomy also there are *devatas* starting from *Mangala* till *Sankata*. Since **She** is in all these forms, **She** is *Yoginee*.

656. ***Yogānandā* - योगानन्दा**

(i) One who is in the form of bliss got through *Yoga*.
(ii) The unison of *Shiva* and *Shakti* is called *Yoga*. The bliss got through this is *Yogānandam*.
(iii) The thought of external world is forgotten during sleep. This is also *Yogānandam* only. *Śreedevee* is in this self-bliss form.
(iv) She is in the form of *Yoganarashimhar* called as *Yogānandar*.
(v) This name can also be split into two as *Ayogā* + *Nanda*. In that case 562nd and 563rd names *Mohinee* and *Mukhyā* have to be merged as a single name.
(vi) The name *Ayogā* means *Asankā* – to be extinct. Or in the form of *Aya*

(iron) mountain. Like a mountain **She** is impartial. **She** takes the devotees along to *Paramashiva.*

(vii) The word *Nanda* indicates river Ganges called as *Alagānanda*. **She** is in that form. The first, sixth and eleventh days of bright lunar fortnight are called *Nanda*. According to *Chanḍi Saptashatee* statement; *Nandā Bhagavatee Nāma Yā Bhavishyati Nandajā* – since **She** was born as daughter of *Nandagopa*, **She** is called as *Nanda*. *Padma Purāṇa* says – The river *Saraswatee*, when flows near *Himāchala*, is called as *Nandā*; *"Nandā Himavat Prushte"*.

(viii) A river flowing near the *Pushkara Kshetra* is called *Nanda*. The reason for this name is mentioned differently in various books;

Yathāgatam Tu Te Jagmu: *Deveem Sthāpya Hime Girou*
Samsthāpyānanditā Yasmāt Tasmān Nandā Tu Sābhavat ll
Nandate Suralokeshu Nandane Vasate'tavā l
Himāchale Mahāpuṇye Nandā Devee Tata: *Smrutā* ll

657. *Yugandharā* - युगंधरा

(i) One who supports the *yuga* (era).

(ii) The word *yuga* has many a meaning - four elbow measures, yoke, *Kruta* and other *yugas* (eras), pair and an herb called *vruddhi*.

(iii) *Kruta* and other *yugas* are supported only by the *Shiva Shakti* form and hence *Yugandhara*.

658. *Ichchāshaktignānashaktikriyāshaktisvaroopiṇee* – इच्छाशक्तिर्ज्ञानशक्तिक्रियाशक्तिस्वरूपिणी

(i) One who is in forms of three energies of desire, wisdom and action.

(ii) To do any task we need these three – the desire to do (*Icchā Shakti*), the knowledge of know-how to do (*Gnāna Shakti*) and the action (*Kriyā Shakti*). All these three forms are *Śreedevee* only.

(iii) These three energies can be seen in the *Chanḍi Saptashatee* in *Mārkaṇḍeya Purāṇa*. In the first book, the destruction of the demons *Madhu* and *Kaidapa* is done just by desire (*Icchā Shakti*). In the second book the destruction of the demon *Mahishāsura* is done by *Śreedevee* directly (the outburst of *kriyāshakti*). In the third book, the king called *Suradā* and the businessman called *Samādi* get the knowledge from *Mahāsaraswatee* (the action of *gnāna shakti*). The serial of the three energies is a little modified here as I*chchā Shakti*, *Kriyā Shakti* and *Gnāna Shakti*.

(iv) Desire is head, wisdom trunk and action feet, thus the three energies are **Her** body organs only.
(v) These three energies are forms of *Brahma*, *Viṣhŋu* and *Shiva* viz., *Vāmā*, *Jeshtā* and *Roudree*. They do the three tasks – creation, protection and destruction. *Śreedevee* is head of these three.

659. ***Sarvādhārā* - सर्वाधारा**

(i) One who is the supporter of all.
(ii) The three energies discussed in the previous name are the supporter of everything happening in this world. Hence **She** is *Sarvādhāra*.
(iii) **She** has all the supports as **Her** form.
(iv) *Sarvā*, the whole world, *dhārā*, gradation, i.e., **She** is one with created things. It is called as *Parampara* (race), since everything originates one after another from the previous one.

660. ***Supratishṭhā* - सुप्रतिष्ठा**

(i) One who is firmly/ propitiously established.
(ii) That means, **She** is established and gives felicity to the entire universe.
(iii) She supports and gives auspicious to everything in this world. Hence eternal.
(iv) *Suprathisṭhā* is a metre of twenty syllables. **She** is of that form.

661. ***Sadasadroopadhāriŋee* - सदसद्रूपधारिणी**

(i) One who is the form of being and non-being.
(ii) *Sat* is eternal and *asat* is impermanent. Both are the forms of *Śreedevee* only.
(iii) *Sat* is *Brahmam*, which is eternal and the *asat* is the universe which originated from *sat* and is destructible. **She** is in the form of this universe and hence impermanent. It does not mean that it is not available from the root. All activities are till the beginning of the universe only. In that case (256th name) *Vishvaroopā* and (934th name) *Vishvamāta*. The form of *Brahmam* is also herself. Hence this combined name.
(iv) When seen from the angle of the soul **She** is split into two both *sat* and *asat*. But seen from **Her** both are same – *sat* only.
(v) *Skanda Purāŋa* says;

Yatyatasti Tayā Bhātiyannāsti Tayabhi Cha I
Tat Tat Sarvam Mahādeva Māyayā Parikalpitam II

(vi) *Māŋikkavāchakar*, a Tamil poet, said; *"Unmaiyumāi Inmaiyumai"* – Both as truth and lie. *Aruŋagirināda* said; *"Ulatāi Ilatāi"* – Both existent and not existent.

662. *Ashṭamoortti*: - अष्टमूर्त्तिः

(i) One who is eight formed.
(ii) The eight forms are given differently. Eight mothers, eight *vāg-devatas*, eight forms of *Shiva s*, eight parts of nature and based on *Matsya Purāŋa* (*Lakshmee* & other eight forms). These are;

Mother	***Vāg Devee***	**Forms of *Shivas***	***Shakti* forms of *Shiva***	**Parts of nature**	**As per *Matsya Purāŋa***
Brāhmee	*Vasinee*	*Bhavan*	Earth	Earth	*Lakshmee*
Mahendree	*Kāmeshwaree*	*Sarvan*	Water	Water	*Medā*
Koumāree	*Mohinee*	*Eesānan*	Fire	Fire	*Darā*
Vaiṣhŋavee	*Vimalā*	*Pashupati*	Air	Air	*Pushṭi*
Vārāhee	*Aruŋā*	*Rudran*	Ether	Ether	*Gowree*
Māhendree	*Jayinee*	*Ukran*	Sun	Mind	*Tushṭi*
Chāmuŋḍā	*Sarveshvaree*	*Bheeman*	Moon	Intellect	*Prabhā*
Mahālakshmee	*Koulinee*	*Mahān*	Master	Ego	*Druti*

(iii) It can also be considered that this name indicates the eight *kulas* (i.e. eight kinds of women) based on *Koulāchāra*. They are - *Ganikā, Shoundikā, Kaivarti, Rajaki, Tanrakāree, Charmakāree, Mātangee* and *Pumschali*;

Ganikā Shoundiee, Chaiva Kaivarttee Rajakee Tathā I
Tantrankāree Charmakāree Mātangee, Pumschalee Tathā II

663. *Ajājetree* - अजाजेत्री

(i) One who is the conqueror of ignorance (*Avidyā*).
(ii) The word *Ajā* means *Avidyā* (ignorance). **She** has won it. Or help the devotees to win over it. **She**, who is the form of knowledge herself, bestows knowledge and wins over ignorance.

664. *Lokayātrāvidhāyinee* - लोकयात्राविधायिनी

(i) One who directs the course of the world's continuous travel.
(ii) The world's travel seems to be endless since every second the world originates, stays and ends.
(iii) the world originates, stays and ends does not mean that in its entirety at a time. In this world some living beings originate and some to an end. In between these two some continue to survive. This seems to be a cyclic travel. She has the capacity to run this show effectively. This cycle includes the various states described by De- Sitter and Einstein.

665. ***Ekākinee* - एकाकिनी**

(i) One who is alone.
(ii) **She** is alone because **She** is without a backup. The 623rd name *Kevalā* may be compared.
(iii) Whether it is destruction of ignorance or (as discussed in the previous name) in effectively running the world's travel, **She** does everything alone.
(iv) *Śree Ādi Śaṇkara* in his commentary of *Vișhṇu Sahasranāma* for the 725th name – *Eka*: mentions; since he is the concluded truth without any kind of differences that are internal or that relates to similar external objects or to dissimilar object, he is *Ekaha*.
(v) *Chāndokya Upansihad* (6-2-1) says; '*Ekamevātvteeyam*'.

666. ***Bhoomaroopā* - भूमरूपा**

(i) One who is the aggregate of all existing things.
(ii) The word *Bhooma* means *Brahmam*. **She** is in the form of *Brahmam*.
(iii) The word *Bhooma* also means many. As mentioned in the previous name "**She** is one", but with this name, "**She** is many".
(iv) Actually what is seen as a single form of *Brahmam* in a supreme state, is seen as many in the nature of this universe.
(v) Many forms of *Śreedevee* have been described in detail in *Devee Purāṇa*.

667. ***Nirdvaitā* - निर्द्वैता**

(i) One who is non-dual i.e., without duality.
(ii) *Dvaita* means the feeling of the existence of another one in addition to self. **She** does not have it.

(iii) When the soul is thought of different from the Supreme Being - it is *dvaita* (duality) condition. Once this is gone, only the *Brahmam* indicated by the names *Ekākinee* and *Kevalā* is seen then it is *advaita* (non-dual). Such is *Śreedevee* or **She** endows such state.
(iv) **She** does not have even an iota of anything as non-dual.

668. *Dvaitavarjitā* - द्वैतवर्जिता

(i) One who removed the state of duality (*dvaita*) i.e., the state of feeling the second one.
(ii) The message conveyed in the previous name is more clearly stressed in this name.
(iii) The names so far read conveyed the sense that there was a feeling of duality and that has been destroyed by **Her**. This name is given to remove such a feeling. The state of duality is an unreal form. That was not there to remove. At any point of time, there was no other thing other than *Śreedevee*, who is the form of *Brahmam*.

669. *Annadā* - अन्नदा

(i) One who is the giver of food for the entire universe.
(ii) Befitting the name "Mother of Universe", **She** protects the entire universe by giving food. In this task of giving food, **She** is called *Annapoorani*. **She** has a vessel full of food in one hand and a ladle, to serve it, in another hand. *Śree Ādi Śaṇkara* prays as;

Annapooraŋe Sadāpoorŋe Shankaraprāŋavallabhe I
Gnāna Vairāgya Sityartam Bhikshām Dehi Cha Pārvati II

Before taking food, if this verse is prayed and imagined that *Śreedevee* only gave us food and that there will be no blemish of food will affect us - body fat, knowledge and zeal will be got.

670. *Vasudā* - वसुदा

(i) One who is giver of wealth to all.
(ii) The word *Vasu* has many a meaning as – wealth, gem, gold, etc., **She** gives all these.
(iii) The very essence of this name is – the necessity of the feeling that any enjoyable wealth we get in this world are all due to her blessings only.
(iv) About this *Annam* and *Vasu*, *Veda* says; "*Sa Vā Esha Mahānaja*

Ātmānnādo Vasudāno Vindate Vasu Ya Evam Veda".

671. ***Vruddhā* - वृद्धा**

(i) One who is senior in age.
(ii) Since **She** is there before everything else, **She** is the most ancient and hence **She** is oldest. According to *Svetāsvatara Upanishad* (IV-3)- Thou, as an old man tottering along on thy staff;
Tvam Jeernā Dandena Vanchasi.
(iii) Or **She** is in the form of completely grown and matured world. It can also be taken that **She** nourishes the world.

672. ***Brahmatmaikyasvaroopiŋee* - ब्रह्मात्मैक्यस्वरूपिणी**

(i) One who in the form of the unified *Brahmam* (supreme being) and *Ātman* (soul).
(ii) The content of *Mahā* statements such as "*Aham Brahmāsmi*" and great *mantras* like '*Soham*' indicate that through the un-chanting *mantra* the *Brahmam* has to be realised in breath of every soul. That is the real form of *Śreedevee*.
(iii) *Aham* indicates the soul and *Sa* indicates *Parameshwara*. The *Hamsa mantra* unites the soul with *Shiva*.
(iv) During inhalation and exhalation of every breath, the feel of *Hamsa*: *Soham mantra* is called *Ajapa* (un-chanting) *mantra*. Instead of chanting the *mantra* separately the breathing itself is considered as chanting of *mantra* and hence it is called un-chanting (*Ajapa*). On the average everyday each of us breath 21600 times. That means we do *Ajapamantra* so many times every day.
(v) The dance of *Thiagarāja* in *Tiruvaroor* is called as *Ajapa* dance. The chest of *Viṣhŋu*, in the lying pose, goes up and down on account of his breathing. *Parameshwar* dances on his chest and hence it is called as *Ajapa* dance.
(vi) 173rd name of *Trishatee – Hamsamantrārttha Roopinee* describes the same meaning.

673. ***Bruhatee* - बृहती**

(i) One who has an immensely great form.
(ii) *Veda* says; *Mahato Maheeyān* – bigger than the biggest.
(iii) Some *Sāma mantras*, called as *Brhatsāman*, are part of *Sāma Veda*.

She is in that form.

(iv) A metre with 36 letters is called *Bruhatee*. **She** is in that form.

(v) *Bruhat* and *Jeshtā* are the words with equal meaning and hence these two indicate *Śreedevee*.

674. *Brāhmaŋee* - ब्राह्मणी

(i) A brahmin lady.

(ii) According to the *Vishva* dictionary the word *Brāhmaŋi* has many a meaning viz., harlot, a brahmin lady, a certain herbal plant, wisdom, etc. **She** is of all these forms.

(iii) The *Samayācāra Smruti* says, *Brāhmaŋi* means divine wisdom crowned with the white flower (*satva*); "*Brāhmani Sveta Pushpādyā Samvitsā Devatātmika*".

(iv) Among the three gods *Shiva* is considered as *brahmin* and *Viṣhŋu* as *kshatriya*. The *Chāndogya Upanishad* (VIII-14-I) says - Thou art *brāhmana* among the *Devas*, I am the *brāhmana* among men, (he who thinks thus) attains *Brahmam*. In the same way, the *Parāsara, Aditya, Koorma, Vāshishṭa* and *Linga Purāŋas* also confirm this – *Shambhu*, the divine consort of *Śreedevee*, is *Brāhmana* and is the deity of *Brāhmanas*. A *Brāhmana* especially should take refuge in *Rudra*, the Lord;

Brahmaŋo Bhagavān Sambo Brāhmanānām Hi Daivatam I
Viseshāt Brāhmano Rudram Esānam Sharanam Vraja II

Being consort of *Shiva,* **She** is *Brāhmanee*, because *Shiva* belongs to the *Brahmin* caste.

675. *Brāhmee* - ब्राह्मी

(i) One who is in the form of *Saraswatee*, the consort of *Brahma*.

(ii) **She** is in the form of speech and hence can be taken as *Vāgeeshwaree*.

(iii) The senior most among the eight mothers. **She** shines alongwith the vehicle swan, the chanting garland (*japamālā*) and *kamaŋḍalu* (a vessel with water used by sages) in hand. **She** killed the enemies just by sprinkling the water from *kamaŋḍalu* through *darbha* (a sacrificial grass).

676. *Brahmānandā* - ब्रह्मानन्दा

(i) One who is in the form of supreme bliss.
(ii) **She** has *Brahmam* itself as bliss for **Her**.
(iii) The form of *Śreedevee* is called as frozen bliss. *Śree Krișhŋa* has been mentioned in many places as; *Sāntrānandatanu* – one who has the supreme bliss as his body. That is applicable to *Śreedevee* also.

677. *Balipriyā* - बलिप्रिया

(i) One who is delighted with the mighty.
(ii) *Dheera* or *Bali*, those who are able to succeed by destroying ignorance. **She** is fond of them.
(iii) One who conquers the enemies like amorousness, desire, etc., can be called as *Bali*. She blesses them with affection.
(iv) During the incarnation as *Vāmanā*, *Vișhŋu* had compassion over the emperor *Bali*. This name indicates that form.
(v) During worship, for the satisfaction of deities, some articles are offered as *bali*. **She** accepts them with hilarity.

678. *Bhāshāroopā* - भाषारूपा

(i) One who is the form of languages.
(ii) Since **She** is the head of speeches, all languages are **Her** form only.
(iii) Based on the phrase; *Bhāshābhi*: *Roopyate* – **Her** form is identified only through languages. **She** can be recognised by speech.

679. *Bruhatsenā* – बृहत्सेना

(i) One who is with a mighty army.
(ii) **She** is very much capable of doing the tasks of creation, protection and destruction by **Herself**. However, just to give a share and pride in the task, **She** creates a huge army and gets her tasks completed through them.
(iii) *Bruhatsenā* is also the name of a certain king's race. **She** is in the form of those kings.

680. *Bhāvābhāvavivarjitā* - भावाभावविवर्जिता

(i) One who is in the form of existence and non-existence.
(ii) **She** neither has an origin nor an end.

(iii) *Bhāvā* means the state existence and *Abhāva* means non-existence. If *Śreedevee* is considered as not to have the existence status, then it may mean that She is non-existent. On the other hand, if **She** is considered as not to have the non-existence status, then it may mean that **She** is existent. If **She** is not in both the states, then what is it? Everything in the world has anyone of the states – existent of non-existent. For instance – rice is existent. After cooking rice is non-existent, but food is existent. Once it is eaten, the food is non-existent and the blood, etc., of the person who consumed the food, is existent. *Śreedevee* does not completely have such states. That Supreme Being is eternal.

681. ***Sukhārādhyā* - सुखाराध्या**

(i) One who can be worshiped comfortably without much effort.
(ii) **She** can be worshipped without bodily pain of fasting, etc. and without restrictions on the mode of meditations putting the body to great strain.
(iii) To worship **Her**, imagining any of the forms in mind as *Śreedevee* is enough. Other restrictions like those required in worshipping any other gods are needed only to change the *rajo* and *tamo* qualities. But to worship *Śreedevee*, only the devotion is required and no other tool is required. Hence worshipping *Śreedevee* is very easy.
(iv) The easiness of *Śreedevee*'s worship has been described in detail in *Tripurasamhimnā Stora*, *Katastava* and *Koorma Purāŋa*.

682. ***Shubhakaree* - शुभकरी**

(i) One who bestows auspicious to **Her** devotees.
(ii) In the previous name it was mentioned that **She** can be worshipped easily. The devotees might get a doubt whether any sin or annihilation will happen by not following the fasting and other requirements. To remove any such doubt this name stresses that **She** grants auspiciousness to **Her** devotees.

683. ***Shobhanā Sulabhā Gati*: - शोभना सुलभा गतिः**

(i) One whose path is lustrous and easy to traverse.
(ii) The word *gati* has many a meaning – the targeted place to reach, goal, way, destiny, knowledge, etc.

(iii) The word *Shobhanā* means great auspicious. *Sulabhā* means easily attainable. *Gati* means salvation. This name is a combination of all these three words. In *archana* this name has to be used as *Shobhanāyai Sulabhāyai Gatyai*.

(iv) To reach the salvation easily, She can be worshipped comfortably.

(v) In this *Sahasranāma* the word *Shobhanā* occurs thrice – 462nd name, this one and 972nd. To remove the criticism of duplication 462nd name is called as *Shobhanayai*, this name as *Shobhanā Sulabha Gati*: and 972nd as *Āshobhana*.

(vi) In this way if this name is split into two as *Shobhanāgati*: and *Sulabhāgati*:. In that case the 827th and 828th names are combined as a single name as *Prachaŋḍagna*.

(vii) This name can also be split into *Shobhanā* + *Asulabhā* + *Āgati*. *Āgati* means without rebirth. *Asulabhā* means difficult to attain. I.e. even the difficult to attain non-rebirth can easily be attained.

(viii) Very rare/ dear human birth becomes auspicious only by the blessings of *Śreedevee*.

(ix) When this name is split into three, 462nd name *Shobhanā* and 463rd*Suranayikā* are combined as a single name by some schools.

684. ***Rājarājeshvaree* - राजराजेश्वरी**

(i) One who is the ruler of the king of kings.

(ii) **She** is the head of the heads of eight directions and also *Brahma*, *Viṣhŋu* and *Shiva*.

(iii) *Kubera* (the god of wealth) is also called as *Rājarāja*. **She** is head of him.

685. ***Rājyadāyinee* - राज्यदायिनी**

(i) One who bestows dominions

(ii) *Rājyam* indicates liberation or *Vaikuŋta* or *Kailasa*. She gives these.

(iii) The heads of directions are indicated by the word *Rājarāja* in the previous name. **She** only gives those posts/ roles to them.

(iv) The word *Rājya* is of three types;

   a. *Vairrajya* – belongs to *Virāt* – the group head of all objects which have physical forms.
   b. *Bhaujya* – the group subtle form *Svarāt* – **She** is head of this.
   c. *Sāmrāt* – indicating unmanifested – unmanifested is the cause of distinction between physical and subtle forms.

686. *Rājyavallabhā* - राज्यवल्लभा

(i) One who is a capable dominion.

(ii) By the word *Rājya* in the previous name indicated all kingdoms and the corresponding heads like *Brahma*, *Indra* and others. *Śreedevee* has affection in all such kings. The sage *Durvāsa* in his book called *Aryā Tvisatee* mentions that these kings wait between the 13th and 14th halls of *Śreepura*, for the sight of *Śreedevee*.

687. *Rājatkrupā* - राजत्कृपा

(i) One who gloriously shines with compassion.

(ii) Since **She** is the form of a mother, **She** is full of compassion.

688. *Rājapeeṭhaniveshitanijāshritā* – राजपीठनिवेशितनिजाश्रिता

(i) One who raises those whose resort to **Her** to royal status.

(ii) **She** gives the posts of *Indra*, etc., to her devotees. There are lots of instances like *Druva*, *Suradha* (*Saptashatee*), etc.

(iii) The real devotees do not accept, treating as mean, such posts of kings or *Devas* when offered by *Śreedevee*. **She** bestows still better status like great *Brahmam* to them.

689. *Rājyalakshmee*: - राज्यलक्ष्मीः

(i) One who is in the form of goddess of sovereignty.

(ii) The word *Rājyalakshmee* indicates the entire wealth of all kings, *devas* like *Indra* and others. **She** is in that form.

(iii) The *mantra* of such *Rājyalakshmee* has been described in *Tantra Rāja*.

690. *Koshanāthā* - कोशनाथा

(i) One who presides over a treasure.

(ii) *Kosha* means a treasure of the government. **She** is the head of all the wealth in it.

(iii) Our physical body is made of five types of sheaths viz., *Annamaya* (food), *Prāṇamaya* (breath), *Manomaya* (mind), *Vignānamaya* (science) and *Ānandamaya* (bliss). **She** being the head of all these sheaths, bless her devotees with origin, life, thought, ego and happiness.

691. ***Chaturangabaleshvaree* - चतुरन्गबलेश्वरी**

(i) One who is the ruler of four types of armies.

(ii) Four types of armies consisting of cavalry, elephants, chariots and infantry; or the four kinds of military arrays. For the soul there are four faculties' viz., mind, intellect, volition and ego. The four aggregates are three gods looking after the task of creation, protection and destruction and the god supervising these three tasks. In general *Brahma, Viṣhṇu, Rudra* and *Eshwara* the four; according to the *Vaishnavas* they are *Pratyumnar, Anirudhar, Sankarshanar* and *Vāsudevar*. According to *Śāktas, Vāmā, Jyeshtā, Roudhree* and *Ambikā* (295th). Thus **She** is the head of everything that are four-fold.

(iii) According to the *Bahvrucho Upanishad*, it means the person in the body, the person in the metre, the person in the *Veda* and the Great Person. **She** is the ruler of all these four.

(iv) 679th name *Bruhatsenā* may be compared.

692. ***Sāmrājyadāyinee* - साम्राज्यदायिनी**

(i) One who bestows imperial dominion to **Her** devotees.

(ii) As indicated in the earlier in (685th name) *Rājyadāyinee*, **She** directly or immediately blesses the devotees with *Sāmrājya*, which is greater than the other three types of *rājyas*.

(iii) That is, **She** bestows the emperor or *Maṇḍaleshwara* status.

693. ***Satyasandhā* - सत्यसन्धा**

(i) One who has unbroken promises or respects.

(ii) The promises of *Śreedevee* and limited respects cannot be broken by anybody. 995th name *Sarvānullanghya Shāsana* may be compared.

(iii) **She** is so adamant in keeping up her words and promises.

(iv) **She** has promised to protect the entire universe and **She** is stubborn in that.

(v) *Śree Ādi Śaṇkara* in his commentary of *Viṣhṇu Sahasranāma* for the 610th name – *Satyasanda*: mentions; *Satya* – truth, *Sandha* – intention – Since he has the intention to keep up the truth, everything will happen according to his thought.

(vi) *Chāndogya Upanishad* (8-1-5) says; *Satya Sankalpa*.

694. ***Sāgaramekhalā* - सागरमेखला**

(i) One who has oceans as girdles.
(ii) Since *Śreedevee* is in the form of this earth, the oceans are treated as girdles around **Her** waist.
(iii) In the midst of the boisterous oceans, **She** in the form of this earth, stays static with unlimited patience.

695. ***Deekshitā* - दीक्षिता**

(i) One who helps others to gain knowledge.
(ii) The *Atharva Samhita* says - Next, therefore, *Deekshā*, from which root *Deekshita* is derived. They call the man who is initiated *deekshita*; Starts as – *"Athāto Deekshā Kasyasvit Hedhor Deekshita Ityāchakshate"* and ends with *"Tam Vā Etam Deekshitam Santam Deekshita Ityāchakshte"*.
(iii) *Deeksha* means destroying the sin of **Her** disciples by invocating the *mantras*. That is the duty of the teachers. Since *Śreedevee* is in the form of *Gurumoortti* (603rd name) **She** is *Deekshita*.
(iv) It has been mentioned earlier also that there is no difference between the teacher, the *mantra* and presiding deity. Hence **She** is integrated with the disciple.
(v) During *yāgās* (sacrificial fire) the master is called as *Deekshitan*. It can be considered that **She** is in that form.

696. ***Daityashamanee* - दैत्यशमनी**

(i) One who quells the demons/ evil forces.
(ii) **She** killed demons like *Bhanḍa*, *Mahisha*, *Shumbha*, *Nishumbha* and many others.
(iii) The word *Shama* means to control. **She** controls the evil thoughts arising in the minds of **Her** devotees.

697. ***Sarvalokavashankaree* - सर्वलोकवशंकरी**

(i) One who keeps all the worlds under her sway.
(ii) *Śreedevee*, in the form of *Ichchā Shakti* (energy of desire) has the power to run all the worlds as per **Her** wish. The world created by **Her**

runs as per **Her** wish.

(iii) **She** makes the world a subjection of **Her** devotees.

698. ***Sarvārthadātree* - सर्वार्थदात्री**

(i) One who bestows all the (four –*dharma* [righteousness], *arttha* [wealth], *kāma* [desires] and *moksha* [salvation]) objects of human endeavour.

(ii) By considering the meaning for the word *Arttha* as wealth, it can be taken as **She** bestows all the wealth for Her devotees.

699. ***Sāvitree* - सावित्री**

(i) One who is in the form of *Sāvithree*, the creator of the world.

(ii) The creator of this universe is called *Savitā*, a form of *Paramashiva.* His consort is *Sāvitree*.

(iii) The world is seen because of Sun – i.e. it is known to all through the light of Sun. Hence he is also called as *Savitā* or *Sāvithree*.

(iv) Since **She** is worshipped through all *Vedas* and since by nature **She** is a pure form, **She** is called as *Sāvithree*.

(v) **She Herself** originates in the form of light and smoothly and continuously flows. Hence **She** is *Sāvithree*.

(vi) According to *Padma Purāṇa*, the presiding deity at *Pushkara Kshetra* is called *Sāvithree*;

Sāvitree Pushkare Nāmnāteertthānām Pravaresubhe.

700. ***Sachchidānandaroopiṇee* - सच्चिदानन्दरूपिणी**

(i) One who is in the form of *Satchitānanda* – existence, knowledge and bliss absolute.

(ii) The form of *Brahmam* has three parts – *Sat, Chit* and *Ānandam* (existence, knowledge and bliss absolute). *Sat* is eternal, *Chit* is knowledge and *Ānandam* is completely filled supreme bliss. All these three forms put together is *Brahmam*. That is *Śreedevee*.

Thus ends the eight *Kalā* called *Bogata*.

*****

Section 9: *Vishvā Kalā*

701. *Deshakālaparichchinnā* - देशकालपरिच्छिन्ना

(i) One who is undivided by space and time.

(ii) Some things are limited by place as they are available in one place and not in other places. Some other things are limited by time as they are available at one time and not in any other time. **She** is eternal and available at all times. Such distinctions do not apply to **Her**.

(iii) The messages conveyed in 136th name *Nityā*, 180th name *Nirnāshā* and 400th name *Vyāpinee* are combined and indicated in this name.

(iv) The *Patanjali Yoga Sūtra* (I-26) says, "He is the teacher even to the ancestors because he is not defined by time". Ancients, *Brahma*, teacher, father, limited by space, etc., means the absolute non-existence of a thing in a certain place. "This is not here". Limited by time; "this was not before and it will not exist in future," a thing having neither antecedence nor precedence; *"Sa: Poorveshāmapi Guru: Kālenāna Vachchedāt"*.

(v) The *Soura Samhita* says "the person is omnipresent like ether, as everything, except himself, is illusory, he is said to be unlimited as to space and things". Since both are **Her** creations. **She** is the same Truth in all times and all places, unlimited by space and time;

Pumān Ākāshavatvyāpee Svātiriktam Mrushāyata: I
Deshata: *Kālatashchāpi Hyananto Vastuta*: *Smruta*: II

702. *Sarvagā* - सर्वगा

(i) One who is omnipresent.

(ii) The message that She is present everywhere conveyed in the previous name is again stressed here. This can be compared to the saying in Tamil, *"Thoonilum Iruppān, Thurumbilum Iruppān"*.

(iii) The *Varāha Purāŋa* says, when *Śreedevee* in the form of the creative *Shakti*, was performing penance in the *Sveta* mountain, *Brahma* said, "Ask a boon". *Śreedevee* replied, "Oh holy one, I cannot bear to remain in one place, hence I beg you to grant me the boon of omnipresence. Thus asked, *Brahma* then replied to the creative *Śreedevee*, Oh thou of all forms, thou shall become omnipresent";

Bhagavannekateshe'ham Notsahe Sthātumanjasā I
Ato'rta Tvām Varam Yāche Sarvagatvamabheepsatee II
EvamuktastadāBrahma Srushtyai Devyai Prajāpati: I

Uvācha Sarvaroope Tvam Sarvagāsi Bhavishyasi II

Since it is mentioned as *Sarvaroope*, in this verse, of all forms, that is separate from **Her**. Omnipresent, your qualified forms will be all bodies or you will become the soul of all. Again it is indicated that those forms are integrated. It is also indicated that the form of *Śreedevee* with attributes in all *kshetras* (in all souls). That is, *Śreedevee* is *Sarvaroopiṇee* (in all forms), *Sarvavyāpinee* (omnipresent) and *Sarvāntaryāminee* (present inside all souls).

(iv) The same message is conveyed in *Devee Purāṇa* also as also; "Oh great wise one, this is the true established doctrine about *Śreedevee*, **She** is certainly the *Vedas*, sacrifices, heaven; this entire universe, animate and inanimate, is pervaded by *Śreedevee*. **She** is sacrificed to and **She** is worshipped, **She** is food and drink. Everywhere *Śreedevee* is present in different forms and names as in the trees, in the earth, wind, ether, water, fire. Thus, this *Śreedevee* is ever to be worshipped according to the rules; one who thus known here, will be absorbed into **Her**";

Devyāvā Esha Siddhānta: *Paramārtho Mahāmate* I
Esha Vedashcha Svakargashchaiva Na Samshaya: II
Devyā Vyāptamidam Sarvam Jagatstāvara Jangamam I
Etyate Pooyate Devee Annapānātmikā Cha Sā II
Sarvatra Shānkaree Devee Tanubhir Nāmabhi Chashsā I
Vruksheshurvyām Tadā Vāyou Vyomnyapsvagnou cha Sarvagā II
Evam Vidā Hyasou Devee Sadā Poojyā Vidhānata: I
Edrusheem Vetti Yatsvenām Sa Tasyāmeva Leeyate II

703 . *Sarvamohinee* – सर्वमोहिनी

(i) One who is all-bewildering.

(ii) How can this *Śreedevee* be said to possess contradictory attributes such as, permanence and impermanence, animation and non-animation, etc., as described in the previous name? This name answers this question. **She** bewilders all the ordinary people, who believe in the reality of the apparent duality; that is **She** makes them devoid of the knowledge of unity. The meaning is that the apparent difference between *Brahmam* and the universe is illusory. In *Saptashatee* (I chapter) also it is mentioned as; *"Gnānināmapi Chetāmsi Devee Bhagavatee Hi Sā Balatākrushya Mohāya Mahāmāyā Prayacchati"*.

(iii) In the *Koorma Purāṇa*, *Shiva* says, "This supreme *Shakti* is in me and is *Brahmam* itself. This *Māyā* is dear to me, infinite, by which this world is bewildered. Oh best of the twice-born ones, I bewilder the whole universe with the *Devas*, demons and men and I create them and I cause them to exist";

Iyam Sā Paramā Shaktir Manmayee Brahmaroopiŋee I
Māyā Mama Priyānantā Yayedam Mohitam Jagat II
Anayaitat Jagat Sarvam Sadevāsuramānusham I
Mohayāmi Dvijasrestā: Srujāmi Visrujāmi Cha II

(iv) In another place in the same *purāŋa*, *Śreedevee* says to *Himavat*, "Whatever different scriptures are found in the world, opposed to *Sruti* and *Smruti*, devoted to the position of duality, namely *Kāpāla*, *Bhairava*, *Sakala*, *Gautama* and many similar ones, they are for the purpose of bewilderment; those who are confused by the false scriptures, also confuse the world, in another cycle; these were all created by me for the sake of bewilderment";

Yāni Shāstrāni Drushyante Loke'smin Vividhāni Tu I
Sruti Smruti Vruddhāni Dvaita Vadaratāni Cha II
Kāpālam Bhairavam Chaiva Shākalam Goutamam Matam I
Evam Vidhāni Chānyāni Mohanārdāni Tāni Tu II
Ye Kushātrābhiyogena Mohayanteeva Mānavān I
Māyā Srushtāni Shāstrāni Mohāyaishām Bhavāntare II

(v) 31st verse of *Soundaryalaharee* starting with *Chatu: Shashṭyā Tantrai:*, says, thus *Shiva* originated 64 *tantras* to bewilder the common people. By the compulsion of *Śreedevee* he also made the 65th*tantra*, which explains the truth.

(vi) The *Soota Samhita* (1-8-38) says, "Sinful men devoid of grace bewildered by *māyā* and suffering birth, death etc. do not know the Lord of Gods";

Prasādaheenā: Papishtā Mohitā Mayaya Janā: I
Naiva Jānanti Devasham Janmanāshādi Peeditā: II

(vii) **She** bewilders *moha* the three worlds *sarva*, or this means **She** is in the form of *Trailokya mohana cakra* in *Śreechakra* and in the form of *Vidya*.

704. *Sarasvatee* – सरस्वती

(i) One who is in the form of *Saraswatee*, the presiding deity of knowledge.

(ii) As mentioned above, there is no difference between *Brahmam* and the universe, both are same. The concept that the *Brahmam* itself seems to be in the form of universe, was explained. Still, due to illusion, people think that Brahmam and the universe are different. Why should we make a difference between a pot and a picture as their apparent difference is simply illusory according to previous rule? This question is answered here.

(iii) The knowledge is surrounded by ignorance. This has been explained in *Śreemad Bhagavad Geeta* (V-15) also as; *Agnānenāvrutam Gnānam Tena Muhyanti Jantava*: - The omnipresent does not take note of the merit or demerit of any. Knowledge is veiled by ignorance; mortals are thereby deluded (pot and picture instance). Knowledge is covered by nescience hence people are bewildered and it is necessary to confuse sinful men because they are devoid of divine grace; to conceal from them the knowledge of non-duality which is the highest human desires and which removes all sorrow. Once he becomes knowledgeable the non-dual thought is highlighted. The salvation also will be reached. This will be only for the devotees of *Śreedevee*. The *moham* (illusion) is necessary for those sinners who are not eligible for such blessings of *Śreedevee*.

(iv) The gist of the meaning of this name is – **She** only creates the illusion and also helps devotees to come out of it. 643rd name *Jnānadā* may also be compared.

(v) In *Saptashatee* (I chapter) also we read the same message;

Gnānimasti Samastasya Jantorvishyagochare I
Vishayāscha Mahābhāga yānti Chaivam Prudak Prudak II

(vi) Again it says;

Tathāpi Mamatāvarte Mohagarte Nipātitā: I
Mahāmāyā Prabhāvena Samsarasthiti Kārinā II
Tannātra Vismaya: *Kāryo Yoga Nidrā Jagatpate*: I
Mahāmāyā Hareschaishā Tayā Sammohyate Jagat II
Gnānināmapi Chetamsi Devee Bhagavatee Hi Sā I
Balatākrushya Mohāya Mahāmāyā Prāyachchati II
Tayā Visrujyate Vishva m Trailokyam Sacharācharam I
Saishā Prasannā Varadānrunām Bavatimuktaye II
Sā Vidyā Paramā Mukter Hetubhootā Sanātanee I
Samsāra Bandhahetuscha Saiva Sarveshvareshvaree II

(vii) *Dhaumyar* says, *Sarasvatee* is a girl of two years age. (In *Kanyā pooja* [worshipping of girls], it is customary to name the girls according to their ages).

(viii) The *Bharadvāja Smruti* says, "*Sarasvatee* is, she who ever resides in the tongues of all beings and who causes speech, hence **She** is called

Sarasvatee by great sages".

Yā Vasetprānijihvāsu Sadā Vāgupavartanāt I
Sarasvateeti Nāmneyam Samākhyātā Maharshibhi: II

(ix) The *Vāsistha Rāmāyana* also says, "She is called *Sarasvatee* because **She** is the stream of sense-impression"; *Saranāt Sarvdrushteenām Kathitashā Sarasvatee*.

(x) The three historical deities in *Saptashatee* and their group names have been mentioned in this *Sahasranāma*. They are;

Durgā	-	190th name
Mahālakshmee	-	210
Sarasvatee	-	704 (this name)
Chanḍikā	-	755

(xi) In *Mahāshoḍa Nyāsam* (*Prapanchanyāsam*), *Sarasvatee* is called as *Panchaprāŋaroopa*.

(xii) **She** is in the form of *Saraswatee* river.

705. *Shāstramayee* - शास्त्रमयी

(i) One who is the full and complete form or form of *Sāstras*.

(ii) The duality in all matters is only due to illusion created by *Śreedevee*. That illusion has to be removed through *Sāstras*. Those *Sāstras* only teach us; *Sarvam Khalvidam Brahma* – the knowledge form of *Śreedevee* is given much importance in *Sāstras*. **She** is in the form of those *Sāstras*.

(iii) The truth of any incident or argument has to be proved through one of the three ways - through eye witness/ enquiries or assumptions (though other evidences) or *Shabdam* (*sāstras*). Out of these the *sāstra* proof is much better than the other two. This is what is mentioned in *Brahma Sutra* (I-1-3). Thus only through *Vedas*, the *Brahmam* can be identified. *Brahadāraŋya Upanishad* (III/9) also says – *"Tamrvo Upanishadam Purusham Pruchchāmi"*.

(iv) The third division of the *Panchadashee mantra* also advises this as other *Vedānta Sāstras*. Contradictorily, the dual method of assumption is due to *Brahmam*, or confusion or illusion. When seen from the earth, the Moon seems to be so small. But in reality it is very big – this is known from *sāstras*. With the recent scientific methods, the actual size of the Moon itself is known and goes with that mentioned in *sāstras*. Hence *sāstras* is stronger than the proof of witness/ enquiries or assumptions methods. In the same way, the knowledge of teaching the *Brahmam* as given in the *sāstras* is better than the things consumed by us in this universe or the knowledge got by assumption. The *sāstra* has to be clearly understood that dual form is only due to illusion and confusion due to *Brahmam*. *Śreedevee* is in the form of such *sāstras*.

(v) The *Brahmāṇḍa Purāŋa* says, "**She** created from her breath, the *Vedas*, namely Rig, *Sāma*, *Yajus* and *Atharva* and the great *mantras* from her egoism (*abhimāna*); from her sweet words **She** created poetry, drama, rhetoric, etc.; from her tongue **She** created *Sarasvatee*. From her chin, whose eyes resemble the *Cakora* bird, the six supplementary of the *Vedas*; from the top of her throat, *Mimāmsā, Nyāya Sāstra, Purāŋas* and *Dharma Sāstras*; from the middle of her throat medicine and archery; from the bottom of her throat the sixty-four sciences; from the rest of her limbs all other *Tantras*; and from her shoulders the science of love";

Ni: *Svāsa Mārutair Vedānrusam Sāma Yajustathā* I
Atarvana Mahāmantranabhimānena Sāsrjat II
Kāvya Nātyādyalankārānasrujan Madhuroktibhi: I
Saraswatee Cha Jihvāyā: *Sasarja Sakalaprashoo*: II
Sulukena Sakorākshee Vedānkāni Sasarja Shat I
Meemamsām Nyāya Shāstram Cha Purāŋam Dharma Samhitām II
Kandordhvarekhā Tantrena Sasarja Sakalāmbikā I
Āyurvedam Dhanurvedam Kandamādhyastharekhayā II
Chatu: *Shashṭi Cha Vidyānām Kandakoopabhuvāsrujat* I
Tantrani Nikhilāngebhyo Dormoolān Madanāgamam II

706. ***Guhāmbā*** **- गुहाम्बा**

(i) One who dwells in a cave.

(ii) The duality is not only common accepted like the idea, the moon is measured by a span, but is also scriptural in *sāstras*. This name explains this further.

(iii) Following the Samskrit grammar; *Madyama Pada Lopee, Śree Bhāskararāya* explains this name. From the phrase; *Guhāyām Sthitā Ambā*, the middle word is removed and this name *Guhāmbā* is obtained. It means that **She** is in the form of a shadow. There are two people shadow and light in the cavity viz., the heart. The *Kaṭopanishad* (III-1) says;

Rutam Pbantou Sukrutasya Loke Guhām Pravishtow Parame Parardhe I
Chāyātapou Brahmavido Vadanti panchāgnayo Ye cha Trināchiketā: II

There are the two, drinking their reward in the world of their own works, entered into the cave of the heart dwelling on the highest summit (the ether in the heart). Those who know *Brahmam* call them shade and light. The meaning is that as both, shadow and light, enter the cavity of the heart and both contradict each other; hence duality is sanctioned by the scriptures. This is called *Poorva Paksha* (technique of raising an objection to expound truth).

(iv) Continuing the *Poorva Paksha* - *guhā* means *Subrahmaŋya* – This name can be taken to mean, **She** is the Mother of *Subrahmaŋya*. In order to destroy the demon *Tārakasura*, at the request of the *Devas*, the wedding/ conjunction of *Shiva* and *Pārvatee* took place and in that union an obstruction was experienced; consequently, *Shiva* became angry and dissipated his seed into the fire, the river *Ganges* and reeds. Thus the story of the birth of *Skanda* is given in all *Purāŋas*. This and other similar stories of him are to be known from the scriptures which support the theory of duality. The other *purāŋas*, which support non-duality are all illogical, because the *Veda* itself says, those house holders who perform the *Trināciketa* sacrifice become the sacrifice itself; *Yajamāna*: *Prastara*:. Non-duality will contract this *veda* phrase.

(v) So far the *Poorva Pakshā* was described.

707. ***Guhyaroopiŋee* - गुह्यरूपिणी**

(i) One who has most secret form.

(ii) The truth is of two types – temporary and permanent. The second type is most secret and is in caves, beyond the phenomenal universe – the knowledge that cannot be perceived by senses. The *Soota Samhita* (IV-47-69) says, we adore *Śreedevee*, who assumes the form of the teacher, in the form of secret knowledge, beloved by her secret devotees, residing in the secret place;

Gurumoorti Dharām Guhyām Guhyavignāna Roopineem I
Guhyabakta Jana Preetām Guhāyām Nihitām Numa: II

(iii) In the previous name whatever was mentioned as shadow light, *Subramanya*, etc., are all for courtesy only. They were explained with individual characteristics leading to duality. In the same way other *Veda* statements also. They are only true for a time, but non-duality is ever true and in the form different from each other. These different forms are all from the single form viz., *Brahmam* Thus the *Brahmam* has to be understood as non-dual.

(iv) This non-dual form of *Brahmam* is the most secret form. **She** is in that form and hence this name.

(v) *Koorma Purāṇa* says, there is an *Upanishad* by the name *Guhyopanishad*; **She** is in that form - the secret form; *Sarvopanishadām Devee Guhyopanishaduchyase* - among the *Upanishads*, Oh *Devee* you are the *Guhyopanishad* - it is not very clear what is meant as *Guhyopanishad*. There is an *Upanishad* called *Shuka Rahasyopanishad*, which could have been meant here. Accepting the request of *Vyāsa*, *Śree Parameshwara* himself did the *Brahmopadesa* (initiation) during the *Upanayana* of *Shuka* (son of *Vyāsa*). At that time he advised this *Upanishad* also to *Shuka* alongwith its sage, meter, meditation verse, etc. It seems that this *Shuka Rahasyopanishad* is indicated here.

(vi) It was explained in 624th name *Guhyā* as - **She** lives in a cave, has most inherent meaning and the union of the soul and the supreme being. It can be reminded here.

(vii) *Śree Ādi Śaṇkara* in his commentary of *Viṣhṇu Sahasranāma* for the 542nd name – *Guhya*: mentions;

a. He who can be understood by secret *Upanishads*.

b. He dwells in the cave in the ether of heart.

708. ***Sarvopādhivinirmuktā* - सर्वोपाधिविनिर्मुक्ता**

(i) One who is devoid of any bases or limitations.

(ii) Every attribute is a limitation that describes the place, time and things. 154th name *Nirupādhi*: and 701st name *Deshakāla-parichchinnā* may be referred.

(iii) The explanation given in the previous (707th) name for the *Poorva Pakshā* mentioned in 706th name was not acceptable – may be argued by the followers of *Poorva Paksha*. This name replies to that argument.

(iv) The argument of the followers *Poorva Paksha* would be as follows; there are statements advocating the duality also in *Veda*. When we take *Veda* as ultimate evidence, how can we ignore these statements?

(v) This name gives reply to this question;

Sarvopādhi, all limitations or attributes such as, the mother of *Skanda*, shadow and light, etc., whatever conditioned or unconditioned. The relation between the qualities and the thing which is qualified is illusory or false, like the relation of the silver in the mother-of-pearl. To establish the authority of the scriptures as truth-indicating, it must be explained that all the *Vedāntas* mean directly or indirectly one and the same supreme *Brahmam*, which is non-duality. The other scriptures which advocates duality are to be taken as explaining the ordinary vision as we find the same in the science of eclipse where it is indicated (by the words) 5 or 6 fingers with regards to the consumption of the sun and moon. So both the scriptures one advocating the duality and the other non-duality, are not to be dealt with equally. Hence this name indicates that *Śreedevee* in the form of *Brahmam* is unrelated to any inherent quality.

(vi) The followers of *Poorva Paksha* may raise an argument for this also. That is being replied in the next name.

(vii) **She** is free from the limitations established by logicians, or **She** is to be known by their real proof (*sathetu*).

709. *Sadāshivapativratā* - सदाशिवपतिव्रता

(i) One who is the devoted spouse of *Sadāshiva.*

(ii) Or **She** is always with the thought as precept consort of *Shiva.*

(iii) The followers *Poorva Paksha* may again raise an argument as - If the above is true, as *Śreedevee* is in the form of energy and as **She** is in the form of supreme egoism (*parāhamtā*) and other qualities, these attributes become illusory.

(iv) This argument is not correct. That is, devoted to *Shiva,* means ever remaining with him in all the three times. The other attributes are imaginary and their qualities are also imaginary. But in this *Shakti* only the qualities are attributed, not the energy itself, hence she belongs to *Brahmam* or **She** is the same as *Brahmam*. This name establishes **Her** equal status with *Shiva.*

710. *Sampradāyeshvaree* - सम्प्रदायेश्वरी

(i) One who is the Queen of the sacred traditions.

(ii) Since it is well (*samyak*) given (*pradeeyate*) to the disciples it is *Sampradāyam*. **She** is the head of it. The knowledge of *Śree Vidyā* worshipping method is to be obtained through a competent teacher (*Guru*) who conveys the traditional wisdom to the disciple. The identity between *Shakti* and *Shiva* cannot be realized by mere book knowledge, but only by the grace of a competent teacher, who will help the disciple have this worship method and resultantly getting the knowledge of *Brahmam*.

(iii) Still the doubt of the followers *Poorva Paksha* is not yet cleared. How, in the absence of special authority, can all qualities except the *parāhamtā*, be said to be imaginary? Rather all the qualities must be unreal and false.

(iv) Answer; *Sampradāya*, the wisdom regularly (*sam*) imparted (*pradāya*) to the disciples by the teachers.

(v) Just as ether and other qualities are attributed to *Brahmam* which is without attributes, again of the ether, etc., when predicated of Brahmam, sound, substance, etc., are attributed, again, when these are predicated of *Brahmam*, other qualities are attributed to them, similarly, as in *Brahmam*, which is without attributes both the visible qualities and the things which are qualified are attributed, one thing becomes both quality and possessor of quality. Here *Shiva* is qualified, *Shakti* is the quality. This is to be known by tradition alone. Those who possess the tradition say that *Brahmam* itself is the *Shakti*. 255th name *Dharmādharmavivarjitā* may be referred. **She** is the Queen or the Ruler/ Controller of that traditional lore, which **She** imparts to the devotees in the form of a teacher.

(vi) Also the *Sampradāya* has been given various meanings for *Panchadashee mantra* as explained in the *Yoginihrudaya* (II-15) and in the *Dattātreya Samhita*. One among these *Sampradāya* meaning. **She** is in that form and head of it. This has been clearly explained by *Śree Bhāskararāya* in *Sethubandam* and *Varivasyārahasya*. In *Varivasyārahasya* it has been mentioned that this *Sampradāya* meaning is more fitted to the *Kādividya*.

711. *Sādhu* – साधु

(i) One who suitable.

(ii) The word *Sādhvee* has been split into two names as *Sādhu* and *Ĕ*. By this the duplication of the name Sādhvee (128) has been avoided.

(iii) It can be taken as - the followers *Poorva Paksha* got their doubts cleared, accepted the above philosophy and said *Sādhu* – good or apt. That is, burning is the inherent quality of fire, so *parāhamtā* is rightly said to be the inherent quality of *Śreedevee*.

(iv) This word is neutral gender and has to be used as *Sādhune Namaha*.

(v) In practice the word *Sādhu* means – one who tolerates the troubles done by others and habitually does only good to others (even for those who has done bad to them). In this sense also it can be taken as *Śreedevee* does good to others.

712. ***Ee* - ई**

(i) One who is in the form of *Ĕ*, the *Kāmakalā* letter.

(ii) *'Ĕ'* is the 4th of the 16 vowels in Samskrit. The first letter *A* indicates *Viṣhŋu*. His sister *Śreedevee* is indicated by the 4th letter. The combined form of these two is indicated by *A* + *Ĕ* = *AE* can be seen in 715th name. This is based on the grammar rule viz., *Yasyeti Cha*.

(iii) It is known to all that when *E* is suffixed with a masculine word, it will denote his wife. Such a suffix will indicate the sister or daughter also. Lot of proofs in this regard – *Subadra*, the daughter of *Vāsudevar* is called as *Vāsudevee*. The daughter of *Indra* is called as Jayantee, by suffixing *Ĕ* to her brother's name. In the same way in the statement; *Nārāyaŋee Sahacharāya Cha* – the word *Nārāyaŋee* indicates the sister of *Nārāyaŋan*. In this *Sahasranāma* itself there are instances – 280 *Padmanābhasahodaree*, 298 - *Nārāyaŋee* and 892 – *Vaiṣhŋavee*.

(iv) Hence through this name, *Śreedevee* is seen as *Viṣhŋuroopiŋee* (893rd name) or sister of *Viṣhŋu*. The story that *Viṣhŋu* only gave *Meenakshee*, in Madurai, as *Kanyakā dānam* (offering the bride to the groom as elder brother) to *Shiva* may be referred.

(v) As already quoted *Em* has been mentioned in many places in *Veda*.

(vi) 41st name in *Trishatee Ĕkāraroopa* may be referred.

(vii) *E* is the third letter in the *Panchadashee mantra* in *Kādi Vidya*.

(viii) According to *Śree Vidyā* practice this letter indicates the *kāmakala*. Its form has been described in *Vāmakeshvara Tantra, Gnānārnavam, Vāyu Purāŋam, Kāmakalā Vilāsam* and Soundaryalaharee (19th verse). This is *Śreedevee*'s subtle form.

(ix) As described in the previous names, the 'one' *Brahmam*, has been split into two viz., the donations and the donor. The donor is *Shiva* and the donation is *Shakti*. In this the donation (*Shakti*) has again split into two and one of them is masculine – *Viṣhŋu* and the other feminine – *Śreedevee*. (That is the reason *Śreedevee* is called as sister of *Viṣhŋu*). This feminine form is called as consort of *Shiva*. The material cause for this world is *Viṣhŋu*. The *Saiva* philosophy is that these three (*Shiva, Śreedevee* and *Viṣhŋu*) put together is the supreme being. This explanation is based on *Koorma Purāŋa*, etc. This has been clearly explained by *Śree Appaiyya Deekshitar* in his book called *Ratnatrāya Pareeksha*. *Śree Bhāskararāya* has often quoted this book.

(x) There are evidences to infer that this *Ĕ* has been indicated by three letters, in earlier days. This can be referred in the explanation for

Lalitā Sahasranāma by *Śree Radhakrişhŋa Sastrigal* (paragraph 1104/4 and its footnote). The *Āyuda* letter in Tamil language is in the form of ஃ. It can be considered that this indicates the group of *Brahmam* split into three.

(xi) The form drawn by *Śree Radhakrişhŋa Sastrigal*, based on inference and description in other *tantra sāstras*, is like this; it resembles a form of a lady. The *bindu* in the head is like a face, the vertical line like the body, the two dots on both the sides like two breasts and the triangle at the bottom like the secret organ.

(xii) *Tantra Sāstras* (with a little modification) explain the creation of *Shabda Brahmam* as follows;

The supreme being can be imagined in two ways viz., with attributes and without. The *Sat Chit Ānanda Shakti* (energy) originated from qualified supreme being. From energy the *nātha* (sound) originated, from sound the *mahābindu*. This *mahābindu* split into three viz., *Bindu, Nātha* (sound – different from the above said *nātha*) and *beejam* (seed). *Bindu* is *Shiva. Beeja* is *Shakti*. Their union is *Nātha*. The same is cryptically mentioned, in *Śree Vidyā* practice as various three-folds like,

- *Prkāsham, Vimarsham and Mishram*
- *Rakta charaŋam, Shukla charaŋam and Misra charaŋam*
- *Moon*, Fire (*Agni*) and Sun
- *Ichā, Gnāna* and *Kriyā*
- *Brahma, Vişhŋu* and *Rudra*

These three are considered as three vertices of a triangle. As per this method Sun has another name as *Kāma* and the other two (Moon and Fire together) called as *Kala*. Hence the cryptic name for this group is *Kāmakala*. Hence the three dot form of letter *Ĕ* is called as *Kāmakalā* letter.

When the *mahābindu* splits into three, a subtle sound is created, which is called as *Parā Vāg*. Later it expands to the stages of *Pashyantee, Madhyamā* and *Vaikharee*. The universe originates from this, is the explanation of creation of *Shabdabrahmam*.

Further explanation about this is available in the book called *Sharadā Tilakam* (first chapter verses 6 to 11). The reason for frequent usage of Sun, Fire and Moon in the method of *Śree Vidyā* worship and in describing the forms of *Śreedevee* can be had here.

(xiii) The below *Veda* statements may be considered;

1. *Chāndokya Upanishad* (VI-2-4); *Tataikshata Bahusyām Prjāyeya So'kāmayata*
2. *Muŋḍako Upanishad*; *Tapasā Cheeyate Brahma.* The

commentary of *Śree Ādi Śaṇkara* for this reads as – the *Brahmam* grows like the seed expands and the sprout comes out.

3. *Brahadāraŋya Upanishad* (I-1-4-3);
Cheeyate, Upacheeyate... Uchchoonathām Gachchati...
Sa Vai Naiva Reme Tasmadekākee Na Ramate Sa Dveteeyamaichchat I
Sa Hatāvānāsa Yathā Stree Pumāmsou Samparishvaktou Sa Immevātmānam Dvedhā'pātayat...
4. *Aitreya Upanishad* (I-1);
Atmā Vā Idameka Evāgra Āseennānyatkinchana
Mishat Sa Ĕkshata Lokānnu Srujā Iti I
5. *Svetāsvatara Upanishad* (IV-1);

Ya Ekovarŋo Bahudhā Shaktiyogād Varŋānane Kānnihitārtho Dadhāti I
Vi Chaiti Chānte Vishva madhou Sa Deva:
Sa No Buddyā Subhayā Samnunaktu II

The words and the method of communicating the same may vary. But message is one and the same in all the *tantra sāstras*.

(xiv) The names indicating the *kāmakala* in this *Sahasranāma* are; 322 – *Kāmakalāroopā*, 453 – *Trinayanā* and 762 - *Tryambakā*

(xv) In practice this name is used as *Yai Namaha*.

713. ***Gurumaŋḍalaroopiŋee* – गुरुमण्डलरूपिणी**

(i) One who is in the form of spiritual teachers.

(ii) The most secret *kāmakala* form of *Śreedevee* has to be learnt through a proper teacher only and not through books. Even if read from books, that knowledge will not be a permanent one – will not help for self-knowledge. This tells about the union of *Shiva -Shakti*. It advises the *mahāvākyās* (great statements) in *Vedāntas*. Hence like *mahāvākyās*, this will result fruits only if learnt through proper teacher.

(iii) *Gurus*, from *Paramashiva* to one's own teacher, *maŋḍala*, the regular succession (of them). The meaning is that this secret was handed down uninterruptedly from teacher to disciple and was not written in books. **She** is in this form of *Gurumaŋḍala*.

(iv) It has been told that the integrated form of the worshipper, self, *mantra*, *yantra*, the deity and the teacher, has to be imagined. There is no difference between the teacher and *Śreedevee*. Hence **She** is *Gurumaŋḍalaroopiŋee*.

(v) *Kādi* and *Hādi mantras* may be different. The race of the teachers (succession) may be different. But **She** is the presiding deity of all the *mantras*. Hence **She** is in the form of all the *Gurumaṇḍala*.

(vi) The *Vāg Devees* mention in the next four names, that the method of this initiation is very secret.

714. *Kulotteerṇā* - कुलोत्तीर्णा

(i) One who is transcending sphere of senses.

(ii) Various meanings have been mentioned for the word *Kula* in earlier names; 90 – *Kulāmrutaikarasikā*, 91 – *Kulasanketapālinee*, 92 – *Kulānganā*, 93 – *Kulāntasthā*, 95 – *Kulayoginee*, 96 – *Akulā*, 439 – *Kuleshvaree*, 440 – *Kulakuṇḍālayā* and 897 – *Kularoopiṇee*.

(iii) In this name the word *Kula* indicates the group of senses. **She** is beyond recognising thorough the senses. 415th name *Manovāchāmagocharā* may be referred. She can be reached only through imagination, devotion and knowledge. 113rd name – *Bhāvanāgamyā*, 119th – *Bhaktigamyā* and 980th – *Gnānagamyā* may be referred.

715. *Bhagārādhyā* - भगाराध्या

(i) One who is to be worshipped in the Sun's disc.

(ii) The word *Bhaga* indicates the Sun's disc. **She** is to be worshipped secretly here. It can be reminded that in 275th name *Bhānumaṇḍalamadhyasthā* it was mentioned that **She** dwells in the midst of Sun's disc. It was also described that one of the dots of the *kāmakalā* form is Sun.

(iii) It can be reminded that during *sandhyāvandana* we meditate the supreme being is in Sun's disc. Also *Gāyatree* is meditated in Sun's disc. The verse; *Nama Savithre..* may be reminded. In the *Śree Vidyā sandhyāvandana*, *Śreedevee* is meditated at all the three times in Sun's disc.

(iv) In Samskrit, the letter *'E'* is written in a triangular form. **She** is worshipped in a triangle.

(v) The letter *A* indicates *Shiva* and *Ĕ* indicates *Shakti*. Accordingly to Samskrit grammar, when these two are merged the letter *E* is obtained. This is the unison of *Shiva* and *Shakti*. The cause of the creation of this world is said to be yoni and its successive word *Bhaga*. I.e. **She** is to be worshipped through the letter *E*. It can be reminded that in almost all the *tantra sāstras*, in the *Sarvasiddhikaree* verses say; *Yadekādashamādhāram Beejam Konatrayātmakam*.

(vi) This also, in continuation of 713th name, has to be learnt through a proper teacher.

716. ***Māyā* – माया**

(i) One who is in the form of illusion.

(ii) The energy which obscures what is plain is *māyā* or illusion. Or to make plain what is not available. Both these are the acts of *māya*.

(iii) In addition the acts of dream or supernatural powers are all due to *māya*. The *Devee Purāŋa* says, "It is called *māyā* because it is the instrument of marvelous actions, producing unheard of results, like dreams or jugglery";

Vichitra Kārya Karanā Achintita Balapradā I
Svapnedrajālavalloke Māyā Tene Prakeertitā II

(iv) The same is set forth at length in the *Varāha Purāŋa* (in 37 verses), where *Viṣhŋu* says to the earth; "The cloud sends forth rain and water is collected. Next the quarters become clear. This is my *māyā*, Oh beloved one, even the moon wanes, again waxes and on the new moon day it is invisible. This is my power of illusion, by it I remain in the water. I create *Prajāpatis* as well as I destroy them".

(v) In *Śreemad Bhagavad Geeta* (VII-14) also it is mentioned that the divine illusion is made up of qualities, is hard to surmount; but those who take refuge in *Śree Kriṣhŋa* alone, can cross over it;

Daivee Hi Eshāguŋamayee Mama Māyā Durātyayā I
Māmeva Ye Prapadyante Māyāmetām Taranti Te II

(vi) The *Sāndilya Sūtra* (86) says, "His energy is *māya*". His - the Lord's energy.

(vii) The power of *māyā* has been explained in *Saptashatee* also. This was already mentioned in 703rd name *Sarvamohinee* and 704th name *Sarasvatee*.

(viii) *Śree Muthuswami Deekshatar* also has sung addressing *Śreedevee* as '*Māye*'.

(ix) The *Śākta Praŋava,* also called as *Bhuvaneshwaree Beeja* or *Hrullekā*, is called as *Māyā Beeja*. **She** is in that form.

(x) According to Śākta method, the 36 *tatvas* (philosophies) are divided as below;

Related body	No. of *tatvas*	Group Name
Physical	24	*Ātma Tatva* or *Ashuddha Tatva*
Subtle	7	*Vidyā Tatva* or *Shuddha Tatva*
Causal	5	*Shiva Tatva* or *Shuddha Tatva*

The *Śree Vidyā* worshippers imagine, in the *Navāvarŋa* worship during an important part called *Tatvasodanam*, that they cross all these 36 *tatvas* and reach the rare supreme being. This is included in the act called *Bindu Tarpaŋa*. 974th name *Bindu Tarpaŋa Santushṭā* may be referred. In this *māyā* is in the group called Mishra *Tatva*. It can be taken as that **She** is in that form.

(xi) In the *Mahāshoḍa Nyāsa* illusion is being appropriated in three places – in *Prapancha Nyāsa* as *Dveeparoopā* and *Guhāroopa* and in *Devata Nyāsa* as *Sahasra Koṭigaŋeshwara Kulasevita*. **She** is in these forms.

(xii) It is being reiterated here that the secret initiations have to done only through appropriate teachers – this was already stressed in 713th name *Gurumaŋḍalaroopiŋee*. Only with the advice of the teacher the illusion is to be reached (according the *Śākta* method) and the illusion is to be crossed (according to non-duality philosophy).

(xiii) According to the non-duality advised by *Śree Ādi Śaŋkara*, only when the illusion is removed the knowledge of *Brahmam* can be obtained. (Many a type of practice is mentioned here – like the darkness is removed once lit or once the knowledge is obtained the ignorance and illusion are removed). According to *Śree Vidyā* practice illusion is the energy (*shakti*) of *Brahmam* only. *Śree Kānchi Kāmakoṭi Paramāchārya*'s talk in this regard is (The book *Deivathin Kural*, 6th Volume, Pages 686 to 689);

The question, that why and how the illusion happened, does not arise according to non-duality principle. *Śākta Sāstra* says that *Chit Shakti* only plays a game by reflecting the illusion in many forms. The soul, in the as is form – having the senses as tools, has to unite with the eternal *Brahmam*.

The *Brahmam* only seems as soul due to illusion. The non-duality principle says that, if the illusion is removed through knowledge then the soul will become the *Brahmam*. Basically the soul and *Shiva* are one and the same. Again it is same at the end of salvation also. This has been clearly accepted in *Śākta* more particularly in *Śree Vidyā tantra*. The difference between the two is the creative duality. No difference about salvation. It has to be simply ignored that it is only illusion which seem to be dual. *Śākta* says that *Śreedevee* created it. All these duality enters into that *Śreedevee* and **She** plays a game. This illusion can be overcome by worshipping and praying to **Her**. Overcome this illusion and merge with the root cause. Again merge with that *Brahmam*, wherein this root cause itself has merged, as a single entity.

(xiv) The *Ĕkshana, Kāmana* and penance of *Parabrahmam* are the cause of creation. This is well understood from the *Veda* statements;

Sa Ekshata Lokānnu Srujā Iti I *So'kāmayata* II *Tapasā Cheeyate Brahma* II *Ĕkshana, Kāmana* and penance are all called as *Shāntāshakti*. This *Shakti* in the combined form of *Ichā, Gnāna* and *Kriyāshaktis* is called illusion. Further details in this regard may be seen in the explanation given in *Soota Samhita*.

717. ***Madhumatee* – मधुमती**

(i) One who is with alcohol.

(ii) The word *Madhu* means honey or alcohol. Alcohol also is one of the offerings during worship. Those who worship in religious manner offer honey, others offer alcohol itself.

(iii) The fact that *Śreedevee* is interested in alcohol has been mentioned in many a name;
330 – *Kādambareepriyā*
333 – *Vārunee Madavihvalā*
432 – *Madaghoorŋitaraktākshee*
433 - *Madapāṭalagaŋdabhoo*:
510 – *Madhupreetā*
575 – *Mādhveepānālasā* and
576 – *Matta*.

When the 235th name - *Catushshashṭiyupacārādhyā* was explained, one of the 64 offerings was mentioned as vessel filled with alcohol.

(iv) It can be reminded that in *Saptashatee* also it has been mentioned that *Śreedevee* consumes alcohol.

(v) *Veda* says that the form of *Śreedevee* itself is like a honey; *Mahtyai Vā Etaddevatāyai Roopam Yanmatu*.

(vi) *Chāndokya Upanishad* says that the honey of *Devas* is Sun; *Āditya Vai Devamadhu*. **She** is in that form of *Madhumatee*.

(vii) *Yoga sāstras* mention about four types of *Yogins*. The fourth type is called *Gatikrāntyabhāvās*. These are the greatest among the four. Still they have to cross (*tāraka*) seven more stages. In that the seventh stage is called *Madhumatee*. **She** is in that form.

(viii) The knowledge obtained at that last stage helps crossing. Hence, since that name is given to *Śreedevee*, it can be considered as *Samsāra Tarikā* (to cross these worldly affairs). *Yoga Sūtra* (*Patanchali Yoga Sūtra* 55) says about this; *"Tārakam Sarvavishyam Sarvathā Vishyakramam Cheti Vivekajam Gnānam"*.

(ix) **She** is in the form of a river called *Madhumatee*.

718. ***Mahee* – मही**

(i) One who is in the form of earth.

(ii) In previous names it was mentioned that **She** is in secret forms. However, this name says that **She** is clearly visible like earth. This makes the devotees, who were anxious and hesitant that "how we can reach the secret *Śreedevee*", interested in worshipping. This name advises that **She** is very clearly visible like earth.

(iii) **She** is like earth, acts as a support for this entire universe. This has been mentioned in *Saptashatee* (XI book) as;

Ādhārabhootā Jagatastvamekā Maheesvaroopena Yata: *Sthitā'si* I
Apām Svaroopasthitayā Tvayaitadāpyayate Krutnasanamalanghya Veerye

(iv) *Devee Purāŋa* says, since it is eternal, the nature is called *Mahee*;

Mahad Vyāpya Sditā Sarvam Maheeti Prakrutitā Matā II

Since **She** is in the form of nature, **She** is also called as *Mahee*.

(v) **She** is in the form of a river called *Mahee*.

719. ***Gaŋāmbā* – गणाम्बा**

(i) One who is the mother of hosts.

(ii) *Gaŋa* means group; **She** is the mother of the *Pramatha* and others groups of *Paramashiva.*

(iii) The head of the hosts or groups of *Paramashiva, Vinayaka* is also called *Gaŋesha* or *Gaŋapati* or *Gaŋan*. It can be taken as **She** is his mother.

720. ***Guhyakārādhyā* - गुह्यकाराध्या**

(i) One who is worshipped by the *Guhyakas*.

(ii) The sage for one variety of *Panchadashee* is *Kubera* (god of wealth). His hosts are called *Guhyakas*. She is worshipped by *Kubera* and his hosts *Guhyakās*.

(iii) According to *Koula* method, *Guhyakā* means being worshipped in a secret place without being known to others.

721. ***Komalāngee* - कोमलाङ्गी**

(i) One whose form is delicate and pleasing.
(ii) The message given in 460th name – *Nalinee* is being stressed here. This reminds the verse in *Shyāmalā Daŋḑaka* of *Kalidāsa* as; "*Shyāmalam Komalam Te Vapu*:"

722. ***Gurupriyā* - गुरुप्रिया**

(i) One who has affection on teacher (*Guru*).
(ii) **She** has great liking over *Parameshwara*, the great teacher of this world.
(iii) **She** has penchant over the teachers, who initiate the *Śree Vidyā* to the eligible disciples and make the worshipping race unbroken.
(iv) **She** is the consort of the teacher or every worshipper. This implies that every worshipper has to treat his teacher's wife as *Śreedevee* herself. In general, the principle and practice of this worshipping method is to treat every lady as *Śreedevee*. In this name, this has been specifically mentioned for the wives of teachers.
(v) *Guru* means, the teacher of *Devas* viz., *Brahaspati*. **She** has care over him.

723. ***Svatantra* - स्वतन्त्रा**

(i) One who acts on **Her** own without the help of others.
(ii) **She** does not expect others' help for doing any activity. **She** does not even need any tool. By declaration itself, **She** does the acts. (There is some difference in principle in this regard between the followers of non-duality and the worshippers of *Śreevidya*).
(iii) **She** owns **Her** consort *Parameshwara*. He owns **Her**. Mutually they own each other. This has been mentioned in *Kālikā Purāŋa* (*Kāmaroopa Kshetra Māhātmya*) as;

Nityam Vashati Tatrāpi Pārvadyā Saha Narmabhi: I
Madhye Deveekruham Tatra Tadadeenastu Shankara: II
Eshānyam Nātake Shaile Shankarasya Sadāsrāyam I
Nityam Vashati Tatresha: *Tadadeenā Tu Pārvatee* II

(iv) **She** is in the form of *Nitya tantra* called *Svatantram*. **She** can also be construed as *Svatantram* mentioned in *Soundaryalaharee* (31st verse). There is some difference of opinion whether it is *Vāmkeshvara Tantra* or *Tantra Rāja Tantra*.

(v) **She** has all the *tantras* as **Her** own *tantras*. The *Shaiva, Vaishnava* and *Gānapatya tantras* describe *Śreedevee*'s pride and hence can be considered as **Hers**. *Gaŋapati* and other gods can be worshipped only after installing (doing *Prāŋaprathishta*) them in the concerned idol or *yantra*. That *Prāŋa* energy is *Śreedevee* only. Only with **Her** help the worship of other gods can be made. One commentator has explained that since the *tantras*, for which presiding deities are other gods, are also **Her** own, **She** is *Svatantra*.

724. *Sarvatantreshee* - सर्वतन्त्रेशी

(i) One who is the head of all the *tantras*.
(ii) **She** installs the 64 *tantras*. **She** makes them meaningful and supports them.

725. *Dakshiŋāmoortiroopiŋee* - दक्षिणामूर्तिरूपिणी

(i) One who is in the form of *Dakhsināmoorti*.
(ii) *Dakshiŋāmoorti* is *Shiva* sitting, well known as the instructor of *Brahma, Viṣhŋu* and others. Since he is facing south, he is called *Dakhhsināmoorti*. He has the capacity to explain complex matters in a simple way (*Dakshiŋā* – abilitity or capacity) and hence he is called so. His *mantra*s are famous in the *Tantra sāstras*.
(iii) *Śree Ādi Śaŋkara*'s *Dakshiŋāmoorti Ashṭakam* preaches clearly the non-dual principles. When properly learning the commentaries on *Prastāna Trāya*, it is the practice, to bow with this and other *Shānti mantras*.
(iv) *Shiva* and *Śreedevee* show in three different forms;
    a. In individual forms.
    b. Integrated form of *Ardhanāree*.
    c. One form merged with the other. *Shiva* is merged in the form of *Kāmākshee*. *Śreedevee* merged in the form of *Dakshiŋāmoorti*.
(v) The *Dakshiŋāmoorti* form is continued in the next two names also.

726. *Sanakādi Samārādhyā* - सनकादि समाराध्या

(i) One who is worshipped by *Sanakar* and others.
(ii) The four sages *Sanakar, Sanandanar, Sanātanar* and *Sanatkumārar* held *Śreedevee* in the form of *Dakshiŋāmoorthi* in the inner self and initiated by *Shiva*. A surprising scene under the banyan tree – a youth

seated as a teacher and advises – the disciples are seniors. Teacher explains in silence and the disciples are relieved of all the doubts;

Chitram Vadataror Moole Vruddhā: Shishyā: Gurur Yuvā I
Gurostu Mounam Vyākyānam Shishyāstu Chinnasamshayā: II

(iii) These four are mental (*mānasa*) sons of *Brahma*, great *Yogins*, highly knowledgeable disciples of *Dakshiŋāmoorthi*. In worshipping *Śreedevee*, there are two methods viz., *Koula mārga* and *Samaya mārga*. It has been mentioned that there are books written by them based on *Samaya mārga* – three *Samhitas* viz., *Sanaka samhita, Sanandana Samhita* and *Sanatkumara Samhita*.

(iv) It has been mentioned in *Brahmāṇḍa Purāŋa* that they are great worshippers of *Śreedevee*.

Tvāmeva Anāḍirakhilā Kāryakāraŋa Roopinee I
Tvāmeva Hi Vichinvanti Yogina: Sanakādaya: II

(v) That is the reason they have been included in the race of teachers.

(vi) It has been mentioned in *Chāndogya Upanishad* (VII-26-2) - *Tripura Rahasyam - Māhātmya Kāṇḍa* – 37th chapter, that *Sanatkumāra* only took birth as Lord *Subramaŋia*.

727. *Shivajnānapradāyinee* - शिवज्ञानप्रदायिनी

(i) One who bestows the knowledge related to *Shiva*.

(ii) *Shiva* – auspicious. **She** provides that knowledge, i.e., the knowledge of *Brahmam*.

(iii) The *Vāshista Rāmāyan* says, wind is recognized by motion, fire by heat, *Shiva* who is the consciousness, purity and tranquility, is known by his vibratory energy. Only through *Śreedevee*, the pure, peaceful and spiritual *Shiva* can be understood. Instances are given to prove that there is no other way to know him;

Spandena Labhyate Vāyurvahni Roushnyena Labhyate I
Chinmātrmamalam Shāntam Shiva Ityuditamtu Yat II
Yatspandamaya Shaktyaiva Lakshyate Nānyathākila I

(iv) The *Vārāha Purāŋa* says, these three Gods (*Trimoortis*) are attained by one who really knows *Rudra*; "*Etāstisropi Siddhayanti Yo Rudram Veththi Tatvata:*" - Hence it has been confirmed that only through *Śreedevee, Shiva* and resultantly the three gods can be realised.

(v) It can also be considered that *Shiva* only gives the knowledge about *Śreedevee*

(vi) The 725th name *Dakshiŋāmoortiroopiŋee* is continued in this name.

728. *Chitkalā* - चित्कला

(i) One who is with divine consciousness.
(ii) *Chit* means knowledge. *Kalā* means a part.
(iii) The *Brahmam* cannot be idolised. The *Sat, Chit* and *Ānandam* symbolises its status. These three are there in *Brahmam*. They are inseparable from one another. But they are parts of *Brahmam* in such a way that each can be individually understood. In this **She** is in the form of *Chit* part.
(iv) It has been mentioned that the *Chaitanya* (consciousness) merged with the inner self of the soul is a part of *Brahmam*.
(v) In *Śreemad Bhagavad Geeta* (XV-7), *Krișhŋa* says – an eternal portion of myself having become the soul;

Mamaivamsho Jeevaloke Jeevabhoota: *Sanātana*:

(vi) *Padma Purāŋa*, while describing the forms of *Śreedevee* says, the energy called *Chitkalā* is there in the minds of the bodies of the souls; "*Chitteshu Chitkalā Nāma Shakti*: *Sarva Shareerinām* II"

729. *Ānandakalikā* - आनन्दकलिका

(i) One who is the bud of divine bliss.
(ii) In the previous name it was mentioned that the consciousness of the soul is a part of the consciousness of the *Brahmam*. Accordingly this name advises that the bliss of the soul is a part of the bliss of the *Brahmam*. The bliss has been described in *Taitireeya Upanishad* (II-8) and *Brahadāraŋya Upanishad* (IV-3-33). Again *Brahadāraŋya Upanishad* (IV-3-32) says;

Etasyaiva Ānandasya Anyāni Bhootāni Matrām Upajeevanti II

(iii) **She** is in the form of the supreme bliss, which is the *Satchitānandam*.
(iv) *Kalikā* means the bud of a flower. It can be construed that **She** is in the form of a bud of the sheath of bliss. The bud has the qualities of a flower in a small way. In the same way the bliss is in a small way within the soul. This name contains the message that - at the appropriate time the bliss in the form of a bud can expand and become the supreme bliss.

730. *Premaroopā* - प्रेमरूपा

(i) One who is in the form of love.
(ii) It is a practice to call the form reflected by any article as the article

itself. For instance we get longevity by consuming ghee. Hence ghee is called as life; *Āyurghrutam*. In the same way the love or devotion of the devotees on **Her** is indicated as *Śreedevee* herself.

(iii) Based on whom we have love its name differs. The love on elders is called as devotion, on peers it is love on children it is affection. **She** is in all these forms.

731. ***Priyamkaree* - प्रियंकरी**

(i) One who grants what is dear to **Her** devotees.

(ii) She does what is sought for by the devotees. Based on the individual mindset, whether it is enjoyment or salvation.

(iii) **She,** in the form of soul consciousness, causes interest in the worldly affairs through the organs like eye, ear, etc. It can also be taken as that **She** creates the knowledge to understand that this interest is also due to the interest on the soul. The *Brahadāraŋyaka Upanishad* (4th and 5th*Brāhmaŋam*) may be referred where *Yāgnavalkeeyar* advises to *Maitreyee*.

732. ***Nāmapārāyaŋapreetā* - नामपारायणप्रीता**

(i) One who is pleased with the litany of her names.

(ii) In one sense the word *Nāma* indicates this *Sahasranāma*. The fruits of this have been explained separately in detail in the results part.

(iii) In worshipping *Śreedevee*, six types of *Pārāyaŋas* are important. They are respectively *Nātha*, *Gatikā*, *Tatva*, *Nityā*, *Nāma* and *mantra*.

(iv) In some other place it was explained that the worshippers of *Śree Vidyā* do *Śree Vidyā Sandhyāvandhana* by dividing the time in *Ashṭānga* (eight) method.

(v) *Nātha* and *Gatikāpārāyaŋams* are part of morning *Sandhyā vandhana*. *Tatva* part of noon and *Nitya* part of evening. The other two have no time restrictions.

(vi) These six *Pārāyanās* are very secretive and energetic. These are very useful to reach *Śreedevee*.

(vii) The book *Laghustuti* is told to be written by *Kālidāsa*. Again there is some debate with the learned whether this is the same *Kālidāsa* who wrote *Raghuvamsa* or a different one. In this book the 18th and 19th verses explain *Mantra* and *Nāmapārāyanās* respectively. *Devee Bhāgavatam* (III book) explains about this *Pārāyanā* that by merging the letters from *A* to *Ksha* with vowels lot many more letters are obtained.

Akārāndi Kshakārāntai: *Svarairai Varŋaistu Yojitai*: I
Asankyeyāni Nāmāni Bhavanti Raghunandana II

(viii) The 19th verse of *Laghustuti* is as follows;

Āĕ Pallavitai: *Parasparayutair Dvitrikramādyaksharai*:
Kādikshāntagatai: *Svarādhibhiratha Kshāntaischa Tai*: *Sasvarai*: II
Nāmāni Tripure Bhavanti Khalu Yānyatyanta Guhyāni Te
Tebhyo Bhiravapatni Vimshati Sahasrebhya: *Parebhya*: *Nama*:

Through this 20,736 names can be obtained. The merging of letters is to be learnt through a proper teacher. There are differences amongst various schools also.

(ix) The method of *pārāyaŋam* is of five types. This can be done in one day, one week, one fortnight, one month or 36 days. This can be known from the statement in the *Kādi* religion;

Dinato Vārata: *Pakshān Māsāt Shattrimshatā Dinai*: II

733. ***Nandividyā* – नन्दिविद्या**

(i) One who is in the form of *mantra* initiated by Lord *Nandikeshvara*.
(ii) Among the sages mentioned in *Śree Vidyā* 12 are important. They are; *Manu*, Moon, *Kuberā*, *Lopāmudrā*, Cupid, *Agasthya*, Fire, Sun, *Indra*, *Skanda*, *Shiva* and *Krodha Battārakar*. In addition *Brahma*, *Viṣhŋu*, *Nandi* and *Yama* are also mentioned as sages deity of *mantras*.

734. ***Naṭeshvaree*** **- नटेश्वरी**

(i) One who is the consort of *Naṭesha*.
(ii) This means that **She** is the consort of *Naṭarāja*, dancing in *Chidambara*. The word *Chidambara* can be taken in two meanings – the place *Chidambara* or the ether of heart. Both are befitting meanings.
(iii) **She** dances alongwith *Naṭesa*. The dance of these two has been mentioned in 41st verse of *Soundaryalaharee*;

Tavādhāre Moole Saha Samayayā Lāsyaparayā
Navātmāna Manye Navarasa Mahātāndava Naṭam I

735. ***Mithyājagadadhishṭhānā*** **- मिथ्याजगदधिष्ठाना**

(i) One who is the locating deity of this false form of the world.

(ii) The sea-shell is wrongly treated as silver – this seems to be real, until it is realised that it is not silver. Once it is understood that it is wrong, the silver goes away and the sea-shell is seen and it is also understood that the false sea-shell was the location for the silver. *Śreedevee* being the real supreme being, but seen as an abstract of the changing universe. There are lots of evidences to prove that **She** is *jagat mityai*.

Māyā Mātramidam Dvaitamadvaitam Paramārthata: II
Gowḍapata Kārikai (I-17)
Neha Nānāsti Kinchana - *Brahadāraṇyaka Upanishad* (IV-4-19)
Sarvam Khalvidamevāham Nānyadasti Sanātanam II
Devee Bhāgavatam
Yatra Trisargo Mrushā II *Viṣhṇu Bhāgavatam*

Once the Supreme Being is known the universe hides itself.

(iii) This can be compared to the Tamil poem;

Maratthai Maraittatu Māmata Yānai
Maratthil Maraintatu Māmata Yānai
Paratthai Maraittatu Pār Mudal Bhootam
Paratthil Maraintatu Pār Mudal Bhootam

(iv) This can be split as *Adhishṭā* + *Ana*: **She** has the *Brahmam*, which supports the universe (*Adhishṭā*) as **Her** breath (*Ana*:). i.e. *Brahmam* is her breath.

(v) According to the followers of *tantras*, the universe is the *Brahmam*. Nothing else from it. The pot made of mud is another dimension of mud. In the same way, the world is another dimension of *Brahmam* only. *Brahmam* is truth and so is the world. In the real sense there is no difference between the universe and *Brahmam*. The policy of the followers of *tantras* is that, whatever difference perceived is abstract. Hence they accept all the *Veda* statements about non-duality. When a difference is seen the evidence shown on the difference is also abstract. Hence there is no reason for the learned to say that this universe is abstract. This has been explained in detail in *Sāmbavānandakalpatai*.

736. *Muktidā* - मुक्तिदा

(i) One who is the giver of salvation.

(ii) *Śreedevee* bestowing salvation for her devotees has been mentioned in many a place. For instance - The *Koormu Puraṇa* says "hence one desirous of salvation should take refuge is *Pārvatee*, *Parameshvaree*, the soul of all beings and also of *Shiva* ".

Tasmādvimuktimanvichchan Pārvateem Parameshvareem I
Ashrayet Sarvabhootānāmātma Bhootām Shivātmikām II

(iii) The *Brahmānḍa Purāṇa* also says, "Those who worship the supreme *Shakti* whether regularly or irregularly, are not entangled in *samsāra*. There is no doubt, they are the liberated souls";

Ye'rchayanti Parām Shaktim Vidhinā'vidhināpi Vā I
Na Te Samsārino Noonam Muktā Eva Na Samshya: II

737. ***Muktiroopiṇee*** **- मुक्तिरूपिणी**

(i) One who is in the form of salvation itself.

(ii) By obtaining knowledge, by destruction of ignorance or by recovering the fifth state, one does not obtain the supreme object of human desire i.e., salvation, but it should be said only when one remains in his own bliss, the real salvation comes to join him. (The subtle difference here is to be noted). 625th name *Kaivalya- padadāyinee* may be referred.

(iii) The form of self is hidden by ignorance. Once that ignorance is gone, the form of self is realised and the self-bliss comes out. This is called salvation. This name stresses that **She** is in the form of this true self bliss.

(iv) The *Saura Samhita* (14th chapter) says, "I will now concisely declare the nature of salvation, by the knowledge of which supreme salvation is attained by all embodied souls" It is said knowledge is the means, then refuting that "the knowledge is not the means, Oh learned, but is merely calling to remembrance," again "knowledge is neither effect nor substance, etc.," refuting the theory that salvation is neither substance, quality, action, nor *sāmānya*, etc., (*samavāya* and *abhāva*). "Hence the supreme salvation is becoming the absolute Self"; thus establishing the real doctrine it concludes, "Hence supreme salvation is of the nature of the Self and this was veiled by ignorance and again revealed by knowledge";

Gnānam Na Kārakam Vidvadbodhakam Khalu Kevalam II
Ata: *Sākshātparā Mukti*: *Svātma Bhootaiva Kevalam* II
Tasmādātma Svaroopaiva Parā Muktira Vidyāyā I
Tirobhootā Vishuddhasya Vidyāyā Vyāgyate'naghe II

738. ***Lāsyapriyā*** **- लास्यप्रिया**

(i) One who is fond of dancing.

(ii) The dance performed by women is called *lāsya* (whereas male's dance is called *tāndava*).

(iii) *Śreedevee* herself dances – We have earlier seen that it has been mentioned in the 41st verse of *Soundaryalaharee*; *Tavādhāre Moole*....

(iv) **She** is pleased by seeing dance of others. In general ordinary people also are pleased with songs and dance. It has been practiced for long wherein artists perform in front of kings and get rewarded. In the court of the empress *Śreedevee* also dance and music performances are given. It is clear that these performances are made in temples also.

(v) For the 184th name in *Trishatee* – *Lāsya Darshana Santushtā*, the commentary of *Śree Ādi Śaṇkara* (according to the translation of *Śree Chidānanda Nātha*) is as follows;

A king, who has got satisfied with all his desires, without attaining any fruits, enjoys hunting, games of children, etc. In the same way *Śreedevee* also enjoys the dance showing four-fold - desirable, undesirable, mixed and abuse and the resultant happiness and sorrow and the consequent facial expressions, the shaking of legs, hands and other organs. Thus enjoyed *Śreedevee* bestows the results of the actions of devotees without any partiality; "*Nā Datte Kshyachipāpam Na Chaiva Sukrutam Vibhu:*". Or She is pleased with the dance according to the tune and drums performed by *Ramba*, *Oorvashee* and other *Devata* ladies.

(vi) 172nd name of *Trishatee* – *Halleesa Lāsya Santushtā* also indicates that **She** is pleased to see the dance of ladies. **She** is also happy to see a type of dance called *Kolāṭṭam* performed by ladies.

739. *Layakaree* - लयकरी

(i) One who is causing absorption.

(ii) *Laya*, a peculiar state of mind, greater than ten meditations.

(iii) The state of mind focusing on seeing, hearing and thinking and do not understand anything else. When we listen to good music, we forget ourselves and do not even know what is happening near us. In the same way the mind absorbs with the Supreme Being also. This happens infrequently and also in a temporary way. For a very few people it is of permanent nature also. She gives that experience.

(iv) Bifurcating the songs and dances according to time of drums is also called as *Laya*. **She** is in that form.

(v) The sage called *Bharata*, treated song and dance as separate arts and a tool for the salvation. The trinity (three geniuses) of classical music also used singing as a tool for salvation.

740. *Lajjā* - लज्जा

(i) One who is in the form of modesty.
(ii) Shyness (shame or modesty) is an important character of ladies especially *pathivratha* ladies. Scare or fear is also part of it. This is the form of *Śreedevee*.
(iii) *Saptashatee* says;

Yā Devee Sarvabhooteshu Lajjāroopena Samsthitā I
Namstasyai Namstasyai Namstasyai Namonama: II

(iv) The word *Hreem* means modesty. Also, this is an important *beejam* of *Śreedevee*. Hence the word *Lajjā* is said to indicate this *beejam* cryptically. 301st and 302nd names *Hreemkāree* and *Hreematee* may be referred.
(v) There are 60 names in *Trishatee* reflecting upon the word *Hreem*.
(vi) Again in *Trishatee* itself we read 79th name *Lajjādyā* and 195th name *Lajjapadasamāradhya*. *Śree Ādi Śaṇkara*'s commentary for these name are (according to *Śree Chidānanda*'s translation);

79th name – *Lajja* is modesty. This is one of the righteousness of the inner self. Hence as a sub-character all the righteousness have to be considered. *Ādyā* means one who has such righteousness as form. On account of shyness, people do not show out completely and hide themselves. In the same way, *Śreedevee* also hides herself with *Tirobhāva* energy and shows up only to her devotees by giving boons.

195th name - *Lajja* is the righteousness of inner self. A (character) tool to loathe. All the righteousness has to be considered as sub-characters. With all the righteousness in the inner self, **She** is well worshipped by the inner mind. Amorousness, desire, skeptical doubt, interest, disinterest, help, disturbance, skepticism, indecisiveness and vacillation are all righteousness of inner self. Out of these skepticism means modesty. **She** is well thought of in these. The below *Veda* statements are evidences of the same;

Ya Ātmaŋi Tishtannandaro yamayati Guhāhitam Gahvareshtam
Purāŋam Tamātmastam E'nupashyanti Dheerā:

(vii) Or the word *Lajja* is a *chakra* of soul. In this, for the development of the bliss, which is the presiding form, **She** is worthy of worship as per the system prevailing in villages.

741. *Rambhādivanditā* – रम्भादिवन्दिता

(i) One who is adored by *Rambhā* and other celestial damsels.
(ii) In the next eight names *Śreedevee*'s form is described.

742. *Bhavadāvasudhāvrushṭi*: - भवदावसुधावृष्टिः

(i) One who is the rain of nectar falling on the wild fire that burns down the jungles of sin.
(ii) The meaning given in (i) above is got by splitting the name as *Bhavadāva* + *Sudhāvrushṭi*:. *Bhava* means worldly existence. *Dāva* means forest-fire. The rain of nectar is to put off this fire. *Dāva* also indicates forest. It can be construed that **She** rains the nectar to grow more and more of the forest of worldly existence. **She** entangles the illusion and ignorant in the worldly existence.
(iii) This name can also be split into three viz., *Bhavadā* + *Vasudhā* + *Vrushṭi*:. *Bhavada* means who gifts *Shiva* – bestows salvation. *Vasu* means wealth or jewel. *Da* indicates *Dhana* i.e., wealth. That means, **She** rains wealth, gems, etc. That is, **She** herself bestows wealth and salvation.
(iv) The *Rudrayāmala* (*Mangalarājastava*) says, "Where there is worldly enjoyment there is no salvation, where there is salvation there is no worldly enjoyment. To the best devotees of *Śreedevee*, salvation and enjoyment are both in their hands";

Yatrāsti Bhogo Na Tu Tatra Moksha: *Yatrāsti Moksho Na Tu Tatra Bhoga*: I
Śreesundaree Sadhaka Pungavānām Bhogashcha Mokshashcha Karastha Eva II

743. *Pāpāraṇyadavānalā* - पापारण्यदवानला

(i) One who is the forest fire that burns down and destroys all the sins.
(ii) The forest fire consuming the forest of sin - i.e., **She** destroys the sins. 167th name *Pāpanāshinee* also conveys the same sense.
(iii) We read the same message in 31st name of *Trishatee* also; *Ena Kooṭa Vināshinee* – the commentary of *Śree Ādi Śaṇkara* (according to the translation of *Śree Chidānanda Nātha*) is as follows; **She** destroys the group of sins. In the society of sins *Prārabdha* (actions from past births that have led to the current birth), *Sanchita* (actions from past births which are set to fructify in future births) and *Āgāmi* (the actions performed after one becomes knowledgeable). If one thinks that these sins can be destroyed by sub-merging in these worldly

enjoyments, it can never happen. But with the blessings of *Śreedevee*, who is in the form of pure self Brahmam integrated with the philosophical knowledge, they are completely ruined. This has been evidenced by the *Veda* statements; *"Aham Tva Sarvapāpebhyo Mokshayishyāmi* and *Ashareeram Vavasantam Priyāpriye Na Sprushata:"*. She destroys the sins, which is caused by deceit and again for which illusion is the root cause. 112th name of *Trishatee* (*Hatyādhi Pāpanāshinee*) says She destroys all the sins including *Brahmahati*.

(iv) The *Brhannāradeeya Purāṇa* says, "The Supreme name of *Gangā* is the fire that consumes the forest of sin because Gangā is the remover of the disease of *samsara*. Therefore it should be sought with much effort. **She** has the great name as *Davānalā* which is the means of destroying sin;

Gangāyā: *Paramam Nāma Pāpāraṇyadavānala*: I
Bhavavyādhiharee Gaṇagā Tasmātsavya Prāyatnata: II

Hence **She** is said to be in the form of *Ganga* also.

(v) By splitting this name as *Pāpāraṇya* + *Tava* + *Ana* + *Lā*, a different meaning can be conveyed. The forest fire called sins (worship and other tools to destroy the sins), *ana* – breath, *Lā* – giver. I.e., it means that **She** outbursts the actions to remove the sins and also preach the same. The *Brahmāṇḍa Purāṇa* says, "The supreme expiation of all sin whether committed knowingly or unknowingly is said to be the remembrance of the feet of the supreme *Śreedevee*";

Krutasyākhila Pāpasya Gnānatognātopivā I
Prāyachittam Param Proktam Parāshakte: *Padasmruti*: II

(vi) In another chapter it is said, "Hear, Oh *Devendra*, this great supreme secret which immediately destroys all sin, possessed of devotion and faith, after bathing, stand in the water and chant the *Panchadashee mantra* one thousand and eight times. Thus worshipping the supreme *Śreedevee*, he is released from all sins";

Idam Cha Shrunu Devendra Rahasyam Paramam Mahat I
Sarveshāmeva Pāpānām Yogapadyena Nāshanam II
Bhakti Shraddhā Samāyukta: *Snādvāntarjala Samsthita*: I
Ashototra Sahasram Tu Japet Panchadashākshareem II
Ārādhya Paramām Shaktim Muchyate Sarvakilbishai: II

744. *Dourbhāgyatoolavātoolā* - दौर्भाग्यतूलवातूला

(i) One who is in the form of cyclone that drives away the cotton bundles of misfortune.

(ii) The results of the actions done in many an earlier birth is the hard luck (misfortune). That is so big like bundles of cotton. That is being driven away by **Her** like the way a cyclone drives the bundles of cotton and hence this name.

(iii) The bundles of cotton are very big by look, but weigh very less. The groups of sins (actions from past births) are very big like heavy bundles. To reduce their weights there are some actions. As a result of those actions, the weights can be reduced like bundles of cotton. Those actions originate from *Śreedevee*. They are related to **Her**. Hence this name.

745. *Jarādhvāntaraviprabhā* - जराध्वान्तरविप्रभा

(i) One who removes by **Her** effulgence, the gloom of infirmities attendant on old age.

(ii) Childhood, boyhood, youth and old age are restricted only to the body and not to the soul. As long as the thought that the body is the self persists, while nearing old age the death is also close by. The fear that it can happen any time continues. On the other hand, the soul is eternal. There are no stages like, childhood, etc., to it. They are limited only to the body. If the thought that, as the worn-out garment is cast off and a new one is put on, when death happens, this body is removed and a new body taken up is firmed up then there is no fear about death. *Śreemad Bhagavat Geeta* (II-22); *Vāsāmsi Jeernāni*.. also conveys the same message. Like the simile that the darkness goes away automatically when the ray of Sun is struck; *Jarai* – for the darkness called old age, **She** is like Sun. That is, **She** bestows knowledge that the body and soul are different and that the youth and old age are only for the body.

(iii) **She** is prayed as *Janma Mrutyujarā Taptajana Vishrāntidāyinee* in 851st name.

746. *Bhāgyābdhichandrikā* - भाग्याब्धिचन्द्रिका

(i) One who is the Moon beam illuminating the ocean of good fortune.

(ii) Welfare happens only by the virtues done in the previous births. Welfare can be enjoyed in peace only by the self. But, when others recognise the welfare of one person, then his happiness multiplies – the total dimension of the welfare does not increase (since it is the

result of virtues of previous births, it has been already fixed).
The ocean boils because of the beams of Moon. The tide waves heavily– but there is no change in the quantity of water in the ocean. Similarly, **She** makes the sea of good fortune swell for **Her** devotees, just as the Moon makes the ocean swell into high tide. **She** is in the form of Moon. With **Her** compassion, **She** makes the others recognise the welfare enjoyed by **Her** devotees.

747. ***Bhaktachittakeki Ghanā Ghanā*** **- भक्तचित्तकेकिघनाघना**

(i) One who is the cloud that excites the peacocks which are the minds of **Her** devotees.
(ii) It is obvious that peacocks dance by spreading the wings once they see black (water) clouds. This name compares the minds of the devotees to peacocks and *Śreedevee* to the black clouds.
(iii) In the name the initial *Ghanā* means cloud as said earlier and *A* is prefixed to the second *Ghanā* and made as *Aghanā*, which means continual without any gap; Hence *Bhaktachittakeki Ghanā Ghanā* means that **Her** life-work like a cloud is the spiritual nourishment for her devotees. Here *Aghanā* – continuous with gap – that is life-works of *Śreedevee* is lot many and they give bliss to the devotees.

748. ***Rogaparvatadambholi***: **- रोगपर्वतदम्भोलिः**

(i) One who is the thunderbolt which shakes the mountain of diseases.
(ii) *Vajrāyudha* (thunderbolt) is the weapon of I*ndra*. It is said that, it is made of the backbone of the sage *Dadeechi*. It is which is very strong and has the energy and pride that it can destroy any heavy things also.
(iii) The *Vasinee Devees*, compare the diseases to mountains and *Śreedevee* to the thunderbolt.
(iv) The same message is conveyed in 551st name *Sarvavyādhi-prashamanee*.
(v) For the 287th name *Oushadha*: and 578th name *Bheshajam* in *Viṣhņu Sahasranāma*, it has commented as medicine for the disease of worldly affairs.
(vi) In usage it has to be said as *Rogaparvatadambholaye Namaha*.
(vii) Further, in *Agni Purāņa* we read as; *Shatakoṭi*: *Svaru*: and *Shambodambholirashanirdvayo*:. Since the word *Dambholi*: comes with the words *Shamba* and *Agni*, it also has to be treated feminine

only. Also the author quotes that the word *Vidhi*: has been used as feminine in *Moksha Dharma* in *Kām Vidhim Samupaskrutya*. He also reasoned it that in the phrase *"Bhāgyam Stree Niyatirvidhi"*, since the word *Vidhi* is conjoined with the word *Niyati*, it is also feminine only. Having these two quotes in mind, it can also be used in feminine form as; *Rogaparvatadambholayai Namaha*.

749. ***Mrutyudāruguṭhārikā* - मृत्युदारुगुठारिका**

(i) One who is the axe that cuts down the tree of death.

(ii) The word *Mrutyu* means death. It indicates 28 types of pains based on the variations of *Ashakti*, *Siddhi* and *Tushṭi* (the commentary of *Śree Bhāskara Rāya* in his original book for the 354th name *Pashupāshavimochanee* may be referred – some of the verses from *Linga Purāŋa* have been quoted there).

(iii) *Dāru*, according to *Vararuchi's Kaṭapayādi* system, means 28 (*Ra*= 2 and *Da*= 8).

(iv) In addition to death, **She** removes, the twenty-eight other kinds of pains also.

(v) Both the words *Mrutyu* and *Dāru* indicate the number 28 and hence it is very apt to say so.

(vi) A tree splits and comes out of the ground. It grows stronger by eating the manures, water, etc., from the ground itself. It can be cut down only by an axe.

(vii) When a man is born his death is fixed – as per saying; *"Jātasya Hi Druvo Mrutyu:"*. Every second of living, the death is nearing – i.e., it can be said as it gets strengthened every second. Everyone is scared of death at any moment. The very reason for that scar is that he does not know what happens to him after death. The important reason for the fear is the doubt whether he may get a lower birth than the current one or will he get more sorrows. However, one does not fear the death, if he has the firm thought that – "I am worshipping *Śreedevee*. I will get salvation. Even if I am reborn, I will be enjoying only the virtues due to good deeds".

(viii) Hence it is very appropriate to compare the death to a tree and the axe to *Śreedevee*.

750 . *Maheshvaree* - महेश्वरी

(i) One who is the supreme sovereign.

(ii) This is different from the 208th name *Māheshvaree* by a letter. On account of long and short nature of *Ma*, it can be taken that this name is not duplicated.

751. *Mahākālee* - महाकाली

(i) One who is great and in the form of *Kālee*.
(ii) One who decides the time is called *Kālee*. One who decides the time for *Kālan* (*Yamā*, the deity of death) is *Mahākālee*.
(iii) The *Mahākālee* is the deity worshipped at Ujjayinee as the consort of *Shiva* in the form of *Mahākāla*.
(iv) **She** as *Mahākālee*, is worshipped as the deity of the first story in *Saptashatee*.
(v) *Kālee* also means one who is black in colour. *Śreedevee* has been mentioned as red in colour in many a place. When **She** takes the rude form, **She** like black in colour. *Śree Kānchi Kāmakoṭi Paramāchārya* has explained this in the book *Deivathin Kural*, 1st Volume, Pages 763 to 772. The gist of it is given below (possibly in his own fashion); It is very apt that *Śreedevee* is red in colour, since **She** is very near to the pure and white Supreme Being and also since **She** is in the form of compassion.

The death is a big sleep. We are peaceful without any sorrows during sleep. In the same way, the soul after death is very peaceful without the fruits (and the corresponding enjoyments) of any of the actions and the related entanglements. Just to give us the peace by removing us temporarily from the bondage of actions, *Shiva* does the role of destroyer. Only the learned who has removed the ego "I do the actions", can permanently come out of the cycle of actions. But, to temporarily remove even the great sinners from this cycle, *Śreedevee* creates the death with compassion. Only when this world is left, one can come out of the worldly movements, reach the salvation and obtain the peace permanently. The feel of that we are in the state of peace and be in peace is called the state of *Samādhi* - the eternal state. This is the result of the task of blessings (*anugraha*) of *Śreedevee*. The next stage is to remain in peace without even this thought – either in sleep or in death. Hence the state even next to *Anugraha* is the death.

(vi) Even in agriculture before even thinking of sowing the new seeds, the previous plants have to be harvested, to be weeded off and the ground ploughed. Death is similar to making the ground ready for next sowing.

752. *Mahāgrāsā* – महाग्रासा

(i) One who is the great devourer.
(ii) The *Kaṭopanishad* (II-25) says - of whom both *Brahmins* and *Kshatriyas* are food, the death is like pickles;
Yasya Brahma Cha Kshatram Chobhe Nhavata Odana: I.
Mrutyuryasyopasechana Kva idthā Veda Yanna Sa: II
(iii) Again the *Brahma Sūtra*; *Attā Charācharagrahanāt* - may also be compared.
(iv) The entire universe is as a huge morsel of food that **She** taking the form of *Parāhantā* swallows all the 36 *tatvas* devours all at once.

753. *Mahāshanā* – महाशना

(i) One who is a great eater.
(ii) According to the previous name, this name indicates that **She** consumes both the animate and the inanimate universe.
(iii) It can be noted that the third letter of this name varies from that of 229th name *Mahāsana*.

754. *Aparŋā* – अपर्णा

(i) One who is without any debt.
(ii) *Runam* – debt, **She** is not indebted to the devotees. **She** bestows more than what is expected by them.
(iii) There is hearsay story – *Śree Bhāskararāya* worshipped *Śreedevee* only through borrowing from others. When the creditors pressed for money, he turned to *Śreedevee* and asked her, "Is it correct that you have a name which means without any debt, but you have not repaid the debt to me". However true this story is, there is a verse in his *Deveestavam*, wherein *Śree Bhāskararāya* conveys such a meaning. It is told that *Śreedevee* went to the creditor's house in disguise of *Śree Bhāskararāya*'s wife and repaid the money.
(iv) *Parna* means leaf. It means that **She** did a penance without eating even a leaf. *Kālika Purāŋa* and *Brahma Purāŋa* say that when **She** did penance as *Parvathi* to marry *Shiva,* **She** did not eat even a leaf. Hence this name;
Āhāre Tyakta parnā'bhoot Yasmāt Himavatu: Sudha I
Tena Devair Aparneti Kathita Pruthiveetale II (*Kālikā Purāŋa*)

Aparnātu Nirāhārā Tām Mātā Pratyabhashata II (*Brahma Purāŋa*)

(v) *Mahā Nārāyaŋopanishad* says *Paramashiva* as; *"Varuksha Iva Stapta:"*. That is, he is like a tree or pillar, without moving, without waving and without any conscious. *Śreedevee* is like a climber around that tree. That climber has no leaves. Hence **She** is *Aparna*.

(vi) According to *Niruktam*, *Parnam* means to fall. This name can be taken as that **She** is without *parnam* (i.e. Falling).

(vii) We read as *Svāsaroopā Aparna* in *Mahāshoḍanyāsa* (*Prapancha Nyāsa*).

755. ***Chaŋḍikā*** **– चण्डिका**

(i) One who is with anger.

(ii) **She** is angry with those who do not have devotion on **Her**.

(iii) Anger is one of the characters of *Brahmam*. Hence, *Śree Bhāskararāya* has described in detail in his commentary on *Saptashatee* that *Chaŋḍikā* is *Brahmam* itself. As an evidence of this he quotes the verses; (1) *Namaste Rudra Manyave – Śree Rudram* and (2) *Bheeshā Asmāt Vāta*: *Bavate – Taitreeya Upanishad*.

(iv) As mentioned in *Devee Bhāgavatam*, it can be construed that **She** is in the form of seven years old girl; *Chaŋḍikā Saptavarshā Syāt*.

(v) **She** is mentioned as *Kalāroopā* in *Mahāshoḍanyāsa* (*Prapancha Nyāsa*).

(vi) From *Saptashatee*, it is understood that the combined form of *Mahākālee*, *Mahālakshmee* and *Mahāsaraswatee* is called as *Chaŋḍika*.

756 . ***Chaŋḍamuŋḍāsuranishoodinee*** **- चण्डमुण्डासुरनिषूदिनी**

(i) One who is the destroyer of demons *Chaŋḍa* and *Muŋḍa*.

(ii) **She**, in the form of *Kālee*, destroyed demons *Chaŋḍa* and *Muŋḍa*, belonging to the group of demons *Shumba* and *Nishumba*. Hence *Śreedevee* gave the name *Chāmuŋḍā* to *Kālee*. This has been mentioned in *Devee Bhāgavatam* and *Saptashatee* (7th book) as;

Yasmāch Chaŋḍam Chamuŋḍam Chagruheetvā Tvamupāgatā I
Tasmāchchāmuŋḍeti Tato Loke Gyātādevee Bhavishyasi II

It can also be reminded what was mentioned in the beginning of this book in part *Śree Vidyā* I.

(iii) But *Varāha Purāŋa* says different reason for the name *Chāmuŋḍa* to *Śreedevee*, "*Devee* struck the demons, *Ruru*, with her trident and cut off his head and because **She** carried off the head (*muŋḍa*) and trunk (*carman*) **She** is called *Chāmuŋḍā*".

Devee Cha Trishikhenā Jou Tam Rurum Samatādayat I
Tayā Tu Tādite Tasya Daidyasya Shubalochane II
Charmamuŋḍe Ubhe Samyak Prudagbhoote Baboovatu: II
Rurostu Dānavendrasya Charmamuŋḍakshnātyata: II
Apahrutyācharad Devee Chāmuŋḍā Tena Samabhavat II

(iv) We also find in the *Amara* dictionary (V-44) – *Charnamoti, Chāmuŋḍā, Charcika* and *Charmamuŋḍā* are all names of *Śreedevee*.

(v) It can also be construed that since **She** killed the demons who had *Muŋḍas* (heads) with *Chandas* (eyes red with anger). It is understood that this indicates the form of *Kālee* who wears the garland of skulls (*muŋḍas*).

(vi) The names of the eight mothers are indicated in this *Sahasranāma* as below;

208 – *Māheshvaree,* 210 – *Mahālakshmee*, 545 – *Pulomajārchitā*, 675 – *Brāhmee*, 756 - *Chaŋḍamuŋḍāsuranishoodinee* (*Chāmuŋḍā* – this name) and 892 – *Vaiṣhŋavee*. The name *Koumāree* can be considered as included in these two names viz.,

70 – *Kirichakrarathārooḍhadaŋḍanāthāpuraskrutā* and

76 – *Vishukraprāŋaharanavārāheeveeryanandita*.

757. ***Ksharāksharātmikā*** **- क्षराक्षरात्मिका**

(i) One who has countless letters/ syllables as **Her** form.

(ii) *Devupanishad* says that **She** is in the form of countless *mantras*; *Mantranām Mātrukā Devee*. *Mantras* are formed with letters and **She** is said as to have the form of countless letters.

(iii) The *Varāha Purāŋa* says, "Though *Śreedevee* is all-syllabled, yet **She** is called mono-syllabled, **She** is the ruler of the universe, **She** alone is all-syllabled"; *Ekākshareti Vikhyātā Sarvāksharamayee Shubhā* I

(iv) In *Trishatee*, for the 23rd name – *Ekānekāksharākruti*:, *Śree Ādi Śaŋkara*'s commentary is (based on the translation of *Śree Chitānanda Nāthar*) –

She is in the form of single letter as well as many lettered. The illusion which is the pure *Satva* form or ignorance is single letter form. The cheap ignorance in the form of *Satva* or ignorance is the limitation of the soul Since there are many souls, so as their limitations also. Hence the word many has been used. According to *Veda* statement; *Māyā Chāvidyā Cha Svayameva Bhavati* – *Śreedevee* is the illusion, which is a limitation of

Eshwara and also the ignorance, which is the limitation of the souls. Again, *Veda* says; *Māyām Tu Prakrutim* – *Śreedevee* is in the form of one and reflecting as many or the limitations of *Eshwara* and the souls.

(v) All living beings are perishable – they are *Kshara* (multiform), *Akhsara* (syllables) and *Ātma* (soul), **Her** body; i.e. **She** is one-syllabled and also multi-syllabled. Or, *khsara* is applied to all beings *akshara* to *Kooṭastha* (Lord), **She** is both - vide *Śreemad Bhagavad Geeta* (XV-16); *Bhootāni Kooṭasthokshara Uchyate* II This name says that *Śreedevee* thus has two different types of forms.

(vi) 480th and 481st names of *Viṣhŋu Sahasranāma* – *Ksharam* and *Aksharam* also convey the same meaning.

(vii) The *Viṣhŋu Bhāgavatam* also says the same message, "There are three forms of *Viṣhŋu* called *purushas*, those who know say, the first is the creator of the *mahat*, the second is the mundane egg, the third is what resides in all beings, by knowing these one is released";

Vishnostu Treeni Roopāni Purushākhyāni Ye Vidu: I
Pratamam Mahata: *Srashṭā Dvteeyam Tvandasamsthitam* II
Truteeyam Sarvabhootastham Tāni Gnātvā Vimuchyate II

758. ***Sarvalokeshee* - सर्वलोकेशी**

(i) One who is the ruler of all worlds - *Ĕshwaree*.

759. ***Vishvadhāriŋee* - विश्वधारिणी**

(i) One who supports the entire universe.

760. ***Trivargadhātree* - त्रिवर्गधात्री**

(i) One who bestows the triad of human values (aspiration to do meritorious acts, the capacity for it and the means for it).

(ii) According to *Amara* dictionary – *Trivarga* indicates the above three.

(iii) It has been indicated in many a place that **She** also bestows salvation. 736th name – *Muktidā* and 764th name – *Svargāpavargada*.

761. ***Subhagā* - सुभगा**

(i) One who has all affluences.

(ii) The *Bhagam* has many a meaning – *Śree* (wealth), *Kāmam* (desire), pride, vigour and effort. According to the *vishva* dictionary;

Bhagamashvaryam Māhātmya Gnāna Vairāgya Yonishu I
Yasho Veeryam Prāyatnechchā Śreerdharma Ravi Muktishu II

She shines with all these.

(iii) **She** gives brightness to the Sun himself. *Śreedevee*, who is in the form of Brahmam, resides within Sun also. This indicates that whatever acts he does are all due to **Her** only. *Viṣhŋu Purāŋa* (2nd book – 11th chapter) from 7th verse starting with *Sarvā Shakti*: till 20th verse ending with *Māsānumāsam Bhāsvantamadhyāste Tatra Samsthitām* – says that all the acts of Sun are due to the *Viṣhŋu* energy within him.
275th name -*Bhānumaŋḍalamadhyasthā* and
715th name –*Bhagārādhyā* may be referred.

(iv) **She** gets the name *Subhagā*, since all the affluences in all the moving or static objects are all due to **Her** only. *Padma Purāŋa* details the eight immobile objects out of these viz., sugarcane, peepal tree, sprouted cumin, coriander, cow's milk (including its variations like curd, butter, ghee, etc.)., yellow cloth, flower and salt. Out of moving objects, *Sumangalis* (ladies living with their husbands) are the important one. The same *Padma Purāŋa* says that if one worships *Śreedevee*, who is called as *Subhagā*, bestowing the affluences to *Devas* and food and liberation (*bakti* & *mukti*) to human, with devotion will get everything in this world;

Trivishtapa Soubhāgyamayeem Bhakti Mukti Pradāmumām I
Aārādhya Subhagām Bhaktyā Nāreem Vā Kim Na Vindati II

That is the reason worshipping *Sumangalis* is an important part of *Navāvarŋa Pooja* and *Chaŋḍi homa*. 970th name – *Suvāsinee* says that **She** herself is in the form of a *Sumangali*. Again 971st name – *Suvāsinyarchanapreetā* says **She** gets pleased when *Sumangalis* are worshipped.

(v) According to *Dhoumya*, a five year old girl is called *Subhagā* and **She** is in that form; *Subhagā Panchavarshāsyāth*.

762. ***Tryambakā* - त्र्यम्बका**

(i) One who is three-eyed.

(ii) *Devee Purāŋa* says - **She** has three eyes - they are the Sun, the Moon and Fire;

Soma Sooryānalās Treeni Yannetranyambakāni Sā I
Tena Devee Trāyambaketi Munibhi: Parikeertitā II

The same meaning was conveyed in the names 453rd – *Trinayanā* and

477th name *Trilochana*.

(iii) It can also be considered as - **She** is in the form of mother of the three gods – *Brahma*, *Viṣhŋu* and *Rudra*.

763. *Triguŋātmikā* - त्रिगुणात्मिका

(i) One who is in the form of the three qualities – *satva*, *rajas* and *tamas*.

(ii) It can be said that – since the three gods have predominantly each of the three qualities, **She** has all the three qualities. 984th name *Triguŋā* may be referred.

(iii) **She** herself is described as without any qualities (*nirguŋā*) in 139th name *Nirguŋā* and 961st name *Guŋāteeta*.

764. *Svargāpavargadā* – स्वर्गापवर्गदा

(i) One who bestows the heaven and the salvation.

(ii) The heaven is the happiness, which is earned through righteous deeds. This does not get corrupted during the enjoyment of happiness or latter. This is the fruit of righteous deeds done with passion. *Veda* says;

Yatra Du:khena Sambhinnam Na Cha Grastamanandaram I
Abhilāshopaneetam Yattatsukham Sva: Padāspadam II

This happiness of heaven is diminishable. *Śree Bhagavad Geeta* (IX-21) says that once the accumulated merit is exhausted the soul has to re-enter the mortal world; "*Ksheene Puŋye Martyalokam Vishanti*".

(iii) *Apavarga* means the permanent salvation. **She** bestows both.

765. *Shuddhā* - शुद्धा

(i) One who is ever pure.

(ii) That is, **She** is without the dirt called ignorance.

(iii) Actual meaning is that **She** is in the form of knowledge.

766. *Japāpushpa Nibhākruti*: - जपापुष्पनिभाकृतिः

(i) One whose form is like the colour of Hibiscus flower.

(ii) The red colour of *Śreedevee* has been mentioned in many names. Even in the meditation verse this has been mentioned and repeated here.

(iii) The letter '*A*' is hidden before this name. There is chance that this can be split into 2 names. In that case, it has to be split as *Ajapā* + *Pushpanibhākruti*:. If it is considered as two names, then some other 2 names have to be treated as a single one viz., merging 955th and 956th names we get *Darādharasutā* (who is in the form of earth and daughter of *Himavān*).

(iv) Let us see the meaning by splitting as *Ajapā* + *Pushpanibhākruti*:.

(v) We get the meanings as; who is in the form of a *mantra* called *Ajapa*. Also **She** is so soft, beautiful and fragrant like a flower.

(vi) The *Ajapā mantra* has been described in *Dakshiṇāmoorti Samhita*; "Without repetition (*japa*), Oh *Devesi*, that which brings to the practitioners of *mantra* the attainment (the result) of the repetition, is called *Ajapā*, which breaks as under the noose of the *samsāra*";

Vinā Japena Deveshi Japo Bhavati Mantrina: I
Ajapeyam Tata: *Proktā Bhavapāsha Nikruntanee* II

This happens while inhaling and exhaling during breathing. The sound thus created, is like cryptic letters indicating *Shiva* and *Shakti*. This indicates the unison of *Shiva* and *Shakti*. The learned say that this is the meaning of *Mahāvākyas*.

(vii) The word *Pushpa*, according to the *Hema* dictionary, means the flowering season, the chariot of *Kubera*, flower and the beauty of the eyes.

767. ***Ojovatee* – ओजोवती**

(i) One who is the vitality (juice of the tissues in the body).

(ii) The juice of the seven tissues in the body like blood, etc., mixes every minute. This mixer is called *Ojan*. This *Ojan* protects the body during the time of emergency or crisis. If this is reduced the consumed food may not give us the necessary strength. **She** is with this energy called *Ojas*. According to interpretations of *Vedas*, *Ojas* is said to be the eight *dhātu* (substances - tissue) of the body.

(iii) The *Vishva* dictionary gives many meanings to the word *Ojas*; light, the vitality of the substance, splendour, strength and radiance; as **She** possesses all these things **She** is called *Ojovatee*.

768. ***Dyutidharā* - द्युतिधरा**

(i) One who is full of splendour.

(ii) The gratification of the mind and body gives brightness to the body.

That is called luster. **She** has it. The same message was communicated in 465th name – *Kāntimatee*.

769. ***Yagyaroopā* - यज्ञरूपा**

(i) One who is the embodiment of sacrifices.

(ii) Five types of sacrifices are fixed for a human being;

1. *Deva Yagnam* – praying to *Devatas*.
2. *Pitru Yagnam* – praying to *antecedents* (father, grandfather, etc.) of the family race.
3. *Brahma Yagnam* – chanting of *Vedas*, teaching it to others and paying gratitude to the teachers and sages.
4. *Manushya Yagnam* – offerings to fellow human beings, especially satisfying the unexpected visitors by offering them food etc., building of temples, construction of tanks – service to the society.
5. *Bhoota Yagnam* – helping the trees, plants, animals, birds, etc., in a proper way.

She is in the form of all these *yagnas*.

(iii) Offering the knowledge and experience got through the senses of the body is called *Gnāna Yagnam*. **She** is in that form also. This has been described in *Mukyāmnāya Rahasya* as;

Indriya Dvārasamgruhyaigandhādyairātima Dhevatām I
Svabhāvena Samārādhyā Gnātu:soyam Mahāmakha: II

(iv) *Śree Bhagavad Geeta* (X-25) says that **She** is in the form of *Japa Yagnam* also; *Yagnānām Japayagnoosme*.

(v) According to *Taitireeya Samhita*; *Yagno Vai Viṣhŋu*: - **She** is in the form of *Viṣhŋu*.

(vi) All the *yagnās* are the form of *Eshwaran*. This has been described in detail in *Harivamsam* and *Padma Purāŋa*.

(vii) *Śree Ādi Śaṇkara* in his commentary of *Viṣhŋu Sahasranāma* for the 445th name – *Yagna*: mentions;

1. He is in the form of all the *yagnās* or.
2. He gives satisfaction to all the *Devas* and offers the fruits of the *yagnās*. *Veda* says; *Yagno Vai Viṣhŋu*:

770. ***Priyavratā* – प्रियव्रता**

(i) One who is fond of vows.

(ii) To start a work with determination to do it and to complete the same is called *Vratha* or vow.

(iii) For instance; *Ekādashee Viratham, Shashṭee Vratham, Varalakshmee Vratham*, etc.

(iv) In the incarnation of *Śree Rāmā,* his vow is to protect the person who catches his feet and says that he has surrendered to him. *Yuddha Kāṇḍa* – 8th chapter;

Sakrudeva Prapannāya Tavāsmeeti Cha Yāchate I
Abhayam Sarvabhootebhyo Dadānyetadvratam Mama II

(v) **She** is fond of all vows even those which are made to other deities. The *Bhavisyottara Purāṇa*, says, "He who makes a vow to any god or to goddess, all is for the delight of *Shiva* and *Śreedevee* who are the creators of the world. There is no difference here because the whole world is of *Shiva* and *Shakti*".

Devam Cha Deveem Cha Voddhshya Yatkaroti Vratam Nara: I
Tat Sarvam Shiva Yos Tushtyai Jagajjanana Sheelayo: II
Na Bhedas Tatra Mantavya: *Shiva Shaktimayam Jagat* II

The same message is read in *Śreemad Bhagavad Geeta* (VII-21);

Yo Yo Yām Yām Tanum Bhakta: *Shraddhayārchitumichchati* I
Tasya Tashyāchalām Shraddhām Tāmeva Vidadhāmyaham II

(vi) **She** is in the form of a king called *Prāyavrata*.

771. ***Durārādhyā* - दुराराध्या**

(i) One who is difficult to worship.

(ii) She is difficult to worship for the incompetent and for those who cannot control their senses and sensory organs. Impossible to be worshipped by the fickle-minded. *Soundaryalaharee* verse 95 says; *Taralakaranānā Masulabha*. To control the senses and to have focus in the mind lot of effort is required and it is very difficult. The same message is conveyed in 871st name - *Bahirmukhasudurlabha*.

772. *Durādharshā* - दुराधर्षा

(i) One who is hard to resist.

(ii) **She** cannot be attracted by luxurious worshipping or strength.

(iii) **She** is to be attained only by devotion. 120th name – *Bhaktivashyā* may be referred.

773. *Pātaleekusumapriyā* - पाटलीकुसुमप्रिया

(i) One who is fond of pale-red trumpet flowers.

(ii) This flower has a mixed colour of red and white. This indicates the unison of *Shiva* and *Shakti*. The verse, which is chanted during the worship of sandals of the teacher, the mixture of red and white is being indicated;

Vande Guru Padadvandvamavānmanasa Gocharam I
Rakta Shukla Prabhāmishramatarkyam Traipuram Maha: II

(iii) *Padma Purāŋa* says *Shiva* most likes the *Vilva* tree (Crataeva religiose) and *Śreedevee* the trumpet flowered tree; *Śree Vrukshe Shankaro Deva*: *Pātalāyām Tu Pārvatee*. (Since, it is a place where *Lakshmee* dwells the *Vilva* tree is called *Śree* tree).

(iv) This *Sahasranāma* indicates other flowers liked by *Śreedevee* in these names; 323 – *Kadambakusumapriyā*, 330 – *Kādambareepriyā*, 435 – *Chāmpeyakusumapriyā*, 776 – *Mandārakusumapriyā* and 919 – *Chaitanyakusumapriya*.

774. ***Mahatee*** **- महती**

(i) One who is very big.

(ii) **She** is the biggest – i.e. bigger than very big. *Mahā Nārāyaŋa Upanishad* (I-1) says; *Mahato Maheeyān*.

(iii) The other things can be measured only with this. Thus says *Shākapoorŋee*; *Mahān Kasmān Manenānyān Jahāti*.

(iv) The meaning of this name according to *Yāskar's Nirukta* is – one that is to be worshipped; *Mahaneeyo Bhavati*.

(v) It can be reminded that, a meaning that it is a tool to measure *Lakshmee* was mentioned for the first name *Śreemāta*.

(vi) The name of the Veena instrument in the hands of *Nārada* is *Mahatee*. **She** is in that form also.

775. ***Merunilayā*** **- मेरुनिलया**

(i) One who dwells in the *Meru*.

(ii) According to the saying; *Meru*: *Sumeru*: *Hemādri*: - *Meru* is a golden mountain. It can be reminded that this was mentioned in the 55th name *Sumerumadhyasrunggastha*. It is said that *Śreedevee*'s *Chintāmaŋi* house is at the top of the centre peak.

(iii) After the demolition of the demon *Bhanḍāsura*, *Devas* ordered their architect *Vishvakarma* and the architect of demons *Mayan*, to construct an appropriate place for *Kāmeshwarā* and *Śreedevee*. It was the *Deva's* wish that in the ocean called *Nitya Gnānam* in the midst of 16 *kshetrās*, *Śreedevee* should dwell in 16 forms, in the 16 cities decorated with gems, for the protection of this universe.

(iv) Accordingly those architects constructed 16 cities in the 16 *kshetrās*. These are on the top of 9 mountains and 7 oceans. These 16 cities were named as *Kāmeshwaree, Bagamālāpuree*, etc., based on the names of *Tithi Nityās*. Out of these there are three peaks to the East, South-west, South-east and centre of *Meru* mountain. In those three peaks there are the residences of *Brahma, Viṣhŋu* and *Shiva* and in the centre the residence of *Śreedevee*.

(v) *Tantrarāja Tantra* (28th chapter) describes such a construction of *Śree* city. *Vidopākyānam* also has details. *Lalithopākyānam, Lalithāstavaratnam* and *Chintāmaŋi Stavam* may be referred for more details about *Śree* city and *Chintāmaŋi* house.

(vi) *Tantrarāja Tantra* (28th chapter) explains that *Nityā Devees* are in the form of the worlds and time and their interchange. Accordingly *Śreedevee* dwells in the *Mahāmeru* during the first year of *Kruta Yuga* (*Kruta* era). *Nityā Devee*s starting from *Kāmeshwaree* till *Jvālāmālinee* live in other *Jambootdveepam, Plaksha Dveepam*, etc. and seven oceans. *Chitra Nitya* lives in the outside ether. In the next years each *Nitya Devee* (including *Śreedevee*) moves to next place. In the same way in the following years they move to adjacent places. In the sixteenth year they return to the original places. Each of the *Nitya Devee*s becomes the Moon of *Meru* in one year. (Further details in this regard can be had from the original book and its commentary called *Manorama*).

(vii) *Śree Chakra* has three imaginative halls called *Bhoo, Kailāsa* and *Meru Prastārams*. Imagining with the eight *Vāg Devee*s starting from *Vashinee* is called *Bhoo Prastāram*. Imagining along with the mother letters (from *'A'* till *'Ksha'*) is called *Kailāsa Prastāram*. Imagining along with the 16 *Nityā Devee*s (*Śreedevee* is also one among them) is called *Meru Prastāram*. This name indicates that **She** has this *Meru Prastāram* as her dwelling place. (*Sanatkumāra, Sanandana* and *Vashishta Samhitas* describes such imagination in three types).

(viii) According to *Gnānārnava Tantra*, a *mantra* with nine letters is called *Meru*. (If the duplications are removed, the *Panchadashee mantra* has only nine letters). **She** has this *Merumantra* as her dwelling place. These nine letters are cryptically indicated;

Bhoomishchandra: Shivo Māyā Shukti: Krushnadhvamādanou I
Ardhachandrashcha Bindushcha Navārno Meruruchyate II

(ix) The gem called *Meru* in the garland of chanting or when counted in fingers, the base line of the middle finger of the palm is called *Meru*. **She** has these places as her dwelling places.

776. ***Mandārakusumapriyā* - मन्दारकुसुमप्रिया**

(i) One who is fond of *Mandāra* flower (shoe flower - Hibiscus Rosa-sinensis).
(ii) *Mandāra* is one of the five trees in the world of *Devas* and also indicates white *Erukka* (white - wild weed).

777. ***Veerārādhyā* - वीराराध्या**

(i) One who is worshipped by the heroics.
(ii) Here a person is called as hero, if he is free from the feeling of duality and its symbols like self, this, etc. and the corresponding imaginations. He should have such mind control and ability. They enjoy the self-form. The icon mentioned in *Panchāshikā* is;

Ahami Pralayam Kurvan Idama: *Pratiyogina*: I
Parākramam Paro Bhunkte Svātmānamshivāpaham II

(iii) The names 836 – *Veeramātā* and 899 – *Veerā* may also be referred.

778. ***Virāḍroopā* - विराड्रूपा**

(i) One who is in the form of *Virāt*, the cosmic whole.
(ii) In the 256th name *Vishvaroopā*, it was mentioned about *Virāt* –the subtle form of the five elements which is the *Brahmāṇḍam* and who is interested in that form called *Hiraŋyagarba*, *Vaishvānara*, *Ĕshwaran* and *Virāt*. **She** is in that *Virāt* form.

779. ***Virajā* - विरजा**

(i) One who is without any stain or sin originated by the *Rajo* character.
(ii) When such meaning is said, the prefix *'Vi'* has to be taken in the opposite sense – i.e. without the character called *Rajo*.
(iii) The verses of *Mahānārāyaŋopanishad* (20th chapter) and *Tatva-soḍanā* may be reminded; *Virajā Vipāpma*...
(iv) The word *Rajas* means splendour, water and world. While accepting these meanings the prefix *'Vi'* has to be specifically considered.
(v) The presiding deity in the place called *Virajā* in Utkala state (present

Orissa) is called *Virāja*. **She** is in that form.

(vi) The usage of this name in *archana* is *Virājase Namaha*.

780. *Vishvatomukhee* - विश्वतोमुखी

(i) One who has faces in all directions.

(ii) **She** is present in all places and directions where the devotees meditate upon. Hence this name says that **She** has faces in all directions. Whichever form the devotee meditates upon **She** is present in that form. *Svetāshvatara Upanishad* says; *Vishvatas Chakshuruta Vishva Tomukha*:. In other places of *Veda* also it is said that; *Sarvata*: *Pānipādam Tatsarvatokshi Shiromukham*. It need not be concluded that these *Veda* statements are contradicting the other statements which say that *Brahmam* does not have hands or legs. The *Veda* statements, which originated later explain the physical form of *Brahmam*. Hence these two different types of statements do not contradict each other.

(iii) *Śreemad Bhagavad Geeta* (IX-15) also says - Some devotees worship Me in various ways as the one, as the distinct and as the all-faced;

Gnānayagnena Chāpyanye Yajanto Māmupāsate I
Ekatvena Pruthaktvena Bahudhā Vishvatomukham II

781. *Pratyagroopā* - प्रत्यग्रूपा

(i) One who is visible to those who see within self.

(ii) The organs or senses are to identify the characters of things outside – i.e. they look outward. Hence they are called *Bahirmukham* or *Parāngmukham*. In the same way looking inward is called *Antarmukham* or *Pratyanmukham*. In the creation, the nature of the organs is only to look outward and not otherwise. This is mentioned in *Kaṭopanishad* (IV-1) as; "*Parānchikhāni Vyatrunat Svayambhoo*: *Tasmātparan Pashyati Nātarātman*".

(iii) **She** is visible to those who control their organs and look inward. The same message is described in 870th name – *Antharmukha-samārādhyā* and 871st name *Bahirmukha Suturlabhā* – She is difficult to be seen by those who have outward looking organs.

(iv) The same message has been mentioned in many places in *Śreemad Bhagavad Geeta* – for instance;

Ananyachetа: *Satatam Yo Mām Smarati Nityasha*: I
Tasyāham Sulabha: *Pārtha Nityayuktasya Yogina*: II (VIII-14)

Mayyeva Mana Ādhatsva Mayi Buddhim Niveshaya I
Nivasishyasi Mayyeva Ata Oordhvam Na Samshaya: II (XII-8)

782. ***Parākāshā*** **- पराकाशा**

(i) One who is the transcendental ether.

(ii) Ether is omnipresent. Its presence can be felt. But its dimension is not visible. Hence it is subtle. **She** is in that form.

(iii) By the word ether, the Supreme Being is indicated. The below *Veda* phrases confirm this. *Brahma Sūtra* (I-1-22); *Ākāshastal Lingāt* and in *Chāndogya Upanishad* (I-9-1); *Ākāsho Itihovā Chākāsho Hyevebhyo Jyāyānākāsha*: *Parāyanam*. This is not the ether, which is one of the basic five elements. *Koorma Purāŋa* confirms that *Śreedevee*, who is the Supreme Being, is in the form superior radiance- space (*parākāsham*) – the great divine energy of Supreme Being is ether; *Yasya Sā Paramā Devee Shaktirākāshasamsthita*. Again it says, **She** is the only origin of the universe, **She** is everything, **She** controls everything, **She** is *Māheshwaree* and *Shakti* and does not have origin, is called as ether and **She** is so bright;

Ittham Hi Sā Jagatee Yoniregā Sarvātmikā Sarvaniyāmikā Cha I
Māheshwaree Shaktiranāḍisiddhā Vyomābhidhānāḍiv Rājateeva II

(iv) *Taitreeya Upanishad* (III-6-1) says that the *Brahmam* is established in the superior radiance-space – fixed there; *Parame Vyoman Pratishṭita*:. This ether is of two types – Macrocosm and Microcosm (*Brahmānḍam* and *Pindāndam*). Both are tools to identify the *Brahmam*. **She** is in that bright form.

(v) The superior radiance-space in the Microcosm is again of two types. *Śree Bhāskara Rāya* quotes a verse (32) from *Kālidāsa*'s (there is difference in opinion whether this is the same *Kālidāsa* who wrote *Raguvamsa*, etc). book called *Chitgagaŋa Chandrika*. According to this, there is fire in the ether between the Sun and Moon in the heart. The ether above the peak of it, is the superior radiance-space;

Hrut (*Druk*) *Kriyātma Shashi Bhānumadhyaga*:
Khe Charatyanaladrushti Dhāmaya: I
Yattadhoordhva Shikaram Param Nabhas
Tatra Darshaya Shiva m Tvamambike II

This has been differently mentioned in *Svachchanda Sangraha*. Above the forehead till the end of the skull is called *Dvādashāntam*. The area two inches from that place is called superior *param* + *vyoma* - radiance-space (*parākāsham*);

Dvadhashāntam Lalātordhvam Kapālordvasānakam I
Dvyangulordhvam Shirodeshāt Param Vyoma Prakeertitam II

Thus **She** is in the form *parākāsham* defined in various ways.

(vi) The ether beyond the seven oceans is called *parākāsham* (the description given in 775th name *Merunilayā*, according to *Tantra Rāja Tantra* – 28th chapter, may be referred). *Śreedevee* is there during the 16th year of *Kruta Yuga* (era). During the first 15 years, other *Tithi Nitya Devee*s dwell there one by one in each year. Since **She** is the form of all the *Tithi Nitya Devee*s, **She** is called as *Parākāsha*.

(vii) *Parāga* indicates a type of penance. *Āshā* means direction or desired thing. Hence the summarised meaning would be that **She** is to be reached through penance.

(viii) Or, **She** enjoys the fruit of the above said penance (it has to be split as *Parāgam* + *Ashnāti*).

(ix) *Agam* means sin or sorrow. **She** eats or destroys great sins and sorrow.

(x) *Pratikāsham* means simile; *Parākāsham* is antonym to that. Hence it means that **She** is without any similarity or comparison. 389th name *Nirupamā* also conveys the same message.

783. *Prāŋadā* - प्राणदा

(i) One who gives life to all.

(ii) The word *Prāŋan* (life) indicates the five breaths viz., *Prāŋa, Apāna, Samāna, Udāna & Vyāna* and again the 11 organs (5 organs of action, 5 organs of knowledge and mind).

(iii) The verb *Da* means to give. Hence it has to be construed that **She** gives the above said life.

(iv) It can also be split as – *Prānān + Dyati – Gandayati* – to obliterate. That is, it means that **She** wipes out the above said *Prāŋan*.

784. *Prāŋaroopiŋee* - प्राणरूपिणी

(i) One who is in the form of breath/ life.

(ii) *Chāndogya Upanishad* says that the word *Prāŋa* indicates the *Brahmam*; *Prāno Brahma Kam Brahma Kham Brahma*. In the *Kousikee Brāhmanam*, in the statement; *Prānosme Pragnātmā Tam Mamayuramrutamupasva*, the word *Prāŋa* indicates the *Brahmam*. This has been evidenced in the *Brahma Sūtra*, *Prānātikaraŋam*.

(iii) The word *Prāŋa* originates from the root word *Prā Poorano* (to fill).

Hence it indicates the completeness. The *Veda* statement; *Poorŋamada*: *Poonamidam*.. also indicates that the word *Prāŋa* means *Brahmam*.

(iv) *Manu Smruti* (XII-123) also says that the word *Prāŋa* indicates *Brahmam*;

Enameke Vadantyagnim Manumanye Prajāpatim I
Indramanye Param Prāŋamapare Cha Maheshvareem II

In some schools this is interpreted as fire, *Manu*, *Prajāpati*, *Indra*, breath and Supreme Being.

(v) These three evidences give the meaning of this name *Prāŋaroopiŋee*.

(vi) One breath is to once inhale and exhale. The calculation of time as day, month, etc., is done by breath only. *Tithi Nityā Devee*s are in the form of time. Since the time origins from breath, it can be taken as that *Tithi Nityā Devee*s are the breath. *Śreedevee* is also one of the *Tithi Nityā Devee*s and hence **She** is *Prāŋaroopiŋee*. The related verses in *Tantra Rāja Tantra* (27th chapter) may be referred; *Athashoḍasa Nityānām Kālena Prāŋatochyate*.

(vii) Also, the 22.5 breaths respectively create the zodiac signs Aries, etc. Thus the zodiac signs, Sun, Moon and the rest, originate from breath only. Hence **She** is *Prāŋaroopiŋee*.

785. *Mārtānḍa Bhairavārādhyā* – मार्ताण्ड भैरबाराध्या

(i) One who is adored by *Mārtānḍabhairava*, a form of *Shiva*.

(ii) In the *Śreepura* between 22nd and 23rd walls there is the devotee of *Śreedevee* named *Mārtānḍabhairava*. This has been mentioned, *Durvāsa's* book called *Lalitāstavaratna* (100th verse): "In my heart I adore *Mārtānḍabhairava*, decked with the jeweled crown, sporting with his wife *Chāvā* who is the energy which supplies light to the eyes;

Chakshus Matee Prakāshana Shaktich Chāyā Samārachita Kelim I
Mānikyamukuṭa Ramyam Manye Mārtānḍabhairavam II

Mārtānḍa is another name for Sun. Sage *Kāshyapa* and *Atiti* worshipped the Supreme Being, in the midst of the solar galaxy and got the boon of a child birth. The pregnant *Atiti* followed ardent vows. When she was weak she gave birth to a child and hence the baby was born as an inert egg. When the couple worshipped the Supreme Being, that egg got life. That baby became Sun by worshipping the Supreme Being in solar galaxy. Since the baby was born when *Atiti* followed ardent vows, the baby had a ferocious form. Hence he is called *Bhairava*. Since he was born from the inert egg, (*mrta* and *anda*) he is called *Mārtānḍa*. He is the Sun who is one in the list of great 12 devotees of *Śreedevee*. He dwells between 22nd and 23rd walls alongwith his consort *Chāyā Devee* and worships *Śreedevee*.

(iii) The fruits or results part of this *Sahasranāma* says that *Mārtāṇḍabhairava* makes the eyes of enemies of the devotees of *Śreedevee* as blind. He is so adamant in protecting the devotees of *Śreedevee*.

(iv) *Bhairava* means *Vatuka* and other different kinds. Concerning the worship of *Śreedevee* by the Sun, the *Padma Purāŋa* says - the Sun after worshipping daily a jeweled image of *Śreedevee* obtained his pure divine lofty position. This has also been described in *Kālikā Purāŋa*.

(v) *Bhiru* means the one who is of frightened nature. The nearness of them is called *Bhairavam*. It implies that *Śreedevee* is worshipped by cowardly people. *Saptashatee* (4th chapter) says that **She** protects them; *Durge Smrutā Harasi Bheetimashesha Janto*:

(vi) In general ladies are fearful in nature. **She** is worshipped by them.

(vii) According to the *Shiva Sūtra* (I-5) "effort is called *Bhairava*"; *Udyamo Bhairava*:. Some of the interpreters give the meaning of *Udyama* as effort. Actually, the word *Udayam* is formed by joining the words *Ud* + *Yam*. In the book called *Vimarshinee* by *Kshemarāja*, this has been explained as the chit that is created without advance intimation. There is also an indication that *Bhairava* is *Shiva*. Since it is a tool that shows *Shiva, Udhyama* is called as *Bhairava*. it is the Sun (*Mārtāṇḍa*) because it destroys the darkness of confusion. This name also indicates that **She** is worshipped by those who got the knowledge of *Shiva* by eradicating the darkness called confusion.

Shiva Sūtra (III-7) says - "By conquering confusion, by the expansion of the endless, victory over innate knowledge";

Mohajayādanantābhogāt Sahaja Vidyā Jaya: II

The *Vārttikakāra* explains the meaning thus - "Confusion means darkness, i.e. inborn egoism, by overcoming this, the Sun of effort is produced; Endless *samskāras* (good mental tendencies); Expansion means the expansion of the *samskāras*. To the *Yogin* who thus understands victory means attainment of *Sahaja Vidya*. The meaning of this can be read in the interpretations of *Sūtras*.

786. *Mantriŋeenyastarājyadhoo*. - मन्त्रिणीन्यस्तराज्यधूः

(i) One who has handed over regal authority to *Mantriŋee Devee*.

(ii) *Mantriŋee Devee* has different names like *Rāja Shyāmalā*, *Rājamātangee*, etc. She is the minister of the empress *Śreedevee*. **She** has delegated the responsibility of administering the state to her. The commander of armies responsibility has been delegated to *Vārāhi Devee* (also called as *Daŋḍanātā*, *Panchamee*, etc).. The participation of these *Devee*s in the battle with *Bhanḍāsura* has been mentioned in the names –

69 – *Geyachakrarathārooḍhamantriŋeeparisevitā*

70 –*Kirichakrarathārooḍhadaŋḍanāthāpuraskrutā*

75 – *Mantrinyambāvirachitavishaggavadhatoshitā* and

76 – *Vishukraprāŋaharanavārāheeveeryananditā*

Also, in the *Panchapanchikā pooja*, they are worshipped in the *Pancharatnāmbākosha* (this has been described in 428th name - *Panjchakoshāntarasthitā*).

(iii) **She** is in the form of *Leela* as per the statement "*Lalanāt Lalita*". She is predominantly pleasure oriented. **She** has delegated the administration to *Mantriŋee* and the in-charge of armies to *Vārāhi*, **She** is involved in gratification. (Even after delegating such tasks, it has to be taken as that **She** supervises them constantly).

(iv) The word *mantri* (minister) indicates those who chant *mantras*. Or a *mantra* is one which is with the character of repeating or protecting with pure mind and a *mantra* is one who has such a mind. An effort to integrate these people with *Śreedevee* is called *Mantriŋee*. The fruit of such an effort makes a union of devotees and *Yogis* and a possession with *Śreedevee*. *Shiva* Sūtra (III-1,2 and3) may be referred in this regard – III-1; *Chittam Mantra*:, III-2; *Prāyatna Sādhaka*: and III-3 *Vidyā Shareera Sphrattā Mantrarahasyam*.

787. ***Tripureshee* - त्रिपुरेशी**

(i) One who is the head of the three *Puras*.

(ii) It was explained in 775th name - *Merunilayā*, that there are three cities belonging to *Brahma*, *Viṣhŋu* and *Shiva* to the East, South-west and South-East directions of the *Meru* Mountain and at the centre *Śreedevee*'s city. **She** is the head of these three cities. (Since **She** only created the three Gods such an analogy is correct).

(iii) *Tripureshi* is also the name of the deity governing *Sarvāsāparipooraka Chakra* i.e., "The circle that fulfills all desires," the second *āvarana* of *Śree Chakra*. Since there is no difference between the presiding deities of *Chakras* and *Śreedevee*, this name calls *Śreedevee* as *Tripureshee*.

788. ***Jayatsenā* - जयत्सेना**

(i) One who is with victorious armies of divine forces.
(ii) In every war with demons or bad elements, the army of *Śreedevee* only wins. Hence this name.
(iii) *Jayatsena* is the name of a king and **She** is in his form.

789. ***Nistraiguṇyā* - निस्त्रैगुण्या**

(i) One who is devoid of the three qualities.
(ii) *Mahat* originated from the nature - Egoism from that *mahat* - The five primary elements from egoism with the help of the three qualities viz., *satva, rajas* and *tamas*. From that originated the universe. This is the order of creation in a nutshell. The three qualities were there with the universe. That is, the universe characterised its qualities into three and helped the egoism. This name indicates that **She** is beyond these three qualities. The names – 139 – *Nirguṇā*, 397 - *Moolaprakruti:*, 398 – *Avyaktā* and 399 – *Vyaktāvyaktasvaroopiṇee* may be referred.

790. ***Parāparā* - परापरा**

(i) One who is in the form of *Brahmam* called *Parā* (absolute), *Aparā* (relative) and *Parāparā* (both absolute and relative).
(ii) *Parā* – the other person, *Aparā* – dependent on self, i.e., it respectively means an enemy and a friend. *Śreemad Bhagavad Geeta* (IX-29) says that the *Brahmam* is of these two types; *Na Me Dveshyosti Na Priya*: - I have neither foe nor friend.
(iii) *Parā* - superior and *Aparā* - inferior. *Sruti* says, "*Brahmam* is the servant. *Brahmam* is ferry-men; and Brahmam is these gamblers";

Brahmadāsā Brahmadāshā Brahmameme Kitavā Uta.

(iv) *Parā* - he who is far off, *Aparā* he who is near. *Śreemad Bhagavad Geeta* (XIII-15) - "I am far and near".
(v) These different meanings are based on the *Vihsva* dictionary; *Parā*: *Syāt Uttama Anātma Vairi Dooreshu Kevale* II
(vi) In general the *Brahmam* is said to be two types viz., pure form and an adulterated form. *Parāparam* is of third type.

a. The *Prashno Upanishad* (V-2) says - "This is indeed, Oh

Satyakāma, para and *apara*"; *Etadvai Satyakāma Param Chāparam Cha*. The *Smruti* also says, "Two Brahmams are to be known, one is *Parā* and the other is *Aparā*"; *Dve Brahmaŋee Veditavye Param Chāparameva Cha*.

b. *Parā* - posterior; *Aparā* - anterior. *Shiva* with the unified form of *Shakti* is *Parāparam or Parabrahmam*. **She** is in that form. To give such meanings for the words *Para* or *Apara* there are enough evidences in *Vedas*; *"Yuje Vām Brahma Poorvyam Namobhi:"* or *"Esho Ushā Apoorvyā Vyachchati Priyā Diva*: II".

c. The author suggests reading *Shivānandalaharee* in this regard.

(vii) *Parā* and *Aparā* are the twofold ether.

(viii) The twofold knowledge, as described in the *Muŋḍaka Upanishad* (I-1-4) *Parā Vidyā* and *Aparā Vidya*. The *Linga Purāŋa* also says, "Two kinds of knowledge should be known, *parā* and *aparā*; the *Vedas* are *Para* and the *Vedāngās* are *Apara*.

(ix) *Skānda Purāŋa* (*Yagna Vaibhava Kānḍa*, 6th chapter) says two types of the *Praŋava* are *Parā* and *Apara*. *Parā* has the qualities of *Sachitānanda* and *Aparā* is pure form, in the form of sound. Since it prays *Parabrahmam*, it is called as *Praŋava* (the word *nava* has such a meaning). Since it is a tool to reach *Parabrahmam*, it is called as *Praŋavam*.

(x) There itself, the interpretation of *Vedas* is of two types – the Supreme Being is *Param* and the tool to reach it is called *Aparam*.

(xi) In the *Yoga Sāstra* also knowledge is divided into three - *Parā, Aparā* and *Parāpara*. For it is said, "Knowledge is said to be threefold by the division of *para, apara* and *parāpara*. Of these, the first is the supreme knowledge and is the cause of cognizing the Lord, the bondage and the Self. The second, *aparā* knowledge, is simply the cause of cognising the bondage. The *parāparā* knowledge is, just as the change of the sight between a man and cat in the night, it does not distinguish the marks *vilakshaŋā*".

(xii) *Nityā Shoḍashikārnava* (8th chapter, 2nd verse onwards) explains that *Śreedevee*'s *pooja* is of three types – *Parā, Aparā and Parāpara. Para* is worshipping with non-duality in mind (however it is done). *Apara* is worshipping *Śree Chakra*. *Parāpara* is worshipping different types of idols.

(xiii) The speech is of two types – *Parā* and *Apara*. *Aparā* includes *Pashyantee, Madyamā* and *Vaikharee*.

(xiv) *Para* is the fourth state. *Aparā* is the three states awaken (*Jāgrath*), dream (*Swapna*) and deep sleep (*Sushupti*).

(xv) The *homa* (sacrificial fire) is of two types *Parā* and *Apara*. The *Parā* is the state after the destruction of all dualistic interpretations respecting the known, the knower and knowledge. The *Parā homa* is said to be that which being absorbed, does not arise again, in the blaze of the great eternal fire of own Self, which burns forever without fuel. This is done in an imaginative way.

The *aparahoma* is again two-fold, gross and subtle. The gross form offering the articles in the form directly. The subtle form is done in the fire in the *Moolādhāra* i.e. *Prānāgnihotra*. In the *Sāmayika Pooja*, which is part of *Navāvarana Pooja* in the *Bindu Tarpaṇa*, there is a verse stating that - in the fire called *Samvit*, which burns without any fuel, all the 36 *tatvas* (from *Shiva* onwards till earth) are offered. By chanting this verse, after getting permission from the teacher the special *argya* from the self-vessel is consumed. That verse is as follows;

Antar Nirantara Nirindhanamedhamāne
Mohāndhakāra Paripanthini Samvidagnou
Kasminchdatbhuta Mareechi Vikāsa Bhoomou
Vishvam Juhomi Vasudhādi Shivāvasānam II

382nd name *Rahastarpaṇatarpitā* may be referred.

(xvi) In the 732nd name *Nāmapārāyaṇapreetā*, six types of *pārāyaṇas* were described. In that the *mantra pārāyaṇa* is one of the types.

(xvii) *Varāha Purāṇa* says when speaking about the *Trimoortis* - The creative energy is said to be *Para* which is the white colour. *Vaishnavee*, which is red and long-eyed is *Apara*. The *Raudri* energy is called *parāpara*.

(xviii) Further relevant meanings may be added.

Note: (to be read in conjunction with (xvi) above; the original book reads as – *"Atra Parāparayorvibhajanena Saptadashārthamelanena Tu Pancheti Dvāvimshati: Anyepi Yathālābham Yojaneyā*: II". *Śree Gaṇesa Iyer* has written this in his foreword to the book written by *Śree RA Sastry*; *Parapara* gives a four syllable *mantra*, this if added to the fifteen syllables, gives a nineteen syllabled *mantra*. If added to the sixteen syllables it gives a twenty syllabled *mantra*.

Śree RA Sastry also gives a foot note; Here the commentator does not show the reason how the *parāparā* is to be taken as four. (The meaning of this part is to be made clear).

791. *Satyajñānānandaroopā* - सत्यज्ञानानन्दरूपा

(i) One who is in the form of truth, wisdom and bliss.

(ii) The meaning is that **She** is in the form of *Satchitānanda*. The *Taitireeya Upanishad* (II-1) says, "The *Brahmam* is truth, wisdom, infinity"; *Satyam Gnānamanandam Brahma*. The *Brahadāraŋya Upanishad* (III-9-28) says - "*Brahmam* is eternal, wisdom, bliss"; *Vignānamānandam Brahma*.

(iii) This name can be split in other way also – *Satee* + *Agnā* + *Anānandaroopa*. I.e. *Sat* - true wisdom, *Ajnā*- those who are ignorant of that, *Ānanda* - such people are without bliss; *Roopa* – form. I.e. **She** causes pain to those ignorant of the true wisdom. The *Isāvasya Upanishad* (9th verse) and *Brahadāraŋya Upanishad* (IV-4-10) says, "Those who worship with ignorance enter into deep darkness".

(iv) Again the name can be split as *Satee* + *Agnā*+*Anānanda* + *Roopa*. That is, **She** gives the world called *Anantā*: for those who do not have the knowledge of *Śreedevee*. This world is full of darkness without any happiness. The *Brhadāraŋya Upanishad* (IV-4-II) says, "Those worlds are called *Ānanda*, which are covered with deep darkness; the ignorant and unwise men go to those worlds after death";

Anandā Nām Te Lokā Andhena Tamasāvrutā: I
Tānste Pretyābhigacchantya Vidvāmsobudhā Janā: II

792. ***Sāmarasyaparāyaŋā* - सामरस्यपरायणा**

(i) One who is the Supreme abode of the co-equal nature with *Shiva.*

(ii) With the co-equal nature is unison. That state of *Shiva* and *Shakti* is the greatest. *Tripuropanishad* describes that equality;

Bhaga: *Shaktir Bhagavān Kām Esha*: *Ubhā Dātārāviha Soubhagānām* I
Sampradhānou Samasttvou Samodayo: *Samshaktrajarā Vishvayoni*: II

(iii) The learned men (*Chandraloka* V-1) say, "We praise the ancient pair, the parents of the universe. Each is the end attained by the penance of the other";

Paraspara Tapa: *Sampat Phalāyita Parasparou* I
Prapancha Mātā Pitarou Prānchou Jāyāpatee Stuma: II

Kālidāsa (*Chitkakana Chandrikā* – 100th verse) also says - "*Shiva* milks out the essence of the co-equal nature when the waves of the enjoyer, enjoyment and the means are calm"; *Bhoktru Bhogya Karanormi Samkshaye Sāmarasya Rasadohinee Shiva.*

(iv) *Sāmarasya*, the worlds of *Devas*, with them, *Parāyana* abode or refuge. **She** is the refuge of the *Devas*.

(v) *Rasya* - songs, *Sāma* - *Sāma Veda* songs, *Parāyana* - fond of. She is fond of *Sāma Veda* songs. The *Vishva* dictionary says, "*Parāyana* means - fond of, devoted to, dependent"; *Parāyanamabheeshtam Syāttat Parāshrāyayo Rapi.*

793. *Kapardinee* - कपर्दिनी

(i) One who is the consort of *Shiva* who is called as *Kapardee.*

(ii) *Shiva* 's raised tuft of lustrous braided hair (matted hair) is called *Kapardam.* One who has it is *Kapardee.* This name is mentioned in *Śree Rudram* for *Shiva* ; *Nama*: *Kapardinee Cha Vyuptakeshāya Cha.* His consort is *Kapardinee.*

(iii) According to the commentator of the *Soota Samhita,* the word *Kapardam* means - earth, mockery and praise. Hence *Kapardinee,* greatly praised.

(iv) *Ka* - water, *Pooram* – the flow, *dai* - sanctifies. I.e. *Shiva* has even the holy Ganges in his hair and further sanctifies it. *Kapardee* is to sanctify even Ganges. His consort.

(v) *Kapardam* - cow-dung cake. When *Shiva* incarnated as *Mailāra,* his wife called *Mahālasā,* was decked with a garland of cow-dung cakes. The *Vishva* dictionary says, "*Karpada* means the matted hair of *Shiva* and cow-dung cakes". In another place instead of cow-dung it is meant as *Chozhi* (a kind of shell).

(vi) *Devee Purāṇa* says that *Shiva,* a deity worshipped at *Chagalānda,* one of the sixty eight sacred places, is called *Kapardee.* His consort is *Karpardinee. Sootha Samhita* (4-43-69) names *Śreedevee* as *Prachaṇḍa.*

(vii) *Śreedevee* also has a form with matted hair. The *Lagustava* (11th verse) of *Kālidāsa* suggests worshipping *Śreedevee* with crescent in her matter hair.

794. *Kalāmālā* - कलामाला

(i) One who wears all the (64) arts as garland.

(ii) Out of the various jewels of *Śreedevee* 64 arts is an important jewel. An indication is made here that *Śreedevee* has lots of prides, plumes and super-bias.

(iii) *Kala* – exquisiteness or beauty, *Mā* – luster or brightness or light, *Lā* – to bring. This can mean that **She** has exquisiteness and luster

795. *Kamadhuk* - कामधुक्

(i) One who fulfills all the desires.

(ii) **She** fulfills all the desires of **Her** devotees. This was mentioned in 63rd name – *Kāmadāyinee* and again will be mentioned in 989th name – *Vānchitārtha Pradāyinee*. In *Trishatee*, 43rd name *Eepsidārtapradāyinee* and 240th name *Sakaleshtadā* may be referred.

(iii) Fulfilling all the desires is the nature of the celestial cow *Kāmadhenu*. She is in that form. Devee Upanishad also preys; *"Sā No Mandreshamoorjam Duhānā Dhenur Vāgasmānu Pashushtotatitu"*.

(iv) It can also be meant that She is in the form of five *Kāmdughāmbā Devees* used in *Pancha Panchikā Pooja*.

(v) 4th verse of *Soundaryalaharee* says that **She** bestows more than what was asked or desired; *Tvadanya Panibhyām*.

796. *Kāmaroopiņee* - कामरूपिणी

(i) One who is in the form of *Kāma*, the supreme *Shiva*.

(ii) **She** is in the form of *Kāmeshvara*. *Śreedevee* and *Kāmeshvara* have the same forms, decorations, weapons, etc., **She** is in his form.

(iii) *Shiva* who desires to create the universe as described in *Taitreeya Upanishad* (II-5), "He desired, let me become many, let me create beings"; *Sokāmayata Bahusyām Prajāyeya*. The *Brahadāraņya Upanishad* (III-9-II) says - "He is the person consisting of desire, it is he, Oh *Sākalya*, who is His deity? He replied, woman is his deity"; *Ya Evāyam Kāmamaya: Purusha: Sa Eva Daivashākalyas Tasya Kā Devateti Striya Iti Hovācha* II

(iv) It can also be construed that **She** assumes any form at will.

797. *Kalānidhi*: - कलानिधिः

(i) One who is the reservoir of arts.

(ii) *Kalās* were described before (in name 236 – *Chatushshashṭi kalāmayee*). **She** is the treasure of those arts.

(iii) *Kalās* are *jeevas* (souls). The *Brahadāraņya Upanishad* (I-5-15) says, "The *ātman* (soul) is the sixteenth *Kalā* of him". I.e. one sixteenth part; *Ātmaivāsya Shoḍasheekala*.

(iv) **She** is the fountain head of *kalās* of Moon. Hence it can be said that **She** is in the form of Moon's galaxy.

(v) According to the *Shiva Sūtra* (I-3 – *Yonivarga*: *Kalāshareeram*), *Kalā* means action (*karmam*); hence all actions end in her; *Śreemad Bhagavad Geeta* (IV-33) also says, "All actions, Oh *Partha*, end in wisdom"; *Sarvam Karmākhilam Pārththa Gnāne Parisamāpyate.*

(vi) In practice this name has to be used as *Kalānidhaye Namaha*.

798. ***Kāvyakalā* – काव्यकला**

(i) One who is the poetic art.

(ii) *Kāvyā*, the work of poets, which is divided into various types, namely poems, drama, etc. They all originate from sounds and words. **She** is in those forms.

(iii) It can also be said that **She** is in the form creating the above said arts and the corresponding ability.

(iv) To write a poem, a creative thought has to originate. By worshipping *Śreedevee* in a particular manner, She blesses with the ability of creating poems. For instance the 15th, 16th and 17th verses of *Soundaryalaharee* may be referred.

(v) *Sukra*, the teacher of demons is a poet. He knows a *mantra* called *Mruta Sanjeevanee* (to give re-birth to the dead). Others do not know this. This can be said as an art. **She** is in that form.

799. ***Rasagnā* - रसज्ञा**

(i) One who knows all the ten tastes (expressions/ emotions)

(ii) The 51st verse of *Soundaryalaharee*; *Shive Srungārārdra*.. may be referred.

(iii) **She** is in the form of the tongue, which recognises the taste.

800. ***Rasashevadhi*: - रसशेवधिः**

(i) One who is the treasure of Supreme Bliss.

(ii) *Rasa*, the nectar of *Brahmam*. The *Taitreeya Upanishad* (II-6-1) says - "He is the rasa, when this essence is obtained one becomes blessed"; *Raso Vai Sa*: I *Rasam Hyevāyam Labdvānandee Bavati* II

(iii) The *Brahmāṇḍa Purāṇa* also says, "*Rasa* is the supreme *Brahmam*. *Rasa* is the supreme way, *Rasa* is the giver of light to man, *Rasa* is said to be the seed. He is the *rasa*, one having obtained the *rasa* becomes blessed. This, on the authority of the scriptures, *rasa* represents the vital breath. Who can live or who can breathe without Him;

Rasa Eva Param Brahma Rasa Eva Parāgati: I
Raso Hi Kāntida: *Pumsām Raso Reta Iti Smruta*: II

(iv) In practice, this has to be used as *Rasashevadhaye Namaha*.

Thus ends the ninth *Kalā* called *Vishva*.

*****

Section 10: *Bodhinee Kalā*

801. ***Pushṭā* - पुष्टा**

(i) One who is well nourished.
(ii) **She** has the 36 *tatvas* as her body and beyond it. Hence complete in all respects without any flaw. Hence *Pushṭa*.
(iii) It can be reminded that in *Saptashatee* (5th chapter) we read as;

Yā Devee Sarvabhooteshu Pushṭiroopena Samsthitā I
Namastasyai Namastasyai Namastasyai Namo Nama: II

(iv) **She** has many qualities and hence *Pushṭa*.
(v) **She** is nourished with the juice of *Brahmam*; bliss only gives completion. Since *Śree Devee* is of the form of *Brahmam*, **She** is *Pushṭa*.
    a. One who is nourished by Brahmins and hence *Pushṭa*.
    b. For instance one *Sruti* and one *Smruti* statements are given;

Brahmaŋai: *Poshitam Brahma*
Brahmayushmat Tadbrāhmanairāyushmat.

802. ***Purātanā* - पुरातना**

(i) One who is the most ancient being; **She** is primordial.
(ii) **She** was there even before creation of all other beings. **She** only created all. Hence *Purātana*. It can be compared to the poem in Tamil – *Thiruvempavai* (9th song) by *Mānickavachagar*; *"Munnai Pazham Porutkum Pazham Porule"*.
(iii) Since **She** has ancient qualities **She** is *Purātana*.
(iv) Instead of *Purātanee* it is *Purātanā*;
    a. Could be due to metre adjustment.
    b. The author mentions that it could be on account of a grammar note.

803. ***Poojyā* - पूज्या**

(i) One who is worthy of worship.
(ii) On account of the above said reasons, (complete, in the form of Supreme Bliss, ancient, filled with attributes, etc.). **She** is being worshiped by all. She is the most fit to be worshiped.
(iii) It can also be treated that **She** is expected by all. The hidden meaning is, since She bestows the four desires, everyone expects and wait for

her to get their desires fulfilled.

(iv) 213th name *Mahāpoojyā* and 580th name *Mahaneeyā* may be referred.

804. ***Pushkarā* – पुष्करा**

(i) One who gives nourishment (bliss or completeness) to all.

(ii) In Samskrit the letter *ra* and *la* are not much differentiated. Hence the word *Pushkam* (nourishment) is split as *Rāti* (*Lāti*) – giver and the meaning is considered.

(iii) In the same way it can be taken as *Pushkalā* – i.e. omnipresent.

(iv) In one of the books it is stated that **She** is one of the consorts of *Iyanar* - *Poorŋā* and *Pushkala*. Both the names mean fullness.

(v) According to *Devee Bhāgavatam* (VII-38-19) the place of *Gāyatree* is called as *Śreemadpushkaram*.

805. ***Pushkarekshaŋā* - पुष्करेक्षणा**

(i) One who has beautiful eyes like lotus.

(ii) It is the practice of the poets to compare the eyes and other organs of the body to Lotus, since it is a beautiful flower. Especially the eyes that are extending till the ears are considered to be so beautiful.

(iii) The *Vishva* dictionary says, "*Pushkara* means lotus, ether, water, elephant's trunk, end, herb, island, bird, place of pilgrimage, a certain musical note, a kind of serpent, the drum, head, sword and a fruit called *Khadgaphala*";

Pushkaram Pankaje Vyomni Paya: *Karikarāgrayo*: I
Oshadhee Dveepa Vihaga Teertha Rāgoragāntare II
Pushkaram Sooryavaktre Cha Kānde Khadkaphalepicha II

(iv) According to the *Padma Purāŋa*, in Astrology *Pushkara* is a certain planetary conjunction. When the Sun is in the asterism called *Vishākhā* and the Moon is in the *Krittikā*, the conjunction is called *Pushkara* and it is a very rare to happening;

Vishākhastho Yadā Bhānu: *Kruttikāsu Cha Chandramā* I
Sa Yoga: *Pushkaro Nama Pushareshvatidurlabha*: II

(v) In the above verse the word *Pushkara* which occurs for the second time means the earth. Again in the *Padma Purāŋa* we read "The *Devas* all the pericarp of the lotus earth, the *sāra* teachers (the meaning is not very clear) in the lotus, they call divine mountains. The upper petals of the lotus became a *Mileccha* (Barbarians) country.

The lower petals are the worlds of the serpents and the demons. Thus by the wish of *Nārāyaŋa*, the earth came out from the lotus – and hence the earth is called *Pushkara*";

Yā Padmakarnikā Devā: *Tām Pritveem Parchakshate* I
Ye Padme Sāraguravas Tān Divyān Parvatāniha II
Yāni Parnāni padmasya Mlechchadeshāstu Tebhavan I
Yānyadhobhāka Patrāni Te Sarpānām Suradvishām II
Evam Nārāyaŋasyarthe Mahee Pushkarasambhavā I
Pradurbhāvocha Chrāyas Tasmānnāmnā Pushkarasamjnitā II

(vi) *Kshaŋa* means remaining inactive. The *Amara* dictionary (V-431) says, "*Kshaŋa* means leisure, a division of time, festivity"; *Nirvyāpārasthithou Kālavisheshotsavayo*: *Kshaŋa*: Hence this means that **She** is idle in the earth and other meanings given above and hence the name *Pushkarekshaŋa*. (Being idle is not easy– only those who are idle know this. There is a saying, "provide double the food for those who are idle").

(vii) *Pushkara* also means the Banyan Tree; because *Matsya Purāŋa* says, "Because there is a Banyan tree in the *Pushkara* island it is called *Pushkara*". The *Vişhŋu Purāŋa* says, "The Banyan tree is in the *Pushkara* country that is the supreme abode of *Brahma*"; *Nyagrodha*: *Pushkaradveepe Brahmaŋa*: *Stānamuttamam*.

(viii) The *Narasimha Poorva Tābinee Upanishad*, (I-1] says, "That one *Prajāpati* was in the Banyan leaf"; *Sa Prajāpatireka*: *Sambhavat*. *Devee Bhāgavatam* says, the *Vişhŋu* in the name of *Bālamukunḍa*, who has the adjective of *Vadabadrasayee* is called as *Pushkara*. **She** looked at him with compassion and advised him the *Brahma Tatva*;

Vadabadrashayānāya Vishnave Bālaroopiŋe I
Shlokārdhena Tada Proktam Bhagavatyākhilārthadam II

(ix) *Pushkara* – water that submerged all the worlds. To create the world **She** sighted (*Ĕkshaŋā*) it. *Sruti* says;

Tāni Vā Etāni Cahtvāryambhāmsi Devāmanushyā: *Pitarosurā*:

(x) *Devee Bhāgavatam* (VII-38-20) says that the presiding deity in *Prabhāsa kshetra* is called *Pushkarekshiŋee*.

806. ***Paramjyoti*****: - परंज्योतिः**

(i) One who is the Supreme light.

(ii) The state without light is darkness. The Ignorance is the darkness in the mind. Once the light is on, the darkness goes away. When there is knowledge ignorance is removed. When it is dark neither inside nor outside the world is seen. The outside darkness is removed by Sun, Moon, stars, fire and other light galaxies. Sound is also light, because we recognise something with the help of sound in darkness also.

(iii) The above said Sun, etc., are illuminated only by **Her**. Hence **She** is called as supreme (*param*).

(iv) The related *Veda* statements;

a. The *Brhadāraŋya Upanishad* (IV-4-16) says, "That is light of light"; *Taddevā Jyotishām Jyotirāya Hopāsadamrutam*.

b. *Kaṭopanishad* (II-2-15) says, The Sun, the Moon and the stars do not shine by themselves; for **She** illuminates the mind that illuminates all of these;

Na Tatra Sooryo Bhāti Na Chandra Tārakam Nema
Vidyuto Bhānti Kutoyamagni: Tameva Bhāntamanubhāti
Sarvam Tasya Bhāsa Sarvamidam Vibhāti

c. *Chāndogya Upanishad* (VIII-3-4) - The sun shines only when he is illuminated by Him; *"Param Jyotirupasampadya"*.

d. The *Brhadāraŋya Upanishad* (III-9-10) "The supreme light one attains" - *Jyotis* here means the illuminator, for we see the same meaning given in such places, "the illuminator of the mind"; *Mano Jyoti*:

(v) *Paramjyotis* is the eight-syllable *mantra* described in the fifth chapter of the *Dakshiŋāmoorti Samhita*.

(vi) Self-eight syllable *mantra* has to be used as *Parasmai Jyotishe Namaha*.

807. ***Parandhāma* - परंधाम**

(i) One who is in the form of Supreme abode above all.

(ii) Here the word *Dhāma* has many a meaning viz., lustre, dwelling place, state (state of mind, etc.). All these meanings fit **Her**.

(iii) Let us consider the meaning lustre – It has been mentioned in many names about the lustre of *Śree Devee*; 414 – *Svaprakāshā*, 452 – *Tejovatee*, 597 – *Trikonāntaradeepikā*, 767 – *Ojovatee*, 768 – *Dyutidharā* and 806 - *Paramjyoti*:

(iv) *Śree Ādi Śaŋkara* in his commentary of *Vişhŋu Sahasranāma* for the 719th name – *Deeptamoorti*: mentions;

a. He who has the bright form of knowledge.

b. He is self-illuminating, bright and lustrous and hence *Deeptamoorti*:

(v) Now let us consider the meaning dwelling place – the great place;

a. The *Śreemad Bhagavad Geeta* (XV-6) says, "The sun never illuminates, nor moon, nor fire. After reaching it when one does not return, that is my supreme abode";

Na Tadbhāsayate Sooryo Na Shashānko Na Pāvaka: I
Yadgatvā Na Nivartante Taddhāma Paramam Mama II

b. *Śree Gouḍapādāchārya* in his book *Māntookya Kārikai* (I-5) advises, "The man who knows both the object of enjoyment as well as the enjoyer is never stained though he enjoys all the three states (awaken, dream and deep sleep)";

Trishoo Dhāmasu Yadbhogyam Bhoktā Yashcha Prakeertita:
Vedaitadubhayam Yastu Sa Bhunjāno Na Lipyate II

c. *Soota Samhitā* (*Yagna Vaibhava Kāṇḍa* – IV-11-32,33) also says, "He who knows the three states, namely waking, dreaming and deep sleeping, he is the Self, that is not the object, the object is super-imposed upon that. I take refuge in the supreme abode which is the evidence of the three abodes, characterized by reality, wisdom, bliss etc. and is the meaning of the word 'I'. *Dhāman*, the states of consciousness, *para*, beyond - **She** is beyond the states of consciousness;

Jāgrat Svapna Sushoptyākhyam Veda Dhāmatrāyam Tu Ya: I
Sa Evātmā Na that Drushyam Drushyam Tasmin Praklpitam II
Tridhāma Sākshinam Satya Gnānānandādi Lakshaṇam I
Tvamaham Shabda Lakshyārtham Param Dhāma Samāshraye II

d. The *Kaṭopanishad* (III-9) says, "That is the supreme abode of *Viṣhṇu*"; *Tadvishno*: *Paramam Padam*. The *Koorma Purāṇa* also says, "My energy is, *Maheshvaree, Gouree*, spotless, tranquil, reality, knowledge, bliss, the supreme abode";

Saishā Māheshvaree Gowree Mama Shaktir Niranjanā I
Shāntā Satyā Sadānandā Param Padamiti Sruti: II

(vi) In practice this name is used as *Parasmai Dhāmne Namaha*.

(vii) Considering the word *param* as indeclinable these two names can be used as *Paramjyotishe Namaha* and *Parandhāmne Namaha*.

808. ***Paramāṇu*: - परमाणुः**

(i) One who is the most subtle Supreme atom.

(ii) The *Kaṭopanishad* (II-20) says "More subtle than the atom", that is, difficult to know; *Anoraṇeeyan*.

(iii) It can be taken as **She** is the root of all commodities mentioned in the science of logic; *"Tārkika Kalpitā*: *Peelavopyasyā Eva Roopamiti Va"*.

(iv) *Aŋu* also means a *mantra*. Hence this name can be construed as to mean that **She** is in the form of great *mantra*.

(v) By quoting a grammatical rule, the author says that it is correct to say *Paramānu*:. For those who are interested in grammar – "*Paramā Cha Sāŋvee Cha Voto Guŋavachanāt Iti Vividhairvaikalpikatvāt Gneebabhāva*:" *Pāŋinee Ashṭātyāyee* – 4-1-44.

809. ***Parātparā* - परात्परा**

(i) One who is the most supreme of the supreme.

(ii) That is, **She** is beyond the very great *Trimoortis* - *Brahma*, *Vişhŋu* and *Rudra*. *Trishatee* 236th name - *Samānādhikavarjitā* says that there is no one equal to or above **Her**;

(iii) According to *Kāli Purāŋa* – one day (one day and night) of *Brahma* is called as *Para*. His day and night are of equal duration and they are called *Parārdham* – (it can be reminded that during any *Sankalpa* [declaring the desire to do *pooja*, etc.] this is being used). But, for the person, who is subtler than the subtle and minute than the minutest there is no bindings like day, night, year, etc., because he only creates the time and he is not controlled by time;

Tasya Brahmasvaroopasya Divārātram Cha Yadbhavet I
Tatparam Nāma Tasyārdham Parārdhamabhidheeyate II
Sa Eshvarasya Divasas Tāvatee Ratriruchyate I
Stoolāt Stoolatama: *Sookshmātyastu Sookshmatamo Mata*: II
Na Tasyāsti Divā Ratri Vyavahāro Na Vatsara: II

810. ***Pāshahastā* - पाशहस्ता**

(i) One who is bearing a noose in her hand.

(ii) Earlier itself in 8th name – *Rāgasvaroopapāshādhyā*, it was mentioned that *Śree Devee* has a noose (in the form desires) in her lower left hand.

(iii) It can also be taken as **She** removes the bonds (*pāsas*) with her hand.

(iv) The author proves through the *Pāŋini Sūtra*; "*Praharaŋārthebhya*: *Pare Nishṭhā Saptamyām*", that the usage *Pāshahastā* is grammatically correct.

811. ***Pāshahantree* - पाशहन्त्री**

(i) One who is the destroyer of the bonds.

(ii) The *Harivamsa* says, "When **She** had broken the bonds, of *Aniruddha* who was bound by the serpent-noose, which was like a thunderbolt, who was distressed in mind, she addressed him, offering to confer boons on him etc.";

Nāgapāshena Baddhasya Tasyopahata Chetasa: I
Trotayitvā Kanarar Nāga Panjaram Vajrasnnibham II
Baddham Bānapure Veeramaŋiruddhamabhāshata I
Sāntvayantee Cha Sā Devee Prasadābhimukhee Tadā II

812. ***Paramantravibhedinee* - परमन्त्रविभेदिनी**

(i) One who is the destroyer of hostile charms – who breaks the spells of one's enemies.

(ii) The enemy kings of **Her** devotees, with their power, influence, status and position, using their energy of *mantra* and force do instigation or witchcraft. *Para*, those who hate her devotees, i.e. kings; *mantra*, certain energies, which are included in the three energies, namely the energy of lordship (*Prabhu shakti*), council (*mantra shakti*) and armed force (*utsāha shakti*). **She** destroys those energies. Here the energy of *mantra* indicates the *mantra* chant by kings about the evil gods and the secret treachery.

(iii) *Para*, by enemies, *mantra*, the magical charms, or the *mantras* of the magical weapons. In the *Harivamsa*, when *Indra* sends words about *Pradyumna*, says, "To destroy those weapons you must now remember *Śree Devee*"; *Tadastra Pratighātāya Deveem Smartumihārhasee* II

(iv) *Parā* - superior, *mantra* - the *Panchadashee mantra, vibhedini* - **She** divides (into twelve kinds). For it is said in the *Tantras* "*Manu*, Moon, *Kubera*, Lopāmudrā, Cupid, *Agastya*, fire, Sun, *Nandi*, *Skanda*, *Shiva* and *Krodhabhattāraka* (*Durvāsa*), these twelve are the devotees of *Śree Devee*";

Manush Chandra Kuberashcha Lopāmudrā Cha Manmatha: I
Agastiragni: *SooryashchaNandee Skanda*: *Shiva Stathā* II
Krodhabhattārako Devyā Dvādashāmee Upāsakā: II

(v) *Para* - superior, *mantra* - those who meditate on *Śree Devee*, *avi* - their sins, *bhedinee* - destroys. The *Linga Purāŋa* says, "The word *avi* in the scriptures means sins, say the *Brahmins*. It is called *avimukta* (freed from sins) because it is freed from that sin and freed from illusion";

Avishabdena Pāpāni Kathyante Srutishu Dvijai: I

Tairmuktam Na Māyā Vyaktamavimuktate: Smrutam ll

813. ***Moortā* – मूर्ता**

(i) One who is with form or shape.

814. ***Amoortā* – अमूर्ता**

(i) One who is without form or shape.
(ii) That which has form is called *moortā*- Earth, water, fire, etc.; *Amoortā* means air, ether, etc., which are formless.
(iii) *Moortā* - the five gross elements mingled with each other; *Amoortā*- the subtle elements which are not mingled with each other. For we see the above two explanations given by the commentators in *Brahadāraŋya Upanishad* (II-3-1), *Brahmam* has two forms, *Moortā* and *Amoortā*;

Dve Vāva Brahmaŋo Roope Moortam Chāmoortam Cha.

(iv) *Moortā* - universe, *Amoortā* - *Brahmam*. The *Vişhŋu Purāŋa* says, "That *Brahmam* has two forms, *Moortā* and *Amoortā*, these two are respectively perishable and imperishable and both are in all beings. The imperishable is the ever remaining *Brahmam*, the perishable is the whole universe". The Logicians explain the word *Moortā* as that which has motion, but we should not adopt their theory as it has no foundation.
(v) *Śree Ādi Śaŋkara* in his commentary of *Vişhŋu Sahasranāma* for the 720th name – *Amoortimān* mention that **he** is formless because he does not have the bondage and actions (*karmās*).

815. ***Anityatruptā* - अनित्यतृप्ता**

(i) One who is satisfied even with our perishable offerings.
(ii) **She** asks for devotion only and not for costly things. These names can also be referred; 118 – *Bhaktipriyā*, 119 - *Bhaktigamyā*, 120 – *Bhaktivashyā*, 353 - *Bhaktimatkalpalatikā*, 372 - *Bhakta Mānasahamsikā*, 567 - *Bhaktanidhi:*, 747 - *Bhaktachittakeki Ghanāghanā*, 918 – *Chaitanyārghya Samārādhyā* and 919 – *Chaitanyakusumapriya*.
(iii) It is not that **She** does not get satisfied with anything (double negative). It actually is, **She** gets satisfied with anything offered provided it is with devotion. The *Śreemad Bhagavad Geeta* (IX-26)

says;

Patram Pushpam Phalam Toyam Yo Me Bhaktyā Prāyacchati I

Tadaham Bhaktryupahrutamashnāmi Prayatātmana: II

Whoever offers me with devotion, a leaf, a flower, a fruit or water, I accept that, the pious offering of the pure in heart. In the story of *Kuchela* and *Kaŋŋappa Nāyanar* this has been made very clear.

(iv) The word *Aniti* indicates breath i.e. the souls. **She** does not get satisfied with the souls. *Kaṭopanishad* (II-25) says, *Brahmins* and *Kshatriyās* are its food;

Yasya Brahma Cha Kshatram Chobhe Bhavata Odana:.

Since everything is digested, not satisfied only with souls.

(v) Everything in the world is perishable, excepting **Herself**. Even if those perishable things are offered to **Her**, **She** gets satisfied.

816. ***Munimānasahamsikā* - मुनिमानसहंसिका**

(i) One who swims like a swan in the rivulets of minds of the saints.

(ii) The explanation given in 372nd name *Bhakta Mānasahamsikā* may be referred.

(iii) The author comments this name as a descendance of *Bhakta Mānasahamsika*. That is, **She** is pleased with the respect and offerings given by the saints and *Hamsakam* – **She,** who wears the foot-bells (worn by dancers) and dances making the devotees happy and through this **She** gets contended.

817. ***Satyavratā* - सत्यव्रता**

(i) One who is vowed to truth.

(ii) A *vrata* (vow) is a self-imposed control to reach a goal. That is to bring the thought, speech and action under control. **She** has the truth itself as **Her** vow. 693rd name *Satyasandhā* may be referred.

(iii) **She** is attainable by following the vow to speak and follow the truth.

(iv) The truth indicates *Brahmam*. *Vrata* (vow) is, some places, used on edible things. For instance, in *Sruti* statement; *"Payovratam Brāhmanasya"* – the word *vrata* indicates eatables. Hence, like eatables, **She** has liking on *Brahmam*.

Satyam (truth) also indicates low hanging fruits (which gives faster results). That is, the vows on **Her** give quick results. For instance, *Śreemad Vişhŋu Bhāgavatam* (X 22) says, the vow followed by *Gopika* ladies to marry *Śree Krişhŋa*, followed the *Kātyāyanee Vrata*.

(v) It can also be construed that **She** has a liking on the place called *Satyavratā* in *Kāncheepuram*.

(vi) *Śree Bhagavān*, in his incarnation as *Śree Rāma – Śreemad Rāmāyanam* (VI-18-33,34) says;

Sakrudeva Prapannāya Tavvsmeeti Cha Yāchate I
Abhayam Sarvadā Tasmai Dadāmyetadvratam Mama II

Like this **She** has very great and un-repeatable vows. (There are some variations in this verse in South India).

(vii) *Shiva Sūtra* (III-27) says developing the body is a *vratha* (vow). This indicates that maintaining the body without any disease and nourishing it is a *vratha*. A commentator of this says; protecting the body which is filled with the nectar in the form of devotion to *Shiva* is a vow. This has to be definitely followed. There cannot be carelessness on this;

Shiva Bhaktisudhāpoorŋe Shareere Vruttirasya Yā I
Vratametatanushteyam Na Tuchcham Tachcha Dhāranam II

For the sake of devotion on *Śree Devee*, such a vow is a must and truth. Hence **She** is *Satyavrata*.

Battotpalar also preys in this regard, "let this body, nourished by the devotion called nectar, be there for a long time for your adoration sake";

Antarullasita Svachchashakti Peeyoosha Poshitam I
Bhavatpoojopabhoghāya Shareeramidamastu Me II

(viii) In *Devee Bhāgavatam* (book 3), *Satyavrata* was earlier an idiot that he shouted loudly 'I', 'I' when he was scared of the forest pig. This shouting was treated as *'Im'* without the *beeja* sound *'M'*. He later became a very big poet by the compassion of *Śree Devee*. This is described in *Lagustuti* also. It can also be said that **She** is no different from that *Satyavrata*.

818. ***Satyaroopā*** **- सत्यरूपा**

(i) One whose form is unaffected at all the three times.

(ii) It is said that for the sake of protecting the good people and destruction of bad people the eternal *Brahmam* originated or created. For instance *Saptashatee* (I chapter) advises;

Nityaiva Sā Jaganmoortis Tayā Sarvamidam Tatam I
Tathāpi Tatsamutpattir Bahudhā Sharooyatām Mama II
Devānām Kārya Siddhyarthamāvir Bhavati Sā Yadā I
Utpanneti Tadā Loke Sā Nityapyabhidheeyate II

(iii) It can also be taken that – **She** protects/ supports the truth (by giving a form to it). *Rig Veda* (VII-104-12) says, "Out of *Sat* and *Asat, Shiva* with *Uma* protects the *Sat* and destroys *Asat*";

Sachchāsachcha Vachasee Pasprughāte I
Tayoryassatyam Yataradru Jeeyastaditsomovati Hantyāsat II

819. ***Sarvāntaryāmiŋee* - सर्वान्तर्यामिणी**

(i) One who is omniscient in the minds of all.

(ii) Or, **She** fixes all the organs or provides the orders. *Brahadāraŋya Upanishad* (III-7-3) says that this is with you and eternal; *Esha Ta Ātmā Antaryāmyamrta*: (the commentaries on *Antaryāmi Brāhmanam* may be referred). *Mānḍukya Upanishad* (6th verse) also conveys the same message; *"Eshontaryāmyesha Yoni: Sarvasya"*.

(iii) Or by splitting the name into *Sarvā* + *Antaryāminee*, it can be construed that **She** is in both these forms. That is it can be said as, **She** is in all forms again inside everybody. *Taitreeya Upanishad* (II-6-1) is an evidence for this; *"Tat Shrushtvā* II *Tadevānuprāvishat Tadanu Pravishya* II *Sachcha Tyachābhavat* II"

Smruti also says;

Sarvasya Sarvadā Gnānātsarvasya Prabhavāpya Yow I
Satosatashcha Kurute Tena Sarveti Kathyate II

(iv) 823rd name *Jananee* may be referred. In some schools, this name is considered as two names viz., *Sarva* + *Antaryāminee*. In that case the 822nd and 823rd names *Brahma* and *Jananee* have to be treated as a single name.

820. ***Satee* - सती**

(i) One who is a great *pativrata*.

(ii) Or **She** is in the form of *Sat*.

(iii) *Satee* is a causal name for *Dākshāyanee*, daughter of *Dakshan*. *Brahma Purāŋa* says about the daughter of *Himavān*, "**She** was earlier as *Satee Devee*, becomes *Uma*, always with *Shiva* and never moves out of him";

Sātu Devee Satee Poorvamāseet Pashchādumābhavat I
Sahavratā Bhavasyaiva Naitayā Muchayate Bhava: II

(iv) *Śree Ādi Śaṇkara*, in his *Soundaryalaharee*, 96th verse starting with *Kalatram Vadhātram*, describes *Śree Devee* as the; *Sateenām Acharame* – first among the *Pativratās*.

(v) Our scriptures well mention about the greatness (energy) of

Pativratās – *Nalāyinee, Damayantee, Aruntatee, Anasooyā, Sitā, Vāsukee* (consort of *Thiruvalluvar*) and others may be reminded.

(vi) *Prapancha Nyāsa* in *Mahāshoḍanyāsa* mentions as;

Muhoortaroopa and *Devatā Nyāsā*as *Sahasra Koṭi Yoginee Kula Sevita.*

821. ***Brahmaŋee* - ब्रह्माणी**

(i) One who gives life to *Brahma.*

(ii) *Ānayati* – gives life, to *Brahma*. Since **She** creates *Brahma* and gives life to him, **She** is *Brahmaŋee. Devee Purāŋā* says; *Brahmaŋee Brahma Jananād Brahmaŋo Jevanena Va.*

(iii) It can also be considered that **She** is in the form of *Saraswatee,* consort of *Brahma* (who is treated as great grandfather of all).

(iv) *Ani* means a tail of a bird. *Sruti* says that *Brahmam* is in the form of a tail at the end of the sheath full of bliss; *Brahmaŋa Āneestha*:. The same message is conveyed in *Brahma Sūtra* (*Ānandamayādi-karaŋam*) also. **She** is in the form of that tail *Brahmam.*

(v) Since he has the sharpness of a trident in his body, the sage *Māndavya* is called as *Anee Māndavya*. The word *Anee* has meanings other than tail also. According to the dictionary called *Shāshvata*, it means sharp edge of a trident. The same is considered here; *"Anirakshāgra Keelesyādani*: *Pucchagni Seemayo*:".

822. ***Brahma* - ब्रह्म**

(i) One who herself is *Brahmam.*

(ii) The one got in salvation and the knowledge that it is no different from the self-soul is called *Brahmam. Vishŋu Purāŋa* (VI-7-53) explains the character of *Brahmam* as – the *Brahmam* is the knowledge which is got by destroying the duality, beyond speech, least in quality and identified only within the self-soul;

Pratyastamita Bhedam Yatsattā Mātra Gochāram I
Vachasāmātma Samvedyam Tajgnānam Brahma Samjnitam II

823. ***Jananee* - जननी**

(i) One who is the mother – the creator of the entire universe.

(ii) These names may be referred – 295 - *Ambikā*, 337 - *Vidhātree*, 457 - *Mātā*, 826 - *Prasavitree*, 934 – *Vishvamātā* and 985 - *Amba.*

(iii) In some schools this name and the previous one are combined and treated as a single name *Brahmajananee*. In that case the 819th name *Sarvāntaryāminee* is split into two as *Sarva* and *Antaryāminee*. *Śree Bhāskararāya* also confirms that there is proper reason for splitting it this way. However, based on the *Paribhāshā* verses treating *Sarvāntaryāminee* as a single name is followed by majority of people. In the same way if *Brahmajananee* is treated as a single name, 966th name has to be split into two viz., *Leelā* and *Vinodinee*.

824. *Bahuroopā* - बहुरूपा

(i) One who has many forms.

(ii) *Devee Bhāgavatam* says – Though **She** is in the form of the Supreme Being, **She** takes the form of *kriyāshakti* (action energy) for killing the demons *Bhanḍāsura* and others;

Aroopāparabhāvatvād Bahuroopā Kryātmika.

Śree Gouḍabadar also in his book called *Śreevidyā Ratna Sūtra* (*Sūtra* 8) – for destroying the demon *Bhanḍāsura*, **She**, in a single form, becomes many; "*Bhanḍāsuro Hananārtha Mekaivāneka*".

Devee Purāṇa also says **Her** forms are many types (moving or static) – *Devas*, human beings and animals, - hence **She** is called *Bahuroopa*;

Bahooni Yasyā Roopāni Sthirānich Charānicha I
Deva Mānusha Tiyanchi Bahuroopā Thatha: *Shivā* II

(iii) In *Sootha Samhitha* (IV-47-64) also it is mentioned that *Śree Devee* is in the form of letters – **She** is the above superlative. **She** is in many forms one, two, sixteen, thirty-two, etc. I bow to her;

Ekadhā Cha Divdhā Chaiva Tathā Shoḍashadhā Sthitā I
Dvā Trimshadbhedabhinnā Vā Yā Tām Vande Parātparām II

a. In this context the number two denotes – vowels and consonants (vowel phonemes and consonant phonemes). By the number sixteen the sixteen vowels from *'A'* to *'A:'* are denoted. While counting the letters from *'Ka'*, since there is no difference between *Ra* and *La* (this was mentioned earlier in 804th name) one has to be left out; *Ha* is the root of all and hence not counted; *Ksha* is a compound letter – not to be counted; remaining we get 32 letters indicated in this name.

b. The names in this *Sahasranāma* start in 32 letters only. It can be taken as this 32 indicates the same.

(iv) Though *Śree Devee* in reality is in a single form, as an actress **She** takes up different characters and shows different forms. This has been mentioned in many places. For instance;

a. *Devee Bhāgavatam –*
Lakshmee Vāgādi Roopena Nartakeeva Vibhāti Yā II
b. *Vāmana Purāŋam -*
Vishvam Bahuvidham Gneyam Sā Chā Sarvatra Vartate I
Tasmātsā Bahuroopatvādbahuroopā Shivā Matā II
c. *Ambāstavam* of *Śree Kālidāsā* (8th verse);
Dākshāyaneeti Kutiledi Kuhāriŋeeti
Kātyāyaneeti Kamaleti Kamalāvateeti I
Ekā Satee Bhagavatee Paramārthatopi
Sandrshyase Bahuvidhā Nanu Nartakeeva II
d. *Kanakatārā Satavam* of *Śree Ādi Śaŋkara;*
Geerdevateti Garuḍa Dhvajasundareeti I

(v) As mentioned in *Sruti, Rudra* has billions of forms. *Śree Bhāskararāya* quotes *Śree Rudram* verses; *Asankhyātā*: *Sahasrānai Ye Rudra Atibhoomyām*. *Śree Devee* is the consort of such a billion forms of *Shiva* and hence **She** is also of many forms. The names of these *Rudrānees* have been mentioned in each of *Mahāpurāŋas* and each of the *tantras* and hence **She** is *Bahuroopa*.

As evidence to this, he quotes *Varāha Purāŋam, Narasimha Upapurāŋam* and *Tripura Sitthāntam*. For the fear of more elaboration, he says, he has stopped the explanation here.

(vi) The relevant meanings of the names in *Viṣhŋu Sahasranāma*; 721 – *Anekamoorti*:, 723 – *Shadamoorti*: and 765 – *Chaturmoorti*:. The commentaries of these names are (from the publication of *Kāmakoṭi Goshastāna*);

Since he takes many forms in the self-imposed incarnations to help the human beings he is *Anekamoorti*:.

On account of various alternatives various forms are created from a single knowledge matter and hence *Shatamoorti*:.

He has four forms viz., *Virāt* (imperishable), *Sootram* (formulae), *Avyākrutam* (unmanifested) and *Tureeyam* (fourth) and hence he is *Chaturmoorti*: II Or since he has four different colour forms as white, red, yellow and black.

(vii) 401st name *Vividhākārā* and 865th name - *Leelā Vigrahadhāriŋee* may be referred.

825. ***Budhārchitā* - बुधार्चिता**

(i) One who is worshipped by the wise.
(ii) In *Śreemad Bhagavad Geeta* (VII-16);

Chaturvidhā Bhajante Mām Janā: Sukrutinorjuna I
Ārto Jignāsurarthārthee Gnānee Cha Bharatarshbha II

Four types of virtuous men worship Me, Oh *Arjuna*!, the man in distress, the man seeking knowledge, the man seeking wealth and the man imbued with wisdom. Out of these, the wise men, even though he has reached the self-attainment, even if untouched by his further actions, he worships for the welfare of the world. This has been mentioned in the fruits/ results part also.

826. ***Prasavitree* - प्रसवित्री**

(i) One who created everything.
(ii) Especially since **She** delivers the entire universe including ether or **She** delivers all the human beings, **She** is *Prasavitree*.
(iii) *Viṣhŋu Dharmotra* says;

Prajānām Cha Prasavanāt Saviteti Nigadyate II

Bhagavati Purāŋa says;

Brahmadyā: Sthāvarāntāshcha Yasyā Eve Samudgatā: I
Mahadādi Visheshāntam Jagad Yasyā: Samudgatam I
Tāmeva Sakallarthānām Prasavitreem Parāmnuma: II

(iv) These names may also be referred; 337 - *Vidhātree*, 457 - *Mātā*, 823 - *Jananee* and 985 - *Amba*.
(v) A mother takes care of her child in five different ways. In each of the type, she takes each of different names;
823 - *Jananee* – For the life given by the father, she gives shape and makes it a baby.
457 – *Mātā*– Protects the life in her womb.
826 – *Prasavitree* (this name) – At the appropriate time, once it has adequately grown, delivers it.
337 – *Vidhātree* – *Dhātree* – Nourishes and brings up the baby.
985 – *Ambā*– During emergency or crisis, she herself protects.

From the *Brahmam*, to create this world **She** takes the form of *Icchā Shakti*, carries the egg (world) called *Moolaprakruti* (the root nature), incubates in the states of *Avyakta* and *Mahat* (unmanifested), in the state egoism deliver that out and participate in its protection by taking the forms of *Brahma*, *Viṣhŋu* and *Rudra*.

827. ***Prachaŋḍā* - प्रचण्डा**

(i) One who is wrathful.

(ii) Anger is a symbol of *Brahmam*. The *Taitreeya Upanishad* (III-8-1) says "For fear of Him the wind, fire and Sun do their respective duties";

Bheeshāsmādvāta: *Bhavate* I *Bheeshodeti Soorya*: I
Bheeshāsmādagnishchandrashcha II *Mrutyurdhāvati Panchama*: II.

The same message is conveyed in *Kaṭopanishad* (II-3-2,3) also - since **She** inspires fear "It is a great terror, a raised thunderbolt"; *Mahadbhayam Vajramudyatam*. *Brahma Sūtra* (I-3-39) explains that thunderbolt (*Vajra*) in this context is *Brahmam*.

(iii) *Kāmāndaka Neeti* also says, "How can, one without possessing even an iota of anger and whom the people do not fear, enforce righteousness?";

Na Yasya Kobonurapi Prajāstasya Na Bibhyati I
Saitām Neetim Katham Rakshet Prjā Yasya Na Bibhyati II

(iv) *Śree Ādi Śaṇkara* in his commentary of *Vişhŋu Sahasranāma* for the below names conveys the same message; 315 – *Krodhakrut*, 776– *Duratikrama* and 833 – *Bhayakrut*.

(v) For the preface in the commentary of *Guptavati* for *Saptashatee*, *Śree Bhāskara Rāya* himself has given the meanings of *Chaŋḍikā* and *Chāmuŋḍa*. There he mentions that these names originate from the root verb *Chadi* – angry. He has quoted the above *Upanishads*. Also he quotes from *Śree Rudram* that initially the anger is bowed; *Namaste Rudra Manyave* and again he quotes the sage *Vālmeeki's* questions in *Śreemad Rāmāyana* – "About whose anger *Devas* also are scared in the battle?"; *Kasya Bibhyati Devāshcha Jātaroshasya Samyuge*.

Further he quotes the verse which says – as ladies will not accept a hermaphrodite as a husband in the same way people will not agree as leader –one whose blessings are unfruitful or whose anger is meaningless;

Prasādo Nishphalo Yasya Kopopi Cha Nrardaka: I
Na Tam Bhartāramichchaŋti Shaŋḍham Patimiva Striya: II

(vi) Or, since the spies of *Śree Devee* are *Prachaŋḍās* (with great anger), **She** is called so.

(vii) *Pra* - fond of, *Chaŋḍā* - a kind of flower called *Shankha* (conch) flower; *Prachaŋḍā* – fond of that flower. The *Vishva* dictionary says, "*Chaŋḍa* means, a kind of perfume (*Dhanahari*), the *Shankha* flower, anger and *Prachaŋḍa* means *Durvaha*, a kind of white *Karavira* and a brilliant man";

Chaŋḍā Dhanaharee Shankha Pushpee Chaŋḍoti Kopane I
Prachaŋḍo Durvahe Shvetakaraveere Pratāpinee II

She is in all these forms.

828. *Āgnā* - आज्ञा

(i) One who is in the form of order.

(ii) **She** is in the form of ordained and prohibited orders in *Veda* statements. As already mentioned in 287th name *Nijāgyāroopanigamā*, these orders are *Śree Devee*'s wishful commands. Now, here it is said that **She** herself is in the form of these orders. *Shiva 's* speech in *Linga Purāŋa* – "**She** is not the nature or soul or unnatural. **She**, with five faces, blesses this world, very great and originated from my face".;

Na Hyeshā Prakrutir Jeevo Vikrutirvā Vichārata: I
Purā Mamāgnā Madvaktrāt Samupannā Sanātanee II
Pancha Vaktrā Mahā Bhāgā Jagatāmabhayapradā I

In *Shiva Purāŋa* also it is said – only by the divine order of *Rudra* the salvation is obtained;

Rudragnaishā Sthitā Devee Hyanayā Muktirambaya.

(iii) This name can also be taken as *Jnā* – the knower. It can be construed as that - **She** has the form of *purusha*, who enjoys the qualities. This has been mentioned in *Linga Purāŋa*;

Kathayanti Gna Shabdena Purusham Guŋabhoginam I

(iv) Or, according to dictionary *Gnā* means *Brahma*, the planet Mercury and wise men; *"Gno Virichow Budhe Soumye"*.

(v) *Svetāshvatara Upanishad* (VI-2) says – *Gna*: - *Ěshwar, Ajna*: - soul; *"Gna*: *Kālakāro Guŋee Sarivavidyā*:".

829. *Pratishṭhā* - प्रतिष्ठा

(i) One who is foundation of the entire universe.

(ii) **She** is the foundation of the whole universe or the entire universe depends on her for support. The *Soota Samhita* (III-28) says; *Vishvasya Jagata*: *Pratishṭhā* and *Brahma Geeta* says;

Prathishtā Sarva Vastoonām Pragnaishā Parameshwaree.

(iii) A type of sixteen syllabled meter is also called *Pratisṭha*. *Śree Bhāskararāya* says that this has been described in his book called *Chaŋḍo Bhāskaram*.

(iv) The arts mapped to the basic five basic elements are;
Earth – *Nivarutti* – To turn out of the desires of the external objects

Water – *Pratishṭhā* – To establish with the supreme being on account of affection on it.

Fire – *Vidyā* – To rationally understand the *paratatva*.

Air – *Shānti* – To dissolute with the supreme being.

Ether – *Shāntyateetā* – Supreme Bliss.

Among this **She** is in the form of the art relating to water *tatva*. *Saivāgamā* says, what is called *Pratishtā* is - to grow the devotion on *Shiva* and dissolute him with *Ĕshwar*;

Shiva rāgānu Raktātmā Sthāpyate Pourushe Yayā I
Sā Pratishtā Kalā Gneyā II

(v) The second of the sixteen *Sadāshiva* arts is called *Pratishṭha*.

(vi) The *Vishva* dictionary says, "*Pratishṭhā* means importance of the attainment of *Yoga* and the four-syllabled division (i.e. one-fourth part of a verse)". Pride, fame and to reach the *yoga* are the various meanings given to *Pratishṭha*. **She** is in all these forms.

830. *Prakaṭākruti*: - प्रकटाकृतिः

(i) One who is visible to all in the manifest form.

(ii) *Prakaṭa* means clear or obvious. **Her** form is clearly visible to all.

(iii) Everyone knows that 'I' is self. But on account of illusion, they do not understand that this I is the *Brahmam*. *Soota Samhita* shows this;

Tamaham Pratyaya Vyājāt Sarve Jānanti Jantava: I
Tadāpi Shiva Roopena Na Vijānanti Māyayā II

(iv) **She** is in the form of *Devees*, in the first hall of the *Śree Chakra*, called as *Prakaṭa Yoginees*.

(v) It can be taken that the letter *'A'* is hidden in front of this name. In that case the name becomes *Aprakaṭākruti*: and it means that **She** has a secret form.

(vi) Again with the word *Aprakaṭākruti*: can be taken as *Apsu* – in the water. That is, **Her** form is visible in water. It implies that **She** in the form of holy rivers. In *Sruti* also we read as; *Apāmekā Mahimānam Bibharti* and again as *Āpo Vā idam Sarvam* (*Mahā Nārāyaŋa Upanishad* XIV–1).

831. *Prāŋeshvaree* - प्राणेश्वरी

(i) One who is the presiding deity of all senses.

(ii) This has been well established in *Vedānta Sūtra* (II-4-14); *Jyotirādyatishṭānam Tu Tadāmananāt* II

(iii) **She** is the deity of the five vital breaths. *Sruti* says; *Prāŋasya Prāŋa*: - "He is the breath of breath"

(iv) *Ana*: - sound, **She** is the presiding deity of very great sound. The *Kaṭopanishad* (II-15) says, All *Vedas* point out the same abode; *"Sarve Vedā Yapadamāmananti"*.

832. ***Prāŋadātree* - प्राणदात्री**

(i) One who bestows the energy of breath and makes the entire universe live.

(ii) *Sruti* says, the word *Prāŋa* indicates the senses; *"Prāŋamanut-krāmantam Sarve Prānā Anootkrāmanti"*. Again the same meaning is given for the *Brahma* Sūtra verse; *"Shabdagater Visheshitativāchcha"*. Hence *Prāŋadātree* means – one who bestows the eleven senses.

833. ***Panchāshatpeeṭharoopiŋee* - पञ्चाशत्पीठरूपिणी**

(i) One who is the form of five *peeṭas*.

(ii) There is a story about the *peeṭas* of *Śree Devee*. These are called as *Shakti Peeṭas* also. *Satee Devee* was born as daughter of *Daksha* and she married *Parameshwara*. *Dakhsha* had an aversion over *Lord Siva*, on account of his pre-birth actions. To insult him he did a sacrificial fire (*yāgā*). He did not invite *Parameshwara* for this *yāga*. Neither did he give any respect to him in the *yāga*. Though not invited *Satee Devee*, even when objected to by *Parameshwara*, visited the *mahāyāga*. She was not treated well by the hosts. *Daksha*, not only insulted *Parameshwara*, but also scolded him. Not able to tolerate this insult, **She** left her body through *yoga* there itself. *Parameshwara* got wild, sent his troupe and destroyed the *yāga*. (This incident was already reminded through the names 598 – *Dākshāyanee* and 600 – *Dakshayajavināshinee*.

Parameshwara, carrying the body of *Sati* on his shoulder moved around like a crazy man. To cure the madness, *Viṣhŋu* with his *Chakra* cut the body of *Sati*. Wherever the parts of the body fell, they all became *Shakti Peeṭas*.

(iii) *Panchāshat* means fifty. In general ten, twenty, hundred, thousand, etc., indicate the approximate numbers around it. The main indication of these words is many. In addition, according to the *Sūtra*; *Sahasreshatam*, in the place *Navāvatāram* the word *Dasavatāram*, in the place *Jagatpati* the word *Ayodyāpati*, the meaning, according to the circumstances, is considered based on the evidences available. *Śree Bhāskara Rāya* reminds that in *Soota Samhita*, the number thirty-two is used to indicate thirty-five (consonants).

(iv) In *Antar Mātrukā Nyasa*, we do *nyāsa* only with fifty letters. In general we say that there are only 50 letters – since there is no difference between *Ra* and *La* (only one is counted); *Ksha* is a compound letter – not to be counted – also in the garland for chanting this letter is considered as a *Meru*. Some schools may think that considering all these *Panchāshat* in this place has to be considered as fifty. That is not correct. *Śree Bhāskara Rāya* says that it has to be taken as fifty-one. As evidence to this he quotes the meditation verse of *Mātrukā Nyāsa*. (*Mātrukā Nyāsa* is not to be used only by those who follow *Śree Vidyā* practice. Those who are interested in other *Veda* practices also have to do this *Mātrukā Nyāsā* – says the *Smruti Muktā Palam* – this is clearly visible from the book by *Śree Vaidyanātha Deekshiteeyam, Āhnika Kānḍa, Poorva Pagā*, page 538. This is part of morning *Sandhyāvandanam* also. Though the word *Panchāshat* is used in this meditation verse, only fifty-one *nyāsās* have been mentioned. The same case in *Gnānārnavam* also. Other *tantras* also unanimously make a mention about fifty-one *nyāsās*. Those are to be done in places where *Mātrukā Nyāsa* is done.

(v) *Harshadeekshita*, who wrote the commentary for *Shāradā Tilaka* also means *Panchāshat* as fifty-one only. Hence in this name, we need to consider fifty-one only for the word *Panchāshat*.

(vi) *Laghu Shoḍanyāsa* was explained earlier in 474th name while describing the *Yoginee* forms of *Śree Devee*. *Peeṭa Nyāsa* is a part in it. The mental appropriation has to be done imagining 51 *Shakti Peeṭas* in one's body. This has been explained in detail in *Brahmānḍa Purāṇa*. Also in *Yoginee Hrudayā*, which is a part of *Nityā Shoḍashikārnava*.

(vii) The author confirms the number 51 with all these evidences – he also criticizes the book *Sundaree Mahodaya* wherein the number 50 is stressed. It has been vehemently opposed that the original verses have been modified to suit his argument. He also quotes the ancient *pooja* practices wherein 51 *peeṭas* have been mentioned.

(viii) He also mentions another reply to those who still insist that *Panchāshat* indicates only 50. According to *Pingala Sūtra*; *Roope Shoonyam – Roopam* indicates the number one. In this name the word *Roopinee* is used. Hence it has to be treated as 50 + 1 = 51.

(ix) There are some differences between schools in doing the *nyāsā* of these 51 *peeṭas*. The taught practice has to be followed.

(x) The *Peeṭa Nyāsa* has been described in detail by *Śree Bhāskara Ray* himself in his book called *Setubandam*, which is the commentary for *Yoginee Hrudayam*.

834. ***Vishrunkhalā* - विश्रृङ्खला**

(i) One who is ever unfettered.

(ii) *Shrunkhalā* means binding chain or fetters. The bonds like actions bind the soul. Hence they are also called as *Shrunkhala*. Action (*karma*) means doing or not doing the ordained ones and doing or not doing the prohibited actions. These are all due to ignorance. There is no bondage of these actions to *Śree Devee*. Hence **She** is *Vishrunkhala*.

(iii) The bondages are the actions that result in sin or virtue. The fetter is a fetter whether it is made up of gold or iron. The wise pray to remove them from these fetters;

Pātaka Prachayavan Mama Dāvat Puŋya Punjama Pinatha Luneemahe I
Kānchanee Bhavatu Lohamayee Vā Shrunkhalā Yadipador Na Vishesha: II

(iv) a. One who is without a dress. Since *Śree Devee*'s idol is in such form in *Alampura* and other places, **She** can be called as *Digambaree*. *Shrunkhalā* means a type of rope (*katee Sūtra*) wound on the dress at the hip. Since it is not there, it is construed that there is no dress on the hip.

b. There is a *Devee* called *Tiraskariŋee*, is in the form of curtain (called *yavanikā*) around the bed of *Śree Devee*. The meditation verse about her says that *Śree Devee* fascinates the idiots and those who involve in erotic actions. The curtain does not need one more curtain. Hence this is apt.

c. The below verses evidencing the above may be referred;

Parito Maŋi Manchasya Pralambamānā Niyantritā Pāshai: I
Māyāmayee Javanikā Mama Duritam Haratu Mechakachchāyā II
(*Lalitā Stavaratnam* - 149th verse)

In 270th name – *Tirodhānakaree*, mention was about *Tiraskariŋee Devee*. The meditation verse of *Tiraskariŋee Devee* says;

Mukta Kesheem Vivasanām, Sarvābharaŋa Bhooshitām I
Svayoni Darshanāt Muhyat Pashuvargām Namāmyaham II

835. ***Viviktasthā* - विविक्तस्था**

(i) One who dwells in secluded places where there is no human being.
(ii) The word *Vivikta* indicates the divine places where there is no human being. That is, a holy place, even if people are there around, is called as *Vivikta*. The secluded place (where there is nobody), even if it is not holy is called as *Vivikta*.
(iii) The holy and secluded (both the qualifications) have been mentioned in this name. *Śree Devee*'s blessings are available to those who meditate in those places and not in other places.
(iv) The other meaning can be – *Śree Devee* is with those who have the knowledge of soul and non-soul.

836. *Veeramātā* – वीरमाता

(i) One who is mother of heroes (*veerās*).
(ii) The warriors who died in the war, i.e. one who died after battling, are praised as *veerās* (heroes). **She** does good to them. (This meaning is considered with the assumption that those who die in a war go to the heaven).
(iii) Great worshippers are called as *veerās*. This was mentioned in 777th name *Veerārādhya*. Again in 899th name *Veerā* may also be referred. Those are called as *Veeras*, who have done *pooja* for 30 years, consumed the special *argyā* for many times and have an uncorrupted mind. *Parāpanchāshikā* says;

Ahami Pralayam Kurvan idam Pratiyogina: I
Parākramapuro Bhunkte Svātmānam Ashivāpaham II

Idam (this) is the base for the differentiated thinking. The opponent to this is *Aham* (self). A *veerā* will fight with valour to destroy this enemy in the battle field, remove the un-auspiciousness and will have great passion over the soul. Such a great worshipper is called *Veera*.

(iv) According to *Vishva* dictionary, the glass of alcohol is called *Veera*. (In the worship of *Śree Devee* five *'Ma's* are offered. *Madhu* [Alcohol] is the primary one. Some of the tantras explain the method of actually offering them [not as imaginary offerings]. *Karma Kāṇḍa* itself explains the meaning of such offerings and says that those who offer them are freed from birth and death, etc. It is again reiterated that those who are interested in the knowledge of self, have to use some representative in the place of alcohol, meat, etc., in reality).

It has been mentioned in various other names that She gets satisfied with alcohol in a vessel; 510 - *Madhupreetā*, 575 – *Mādhveepānālasā* and 717 - *Madhumatee*.

(v) There is a story in *Padma Purāŋa* that *Śree Devee* has adopted, of course with the permission of *Parameshvara,* a person by name *Veera* (head of a group), as **Her** son. Mother of that *Veera.*

a. **She** accepted the *Veerabāhu, Veerakesari* and others (nine *veerās*) as **Her** own sons, as younger brothers of Lord *Muruga.*

The origin of these nine *veerās* has been described in *Śree Skanda Mahā Purāŋa - Sambava Kāṇḍa* - 27th chapter. By seeing the luster originating from the eyes of *Śree Parameshwara,* the *Devas* got frightened and ran here and there. *Śree Devee* also got scared and got up from the lap of *Śree Parameshwara* and walked towards her palace. While doing so, **She** slipped and the nine gems from the anklets scattered on the way. Once **Her** fear got removed, **She** came back to *Śree Parameshwara* and **Her** form reflected in the nine gem stones and they all became ten *Devees* (including *Śree Devee*). *Śree Parameshwara* asked the other nine *Devees* to come fast. At once, they got the respective gem stone names and reached him fully decorated. They looked at *Śree Parameshwara* and got pregnant immediately. The nine *veeras* are the children of these *Devees.*

Gem stone	Reflected *Devee*	Name of the *Veera*
Ruby	*Raktavalli*	*Veerabāhoo*
Pearl	*Taralavalli*	*Veerakesari*
Natural Pearl	*Pousheevalli*	*Veeramahendra*
Hessonite	*Kometatilakā*	*Veeramaheshvara*
Cat's eye	*Vaidooryavalli*	*Veerapurandra*
Diamond	*Vajravalli*	*Veerarākshasa*
Emerald	*Maragatavalli*	*VeeraMārtāṇḍa*
Coral	*Pavazhavalli*	*Veerāntakā*
Blue Sapphire	*Neelavalli*	*Veeradeera*

b. The hidden message of this story has been explained by *Śree Chidānandanāthar* in his book called *Śree Subramanya Tatva* – pages 63 & 64). The gist of it is;

The *Chit Shakti,* which is not different from *Parameshwara* is the knowledge-luster. Once the *Chit Shakti* came out, *Śree Devee* became static *Shakti.* Can a single object be static as well *Chit*? May be – the *Upanishad* statement is an evidence for this – *Vidyām Chāvidyām Cha Svayameva Bhavati.* In this *Sahasranāma* itself, the below names insist on this; 416 - *Chichchakti:*, 417 - *Chetanāroopā*, 418 – *Jadashakti* and 419 - *Jadātmika*

Since *Śree Devee* was in the illusionary form, having feared from the form of *Brahmam* and moving towards her palace is acceptable by the *sāstras* only – an evidence would be; *Atishtānāvashesho Hi Nāsha: Kalpitavastuna:*.

The learned says that the ankle rings of the *Chit Shakti,* who is the *Brahmavidyā,* is only the four *Vedas* and *Upanishads* and the gem stones in it are the *Mahā* sayings. The truth of advising, for nine times, is to be read from *Chāndokya Upanishad; Tatvamasi Shvetaketo*. The nine gems scattered from the ankle rings reflected in the illusionary half as nine *Devees*. The *sāstras* call them as nine *Durgās* or nine *Shaktis*. Earlier it was mentioned that they are the reflected forms of *Gowree* (*Śree Devee*). *Gowri* means speech. *Upanishads* and *Mahāvākyās* are in the form of sound. Sound is the character of ether. *Sāstras* confirm that the integrated (un-differentiated) knowledge is due to sound, in the form of *Mahāvākyās*, only.

The *Mahāvākyās* are sounds with the character of *Chit* ether. Hence with this sound the universal expansion happens and the broad form of the non-differentiated knowledge happens. With this knowledge the differentiated forms like demons get destructed. This type of knowledge form is that nine *veerās*.

c. *Śree Chidānanda Nātha* has described these nine *veerās* in his other books as below. That is, these nine *veerās* are compared to the expanded forms of knowledge, the *tatvas* of the nine halls of *Śree Chakra* or *Yoginees*. The list goes as;

Nine *Veerās*	**The development of knowledge**	***Śree Chakra***	
		Hall	***Tatva, Yoginee***
Veeradeera	Knowledge in arguments	*Poopuram – Trailokya Mohana Chakra*	Awakened state – *Prakata Yoginee*
Veerāntakā	Knowledge in actions	Sixteen petalled – *Sarvāshāparipooraka Chakra*	Dream state – Gupta *Yoginee*
VeeraMārtānḍa	Knowledge in *Yogas*	Eight petalled – *Sarva Samkhopana chakra*	Deep Sleep state – *Guptatara Yoginee*
Veerarākshasa	Knowledge of knowledge – *Bāhya Drushyānuvitta Samādhi*	*Chaturtashāram – Sarva Soubhāgya Tayaka chakra*	The state of thinking about *Ěshwara*, who is the reason for this world– *Sampratāya Yoginee*
Veerapurandra	Knowledge of knowledge – *Bāhya*	*Bahirdashāram – Sarvārta Sadaka Chakra*	The state of reaching a good teacher –

Nine *Veerās*	**The development of knowledge**	***Śree Chakra***	
		Hall	***Tatva, Yoginee***
	Shabdānuvitta Samādhi		*Kulottheerna Yoginee*
Veeramaheshvara	Knowledge of knowledge – *Bāhya Nirvikalpa Samādhi*	*Antardashāram – Sarva Rakshākaran Chakra*	The state of hearing – *Nikarpa Yoginee*
Veeramahendra	Knowledge of knowledge – *Āndhra Drushyānuvitta Samādhi*	Eight cornered – *Sarvārta Rohahara Chakra*	The state of remembering – *Rahasya Yoginee*
Veerakesari	Knowledge of knowledge – *Āndhra Shabdānuvitta Samādhi*	Triangle – *Sarvasiddhiprata Chakra*	*Nitiyāsanam – Atirahasya Yoginee*
Veerabāhoo	Knowledge of knowledge – *Āndhra Nirvikalpa Samādhi*	*Bindu – Sarvāndamaya Chakra*	*Savikalpa Samādhi – Parāparāti-Rahasya Yoginee*

(vi) Out of the nine places above the *Agnā Chakra* till *Brahmarandram*, (*Bindu*, crescent moon, *Rodinee, Nātham, Nādāntam, Shakti, Vyāpikā, Samanā*and *Unmanee*), *Unmanee* is beyond our mind and speech. Hence merging that with *Samanā*, it is counted as eight only and indicated with eight *beejas*. The combination of all these eight *beejas* is called as *Ānanda Bhairava Beeja*. This is included in the *Panchadashee Guru Pātukāmantras*. This *beeja* is called as *Navanātha Beeja*. Since it is nine *veerās*, this nine *nādābeeja* is being indicated. **She** is the mother of these nine *beejas* (they originated from **Her** only).

837. *Viyatprasoo*: - वियत्प्रसूः

(i) One who delivered the ether.

(ii) *Sruti* statements which explain the evolution say that - air from ether, fire from air, water from fire and earth from water originated. That ether originated from *Brahmam*. *Taitireeya Upanishad* (II-1) says; *Ātmana Ākāshа: Sambhoota*:. **She** is called as that *Brahmam*, which created the ether. 550th name *Viyadādijagatprasoo*: may be referred.

838. ***Mukundā* – मुकुन्दा**

(i) One who bestows salvation.
(ii) *Muku*: means salvation. **She** bestows it. *Śree Ādi Śaṇkara* also conveys the same message, in his commentary of *Vişhŋu Sahasranāma* for the 515th name – *Mukunda*:.
(iii) a. *Mukunda*: is one of the names of *Vişhŋu*. It has been well mentioned in *Śreemad Bhāgavatam* and other *tantra* books that there is no difference between *Śree Devee* and *Vişhŋu*. For instance these verses are read from *Tantra Rāja Tantra* while explaining the differences of *Gopala Mantra*;

Kadā Chidādyara Lalitā Pumroopā Krushna Vigrahā I
Sva Vamsha Vādanārambāda Karodvivasham Jagat II
Tata: *Sagopee Samgnābhirāvrutobhhotsvashaktibhi*: I
Tadā Tena Vinodāya Svam Shoḍākalpayadvapu: II

Once *Śree Devee* wanted to take a male form. The form taken by **Her** was *Śree Krişhŋa*. **She** attracted the world through the sweet music from **Her** flute. **She** created the *Gopika* ladies from her energies and shined beautifully with them around.

c. These names may be referred; 892nd – *Vaishŋavee,* 893 - *Vişhŋuroopiŋee* and 949 - *Panchabhooteshee*.

(iv) According to *Vishva* dictionary, *Mukundā* means a special gem stone or mercury; *Mukunda*: *Pundareekākshe Ranabhedepi Pārade*.

839. ***Muktinilayā* - मुक्तिनिलया**

(i) One who is abode of salvation.
(ii) Depending on the eligibility of the devotees, based on their worship with quality, **She** bestows salvation of four types; *Sālokyam, Sāmeepyam, Sāroopyam* and *Sāyujyam* (Seeing the *Brahmam,* nearing the *Brahmam*, having the vision of the form of the *Brahmam* and merging in the *Brahmam*). Hence She is the abode of liberation. **She** also bestows *Paramukti* or *Nirvānā*, (absolute closure – form formless) – integrating with *Brahmam*, without limitations, without qualities, without any specialties, etc., to **Her** eligible devotees. Just to bestow these five types of salvations to **Her** devotees, **She** has them with her.

840. ***Moolavigraharoopiŋee* - मूलविग्रहरूपिणी**

(i) One who is the root from where all other energies (*Shaktis*) originate.

(ii) **She** is of the form indicated by *Rājarājeshwaree, Lalitā, Mahātripurasundaree* and many other names.

(iii) *Bala, Bagalā* and all other *Shaktis* originate from the three forms *Shāmbavee, Vidyā* and *Shyāma*. Those three forms originate from *Śree Devee*. This has been described in detail in the book called *Śreevidyā Ratna Sūtra* by *Śreegowḍapadar* and in *Bahvrocho-panishad*. That form of *Rājarājeshwaree* is mentioned in this name.

(iv) The *Sūtras* of *Śreegowḍapadar*; *SaiveyamanāmākyāŚreevidyā* I *Tatvatrayena Trividhā* I *Sā Shāmbhavee Vidyā Shyāmā Tatvatrāyakrti*: I *Trividhā Jātā Vidyāyā*: *Poorvottarābhyām Aneka Vidyā Jātā*: II

(v) From *Bahvropanishad*;

Saishāshoḍashee Śreevidyā Panchadashākysharee
Śreemahātripursundaree Bālāmbiketi Bagaleti Vā
Mātankeeti Svayamvarakalyāneeti Bhuvaneshvareeti
Chāmuŋḍeti Chaŋḍeti Vārāheeti Tiraskariŋeeti
Rājamāntankeeti Vā Shukashyāmalaeti Vā Laghushyāmaleti Vā
Ashvārooḍheti Vā Pratyangirā Dhoomāvatee Sāvitree Gāyātree
Sarasvatee Brahmanandakaleti II

841. ***Bhāvajnā* - भावज्ञा**

(i) One who knows all thoughts and sentiments.

(ii) The word *Bhāva* has lots of meanings. According to *Amara* dictionary (III-3-207); *Sattā Sajāteeyavijāteeya Svagatabheda Rahitā Anubhooti*: *Sattā* – to stay, nature (of qualities), idea (or goal), action, soul and birth; *Bhāva*: *Sattāsvabhāvābhiprāya Cheshtātmajanmasu*:. In some other dictionaries the following additional meanings are also provided – pregnancy (vagina), wise men, wealth, mercy, sports and grandeur. According one other *Sūtra*, *Bhava* means righteousness. In *Smrutis* this has been used to mean meditation. If it is considered as a verb, it can be taken to mean, pure, without any other and Supreme Being. According to *Yāskarā's Nrukta* (I-1-2), six types of stages (changes or states) is called as *Bhava* – they are – to stay, to be born, to grow, to wane, etc.

(iii) Logicians call these six as *Bhāvas*;

- Pious or devotion
- Family people (*bhava* indicates family and hence *bhāvā* should indicate family people)

- Those who follow *Shiva* (*bhava* indicates *Shiva* and hence *bhāvā* means who follow *Shiva*),
- Sun and other bodies which provide light (*bha* means light or luster and hence *bhāvā* is illuminating body)
- *Yoginee Hrudaya* gives six different meanings to *Panchadashee mantra*. One among them is *Bhāvārta*.

(iv) Thus, the summary is that **She** shines with various meanings.

842. *Bhavarogaghnee* - भवरोगघ्नी

(i) One who cures the disease of trans-migratory existence (*samsārā*).

(ii) Being born again and again is a disease. *Shiva Purāŋa* and *Śreemad Rāmāyana* say that *Shiva* has the capability of curing it.

In *Shiva Purāŋa*;

Vyādheenām Bheshajam Yadvat Pratipaksha Svabhāvata: I
Tadvat Samsārarogānām Pratipaksha: *Shivādhava*: II

In *Śreemad Rāmāyana*;

Nānyam Pashyāmi Bhaishajyamantrena Vrushdhvajam I

(iii) *Śree Ādi Śaṇkara* in his commentary of *Vişhŋu Sahasranāma* for the 578th name – *Bheshajam* says – The medicine for the disease called *samsārā* is **he** only.

843. *Bhavachakrapravartinee* - भवचक्रप्रवर्तिनी

(i) One who controls the wheel of trans-migratory existence (*samsārā*).

(ii) *Manu Smruti* (XII-124) says – he rotates, like a wheel, all the living beings, in the form of the five primary elements earth, water, fire, air and ether, through birth, growth and waning;

Esha Sarvāni Bhootāni Panchabhirvyāpya Moortibhi: II
Janma Vruddhi Kshayair Nityam Samsārāyati Chakravat II

(iii) In *Vişhŋu Bhāgavatam* also we read as – you are the head of all the bondages in the world and also the remover of those bondages. The wise and those who surrender to you, worship you to get rid of the pains;

Tvameva Sarvajagatām Eshvaro Bandhamokshayo: II
Tam Tvām Archaŋti Kushalā: *Prapannārtiharam Haram* II

(iv) It can be reminded that earlier in 568th name – *Niyantree* – one who controls the entire world under rule and 569th name – *Nikhilesvaree* – one who has such controlling capability. The summary meaning of it is that since **She** is the form of *Brahmam*, **She** controls everything in the world by giving birth, protecting and destroying. This has been mentioned in *Saptashatee* (12th chapter) also;

Evam Bhagavatee Devee Sā Nityāpi Puna: Puna: I
Sambhooya Kurute Bhoopa Jagata: Paripālanam II

Śreemad Bhagavad Geeta (XVIII-61) says;

Ĕshwara Sarvabhootām Hruddesherjuna Tishtati I
Bhrāmayansarvabhootāni Yantrārodāni Māyayā II

97th verse of *Soundaryalaharee* says;

Tureeyā Kāpi Tvam Duradhigamaŋisseemamahimā I
Mahāmāyā Vishvam Bhramayasi Parabrahmamahishi II

(v) Since *Anāhata chakra* is the place of *Shiva, Bhavachakra* indicates *Anāhatam*. A doubt may arise here. As per *Tantras* those which have corners and petals are called *chakras*. Since *Anāhatam* does not have corners, it does not qualify to be called as a *chakra*. That is the reason in 485th name it was mentioned as *Anāhatābjanilaya*. That which has only petals, is called as Lotus. That which has only corners is called as *yantra*. Hence *Śree Bhāskararāya* clarifies that *Anāhata* cannot be called as *chakra*, by quoting the commentary of *Vidyā Ratna Bhāsyakāra*. Since the pericarp of lotus (in the *Moolādhāra* and other *chakras*) has corners, it is apt to call them as *chakras*.

(vi) In *Śreechakra, bindu*, eight petalled, sixteen petalled, triangle and *Poopuras* are called as *bhavachakras*. It can be recalled that they are called as *Shiva Kona*s (corners) in the results part of *Trishatee*. (Three circles are not being mentioned se*para*tely). By integrating with the *Shakti Chakras* they get pride. The first verse of *Soundaryalaharee* also conveys the same message.

(vii) According to *Vişhŋu Purāŋa, chakra* indicates the mind. It says that *Vişhŋu*, in his hand, has the form of a *chakra*, which revolves faster than mind;

Chalatsvaroopamadyantam Javenāntareetānilam I
Chakrasvaroopam Cha Mano Dhatte Vişhŋu: Karesthitam II

Hence the meaning of this name can be taken as that **She** drives the mind of *Shiva*.

844. ***Chanda:sārā* - छन्दःसारा**

(i) One who is the essence of all *Vedas*.

(ii) The word *Chaŋḍa*: would mean – word, *Veda, Gayatree*, metre, *Paingala tantra* which explains the prosody. **She** is the essence (strength, permanency and greatness).

(iii) *Gāyatree mantra* is the essence of all *Chaŋḍa*: That is of two types. One is explicitly mentioned in *Vedas* and the other is the *Panchadashee mantra*, indicated through code words. This name is fitting since there is no difference between *Śree Devee* and *Śreevidya*. In this regard *Śree Bhāskararāya*'s book called *Varivasya Rahasya* (verses 6 to 8) and *Tripuropansishad* may be referred. For *Tripuropanishad* also *Śree Bhāskararāya* has written his commentary. *Kādi Vidyā* has been explained in this.

(iv) The description of *Śree Chakra* has been made in two *Sūtras* of *Paingala tantra*; *Dvikou Glou* and *Mishroucha*. *Śree Bhāskararāya* also mentions that he has explained this in his book called *Chaŋḍobhāskaram*. Already it was mentioned that the word *Chaŋḍa*: indicates *Paingala Tantra*. *Śreechakra* is considered as the essence of it. Hence this meaning is very much apt for this name.

(v) *Sāra* means strength, greatness i.e. *Śree Devee*'s greatness is explained through *Chaŋḍa*: (speech in the form of *Vaikharee*). Hence *Chaŋḍa:sāra*.

(vi) *Chaŋḍa*: also means to act according to one's own wish (*Vishwa* dictionary is the evidence for this also). *Vignāna Bhairava Battāraka* says wherever the mind becomes happy, it has to be focused in those places – then the supreme bliss shines. Accordingly whatever the initiated worshipper wants to do it is right and whatever he does not want to do, it is not right. In this regard the famous verse in the *Shākuntala* may be reminded. Wherever doubt arises the inner self of the learned is the proof; *Satām Hi Sandehapadeshu Vastushu Pramāŋamanta*: *Karaŋapravrttaya*:.

According to *Parasurāma Kalpa Sūtra* also till one reaches the stage of emancipation he has to follow the righteous rules defined in the *Smrutis*; *Proudāntam Samayāchārā*:.

Koula Upanishad says – righteousness is wickedness and the wickedness is the righteousness. The same message is conveyed in *Yoginee Hrudaya* also.

In *Manu Smruti* (II-6) also the righteousness is that what is mentioned in *Vedas* and *Smrutis*, the practice of good people and things or thoughts that make the mind happy. There is one important aspect to be noted here. Whatever was mentioned here is applicable only to great worshippers and those who have felt the meaning of *Mahāvākyās* by experience. Others (who have not yet come to that stage) have to follow what is mentioned in *Vedas* and *Smrutis*. They should not act as per their own wish.

Thus behaving according to one's own wish is *Chaŋḍa*:. **She** has that as her *Sārā* (justice). Hence *Chaŋḍa:sāra*.

(vii) *Chaŋḍa*: indicates willingness. It means that **She** is in the form if *Icchā Shakti*.

845. ***Shāstrasārā* - शास्त्रसारा**

(i) One who is the essence of all *Sāstras* (scriptures).

846. ***Mantrasārā* - मन्त्रसारा**

(i) One who is the essence of all *mantras*.
(ii) These two names have to be explained as the previous name.
(iii) *Sāstra* indicates *Vedas*. Thus explains the *Brahma Sūtra* (I-1-3); *Shāstra Yonitvāt*. Those who follow *tantras* also accept *sāstra* as it defines the rules.
(iv) *Sāstra* also indicates (old) *Meemāmsa sāstra*. In the book called *Bāmti* written by *Śree Vāchaspati Mishra*, as mentioned in *Vedas*, *sāstras* advise ordained and prohibited actions;

Pravruttir Vā Nivruttirvā Nityena Krutakena Vā I
Pumsām Yenopadshyeta Tachchāstramabhidheeyate II

(v) The word *mantra* indicates *Veda* also. Again the *mantras* included in the *tantras* also indicate the same *tantras*. **She** is the essence of all these.

847. ***Talodaree* – तलोदरी**

(i) One who has a slender waist.
(ii) It can be reminded that earlier in 35th name *Lakshyaroma Latādhāratāsamunneyamadhyamā*, it was mentioned that **She** has a very subtle waist.
(iii) If the syllable *'A'* to be added the name becomes *A-talodaree*; the *atala* world is her abdomen when **She** assumes the *virāt* form. In **Her** anthropomorphic form, **She** is beautiful, having a slender waist. Following the *Devee Geeta*; *Stalāti Mahālokā*: *Katyadho Bhāgatām Katā*: - the meaning of *Lalitā Stavarājam* (13th chapter) in the *Lalithopākyānam* is the world *Rasātala* only;

Atalamtu Bhavet Padou Vitalam Jānur Tava I
Rasātalam Katithesha: *Kukshiste Dharaŋee Bhavet* II

848. *Udārakeerti*: - उदारकीर्तिः

(i) One who has great fame extending everywhere.

(ii) *Ut* – very great, *Ā* – spreading in all places, *Ara* – reachable early, *Keerti*: - fame or pride – That is, **She** bestows fame to the devotees soon. **She** herself is with very great pride.

(iii) *Ru* – mother of *Devas*. Hence the name is *Arā*: of *Devas*. **Her** pride is much greater than that of *Devas*.

(iv) *Āra* – the bad planets like Mars, etc. **Her** fame is much higher than theirs. That is, **She** removes the blemishes due to the planets like Mars, etc.

(v) *Ud* – The manifested form with attributes in the Sun galaxy. *Chāndogya Upanishad* (I-6-6,7) says the golden *purush* lives in Sun and his name is *Ud*; *"Ya Eshontarāditye Hiranmaya*: *Purusha*:.. *Tasyoditi Nāma..."*.

Ārā is a kind of weapon. The fame gained through worshipping *Śree Devee*'s is greater than the fame of the golden *purush* in Sun. Hence **Her** name is *Udārakeerti*:

(vi) *Chāndogya Upanishad* (VIII-5-4) says that there are two lakes of nectar called *Ara* and *Nyam* (big like oceans) in the *Brahma* world.

Śree Ādi Śaṇkara in his commentary for *Brahma Sūtra* (IV-4-22); *Anāvrddhi Shabdāt* – explains this. **She** is so pride like these lakes.

849. *Uddhāma Vaibhavā* - उद्धाम वैभवा

(i) One who has boundless glory.
Dhāma means binding rope. *Ud* – beyond it. That is, **She** has, beyond any bindings, boundless glory.

850. *Varŋaroopiŋee* - वर्णरूपिणी

(i) One who is of the form of letters.

(ii) *Varŋa* means letters. **She** is of that form. 529th name *Sarvavarŋopashobhitā* and 577th name *Mātrukāvarŋaroopiŋee* may be referred. The *Pāŋini sikshā* says, "According to the *Sāmbhava* school there are sixty-four letters, these are promulgated by *Svayambhu* (self-originated) in the *Prākrut* or Samskrit language"; **She** is of that form.

(iii) *Varŋam* means caste – **She** is in the form of *Varŋam* in *Varŋāshramam*. Crossing of castes will result in great danger. It can be read in *Śreemad Bhagavad Geeta* (I-41) as *Arjuna* explains. The real meaning of this name is *Śree Devee* is in the form of controls like *varŋas*.

851. *Janma Mrutyujarā Taptajana Vishrāntidāyinee* –
जन्म मृत्युजरा तप्तजन विश्रान्तिदायिनी

(i) One who is bringing rest, clear self-happiness and peace to human beings, consumed by birth, death and decrepitude.
(ii) The period after the death till next birth is a type of temporary rest – the permanent rest is being without any more births. **She** bestows both.

852. *Sarvopanishadudghushṭā* - सर्वोपनिषदुद्घुष्टा

(i) One who is proclaimed in all the *Upanishads*.
(ii) Since it takes along near the manifested *Brahmam*, it is called as *Upanishad*. *Śree Ādi Śaṇkara*, says, since the soul is merged with the non-dual *Brahmam* and the ignorance and its results are destroyed, it is called as *Upanishad*; *"Upaneeya Immātmānam Brahmapāsta Dvayam Sata*:I *Nihantyavidyām Tajjām Cha Tasmad Upanishanmatā*II" Hence, *Itreyam* and others are secret and as the head parts of *Vedas*. They are called as *Upanishads*.
(iii) *Ghusta* - loudly proclaimed, *ud* - exalted, in this context it has to be considered as a single form. There is no difference between the Upanishads when they talk about worshipping with attributes. They are all one and the same. This has been clearly mentioned in the commentary of Brahma Sūtra (III-3-1); *Sarvavedānta Pratyayam Chodanādyavisheshāt*.

853. *Shāntyateetakalātmikā* - शान्त्यतीतकलात्मिका

(i) In some schools this is used as *Shāntyateetākalātmikā* – शान्त्यतीताकलात्मिका.
(ii) Out of the *kalās* of the five primary elements, the *kalā* of ether *tatva* is called *Shāntyateeta*. (829th name *Pratishṭhā* may also be referred). The *Saiva Agamas* describe its nature thus "*Sāntyatitakalā* annihilates duality and bestows bliss"; *Shāntyateetakalā Dvatanivānānandabodhada*. **She** is of that form. It can be noted that

this *kalā* has been indicated in the special *mantras* for the worshippers of *Shoḍashee* in the *Navāvarŋa Pooja*, as a continuity of the ninth *Āvarŋa*; *Sarvānandamaye Chakre Mahodyānapeedecharyānanda Nāthātmaka Tureeyāteeta-dashādhishdāyaka Shantyateetakalātmaka Prakāsha Vimarsha Sāmarasyātmaka Parabrahmasvaroopiŋee*.

(iii) 905th name – *Baindavāsanā* may be referred. Above the eye-brows in the circular place called *Bindu*, *Shāntyateetā* lives in the left side of *Shiva*. *Svacchandra* says; *"Vāmabhāge Samāseenā Shāntyateetā Manonmanee* II". That form is also part of *Śree Devee* only, i.e. a *kala*.

854. ***Gambheerā* - गम्भीरा**

(i) One who is fathomless or one whose depth cannot be measured.
(ii) Her limits cannot be identified; *"Adimudi kāŋa mudiyāthattu"* – neither the feet nor the head can be seen.
(iii) **She** is in the form of *Mahāhrada* (a large tank). The *Shiva* Sūtra (I-23) says, "By meditating on *Mahāhrada*, one derives the experience of the power of the *mantra*"; *Mahāhradānu Sandhānān Mantra Veeryānubhava*: II

That is - "*Mahāhrada* means the supreme divine energy. Meditation (*anusamdhāna*) means the feeling of being merged in that. *Mantraveerya*- the power of *mantra* is the cognition of the *poorŋāhamsā* (complete egoism). Experience, the clear manifestation, of the Self;

Mahāhrada Iti Proktāshaktibhagavatee Parā I
Anusandhānamityuktam Tattādātmya Vimarshanam II
Mantraveeryamiti Proktam Poonāhantā Vimarshanam I
Tadeeyonubhavastasya Sphuranam Svātmana: *Spuhutam* II

In another place also, "The Supreme Queen is knowledge. **She** first emanates the energy of desire and then gross objects as well as souls with their qualities of activity, purity and infinity etc. Hence *Mahāhrada* means *Śree Devee* who pervades the universe and is beyond space and time";

Parā Bhattārikā Samvitcchā Shakti Purassaram I
Sthoola Prameya Paryantam Vamantee Vishvamāntaram II
Pramātrantar Baheeroopā Hrusheekavishayātmanām I
Pravartakatva Svacchatva Ghambheeratvādi Dharmata: II
Mahāhrado Jagadvyāpee Desha Kālādyagochara: II

(iv) *Gam* is the *Gaŋapatibeeja*, *bhee* - fear, *ra* - drives out.
   a. One book says, since **She** removes fear of *Gaŋapati*, **She** is

Gambheera.

b. It seems, it can be said that **She** removes the fear by worshipping *Gaŋapati*. The first step in worshipping *Śree Vidyā* is *Gaŋapati* worship. Through this any obstruction or fear during the worship is removed. 451st name *Vighnanāshinee* may be referred. It can be noted that in *Gaŋapati Sahasranāma* also we read some names relating to *Śreevidyā* (*Śree Bhāskararāya* himself has written commentary for in his book *Khadyotam*). In another *Gaŋapati Sahasranāma*, which is most secret, there is a lot about *Śreevidya*.

(v) *Śree Ādi Śaṇkara* in his commentary of *Viṣhŋu Sahasranāma* for the 543rd name – *Gambheera*: mentions; he is so gigantic with his knowledge, wealth, strength, vigor, etc.; *Gnānaishvaryabala-veeryādibhirgambheero Gambheera*:

855. *Gaganāntasthā* - गगनान्तस्था

(i) One who pervades in the midst of the ether.

(ii) The ether indicates three types – *Daharākāsh* – the ether in the heart, *Bhootākāsh* – one of the five primary elements and *Parākāsh* – the great ether.

The word *Anta*: may mean midst, till the end and inside-outside. Hence **She** is prevalent in all these three ethers in the midst, inside, outside and till the end.

Svetāsvatara Upanishad (III-9) says - like a tree in ether; "*Vruksha Iva Stabdho Divi Tishtatyeka*: II" *Mahānārāyaŋopanishad* also conveys the same message.

(iii) *Gagana*: - ether, *anta* – its end, *sthā* – one who is. That is, one who continues to be even after the end of the ether, i.e., after the great dissolution.

(iv) *Gagana*: - *Ha*, the *beeja* which indicates ether. Since the other basic elements (like air, etc.) originated from ether, those *beejams* are all included in this. The other perspective is – according to grammar the letters *ya*, *ra*, *la* and *va* are called as *antasta*. They are the *beejas* of other four elements. Hence the summarised meaning would be that **She** is in the form of all the five primary elements.

856. *Garvitā* - गर्विता

(i) One who is with pride.

(ii) **She** has the great ability of creating this world, protecting it and finally merging it with herself. Hence **She** is pride. The combined form of self-ego found in each of the souls is called *Parāhanta*. **She** is in the form of *Parāhanta*.
(iii) It can be recollected that in the 508th name *Atigarvitā*, we read that **She** is proud on account of her beauty.

857. ***Gānalolupā* - गानलोलुपा**

(i) One who is fond of music.
(ii) **She** is interested in vocal music, instrumental and *Sāma Gānam*.
(iii) *Kālidāsa* says in his *Shyāmalādaṇḍaka* as; *"Jaya sangeeṭa Rasike"*.
(iv) 66th verse of *Soundaryalaharee* says that **She** sings the stories of *Parameshwara*. *Saraswatee* sings the stories of *Parameshwara* in his Veena. You enjoy it and happily praise her. By hearing the sweetness of your voice, feeling shy, she puts her Veena in its cover; *"Vipanchyā Gāyantee"*.

858. ***Kalpanārahitā* - कल्पनारहिता**

(i) One who is without imagination or dexterity.
(ii) *Kalpana* (imagination) is those thoughts about the world relating to senses. Those are experience based – i.e., imagining the new ones based on the previous experience or known facts. The souls imagine these themselves. It does not apply to *Śree Devee* – **She** knows everything. Everything originated from **Her**– nothing to imagine.
(iii) This name can be read with stress on different syllable – *Kalpa* + *nārā* + *hita*. *Kalpa* indicates the great dissolution. **She** does well to the souls at that time. **She** keeps the souls with her during the dissolution and gives re-birth later. Thus **She** does what is good to the souls even during the dissolution period. It has been hinted here that when **She** does good things to the souls even during dissolution period, definitely **She** will do much better during other creation and protection times.
(iv) *Ashṭāvakra Samhita* (*Geeta*) (II-25) says – "It's surprising. The souls originate from me, in the form of boundary-less ocean, as natural waves. They hit each other, play for some time and abscond after some time;

Mayyanante Chidambhodhāvāshcharyam Jeevavĕshwaya: I
Udyanti Gnanti Khelanti Pravishanti Svabhāvata: II

859. ***Kāshṭhā* - काष्ठा**

(i) One who is in the form limited by the statements in *Vedānta*.

(ii) *Kaṭopanishad* (III-11) says – **She** is in the form conclusively mentioned in *Vedānta* statements; "*Sākāshta Sā Paragati:*".

Sootha Samhita says – whether true or not, whether visible or not, it is *Shiva.* The conclusion of *Vedāntas* is called *Kāshṭhā*;

Prateetamaprateetam Vā Sadasachcha Para: Shiva : I
Iti Vedānta Vākyānām Nishtā Kāshteti Kathyate II

(iii) *Kalā* and *Kāshṭhā* are measurements of time. *Śree Bhāskararāya* says that *Kāshṭhā* is 18 minutes. He quotes the below statements while giving the meanings for verses 16 and 17 of *Varivasya Rahasya* – The time taken by a sharp needle to pierce a subtle pericarp of Lotus is called *lavam*. There is no time duration less than this;

Nalinee Patra Samhatyā: Sookshma Soochyabhivedhane I
Daladale Tu Ya: Kāla: Sa Kālo Lavasamgjni: II
Ata: Sookshmatama: Kāla: Nopalabhyo Bhrugodvaha II

Tantra Rājam (XXXVI-44) also indicates *lavam* in the same way. However, mathematical books mention the below table;

100 *drushti*	=	1 *Veda*
3 *Vedas*	=	1 *Lavam*
3 *Lavas*	=	1 *Nimesham*
3 *Nimeshams*	=	1 *Kshanam*
5 *Kshanams*	=	1 *Kāshṭhā*
15 *Kāshṭhās*	=	1 *Lagu* (minute)
15 *Lagus* (minutes)	=	1 *Nāḍi*
2 *Nāḍis*	=	1 *Muhoorta*
6 *Muhoortas*	=	1 *Yāma*
8 *Yāmas*	=	1 day

This indicates that **She** is in the form of a minute time period. This has been mentioned in *Deveeupanishad*;

Saishā Grahanakshatra Jyoteemshi Kalā Kāstāti Kālaroopaṇee I

The same meaning is conveyed in *Saptashatee* (XI chapter) also;

Kalā Kāstādi Roopena Parinām Pradāyinee I
Vishvasyoparatou Shakte Nārāyaṇi Namostu Te II

While commenting on the meaning of this verse, the authors say –

18 *Nimeshams* = 1 *Kāshṭhā*

(some others say 15 *Nimeshams* make one *Kashthu*. *Viṣhṇu Purāṇu* (II-8-60) also says 15 *Nimeshams* make one *Kāshṭhā*;

Kāshṭhā Nimeshā Dasha Pancha Chaiva

Trimshachcha KāshṭhāGaŋayet Kalāmcha I
Trim Shatkalashchaiva Bhavenmuhoortas
Taisrimshatā Rātryahanee Samete II

(iv) The ether form of *Parameshwara* is called *Bheemam*. In that form his consort is *Kāshṭhā*, mother of heaven. **She** has the form of ten directions. *Linga Purāŋa* says;

Charācharānām Bhootānām Sarveshāmavakāshata: I
Vyomātmā Bhagavān Devo Bheema Ityuchyate *Budhai*: II
Mahāmahimno Dhevasya Bheemasya Paramātmana: I
Dasha Svaroopā Dig Patnee Suta: *Svargashcha Sooribhi*: II

Vāyu Purāŋa also says;

Nāmnā Shashṭasya Yābheemā Tanurāgāsha Uchyate I
Disha: *Patnya*: *Smrutās Tasya Svargas Tasya Soota*: *Smruta*: II

She is omnipresent, will seem to be very close by, but will be unreachable.

(v) Beyond one thing is called as *Kāshṭhā*; *Krāntavā Tishtateeti Kāshṭha*. *Veda* also says he was ten inches long. *Svetashvatara Upanishad* (III-14) says; *Atyatishtād Dashāngulam*. We read the same message in *Śreemad Bhagavad Geeta* (X-42) also;

Athavā Bahunaitena Kim Gnātena Tavārjuna I
Vishtabhyāhamidam Krutsnamekāmshena Stito Jagat II

(vi) *Kāshṭhā* indicates a kind of tree called *Tāruharitra*. *Mairāla Tantra* says that is integrated with *Shiva Shaktis*. The colour of the inside of the skin of this tree is yellow in colour. Its dimension is like an umbilical cord. Hence it is mentioned as part of *Shiva -Shakti*.

(vii) *Kāshṭhā* indicates a dried tree. That is, **She** does not change on account of growth, etc. That may be reason when ascetics follow ardent silent vow, it is said that they are in *Kāshṭhā* silent vow.

860. *Akāntā* - अकान्ता

(i) One who removes sins.
(ii) *Aka* - sin or sorrow. **She** destroys them. Hence *Akānta*.
(iii) 167th name *Pāpanāshinee* and 743rd name *Pāpāraŋyadavānalā* may be referred.
(iv) In *Trishatee* also for the 31st name *Ena*: *Kooṭavināshinee* and 112th name *Hatyādi Pāpashamanee* the meaning is destroyer of sins.
(v) This verse is split as 859th name *Kāshṭhā* and 860th name *Akānta*. Earlier we read the 329th name as *Kānta*.

861. ***Kāntārdhavigrahā* - कान्तार्धविग्रहा**

(i) One who has the half body of her consort.
(ii) *Ardhanāree* form is being considered here. It can be taken in two ways – **She** has taken half body of *Parameshwara* or He has taken half body of **Hers**. Both are correct according to grammar.
(iii) 23rd verse of *Soundaryalaharee* may be referred – *Tvayā Hatvā Vāmai Vapuraparitrutena Manasā* I
(iv) 392nd name *Shreekanthārdhashareeriɲee* may also be referred.
(v) The end of letter *ka* is *kha*. *Kha* means heaven. Heaven is also a part of **Her** body. *Chāndogya Upanishad* (III-12-6) describes – all the living beings are one fourth of **Her** only and other three immortal portions are in the heaven; *"Pādosya Sarvā Bhootāni Tripadasyāmrutam Diveeti* II".
(vi) For those who are interested in Samskrit grammar, *Śree Bhāskararāya* has given some grammatical notes.

862. ***Kāryakāraɲanirmuktā* - कार्यकारणनिर्मुक्ता**

(i) One who free from cause and effect.
(ii) *Kāraɲa* (cause) – *Moolaprakruti*. *Kārya* (effect) - the categories, *mahat*, etc., since they originate from *Moolaprakruti* in an orderly way. This was already explained in 397th name - M*oolaprakruti:*. *Veda* says that the *Chaitanya* (*Brahmam*) has neither cause nor effect; *Na Tasya Kāryam Kāraɲam Cha Vidyāte* II

In *Śreemad Bhagavad Geeta* (III-22) *Śree Krişhɲa* says – there is naught in three worlds that has not been done be me; *"Na Me Pārthāsti Kartavyam Trishu Lokeshu Kinchana"*.

863. ***Kāmakelitarangitā* - कामकेलितरङ्गिता**

(i) One who has succession of waves constituting the play of erotic.
(ii) The word *Lalitā* itself indicates erotic. The saying goes; *Lalanāth Lalitā*. The meaning is to prattle. It can be reminded that earlier in 376th name *Shrungārarasasampoorɲā*, it was mentioned that **She** is full of the essence of love.
(iii) *Śree Devee's* erotic games flow like waves.
(iv) It can also be construed that *Parameshwara's* love game reaches *Śree Devee* as waves.

864. ***Kanatkanakatāṭankā* - कनत्कनकताटङ्का**

(i) One who wears shining gold ear-rings
(ii) In the 22nd name *Tāṭangkayugaleebhootatapanodupamaŋḍalā*, it was mentioned that Sun and Moon are the two ear studs of *Śree Devee*.
(iii) An ornament in the ears is very important. In Tamil, *Shiva* is described as *Thodudaiya Seviyan* – one who has studs in his ear.
(iv) It is said that *Śree Ādi Śaṇkara* has installed ear studs to *Śree Devee* in most of the important temples.
(v) From the statement (flowing smoothly like water) *Kātilolakātilola*, it is very clear that the ear studs enhance the beauty of a lady – Two ladies talk to each other;

First lady: *Kā Atilola* – who is very beautiful?
Second lady: *Kātil lola* – one who wears rings in ears.

(vi) 28th verse of *Soundaryalaharee* says that – even after consuming the great venom *Shiva* continued to live, on the other hand, even after consuming nectar, *Devas* get destroyed (during dissolution); *Sudhāmaptāsvādhya*...

865. ***Leelā Vigrahadhāriŋee* – लीला विग्रहधारिणी**

(i) One who, playfully and without much of effort, takes various incarnations.
(ii) **She** assumes different forms just like that by her thought alone. 401st name - *Vividhākārā* and 824th name *Bahuroopā* may be referred.
(iii) **She** is mentioned in the *Yogavāsistha* as - "There was in this royal family one name *Padmarāja*, he had a beautiful chaste wife named *Leelā*". Again this *Leelā Devee* is mentioned in 966th name *Leelāvinodinee*.

866. ***Ajā* - अजा**

(i) One who is unborn.
(ii) The same message is conveyed in136th name *Nityā* - **She** is eternal and in 174th name *Nirbhavā* - without origin.
(iii) The *Svetashvatara Upanishad* (IV-5) - The one, unborn; was not born, will not be born;

Ajāmekām Lohita Shukla Krushnām Bahvee: *Prajā*: *Srujamānām Saroopā*: I
Ajo Hyoko Jushamānonushete Jahātyenām Bhuktabho Gamajonya: II

In another *Sruti* we read as – unborn and will not be born again;

Najāto Najanishyate.

In *Devee Upanishad* also (26th *rig*) we read as;

Yasyā Anto Na Vidyāte Tasmāduchyatenantā I
Yasyā Jananam Nopalabyate Tasmātuchyatojā II

The *Mahābhārata* also the same meaning is conveyed: "I was not, am not and will not be born at any time, I am the *Kshetrajna* of all beings and hence I am called as *Aja*";

Na Hi Jāto Na Jāyeham Najanishye Kadāchana I
Kshetragna: *Sarvabhootānām Tasmadahamaja*: *Smruta*: II

Śreemad Bhagavad Geeta (II-27) says, "Death is certain of that which is born; birth is certain of that which is dead. You should not therefore lament over the inevitable;

Jātasya Hi Druvo Mrutyu: *Druvam Janma Mrutasya Cha* I
Tasmādaparihāryerthe Na Tvam Shochitumarhasi II

When there is no birth, there is no death also. This is being mentioned in the next name.

867. ***Kshayavinirmuktā* - क्षयविनिर्मुक्ता**

(i) One who frees from decay (death).
(ii) One who does not have birth itself; hence there is no growth, decay or death.
(iii) *Kshaya* also means house. The devotees of *Śree Devee*, need not go leaving their house to forest in search of salvation or doing penance. While living as householder (enjoying the household activities), by the blessings of *Śree Devee* can reach the salvation. It is said that, the devotees of *Śree Devee* have both the *Bhoga* (enjoyment) and *Moksha* (salvation) together in their hands;

Yatrāsti Bhogo Na Cha Tatra Moksha: *Yatrāsti Moksho Na Cha Tatra Bhoga*: I
Śreesundaree Sādhaka Pugavānām Bhogashcha Mokshashcha Karastha Eva II

The results part of this *Sahasranāma* itself we read as;

Nānena Sadrusham Stotram bhogamokshapradam Mune I
Keertaneeyamidam Tasmād bhoga Mokshārthipir Narai: II

868. ***Mugdhā* - मुग्धा**

(i) One who is beautiful.
(ii) According to Vishva dictionary this word indicates beauty and

ignorance. In this context only the meaning beautiful is apt. As discussed in the 48th name *Mahālāvaŋyashevadhi*: - **She** is the treasure of beauty. **She** is *Mahātripurasundaree* (234th name) and **She** is *Shobhanā* (462nd name).

(iii) Some schools prefix *'A'* - making the name *Amugdha*. In that case it has to be construed as, not ignorant, i.e., her devotees are not ignorant and they are full of knowledge.

869. ***Kshipraprasādinee*** **- क्षिप्रप्रसादिनी**

(i) One who blesses early.

(ii) The *Saura Purāŋa* says, "Oh *Dvijās* (brahmins), by worshipping other deities salvation is gradually, but by worshipping the *Umapathi* one is freed in the same birth". This evidence is considered since *Shiva* and *Śree Devee* are one and the same this will apply to *Śree Devee* also;

Kramena Labhyatenyeshām Muktirārādhanāddvijā: I
Ārādhanādumeshasya Tasmin Janmaŋi Muchyate II

This refers to those who practice excessive devotion. Regarding others, the *Shiva Purāŋa* says, "Though he has only little faith that mortal will not surely undergo the pain of the womb after the third birth";

Alpabhāvepi Yo Martya: *Sopi Janmatrayātparam* I
Na Yoniyantrapeedāyai Bhavishyati Na Samshaya: II

Confirming this, the *Tantrarāja* says, "The prayers, oblations, worship, etc., performed without regularity make one fit (for salvation) in the next birth";

Anyathāsamprdāyena Japahomārchanāḍikam I
Krutam Janmāntare Samyak Sampratāyāya Kalpate II

383rd name *Sadya*: *Prasādinee* may be referred.

870. ***Antarmukhasamārādhyā*** **- अन्तर्मुखसमाराध्या**

(i) One who is well adored by those who are inward looking.

(ii) **She** is worshipped in a grand way, by those who have diverted their mind from other activities and have inward looking power.

(iii) **She** is *Hrudayasthā* (595th name) and *Daharākāsharoopiŋee* (609th name).

(iv) In *Śreemad Bhagavad Geeta* (IV chapter) *Śree Krişhŋa* clearly advises the inward looking powers.

(v) We see in the practices of *Navāvarŋa Pooja* also inward looking worship is very great (*parā*);

Paramāmrutavarshenna Plāvayantam Charācharam I
Sanchintya Paramadvaidabhāvanāmrutasevayā II
Modamāno Vismrutānyavikalpavibhavabhrama: I
Chidambudhimahābhangachchinna Sankocha Sankata: I
Samullasan Mahānāthalokanontarmukhāyana: II
Mantramayyā ManovruttyāParamadvaitameehate I
Saparyā Sarvabhāveshu Sā Parā Parikeertitā II

(vi) *Pavanopanishad* also advises that the body itself has to be imagined as *Śreechakra*. *Śree Bhāskararāya* himself has written the usage method for this. 113rd name *Bhāvanāgamyā* may be referred.

871. ***Bahirmukhasudurlabhā* - बहिर्मुखसुदुर्लभा**

(i) One who is rare for those whose mental gaze goes on outward things.
(ii) In the previous names it was mentioned that **She** is worshipped by inward looking people. The real meaning is that **She** gets satisfied with that **She** blesses them. On the other hand, those who have wavering mind, it is very difficult to reach **Her** (*Su – Durlabhā*) – says this name. Only following this, *Śree Ādi Śaṇkara* says in 95th verse of *Soundaryalaharee* as; "*Tarana Karanānāmasulabhā*" – **She** is not reachable by those who have uncontrolled mind.
(iii) Earlier in 188th name said *Durlabhā* (difficult to reach) and this name says *Sudurlabhā* (very difficult to reach).

872. ***Trayee* - त्रयी**

(i) One who is in the embodiment of three *Vedas* - *Rig*, *Yajus* and *Sāma*.
(ii) Including the *Atharva*, *Vedas* are four in number. However, *Atharva Veda* is not very popular; it has become a practice to address these three *Vedas* as triple revelation. She is mother of *Vedas*. 338th name *Vedajananee* may be referred. Hence it is apt to call **Her** as *Trayee*.
(iii) In some schools, based on the commentary for *Shāradhā Tilak*, it is felt that this name indicates the three *kāndās* (sections) of the four *Vedas* - *karma* (action), *upāsanā* (devotional practice) and *gnāna* (knowledge).
(iv) The verses of *Rig*, *Yajus* and *Sāma Vedas* (*Agnimeele*, *Ishctvā*, *Agna Ayāhi*) begins with the syllables *A*, *E* and *A*. According to Samskrit grammar, if these letters are merged we get the letter I. This is the *Vāgbhava beeja* without *bindu*. According to *tantras* it is called as

Trayee. (It can be noted that if the first syllable of *Atharva Veda* is also added we get the *bindu* also). *Devee Bhāgavatam* (III chapter) describes in detail the story of *Sudarsan*, who got the blessings of *Śree Devee*, by worshipping the *Vāgbhava beeja* without the *bindu*. **She** is in the form of that *Vāgbhava beeja*.

(v) This has been clearly explained in the *Shakti Mahimna Stotra* by *Śree Durvāsa* (according to the commentary of *Śree Nityānanda Nātha*). This explanation of *Śree Chidānanda Nātha* is based on this book only.

873. ***Trivarganilayā* - त्रिवर्गनिलया**

(i) One who is abode of the three objects of desire.
(ii) According to dictionary *Trivarga*: means three types of desire – (righteousness, desired objects and bliss). **She** is there in all these desires. Since **She** is the fourth desire viz., salvation also, this name mentions that **She** is in these three. 760th name *Trivargadhātree* may be referred.

874. ***Tristhā* - त्रिस्था**

(i) One who resides in all the trinities.
(ii) This can be split in various methods;
   a. **She** is in all the times – past, present and future.
   b. **She** is in three syllables of *Praŋava* - *AUM* (*Om*).
   c. **She** is in all the three worlds. The *Markandeya Purāŋa* says, "There are three worlds, three *Vedas*, three *vidyās*, three fires, three lights, three objects of desire, namely virtue, etc., three qualities, three sounds, three sins, three conditions of life, three times, three states of consciousness, three *pitrus*, day, night and twilight, three *Mātrās* the three *Guŋas*, the three phases of time and the three letters in *Trivarga*;

Trayee Lokās Trayodevās Traividyām Pāvakatrāyam I
Treeŋei Jyoteemshi Vargāshcha Trayo Dharmādayas Tathā II
Trayo Guŋas Trāya: *Shabdās Trayo Doshās Tadāshrayma* I
Trāya: *Kālās Tathāvasthā*: *Pitarohar Nishādaya*: I
Mātrātrāyam Cha Te Roopam Tristhe Devee Saraswatee II

875. ***Tripuramālinee* - त्रिपुरमालिनी**

(i) One who is in the form of *Tripuramālinee*.
(ii) The sixth hall of *Śree Chakra* is called *Sarva Rakshākara Chakra* (*Antardasāra Chakra*). In that *chakra* **She** is *Tripuramālinee Devee*, head of *Nikarpa Yoginee Devees*.

876. ***Nirāmayā* – निरामया**

(i) One who is without any disease.
(ii) Sickness affects both body and mind. **She** is without any disease. Since **She** is the medicine for all the diseases, how can any disease affect **Her**? 551st name *Sarvavyādhiprashamanee* may be referred.

877. ***Nirālambā* – निरालम्बा**

(i) One who is without any support.
(ii) Everything in the universe depends on **Her**. **She** is unsupported, as **She** supports everything.
(iii) In *Saptashatee* also in the 10th chapter describing the battle with *Shumba* we read as; **She** fought with Shumba staying in the air without any support;

Utpatya Cha Pragruhyochchair Deveem Gagaṇamāsthita: I
Tatrāpi Sā Nirādhārā Yuyudhe Tena Chaṇḍikā II

878. ***Svātmārāmā* - स्वात्मारामा**

(i) One who is rejoicing in herself.
(ii) **She** rejoices in **Her** own Self. She splits herself into two and plays with each other. The *Brahadāraṇya Upanishad* (I-4-3) says, *Brahmam* was not happy; therefore the lonely one is never happy. He desired a second and he became thus; *"Sa Vai Na Reme Tasmādekākee Na Ramate Sadviteeyamachchat Sa Hyetāvānāsa Yadā Streepumāmsou Sāmparishvaktou Sa Imame Vātmānam Dvedhā Patayattata: Patishcha Patneechābhavatām..."*
(iii) It is said that during the time of creation, the universe originates in the minds of *Śree Devee* and again during the time destruction it submerges in her mind itself. This universe is like a grove or orchard. Since the universe is in **Her** mind, it has to be construed that **Her** mind is like an orchard. The *Vāyu Purāṇa* says, "**She**, one Lord through the energy of dominion, becomes many. Having become many **She** again

becomes one";

Ekastu Prabhushaktyā Vai Bahudhā Bhavateeshvara: I
Bhootvā Yasmāchcha Bahudhā Bhavatyeka: *Punastu Sa*: II

(iv) **She** plays in her *Svātman*, herself alone, *Arāma* (artificial garden), i.e. the various worlds are nothing by **herself**. That is, **She** herself is the universe and *Brahmam* as well. The *Mārkaṇḍeya Purāṇa* says, "Thou art the supreme and eternal Devee in whom all are established. *Brahmam* is supreme and imperishable and the universe is perishable. Just as the fire is in the fire stick and atoms in the earth, so remain *Brahmam* and the whole universe in thee";

Tvamaksharam Param Devee Yachcha Sarvam Pratishtitam I
Tathā Tvati Sthitam Brahma Jagachchedamasheshata: II

879. ***Sudhāsruti*: - सुधाश्रुतिः**

(i) One who is like a stream of nectar.

(ii) **She** is the ambrosial stream, or flow of bliss, that results from meditation on *Śree Devee* in *sahasrāra*. **She** is the continuous flow of the experience of divine bliss in devoted spiritual practice. The nectar which is in the moon of the pericarp of the *Sahasrāra* lotus flower through the *Kunḍalinee*. The circles of the *Dākini* and other deities are watered by this stream whence the *Kunḍalini* becomes the energy of action.

(iii) In this regard 106th name *Sudhāsārābhivarshinee* may be referred. *Śree Ādi Śaṇkara*, in his *Soundaryalaharee* – verses 9 and 10 conveys the same message; *"Maheem Moolādhāre, Sudhādhārāsārai:"*.

(iv) The *Vāyu Purāṇa* says, "The *Devas* become fat by drinking the fifteen streams of nectar which flow from the moon in the dark fortnight of the lunar month. *Shākta Tantras* also communicate the same meanings. All these are due to the *Shāmbhavee Māyā*";

Dashbhi: *Panchabhishchaiva Sudhāmruta Parisravai*: I
Krushnapakshe Satā Peetvā Jāyante Peevarā: *Surā*: II

(v) *Sudhāsruti* according to the *Jnānārnava Tantra* (19th chapter, verses 29.5 to 31 – this will rescue from poisonous fever) means a kind of meditation on *Śree Devee* causing flow of nectar and removing the position, when one is aspiring to attain the *Shakti Beeja*;

Sravatpeeyooshadhārābhir Varshanteem Vishahāriṇeem II
Hemaprabhā Bhāsamānām Vidyunikarasuprabhām II
Spurat Chaṇḍrakalā Poorṇakalasham Varadābharou II
Gnānamudrām Chadadhāteem Sākshādamruta Roopineem

Dhyāyanvisham Haren Mantree Nānākāravyavasthitām II

Thus removing the venom has been mentioned in 20th verse of *Soundaryalaharee* also;

Kirantee Mangebhya: Kirana Nikurumbāmrutarasam
Hadi Tvāmādhatte Himakarashilā Moortimiva Ya: I
Sa Sarpānām Darppam Shamayati Shakuntādhipa Iva
Jvaraplushtān Drushyā Sukayati Sudhādhārasirayā II

880. *Samsāra Panka Nirmagna Samuddharaŋa Paŋḍitā*–
संसार पङ्क निर्मग्न समुद्धरण पण्डिता

(i) One who is skilled in bringing out those sunk in the mire of the transmigratory life.
(ii) If **She** herself is sunk in the quagmire, then how can **She** save others who are sunk in it? **She** has no connection with the cycle of births and deaths. Hence **She** can rescue others drowning in the quagmire of the cycle of births and deaths called *Samsāra*. **She** is well skilled in this.
(iii) In the same way the *Koorma Purāŋa* also says, "Those who once remember *Śree Devee* invoking **Her** protection do not fall into the endless ocean of *Samsāra*, which is difficult to be crossed";

Ye Manāgapi Sharvāneem Smaranti Sharanārdina: I
Dustarāpāra Samsārasagare Na Patanti Te II

881. *Yajnapriyā* - यज्ञप्रिया

(i) One who is fond of sacrifices.
(ii) That is **She** is fond of sacrifice, such as of penance, etc. Sacrifice here may be taken as the sacrificial offering of the devotees. Upon concentrating on the meanings of the *mantras*, the *Navāvarŋa Pooja* itself is a sacrifice. This has been explained by *Śree Sidānanda Nātha* in his book called *Saparyā Pattati Vāsana*. It can be considered that **She** is interested in the *Navāvarŋa Pooja*.
(iii) *Veda* says that *Śree Vişhŋu* himself is *yagnā* (sacrifice); *Yagnoo Vai Vişhŋu*. Hence it can also be taken as that **She** is interested in *Vişhŋu* or *Vişhŋu* is interested in **Her**. This is apt since **She** is part of *Vişhŋu* as per the below names;
267 - *Govindaroopiŋee*, 280 - *Padmanabhasahodaree*,
298 - *Nārāyaŋee*, 892 –*Vaishŋavee*and 893 - *Vişhŋuroopiŋee*.
Saptashatee (11th chapter) also says; *Tvam Vaishŋavee Shaktirananda Veerya.*

882. *Yajnakartree* - यज्ञकर्त्री

(i) One who is the consort of doer of sacrifices.

(ii) One who has desired and initiated to do a sacrifice is called a *yajamānar* (master). He is said to be of the form of *Paramashiva.* His consort is called *Deekshā* and their son is called *Santānan*. **She** is in that *Deekshā* form.

Linga Purāŋa says;

Yajamānātmako Devo Mahādevo Budhai: *Prabhu*: I
Ugra Ityuchyate Sadbhireeshānashcheti Chāparai: II
Ugrāhvayasya Devasya Yajamānātmana: *Prabho*: I
Deekshā Patnee Budhairuktā Santānākhyastadātmaja: II

In *Vāyu Purāŋa*;

Ugrā Tanu: *Samptamee Yā Deekshitair Brahmaŋai*: *Saha* I
Deekshā Patnee Smrutā Tasya Santāna: *Putra Uchyate* II

(iii) In one of the books, it has been mentioned that **She** is of the form of the teacher who conducts the sacrifice.

883. *Yajamānasvaroopiŋee* – यजमानस्वरूपिणी

(i) One who is in sacrifice.

(ii) The last form of the eight forms of *Parameshwara* is called *Yajamāna Moorti*. This form itself, in some schools, is called as soul. *Linga Purāŋa* says;

Panchabhootāni Chandrārkāvātmeti Munipungavā: I
Moortirashṭou Shiva Syāhoor Devadevasya Dheemata: II
Atma Tasyāshtamee Moortir Yajamānāhvayā Parā II

This name says both the names master (*yajamāna*) and the self-soul (*Sva ātmā*) and says that *Śree Devee* is in both the forms. This name reiterates that *Śree Devee* and *Parameshwara* are one and the same.

(iii) Earlier said name 662nd *Ashṭamoortti*: may be referred.

(iv) During any worship, the worshipper has to imagine a lot of forms on his own – self, his teacher, *mantra*, the presiding deity and *yantra*. It can be taken that those who do *Navāvarŋa Pooja* is also *Śree Devee,* since it is also treated as a sacrifice.

(v) It can be noted that *Śree Devee* has been mentioned as *Yajnyaroopā, Yajnayapriyā* and *Yajnakartree* (769, 881 and 882).

(vi) The names in *Vişhŋu Sahasranāma* are also worth comparing; 445 – *Yagna*: - in the form of all sacrifices and 973 – *Yajvā* – in the form of one who does the sacrifice.

884. ***Dharmādhārā*** **- धर्माधारा**

(i) One who is as a support for *Dharma* (righteousness).
(ii) Righteousness can be defined as the mode of life laid down in each country, by the tradition of the wise and not contrary to the *Vedas*.
(iii) The *Taitreeya Upanishad* (I-11-3,4) says;

Atha Yadi Te karmavichikitsā Vā Vrutta Vichikitsā Vāsyāt I
Ye Tatra Brāhmanā: *Sammarshina*: I *Yuktā Āyuktā*: I
Alookshā Dharmakāmā: *Syu*: I *Yathā Te Tatra Varteran* I
Tathā Tatra Vartethā: I *Athā Bhyākhyāteshu Ye Tatra* I
Brāhmaṇā: *Sammarshinai Yuktā Āyuktā*: I
Alookshā Dharmakāmā: *Syu*: I *Yathā Te Tatra Varteran* I
Tatā Tatra Vartethā: II

(iv) The *Samvarta Smruti* also says, "In each country that rule of conduct, which is handed over by tradition and is not contrary to the *Vedas* is distinguished as righteousness":

Yasmin Deshe Ya Āchāra: *Pāramparyakramāgata*: I
Āmnāyaira Viruddhashcha Sa Dharma: *Parikeertita*: II

(v) Those righteousness, *A* - in all directions or in all countries, *Dhārā* - flowing stream. Hence **She** can be called as in the form of omnipresent righteousness.
(vi) Righteousness is her support. Because the *Mahānārāyaṇa Upanishad* (XXII- 1) says - "Everything is established in *dharma*" or by whom *dharma* is supported, i.e., *dharma* becomes the support of all things by **Her;** *"Dharme Sarvam Pratishtitam"*.
(vii) **She** makes the righteousness to be the support for everything.

885. ***Dhanādhyakshā*** **- धनाध्यक्षा**

(i) One who is the head of wealth.
(ii) *Kuberā* is said to be the presiding deity of wealth. He is one of the famous worshippers of *Śree Devee*. The scriptures say that there is no distinction between the worshipper and the worshipped deity. In that fashion *Śree Devee* is in the *Kubera*. Hence **She** is the head of wealth.

886. ***Dhanadhānya Vivardhinee*** **- धनधान्य विवर्धिनी**

(i) One who is increasing the wealth and grain.

887. ***Viprapriyā* - विप्रप्रिया**

(i) One who is fond of those who know *Vedas* and *Sāstras*.

(ii) The *Brahma Vaivarta Purāŋa* says - "A Brahmin should be known by his birth. He is called *Dvijā*, (twice born) on account of his purification ceremonies. He becomes a *vipra* by knowledge. One who possesses all these is called *srotriya*";

Janmanā Brahmaŋo Gneya: *Samskārair Dvija Uchyate* I
Vidyāyā Yāti Vipratvam Taribhi: *Shrotriya Uchyate* II

Lord *Śree Krişhŋa* says, "whether he has attained the *Vidyā* or not, all the *Brahmins* are my body only". In that case is there any doubt to have more affection of god, for those who have become a *Vipra*.

(iii) *Śree Ādi Śaņkara* in his commentary of *Vişhŋu Sahasranāma* for the 670th name – *Brahmaŋa Priya*: mentions;

a. He is fond of Brahmins – those who have the knowledge of *Brahmam*.

b. He is liked by Brahmins.

(iv) The author quotes the Lord *Śree Krişhŋa's* sayings as above;

Gnandam Shapantam Parusham Vadantam
Yo Brahmaŋam Na Pranamedyathārham I
Sa Papakrud Brahma Davāgni Dagdho
Vadhyashcha Dandyashcha Na Chāsmateeya:

(v) Again the statement from *Mahābhārata* is quoted;

Yam Devam devakee Devee Vasudevādajeejanat I
Bhoulamasya Brahmaŋo Guptyai Deeptamagnimivārani: II

888. ***Vipraroopā* - विप्ररूपा**

(i) One who is of the form of the *vipras* (the learned).

(ii) This is evidenced by the saying the Lord *Śree Krişhŋa* quoted in the previous name.

(iii) That is the reason *Veda* says that – all *Devas* are with the Brahmins who know *Veda*;

Yāvateervai Devatāstā: *Sarvā Vedavidi Brahmaŋe Vasanti*.

(iv) *Parāsara Smruti* also says that – Brahmins are mobile holy waters; The dirty people get purified by the water in the form of their speech; *Yeshām Vaktodakenaiva Sheeddhyanti Malinā Janā*: II

(v) **She** makes the *viprās* more nourished. I.e. by the repetition of *mantras* (of *Śree Devee*) and *homa* (oblation), etc., Brahmins are nourished. The *Āpastamba Smruti* says "By disgrace their penance is increased, by adulation their penance is destroyed. If the Brahmin is adored and worshipped he becomes exhausted like a cow after milking. Just as the cow is nourished during the day by tender grass, so the Brahmin is nourished by repetition of the *mantras* and by *homa*";

Apamānāttapo Vruddhi: *Sanmānāttapasa*: *Kshaya*: I
Archita: *Poojito Vipro Dugdhā Gouriva Seedati* II
Āpyāyate Yathāhassoo Trunairamruta Sambhavai: I
Evam Japaishcha Homashcha Punarāpyāyate Dvija: II

889. ***Vishvabhramaṇakāriṇee* - विश्वभ्रमणकारिणी**

(i) One who is causing the revolution of the earth.

(ii) *Vishva* - all the *Brāhmic* eggs, *Bramana* - their creation, preservation and destruction. The *Svesvatara Upanishad* (VI-1) says, Some wise call it nature, some confused call it time, that by which the wheel of *Brahmam* is revolving, is the glory of the Lord";

Svabhāvameke Kavayo Vadanti Kālam Tathānye Parimuhyamāna: I
Devasyaisha Mahimā Tu Loke Yenedam Bhrāmyate Brahmachakram II

Śreemad Bhagavad Geeta (XVIII-61) also says, All beings which are fixed on the wheel of the universe which he causes to revolve by his illusion;

Bhrāmayam Sarva Bhootāni Yantrāroodhāni Māyāyā II

(iii) *Vishvam* means *Vişhṇu*, for the word *Vishva* is explained thus when it occurs in the *Vişhṇu Sahasranāma* (1st name) "causing confusion to him". This story occurs in the *Kālika Purāṇa* - "*Vişhṇu* once travelling through the sky, mounted on his vehicle *Garuḍa* (the bird Eagle), passed by the *Devee* named *Kāmakyā*, residing in the *Nilāchala* mountain in the *Kāmaroopa* country, without saluting her; then by the force of her anger he fell into the ocean and there he remained confused; after a long time *Lakshmee* (his consort) began to look for him and hearing of this event from *Nārada*, she appeased *Śree Devee*, by penance and freed *Vişhṇu* from his confusion. Afterwards he worshipped *Śree Devee* and reached *Vaikuṇta*.

890. ***Vishvagrāsā* - विश्वग्रासा**

(i) One who is the consumer of the universe.

(ii) She swallows all the fixed and moving objects - animate or inanimate.

(iii) The *Kaṭopanishad* (II-25) says, "The Brahmins and Kshatriyas are both His food, death is His condiment, who is able to know where he is";

Yasya Brahma Cha Kshatram Cho Bhe Bhavata Odana: I
Mrutyur Yasyopasechanam Ka Itthā Veda Yatra Sa: II

(iv) The *Brahma Sūtra* (I-2-9) also reflects this - the ether (is the highest Self) since what is moveable and what is immovable is mentioned as his food; *Attācharācharagrahanāt* II.

(v) 752nd name *Mahāgrāsā* may be referred.

891. ***Vidrumābhā* - विद्रुमाभा**

(i) One who has the luster of coral.
(ii) She is red in colour like coral.
(iii) *Vid* - knowledge, *druma* – tree. I.e. **She** is like a tree of knowledge.
(iv) A tree originates from another tree. A teacher provides knowledge through his teachings to various disciples. Hence the knowledge is compared to a tree.

892. ***Vaishŋavee* - वैष्णवी**

(i) One who is the power of *Vişhŋu*.

893. ***Vişhŋuroopiŋee* - विष्णुरूपिणी**

(i) One who is in the form of *Vişhŋu*.
(ii) **She** depends on *Vişhŋu*. The *Devee Purāŋa* says, "She is sung as *Vaishŋavee* because **She** bears the conch, disc and club, the mother of *Vişhŋu* and the destroyer of foes";

Shankha Chakra Kadā Dhatte Vişhŋumātā Tathārihā I
Vişhŋuroopāthā Devee Vaishŋavee Tena Geeyate II

(iii) Four meanings are provided here. By the word *Arihā*, it is said like *Vişhŋu*, **She** destroys the demons. The other two are self-clear. For the last one *Vişhŋuroopā* let us consider the following;
   a. In the *Brahmānḍa Purāŋa*, in the *Lalitopākhyāna*, *Śree Devee* says – my male form bewildering the milk-maids;

Mamaiva pourusham Roopam Gopikā Janamohanam II

In the same place *Vişhŋu* says to *Veerabhadra*, "The ancient *Shakti* of the Lord is divided into four forms, that *Shakti* becomes *Bhavāni* in its ordinary form, in battle she takes the form of *Durga*; in anger that of *Kālee*; and she is also my female form";

Ādyāshaktir Maheshasya Chaturdhā Bhinna Vigrahā I
Bhoge Bhavāneeroopā Sā Durgāroopā Cha Samgare II

Kope Cha Kālikāroopā Pumroopācha Madātmikā II

In the same meaning;

Kadāchil Laliteshānee Pumroopā Krişhna Vigrahā
Ekaivāshakti: *Parameshvarasya Bhinnā Chaturdhā*
Viniyoga Kāle Bhoge Bhavanee Purushetu
Vişhŋu: *Kope Kālee Samare Cha Durgā*

949th name *Pajnchabhooteshee* may also be referred.

b. In the *Koorma Purāŋa* when *Himavān* praises *Śree Devee* says, "I salute thy form called *Nārāyaŋa*, Oh *Lalitā*, which has a thousand heads, which is of infinite energy, having a thousand arms, the ancient person, reclining on the waters";

Sahasra Moordhānamanandashaktim Sahasrabāhoom Purusham Purāŋam I
Shayānamabdhou Lalite Tavaiva Nārāyaŋākhyam Pranatosmiroopam II

c. In the *Koorma Purāŋa* itself, when *Shiva* showed his universal form to *Mankanaka*, the latter said - "What is the terrible form of thy, facing every side; who is she shining by your side?" Thus questioned, *Shiva,* after explaining the glory of his own nature, says, "She is my supreme *Māyā* (illusion) and *Prakruti* (nature) of triple qualities. She is said by sages to be the ancient womb of the universe. He bewilders the universe by the illusion, he is the knower of the universe, *Nārāyaŋa*, supreme, unmanifested, in the form of illusion - thus says the *Vedas*";

Mama Sāparamā Māyā Prakrutis Triguŋātmikā I
Prochyate Munibhi: *Shaktir Jagadyoni*: *Sanātanee* II
Sa Eva Māyāyā Vishvam Vyāmohayati Vishvavit I
Nārāyaŋa: *Parovyakto Māyāroopa Iti Sruti*: II

d. In the *Sanatkumāra Samhitā*, describing to king *Prabhākara*, the devotion to *Vişhŋu* and describing to his wife *Padminee*, the devotion to *Pārvati*, it is said - *Janārdana* is thus in the form of *Devee* as well as in his own form, for the husband and wife being one production, the only one is worshipped as two;

Evam Devyātmanā Svena Roopena Cha Janārdana: I
Dampatyoreka Gāyatvādeka Eva Dvidhārchita: II

e. The *Bruhat Parāsara Smruti* also says, "He who with delighted mind worships *Durga*, *Kātyāyanee* and *Vāgdevatā* obtains the world of *Vişhŋu*";

Durgām Kātyāyaneem Chaiva Yajan Vāgdevatāmapi I
Chetasā Suprasannene Vişhŋulokamavāpnuyāt II

f. In the *Padma Purāŋa* also "One who bathes the image of *Chaŋḍikā* with the juice of the sugarcane and places her on a

golden vehicle, enjoys the presence of *Vişhŋu* after death";
Chaŋḍikām Snapayedyastu Ikshavena Rasena Cha I
Soupariŋena Cha Yānena Vişhŋunā Saha Modate II

g. The *Āditya* and *Shiva Purāŋas* say - "she who dwells by his side is the young *Pārvati* and *Hari* also is a part of him";
Yā Tasya Pārshvagā Bālā Sā Pārvatyamshajo Hari: II

h. The *Vāmana Purāŋa* also says, "One who on the full moon day of the month *Māgha* worships *Śree Devee* according to rule, he obtains the benefits of the *Ashvamedha* sacrifices and after death he shines in the world of *Vişhŋu*";
Pourŋamāsyām Tu Yo Māghe Poojayedvidhivachchivām I
Sooshvamedhamavāpnoti Vişhŋuloke Maheeyate II

i. In Tamil, *Thirumazhisai Alwar* (65th verse) says; *"Mātāya Mālavanai... Mādhavanai"*.

894. ***Ayoni*: - अयोनिः**

(i) One who has not originated from anything.
(ii) **She** is the original cause of everything, original place, supreme being, etc.
(iii) *Yoni* means abode, because *Sruti* says, I prepared a place of abode for thee, Oh *Indra*; *"Yonishta Indras Nishate Akāri"*. *Ayoni* means having no abode, i.e. omnipresent.
(iv) *Asya* – this *Vişhŋu's*, *Yoni* – mother. That is **She** is mother of *Vişhŋu*.

895. ***Yoninilayā* - योनिनिलया**

(i) One who houses the origination and merging place of the universe.
(ii) The universe originates from *Śree Devee*. Hence **She** is the *yoni* (mother) of it. During dissolution it merges with **Her**– i.e. *Nilaya*. That is **She** is both *Yoni* and *Nilayā* and hence *Yoninilaya*.
(iii) *Yoni* indicates nature also. As an evidence for this, *Muŋḍakopanishad* (III-1-3) may be referred; *"Kartāram Ěshwam Purusham Brahmayonim"*. Again *Brahma Sūtra* (I-4-27) says; *"Yonishcha Hi Geeyate"*.
(iv) *Shvetashvatara Upanishad* (IV-11) says *Yoni* as illusion; *"Yo Yonim Yonimadhitishtatyeka:"*.
(v) It can also be construed as – the merging place for *Brahma* and others, who are the cause of this universe, is *Śree Devee* only.
(vi) *Śree Devee*, in the form of *Bindu*, having the centre of *Śree Chakra* as

Her abode, is indicated here. *Śree Bhāskararāya* quotes some *Atharvaṇa Veda* statements as evidence here;

Ashṭāchakra Navadvārā Devānām Poorayodhyā I
Tasyām Hiranmaya: *Kosha*: *Svargopi Jyotishā Vruta*: II
Tasmin Hiranmaye Koshe Tryakshare Tripratishtite I
Tasmin Yadyakshamātmanvattadvai Brahmavido Vitu: II

(vii) In *Aruṇa Prashnai* also the same meaning is conveyed; *Imā Nukam Bhuvanā Seeshwatema*.

(viii) *Soundaryalaharee* (verse 11); "*Chaturbhi*: *Śreekanṭai*:" - the commentary of *Lakshmeedhara* can be read.

896. ***Kooṭasthā*** **- कूटस्था**

(i) One who is the location of ignorance.

(ii) *Kooṭa* means – cheating, hidden, lie, etc. The true bliss form of the soul, is hidden by ignorance and made to whirl in the cycle of births and deaths. **She** only is the head of this ignorance and deludes the souls. *Saptashatee* (5th chapter) says;

Yā Devee Sarvabhooteshu Brantiroopena Samsthitā I
Namstasyai Namstasyai Namstasyai Namonama: II

Śreemad Bhagavad Geeta (XII-3) also says; "*Kooṭasthamachalam Dhruvam*".

(iii) It means that **She** is the abode of the above said ignorance.

(iv) In addition, *Kooṭa* also means – peak of a hill, a smith's large hammer, etc.

a. She is idle like a peak of a hill, without any work and immobile.

b. The lathe of an iron smith is called as *kooṭa*. To change the shape of anything, it will be beaten with a huge hammer after heating it with high temperature. But the shape of the lathe does not change. In the same fashion **She** is without any change.

(v) **She** is in the halls (*kooṭas*) like *Vāgbhava*, etc.

(vi) *Kooṭa* also indicates the entrance of a city. Taking it to indicate the triangle of a *Śree Chakra*, it can be considered that **She** resides there.

(vii) *Kooṭa* means society, meeting, etc. The entire society of this universe is with *Śree Devee* and hence this name.

897. ***Kularoopiṇee*** **- कुलरूपिणी**

(i) One who is in the form of *Kula*.

(ii) *Kula* means *Moolādhāra*, the path of the sect called *Koulas*, external worship, race or conduct. She who assumes all these forms. These names may also be referred; 90 to 96, 439 to 441 - *Kulāmrutaikarasikā, Kulasanketapālinee, Kulānganā, Kulāntasthā, Koulinee, Kulayoginee, Akulā, Kuleshvaree, Kulakuŋḍālaya* and *Koulamārga Tatparasevita.*

898. ***Veeragoshṭheepriyā* - वीरगोष्ठीप्रिया**

(i) One who is fond of the society of worshippers (*veerās*). In 836th name *Veeramātā* the meaning of *Veera* was given in various ways. **She** is fond of the assembly (or conversations) of such *Veeras*.

899. ***Veerā* - वीरा**

(i) One who is valorous.
(ii) As mentioned earlier, **She** herself is a warrior in battles, has valour and has killed lots of demons.
(iii) A *veerā* is a lady living with her husband and sons.
(iv) *Śree Ādi Śaṇkara* in his commentary of *Vişhŋu Sahasranāma* for the 658th name – *Veera*: mentions; to go, to spread, to create, to enlighten, to throw, to eat, etc. The meaning of the verb *Vee* is a person who does all these actions.

Śree Ādi Śaṇkara says that the 643rd name is to be read as *Soora* and the 401st name as *Vikramashāli*.

900. ***Naishkarmyā* – नैष्कर्म्या**

(i) One who does not have any relationship with actions.
(ii) The real meaning of this name is, though it seems that **She** does the actions of creation, protection and destruction, in reality **She** is unrelated to all these actions. The results of doing or not doing any actions do not affect **Her**. **She** is in the pure knowledge form unrelated to any of the actions. There is no action in knowledge. The knowledgeable person, even if he does some actions it will not affect him.
(iii) The *Kaivalya Upanishad* (I-22 or according to some books II-3) says, I am neither sinful nor righteous; "*Na Puŋya Pāpe Mama*".
(iv) In *Śreemad Bhagavd Geeta* (V-10) also it is said as, He is free from the taint of action; "*Lipyate Na Sa Papena*".
(v) The *Patanjali Yoga Sūtra* (I-24), *Eshvara* is a person untainted by pain,

action, the result of action and mental impression;
Klesha Karma Vipākāshayaira Parāmrushta: *Purusha Vishesha*: *Eshwara*:

Thus ends the tenth *Kalā* called *Bhodinee*.

*****

Section 11: *Dhāriṇee Kalā*

901. ***Nādaroopiṇee* – नादरूपिणी**

(i) One who is the primal mystic sound.
(ii) While pronouncing the words *Om, Hreem,* etc., the last syllable *m* sounds in an elongated way. After plucking the strings of Veena, or after ringing the bells in temples, if we allow the sound to subside on its own, it subdues mildly in a reverse telescopic way. The pronunciation of the sound *m* also should subdue in the same way. This sound is the head portion of the *pranava*. This is called *nātha*.
(iii) The sound/ vibration created without hitting of heart with the *Anāhata chakra* is called *Anāhata*. This can be identified only by the inward looking *Yogis*. Those who identify this get high glee, with Goosebumps and tears of delight. They are the lucky ones, says *Ambāstava* (19th verse);

Ānanda Lakshŋamanāhata Nāmini Deshe
Nādātmana Parinatam Tava Roopameeshe
Pratyanmukhena Manasā Paricheeyamānam
Shasanti Netrasalilai: Pulakaishcha Dhanyā: II

(iv) The *'m'* sound is enjoyed with little by little reduction in the nine places from *Agnā Chakra* till *Brahmarantram*. The third in those nine places is called *Nātha*. From there *Śree Devee* moves upwards. This has been mentioned in *Svacchanta Tantra*.

Rodhinyākhyam Yaduktam Te Nāthas Tasyordhva Samsthita:
Padma Kinjalka Sankāsha: Sooryakoṭi Samaprabha:

Thus describing, it advises to meditate upon *Śree Devee* in that place;

Tasyosangatāmoordhvagāmineem Paramām Shivām Dhyāyet II

(v) 299th name *Nātharoopa* and 836 – *Veeramātā* may be referred.

902. ***Vijnānakalanā* – विज्ञनकलना**

(i) One who is the realisation of supreme absolute.
(ii) That is, **She** arranges the perception of *Brahmam*. 643rd name *Gnādā* and 727th name *Shivagnānapradāyinee* may be referred.
(iii) According to the *Koorma Purāŋa, Vijnāna* means retaining in the mind the fourteen *vidyās* with their meanings; *"Chaturdashānām Vidyānām Dhāranam Hi Yathārthata:* I *Vignānamiti Tadvidyāt* II"
(iv) **She** gives this.

903. ***Kalyā* - कल्या**

(i) One who is skillful in arts.
(ii) The *Vishva* dictionary says, "*Kalyā* means creation, dawn, one without disease, a skillful man, auspicious speech, liquor". Accordingly it can be considered that **She** has the concerned qualities and takes the relevant forms. That dictionary says;

Kalyam Sarge Prabhāte Cha Kalyo Neerogadakshayo: I
Kalyā Kalyānvachee Syāt Kādambaryāmapi Smrutā II

904. ***Vidagdhā* - विदग्धा**

(i) One who is adept and skillful.
(ii) The skill is not only ability, but also understanding or anticipating others' mind and behaving according to it.

905. ***Baindavāsanā* - बैन्दवासना**

(i) One who is seated on *Bindu*.
(ii) The *bindu*, called as *Sarvānandamaya Chakra*, in the centre of the triangle in the middle of the *Śree Chakra*. This is called *Baindava* place. **She** resides there.
(iii) The *Baindava* resembles the round spot above the eye-brows. Earlier in these names the places from *Āgnā chakra* till *Brahmarandandram* was explained – 299 – *Nātharoopā*, 836 – *Veeramātā*and 901 - *Nātharoopiŋee*. The *Svacchaŋḍa Tantra* says, above the *Hākini* circle there is a disc called *Bindu*; *"Hākinee Maŋḍalādoordhvam Bindu Roopam Tu Vartulam"*.

There, after describing the lotus and *Shiva,* there is the energy *Manonmaŋi*, which is above the *Shanti*, on the left side, etc".;

Vāmabāge Samāseenā Shāntryateetā Manonmanee II

(iv) 853rd name *Shāntyateetakalātmikā* may also be referred.
(v) In addition *Bindu* indicates the below seats and She dwells in all these.
    a. *Sudhā Sindu*
    b. The moon's disc in the *karnikā* of *Sahasrāra Kamala*.
    c. The lap of *Kāmeshwara*.
(vi) She has the collection of bindus, as her seat or form. She is the support for all those indicate by these words. The *Jnānārnava* says, "Oh fair one, I will explain to you the collection of *bindus* which are

in the form of *beeja*, know, Oh! *Pārvatee*, ha with *bindu* as *Brahma*, *sa* with *bindu* and *sarga* as *Hari* and myself, Oh Queen of *Devas*, the relation between Hari and Hara is that of inse*para*ble association". After describing *Vāmā* etc., *Icchā*, etc., awakened state, etc., all those are in the form of *bindus*, thus it is concluded by explaining, "thus since *Śree Devee* is conjoined to the three *bindus*, **Her** name is *Tripurā*".

The verses start with;

Bindu Vyooham Pravakshyāmi Beejaroopam Varānane I
Hakāram Binduroopena Brahmanam Viddhi Pārvati II
Sakāram Bindu Sargābhyām Harishchāham Sureshvari I
Avinābhāva Sambandhou Loke Hariharou II

And ending with;

Evam Bindu Trāyai Yokāt Tripurā Nāmaroopiṇee II

(vii) It can also be considered as the *Kāmakala* form of *Śree Devee*. 88th name *Moolamantratmikā*, 89th name – *Moolakooṭatrayakalebarā* and 322nd name *Kāmakalāroopā* may be referred. *Kāmakala vilasam*, *Varivasyārahasyam* and 19th verse of *Soundaryalaharee* may also be referred.

(viii) This name can be split by prefixing *A* to it, it becomes *Abaindavāsanā* (this may not fit according to *paribāsha* verses) - *Ap* - water, *aindava* - the multitude of moons, i.e., of the souls, *Āsana* - **She** remains. The meaning is **She** remains alone by non-difference, in the multitude of the souls which are **Her** different reflections like the various reflections of one moon in different water bodies; *Ekadhā Bahudhā Chaiva Drushyate Jala Chandravat* II The *Bruhat Bindoo Upanishad* (12) says, "*Brahmam* is seen as one and as many like the moon in the water".

906. *Tatvādhikā* - तत्वाधिका

(i) One who is beyond the *Tatvas*.

907. *Tatvamayee* - तत्वमयी

(i) One who is in the form of *Tatvas* (the literal meaning of *tatva*, in Samskrit, is philosophy).

(ii) Those that last till great dissolution and be enablers of the souls to enjoy are called *Tatvas*. The objects like body, pot, etc., do not qualify to be called as *tatva*. *Soota Samhita* says;

Ā Pralayam Yat Thistati Sarveshām Bhogadāyi Bhootānām I
Tat Tavamiti Proktam Na Shareera Ghatādi Tatvamata:.

According to various principles the number of *tatvas* vary – 25, 36, 51 and 94.

(iii) According to the *Śreevidyā* practice (even in *Saiva* practice) *tatvas* taken as 36 in number. This can be split into three groups. The list below details it. What is in reality indicates *Atma* (self) *tatva*. Hence this is also called as *Sat Tatva*. It includes;

Primary elements	-	5
Subtle elements	-	5
Actions organs	-	5
Sense organs	-	5
Nature, ego, intellect and mind	-	4
Total	-	24

Vidyā tatva indicates knowledge. Hence it is called as *Chit Tatva* also.

Illusion, art, illiteracy, desires, time, rules and *purush* - 7

Shiva tatva indicates salvation. Hence it is called as *Ānanda Tatva* also.

Shiva, Shakti, Sadāshiva, Eshwara and *shuddha Vidyā* - 5

Total - 36

(iv) Since **She** is in the form of the self, *Vidyā* and *Shiva tatvas* mentioned above, **She** can be called as *Tatvamayee*. Since **She** is in the combined form of all these *tatvas*, **She** can also be called as *Tatvādhika*. **She** continues to be even when these *tatvas* get destroyed during great dissolution. Hence **She** is greater and beyond the *tatvas*. 424th name *Tatvāsanā* may also be referred.

(v) The combination of the *Sat* (eternal), *Chit* (energy) and *Ānanda* (bliss) *tatvas* is the supreme bliss. It indicates *Satchitānanda*. Hence **She** is called as *Satchitānanda Roopinee* (in the form of *Satchitānanda*).

(vi) In these types of *tatvas*, the *chit* and *ānanda* types are hidden. The below list explains them;

Tatva	**The hidden part**	**The explicit part**	**Other names on account of this reason**
Ātma (self)	*Chit* and *Ānanda*	*Sat*	*Ashuddha* (impure)
Vidyā	A small portion of *Ānanda*	*Sat* and *Chit*	*Shuddhāshuddha* (pure and impure as well) or *Mishra*
Shiva	Nil	*Sat, Chit* and *Ānanda*	*Shuddha* (pure)

(vii) To worship *Śree Devee* in the form of *Paramātmā* there are six different ways. They are *Varŋa* (race), *Pada, Mantra, Kalā, Tatva* and *Bhuvana* (world). *Śree Devee* is beyond all these. This will be explained further later in 991st name *Shaḍadhvāteeta Roopiŋee*. It can said as – considering these six routes as the body of *Paramātmā* and treating the *tatva* as an organ of that body, the name *Tatvamayee* has originated.

(viii) The author gives a different meaning for this name. *Tatva* will mean *Shiva Tatva*. *Tatvamayee* means something above *Shiva tatva* – i.e. *Chinmayee*. The *Samādhi* (concentrated meditation – not aware of the external happenings) state obtained by the worshipper by crossing the *Shiva Tatva* is called *Samprāgna Samādhi*. Without crossing the *Shiva Tatva*, but being along with it is called *Asam Pragnāta Samādhi*. The characters of these are explained in *Gnānārnava Tantra*. These states of *Samādhi* are differentiations of light. *Śree Bhāskararāya* ends the explanation here with the remark that further details are to be obtained from a competent teacher. The 6th chapter of *Geeta Bhāshyam* by *Śree Madusoodana Saraswatee* may be referred.

The 16th chapter of *Gnānārnava* has the verses explaining these.

Eeshwara Uvācha;

Shruŋu Devee Pravakshyāmi Yajanam Chā''ntaram Mahat I
Shru Moolādibrahmarandhrāntam Bisatantutaneeyaseem II 2
Udyatsooryaprabhājāla Vidyutkotiprabhāmayee I
Chandrakotiprobhādrāvām Trailokyaikaprobhāmayeem II
3
Asheshajagadutpattisthitisamhārakāriŋeem I
Dhyāyenmano Yathā Deveem Nishchalam Jāyate Tathā II 4
Sahajānandasandohamandiram Bhavati Kshaŋāt I
Mano Nishchalatām Prāptam Shiva shaktiprabhāvata: II
5
Samādhirjāyate Tatra Samgyādvayavijrumbhita: I
Svayampragnāmaiko Hyasampragnānāmdrut II 6
Svayampragnātasangnastu Shaktyādhikyena Jāyate I
Asampragnātanāmaiko Shivādhikyena Vai Bhavet II 7
Svayampragnātabhedastu Teevrasteevrataro Bhavet I
Asampragnātabhedastu Mando Mandatarastathā II 8
Sangnā Pragnā Na Yatraivam Svayampragno'bhidheeyate I
Asampragno Hi Bhooyastu Sthitapragna: *Pratishṭhita*: II 9
Pragnāpragnānamevedamasamsmayamiti Dvayam I
Sangnādvayammidam Devee Shiva tatvena Vaibhavet II
10

Hāsya Rodan Romānchakampa Svedādvilakshaŋa: I
Teevrasteevrataro Devee Samādhiroopalakshita: II 11
Nimeshavarjite Netre Vapustallakshŋam Sthiram I
Mando Mandataro Devee Samādhi: *Parikeertita*: II 12
Shāmbhavena Cha Vedyena Sukhee Bhooyānnirantaram I

908. ***Tatvamarthasvaroopiŋee* – तत्वमर्थस्वरूपिणी**

(i) One who **Herself** is the meaning of the great statement *Tatvamasi*.
(ii) *Tat* means *Shiva* (*Paramātma* – the supreme being) and *tvam* means the soul. This great statement advises the unison of these two. **She** is the meaning of it.

909. ***Sāmagānapriyā* - सामगानप्रिया**

(i) One who is fond of *Sāmaveda* songs.
(ii) Hearing *Sāmaveda* will be so sweet to the ears like music. It is also said that the music originates only from *Sāmaveda*. *Parameshwara* is also very much interested in *Sāmaveda* songs. It is told (*Śreemad Rāmāyana, Uttara Kāṇḍa* – 16-33) that *Rāvanā* sang *Sāmaveda* and pleased *Parameshwara*. Since *Śree Devee* is an integral part of *Parameshwara*, **She** is also very much fond of *Sāmaveda* songs;
Evamuktastadāmātyaistushtāva Vrushbhadhvajam I
Sāmabhirvividhai: *Stotrai*: *Pranamya Sa Dashānana*: II
(iii) It can also be said that those who follow *Sāmaveda* are so dear to **Her**, as **Her** own life. This meaning is taken by splitting the name as *Sāmagā* + *Ana* + *Priyā* (*Ana* means life). Like **Her** life force, **She** is interested in those who sing *Sāmaveda*.

910. ***Somyā* (*Soumyā*) - सोम्या (सौम्या)**

(i) One who is fit to be adored in the *Soma* sacrifice.
(ii) The word *Soma* means moon or camphor. Hence *Soumyā* means one that pleases the mind like Moon.
(iii) *Soma* means *Shiva* accompanied with *Uma* – another meaning is - one who has *Paramashiva* as a part of her own body. This was earlier mentioned in 392nd name *Shreekanthārdhashareeriŋee*.
(iv) *Śree Bhāskararāya* quotes various rules of grammar to justify suffixing '*ya*' with the three meanings mentioned above.
(v) If the variation *Soumyā* is considered it means, **She** is beautiful,

peaceful and affectionate.

911. *Sadāshivakuṭumbinee* - सदाशिवकुटुम्बिनी

(i) One who is the consort of *Sadāshiva.*
(ii) The same name and meaning is seen in *Trishatee* also - 231st name *Sadāshivakuṭumbinee*.
(iii) It also means the *Devees* - *Shyāmalā, Shuddha Vidyā* and *Ashvāroodha*.

912. *Savyāpasavyamārgasthā* - सव्यापसव्यमार्गस्था

(i) One who is standing in the right (*savyā*) and left (*apasavyā*) paths.
(ii) The author gives various types of meanings to this name.
(iii) *Savya* - creation, *Apasavya* - destruction, *Mārga* – in the middle viz., protection. **She** is engaged in all these three tasks. It can be reminded that the same meaning was conveyed in names 264 - *Srushṭikartree*, 266 - *Goptree*, 268 – *Samhāriṇee* and 317 - *Rakshākaree*.
(iv) *Savya* – worship according to *Vedas* and *Apasavya* - worship according to *Tantras*. **She** is there in both the ways.
(v) There are three paths of the solar disc distinguished as north, south and middle. It has been said that - the 27 constellations (*Nakshatras*) make the lines (*veethis*) for the movement of Sun and three of these lines make one path and these three paths are defined. Their names are;

Path	Star constellations
	1. North
Nāga (snake)	*Ashvini* (Castor and Pullox), *Bharaṇi* (Arietis or a Muscae) and *Kruttikā* (Tauri or Alcyone)
Gaja (elephant)	*Rohiṇee* (Aldebaran), *Mrigaseersha* (Orionis) and *Ārudra* (Betelgeuse)
Irāvata (the white elephant with *Indra*)	*Punarvasu* (Geminorium), *Pushyami* (*Cancri*) and *Aslesha*
	2. Middle
Ārshata	*Magha* (Hydarae), *Poorvaphalguni* (*Leonis*) and *Uttaraphalguni* (Lionis)
Go (cow)	*Hasta* (Corvi), *Chitrā* (Virginis or Spica) and *Swati* (Bootis or Arcturus)
Jāradgavee	*Vishakha* (Librae), *Anurādha* (Scorpionis) and *Jyestha* (Antares)
	3. South

Path	Star constellations
Aja (goat)	*Moola* (Scorpionis), *Poorvashadha* (Sagittari) and *Uttarashadha* (Sagigtarii).
Mruga (deer)	*Shravaŋa* (Aquarii), *Dhanishta* (Capricorni or Delphini) and *Satabhistha* (Aquarii)
Vashvānara	*Poorvabhadra* (Pegasi), *Uttarabhadra* (Andromedae) and *Revati* (Piscium)

She controls the movement of Sun by staying in these three routes/ paths. That is, the summary meaning is that **She** administers the worldly affairs by staying in these three paths.

This meaning has been derived by taking evidences from *Vāyu Purāŋa* (the verses are not quoted).

Note: In general *Savya* means right and *Apasavya* means left. But at times the meanings are interchanged. This is also mentioned by *Śree Bhāskara Rāya*. Again, in the original verses the word *Mārgee* can be taken as related to *Mrigaseer*. In that case directions of these three paths will be changed.

(vi) *Sāstras* say that after one's death, depending on the virtues and sins done, the soul reaches the other worlds.

Savya indicates the "path of light" called *Archirāti* or *Devayāŋa*. This is the path used by those who worship with renunciation, to go to *Deva's* world, after death. The path used to cross the worlds related to the five primary elements, leaving the body, after the body is over, with the self-tools and trials as advised in the *gnāna* (knowledge) *kāndā* of *Vedas*. This is called as salvation or extinction.

Apasavya is called as *Pitruyānam* – the "path of smoke". Those who worship with iniquity go to the world of *pitrus* after leaving this body, use this path. After fulfilling the actions defined by the *Karma* (action) *Kāṇḍa* of *Vedas,* having been attained the results of taking this body, reach the upper world through this path. After enjoying the fruits of the actions, they take re-birth in this world.

Mārgasthā indicates the world of *Vişhŋu*, the residing place *Druva* star.

Druva is the pole star on which depend the established paths of the sun and the planets; hence *Mārgastha* means *Dhruva.*

One meaning could be, thus **She** is in the form of *Savya, Apasavya* and *Mārgastha*. (The evidenced verses are not written here).

(vii) Another meaning is that **She** is in the form of the three words viz., *Pitru, Deva* and *Vişhŋu*. These have been described in *Vişhŋu Purāŋa* (II part) and *Matsya Purāŋa*. Those who follow the *Karma* (action) *Kāṇḍa* of *Vedas* which advises the iniquity path go to the world of *pitrus*. The great among them again take birth in their races, in every era (*yuga*) or whenever need arises, show the respect and the paths of *Veda* to all and return to the world of *Pitrus*.

In the world of *Devas*, those who have controlled their senses, who do not have stinginess, who do not have disgust, etc., who have won the erotic desires and who do not go in the path of iniquity, will be there till great dissolution with further birth or death.

In the world of *Vişhŋu*, those who do not have any blemish, who have control over their senses, who do not have any sin or virtue and the sages who do not have any cause for sorrow, will reside. They are integrated with *Vişhŋu* and will be there with their minds always in the thoughts of *Vişhŋu*. (The evidenced verses are not written here).

(viii) a. In worshipping Gods there are two methods viz., *Vāma* (left) and *Daskshina* (right). These are the sub-divisions of the *Samaya* religion. There is one other called *Koula* religion. The names 97 – *Samayāntasthā*, 98 – *Samayācāratatparā* and 441 – *Koulamārgatatparasevitā* may be referred.

b. The left path means one should always meditate upon his own deity in all ceremonies such as Agnihotra, etc., described in the *Vedas* or in the ceremonies such as *Ashṭakā*, etc., enjoined in the *Smrutis* or in the *mantra, siddhis*, etc., described in the *Tantras*, whatever chief deities or secondary deities are invoked he should add his own deity; that is in every ceremony one should add or repeat his particular or chosen deity after repeating the deities which belong to each *mantra*. He who goes by this path will have with him the sin as he does not discharge his (three) debts to *Devas, rishees* (sages) and *pitrus*.

c. This is explained at length in *Kālika Purāŋa* - "Everywhere whether in the *Devee mantras* or in the *Vedic mantras* and in all the *mantras* to gods he should duly meditate on *Bhairavee, Tripura*. One should add the suffix *Bhairavee* to all the names of the deities as a subject. The *Devee* name should not be recited without the names of other deities as qualified.

d. Many persons of higher-level follow the *vāma* path, for they should wait a little time to finish all their *karmās* (actions) whether high or low by the enjoyment in the same body. They have the desire to enjoy a lot in this world itself. They live smart and with all the facilities in the world.

e. But in the right hand path, in the place of the deities of the ceremonies as enjoined in *Sruti* and other works, his chosen deity (i.e. the deity whom he worships) should be necessarily substituted and worshipped. As he observes all the rites described in different scriptures, (i.e. he worships his chosen deity) in the place of other deities of different ceremonies, he has no sin with him of that (left hand path) as he has discharged the debts of *Devas*, etc., by the meditation on one supreme gods. Hence he attains the salvation soon.

f. Out of these two paths, the *Vāma* path does not fulfill the wishes of other gods and *Dakshiŋā* path satiates all the gods. Hence people say that the later path is great.

g. The deities *Mahāmāyā*, *Shāradā* and *Shailaputree* have to be worshipped only through *Dakshiŋā* method. The other deities may be worshipped through any method.

h. The summary of all the above is that *Śree Devee* can be worshipped in either of the methods. **She** is there in both.

(ix) According to *Shiva Sūtra* (44); *Savyāpasavya Soushumneshu* – *Savya* indicate *ida nāḍi* (pulse) and *Apasavya* indicates *Pingala nāḍi*. *Mārga* indicates *Shusumna nāḍi*. **She** dwells in all these. That is, **She** can be reached with practice of Yoga relating to all these three. (In this context the *yoga* practice indicates what is mentioned in *Kāshmeera Shaiva* and not the *Haṭayoga*).

It can be reminded that in 110th name *Kunḍalinee*, it was mentioned that *Haṭayoga* practice is not suitable for ordinary people. *Śree Devee* has to be tried and reached through devotion only – says *Śree Kānchi Kāmakoṭi Paramāchārya*.

913. ***Sarvāpadvinivāriŋee* - सर्वापद्विनिवारिणी**

(i) One who removes every type of danger.

(ii) By not following either of the *Savya* or *Apasavya* worshipping methods, as discussed in the previous name, one may end up with great dangers. *Chāndogya Upanishad* says that those who do not follow either of these 2 methods will become a worm or a bird;

Atha ya Ethou Panthānou Na Viduste Keetā:
Patangā: *Yadidam Daŋḍashukam*.

Śree Devee removes the their dangers by **Her** compassion through other tools like *Nāma Keertanam*, etc.

(iii) In *Koorma Purāŋa*, *Śree Devee* says – I protect all those, who come to my refuge leaving all the desires, who worship with devotion, who have compassion with all beings, who are with pacification, who have control over senses, who have no jealous on others, who are modest, who are intelligent, who do penance, who complete the desired vows, who think on me alone and who have interest in propitiating my knowledge, irrespective they being young boys (*brahmachāri*) or married or *vānaprastās* or *sanyāsins*. Even those who do have any of these characteristics, but if they chant my name, I save them soon from mountain like dangers like a light.

Ye Tu Sangān Parityagya Māmekam Sharanm Gatā: I
Upāsate Sadā Bhaktyā Yogamaishvaramāshritā: II
Sarvabhoota Dayāvanta: *Shāntā Dāntā Vimatsarā*: I
Amānino Buddhi Mantas Tāpasā Samyatavratā: II
Machchittā Madgata Prānā Majgnānakathane Ratā: I
Sanyāsino Gruhasthāshcha Vanasthā Brahmachārina: II
Ye Choktair Lakshaṇair Heenā Api Manāmajāpakā: I
Teshām Nityābhiyuktānāmpatām Parvatānapi I
Nāshayāmitarām Gnānadeepena Na Chirādiha II

(iv) *Hari Vamasa* says that *Śree Devee* protects from the dangers of loss of wealth, death of children, death and other dangers;

Āpatsu Nikhilāsu Tvam Rakshasyeva Na Samshaya: II

(v) In *Varāha Purāṇa* also, we read that those who have surrendered to *Śree Devee* do not meet with any danger or troubles;

Sharanam Tvām Prapadyante Ye Devee Parameshvari I
Na Tashāmāpada: *Kāshchij Jāyante Kvāpi Sankata*: II

(vi) The learned advise;

What to do while in danger? Think of the two feet of *Śree Devee*.

What will do such thinking? It will make *Brahma* and others also as servants;

Āpadi Kim Karaneeyam Smaraneeyam Charaṇayukalambāyā: I
Tatsmaranam Kim Kurute Brahma Deenapi Cha Kareekurute II

(vii) In *Saptashatee* also *Śree Devee* is prayed as; *Sharanāgata Deenārta Paritrāna Parāyane*. There itself in (12-22) *Śree Devee*'s divine speech goes;

Shrutam Harati pāpāni Tathārogyam Prāyachchati I
Rakshām Karoti Bhootepyo Janmanām Keertanam Mama II
Yuddheshu Charitam Yanme Dushṭadaitya Nibarhanam I
Tasmin Shrute Varikrutam Bhayam Pumsām Na Jāyate II

Again

Aranye Prāntare Vāpi Dāvākni Parivārita: I
Dasyubhirvā Vruta: *Shoonye Gruheeto Vāpishatrupi*: II

Simha Vyaghrānuyāto Vā Vane Vā Vanahastibhi: I
Ragnā Kruddhena Chāgnapto Vadhyo Bandhagatopi Vā II
Āghoornito Vā Vātena Sthita: *Pote Mahārnave* I
Patatsu Chāpi Shastreshu Sangrāme Bhrushadārune II
Sarva Bādhāsu Ghorāsu Vedanābhyāditopi Vā I
Smaran Mamatach Charitam Naro Muchyeta Sankatāt II

914. ***Svasthā* – स्वस्था**

(i) One who does not have mind agitation or trembling on account of sorrows.

(ii) **She** is in the form of happiness/ bliss. How can **She** have sorrows?

(iii) **She** is settled in self (*sva* – self, *sthā* – to settle or to stay). Only from the second the sorrow and fear originate. When it is related to self, it is a state of no-sorrow. This is the healthy and no-disease state. *Chāndogya Upanishad* (VII-24-1) says – where no other thing is seen, no other thing is heard and no other thing is identified that is limitless. However, where anything else is seen or heard or identified that is small; that which is limitless is eternal. That which is insignificantly small is destroyable. In which of these it stays, with the self-pride?; *Yatra Nānyati, Nānyat Shrunoti, Nānyat Vijānāti, Sabhoomātha Yatrānyat Pashyatyanyach Chrunotya Nyadvijānāti Tadalpam Yo Vai Bhoomā Tadamruthamatha Yadalpam Tan Martyam Sa Bhagava*: *Kasmin Pratishtita Iti Sve Mahimni.*

(iv) It can also be recollected what is given in *Kaṭopanishad* (3-11);
Sā Kāshṭhā Sā Parā Gati.

(v) *Sva*: - heaven. **She** is the head of it.

(vi) *Soo* – auspicious, *Asthā* – without staying. That is, it means that **She** bestows auspicious.

915. ***Svabhāvamadhurā* – स्वभावमधुरा**

(i) One who is sweet by nature and hence liked by all.

(ii) **She** is sweet by nature. It is not that **She** becomes sweet by mingling with or adding anything else. This is construed by considering the sweetness as meaning for the word *Madhuram*. The *Madhurāshtakam* – *Adharam Madhuram*... - can be reminded.

(III) The word *Madhuram* also means room for affection. Hence it can be taken as that - **She** is loved and liked by all.

(iv) It can also be taken as; *Sva* – self, *Bhāva* – dwelling place, *Madhura* –

the city Madurai. That is, **She** is *Meenākshee Devee,* who has the city Madurai, which is called as *Hālāsya* city, as her dwelling place. This *Meenākshee Devee* was mentioned in 18th name *Vaktralakshmee Pareevāhachalanmeenābhalochana*. Or **She** is in the form of that city itself. It can also be reminded that 323rd name *Kadambakusumapriyā* also mentioned above *Meenākshee Devee.*

(v) *Sva* – self, *Bhā* – in the lustre, *Avamā* – among the top most, *Dhurā* – one who supports the weights. That means, **She** takes along all the responsibilities of the people great in self-knowledge. For instance, the yoke is an important part of a cart. Being a great part, it supports the entire weight of the cart. In the same fashion, *Śree Devee* supports the weight of the self-knowledgeable people.

The author quotes some of the verses from results part as evidence to interpret this meaning. He also quotes a grammar rule convincing that it is correct that this name ends with *A*.

(vi) The name is split in other way also – *Svabhā* – self lustre or self-knowledge, *Vama* – to make available, *Dhoo* – great. That is, **She** is the greatest among those who can provide self-knowledge; *Svabhāvātpragnānam Ye Vamanti Srujanti Sādhayanti Teshu Dhooruttameti* – the author gives some grammatical explanations.

(vii) Desire and responsibility are called as *Bhāvas*. Without those – *Abhāva Soo* – cute or auspicious. Hence **She** is so auspiciously sweet without any desire or responsibility.

(viii) *Sva* – own people (devotees of self), *Bhāva* – stays, *Madhurā* – **She** is sweet. That is **She** is sweet because, **She** dwells in her own devotees.

(ix) *Sva* – own people (devotees of self), *Bhāva* – the state of devotion, *Madhu* – great strength (fruit like knowledge) and *rā* – gives. That is **She** gives the knowledge as a fruit, as a strength to her devotees who have pious on her.

(x) The word *Bhāva* also means opinion or incarnation. Hence, by adding these meanings also, this name can be interpreted.

916. ***Dheerā* - धीरा**

(i) One who is learned and knowledgeable.

(ii) Or one who has courage.

(iii) Or, one who bestows the non-dual intellect. *Avadhootha Geeta* (1st verse) says – "the non-dual knowledge happens only with the blessings of *Eshwar; Eshwarānugrahādeva Pumsāmadvata Vāsana*.

(iv) **She** is the presiding deity of the tenth day, in Moon's fortnight, called

Irā, which will provide intellect.

917. ***Dheerasamarchitā* - धीरसमर्चिता**

(i) One who is well worshipped by the clever and learned.
(ii) *Sruti* says; *Tam Dheerā*: *Kavaya Unnayanti* – the clever learned and poets praise her. Further we read as; *Tasya Dheerā*: *Parijānanti Yonim*.
(iii) *Śree Bhāskararāya* quotes what was said by *Śree Kalyāna Charaŋās* – "whether I am pushed into the *pātālā* world (under world beneath the earth) or I am made as a head of all the worlds, I will not leave your feet";

Pātaya Vā Pātāle Sthāpaya Vā Nikhilaloka Sāmrājye
Matas Tava Padayugalam Nāgam Munchāmi Naiva Munchāmi II

(iv) The meaning of this name is said as – **She** is worshipped aiming the essence of happiness called *Dhee*. (*Dhee* – nothing different from knowledge, *rasam* – happiness [aiming at], *architā* – being worshipped). That is, those who aim at knowledge worship **Her**.

918. ***Chaitanyārghyasamārāadhyā* – चैतन्यार्घ्यसमाराध्या**

(i) One who is best worshipped with the offerings of the consciousness (*chaitanya*) as *Arghya*.
(ii) Consciousness is the form of mind. Self-consciousness is the form mind of the soul. The mind form of soul. *Shiva Sūtra* (I-1) says that this is the soul; *Ātma Chaitanyamātma*.

Arghya is water, etc., used in any *pooja*. Imagining self as the *Brahmam* is called *Nirādhāra Pooja*. *Pāvanopanishad* advises as; *Gnānam Arghyam* – the knowledge is *arghyam*. That knowledge is *Chaitanyārghyam*, which is – thinking the three, the knower, the knowledge and the object of knowledge, which seem to be different from consciousness, as one and the same.

Tantra Rāja says;

Gnātā Svātmā Bhavet Gnānam Arghyamgneyam Havi Sthitam I
Śree Chakrapoojanam Teshām Ekeekaranmeeritam II

The summary meaning of this name is that **She** is well worshipped with such offerings.

In *Shiva Purāŋa*, *Māŋickavāchaka* also says – the acute intellect, is to identify the sharp and true knowledge.

(iii) *Soota Samhita* (I-5-19) says – worshipping *Maheshwaree* with support, will get beneficence. **She** is worth worshipping in that way;

Svānubhootyā Svayam Sākshāt Svātmabhootām Maheshwareem
Poojayedādarenaiva Pooja Sā Purshārthadā

(iv) According to *Vishva* dictionary, *Arghya* means the holy water used in *pooja*, knowledge, *Vidyā* and root of a tree. The *mantra* which has goddess as presiding deity is called *Vidya*. The meaning of this name is obtained as - **She** is being worshipped with the *Vidyā* called *chaitanya* (consciousness).

Soota Samhita says that if one chants the *mantra* called *chaitanya* for 10000 times, he is removed from all groups of sins and other sins;

Japitvā Dashsāhasram Mantram Chaitanyavāchakam I
Mahāpātakasanghaishcha Muchyate Pātakāntarai: II

The commentary for this verse says that the *mantra* called *Chaitanya* is said to be *Bhuvaneshwaree mantra*. Hence we get the meaning for this name as She is to be worshipped by *Bhuvaneshwaree mantra*.

(v) *Chaitanya* (consciousness) means the essence of the form of the potency of knowledge. This is the one – in the *arghya* used in the *pooja* of *Śree Devee* in two ways viz., ordinary and special. The vessel of special *arghya* is to be filled with *chaitanya* mentioned here – with many of the offerings it has to be made eligible for *pooja*. The meaning of this name is that – **She** is being worshipped with offering of this special *arghya* (water). *Rudrayāmala* says that instead of filling this vessel with alcohol etc., it is great to fill it with this special *arghya*.

(vi) The fifth essence mentioned as *Kuṇḍagolodbhava* by *Tāntrikās* is called as *Chaitanya* (since it originates from the body). **She** is being worshipped with this. This is a matter of *Koula* path.

919. *Chaitanyakusumapriyā* – चैतन्यकुसुमप्रिया

(i) One who loves the flower of consciousness (*chaitanya*).

(ii) The *chaitanya* (consciousness) itself is mentioned as a flower here. If it is offered to *Śree Devee*, **She** bestows great results. *Śree Ādi Śaṇkara*, in his *Soundaryalaharee* 3rd Verse considers *chaitanya* as a flower;

Jadānām Chaitanya Stabakamakaranda Srutijaree I

(iii) Consciousness (*chaitanya*) is an intuition. It spreads and comes out through the intellect and mind. When it comes out, through control of senses, it has to be converted into good feelings and offered to *Śree Devee*. The learned say that there are eight such flowers in *Chaitanya*. They are; non-violence, control of senses, compassion, knowledge, penance, truth and meditation;

Ahimsā, Prathamam Pushpam, Indriyānām Cha Nigraha: I
Kshānti: *Pushpam Dayā, Pushpam Gnānapushpam Param Matam* II
Tapa: *Pushpam Satya Pushpam Bhāva Pushpam Athāshtamam* II

The *chaitanya* containing these eight flowers if very much liked by *Śree Devee*.

(iv) The gist of the above is that, *Śree Devee* expects only the mind of the devotees and not the costly offerings in the *pooja*. In *Śreemad Bhagavad Geeta* (IX-26) also we read the same message. Lord *Śree Krişhŋa* accepts whatever is offered to him with devotion. *Sabari, Kuchela, Kaŋŋappa Nāyanar* and others are evidences for this;

Patram Pushpam Phalam Toyam To Me Bhaktyā Prāyachchati I
Tadaham Bhaktyupahrutamashnāmi Prāyatātmana: II

920. ***Sadoditā* - सदोदिता**

(i) One who is ever raising by self-illumination.
(ii) These names can be reminded. 6th name - *Udyadbhānusahasrābhā* - **She** is as bright as thousands of rising Suns. 275th name – *Bhānumaŋḍalamadhyasthā* – **She** is in the midst of solar orbit. 596th name – *Raviprakhyā* – **She** is as bright as Sun.
(iii) **She** shines in the minds of good people.

921. ***Sadātushṭā* - सदातुष्टा**

(i) One who is ever pleased.
(ii) **She** has the great bliss as her form. This message was already mentioned in these names and has been repeated here; 252 – *Paramānandā*, 365 - *Svātmānandalavee Bhootabrahmadyānanda Santati*:, 676 – *Brahmananda*.
(iii) It can be meant that - as mentioned in the previous name, **She** dwells in the minds of good people with complete bliss and She makes them *Ātmārāmas*.

922. ***Taruŋādityapāṭalā* - तरुणादित्यपाटला**

(i) One who is crimson coloured like the morning rising Sun.
(ii) **She** assumes different colours according to the form under which **She** is contemplated, meditating methods and intending desires.
(iii) Those who seek salvation, have to meditate a peaceful form white in

colour. Those who want to attract ladies, kings and other people have to mediate with white and red mixed colour. Those who seek wealth have to meditate yellow in colour. Those who want to win over the enemies have to meditate black in colour;

Shāntā Dhavalavarṇābhā Mokshadharma Prakalpane I
Streevashye Rajavashye Cha Janavashye Cha Pātalā II
Peeṭa Dhanasya Sampatthou Krushnām Māranakarmaṇi I
Babhrur Vidveshne Proktā Shrungāre Pātalākruti: II
Sarvavarṇā Sarvalābhe Dyeyā Jyotirmayee Parā II

923. ***Dakshiṇādakshiṇārādhyā* - दक्षिणादक्षिणाराध्या**

(i) One who is fit to be worshiped by the educated (who has capability) and the uneducated (who do not have capability) alike.

(ii) *Dakshiṇa*: means able people. (it can be reminded that *Śree Ādi Śaṇkara*'s *Dakshiṇāmoorti Ashṭaka* says so). For adoring *Śree Devee* only the interest and devotion are important and not education.

(iii) She is fit to be worshipped by - *Dakshiṇa* – the things that are used while worshipping or the charge that is paid to the teacher or the learned people.

(iv) *Sruti* says – through knowledge the sages reach the place where there are no desires. The idiots and *Dakshiṇās* do not reach this place.

Vidyāyā Tadārohanti Yatra Kāmā: *Parāgatā*: I
Na Tatra Dakshiṇā Yanti Nāvdvāmsas Tapasvina: II

This implies that those who follow the *karma* (action) path of *Vedas* are *Dakshiṇās* and those who follow the *gnāna* (knowledge) path of *Vedas* are *Adakshiṇās*. **She** is fit to be adored by these two types of worshippers. She is fit to be worshipped, since **She** bestows the results based on the actions of individuals – says 20th name of *Trishatee*; *Karmaphalaprada*.

(v) **She** is adored by right and left hand followers – i.e. **She** is worshiped by both *Dakshiṇāchārās* and *Vāmāchārās*. 912th name *Savyāpasavyamārgasthā* may be referred.

924. ***Darasmeramukhāmbujā* - दरस्मेरमुखाम्बुजा**

(i) One whose lotus face is radiant with a sweet smile.

(ii) 460th name *Nalinee* compared the beauty of *Śree Devee* herself with that of Lotus. It is the practice of poets to compare the face, feet, hands and eyes to Lotus flower. The following famous verse can be reminded;

Karāravidena Padāravidam Mukhāravinde Viniveshayantam I
Vatasya Patrasya Pute Shayānam Bālam Mukunḍam Manasā Smarāmi

The smile of *Śree Devee* has enhanced the beauty of the already beautiful face. **She** has attracted *Kāmeshwara* with this smile. 28th name may be referred; *Mandasmitaprabhāpoora Majjatkāmeshamānasā*.

(iii) **She** is already in the form of happiness 878th name *Svātmārāma*. A drop of the happiness enjoyed by **Her** is seen as smile. In *Trishatee* the 60th name – *Eshatsmitānanā* and 280th name - *Laptaharshā Bhipooritā* also convey the same message. The *Mantasmita Chatakam* of *Mookapanchashatee* completely describes the smile of *Śree Devee* only.

(iv) *Dara* – conch. Like the stem for Lotus flower, **Her** conch like neck forms the stem of lotus like face. That neck shines well like conch. It is the practice of poets to compare the neck to a conch. 157th name of *Trishatee – Kambukantee* says there are three lines in **Her** neck. The commentary for this describes that these three lines can be compared to the three letters of *Praŋava* and *Pashyantee, Madhyamā, Vaikharee* speeches.

The summary of this meaning – the head (the knowledge of *Brahmam*) is supported by the neck (*Praŋava*) is being advised by this name.

69th verse of *Soundaryalaharee – Gale Rekhāstisro* - also describes these three lines.

(v) *Dara* - in time of fear, *smeramukha* - **Her** face is always shinning, even in time of fear. The meaning is even at the time of final dissolution when all beings including the tri-gods are being destroyed, **She** without any fear on **Her** face, continue to smile. **She** does not have fear. Even at that time, **She** witnesses the *tāndava* of *Maheshwara*. It can be reminded that this has already been described in 232nd name *Maheshvaramahākalpa Mahātāndava sākshinee*.

(vi) *Dare* – when it comes to protecting the devotees, **Her** face is always gracious.

925. *Koulinee Kevalā* - कौलिनी केवला

(i) One who has pure knowledge called *Kevala* and follows the religion called *Koula*.

(ii) According to those who follow *Salākshara Sūtra*, this name is considered as *Koulinee* and the next name is taken as *Kevalānarghyakaivalyapadadāyinee*. The *Paribhāshā* verses created by *Śree Nrusimhānandanātha*, the teacher of *Śree Bhāskararāya*, differ from *Salākshara Sūtra* and consider *Koulinee Kevalā* as one name and *Anarghyakaivalyapadadāyinee* as another name. In the same way, he has differed from *Salākshara Sūtra* in two other places. That is, according to *Salākshara Sūtra*, *Koulinee Kulayoginee* is a single name, but in this *Paribhāshā* verses this has been considered as two names *Koulinee* and *Kulayoginee* (94th and 95th).

Again in *Salākshara Sūtra*, *Prakaṭa* and *Ākruti*: are two different names, but considered as a single name as *Prakaṭākruti*: (830th) in *Paribhāshā* verses.

Śree Bhāskararāya considers the names based on the *Paribhāshā* verses only explaining reasons for the same. We also follow the same. Those who are interested in understanding the reasons may refer the original book.

(iii) The description given for the 623rd name *Kevalā* may also be referred.

(iv) *Kevala* - the knowledge of *Eeshvara*, because it has been thus used in the *Jaina* tantras.

(v) *Kevala* - devoid of all attributes, or freed from pleasure and pain.

(vi) In the *Shiva Sūtras* (III-35) *Shiva* is named as "*Kevalin* who is free from happiness and sorrows"; *Sukhāsukhayor Bahir Mananam* and *Tadvimuktistu Kevalee*.

(vii) The *Vishva* dictionary gives various meanings to the word *Kevala* - a certain kind of knowledge, one, complete, decision and deception. Hence it can be construed that **She** is decided, *kevala*, by the *Kualās*.

(viii) a. The ladies who follow the *Koula* religion are called as *Koulinees*. Hence it can be taken as – *Śree Devee* is by whom they become *Kevalas* – consorts of knowledge. That is, **She** gives knowledge to those ladies who follow *Koula* religion.

b. It can also be taken as - one who is decided by the *Koulinees* and hence *Koulinee kevala* (the author quotes various grammar rules to split this name in this way and mean it).

(ix) Two other books (in this the second one seems to be based on the first one) say that this name is *Kālineekevala*. *Śree Bhāskararāya* has not mentioned this. If such a version is available, then there is no need for arguments about *Nāmavibhāga*.

According to this the meaning is – **She** is beyond all things that can be fixed by time or **She** is without any religion.

926. *Anarghyakaivalyapadadāyinee* – अनर्घ्यकैवल्यपददायिनी

(i) One who confers the abode of priceless salvation.

(ii) That is, *Anargha* - priceless, *kaivalya* – one who bestows the fifth state of salvation. 625th name *Kaivalyapadadāyinee* may also be referred. The four kinds of salvation, namely *sālokya, sāroopya, sāmeepya* and *sāyujya* are results of actions, dependent on each other and temporary. It has been explained that, hence they have name as status. Further there itself it has been described that the salvation called *Kailvalya* is the result of knowledge, has bliss as its character and is eternal. It has been reiterated here that **She** bestows that fifth type of salvation called *Kaivalya* (priceless has been added as an adjective). 948th name *Panchamee* may also be referred.

(iii) One variation of this name is *Anarghyā Kaivalya Pada Dāyinee*. In this case this name can be split in two ways –

a. *Anarghya Ākaivalya Pada Dāyinee* – *Ā* means omnipresent. Hence the priceless and omnipresent Kaivalya salvation is being offered to the devotees.

b. *Anarghya Akaivalya Pada Dāyinee*– *Akaivalya* status – Without anything else, that is, reaching **Her** only is *Kaivalya*. There is nothing else called as *Kaivalya* status. The real meaning is that - thus reaching **Her** is a priceless great status.

927. ***Stotrapriyā* - स्तोत्रप्रिया**

(i) One who is fond of praises (*stotras*).

(ii) The praises are of two types – *Vaidheeka* (based on *Vedas*) and *loukeeka* (not based on *Vedas*).

(iii) The characters of *loukeeka stotras* have been divided into six types by learned. They are, "Salutation (*namaskāra*), blessing (*Āshirvāta*), praising the attainments (telling about the *siddhāntās*), praising exploits (*parākrama*), rehearsing glory (*vibhooti*) and prayer for prosperity (*prārthanā*);

Namskāras Tathāsheeshcha Siddhāntokti: *Parākrama*: I
Vibhooti: *Prarthanā Cheti Shdvidham Stotra Lakshaṇam* II

In this *Sahasranāma*, all these six types are covered. The below names are shown as instances – one for each of the types;

627 – *Trijagadvandyā*, 448 – *Svastimatee*,
735 – *Mithyājagadadhishṭhānā*,
79 – *Bhanḍāsurendranirmukta ShastrapratyastraVarshinee*,
658 - *Ichchāshaktijnānashaktikriyāshaktisvaroopiṇee*,
692 - *Sāmrājyadāyinee*.

The 1000 names entirely fit in any one of these 6 types.

(iv) It refers to the *Vedic* praise, namely chanting the Vedic verses relating to *Śree Devee* like *Rātri Sookta*, etc. **She** is very fond of it.

(v) The word *'Ap'* indicates all the four types' viz., *Devas*, human beings, *Pitrus* and demons. There are lots of evidences in this regard in *Vedas*. For instance;

Tāni Vā Etāni Chatvāryambhamsi...
Panchamyāmāhootāvāpa: *Purushavachaso Bhavanti* – *Chāndokya Upanishad* (V-3-3)
Āpo Vā Idam Sarvam – *Mahānārāyaṇa Upanishad* (XIV-1) –
All these indeed are water.

In this sense, this name indicates that **She** is fond of *Deva*, human, *Pitru* (ancestors) and demon who praise **Her**. To suit this interpretation the name is split as *Stotree* + *Āpa*: + *Priya*.

(vi) *Śree Ādi Śaṇkara* in his commentary of *Viṣhṇu Sahasranāma* for the 679th - *Stavya*: and 680th - *Stavapriya*: says – **He** is praised by all, but **he** does not praise anybody and hence *Stavya*:. Because of this he is interested in praising – *Stotrapriyā*:

928. *Stutimatee* - स्तुतिमती

(i) One in about whom lots of praises have been sung.
(ii) There are lots of praises about her – both *Vaidheeka* and *Loukeeka* and hence *Stutimatee*. Among the *Loukeeka* praises, the top ones are – *Lalitā Stavaratnam* by *Śree Durvāsa*, *Mooka Panchashatee* by *Śree Mooka* and *Soundaryalaharee* by *Śree Ādi Śaṇkara*.
(iii) By splitting the name as *Stuti* + *Mati* + *E*, it can be construed as – by worshipping **Her**, one can get knowledge (*mati*) and dominion (*E*).

929. *Srutisamstutavaibhavā* - श्रुतिसंस्तुतवैभवा

(i) One whose glory is praised in *Vedas*.
(ii) Earlier it was mentioned that there are *Vaidheeka* praises. **She** is praised through them.
(iii) According to the *Amara* dictionary (III-2-23), *samstuta* means experience; *Samstava*: *Syāt Parichaya*: i.e. **Her** greatness is enjoyed by the *Vedas* themselves.
(iv) *Veda* indicates the number four – evidence; *Chanda*: *Sudhākaram*. **She** experiences **Her** glory as the four *Shaktis*. As mentioned in *Bahvruchopanishad*, She is in the form of the four groups' viz. *Shareerapurush* (body), *Chanta:purush* (metre), *Vedapurush* and

Mahāpurush (great). i.e. **Her** glory is experienced in four ways, the person in the body, the person in the meters, the person in the *Vedas*/ scriptures and the great person.

(v) The *Koorma Purāṇa* also says - "*Devee* has four *shaktis*; they declared to be her own nature and **She** is the support of these four; Listen to me, Oh best of sages, these are *shānti* (peace), *vidyā* (knowledge), *pratiṣṭā* (fixity) and *nivrutti* (restraint). Hence the supreme Lord is said to be four-formed. By these four *shaktis* the supreme Lord enjoys **his** own bliss";

Chatasra: *Shaktyo Devyā*: *Svaroopatve Vyavasthitā*: I
Adhishṭānavashāttasyā: *Shrunudhvam Munipungavā*: II
Shāntirvidyā Pratishṭā Cha Nivruttishcheti Tā: *Smrutā*: I
Chaturvyoohastato Deva: *Prochyate Parameshwara*: II
Anayā Paramo Deva: *Svātmānandam Samashnute* I
Chatursvapi Cha Deveshu Chaturmoortir Maheshwara: II

930. ***Manasvinee* - मनस्विनी**

(i) One who has self-possessed mind.
(ii) **She** does not have a mind dependent on others. **She** has it on her own.

Note: The author quotes a grammar note to convince that this name ends with *Vinee*.

931. ***Mānavatee* - मानवती**

(i) One who has high/ broad minded.
(ii) *Māna* may mean the elevation of mind, regard, the expression indicating the forgiveness of sin, proof, or measurement. **She** has all these and hence *Mānavatee*.

932. ***Maheshee* - महेशी**

(i) One who is the consort of *Maheshvara*.
(ii) 208th name - *Māheshvaree* and 750th name - *Maheshvaree* may be referred.
(iii) The *Devee Purāṇa* says, "As **She** was born from *Mahādeva* and worshipped by great men and as **She** is the consort of *Mahesha*, **She** is called *Maheshee*";

Mahadevāt Samupannā Mahadbhir Yata Ādrutā I
Maheshasya Vadhooryasmānmaheshee Tena Sā Smrutā II

(iv) A part of *Śree Ādi Śaṇkara*'s commentary for the 257th name in *Trishatee – Kāmeshwara Maheshwaree* – very great, with blemish-less wealth – *Maheshwaree;*

Mahatee Cha Sā Eshwaree Nirupādhikaishvaryavatee,
Mahānprabhurvai Purusha: Iti Srute: II

933. ***Mangalākruti:* - मङ्गलाकृतिः**

(i) One who has a beneficent form.
(ii) 116th name - *Bhadramoortti:* and 200th name – *Sarvamangalā* may be referred.

934. ***Vishvamātā* - विश्वमाता**

(i) One who is the mother of the universe.
(ii) This has been accepted by all right from *Moolaprakruti* till the creation of this universe.
(iii) *Vishva* means *Viṣhŋu*. *Viṣhŋu Sahasranāma* itself begins with the name *Vishva*. *Śree Bhāskararāya* quotes the statement from *Veda* starting from *Soma: Pavate* till *Janitota Viṣhŋu*.

935. ***Jagaddhātree* - जगद्धात्री**

(i) One who is the sustainer and protector of the world.
(ii) *Dhātree* means mother or nurse. As mother nourishes her child, **She**, in the form of earth, protects the living beings.
(iii) 337th name *Vidhātree* may be referred.

936. ***Vishālākshee* - विशालाक्षी**

(i) One who has long and large eyes.
(ii) The eyes leading upto the ears will be beautiful.
(iii) In *Soundaryalaharee* there are many verses describing the beauty and greatness of eyes of *Śree Devee*. Specifically these verses may be referred; 52 to 57 – *Gate Karnābhyarnam, Vibhakta Traivarŋyam, Pavitreekartum Na:, Nimeshon Meshābhyām, Tavāparne Karne* and *Drushā Dragheeyasyā*.

(iv) In this *Sahasranāma* itself these names describe the beauty of the eyes of *Śree Devee*; 18 – *Vaktralakshmee Pareevāha Chalanmeenābha Lochanā*, 332 - *Vāmanayanā*, 561 – *Mrugākshee* and 601 - *Darāndolitadeerghākshee*.

(v) In *Trishatee* also **She** is addressed as *Kamalākshee* (7th name). That is, her eyes are like blossomed Lotus.

(vi) According to *Padma Purāṇa, Vishālākshee* is the name of the deity worshipped at *Benaras*. **She** is of that form.

(vii) 49th verse of *Soundaryalaharee* beginning with *Vishālā Kalyanee* may also be referred. *Vishālā* means blossomed sight. In commentaries this has been mentioned as energy that creates confusion.

(viii) The word *Vishālā* indicates *Badrikāshrama*. Since it is in the Himalayas, it also indicates *Nepala Peeṭa*. In *Laghu Shoḍa Nyāsa* (*Peeṭa Nyāsā*), *Brahmāṇḍa* and other *Purāṇas* say, that the *Nepala Peeṭa* should be meditated upon as situated in the eyes. The word *Akshee* indicates both the eyes. Hence it can be considered that **She** has *Vishāla Peeṭa* as her eyes.

937. ***Virāgiṇee* - विरागिणी**

(i) One who is dispassionate.

(ii) That is, one who is with zeal.

(iii) Already it was mentioned in 156th name as *Neerāga*.

938. ***Pragalbhā* - प्रगल्भा**

(i) One who is daring and powerful.

(ii) A lady who has courage and strength is called *Pragalbha*. **She** is strong in the action of creation, etc. and hence *Pragalbha*.

939. ***Paramodārā* - परमोदारा**

(i) One who is extremely generous.

(ii) **She** is supremely generous, readily responding to the prayers of **Her** devotees.

(iii) *Udārā* also means very big. **She** is very big both in space and time. Since **She** is very big, **She** is called as *Paramodāra*.

(iv) This name can be split as – *Para* - supreme, *moda* - bliss, *Āra* – complete. That is, **She** bestows complete and supreme happiness to **Her** devotees.

(v) If the name is split as – *Parama* + *Uda* + *Āra*. In that case, very great water i.e. ocean; ocean here meaning the ocean of worldly existence; *Ārā* - weapons. **She** is the destroyer of the worldly existence of her devotees.

(vi) By prefixing *A* to the name we get *Aparamodārā*; if this is split as *Aparama* + *Udāra*. *Apa* - gone, *Rama* – wealth or joy. i.e. for the poor and miserable people, **She** is, *Udāra*.

940. *Parāmodā* - परामोदा

(i) One who is supremely reputed.
(ii) *Para* – great, *Āmoda* - sweet smell, i.e. fame.
(iii) *Para* - great, *Ā* – spread on all sides, *moda* - happiness. **She** embodies the ultimate bliss of realisation.

941. *Manomayee* - मनोमयी

(i) One who has the mind itself as her form.
(ii) The *Mahā Vāshishṭa Rāmāyana*, says, "That *Bhairava, Shiva,* is said to be *Chidākāsha*, his own active energy (*spandashakti*) known as *Manomayee*";

Sa Bhairava: *Chidākāsha*: *Shiva Ityabhidheeyate* I
Ananyām Tasya Tām Viddhi Spandashaktir Manomayee II

(iii) The *Brhadāraŋya Upanishad* (IV-4-19) says "By mind alone it is to be seen"; *Manasaivānudrashṭavyam*. According to this, mind is the chief instrument in creating self-knowledge.

942. *Vyomakeshee* - व्योमकेशी

(i) One whose hair is the form of ether – that is the form of *Virat*.
(ii) Or *Vyomakesha*, i.e. *Shiva,* his consort. Since it is being said that the directions are his wives, it can be considered that **She** is in the form of directions.
(iii) If the letter *ka* is suffixed to a word it makes it small. For example *Balaka*:, *Udaka*:, etc. *Vyoma* means ether. If *ka* is suffixed, it becomes small sky or ether. **She** is the head of that also (the ether in the pot etc.). **She** is present in those also i.e. omnipresent.

943. *Vimānasthā* - विमानस्था

(i) One who is no different from *Devas* in the celestial chariot i.e. flights.
(ii) **She** is omniscient. Since **She** herself is in the form of *Devas*, this meaning is derived.
(iii) *Vi* – Especially or in a great way, *Māna* –in supporting her devotees, *Sthā* – one who is stubborn. That is, **She** is stubborn and has great interest in supporting her devotees.
(iv) It can be split as – *Vi* – great, *Mā* – with lustre, *Ana* – cart or chariot, *Sthā* – **She** is there. That is, **She** is in various chariots like *Geyachakra*, *Girichakra* and *Chakrarāja*. That **She** herself is in the form of *Mantriŋee* and *Ḍanḍinee Devees*.
(v) If it is split as *Vimāna* – immeasurable + *sthā* – is there. **She** resides in the immeasurable *Brahmam*.
(vi) *Māna* – dimension or measurement. The author says that *Stā* has to be taken as *stiti* and meant to be originated from status. *Vi* indicates the antonym. Hence **She** is not in a position to be measured i.e. immeasurable.
(vii) Since it provides especially the true knowledge, the *Veda* can be considered as a flight. **She** is there, described by *Vedas*.
(viii) **She** remains in the evidences, which are not opposed to the *Vedas*, in the form of righteousness.
(ix) It can specially be taken as that, **She** lives in the fourteen *Vidyās*, (the scriptures, *nyāyās*, *meemāmsās* and others), which describe the form of limitations.

944. *Vajriŋee* - वज्रिणी

(i) One who is the consort of *Indra*, the possessor of the weapon *Vajra*.
(ii) Or one who has the thunderbolt in hand.
(iii) Or adorned with jewels like diamond and other gems.
(iv) Or *Kaṭopanishad* (VI-2) says, "The great terrible *Vajra*". *Vajra* means *Brahmam*. *Śree Devee* is called *Vajriŋee* as **She** is related with *Brahmam* as its limitator; *Mahadbhayam Vajramudyatam*.
(v) In *Mahāshoḍanyāsa* (*Moorti Nyāsa*), **She** is called as *Parameshṭin*.

945. *Vāmakeshvaree* - वामकेश्वरी

(i) One who is in the form of *Vamakeshvarą tantra*.
(ii) This *tantra* is about *Śree Devee*. In this in the part called *Nityāshoḍashikārnava* (*Śree Bhāskararāya* himself has written commentary for this in his book called *Sethu Bandam*), lot of

important matters about *Śree Devee* (its importance and meanings), the method of worshipping her, etc., have been described. The 31st verse of *Soundaryalaharee* (beginning with *Chatu*: *Shashṭyā Tantrai*:) says – *Parameshwara*, has cheated people, by creating 64 *tantras*, attracting them towards it and has entangled them in the cycle of births and deaths. However, because of your compulsion, he has made one *tantra* which bestows all the desires. *Śree Bhāskara Rāya* in his *Sethu Bandam*, has categorically mentioned that it is the 65th *tantra* viz., *Vāmakeshwara Tantra*.

(iii) Those who follow the left path are called *Vāmakās*. They do not perform the five sacrifices viz., *Panchayajnās*. They do not repay the credits to *Devas*, sages (*rishis*) and *pitrus* (ancestors). The description given for the 912th name *Savyāpasavyamārgasthā* may be referred. **She** is head of them – i.e. **She** is worshipped by them.

(iv) *Vāmana* indicates creation. *Daksha* and other *prajāpatis* who create the world are called *Vāmakās*. **She** is head of them.

946. ***Panjchayajnapriyā* - पञ्चयज्ञप्रिया**

(i) One who loves the five types of sacrifices.

(ii) Different books differently list down the five sacrifices. **She** is fond of all those.

(iii) *Veda* lists – *Agnihotram*, *Darshapoorṇamāsam*, *Chāturmāsyam*, *Pashuyāgam* and *Somayāgam*.

(iv) *Smruti* lists – *Deva, Pitru, Brahma, Bootha* and *Manushya* sacrifices.

(v) *Pāncharātra Āgama* lists – *Abhigamanam* (nearing the God), *Upādhānam* (compiling the things needed for worship), *Ijyam* (worship), *Svātyāyam* (repeating *Veda*, etc). and *Yogam* (meditation).

(vi) *Kulāgama* lists – *Kevala*, *Yāmala*, *Mishra*, *Charayug* and *Veerashankara*.

(vii) *Nityā Tantra* explains the five types of worshipping methods with alcohol and others.

(viii) Five types of ladies are explained in *Bruhattantra Mahotati* (and *Mantra Mahodadi* which was based on it) as – *Āturee, Soutakee, Tourpotee, Trāseesātanā* and *Bhavānee*.

(ix) Five types of offerings in *Agnihotram* is also called as five sacrifices. Its meaning has been given in *Chāndogya Upanishad* (V-3-3). In the last sacrifice it becomes the human body itself. The places where these sacrifices are done are; *Soma world, Tyu world*, earth, male and female.

(x) One of the meanings of *Pancha* is – to expand. Hence, it can be considered as the place of dwelling for those who create the universe.

947. ***Panchapretamanchādhishāyinee* – पञ्चप्रेतमञ्चाधिशायिनी**

(i) One who is reclining on a couch made of five corpses.

(ii) To indicate that **She** is greater than the five tasks (creation, protection, destruction, *tirodhāna* and *anugrahā*), the persons who do those tasks have been compared to the legs of the cot and its plank. *Brahma, Vişhŋu, Rudra* and *Eshvara* are the four legs of the couch and the *Sadāshiva* is the pure white sheet". **She** shines in that cot. These five are mentioned as corpses. They do their tasks through their respective *Shaktis* (energies) viz., *Vāmā, Jyeshtā*, etc. If the energies are not there, they cannot do anything. Hence they are indicated as corpses.

(iii) The *Bhairavayāmala* says in the *Bahuroopā Shatakaprastāra* - "On that great and pleasant couch whole pillow is *Mahesāna*, of whose four legs are *Brahma*, etc. and whose mattress is *Sadāshiva,* reclines the great *Tripurasundaree*, the Great Queen";

Shivātmake Mahāmanche Maheshānopa Barhane I
Mrutakāshcha Chatushpadā: *Kashipushcha Sadāshiva* : II
Tatrashete Maheshānee Mahātripurasundaree II

(iv) *Lalitā Stavaratnam* (verses 151 and 152) also describes this bed;

Paryankasya Bhajāma Pādān Bimbāmbudendu Hemarucha:
Ajaharirudrechmayān Anlāsuramārutesha Konasthān I
Phalakam Sadāshiva mayam Pranoumi Sindoora renu Kiranābham II

(v) In *Soundaryalaharee* also (92nd verse) we read as – the four gods *Brahma* and others, though being the heads of their worlds, with the intention of being near *Śree Devee* and to serve her, take the form of the legs of the cots;

Gatāste Manchatvam Druhina Hari Rudreshvara Bruta:
Shiva: *Svachchachchāyā Gatitakapata Prachchadapata*: I

(vi) The commentators quote the below verse from *Rudrayāmala*. The details of this can be obtained from the explanations of *Śree Lakshmeedhara* and from the book called *Tatparyateepinee*;

Brahma Vişhŋushcha Rudrashcha Ěshwarashcha Sadāshiva : I
Ete Pancha Mahāpretā: *Bhootadhipatayo Matā*: I
Chatvāro Manchacharaŋā: *Panchama*: *Prachchadha*: *Pata*:
Sākshi Prakāsharoopena Shivenābhinna Vigrahā I

Tatrāsane Samāseenā Nirbharānandha Roopinee ll

This bed has been described in detail in *Lalitopākyāna*. Further 952nd name *Shāshvataishvaryā* may be referred.

(vii) It is being explained in the book called *Saparyāpattati Vāsanā* by *Śree Chidānanda Nātha* (page 67) as below;

1. *Brahma Maya Manchapāda* = Energy of creation = *Moolādhārā* = the seat of *Brahma*.
2. *Vişhŋu Māyā Manchapāda* = Energy of protection = *Swādishtānāna* = the seat of *Vişhŋu*.
3. *Rudra Maya Manchapāda* = Energy of destruction = *Maŋipoorakam* = the seat of *Rudra*.
4. *Ĕshwara Maya Manchapāda* = Energy of complete annihilation = *Anāhata* = the seat of *Ĕshwara*.
5. *Sadāshiva Manchapalakam* = Energy of *anugraha* = *Vishuddhi* = the seat of *Sadāshiva*.

(viii) The corpse form of *Brahma, Vişhŋu* and others has been explained in *Gnānārnavam* (verses 12 to 27);

Śree Devee said;

Pancha Pretān Maheshāna Bhroohi Teshām Tu Kāraŋam l
Nirjeevā Avināshāste Nityaroopā: *Kadam Vibho* ll
Nirjeeve Nāsha Evāsti Te Katham Nityatām Gatā: l

Eshwara said;

Sādhu Prushtam Tvayā Bhadre Panchapretamayam Katham ll
Brahma Vişhŋushcha Rudrashcha Ĕshwarashcha Sadāshiva : l
Panchapretā Varārohe Nishchalā Eva Sarvadā ll

948. ***Panjchamee* - पञ्चमी**

(i) One who is the consort of *Sadāshiva*.

(ii) We read in *Soota Geeta* that *Brahma, Vişhŋu, Rudra, Ĕshwara* and *Sadāshiva* are one greater than the previous in that order;

Trishu Rudro Varishta: *Syātteshu Māyee Para*: *Shiva* : l
Māyāvishishtāt Sarvagnāt Sāmba: *Satyādi Lakshaŋa*: ll
Sadāshivo Varishta: *Syānnātra Kāryā Vichāranā* ll

Among them **She** is the consort of *Sadāshivā*, the fifth god.

(iii) *Vārāhi Devee* is also called as *Panchamee*. It can be said that **She** is in that form. *Vārāhee* is the fifth of the eight *Matru Devee*s (*Brāhmee* and others). *Vārāhee* is the last in *Pancharatna Devees*. *Vārāhee* is the last in *Pancha Kosha Devees*. In this way also, **She** can be called as *Panchamee*, the fifth. Further, *Dakshiŋāmoorti Samhita* indicates in more than one place that *Panchāmee* is the natural name of *Vārāhee*.

(iv) The last in the five 'M's is the bliss form. It can be said that **She** is in that form. Or, it can also be said that **She** is the group of five *M*s. *Tripuropanishad* describes all these. *Śree Appayya Deekshitar*, who has written commentary for this has specified that this has to be used only for reading and the things mentioned, Brahmins should not think of using it even in their dream. Even though this was mentioned earlier in 330th name *Kādambareepriyā*, it has just been reiterated here.

(v) The five sacrifices are mentioned in 946th name *Panchayajnapriya*. The fifth one in that is a lady and it can be taken that **She** is in that form.

(vi) It can also be taken that **She** is in the form of the fifth type of salvation called *Kaivalya*. 625th name - *Kaivalyapadadāyinee* and 926th name - *Anarghyakaivalyapadadāyinee* may also be referred.

949. *Panjchabhooteshee* - पञ्चभूतेशी

(i) One who is head of five elements (earth, etc)..

(ii) Since *Śree Devee* is in the form of essence of all the five basic elements, it can be said that **She** is the head of them. This can further be read in *Panchadashee* and *Panchaboota Viveka* by *Śree Vidyāraṇya*.

(iii) It can also be considered that since **She** is in the form of five or **She** originated in five ways. She is the head of *Panchabhoota*, fivefold, because that is the garland called *Vaijayanti* formed of five elements and five gems. 267th name - *Govindaroopiṇee*, 838th – *Mukundā* and 893rd – *Viṣhṇuroopiṇee* may also be referred.

It has thus been mentioned, since this garland is made of Pearl, Ruby, Diamond, Emerald and Blue Sapphire and since these gems originated from earth. As evidence to this, the author quotes the verses from *Viṣhṇu Purāṇa* and *Viṣhṇu Rahasyā*, "The club-bearer's (*Viṣhṇu's*) garland called *Vaijayanti* consists of five elements, it is also called the element garland, Oh twice born one";

Prutivyām Neela Samgnānamadbhyo Muktāphalāni Cha I
Tejasakoustubho Jāto Vāyor Vaidoorya Samgnakam II
Pushkarāt Pushparagastu Vaijayantyā Harerime II

950. *Panchasankhyopachāriṇee* - पञ्चसंख्योपचारिणी

(i) One who is worshipped with five offerings.
(ii) Sandal, flowers, incense, lamp and food are the five offerings mentioned here. By offering them it is imagined that the five elements are offered to *Śree Devee*. It is the practice that these five objects are offered mentally by pronouncing their five *beejas*.

951. *Shāshvatee* - शाश्वती

(i) One who is omnipresent.
(ii) 136th name *Nityā* may also be referred.
(iii) According to *Amara* (III-6) dictionary, *Shāshvatā* means definite or always.
(iv) *Shashvat* means often/ frequently. **She** is often worshipped by devotees and hence *Shāshvatee*.

952. *Shāshvataishvaryā* - शाश्वतैश्वर्या

(i) One who is possessing eternal dominion. She is ever the giver of Eternal Bliss, which is the greatest of eternal kingdoms and dominions.
(ii) It can be said that the prefixed syllable *E* is hidden in this name (it has gone as the last syllable of the previous name). In that case, the *Ĕsas* - the rulers of the universe (*Brahma*, etc)., the five corpses, *Ashvatā* - the condition of being a horse (vehicle), *aishvarya* - dominion, i.e. the five corpses (*Brahma* and others) form her seat. This message was already mentioned in 947th name *Panjchapretamanjchādhishāyinee* and is being reiterated here.

953. *Sharmadā* - शर्मदा

(i) One who is the bestower of happiness.
(ii) *Sharma* means the eternal bliss. After this there is no question of sorrow.
(iii) 125th name - *Sharmadāyinee*, 192nd – *Sukhapradā* and 968 - *Sukhakaree* may be referred.
(iv) *Śree Ādi Śaņkara* in his commentary of *Vişhŋu Sahasranāma* for the 459th name – *Sukhadā*: mentions – Since he bestows happiness to those who have good habits and destroys the happiness of those who have bad habits, **He** is *Sukhadā*:.

The 889th name *Sukhadā*: - **He** gives the happiness of salvation to the devotees.

954. ***Shambhumohinee* - शम्भुमोहिनी**

(i) One who bewitches even *Paramashiva.*
(ii) Since he bestows well beings to the devotees, he has the names *Shambhu* or *Shankaran*.
(iii) He is renowned for his self-control, but still he is bewitched by *Śree Devee.*
(iv) It can be reminded that **She** has a succession of waves constituting an erotic play, which was mentioned in the 863rd name *Kāmakelitarangita*. **She** bewitches *Kāmeshwara* also.
(v) The same message is being conveyed in the below names in *Trishatee*; 243 – *Kāmeshwara Manoharā*, 251 - *Kāmeshvara Mana*: *Priyā* and 253 – *Kāmeshwara Vimohinee.*

955. ***Dharā* - धरा**

(i) One who is in the form of Earth.
(ii) It can be taken that cryptically this has cryptically indicated all the other four primary elements also.
(iii) **She** is in the form of *La*, which is the *bheeja* letter of earth.
   a. This will indicate the Earth *Devee* including the mountains, forests and 51 *peeṭas*.
   b. **She** is in the form of letter *La* in every hall of the root *vidya.*
(iv) Since **She** supports the entire universe, **She** got this name.

956. ***Dharasutā* - धरसुता**

(i) One who is the daughter of *Himalaya.*
(ii) 246th name *Pārvatee* also conveyed the same message.

957. ***Dhanyā* - धन्या**

(i) One who is grateful.
(ii) As means of expressing gratitude to the devotees who worship **Her, She** bestows the results.
(iii) **She** bestows wealth. It can also be taken that **She** has wealth. The author quotes a grammar rule to confirm that this name ending with *ya*.

(iv) *Dhanya* is a certain *Yogini* as mentioned in the *Jyotisha sāstra*, namely *Mangalā*, *Pingalā* and *Dhanya*.

(v) The *Bhavishyottara Purāṇa* says, during the last period when the soul goes out of the body, four types of thought process may happen. Accordingly the results may vary. The gist of it is as below;

   a. **Thought *Ārta*;** *Ārta* is the meditation, which arises through illusion, the desire to possess dominion, pleasure, beds, seats, women, scents, garlands, jewels, cloths and ornaments.

   b. **Thought *Raudra*;** *Raudra* is said by the wise to be that meditation, in which arises the desire and not indifference, though he had wounds, fire, beating, cruelty, bodily injury, breaking limbs, etc.

   c. **Thought *Dhanya*;** – *Dhanya* is said by the wise to be that meditation in which arises a thought by the following of the meaning of the *Upanishads* and by the performance of great vows, etc. about the causes of bondage and liberation and going and coming (reincarnation) and of the tranquility of the five senses and compassion in all beings.

   d. **Thought *Shuklā***; *Shuklā* is said by the wise to be that meditation in which by practice of Yoga which destroys the constructive imagination the senses are not tainted by material objects, the inner self is fixed on its unity with one reality i.e. *Brahmam*.

(vi) *Śreemad Bhagavad Geeta* (VIII-6) says – whatever being a man thinks of at the last moment when he leaves his body, that alone does he attain, Oh Kaunteya, being ever absorbed in the thought thereof;

Yam Yam Vāpi Smaranbhāvam Tyajatyante Kalevaram I
Tam Tamevarlti Kounteya Sadā Tadbhāvabhāvita: II

958. ***Dharmiṇee* - धर्मिणी**

(i) One who is with righteousness.
(ii) Or **She** is with the experience of righteousness like bliss and eternity.

959. ***Dharmavardhinee* - धर्मवर्धिनी**

(i) One who promotes righteousness.
(ii) *Vāmana Purāṇa* says – *Śree Devee* promotes righteousness in her devotees, like control of senses, cleanliness, wealth and devotion to god;

Jitendriyatvam Shoucham Cha Māngalyam Bhaktireva Cha I

Shankare Bhāskare Devyām Dharmoyam Mānusha: Smruta: II
Dyāta: Samba Imān Dharmān Vruddhim Nayati Dehinām II

(iii) The verb *Vrudh* means to cut or to destroy. Righteousness indicates everything visible, for which *Brahmam* is the basis. **She** makes the *Brahmam* visible by cutting things, that is, by cutting the visible things, **She** is called as *Dharmavardhinee*.

(iv) The presiding deity at *Thiruvaiyāru*, which is a city of five rivers, is *Dharmasamvardhinee*.

960. *Lokāteetā* - लोकातीता

(i) One who transcends the worlds – **She** is beyond all the worlds.

(ii) After crossing all the worlds from *Indra* to *Viṣhṇu, Mahā Kailāsa*, the world of *Paramashiva* can be seen. **She** resides in this world. The *Shivadharmottara* says that the world of *Paramashiva* transcends all other worlds. It has been mentioned that those who reach here do not have re-birth. The original verses have not been mentioned. About *Kailāsā*, it has already been mentioned in 578th name *Mahākailāsanilaya*.

(iii) It can also be considered as that **She** is beyond all worlds or souls (the souls originate from her only).

961. *Guṇāteetā* - गुणातीता

(i) One who transcends the three qualities.

(ii) **She** is in the form of *Brahmam*. **She** is earlier to root nature (*moolaprakruti*). Hence **She** is also earlier to the three attributes.

962. *Sarvāteetā* - सर्वातीता

(i) One who transcends all.

(ii) **She** transcends everything, including the Universe of name and form. *Sarva* - all. Since **She** transcends all that includes transcends speech. 415th name *Manovāchāmagocharā* can be reminded.

963. *Shamātmikā* - शमात्मिका

(i) One who is in the form of tranquility.

(ii) The *Māṇḍukya Upanishad* (7) and *Narasimha Tāpinee Upanishad* (2) say, "They hold that it is tranquility of the activity of the world, peace, non-dual and the fourth"; *Prapanchopashamam Shiva m Shāntam Advaitam Chaturtham Manyante* II **She** is that *Brahmam*.

(iii) *Sham* – bliss. **She** has bliss as **Her** soul.

964. *Bandhookakusumaprakhyā* - बन्धूककुसुमप्रख्या

(i) One who has the lustre similar to the *Bandhooka* flower.

(ii) *Bandhooka* (*Bandhujeeva*) is a famous big tree in Bengal. This belongs to Vengai race of trees (pterocarpus bilobus). This blossoms pretty yellow mixed with red coloured flowers. **Her** lustre is similar to that of this flower.

965. *Bālā* - बाला

(i) One who is in the form of girl or *Śree Balatripura Sundaree*.

(ii) *Bālāmbikā* is a girl of nine years, similar to the form of *Śree Devee* and *Śree Devee* is fond of her. (*Lalithopākyānā* may be referred). In 74th name – *Bhanḍaputra Vadhodhyuktabālāvikramananditā*, we read as – *Śree Devee* was pleased by killing of the sons of *Bhanḍa* by *Bāla*.

(iii) Like a girl **She** is interested in games and *Śree Devee* is called as *Bālā*, says *Tripurā Sittāntam*; *Bālaleelā Vishishṭadbāleti Kathitāpriye* II

(iv) 172nd name of *Trishatee* – *Halleesa Lāsya Santushṭā* – **She** is pleased by looking at the girls playing *Kolāṭṭam* (a group dance game played with sticks according to rhythm).

(v) The *Svetāshvatara Upanishad* (IV-3) says - Thou art boy or girl;

Tvam Kumara Uta Vā Kumāree.

(vi) *Mahāshoḍa Nyāsa* also says;

Pumroopam Vā Smaret Deveem Streeroopam Vā Vichintayet I
Athavā Nishkalam Dhyāyet Sachchitānanda Lakshaṇam II

966. *Leelāvinodinee* – लीलाविनोदिनी

(i) One who gets pleasure in amusement.

(ii) *Leelā* is related to the Universe; **She** playfully does the activities like creation, protection and destruction and is happy with that. *Manu Smruti* (I-80) also says so.

Manvantarānyasankhyāni Sarga: *Samhāra Eva Cha* I
Kreedannivaitat Kurute Parameshtee Puna: *Puna*: II

A sport is played for happiness. But, *Brahmam* does not do this for happiness, since it is *Āptakāman*. *Śree Kullooka Battar* in his commentary explains this that it is said as like (*Iva*) a sport.

(iii) In *Brahma Sūtra* (II-1-33) also it is said as; *Lokavattu Leelā Kaivalyam*.

(iv) In *Yogavāsishtha* the story of *Leelā* is given thus; *Leelā Devee*, the wife of king *Padmarājā*, worshipped *Sarasvatee* and pleased her and received knowledge from *Sarasvati* and brought her husband back to life. If the word *Leelā* is taken as a separate name, it means *Lakshmee*. 865th name *Leelā Vigrahadhāriŋee*.

(v) The *Devee Purāŋa* explains it thus: "*Lakshmee* is called *Leelā* because **She** fondles (*Lālana*)"; *Lakshmee Lālanato Leela*.

(vi) This name can be split into two as *Leelā* and *Vinodinee* and in that case the names 822 and 823 have to be combined and read as *Brahmajananee*.

967. *Sumangalee* - सुमङ्गली

(i) One who is very auspicious.

(ii) **She** has great auspicious. One whose husband is alive is called *Sumangalee* or *Suvāsinee*. (The author gives the grammar rules for the word ending with *E*).

(iii) Auspicious indicates *Brahmam*. Hence it means that She is in the form of auspicious *Brahmam*.

(iv) We read in *Vişhŋu Purāŋa* – the auspicious, which removes the sorrows and gives happiness, is called *Brahmam*;

Ashubhāni Nirāchashțe Tanoti Shubhasantatim I
Sruti Matrena Yatpumsām Brahma Tanmangalam Vidu: II

(v) In *Atri Smruti* also says – the sages who talk about *Brahmam* say that by not doing the wrong deeds and doing the commendable deeds is called auspicious;

Prashastācharaŋam Nityamaprshasta Vivarjanam I
Etaddhi Mangalam Proktamrushibhir Brahmavādibhi: II

(vi) 970th name *Suvāsinee* also conveys the same meaning.

968. *Sukhakaree* - सुखकरी

(i) One who gives the happiness.

(ii) It may be seen that the same message has been mentioned 125th name *Sharmadāyinee*, 192nd – *Sukhapradā* and 953rd – *Sharmada*.

969. *Suveshāḍhyā* - सुवेषाढ्या

(i) One who is the decked with beautiful raiment and ornaments.
(ii) Since **She** is *Sumangalee*, **She** is adorned with beautiful and auspicious raiment and ornaments.
(iii) **She** is adorned with jewels - 51st name *Sarvābharaŋabhooshita*. **She** wears gold jewels – 163rd name of *Trishatee – Hāṭakābharanojvala*.

970. ***Suvāsinee* - सुवासिनी**

(i) One who lives with her husband.
(ii) Living with their husbands is a great thing for ladies and it is also the breath for them. They only can wear gorgeous dress (*vāvāmsi*).
(iii) In *Śreemad Rāmāyana* (*Ayodhyā Kāndā* – 117th chapter) – *Anasooyā Devee* says; *Streenāmāryasvabhāvānām Paramam Daivatam Pati*: II

39th chapter;

Sādhveenām Tu Sthutānām Hi Sheele Satye Shrute Sthite I
Streenām Pavitram Paramam Patireko Vishishyate II
Nātantree Vādyate Veenā Nāchakro Vartate Ratha: I
Nāpati: *Sukhmedheta Yā Syādapi Shatātmajā* II
Mitam Dadāti Hi Pitā Mitam Mātā Mitam Suta: I
Amitasya Hi Dātāram Bhartāram Kā Na Poojayet II
Ārye Kimavamanyeya Streenām Bhartā Hi Daivatam II

971. ***Suvāsinyarchanapreetā* - सुवासिन्यर्चनप्रीता**

(i) One who is pleased with the *archanā* done by *Suvāsinees*.
(ii) Or one who is pleased by doing *archanā* to *Suvāsinees*.
(iii) One of the important parts of worshipping *Śree Devee* is worshipping *Suvāsinees*.
(iv) In *Saptashatee* (11th book) also we read as – all the ladies in all the worlds are to be treated as *Śree Devee*. Hence worshipping them is equal to worshipping *Śree Devee*; "*Vidyās Samastās Tava Devee Bhedā*: *Striya*: *Samastā*: *Sakalā Jagastu* II"

972. ***Āshobhanā* - आशोभना**

(i) One who is always and everywhere beautiful.
(ii) The beauty of *Śree Devee* has been mentioned in many a place in this *Sahasranāma* itself.
(iii) The second part of *Soundaryalaharee* (verses 42 to 100) is entirely devoted to describe the beauty of *Śree Devee*.

973. ***Shuddhamānasā* - शुद्धमानसा**

(i) One who is pure minded.

(ii) *Śree Devee* neither has birth nor death. There are no actions and the corresponding results.

974. ***Bindutarpaŋasantushṭā* - बिन्दुतर्पणसन्तुष्टा**

(i) One who is pleased when **Her** devotees do *Bindu Tarpanā* (offerings).

(ii) The worshippers do *tarpaŋa* in the *Sarvānandamaya Chakra* (*Bindu*). **She** is pleased with the same.

(iii) **She** is happy with the special *arghyabindus*.

(iv) The details of *Bindu* offerings can be found in *Parasurama Kalpa Sūtra*, *Paramānanda Tantra* and *Lagu Stuti*.

(v) *Śree Chidānanda* streamlined the method of *bindu* offerings by the worshippers other than the main devotee.

(vi) According to the saying; *Binduricchu*: - *Bindu* also means the wise men and **She** is pleased by their offerings.

975. ***Poorvajā* - पूर्वजा**

(i) One who is the first born.

(ii) **She** is the first movement of consciousness towards creation, as *Iccha Shakti*, also known as *Avyakta*. *Ahamasmi Prathamajā Rutasya* - I am the first born of the truth – says *Taitreeya Upanishad* (III-10-6).

(iii) It can be said that **She is** the first creation or *Moola Prakruti* (the root nature).

976. ***Tripurāmbikā* - त्रिपुराम्बिका**

(i) One who is in the form of *Tripurā Devee*.

(ii) *Tripurāmbikā* is the name of the deity of the eighth *chakra* of *Śree Chakra*. **She** is not different from **Her**.

(iii) **She** creates the three states awaken, dream and deep sleep. **She** also creates the soul which enjoys these three states.

(iv) She originates the *Vāmā* and other *shaktis*. *Tantra sāstras* mention that *Vāmā*, *Jyeshtā* and *Roudhree shaktis* take the male form, *Brahma*, *Viṣŋu* and *Rudra* and their corresponding *Devees*, *Bhāratee*, *Lakshmee* and *Rudrani*. They only take the form *Icchā* (desire), *Gnana* (knowledge) and *Kriyā* (action) *shaktis* and the three qualities *Satva*, *Rajas* and *Tamas*.

(v) *Śree Devee*, who delivered them, shines in their combined form and the *Shakti* called *Shāntā* with the name *Ambika*. *Vāmakeshvara Tantra* and *Prātānika Rahasya* of *Saptashatee* describe these.

(vi) They only are being worshipped in *Bindu*, in the eighth hall as *Kāmeshwaree*, *Vajreshwaree* and *Bagamālinee*. Again in the ninth hall as *Śree Devee* and in combined form as *Mahātripurasundaree*.

977. *Dashamudrāsamārādhyā* - दशमुद्रासमाराध्या

(i) One who is well worshipped by ten *mudras* (signs or symbols of hands).

(ii) Some schools say in worshipping method, in the *Navāvarŋa Pooja*, at the end of each *pooja*, a symbol has to be shown. Some other schools say, at the end of every *pooja* all the symbols have to be shown. The tenth symbol mentioned here is called as *Trikanta*. This has to be shown by those who are initiated with *Shoḍasee mantra*. (However, even those who are not initiated with *Shoḍasee mantra* can show this symbol by filling it with flowers and stabilising *Śree Devee* in *Śree Chakra* from their hearts). This *Trikantā* symbol is the combined form of all the symbols.

(iii) In general to be known – this has to be done using both the hands. Since the right side of the body indicates *Shiva* and the left side indicates *Śree Devee*, both the hands put together indicate the unison of *Shiva -Shakti*. The symbols shown in dance have relevant meanings. In the same way, these symbols also have characters and meanings. These are explained in *tantra sāstras* particularly *Tantra Rāja Tantram* and *Nityā Shoḍashikārnavam*. But, these are to be learnt only through a proper teacher.

(iv) If these symbols are correctly shown the presiding deities of the concerned halls get satisfied and permit the worshipper to move on to the next hall. *Mudham* – happiness, *rādhi* – to give or to create, hence it is *Mudra*. A *mudrā* is like an identity to be shown to the concerned deit*i*es that the worshipper is our person.

(v) Depending on the doing method, *mantra* and *tatva*, these *mudrās* differ in meaning like *Stoola* (physical), *sookshma* (subtle) and *para*. They also have individual *beeja* letters.

(vi) In *poojas* there are various *mudrās* viz., *āvahanādhi* (installation), *nyāsa*, to be done during fixing of vessels, *bāna*, *nivedana* (offering food) and *yoni*(praying).

(vii) All the *mudras* are to be shown in a secret way – not in a public place or when others are looking at.

978. ***Tripurāshreevashankaree* - त्रिपुराश्रीवशन्करी**

(i) One who has attracted *Tripurāshree Devee* towards **Her**.

(ii) The presiding deity of the *Sarvārtha Sādaka Chakra*, the fifth one in *Śree Chakra* is called as *Tripurāshree*. **She** is in that form.

(iii) The philosophy of the fifth hall is *guroopasādanam* (reaching a proper teacher) – i.e. to understand the philosophy of *Brahmam* to be taught by him. The learned worshippers of *Śreevidyā* do the *pooja* for the fifth hall twice, with the feeling - to get self-knowledge by the blessings of the teacher and that knowledge to be permanent with them. It is believed similar to the belief of *Āvahanti* sacrifice to have continuous teacher-student race.

(iv) The names of all the presiding deit*ies* of all the halls have been mentioned in this *Sahasranāma* either explicitly or implicitly. It seems, *Vasinee Devee*s reiterate and confirm again that only *Śree Devee* is in the form of all the presiding deit*ies*.

Number of the name	Name	Number of the *Chakra*	Presiding Deity of the *Chakra*
626	*Tripurā*	1	*Tripurā*
271	*Ishvaree*	2	*Tripureshee*
997	*Shreemattripurasundaree*	3	*Tripurasundaree*
970	*Suvāsinee*	4	*Tripuravāsinee*
978	*Tripurāshreevashankaree*	5	*Tripurashree*
455	*Mālinee*	6	*Tripuramālinee*
471	*Siddheshvaree*	7	*Tripurasiddhā*
976	*Tripurāmbikā*	8	*Tripurāmbikā*
234	*Mahātripurasundaree*	9	*Mahātripurasundaree*

979. ***Jnānamudrā* - ज्ञानमुद्रा**

(i) One who is in the form of *Gnānamudra* (symbol of knowledge).

(ii) This is called as *Chin mudra*. It has been told that *Śree Dakshiṇāmoorṭi* shows the *chin* sign and teaches the knowledge to *Sunaka* and others. Joining the ends of thumb and fore fingers of the right hand is called as *chin* sign.

(iii) It can also be considered as – **She** bestows happiness through knowledge. *Sāstras* say that those who have got the self-knowledge enjoy the bliss.

(iv) It can also be told that **She** hides both knowledge (part of *chit*) and bliss.

980. ***Jnānagamyā* - ज्ञानगम्या**

(i) One who can be reached through knowledge.

(ii) Though it has been mentioned in 113th name - *Bhāvanāgamyā* and 119th name – *Bhaktigamyā*, devotion and meditation lead to knowledge and **She** can be reached only through knowledge. In *Śreemad Bhāgavatam* (I-7-10) it has been mentioned that even after getting the knowledge devotion can be there – the sages who enjoy in the soul, even if all the desires are removed they have devotion over gods without any reason;

Ātmārāmām Cha Munayo Nirkrantā Apyurukrame I
Kuvantyahetukeem Bhaktimittham Bhotaguṇo Hari: II

(iii) *Śreemad Bhagavad Geeta* (X-10, 11) says;

Teshām Satatayuktānām Bajatām Preetipoorvakam I
Dadāmi Buddhiyogam Tam Yena Māmuyayānti Te II
Teshāmevānukampārthamahamagnānajam Tama: I
Nāshyāmyātmabhāvastho Gnānadeepena Bhāsvatā II

Śreemad Bhagavad Geeta (IV-33) says;

Sarvam Karmākhilam Pārtha Gnane Parisamāpyate II

Śreemad Bhagavad Geeta (IV-39) says;

Gnanam Labdhvā Parām Shāntimachirenādhigachchati II

Śreemad Bhagavad Geeta (VII-19) says;

Bahoonām Janmanāmante Gnanavānmām Prapadhyate II

(iv) *Koorma Purāṇa* says – the blemish-less form of *Śree Devee* can be reached only through knowledge;

Yattu Me Nishkalam Roopam Chinmātram Kevalam Shiva m I
Sarvopādhivinirmuktamanandamamrutam Param II
Gnanenaikena Tallabhyam Kleshena Paramam Padam I
Gnanameva Prapashyanto Māmeva Pravishanti II

981. ***Jnānajneyasvaroopiṇee* - ज्ञानज्ञेयस्वरूपिणी**

(i) One who is in the form of knowledge and the object of knowledge.

(ii) This can be compared to what is mentioned in *Śreemad Bhagavad*

Geeta (XIII-17); "*Gnānam Gneyam Gnānagamyam Grudi Sarvasya Vishtitam* I". He, in the form of the knowledge, the knowable and the goal of knowledge, seated in the hearts of all.

(iii) This is called as the object and the sight. (There is a book by name *Drik Drishyam Vivekam*, the author of which is not clearly known. Someone has mentioned that this is written by *Śree Ādi Śaṇkara*).

(iv) It can also be mentioned that **She** is reachable only through knowledge.

982. *Yonimudrā* - योनिमुद्रा

(i) One who is in the form of *Yoni Mudra*.

(ii) Out of the ten symbols mentioned earlier this is to be done in the ninth hall. Even at the end of every hall one has to bow with *Yoni mudra*. This is also told as the first *mudra*. The character and the results of this *mudra* can be read from the book called *Sethu Bandam* by *Śree Bhāskara Rāya*.

(iii) It can also be considered that **She** gives happiness in *Yoni*.

(iv) It can also be stated that **She** is in the form of *Bindu*, which is veiled behind *Yoni*.

(v) *Yoni* is that part between anus and the genital organs in the body. *Śree Bhāskararāya* mentions that the use of this *mudra* is to remove mistakes in the *mantra* and must be learned from a proper teacher. (This *mudra* is done to get the *mantra*s initiated, by controlling the breath with pressure).

983. *Trikhaṇḍeshee* - त्रिखण्डेशी

(i) One who is the head of *Trikhanḍa mudra*.

(ii) This is the tenth one of the *mudras* mentioned above. This is being used to stabilise *Śree Devee* in the *Śree Chakra*.

(iii) It can also be said as that **She** is the presiding deity of the three halls of *Śree Vidya*.

984. *Triguṇā* - त्रिगुणा

(i) One who is endowed with the three qualities.

(ii) The *Vāyu Purāṇa* says, "This *Yogeshvaree* creates as well as destroys forms, **She** has many forms, many functions and many names, by function and by **Her** sport **She** is threefold in the world, hence **She** is called *Triguṇā*";

Yogeshvaree Shareerāni Karoti Vikaroti Cha I
Nānākrutikriyā Roopa Nāma Vrutti: Sva Leelayā II

(iii) The *Viṣhṇu Purāṇa* also says, "I admire that eternal energy, which is thy energy which is in all beings and in all souls, the basis of the qualities";

Sarbhooteshu Sarvātmanyā Shaktiraparā Tava I
Guṇāshrayā Namstasyai Shāshvatāyai Sureshvaree II

(iv) In 139th name *Nirguṇā*, **She** was mentioned as without qualities. Depending on the qualities of the worshippers, **She** can be worshipped with or without qualities.

(v) *Devee Purāṇa* explains in another way - "As **She** has three steps, the three paths of Ganga, the three qualities, etc"; for it says, "Bali was bound by three steps, the Ganga came from three places, heaven, etc., by the three qualities *satva*, *rajas* and *tamas*. **She** performs the functions of creation, preservation and destruction, hence **She** is called *Triguṇā*";

Padastribhir Balir Baddha: Svargādi Tripathāngatā I
Utpatti Sthlti Nāshashacha Sattvādyais Triguṇochyate II

985. *Ambā* – अंबा

(i) One who is the mother.

(ii) **She** is the mother of the three qualities mentioned above. That is, these qualities originate from **Her**. This form is called in the *Tantras* as the soul of the *mantras* (*mantrajeeva*). The *Tantrarāja* says, "The three qualities are the cause of *tejas*, of the forms of *Shakti* and of the universe. The cause of these qualities is *Śree Devee*; that *samyuktva* (rightly) means the attainment of perpetual contemplation of the nature of that;

Tejesām Shaktimooteenām Prapanchasyāpikāraṇam I
Guṇatrāyamameeshām cha Yatkāraṇamudāhrutam II
Tat Svaroopānu sandhāna Siddhi: Samyaktvameeritam I
Tan Mantraveeryamuddishtam Mantranām Jeeva Ĕrita: II

(iii) Already we read many names in this *Sahasranāma* giving the meaning of mother; 1 - *Shreemātā*, 295 - *Ambikā*, 337 - *Vidhātree*, 457 - *Mātā*, 823 - *Jananee*, 826 – *Prasavitree* and 934 - *Vishvamāta*. **She** is the mother of the entire universe.

986. *Trikoṇagā* - त्रिकोणगा

(i) One who resides in the *Yoni chakra*, which is in the form of a triangle.

(ii) The innermost triangle of *Śree Chakra* is the *Yoni chakra* in a triangle form. **She** is in that form. This has been mentioned in *Trishatee*;

Trikoŋaroopiŋee Shakti: *Bindu Roopa*: *Para*: *Shiva* : *Smruta*: I

Avnābhāva Sambandha: *Tasmāt Bindu Trikoŋayo*: II

(iii) It can also be told as – The second letter of *Panchadashee mantra* is in the form of a triangle - **She** is in that letter form. 21st name of *Trishatee* – *Ekāra Roopā* – may be referred.

987. ***Anaghā* - अनघा**

(i) One who is without any *Agham* (sorrow or sin).

988. ***Adbhutachāritrā* - अद्भुतचारित्रा**

(i) One who has surprising stories (history).

(ii) Many sports (stories) like killing of *Bhanḍāsurā*, blessings to Cupid, etc.

(iii) It can also be taken that **She** protects all from the ill effects of earthquake and other similar dangers.

989. ***Vānchitārthapradāyinee* - वाञ्छितार्थप्रदायिनी**

(i) One who bestows what was sought for by the devotees, in plenty.

(ii) The devotees need not ask for, just thinking is enough. **She** bestows those things. This is clear from the usage of the word *Vānchita*.

(iii) In *Trishatee*, in the names 43 – *Ĕpsitārtha Pradāyinee*, 144 – *Kāmitārthadā* and 260 – *Kānkshitārthatā* – it has been commented that **She** bestows whatever asked for by the devotees both in this and the other worlds including the salvation.

(iv) Unlike other gods, *Śree Devee* does not have *varada* (bestowing boons) *mudra*. No need for it. *Śree Ādi Śaṇkara*, in his *Soundaryalaharee* 4th *verse* mentions as - **Her** Lotus feet itself bestows more than what is sought for, by the devotees;

Tvadanya: *Pānibhyām Abhayavarado Daivatagaŋa*:

Tvamekā Naivāsi Prakatita Varābheetyabhinayā I

Bhayāt Trātum Dātum Phalamapi Cha Vānchāsamadhikam

Sharanye Lokanām Tava Hi Charaŋaveva Nipunou II

990. ***Abhyāsātishayajnātā*** **- अभ्यासातिशयज्ञाता**

(i) One who can be recognised through frequent practice.

(ii) According to the saying; *Āsoopte*: *Āmrute*: *Kālam Nayet Vedānta Chintayā* – Till going to sleep, even till death, the thought of *Vedānta* should continue. Continuously – without any gap – it has to be meditated that *Brahmam* and the self are one and the same. Its summary meaning is that once this meditation increases/ progresses, the knowledge about *Śree Devee* is obtained. The same message is conveyed in *Brahma Sūtra* (IV-1-1) and *Kapila Sūtra*; *Āvruttirasakrudupateshāt*.

(iii) We read the same message in *Brahmāṇḍa Purāŋa* also;

Dhyānaika Drushyā Gnānānkee Vidyātmā Hrudayāspadā I
Ātmaikyādvyaktimāyāti Chirānushṭāna Gouravāt II

(iv) In *Śreemad Bhagavad Geeta* (IX-22) Lord *Śree Krişhŋa* himself confirms;

Ananyāshchintayanto Mām Ye Janā: *Paryupāsate* I
Teshām Nityābhiyuktānām Yogakshemam Vahāmyaham II

991. ***Shaḍadhvāteetaroopiŋee*** **- षडध्वातीतरूपिणी**

(i) One who transcends the six modes of devotion.

(ii) It is told that there are six methods of worshipping *Śree Devee* viz., *Varŋa* (race), *Pada*, *Mantra*, *Kalā* (art), *Tatva* and *Bhuvana* (world). 203rd name *Sarvamayee* may be referred.

   a. *Varŋātvā* is formed with the letters beginning from *A* till *Ksha*.
   b. *Padātvā* is of words - are group of letters.
   c. *Mantratvā* is of *mantra* – a group of words.
   d. *Kalātvā*is of *kalās* – abolition, etc.
   e. *Tatvādhvā* is of *tatvās* – *tatvās* are being mentioned differently in *Sivāgamam*, etc.
   f. *Bhuvātvā* is of *Bhuvanas* (worlds).

(iii) Out of the above, the first three are in the form of sounds and hence they are part of *Vimarshās* i.e. part of *Shaktis*. The other three are in *artha* (meaning) forms and hence they are part of brightness, i.e. part of *Shiva*. This has been mentioned in *Vāyaveeya Samhita* and *Viroopāksha Panchāshika*.

(iv) While describing the imagination of *Śree Chakra* these are mentioned in *Dakshiŋāmoorti Samhitā* (published by *Tanjore Saraswatee Mahal* – 26th chapter). These are mentioned while detailing the be images to be deified in *Śree Chakra*;

Padādhvā Chakrapatreshu Bhuvanādhvā Trisandhishu I
Varŋādhvā Matrukāpeeṭhe Sarvamantravijrumbhite II
Shaṭtrimshattatvabharitam Chakram Moolārŋaroopata: I
Panchasimhāsanonnaddha: *Kalādhvā Chakrashāsanāt* II
Navadhāchakrabharitām Tathāntyaparayā Yutām II
Shoḍashārŋasvaroopā Cha Chakram Vyāpya Vijrumbhite II
Mantradhveti Tadākhyāta: *Neerajāyatalochane* I
Evam Shaḍadhvabharitam Śreechakram Parichintayet II

(v) This has been explained still in detail in *Gnānārnava* (X chapter verses 89 to 98).

(vi) *Śree Padmapādāchariyar* tells about the *tatva* examining to be done by the teacher to his disciple before initiation, in *Prapancha Sārā* (VI chapter 119th verse). Still further in detail this has been described in *Paramānanda Tantra* – 12th*Ullāsā*, verses 170 to 177 and again in 15th*Ullāsā* verses 98 to 100.

(vii) *Śree Raghunāta Mishrā* wrote commentary for *Chitkakana Chandrikā* of *Kālidāsā* (published by *Sampoorŋānanda* Samskrit University, Varanasi). He describes about these 6 *atvās* in the start of the 36th verse.

(viii) **She** transcends all these 6 *atvās*.

(ix) Worshipping of *Shiva, Vişhŋu*, *Shakti*, Sun, *Gaŋapati* and *Kumāra* (or *Indu*, which means Jainism) can be taken as six *atvās*. It has been mentioned that those who got his mind cleaned by these worships in the previous births, gets to worship *Śree Devee* in this birth. Hence it can be said as **She** transcends all these 6 *atvās*.

992. ***Avyājakaruŋāmoorti*: - अव्याजकरुणामूर्तिः**

(i) One who has compassion without partiality.

(ii) *Avyāja* means without gambling or deceit or partiality. **She** has so much compassion.

(iii) In some other book, *Avyāja* has been used to mean interest on the loans. Hence this name is interpreted as - **She** has compassion towards her devotees without any expectations.

(iv) The compassion of *Śree Devee* has been mentioned in various names. Even in the meditation verse we read as – *Aruŋām Karuŋātarangitākshcem*. In the meditation verse of *Trishatee* we read as – *Athishaya Karuŋām*. These names may be referred –197 - *Sāndrakaruŋā*, 326 - *Karuŋārasa Sāgarā* and 581 - *Dayāmoorti*:.

These names in *Trishatee* are also worth noting – 9 – *Karuŋāmruta Sāgarā*, 151 – *Kaṭākshasyandikaruŋā* and 153 – *Kārunya Vigraha*.

(v) All devotees have sung praises about the compassion of *Śree Devee*. For instance; *Jayati Karuŋā Kāsitaruŋā* - Glory to *Śree Devee*, the compassionate one.

993. ***Ajnānadhvāntadeepikā* - अज्ञानध्वान्तदीपिका**

(i) One who dispels the darkness of ignorance.

(ii) As mentioned above, **She** is so compassionate to her devotes that **She** removes the darkness called ignorance around the beings and bestows them with wellbeing. Once a light is lit, the darkness goes away. The light does its duty of encompassing brightness, immediately the darkness escapes. That is, once knowledge is lit, the ignorance runs away.

(iii) In *Śreemad Bhagavad Geeta* (X – 11) also we read as;

Teshāmevānukampārthamahamagnānajam Tama: I
Nāshayāmyātmabhāvastho Gnānadeepena Bhāsvatā II

994. ***Ābālagopaviditā* - आबालगोपविदिता**

(i) One who is known even to children and cowherds.

(ii) Even immature children and lay men who do not have the thought of *Brahmam*, since they have their complete focus in managing the cattle, can recognise **Her**. In this context, managing the cattle should be taken as sub-character of any task. That is, it has to be taken as that those who have their complete focus only on their tasks, who do not think of *Brahmam*. In *Śree Rudram*, we read;

Uthainam Gopā Adrushannadrushannudahārya: II

(iii) The words in this name are interestingly split by the author;
Who supports children and *Brahma* (and others) is called *Bālagopa*.
One who is like children and as cowherd is called *Bālagopa*.
In the above two definitions of *Bālagopa*, one indicates *Shiva* and the other the *Krişhŋa* incarnation (above *Brahma*, *Vişhŋu* and *Rudra* – these three are like his children or young boys). The second indicates lay men.

(iv) The same meaning is conveyed in *Soota Samhita* (I-8-36) – All beings recognize Him in the shape of the idea of, 'I' (self). That is, *Śree Devee* in the inner self is recognised as 'I' (myself) instead of **Herself**;

Tām Aham Pratyaya Vyājāt Sarve Jānanti Jantava: II

(v) Is that **Her** respect is reduced among the people, since **She** is known to all? No, **Her** orders cannot be disobeyed by anybody, says the next name.

995. ***Sarvānullanghyashāsanā* - सर्वानुल्लङ्घ्यशासना**

(i) One whose commands cannot be disobeyed by anybody.

(ii) **She** is understood by learned and lay men as well. However, nobody can exploit the nearness and disobey **Her** orders. Even the three Gods *Brahma*, *Vişhŋu* and *Rudra* understand the commands of *Śree Devee* just by her blinking of eye brows and execute the same. 24th verse of *Soundaryalaharee* conveys the same meaning -*Brahma* creates the universe, *Vişhŋu* protects it and *Rudra* destroys it. *Shiva* annihilates all these three as well as himself and finally, under thy order indicated by the movement of thy creepers-like brows, *Sadāshiva* approves the same;

Jagatsoote Dhātā Hariravati Rudra: *Kshapayate*
Tirskurvannetat Svamapi Vapurĕshwastirāyati I
Sadā Poorŋa: *Sarvam Tadidamanugruhnāti Cha Shiva*
Stavāgnā Mālambya Kshanachalitayor Bhroolatikayo: II

996. ***Shreechakrarājanilayā* - श्रीचक्रराजनिलया**

(i) One who is abiding in the royal *Śreechakra*.

(ii) **She** abides in *Śree Chakra*, in the form of *Bindu*, triangle, etc.

(iii) *Trishatee* says that, "*Śreechakra* is the body of *Shiva* and *Śree Devee*". The meaning is that just as the soul resides in the body so they reside in the *Śreechakra*; *Śreechakram Shiva yor Vapu*:.

(iv) Since it is the greatest of all the *chakras*, it is called as *Śree Chakram*, *Chakra Rājam* and *Śree Chakrarājam*.

997. ***Shreematripurasundaree* - श्रीमत्रिपुरसुन्दरी**

(i) One who is the consort of the great *Tripura*.

(ii) The bodies of *Brahma*, *Vişhŋu* and *Shiva* are called as *purās*. The *Paramashiva* who has three *purās* as part of his body is called as *Tripura*. This has been mentioned in *Kālikā Purāŋa* as, - by the will of the *pradhāna* the body of *Shiva* become triple. Then the upper part became *Brahma* with five faces, four arms and whose body had the colour of the pericarp of the lotus. His middle part became *Vişhŋu* with the blue colour, having one face, four arms, bearing the conch, disc, club and lotus. The lower part became *Rudra* having five faces, four arms and the colour of a white cloud and the Moon as a crest jewel. As these three *Puras* are in him, he is called *Tripura;*

Pradhānecchā Vashācchambho: *Shareeramabhavattridhā* I
Tatrordhva Bhāga: *Sanjāta*: *Panchavaktrash Chaturbhuja*: II
Padma Kesara Gorānga: *Kāyo Brāhmo Maheshware* I
Tanmadhya Bhāgo Neelānga Ĕkavaktrash Chaturbhujai I
Shankha Chakra Kadā Padma Pāŋi: *Kāya*: *Sa Vaishŋava*: I
*Abhavattadhobhāge Panchavaktrash Chaturbhujai*I
Sphaṭikābhramaya: *Purair Shukla*: *Sa Kāyashchāndrashekhara*: I
Evam Tribhi: *Purair Yogāt Tripura*: *Paramashiva* : II

(iii) **She** is *Śreemathi* (one with wealth), further **She** is *Tripurasundaree* or one with *Śree* (*Lakshmee*) and the consort of the above said *Tripura.*
(iv) **She** is *Chakreshvaree*, the presiding deity of the 3rd hall. 978th name *Tripurāshreevashankaree* may also be referred.

998. *Shree Shivā* - श्री शिवा

(i) One who is the blessed *Śree Shiva.*
(ii) **She** is *Shiva* I with *Śree* (wealth). Since **She** is the sacred consort of *Shiva* and since **She** is an integral part of *Shiva,* **She** got the name as *Shiva.* Hence whatever meaning applicable to *Shiva* is applicable to **Her** also. The verses like; *Yā Te Rudra Shivā Tanooraghorāpā-pakāshinee* in *Śree Rudram* may be refereed.
(iii) 53rd name *Shivā* may also be referred.
(iv) **She** is called as *Nimesha Roopā* in *Mahā Shoḍa Nyāsā* (*Prapancha Nyāsa*).
(v) *Śree Ādi Śaṇkara* in his commentary of *Vişhŋu Sahasranāma* for the 27th name – *Shivā* mentions;

Since he is pure and not influenced by the three qualities, he is called as *Shiva. Nārāyaŋopanishad* advises the integrated form, *Vişhŋu* only is being worshipped as;

Shivā; Nistraiguŋyatayā Shuddhatvāt Shiva : I *"Sa Brahma Sa Shiva :"*
Ityabhedopadeshāt Shivādināmabhi: *Harireva Stooyate* II

999. *Shivashaktyaikyaroopiŋee* - शिवशक्त्यैक्यरूपिणी

(i) One who is the unison of *Shiva* and *Shakti.*
(ii) **She** embodies the union of *Shiva* and *Shakti.*
(iii) **She** is the universal absolute and cannot be considered as individual

Shiva or *Shakti* forms – must be considered in the integrated unison form. Many an example can be given in this regard – light and illumination, word and its meaning, Sun and heat, Moon and coolness, till and oil, match box and fire, etc.;

Bhāvakasyoshnateveyam Bhāskarasyeva Dheedhiti: I
Chandrasya Chandrikeveyam Shiva Sya Sahajā Shivā II
Shivechayā Parāshakti: *Shiva Tatvaikatām Gatā* I
Tata: *Parisphuratyādou Sarge Tailam Tilādiva* II

(iv) Here 'union' means the supreme equality, the being of absolute unity without any differences. The *Saura Samhita* says, "The *Shakti*, which is separate from *Brahmam* is not different from *Brahmam* itself. Such being the case it is only called *Shakti* (as separate) by the ignorant. It is impossible to distinguish the difference, between the *Shakti* and the possessor of *Shakti*";

Brahmaŋobhinna Shaktistu Brahmaiva Khalu Nāparā I
Tathā Sati Vruthā Proktam Shaktirityavivekbhi: II
ShaktiShaktimator Vidvan Bhedābhetastu Durghata: II

(v) In *Vāsishṭa Rāmāyana*, also it is mentioned as, "as there is only one movement of air, only one *oḍyāna Peeṭa* (in the world) and only one manifested *Chitshakti*, also there is only one union (of *Shiva* and *Shakti*);

Yathaikam Pavanaspanda Meka Moushnyāna Lou Yathā I
Chinmātram Spanda Shaktishcha Tathavaikātma Sarvadā II

(vi) We read the same message in *Tripuropanishad* also;

Bhaga: *Shaktir Bhagavān Kāma Esha Ubhā Dātārāviha Soubhagānām* I
Samapradhānou Samasttvour Samotayo: *Samshaktrarājarāvishvayoni*: II

(vii) The commentaries for *Soundaryalaharee* (34th verse) mentions that there are five different characteristics for *Shiva -Shakti*. They are;

a. Equality in worshipping with *chakra*, etc.,– *Atishṭāna Sāmyam* (quality in installation)
b. Equality in tasks like creation, protection, etc., - *Anushtānā Sāmyam* (quality of tasks)
c. Equality in actions like dance, etc., - *Avastāna Sāmyam* (quality of actions)
d. Equality in names like *Shivā-Shiva, Bhairavee-Bhairava*, etc., - *Nāma Sāmyam* (quality of names)
e. Equality in Red colour (this has originated from white), three eyes, crescent Moon, etc., *Roopa Sāmyam* (quality of form)

Shareeram Tvam Shambho: *Shashimihira Vakshoruh Yugam*
Tavātmānam Manye Bhagavati Navātmāna Managham I

Ata: *Shesha*: *Shesheetyayam Ubhayasādhāranatayā*
Sthita: *Sambandho Vām Samarasa Parānanda Parayo*: II

(viii) In *Śree Chakra*, **Her** form is the union of *Shiva Chakra* and *Shakti Chakra*. In *Śree Chakra* the upward four *chakras* are *Shiva Chakras* and downward five *chakras* are *Shakti Chakras*. This has been described in the 11th verse of *Soundaryalaharee* (*Chaturbhi*: *Śreekantai*:.).. The commentary may be referred for further details.

(ix) It can be noted that *Trishatee* describes in details about the formation of *Śree Chakra* and its parts – which are integrated and mingled with each other.

(x) It can also be construed that **She** is in the form of *Hamsa mantra*, which indicates the union of *Shiva -Shakti*, for in this *mantra* is declared that union of *Shiva -Shakti*. This *mantra* has the inner meaning of the *Mahāvākyās*. This has been cryptically indicated in *Soota Samhita*, (IV-7-2) - "*Shakti* of *Shiva* is said to be the end of the syllable *Sā* and end of that *ha*, which is called *Beeja*. The *Beeja* is the *Vidyāshakti*. That itself is *Shiva*. Therefore this supreme *mantra* is said to signify *Shiva* as well as *Shakti*";

Shāntāntam Shaktrasyoktā Tadantam Bheejamuchyate I
VidyāShaktibhavedbheejam Shiva Eva Na Chānyathā II
Tenāyam Paramo Mantra: *Shiva Shakyātmaka*: *Smruta*: II

(xi) The *Viroopāksha Panchāsikā* (verses 27 and 28) says **She** is the collective form of the five *Shaktis* (*Dhoomāvatee* and other 4) of *Shiva*. The list of their names, action, place, etc., goes as below;

Name	**Action**	**Place**
Dhoomāvatee	*Tirodānam* – veiling	Earth
Bhāsvati	Revealing	Fire
Spanda	*Kshopana* - Stimulation	Air
Vibhvee	*Vyāpakam* – pervading	Ether
Hlādā	*Pushṭi* – nourishing	Water

(xii) *Śree Kānchi Kāmakoṭi Paramāchārya*'s talk in this regard is worth noting (The book *Deivathin Kural*, 6th Volume, Pages 690);

Śreevidyā does the role of merging non-duality and duality themselves as non-dual. It says that *Shiva* (who is so peaceful and not known to the second) and *Shakti* (who is the cause of duality) are unified without being able to be split.

(xiii) Before ending this *Sahasranāma* with the name *Lalitāmbikā*, this name *Shivashaktyaikyaroopiṇee*, is a befitting last but one.

1000. ***Lalitāmbikā* – ललिताम्बिका**

(i) One who is a beautiful mother called *Lalitā*.
(ii) This is the end of 1000 names. In some other schools we read more than 1000 names. However in this book we have exactly 1000 names.
(iii) The message of a book has to be decided with 6 characters viz., commencement, conclusion (summing up), explanatory remarks, communicating quiet a new things, practice and strength. In this book, in the first three names, *Vasinee Devee*s tell us that *Śree Devee* does the three tasks of creation, protection and destruction. They themselves say in other names that *Śree Devee* does the other two tasks of complete dissolution and re-creation which are the cause of bondage and salvation. In some other places, the first three tasks are again reiterated. For instance 264 - *Srushṭikartree*, 266 – *Goptree* and 268 – *Samhāriṇee*. After advising the state of *Brahmam* without any qualities and secret of *Śree Chakra*, now they advise what are not available with other gods and what is special of *Śree Devee* and the great name of *Śree Devee*.
(iv) *Parameshwara*, gave the initiation as *Pittā* (Tamil word which means lunatic), for the devotee who wanted to sing prayers on **him**. We read in the *Poorva* (first) part itself that *Śree Devee* ordered *Vasinee Devee*s to sing about **Her**– this can be reminded now. *Śree Devee* ordered *Vasinee Devee*s with the intention of doing good to the devotees and since they
    - Are *Vāg* (speech) *Devee*s,
    - Have great oratory competency with the blessings of *Śree Devee*,
    - Have been appointed by *Śree Devee* to bestow speaking capability to others,
    - Know the secret of the *chakra* of *Śree Devee* and
    - Have passion towards the names, which are in the form of *mantra*s, of *Śree Devee*.

She has cryptically indicated that the above characters should be in this *Sahasranāma*. That is, this *Sahasranāma*, should cover the secret of the *chakra* and other *mantras*. The message is that this should be understandable by those who read with interest and their oratory competency should improve. According to the saying; *Kurudhvam Ankitam Stotram* - it should be the flagship (*ankitam*) verse about *Śree Devee*. Keeping the primary name as the last one is called *ankitam*. *Śree Devee* has countless names, but *Lalitā* is an important one. Hence as a befitting finale, *Vasinee Devee*s have kept this name at the end. Though

She is of the form of *Brahmam*, devotees can easily access **Her** as a mother. As it started with the name *Śreemātā* (mother) at the end also *Vāg Devee*s mention **Her** as *Ambikā* (mother).

(v) This *Sahasranāma* advises *Brahmam*. Hence it is a secret. Each name has many a meaning. There is no duplication of names. There are no meaningless words like *Cha*, *Vai*, etc. All the names begin with one of the 32 blemish-less letters. It includes *mantras*. It mentions about the secret of *Śree Chakra*. It has all the six characters mentioned in 927th name – *Stotrapriya*. On account of all these reasons, those who heard this for the first time in the assembly of *Śree Devee*, they were much surprised.

[The footnote of the book by Śree R Ananda Krişhŋa Sastry in English (page 28) is worth noting here;

"The science showing the potency and virtues of the letters says that the selected 32 letters for the beginning *Sahasranāma* are good and the rejected 19 letters are bad. This indicates according to *Nrsimha*, the author of the *Paribhāshā*, that the compiler of this hymn had great responsibility in selecting auspicious letters for the beginning of the 1000 names of this collection].

(vi) Since **She** is the mother of the entire universe, **She** is *Ambika*. Since **She** is also *Lalitā*, **She** is called as *Lalitāmbika*.

(vii) Since **She** is always playing (in 648th name - *Leelākluptabrahmaŋḍa-maŋḍalā* - it was mentioned that the tasks like creation, etc., are themselves like sports for **Her**), **She** is called as *Lalitā*.

Padma Purāŋa says; *Lokānateetya Lalate Lalitā Tena Sochyate* II – in this context the word *Lokā* indicates rays or presiding deit*i*es. Controlling all of them, *Śree Devee* occupies the place *Bindu* with a unexplainable lustre. Hence the name *Lalita*.

(viii) Any imagination that gives happiness to the mind can be indicated by the word *Lalitām*. Wise men say that these eight constitute *Lalitām* - brightness, origination, sweetness, depth, stability, energy, flattering and magnanimity;

Shobhā Vilāso Madhuryam Gāmbheeryam Sthairya Tejasee I
Lālityam Chatathoudāryamityashṭou Pourushāguŋā: II

(ix) It is so famous in *Kāma Sāstra* that softness and eroticism are *Lalitām*. **She** is great in eroticism and compassion as well.

(x) Since **She** has all these qualities, **She** is called as *Lalita*.

(xi) Further, wise men say, everything depending on **Her** is *Lalitām* and hence this name is very much apt for **Her** – everything with you like nine divine services, sugarcane bow, flowers as arrows, etc., are

Lalitām;

Laliteti Nāma Yuktam Tava Kila Divyā Navāvrutaya: I

Dhanuraikshavamastrānyapi Kusumāni Tathākilam Lalitām II

(xii) In *Shabdārnavam*, it has been mentioned that *Lalitā* means beautiful.

(xiii) According to *Padma Purāŋa*, **She** is the deity worshipped in *Prayāga*.

(xiv) There is a temple for *Lalitā* in Tirumeeyacchoor. In the beginning of this book, the description of the specialties of this book may be referred.

(xv) At the end of this name *'Om'* has to be pronounced.

Thus ends the eleventh *Kalā* called *Dhāriŋee*.

Thus chanting all the 1000 names again the *Shadanga* (six organs) *nyāsa*, chanting of meditation verse and *Pancha-pooja* (five-poojas) are to be done. Then this chanting itself has to be dedicated to *Śree Devee*. Then it has to be prayed to get the fruits of this *mantra*. There ends the 182½ verses as chant by *Vasinee* and other *Vāg Devees*.

Thus ends the second chapter of *Brahmānḍa Purāŋa* in the form of dialogue between *Śree Hayagreeva* and sage *Agasthya*.

*****

Śree Lalitā Sahasranāma

***Uttara Bhāga* (End part)**

***Phalaśruti* (The fruits)**

Section 12: *Kshamā Kalā*

The results that can be obtained or results of chanting this *Sahasranāma* are described in the below verses.

1. *Ityetannāmasāhasram Khathitam Te Ghaṭodbhava* I

(i) Thus this *Sahasranāma* was told to you Oh *Agastya*!

(ii) This sentence if read in conjunction with what *Śree Hayagreeva* said "I told you as told by *Vāgdevees*" in the previous chapter. The word *Nāmasāhasram* is repeated many a time - this repetition reiterates that this hymn has exactly 1000 names, not even one more or less.

2. *Rahasyānām Rahasyam Cha Lalitāpreetidāyakam* I
***Anena Sadrusham Stotram Na Bhootam Na Bhavishyati* II**

(i) These 1000 names are secret of the secrets and are very dear to *Śree Lalitā Devee*. Hence this type of hymn has never existed in the past or neither will exist in the future.

(ii) The following verses describe some of the specialties of this hymn. In the same way various benefits of chanting this are also explained.

(iii) Since this has to be read only with *Nyāsa*, *japa*, etc. and also since it contains the meanings of lot of *mantras*, it has to be treated as most secret.

(iv) Two special characters viz., secret and most dear to *Śree Devee* are mentioned in this verse. These will be reiterated in the following verses again and again.

3. *Sarvarogaprashamanam Sarvasampatpravardhanam* I
***Sarvāpamrutyushamanam Kālamrutyunivāranam* II**

(i) This cures all diseases and helps in creating all types of wealth. It prevents all accidental deaths and is an antidote to untimely death.

(ii) To start with it cures all the diseases resulting in a healthy life. Poverty is also considered as a disease and it removes it by bestowing all wealth.

(iii) The word *Apamrutyu* means untimely death due to accident, snake bite, forest animals, etc. One result is, this avoids such deaths. *Kālamrutyu* indicates the whole life defined for a person. That is, it gives long life. How can this be mentioned as *Kālamrutyu nivāranam*? Who can prevent the death at the end of the life? Prevention of death does not mean to evade death. The 100 years lifetime mentioned in *Vedas* is called long life and death at the end of it is indicated as *Kālamrutyu*. Further according to *Vedāntas* death is for the body and not for the soul. Death after living a complete life and not undergoing rebirth, etc., can be considered as *kālamrutyunivāranam* (protecting from regular death also).

(iv) *Śree* G.V.*Gaŋesaiyer* explains the words *apamrutyu* and *kālamrutyu* in an interesting manner as below. If a lamp having oil and wicket is puts off itself, it is equivalent to *kālamrutyu*. If the same lamp is put off by wind even when it has adequate oil and wicket, then it can be equated to *apamrutyu*.

(v) The word *sarva* appears in the first three parts of this verse. It is considered with the meaning 'all'. The same can be considered to 'mean to all' or 'belonging to all'. This is also an apt meaning only. That is, it implies - all diseases or diseases of all.

4. *Sarva Jwarārtishamanam Deergāyushyapradayakam* I
***Putrapradamaputrānām Purushārthapradayakam* II**

(i) It is a cure for the sufferings from all types of fever. It gives rise to long life. It bestows the issueless with child. *Purushārtham* – that is, it gives the salvation, which is greatest need among all.

(ii) In the previous verse it was mentioned as all types of diseases. Now the fever is se*para*tely mentioned. This implies that fever is a special type or an important disease. Further since there are many types of fevers, it has to be mentioned as all fevers.

(iii) Not only is this – later in the 24th verse, the chanting method of this *Sahasranāma*, for getting rid of a fever is again described. In that verse, the word *jwarārtthi*, which indicates all sufferings like headache, etc., on account fever is separately mentioned.

(iv) Long life mentioned here is 100 years as mentioned in *Vedas*. Chanting of this *Sahasranāma* will bestow long life. If that has to be given, isn't that the obstructing diseases have to be wiped off?

(v) Since long life does not specifically mention any number, it can further extend beyond 100 years as a result of this *Sahasranāma*.

(vi) Those who chant without any specific expectation or wish will get the salvation. This has been reiterated in all hymns describing worshipping of *Śree Devee* – this stresses that only in the last birth, one will get interest in worshipping *Śree Devee*.

5. ***Idham Visheshāchreedevya*: *Stotram Preetividhayakam* I**
***JapenNityam Prāyatnena Lalitopāstitatpara*: II**

(i) This special prayer of *Śree Devee* has to be chant by the devotees with full focus, concentration and interest and with an aim to please **Her**, after worshipping **Her**.
(ii) The word *Visheshāt* mentioned in this verse indicates some of the special characteristics of this hymn. Especially giving great fruits is its one specialty. That too, *Śree Ādi Śaṇkara* mentions two characters; *Sakalapurushārttha Sādhanam Sukhasampādyam, Alpaprayāsam* – with least effort most benefit is reaped.
(iii) *Lalitāpreetividhāyakam* – the hymn which gives limitless enjoyment to *Śree Devee*. Earlier in 2nd verse it was mentioned as *Lalitāpreetidhāyakam*. Further again this will be stressed.
(iv) It is often indicated that the happiness got by *Śree Devee*, from this *Sahasranāma* is not got by her from any other hymn or worship.
(v) According to *Karma Kāṇḍa*, depending on the strength of the actions the results will also vary. *Meemāmsā* argues that there are variations even in heaven. There are no such partialities/ variations in this *Sahasranāma*. It is the most befitting character "very less effort leading to maximum result".
(vi) If the statement that "if the effort is more than the result will also be proportionately higher" is considered to be true, then more effort than chanting of this *Sahasranāmā* may lead to higher fruits. The specialty of this verse is that it says "that is not the case".

6. ***Prāta*: *Snatwā Vidhānena Sandhyakarma Samāpya Cha* I**
***Poojāgruham Tato Gatvā Chakrarājam Samarchayet* II**

(i) After taking bath in the morning, finishing the oblations like *Sandhyāvandanam*, etc., according to the individual's tradition, the prayer room has to be entered and worship to the *Śree Chakra* has to be done first.
(ii) The summary is bathing and *Sandhyāvandanam* have to be done according to tradition/ practice (*vidhānena*). For the tri-castes two

Sandhyāvandanams are prescribed – *Vaidheeka* and *Tāntreeka*. For others only the latter.

(iii) Entering the prayer room is one of the actions part of worshipping *Śree Chakra*. *Samarchayet* – i.e. *Samyak* + *Archayet* – *Archana* has to be done in a proper way. It is also acceptable, if it is done by others, but only when it is not possible by self.

7. ***Vidyām Japetsahasram Vā Trishatam Shatameva Vā* I**
***Rahasya Nāmasāhasramidam Paschchāt Patennarai* I I**

(i) *Śree Devee's mantra* has to be chant 1000 or 300 or 100 times and then this *Sahasranāma* should be read.

(ii) The word *Vidyām* means *mantra* - that is, *Panchadashee* or *Shoḍashee mantra*.

(iii) Whether it is 1000 or 300 or 100 times, 8 times have to be added in chanting.

(iv) The word *Pashchāt* means 'later'. That is after chanting this hymn and before offering flowers – that is to be done in between these two. This rule is applicable only when all these three are done - chanting of *mantra*, reading this hymn and offering of flowers. If only the reading of this hymn is done, it is not applicable.

8. ***Janmamadhye Sakruchchāpi Ya Yetatpaṭhathesooudhee*: I**
***Tasya Puŋyaphalam Vakshye Srunutvam Kumbhasambhava* II**

(i) Oh, sage *Agastya*! Please hear the results of reading this hymn in the middle of his life even once by devotees.

(ii) *Śree Hayagreevā* insists to hear in an attentive manner, since if these are going to be results for reading once in the life time, what would be results for regular reader of this hymn.

9. ***Gangādisarvateertheshu Ya*: *Snāyātkoṭijanmasu* I**
***Koṭi Lingapratishtām Cha Ya*: *Kuryādh Avimuktake* II**

10. ***Kurukshethre Tu Yo Dadhyātkoṭivāram Ravigrahe* I**
***Koṭim Sournabhārānām Srotreyeshu Dwijanmasu* II**

11. ***Ya:Koṭim Hayamedhānām Āharedgāngarodhase* I**
***Ācharethkoopa Koṭiryo Nirjale Marubhootale* II**

12. ***Durbhikshe Ya*: *Pratidinam Koṭibrāhmanabhojanam* I**
***SraddhayāParaya Kuryāt Sahasraparivatsarān* II**

13. ***Thatpuŋyam Koṭiguŋitam Labhetpuŋya Manuthamam* I**

***Rahasya Nāma Sāhasre Nāmnāpyekasya Keerthanāth* II**

(i) If a devotee chants even one name out of these 1000, he gets crore times the benefits of doing all the actions mentioned below:
  a. Taking bath in sacred rivers like Ganges and others for one crore births
  b. Consecrating one crore *Shivalingas* in Benaras, which is called as *Avimukta* place.
  c. Giving one crore *bhāra* (a weighing measure – detailed below) of gold ornaments to Brahmins who have learnt *Vedas*, one crore times in *Kurukshetra*, during solar eclipse
  d. Performing one crore *Ashwamedha* sacrifices in the shores of the Ganges.
  e. Digging one crore wells with water in the deserts.
  f. Feeding one crore Brahmins daily during the time of famine.

(ii) Since it is mentioned as Ganges and other (all) holy waters, it includes all holy lakes/ tanks also. Again since it was mentioned as Ganges and other rivers, it includes all the holy rivers in all the three worlds.

(iii) The result of taking bath in the holy rivers daily in one crore births.

(iv) *Avimuktam* is another name for Banares. It has been mentioned that in Banares, there are four holy places viz., Kāsi, Vāranāsi, *Avimuktam* and *Antargruham* inside one another like five sheaths. Among these *Antargruham* is the most holy, innermost and sacred place. This is really the body of *Paramashiva.*

(v) The word *Avi* means sins. *Linga purāŋa* says that since the sins are removed and *Paramashiva* himself dwells there, that place is called *Avimuktam*. By inserting the letter *ka* we get *Avimuktakam*. This word indicates unidentified *Antargruham*. Hence it refers the most holy virtual *mānastalam*.

(vi) *Kurukshetra* is the place where the *Mahābhāratā* battle did happen. This is also indicated as place of *Dharma* (righteousness). Hence the results of the action of given away things is much more than the same action in other places.

(vii) The virtue that is got by the giver is equal to the sin got by the receiver. Hence he has to do adequate expiation to remove the sin. But, it has been mentioned that if he receives anything in *Kurukshetra*, there is no expiation for this and hence the giver gets limitless virtue.

(viii) Cows, earth and the knowledge are said to be the great things that can be given away. These three can be attained through gold and hence giving away gold is said to be the greatest one.

(ix) Here is the calculation for one *bhārā* (of gold mentioned above) – 100 *palam* equal 1 *tulām* and 20 *tulāms* equal one *bhāra*. That is one *bhārā* equal 2000 *palams* (approximately equal to 70 kilograms).

(x) It has been mentioned that we have to give away to *srotrias*. *Brahmavaivartta Purāṇa* defines *srotria* with three characteristics viz., birth, *Upanayanam* (the sacred thread is first worn) and knowledge.

(xi) *Ashwamedha* sacrifice is said to be the greatest of all sacrifices. It removes the sins in Toto. The virtue got by performing one crore *Ashwamedha* sacrifices in the banks of river Ganges with great *purohits* is mentioned here.

(xii) The gist of this verse is that by just chanting one name out of 1000, a devotee gets one crore times the results of all the above summed up.

(xiii) Repeatedly mentioning the numbers crore, thousand etc., is just to indicate that it is infinite or countless.

14. *Rahasyanāmasāhasre Nāmaikamapi Ya*: *Patet* I
***Tasya Pāpāni Nashyanti Mahāntyapi Na Samshaya*: II**

(i) Even if one among the thousand secret names is chant, all the sins committed by the devotee would be destroyed – there is no doubt about it.

(ii) The earlier verses talked about the virtues and this verse talks about destruction of sins.

(iii) By the word *Mahāntyapi*, even very great sins are indicated. In that case, is there no need to separately talk about ordinary sins.

15. *Nityakarmānushṭāna Nishiddhakaraṇādhapi* I
***Yatpāpam Jāyate Pumsām Tatsarvam Nashyatidhruvam* II**

(i) The sins caused by the very bad act of not doing the ordained daily sacred routines and the sins caused by doing objected actions, would go away and all the sins would be destroyed speedily.

(ii) If the ordained actions are not done at the appropriate time sins will accrue. This depends on the race/ caste one follows.

(iii) The daily routines will also include the special occasions like New Moon Day, the eclipse time, etc.

(Iv) By the word *druvam*, it has been indicated that no other expiation is needed. Just chanting of one name will do.

(v) In addition to these two types of sins, there is a third type – non-control of organs. This is the root cause of the other two types and hence not been mentioned explicitly.

16. *Bahunātrakimuktena Srunutvam Kumbhasambhava* I

(i) Why talk too much? Oh *Agastya*! Hear what I say.

Ātraika Namno YāShakti: *Pātakānām Nivarttane* I
Tannivartyam Agam Kartum Nālam Lokachchadurdasha II

(ii) The capability of removing the sins by chanting one name from this hymn is that much –that as many sins cannot be done by fourteen worlds.

(iii) All the living beings in all the fourteen worlds cannot do as many sins, which cannot be removed by the single name from this hymn.

17. *Yastyaktvā Nāmasāhasram Pāpahānimabheepsati* I
***Sa Hi Sheetanivrtyarttam Himashailam Nishevate* II**

(i) If a person is desirous of getting rid of the sins, but hates to chant this hymn, it is like going to Himalayas to avoid cold.

(ii) If a worshipper of *Śreevidyā*, does not reach to *nāmasangeertanam* for expiation but tries some other methods, he gets one more sin. That is, with any other expiation methods, the sins cannot be got destroyed.

18. *Bhakto Ya*: *Keertyan Nityam Idam Nāmasāhasrakam* I
***Tasmai Śree Lalitā Devee Preetābheeshtam Prāyachati* II**

(i) Devotees, who sing these thousand names daily, would be blessed and their wishes fulfilled by very much pleased *Śree Devee*.

(ii) That is the reason it was earlier mentioned as *Śreedevyā*: *Preeti Vidāyakam*. That is the chanting of this hymn has to be done by the devotees on a daily basis. Chanting of the complete hymn has to be done till the life time. It has been mentioned that this has to be added to the daily chore of actions like early morning bath, etc.

(iii) Since it has been repeatedly mentioned as *Nāmasāhasrakam*, it implies the entire 1000 names in Toto. The word *Nityam* indicates daily as well as till the life time.

19. *Akeertayennidam Stotram Kathambhakto Bhavishyati* I

(i) How can one become a devotee without chanting this hymn? The implied meaning is that he cannot.

(ii) For a worshipping devotee, only the happiness of the presiding deity is important. Since that happiness is reached by chanting of this hymn, it becomes important for him.

(iii) In *Śreemad Bhagavad Geeta*, *Śree Krişhŋa* says that there are four types of devotees - *"Ārtto Jignāsu*: *Arttārttee Gnānee"*.

Ārtto is – one who is suffering from sorrows on account of sinful actions.

Jignāsu: is – one who wants to get knowledge. Since he does not have any interest in anything he gets his mind purified by chanting this *Sahasranāmā* and gets knowledge.

Arttārttee is - one who likes things. The chanting of this hymn is capable of giving more things and happiness than what is sought for.

Gnānee is – one who has reached the knowledge of *Brahmam*. He does devotion and chanting of this hymn just to show this world.

In all these four types, chanting of this hymn is necessary for the devotees.

20. *Nityam Sankeerttanāshakta*: *Keerttayet Puŋyavāsare* I
***Sankrantou Vishuvechaiva Svajanmatritaye Ayane* II**
***Navamyām Vā Chaturdashyam Sitāyām Sukravāsare* II**

(i) People who cannot sing it daily should chant it on the special occasions, viz., first day of every month, first of the New Year and the three birthdays, on ninth and/ or on fourteenth days or Fridays of the waxing moon and on the full Moon day - singing this hymn is very special.

(ii) Special days include *Arddhodayam*, *Mahodayam* and the below detailed days.

(iii) *Vishnu* means the first day of the months *Chaitra* and *Tula*.

(iv) Three birth days include self, spouse's and son's.

Or the three days - self birth day, the initiation day and the day of *poorŋābhishekam*.

Or the three days - self birth day, the previous and the next days.

Or the three days - self birth day, the 10th and the 19th stars (*janmānujanmam*).

(v) *Ayane* means the first day of the *Kataka* and *Mukura* months.

(vi) It can be construed that the word *Navamyām Vā* (ninth day) includes the eight day also.

21. *Keertyen Nāmasāhasram Pourŋamāsyām Viseshata*:

(i) The chanting of this hymn has to be done especially on the full Moon days.

(ii) If the days, stars, etc., mentioned so far fall on the same day, it is enough if the chanting is done once.

22. *Pourŋamāsyām Chandrabhimbhe Dyatvā Śree Lalitāmbikām* I
***Panchopacharai*: *Sampoojya Paṭhennāma Sahasrakam* II**

(i) On the full Moon day, one should meditate by imagining *Śree Devee* on the full Moon, after offering the five oblations and these thousand names should be read.

(ii) The night of the full Moon day is the last night of bright fortnight of the Moon. This has to be chant in the night only when the full Moon *thithi* spans at that time.

(iii) On the full Moon day, *Śree Devee* has to be imagined on the full Moon. All the fifteen *thithi nityā Devees* and the sixteenth *kalā* called *Sādā* also shine in the form of full Moon. The evidence for this is the 240th name *Chandramaŋḑalamadhyaga*.

(iv) *Śree Vişhŋu* and *Śree Shiva* are always present in *Sāligrāma* and *Bhānā* respectively. Hence no need of establishing them through *Āvāhana* (deifying), *Prāŋa Prathishtā*, etc., in those idols. In the same manner, *Śree Devee* is always there in the form of a Moon and hence no need of *Āvāhana* (deifying) and related *mudrās* (signs of hand).

(v) Since it has mentioned as *Dyatvā*, *Śree Devee* has to be imagined as mentioned in meditation verses.

(vi) The five oblations are – the offerings of sandal, flower, fragrant smoke, light and food.

(vii) The word *Sampoojya* stresses the integrated feeling of non-duality between self and *Śree Devee*.

23. *Sarve Rogā*: *Pranashyanti Deergāyushchchavindati* I
***Ayamāyushkaro Nāma Prayoga*: *Kalpachodita*: II**

(i) Such usage will make all the diseases vanish. It gives long life. That is the reason this usage has been mentioned as *Āyushkāra* (rite to get long life) in the *kalpa Sūtras*.

(ii) The usage *Pranashyanti*, instead of *Nashyanti*, stresses that no disease will affect (not about getting cured).
(iii) The word *Deergāyul* indicates that both type of deaths *Apamrutyu* and *Kālamrutyu* will not happen.
(iv) The word *cha* indicates that in addition good things also will happen.
(v) The word *Kalpanodita*: indicates that *Parasurama Kalpasūtra*. But there is no such usage in *Parasurama Kalpasūtra*. But it is said that it has been subtly indicated. It can be construed as that this has been mentioned in some other *kalpasūtras*.
(vi) This and other usages detailed in the following verses can be done only by those who do their daily chores regularly. It can be for self or for others. The method of this usage has been detailed in the original commentary book.

24. ***Jwarārttam Shirasi Sprushtvā Patennāma Sahasrakam* I**
***Tatkshnāth Prashamam Yāti Shirastodo Jvaropi Cha* II**

(i) If one has fever, if the other person touches his head and chants this hymn names, the fever and the consequent headache would descend away immediately.
(ii) This usage is also explained in detail. The first part of this hymn has to be read, the 1000 names has to be read with a hand on the diseased person and again after removing the hand this last part has to be read.
(iii) If a person is attacked with fever, he himself can also chant this hymn by having his own hand on his head. Any number of times this can be chant, till the fever is cured.

25. ***Sarvavyādhi Nivrutyartham Sprushtvā Bhasma Japedidam* I**
***Tadbhasmadhāranādeva Nashyanti Vyādhaya: Kshanāt* II**

(i) For getting rid of all diseases this has to be chant by touching the holy ash. And by smearing that ash on the body all diseases would immediately be cured.

26. ***Jalam Samantrya Kumbhastham Nāmasahasrathomune* I**
***Abhishinched Grahagrastān Grahā Nashyanti Tatkshanāt* II**

(i) Oh *Agastya*! Storing the water in a pot and chanting this hymn and anointing the person affected by any planet with that water would remove all problems created by planets.

(ii) The word planets imply the planets that are in affecting positions, the sinful planets and evil beings.

27. ***Sudhāsāgaramadhyastham Dhyatva Śreelalitāmbikām* I**
***Ya: Patennāmasāhasram Visham Tasya Vinashyati* II**

(i) Meditating on *Śree Devee* as **She** is in the ocean of nectar and chanting this hymn will remove any effect of poison.

(ii) 61st name *Sudhāsāgaramadhyasthā* may be referred.

28. ***Vandhyānām Putralābhāya Nāmasāhasramantritam* I**
***Navaneetham Pradadhyattu Puthralābho Bhaveddhruvam* II**

(i) For blessing with a male issue, for those who do not have, chant this hymn and make them eat the butter offered *Śree Devee*. By this they will be blessed with a son soon.

(ii) The word *Vandhyā* indicates four types of issueless ladies – one who has not conceived at all, one who got a baby and it has died, one who has got only girl children and one who has got a single child. All these type of ladies will get the baby of their choice.

(iii) *Putralābhāya* means not necessarily male child, but any child.

(iv) If the issueless lady herself is a worshipper, she can do this usage for herself.

(v) The word *dhruvam* stresses that it is definite to have a child.

29. ***Devyā: Pāshena Sambaddhāmākrushtāmangushena Cha* I**
***Dhyātvābheeshtām Striyam Ratrou Japennāmasahasrakam* II**

30. ***Āyāti Svasameepam Sā Yadhyapyanta:puram Gatā* I**

(i) If a worshipper chants this hymn in the night with a lady of his liking, as binding with a noose and attracted by a goad, then she will come near him, even she is in the queen's wing of a palace.

(ii) The queen's wing, in a palace, is a secluded place, where men are not allowed. Even if the lady is in that place, by the attraction of this hymn, she will come out and reach the worshipper.

31. ***Rajākarshana Kāmaschedrājā Vasathadingmukha:* I**
***Triratram Ya: PatedetachchreeDevee Dhyāna Tatpara:* II**

32. ***Sa Rājā Pāravashyena Turangam Vā Matangajam* I**

***Āruhyāth Nikatam Dāsavat Prānipatyacha* I**
***Tasmai Rājyam Cha Koshamcha Dadyādeva Vasam Gata*: II**

(i) If a worshipper wants to attract a king, he can face the palace of the king and chant this hymn for three days, meditating on *Śree Devee*. Definitely then the king would be under the control of the worshipper. He would ride a horse or elephant, come near the worshipper and would salute and serve him as a slave. He would even offer his country or a state of his country or a treasure.

(ii) *Rājāvasathadingmukha*: - the direction in which the king resides from the dwelling place of the worshipper.

(iii) *Trirātram* – to be chant for three nights and days continuously. There is no limit on number of times.

33. ***Rahasyanāma Sāhasram Ya*: *Keertayati Nityasha*: I**
***Tan Mukhāloka Matrena Muhyellokatrāyam Mune* II**

(i) Oh sage! The three worlds immediately faint, as soon as the face of a person, who chants this secret hymn daily, is seen.

(ii) It need not be the aim of the worshipper that all the worlds be attracted to him. Even then, if he is regularly chanting this hymn, this fruit will automatically be reaped.

34. ***Yastvidam Nāmasāhasram Sakrutpatati Bhaktimān* I**
***Tasya Ya Shatrava*: *Theshām Nihantā Sharabheshwara*: II**

(i) The enemies of the devotee, who reads this hymn once, would be killed by arrows by *Sharabheshwarar*.

(ii) *Sakrut* means once. The word *Nityacha*: mentioned in the previous verse should be read with this and has to be considered as once daily.

(iii) *Sharabheshwarar* is one of the incarnations of *Shiva*. *Linga Purāŋa*, *Kālikā Purāŋa*, etc., say that when *Śree Vişhŋu* took the incarnation of *Narasimha* and killed the demon *Hiranyakasipu*. Even after this his anger did not subside and he was about to destroy the entire world. At that time *Shiva* took the incarnation of *Sharabheshwarar* and controlled *Narasimha*. *Narasimha* is a combined form of man and lion. In the same manner *Sharabheshwarar* is a combined form of man, lion and a bird.

(IV) *Āmnāya* worship is a part at the end of *Śreechakra nāvāvarŋa* worship. In general it is a practice that this is done in a group in an abridged form with all the *mantras* in it. For those who are initiated with *Panchadashee mantra*, four *Āmnāya* worships and for those who are initiated with complete *Shoḍashee* worship, six *Āmnāya* worships are prescribed. Four for the four directions – East, South, West and North. In addition above and below are two more. It can be said that there is no *mantra* or deity, which is not there in these *Āmnāyās*. In the *Āvarŋa Pooja* itself, all the dei*ti*es happen to be worshiped with their respective *mantra*s. That is the reason it has been mentioned that *Sharabha* kills the enemies of those who chant this hymn. The devotee does not worship *Sharabheshwarar* directly. Further it has been mentioned that some more dei*ti*es themselves do what is needed for the devotees who chant this hymn.

(v) The *mantra*s of *Sharabheshwarar* mentioned here occur as a group of *mantras* for the 8th deity in the South *Āmnāya*. There are two *mantra*s – one indicating *Sharabhar* and the other indicating *Sharabhasālva*, a king of birds. Both these dei*ti*es are for usage of highly vehement *mantras* and for saving from such *mantras* also. These two *mantra*s have high vigor. Even a person who do not chant these *mantras*, but just chant this hymn, will get the results of those *mantras*.

35. *Ye Vābhichāram Kurute Nāmasāhasrapatake* I
***Nivartya Tatkriyām Hanyat Tamvai Pratyangirasvayam* II**

(i) He who does black magic against the person, who reads this hymn, would automatically be killed by *Pratyangira Devee* herself for protecting the devotee, by returning the black magic to the person, who used it.

(ii) Black magic is one, for which the source cannot be identified, but does a lot of hardship on the person, whom it was aimed at – including death - witchcraft, conjuring, sorcery, an elf, imp, etc., are forms of black magic.

(iii) If anybody tries black magic on a devotee of *Śree Devee*, *Pratyangira Devee* will return it on the person who originated and will even kill him.

(iv) *Pratyangira Devee* is *Kālee* herself. As mentioned earlier, the *mantra*s of *Pratyangira Devee* occur as a group of *mantras* for the 12th deity in the East *Āmnāya*. According to what is said in this *Āmnāya*, there are five dei*ti*es – *Brāhmee, Nārāyaŋee, Roudhree, Ugrakrutyā* and *Atharvabadrakālee*. We read as in these *mantras* themselves as;

Pratyakkarttāram Ruchchtu – will destroy who originates it.

(v) This *Atharvaṇabadrakālee Pratyangira Devee* has a rude (fearful) form and the deity is strong and fervent. There are 32 *mantras* in the *Sounaka* branch of *Atarva Veda* and 48 *mantras* in the *Pippalāta* branch about this *Devee*. The usage of these *mantras* has been described in *Nārada Tantra*.

(vi) *Pratyangira Devee* and *Shoolinee* are the consorts of *Sharabheshwarar* mentioned earlier.

36. ***Yo Krooradhrushtyā Veekshyante Nāmasāhasrapatakam* I**
***Tān Andhān Kurute Kshipram Svayam Mārtandabhairava*: II**

(i) He, who sees, with cruelty, the one who reads these thousand names, would be made blind, immediately by *Mārtanḍa Bhairava* himself.

(ii) This was mentioned in the 785th name *Mārtānḍa Bhairavārādhya*.

(iii) The name *Mārtanḍa Bhairava* indicates the Sun. The Sun rays have the capacity of giving or taking away the eye-sight. If Sun is worshipped with devotion, eye-sight will improve. On the other hand, if anybody sees the Sun directly his sight will be affected.

(iv) A deity called, *Mārtanḍa Veerabhairava*, has been mentioned as one among the 10 *Veerabhairavas* in the West *Āmnāya*.

37. ***Dhanam Yo Harate Chorai*: *Namasāhasra Jāpina*: I**
***Yatra Kutra Stitam Vāpi Kshetrapālo Nihanti Tām* II**

(i) He, who tries to steal the wealth of the devotee, who reads these thousand names, through thieves, would be killed by *Kshetra Pālā*, wherever he is.

(ii) It has to be noted that it is not been mentioned as "one who steals", but it has been mentioned as "one who steals through thieves".

(iii) *Kshetra Pālā* is a form of *Shiva* only. The details may be seen in the commentary for 345th name – *Kshetrapālasamarchita*.

38. ***Viddhyasu Kurute Vādam Yovidvān Nāmajāpeena*: I**
***Tasyavāk Stambhanam Sadhya*: *Karoti Nakuleshwaree* II**

(i) He who argues with the learned man, who reads these thousand names, would be made dumb immediately by *Nakuleshwaree*.

(ii) *Nakuleshwaree* is one of the organ deit*ies* of *Shyāmalā*, the minister of *Śree Devee*. She is in-charge of speech. Hence she makes the person dumb or causes speech obstructions. Her *mantra* is available in *Parasurāma Kalpasūtra*. **She**, who is one of the army deit*i*es of *Śree Devee*, is being worshipped in the *Navāvarŋa Pooja*.

39. ***Yo rāja kurute vairam nāma sāhasra japina*: I**
***Chaturanga balam tasya ḍanḍinee samharet svayam* II**

(i) The four armies (chariots, elephant, horse and human) of the king, who shows enmity on the devotee, who chants this hymn, would be immediately destroyed by *Ḍanḍinee Devee* herself.
(ii) *Ḍanḍinee Devee* is commander-in-chief of *Śree Devee*. She heads the army in the battle between *Śree Devee* and the demons. She herself fights with the enemy of the devotee of *Śree Devee* and kills him.
(iii) *Ḍanḍinee Devee* is *Vārāhee* only. She is also worshipped in the *Navāvarŋa Pooja* alongwith other the army deit*i*es of *Śree Devee*.
(iv) By the word *samharet* – hostility, cursing and killing are indicated.

40. ***Ya Paten Nāma Sāhasram Shanmāsam Bhaktisamyuta*: I**
***Lakshmee*: *Chānchalya Rahita Sadathishtati Tadgruhe* II**

(i) He, who reads these thousand names daily for six months with devotion, will have *Lakshmee*, the Goddess of wealth, live in his house permanently.
(ii) It has been mentioned everywhere that *Lakshmee* or wealth is fickle minded and never stays continuously in one place. She herself stays permanently in house of the devotee who chants this hymn daily for six months.

41. ***Māsamekam Pratidinam Trivāramya*: *Paten Nara*: I**
***Bharathee Tasya Jihvāgre Range Nrutyati Nithyasha*: II**

(i) He, who reads it daily three times for a month, will have *Saraswatee*, the goddess of knowledge, always dancing on the tip of his tongue.
(ii) *Rangam* means the dancing platform. *Saraswatee Devee* will be dancing with his tongue as the platform.

42. ***Yastvekavāram Patati Pakshmātram Atandrita*: I**
***Muhyanti Kāmavashagā Mrugāshyastasya Veekshanāt* II**

(i) If a devotee chants this hymn at least once in a day, without feeling lazy, for a fortnight, he will have ladies attracted and gets erotic towards him just by his sight.

(ii) *Atandrita*: means one who is without laziness, tiredness or sleep. This indicates that this usage has to be done in the night.

(iii) So far the results like succeeding the enemies, getting back the lost things, attracting ladies, knowledge, etc., were discussed. Further the results like righteousness, etc., are being discussed.

43. *Ya Paten Nāmasāharamjanmamadhye Sakrunnera*: I
***Thaddhrushtigocharā*: *Sarve Muchyanthe Sarvakil Bishai*: II**

(i) If a person reads these thousand names at least once, in the middle of his life, whoever is sighted by him would be pardoned of all the sins.

(ii) The word *Thaddhrushṭigocharā*: indicates – whoever is seen by him, all their sins would be pardoned off. Since it is mentioned as *Sarve* – this not only means human being, but all living beings.

(iii) So far it was mentioned as entire life time, six months, one month, one fortnight and that too daily once, three times, unlimited times continuously, etc., were mentioned. Now it is mentioned even if it is once in a life time, so much results will reaped.

44. *Yo Vetti Nāmasāhāsram Tasmai Dheyam Dvijanmane* I
***Annam Vasthram Dhanam Dhanyam Nānyebhyastu Kadāchana*II**

(i) The Brahmin, who has completely understood this hymn, should be given food, clothes, wealth, cereals and all that he wishes and definitely not others.

(ii) The capacity of the receiver is very important when anything is given. One of the must qualities of the receiver is the knowledge of this hymn.

(iii) A Brahmin gets the quality of receiving anything by chanting this hymn.

45. *Śreemantrarājam Yovetthi Śreechakram Ya*: *Samarchati* I
***Ya*: *Keertayati Nāmāni Tam Satpātram Vidu*: *Budha* II**

(i) He who has learned *Śreevidyā*, one who does worship to *Śreechakra* and one who chants these thousand names, would be considered as holy by the learned.

(ii) *Mantrarājam* means *Śreevidyā mantra*.

(iii) For a person to be considered as *Satpātram* (holy) three qualities have been mentioned *Śreevidyā*, worshipping *Śreechakra* and chanting this hymn. Such a Brahmin is great and holy. In these, if the first two are individually or both together are known then it is the next stage. One who chants this hymn is still in a higher stage than the other two. It is normally not possible to have one such person. Because one do not get a right to learn this hymn without *Śreevidyā mantra*. That is the reason all the three specialties are mentioned together.

46. *Tasmai Deyam Prāyatnena Śree Devee Preetimichatā* I

(i) A devotee, who likes to the blessings of *Śree Devee*, should take effort to search for such an eligible Brahmin and give him anything.

47. *Na Keertayati Nāmāni Mantrarājam Na Vetti Ya*: I
***Pashutulya*: *Sa Vijneya*: *Tasmai dattam Nirarthakam* II**

(i) One who does not chant this hymn or one who does not know *Śreevidyā* is equal to an animal. Nothing should be given to such a Brahmin.

(ii) Though only two qualities are mentioned here, all the three qualities mentioned earlier are to be considered.

(iii) *Nirarthakam* means useless. That is, since it was earlier mentioned that the result of such a giving is for satisfying *Śree Devee*, **She** does not get satisfied with this.

(iv) Since *sāstras* say; *Vidhyāviheena*: *Pashu*: - he has to be considered as an animal;

Pareekshya Viddhyā Vidhushastebhyo Daddhyādvichakshana: I

(v) Hence anything has to be given only to those who have knowledge and that too after proper evaluation.

(vi) To properly evaluate and choose the holy man to give anything is the duty of the giver.

(vii) Once who has the capacity to evaluate and choose the holy man has been mentioned as *Vichakshaṇa*:.

48. *Śreemantrarāja Sadrusho Yatha Mantro Na Vidhyate* II

49. *Devatha Lalitātulyā Yathā Nāsti Ghaṭodhbhava* I
***Rahasya Nāma Sāhasratulyā Nāsti Tatha Stuti*: II**

(i) There is no other *mantra* equal to *Śreevidya*.
(ii) *Śreevidyā mantra, Śree Devee* and this hymn are the three very great things and nothing else equal or higher or even com*para*ble exists.
(iii) *Śreevidyā* means *Panchadashee* or *Shoḍashee*.
(iv) In this verse again *Agastya* has been addressed as *Ghaṭodhbhava* or born out of a pot.

50. ***Likhitvā Pustake Vasthu Nāmasāhasra Muthamam* I**
***Samarchayedsada Bhaktya Tasya Tushyati Sundaree* II**

(i) He who writes this great hymn in a book and worships it with devotion, *Śree Devee* becomes very much satisfied with him.
(ii) As it is indicated as "one who" – it may be a worshipper or otherwise – whoever it is. If he is a worshipper he has the qualification and duty to chant and this type worshipping the book is not a must for him. It has been mentioned earlier that chanting of this hymn is a daily chore for him.
(iii) It is enough if he worships the book, if he is not initiated with the *mantras*. Even then *Śree Devee* is much pleased.
(iv) The word *Sundaree* is the short form of *Śreelalitā Mahātripurasundaree*.
(v) The word *sadā* indicates always;

Bahunātra Kimuktena Shrunutvam Kumbhasambhava I

(vi) Why to tell again and again? Oh Agastya! Hear what I say.
(vii) This statement has been mentioned in the 15.5th verse also.

51. ***Nānena Sadrusam Stotram Sarvatantreshu Drushyathe* I**
***Tasmādupāsako Nityam Keertayedhida Mādarāt* II**

(i) There is no such prayer anywhere in literature of *Tantra* and hence the worshipper has to practice it with devotion on a daily basis.
(ii) The word *Keertayed* indicates chanting after understanding the meaning. *Devee Bhāgavatam* says "if the worshipper understands the meaning of at least one name and chants it, he lives in the *Śreepuram* for crores of years".

Abhyekam Nām Yovetti Tātvartta Nigamatibhi: I
Sopi Śreelalitā Loke Kalpakoteervaset Nara: II

(iii) Further, chanting it without knowing the meaning is equal to adding fuel (a wooden stick) to a fire after it is put out.

Anateetam Avignātam Nigatenaiva Patyate I
Anagnāviva Shushkaito Natatdvalatikarihichit II

(iv) One who does not have the capacity or ability to know the meaning can read it as it is. He gets some benefits based on the knowledge of sounds. In the same manner, one who is a literate can just worship the book. In the next birth he will get the knowledge to read and further to know the meaning step by step.

(v) This hymn will bestow its blessings even for those who do not worship.

52. *Yebhir Nāma Sahasraistu Śreechakramyorārchayedh Sakruth* I
***Padmair Vā Tulaseepushpai*: *Kalhārair Vā Kadambakai*: II**

53. *Champakair Jāti Kusumai*: *Mallika Karaveerakai*: I
***Utpalair Bilvapatrairvā, Kunḍakesara Patalai*: II**

54. *Anyai*: *Sugandhi Kusumai*: *Ketakee Mādhaveemukhai*: I
***Tasya Puŋya Phalamvaktum Nasaknoti Maheshvara*: II**

(i) Even Lord *Shiva* would not be able to tell comprehensively, the effect of worshipping the *Śreechakra* using the thousand names at least, with lotus flower, flower of basil, *Kalharrā*, *kadamba* flowers, Jasmine, *Champak*, *Karaveera*, *Uthpala* leaves of *Bilwa* (cratava religious), Jasmine buds, Kesara flowers and other scented flowers like, *Ketakee*, *Mādavee*, *Mukha*, etc.

(ii) *Archanā* means – chanting each name with the fourth case ending by prefixing *Om* (*praŋava mantra*) and suffixing with *Om Nama*: (I bow) and offer one flower at the feet of *Śree Devee*. For instance *Om Śreemātre Om Nama*:, *Om Śree Mahāragnai Om Nama*:, *Om Śreelalitāmbhikāyai Om Nama*: and so on.

(iii) Fifteen types of flowers have been mentioned as a sample. Other than these any fragrant flower can be used.

(iv) When it is mentioned as flower of basil, it is not the leaves or tri-leaves. It is the flower per se.

(v) Ordained or restricted flowers can also be used for this purpose.

(vi) The flower of European Saffron tree is very much significant to use.

(vii) When many a flower is being used, it has to be offered one by one after sorting and not in a group in a combined fashion. After completing one set of flowers, the sets have to follow.

(viii) Even *Maheshvarā* does not have the capability or capacity, to convey the results of such an *Archana*.

55. ***Sā Vetti Lalitā Devee Svachakrarjanajam Phalam* I**
***Anye Katham Vijāneeyu: Brahmaddhyā Svalpamedhasa:* II**

(i) Only *Śree Devee* can tell something about the result of worshipping **Her** *chakra*. How Lord Brahma and others, who have lesser intellect can may be able to.

(ii) The reason that *Brahma* and others could not know this is that they have lesser intellect (*medhā*). Here *medhā* means the capacity of understanding and retaining things.

(iii) One specialty of this *Archanā* is that in the *sankalpa* (declaration of intention to do a *pooja*) itself it can be declared that such-and-such flower is going to be used and the same flower used for all the 1000. Like chanting, the declaration has to be made, the three *nyāsās* to be done and the names have to be pronounced as described above. The flowers are to be used looking above, as it was in the tree. At the end again the *nyāsās* to be performed and this last part has to be read.

56. ***Pratimāsam Pourŋamāsyām Ebhir Nāmasahasrakai:* I**
***Ratrou Ya: Chakrarājastām Archayet Paradevatām* II**

57. ***Sa Yeva Lalitā Roopastadroopā Lalitā Svayam* I**
***Na Tayor Vidhyate Bhedho Bhedhackrut Pāpakruthbhavet* II**

(i) In every month during the full moon day, if **She** is worshipped, with the thousand names as described above, in the night by imagining *Śree Devee*'s form on the *Śreechakra*, the worshipper would himself have the form of the goddess *Lalitā* and he cannot be seen as another one, for it is a sin to see him as anything else.

(ii) In earlier verses it was mentioned that the result of once worshipping *Śree Devee* would be known only to **Her**. Here it is mentioned that if the devotee worships **Her** every month, he himself becomes the form of *Śree Devee*. That is the unity/ integrity. That is why it was detailed as; *Sa Yeva Lalitā Roopa: Tad Roopā Lalitā Svayam.*

(iii) It is mentioned that those who do not see him in the form of *Śree Devee* becomes a sinner.

58. ***Mahānavamyām Yo Bhakta: Śrī Deveem Chakramadhyagām* I**
***Archayen Nāmasāhasrai: Tasyamukti: Karesthitā* II**

(i) That devotee who worships **Her** on a *Mahānavami* day, on the *Śreechakra* using these thousand names, the salvation is in his hands.

(ii) *Mahānavami* is the last two days of *Shāradā Navarātri*. *Māhanavami* is the form of unison of *Shiva-shakti*.

(iii) This worship is also to be done in the night only. There is another school of thought that the eighth day worship has to be done in the night and the ninth day done in the day time.

(iv) It has been said that the eighth day is special to *Shiva* and the ninth day to *Śree Devee*. If in a particular if both these *thithis* are conjoined then that day is special to *Ardha Nāreeshwaran* (the combined form of *Shiva* and *Shakti*, with *Śree Devee* in the left half).

(v) People of all caste have the right to do this worship.

59. ***Yastu Nāma Sahasrena Shukravare Samarchayeth* I**
***Chakrarājemahā Deveem Tasya Puŋyaphalam Shrunu* II**

(i) If a person does the *Archanā* in a great manner, using these thousand names on a Friday, to the *Śreechakra* of *Śree Devee*, please hear the benefits he would reap.

(ii) By Friday, it has to be construed as many weeks.

60. ***Sarvān Kāmānavāpyeha Sarvasoubhāgya Samyuta*: I**
***Putrapouthrādhisamyukto Bhuktvā Bhogān Yathepsitān* II**
61. ***Anthe Śreelalitādevyā*: *Sāyujyamatidurlabham* I**
***Prārthaneeyam Shivādhyaischaprapnotyeva Na Samshaya*: II**

(i) The devotee mentioned in the previous verse gets all his desires fulfilled here (in this world) itself. He would lead a life with all the blessings, would be surrounded by children and grand-children and enjoy all the pleasures of life more than what he expected. At the end he would get the salvation, which is very difficult to obtain and there is no doubt in this.

(ii) *Iha* means in this world itself. He enjoys all the pleasures with children and grand-children means, not only he is benefitted, but also his entire family/ race.

(iii) *Anthe* means at the end when the body falls down, he reaches the salvation of *Śree Devee* by taking the route of *Devas*. The details can be seen in 912th name *Savyapasavyamārgastha*.

(iv) *Sāyujyam* (salvation) also indicates the *Kailvalya* stage. *Śree Devee* is *Kaivalyapadadāyinee*.

62. ***Ya*: *Sahasram Brāhmanānam Ebhirnāma Sāhasrakai*: I**
***Samarchaya Bhojayedh Bhaktyā Pāyasāpoopashadrasai* II**

63. ***Tasmai Preenāthi Lalitā Svasāmrājyam Prāyachathi* I**
***Natasya Durlabhamvasthu Trishulokeshu Varddhte* II**

(i) Dedicating these thousand names to thousand Brahmins, feeding them with sweet *Pāyāsam*, *Vada* made out of black gram and a meal with all the six tastes, would make one dear to *Śree Devee*. **She** would bless him with her kingdom and there would be nothing in the three worlds that would be difficult to get for this man.
(ii) It is enough if this type of feeding the Brahmins is done once.
(iii) By the word *Brāhmanānam* it has to be construed as worshippers of *Śreevidya*.
(iv) The word *Svasāmrājyam* means it is un-distinguishable stage of *Kaivalyam* only. In this stage of *Sāmrājyam* in the path of *Vedānta*, even ruling of a world is not possible for a devotee who has reached this *Sāmrājyam*. Though *Vedāntam* through *Brahma Sūtra* (4-4-17) says; *Jagatvyā Bhāratvavarjam Prakaranāt Asannihi Tatvātch* – since the *Śreevidyā* devotees are integrated with *Śree Devee*, they get all the *shaktis* of *Śree Devee*. *Śree Bhāskara Rāya* has proved this through various arguments.
(v) The method of feeding of 1000 Brahmins has not been described here. However, it has been explained as below in the results part of *Trishatee*:. It has been explained in 7 verses starting with;

Nityāshoḍashikāroopānprānātoutu Bhojayet I
Nityāshoḍashikāroopānvibrānātoutu Bhojayet II

And ending with; *Tasyaivam Sabalam Tasyamuktistasya Karestitā* II

The method follows:

After doing regular *Prānāyāmā*, details of the place, time, etc., in the declaration, it has to be announced that I feed 1000 Brahmins through *Lalitā Saharanāmā* for the satisfaction of *Śree Devee*. Then for purity of the place and all the things used, *Punyāhavāchanam* has to be performed. Sixteen Brahmins have to be chosen and offered water, cleaning of feet, seat, oil bath in hot water, etc. The 15 *thithi nityā Devees* and *Mahānityā* have to be imagined on these 16 Brahmins. Worshipping them with 16 offerings has to be completed. All the 16 Devees have to be worshipped like *Hreem Śreem Kāmeshwaryai Namahā*, *Hreem Śree Bagamālinyai Namahā* and so on. *Tarpaṇa* has to be done by them. These 16 Brahmins are made to sit facing East or North. They have to be offered clothes, sandal paste, jewels, flowers, other fragrant materials, fragrant smoke, light, etc. Then they have to be fed with food with sweet, fruits, etc. They have to be bowed after given betel leaves and money. Such worship is called *Nitya Bali*. This has to be followed with feeding of 1000 Brahmins. If it could be done on a single day that would be great, else, it could be for 100 days at the rate of 10 per day. Thus the count of 1000 has to be completed. If it is *Lalitā Trishatee* based feeding it could be for 15 days at the rate 20 per day – this is also a great accomplishment. That too it can be from the first day of the bright lunar fortnight till the full Moon day – the Brahmins have to be imagined with the 300 names in *Trishatee*. All these days the worshipper has to follow the vow obligations. The *Niyābali* worship has to be done on the starting day.

(vi) The feeding of 1000 Brahmins has been mentioned in the *Dharma Sūtra* of *Bhodhāyana*. It is understood that *Śree Bhāskararāya* has written his commentary for this. Whatever mentioned here is based on it.

(vii) The feeding of 300 Brahmins has been described in the results part of *Trishatee* and it has been mentioned that feeding of 1000 Brahmins also to be done in the same manner;

Rahasyanāmasāhasrabhojanepyevamevahi I
Ādounityābalim Kuryāt Pashchāt Brahmaṇa Bhojanam II

64. *Nishkāma*: *Keertayedhyasthu Nāma Sāhasramuttamam* I
***Brahmagnānamavāpnoti Yenamuchyatebandhanath* II**

He, who chants these thousand names, without any specific desires or attachments, would get the knowledge of *Brahmam* and would be released from the bonds of life.

(i) *Nishkāmanai* means – nothing is sought by self – the chanting is done thinking only the satisfaction of *Śree Devee*.

(ii) The knowledge of *Brahmam* is that the stage of the soul getting integrated with the supreme being. That is the stage of *Kaivalya*.

65. *Dhanārthee Dhanamāpnoti Yashortheechāpnuyādyasha*: I
***Vidhyārtheechāpnuyad Vidhyam Nāmasāhasra Keertanāt* II**

(i) By singing these thousand names, one who wants money would get money, one who wants fame would get fame and one who wants knowledge would get knowledge.

(ii) The word knowledge (*vidyā*) here does not mean the knowledge of *Śreevidyā*, since one cannot chant this hymn without the knowledge of it. It can be construed as 18 types of knowledge.

(iii) Or by the word *vidyā*, it can be taken as the knowledge of *Brahmavidyā* or *Brahmam*.

66. ***Nānena Sadhrusham Stotram Bhogamokshapradhammune* I**
***Keerthaneeyam Idham Tasmādbhoga Mokshārthibhir Narai*: II**

(i) Oh Sage! There is no prayer similar to this one, which would give pleasures as well as salvation, for human beings chanting this hymn, would get both pleasures and salvation.

(ii) The word *Vidyā*, in the previous verse, was given the meaning as knowledge of *Brahmam*. Hence to get the zeal, which is a tool to reach that knowledge, the pleasure as well as the salvation are bestowed.

(iii) The pleasure and salvation can be considered with a special meaning. If an action is aimed at the pleasure and some mistake happens, it may lead to salvation or vice versa.

(iv) If the word *Vidyā*, in the previous verse, is given the meaning as knowledge of *Brahmam*, then the zeal can be considered as its previous step - to get the eligibility to reach the salvation by moving away from the pleasures.

67. ***Chaturāshrama Nishtaichcha Keertaneeyamidam Sada* I**
***Svadharma Samānushṭāna Vaikalya Paripoortaye* II**

(i) In all the four stages of life, chanting these thousand names and also following one's own tradition, would help reach his goal without any obstacles.

(ii) The four stages are - bachelors (*brahmacharyam*), married (*grahastam*) or *vānaprastās* or ascetics (*sanyāsins*). For each of these stages various chores are prescribed. Only if those are followed according to *sāstras*, without any flaws, the full result can be obtained. To follow everything without any flaws, especially under the present day circumstances is next to impossible. That is the reason, as expiation, this hymn has been prescribed.

68. ***Kaloupapalkabahule Dharmānushṭāna varjate* I**
***Nāmasankeerthanam Muktvā Nrunam Nānyalparāyanam* II**

(i) In the era of *Kali*, when sins have increased and following the prescribed chores by *sāstras* have been forsaken, there is no other alternative for human beings other than singing these names.

(ii) It is very common to make flaws while doing the actions. Lot of other actions are prescribed as expiation for them. At lease these expiation actions are to be done 100% perfect to get the full results. Otherwise some other expiation actions have to be searched for it. It will become endless vicious cycle. That is the reason, if the expiation is done through this hymn; there is no chance for making flaws. Just by thinking these names, all the sins are pardoned and hence this hymn is the only expiation for all sins. The same message is conveyed by this verse also. It has been said that even if the name of *Śree Devee* is unintentionally or unconsciously uttered, the sins are pardoned;

Aspashṭa map Yannāma Prasankopi Bāshitam I
Tatāti Vānchitānarttān Durlapānapi Sarvadā II (*Devee Bhāgavatam*)
Matātpramātāt unmātāt utsvapnāt Skalanātapi I
*Katitam Nāma Te Gouri Nrunām Pāpāpanuttaye*II
(*Shakti Rahasyam*)

(iii) *Matam* is unconsciousness due to alcohol, the *pramātam* is carelessness, *unmātam* is specter, *utsvapnam* is clamor during sleep and *skalanam* is talking differently due slip of tongue – If the name of *Śree Devee* is told due to any of these, even then the sins are removed.

(iv) This logic called *koopa kānakam* (well logic) has been explained here - When a well is being dug, the person working on it may get dirty with mud. He will use the well water itself for cleaning his body and other purposes, may be not for drinking. In the same manner, to remove other sins this hymn is used. While doing so, if any flaws happen then the same hymn is used to remove those sins also.

(v) The same message is communicated at the end of the commentary also as below;

Tatāpyanta: *Santa*: *Satayahrutayā Nāma Mahimā* I
Pyapoorvastasmānme Nakalu Kalapāpopayamayam II

(vi) *Śree Bhāskararāya* does not vouch for the statement that singing of these names will be the expiation for the flaws happened in other expiation activities. Hence he says in his book called *Shiva stavam* as: "*Purāŋas* say that chanting the name of *Shiva* twice as *Shiva -Shiva* with devotion, is the expiation for the sins that occur due to not properly doing ordained actions and doing restricted actions. Hence instead of doing the ordained actions, not doing the restricted actions and doing expiation for all these, why can't I say your name right from the beginning? Will it not take me to the shore? Hence I have renounced all my actions".

(vii) If singing these names is the way out for getting the sins removed, what is the specialty of these 1000 names over others? This question is replied in the following verses. All these viz., electric-fly, Sun, Moon and fire are used to remove the darkness. However, there is difference in their energies. In the same way this hymn differ is treated as the greatest when compared to all the others.

69. *Loukikādvachanān Mukhyam Vişhŋu Nāmanu Keerthanam* I

(i) Singing the names of *Vişhŋu* is more important than the unwanted chit-chat;

Eka: *Shabda*: *Samyak Gnāta*: *Sushtu Prayukta*:
SvarggheLoke Kāmaduk Bhavati.

A single word, completely comprehended and used at the appropriate place, has the capacity to reach the heaven, get everything wanted and enjoy them. The fundamental reason for this is that all the words originated from the sound of *udukkai* (a small percussion instrument tampered in the middle) in the hands of Lord *Parameshvara*. Hence all of them have divine energy.

(ii) Singing the names of *Vişhŋu* is much greater than such ordinary 1000 words.

70. *Vişhŋu Nāma Saharāchcha Shiva Nāmaikamuthamam* II

(i) Thousand names of *Shiva* are much greater than 1000 names of *Vişhŋu*.

71. *Shiva nāma Sahasrāchcha Devyā Nāmaikamuthamam* I

(i) Better than the thousand names of *Shiva* are the name of *Śree Devee*.

(ii) The word *Devyā* indicates *Tripurasundaree Devee*.

(iii) All these statements are made to explain the greatness of this hymn. In any hymn, it is quiet natural that not only the presiding deity is placed at the highest stature and there are some words which bring down the greatness of other deities. This is being accepted by the learned with various reconciliations. The first route Is the argument called *Nahi Nintānyāyam*. That is, the aim of those statements is not to degrade others, but place the presiding deity in a higher platform.

In Tamil literature this is called as *Ikazchchi Navilal.*

(iv) The second method is based on officer argument. This is the method *Śree Bhāskararāya* also followed in his commentary called *Setubandam*. In early childhood a father encourages his son to play. But the same father after some years, at the age when he has to learn *Vedas* and *sāstras*, obstructs him from playing and encourages reading. In reality in the life of a boy there is some period for playing. During that time it gets priority over other activities. In the next stage only learning is important. During childhood whoever is in-charge of playing becomes the in-charge of epics during the start of education. This is what mentioned in *sāstras* as *Guŋavat Kāvyam* – epics are to be read and again as *Kāvyālā Pāncha Varjayet*– epics are to be restricted – we read contradicting statements. Then the books, which will lead to self realisation are only to be read. The argument here is that worship of whichever Lord or *mantra*, one is for, that is the priority or important for him when compared to all other *mantras*. Every human has crossed many a birth and hence depending on the self-perspective or dimension, he gets interest and capacity to learn and follow one or more *vidyās*. With respect to him the other things are not important.

(v) The third method is explained with an example. If a person looks at the same turning and object in a bridge once at a distance of one kilometer and again from at the other end of the bridge, it will look differently in size, but the object and the turning remain the same. In the same manner the matter on hand looks greater than anything else.

(vi) The reconciliations given so far lead to the assumption that the statement that *Lalitā Sahasranāma* is greater than other hymns and this needs some explanation. But in reality, the argument that whatever mentioned, about the greatness of this hymn so far are completely true, is put forth. The presiding deity of this hymn is *Śree Lalitāmbika*. Each name indicates **Her** only. This *Lalitā Devee* is called as *Shakti* because, all the other various deit*ies* indicated by *tatvas* explain worshipping method of the concerned deit*ies*, their forms, symbols, idols, etc. But this *tatva* called *Shakti* indicate the *Shakti* (energy) of so many great deit*ies*. This energy is integrated in all the forms and hence there is no difference. Isn't that the names, which explain the separate internal *tatvas* is better than all other descriptions?

Devee Nama Sahasrāni Koṭisha Santhi Kumbhaja II

(vii) Oh Agastya! There are crores of thousand names of *Śree Devee*.

72. ***Teshu Mukhyam Dashavidham Nāmasāhasramuchyate* I**
***Rahasya Nāmasāhasramidam Sastamdashasvapi* II**

(i) It is said that there are ten important thousand-names out of those crores of thousand-names. Among those ten this hymn is the greatest one.

(ii) The ten important thousand-names indicated here are "*Gan, Gāshyā, La, Kā, Bā, La, Rāsa* and *Ba*" viz., *Ganga, Gāyatree, Shyāmalā, Lakshmee, Kali, Bālā, Lalitā, Rājarājeshvaree, Saraswatee* and *Bhavanee*).

(iii) It can also be taken that all the ten thousand-names are in the name of *Lalitā* **Herself**.

(iv) Only this *Lalitā Sahasranāma* has got an adjective as secret.

73. ***Tasmat Sankeerttayen Nityam Kalidosha Nivruttaye* I**

(i) Singing this hymn daily would cure the ill effects of *Kali* era.

(ii) The major flaw of Kali era is that the daily chores prescribed will not be followed regularly and doing prohibited actions will increase.

(iii) This is what mentioned earlier as; *Kaloubhā Bhoubagabahule*.

74. ***Mukhyam Śreemātrunāmeti Na Jānanti Vimohitā*: II**
***Viṣhŋu Nāmaparā*: *Kechichchivanāma Parā*: *Pare* I**
***Na Kashchidapi Lokeshu Lalitānāma Tatpara*: II**

(i) People, who are confused, do not understand that only *Lalitā Sahasranāma* is the greatest. Some people sing *Viṣhŋu Sahasranāma* and some else sing names of *Shiva*. No one is to sing *Lalitā Sahasranāma*.

(ii) Those, who are bewildered on account of illusion, try to devote various deit*i*es. The do not recognise that this *Lalitā Sahasranāma* aims at the integrated form of the energies of all those deit*i*es.

75. ***Yenānya Devatānāma Keertitam Janmakoṭishu* I**
***Tasyaiva Bhavatishraddhā Śree Devee Nāma Keertane* II**

(i) Only the person, who has sung the names of other deit*i*es in crores of births, will get interest in this hymn.

76. *Charame Janmaŋiyatha Śreevidyopāsakobhavet* I
***Nāma Sāhasra Pātascha Tatha Charame Janmaŋi* II**

(i) A person becomes the worshipper of *Śreevidyā* only in his last birth. In a similar fashion reading these thousand names would also happen only in the last birth.
(ii) This *Sahasranāma* is equal in all respects to the *mantra* of *Śree Devee* and hence this will happen only in the last birth.

77. *Yataiva Virala Loke Śreevidyārājavedina*: I
***Tathaiva Viralo Guhya Nāma Sāhasra Pataka*: II**

(i) In this world it is very rare to find the people who know the methods of *Śreevidyā* and it is also rare to find those who read these thousand secret names.
(ii) In worshipping *Śreevidyā*, chanting of *Śreevidyā mantra*, which is the king of *mantras* and worshipping *Śreechakra*, which is the king of *chakras*, are two important parts. This is very rare. In the same manner chanting of this hymn is also rare and hence both are equal.

78. *Mantrarāja Japashchaiva Chakrarājārchanam Tathā* I
***Rahasya Nāma Patashcha Nālpasya Tapasa*: *Phalam* II**

(i) Chanting the king of *mantras* viz., *Śreevidyā mantra*, followed by worship of *Śree Chakra* and reading these thousand names is not the results low-end penance.
(ii) All these three will be got only with great results of penance. They will not be got by ordinary people.

79. *Apatannāmasāhasram Preenayedhyo Maheshvareem* I
***Sa Chakshushā Vinā Roopam Pashyedeva Vimoodadhee*: II**

(i) Without reading these thousand names and trying to please *Śree Devee*, is like a fool trying to see a form without eyes.
(ii) A blind person cannot see any form. In the same manner one who has not chant this hymn cannot satisfy *Śree Devee*.

80. *Rahasyanāma Sāhasram Tyaktvā Ya*: *Siddhikāmuka*: I
***Sa Bhojanam Vinānoonam Kshunnivruttim Abheepsati* II**

(i) Forsaking the thousand names and trying to get occult powers, is like satiating hunger after forsaking all food.

(ii) For the disease of hunger food is the only medicine. In the same fashion to get the worshipping initiation, chanting of these 1000 names is the only way out.

81. ***Yo Bhakto Lalitā Devyā: Sa Nityam Keerthayedidam* I**
***Nānyathā Preeyatā Devee Kalpa Koṭishatairapi* II**

(i) One who is a devotee of *Śree Devee* has to sing these 1000 names of *Lalitā Devee*, else **She** does not get pleased with anything else even for hundreds of eons.

(ii) Only those who chant this hymn become the devotee of *Śree Devee* and nobody else.

82. ***Tasmādrahasya Nāmāni Śreemātu: Prāyata: Patet* I**

(i) Hence these secret thousand names of the mother are to be read with repression.

(ii) The word *Prāyata*: will mean – with repression, with devotion, with holy thought, with interest and with control of organs. It has to be chant with all these.

Iti Tey Kathitam Stotram Rahasyam Kumbha Sambhava II

(iii) Thus these 1000 names were told to you, Oh sage Agastya!

83. ***Nāvidyāvedine Brooyānnābhaktāya Kadachana* I**
***Yathaiva Gopyā Śreevidyā Tathā Gopyamidam Mune* II**

(i) This should never be taught to those who do not have the knowledge of *Śreevidyā* and who is not a devotee. Oh sage! Just as *Śreevidyā*, this hymn also has to be protected as a secret.

(ii) The inherent meaning is – even if he is a devotee, if he does not have the knowledge of *Śreevidyā*, he should not be taught with this.

(iii) This has to be protected from non-devotees and who do not know the *mantras*.

84. ***Pashutulyeshu NabrooyājJaneshu Stotramuttamam* II**

(i) This hymn should not be told to people who are like animals.

(ii) Earlier in the 46th verse it was mentioned that a person who do not know this hymn and *Śreevidyā mantra* is equal to an animal. In this verse it is mentioned that animal like people are ineligible to learn this hymn.

85. ***Yodadāti Vimoodātmā Śreevidyā Rahitāyacha* I**
***Tasmai Kupyanti Yoginya*: *Sonartha*: *Sumahān Smruta*: II**

An idiotic soul only will teach this hymn to a person who does not have the knowledge of *Śreevidya*. The *Yogis* would be very angry with that fool. It has been mentioned that the anger of a Yogi will have adverse effects.

(i) The word *cha* in this verse will mean that the teacher and the student will be aimed at by the anger of *Yogis*.
(ii) The bad result means sorrows, accident, bad luck, etc.
(iii) This verse indicates what will happen if the secrecy mentioned earlier is not protected.
Rahasyanāma Sāhasran Tasmāt Sangopayedidam II
(v) Hence the secrecy of this hymn has to be well protected.

86. ***Svatantrena Māyānoktam Tavāpi Kalashodbhava* I**
***Lalitā Preraŋenaiva Mayoktam Stotramuttamam* II**

(i) Oh Agastya! Even to you, I have not told this on my own. I have told you about this great hymn, only by the order of *Śree Devee*.
(ii) *Śree Hayagreevā* reminds that to protect the secrecy of this great hymn, he did not reveal this till he got the order from *Śree Devee*.
(iii) According to the saying; *Sarvottame Chottamānke Kumbhesha Kalasadvani* – it can be considered by the word *Kalasee* that *Śree Devee* **Herself** was indicated. Hence with the word *Kalaseesudha*, *Agastyā* was addressed as son of *Śree Devee*. It is not a mistake to address a great devotee of *Śree Devee* as son of *Śree Devee*. Only because of the affection *Śree Devee* had on *Agastyā*, he was taught with this hymn, by **Her** order, by *Śree Hayagreeva*.
(iv) The word *Preranā* indicated order. Since *Śree Devee*'s order cannot be disobeyed, *Śree Hayagreevā*, most obediently, told this hymn to *Agastya*. Isn't that *Lalitā* is *Sarvānullankya Shāsana* (995th name)?

87. ***Keertaneeyam idam Bhaktyā Kumbhayone Nirantaram* I**
***Tena TushtāMahādevee Tavābheeshtam Pradāsyati* II**

(i) Hence this hymn has to be chant by you continuously. Oh sage *Agastya*! *Śree Devee* will be very much pleased and fulfill your desires.
(ii) The word *Nirantaram* indicates continuous, permanent and an integrated mind (without differentiating self and *Śree Devee*)

88. ***Śree Soota Uvacha*:**
***ItyuktvāŚree Hayagreevo Dhyātvā Śreelalitāmbikām* I**
***Ānandamagna Hrudaya*: *Sadhya*: *Pulakitobhavat* II**

Śree Sootha said:
(i) After telling thus, *Śree Hayagreevā* meditated on *Śree Devee*, was drowned in bliss and became enraptured.
(ii) *Ānanda* means the state of supreme bliss. *Śree Hayagreevā* reached this state by the thought of *Śree Devee* in his mind. Because of this state of bliss, his body was enraptured. This is what was indicated as *Pulakit*.
(iii) The last name in the list of 1000 names was *Śreelalitāmbika*. In the same manner this end part also closes with the word *Śree Lalitāmbika*.

***Iti Śree Brahmāṇḍa Purāne Uttarakānde Śree Hayagrrevāgastya Samvāde Śree Lalitā Rahasyanāmasahasre Phalaniroopanam Nāma Trutiyodhyāya*:**

Thus ends the narration of fruits of reciting *Lalitā Sahasranāma* in *BrahmāṇḍaPurāṇa*, in the form of dialogue between *Śree Hayagreeva* and *Sage Agastya*.
Thus ends the twelfth *Kalā* called *Kshama*.

*****

Appendix 1

The 1000 names in alphabetical order

No.	Name in English	Name in Samskrit
994	*Ābālagopaviditā*	आबालगोपविदिता
990	*Abhyāsātishayajnātā*	अभ्यासातिशयज्ञाता
285	*Ābrahmakeeṭajananee*	आब्रह्मकीटजननी
554	*Achintyaroopā*	अचिन्त्यरूपा
988	*Adbhutachāritrā*	अद्भुतचारित्रा
615	*Ādishakti:*	आदिशक्ति:
649	*Adrushyā*	अदृश्या
828	*Āgnā*	आज्ञा
521	*Āgnāchakrabjanilayā*	आज्ञाचक्राब्जनिलया
103	*Āgnāchakrantarālasthā*	आज्ञाचक्रान्तरालस्था
553	*Agragaŋyā*	अग्रगण्या
866	*Ajā*	अजा
663	*Ajājetree*	अजाजेत्री
993	*Ajnānadhvāntadeepikā*	अज्ञानध्वान्तदीपिका
860	*Akāntā*	अकान्ता
489	*Akshamālādidharā*	अक्षमालादिधरा
96	*Akulā*	अकुला
537	*Amati:*	अमति:
985	*Ambā*	अंबा
295	*Ambikā*	अंबिका
616	*Ameyā*	अमेया
814	*Amoortā*	अमूर्ता
483	*Amrutādimahāshaktisamvrutā*	अमृतादिमहाशक्तिसंवृता
296	*Anādinidhanā*	अनादिनिधना
987	*Anaghā*	अनघा
485	*Anāhatābjanilayā*	अनाहताब्जनिलया
29	*Anākalitasādrushyachibukashree virājitā*	अनाकलितसादृश्यचिबुकश्री विराजिता
729	*Anandakalikā*	आनन्दकलिका
926	*Anarghyakaivalyapadadāyinee*	अनर्घ्यकैवल्यपददायिनी

No.	Name in English	Name in Samskrit
50	*Anavadyāngee*	अनवद्याङ्गी
620	*Anekakoṭibrahmaṇḍajananee*	अनेककोटिब्रह्माण्डजननी
517	*Angkushādipraharanā*	अङ्कुशादिप्रहरणा
815	*Anityatruptā*	अनित्यतृप्ता
669	*Annadā*	अन्नदा
870	*Antarmukhasamārādhyā*	अन्तर्मुखसमाराध्या
273	*Anugrahadā*	अनुग्रहदा
541	*Anuttamā*	अनुत्तमा
642	*Aparicchedyā*	अपरिच्छेद्या
754	*Aparnā*	अपर्णा
413	*Aprameyā*	अप्रमेया
476	*Āraktavarṇā*	आरक्तवर्णा
37	*Aruṇārunakousumbhavastrabhāsvat -kaṭeetaṭee*	अरुणारुणकौसुम्भवस्त्रभास्वत् –कटीतटी
972	*Āshobhanā*	आशोभना
15	*Ashṭameechandra Vibhrājadalikasthala Shobhitā*	अष्टमीचन्द्र विभ्राजदलिकस्थल शोभिता
662	*Ashṭamoortti:*	अष्टमूर्त्तिः
67	*Ashvārooḍhādhishṭitāshvakoṭikoṭi Bhirāvrutā*	अश्वारूढाधिष्ठिताश्वकोटिकोटि भिरावृता
516	*Asthisamsthitā*	अस्थिसंस्थिता
508	*Atigarvitā*	अतिगर्विता
617	*Ātmā*	आत्मा
583	*Ātmavidyā*	आत्मविद्या
639	*Avaradā*	अवरदा
992	*Avyājakaruṇāmoorti:*	अव्याजकरुणामूर्तिः
398	*Avyaktā*	अव्यक्ता
427	*Ayee*	अयी
894	*Ayoni:*	अयोनिः
871	*Bahirmukhasudurlabhā*	बहिर्मुखसुदुर्लभा
824	*Bahuroopā*	बहुरूपा
905	*Baindavāsanā*	बैन्दवासना
965	*Bālā*	बाला
677	*Balipriyā*	बलिप्रिया

No.	Name in English	Name in Samskrit
546	*Bandhamochanee*	बन्धमोचनी
511	*Bandhinyādisamanvitā*	बन्धिन्यादिसमन्विता
964	*Bandhookakusumaprakhyā*	बन्धूककुसुमप्रख्या
547	*Bandhurālakā (Barbarālakā)*	बन्धुरालका (बर्बरालका)
116	*Bhadramoortti:*	भद्रमूर्त्तिः
115	*Bhadrapriyā*	भद्रप्रिया
277	*Bhagamālinee*	भगमालिनी
715	*Bhagārādhyā*	भगाराध्या
279	*Bhagavatee*	भगवती
746	*Bhāgyābdhichandrikā*	भाग्याब्धिचन्द्रिका
276	*Bhairavee*	भैटबी
747	*Bhaktachittakeki Ghanā Ghanā*	भक्तचित्तकेकि घना घना
404	*Bhaktahārdatamobhedabhānu -madbhānusantati:*	भक्तहार्दतमोभेदभानुमद्भानुसन्ततिः
372	*Bhaktamānasahamsikā*	भक्तमानसहंसिका
567	*Bhaktanidhi:*	भक्तनिधिः
117	*Bhaktasoubhāgyadāyinee*	भक्तसौभाग्यदायिनी
119	*Bhaktigamyā*	भक्तिगम्या
353	*Bhaktimatkalpalatikā*	भक्तिमत्कल्पलतिका
118	*Bhaktipriyā*	भक्तिप्रिया
120	*Bhaktivashyā*	भक्तिवश्या
593	*Bhālasthā*	भालस्था
275	*Bhānumaŋḍalamadhyasthā*	भानुमन्डलमध्यस्था
74	*Bhaŋḍaputravadhodyuktabālā -vikramananditā*	भण्डपुत्रवधोद्युक्तबाला –विक्रमनन्दिता
72	*Bhaŋḍasainyavadhodyuktashakti -vikramaharshitā*	भण्डसैन्यवधोद्युक्तशक्तिविक्रमहर्षिता
65	*Bhaŋḍāsuravadhodyuktashaktisenā -samanvitā*	भण्डासुटबधोद्युक्तशक्तिसेनासमन्विता
79	*Bhaŋḍāsurendranirmuktashastra -pratyastravarshiŋee*	भण्डासुरेन्द्रनिर्मुक्तशस्त्र– प्रत्यस्त्रवर्षिणी
678	*Bhāshāroopā*	भाषारूपा
680	*Bhāvābhāvavivarjitā*	भावाभावविवर्जिता
843	*Bhavachakrapravartinee*	भवचक्रप्रवर्तिनी
742	*Bhavadāvasudhāvrushṭi:*	भवदावसुधावृष्टिः

No.	Name in English	Name in Samskrit
841	*Bhāvajnā*	भावज्ञा
113	*Bhāvanāgamyā*	भावनागम्या
175	*Bhavanāshinee*	भवनाशिनी
112	*Bhavānee*	भवानी
114	*Bhavāraŋyakuṭhārikā*	भवारण्यकुठारिका
842	*Bhavarogaghnee*	भवरोगघ्नी
121	*Bhayāpahā*	भयापहा
179	*Bhedanāshinee*	भेदनाशिनी
293	*Bhoginee*	भोगिनी
666	*Bhoomaroopā*	भूमरूपा
294	*Bhuvaneshvaree*	भुवनेश्वरी
380	*Bindumaŋḍalavāsinee*	बिन्दुमन्डलवासिनी
974	*Bindutarpaŋasantushṭā*	बिन्दुतर्पणसन्तुष्टा
111	*Bisatantutaneeyasee*	बिसतन्तुतनीयसी
822	*Brahma*	ब्रह्म
100	*Brahmagranthivibhedinee*	ब्रह्मग्रन्थिविभेदिनी
676	*Brahmanandā*	ब्रह्मानन्दा
821	*Brahmānee*	ब्रह्माणी
674	*Brāhmanee*	ब्राह्मणी
265	*Brahmaroopā*	ब्रह्मरूपा
672	*Brahmātmaikyasvaroopiŋee*	ब्रह्मात्मैक्यस्वरूपिणी
675	*Brāhmee*	ब्राह्मी
83	*Bramopendramahendradideva samstutavaibhavā*	ब्रमोपेन्द्रामहेन्द्रदिदेवसंस्तुतवैभवा
673	*Bruhatee*	बृहती
679	*Bruhatsenā*	बृहत्सेना
825	*Budhārchitā*	बुधार्चिता
919	*Caitanyakusumapriyā*	चैतन्यकुसुमप्रिया
918	*Caitanyārghya Samārāadhyā*	चैतन्यार्घ्य समाराध्या
245	*Cakrarājaniketanā*	चक्रराजनिकेतना
68	*Cakrarājarathāroodhasarvāyudha -parishkrutā*	चक्रराजरथारूढसर्वायुध –परिष्कृता
13	*Campakāshokapunnāgasougandhi kalasatkachā*	चम्पकाशोकपुन्नागसौगन्धि– कलसत्कचा

No.	Name in English	Name in Samskrit
435	*Cāmpeyakusumapriyā*	चाम्पेयकुसुमप्रिया
434	*Candanadravadigdhāngee (ngā)*	चन्दनद्रवदिग्धाङ्गी (ङ्गा)
240	*Candramaŋḍalamadhyagā*	चन्द्रमन्डलमध्यगा
592	*Candranibhā*	चन्द्रनिभा
239	*Candravidyā*	चन्द्रविद्या
756	*Caŋḍamuŋḍāsuranishoodinee*	चण्डमुण्डासुरनिषूदिनी
755	*Caŋḍikā*	चण्डिका
244	*Carācarajagannāthā*	चराचरजगन्नाथा
243	*Cārucandrakalādharā*	चारुचन्द्रकलाधरा
242	*Cāruhāsā*	चारुहासा
241	*Cāruroopā*	चारुरूपा
236	*Catu:shashṭikalāmayee*	चतु:षष्टिकलामयी
235	*Catu:shashṭiyupacārādhyā*	चतु:षष्टियुपचाराढ्या
691	*Caturangabaleshvaree*	चतुरन्गबलेश्वरी
7	*Caturbāhusamanvitā*	चतुर्बाहुसमन्विता
505	*Caturvaktramanoharā*	चतुर्वक्त्रमनोहरा
417	*Cetanāroopā*	चेतनारूपा
844	*Chanda:sārā*	छन्द:सारा
416	*Cicchakti:*	चिच्छक्ति:
4	*Cidagnikuŋḍasambhootā*	चिदग्निकुण्डसंभूता
364	*Cidekarasaroopiŋee*	चिदेकरसरूपिणी
251	*Cinmayee*	चिन्मयी
57	*Cintāmaŋigruhāntasthā*	चिन्तामणिगृहान्तस्था
362	*Citi:*	चिति:
728	*Citkalā*	चित्कला
512	*Dadhyannāshakahrudayā*	दध्यन्नासक्तहृदया
560	*Dāḍimeekusumaprabhā*	दाडिमीकुसुमप्रभा
609	*Daharākāsharoopiŋee*	दहराकाशरूपिणी
599	*Daityahantree*	दैत्यहन्त्री
696	*Daityashamanee*	दैत्यशमनी
484	*Ḍākineeshvaree*	डाकिनीश्वरी
600	*Dakshayajnavināshinee*	दक्षयर्ज्ञविनाशिनी
598	*Dākshāyanee*	दाक्षायणी
923	*Dakshiŋādakshiŋārādhyā*	दक्षिणादक्षिणाराध्या

No.	Name in English	Name in Samskrit
725	*Dakshiŋāmoortiroopiŋee*	दक्षिणामूर्तिरूपिणी
498	*Ḍāmaryādibhirāvrutā*	डामर्यादिभिरावृता
488	*Damshṭrojvalā*	दंष्ट्रोज्वला
608	*Daŋḍaneetisthā*	दण्डनीतिस्था
602	*Darahāsojvalanmukhee*	दरहासोज्वलन्मुखी
601	*Darāndolitadeerghākshee*	दरान्दोलितदीर्घाक्षी
924	*Darasmeramukhāmbujā*	दरस्मेरमुखाम्बुजा
977	*Dashamudrāsamārādhyā*	दशमुद्रासमाराध्या
581	*Dayāmoorti*:	दयामूर्तिः
695	*Deekshitā*	दीक्षिता
701	*Deshakālaparicchinnā*	देशकालपरिच्छिन्ना
5	*Devakāryasamudyatā*	देवकार्यसमुद्यता
64	*Devarshigaŋasamghātastooya-mānātmavaibhavā*	देवर्षिगणसंघातस्तूय–मानात्मवैभवा
607	*Deveshee*	देवेशी
886	*Dhanadhānya Vivardhinee*	धनधान्य विवर्धिनी
885	*Dhanādhyakshā*	धनाध्यक्षा
957	*Dhanyā*	धन्या
955	*Dharā*	धरा
956	*Dharasutā*	धरसुता
884	*Dharmādhārā*	धर्माधारा
255	*Dharmādharmavivarjitā*	धर्माधर्मविवर्जिता
959	*Dharmavardhinee*	धर्मवर्धिनी
958	*Dharmiŋee*	धर्मिणी
916	*Dheerā*	धीरा
917	*Dheerasamarcitā*	धीरसमर्चिता
446	*Dhruti*:	धृतिः
254	*Dhyānadhyātrughyeyaroopā*	**ध्यानध्यातृध्येयरूपा**
641	*Dhyānagamyā*	ध्यानगम्या
631	*Divyagandhāḍhyā*	दिव्यगन्धाढ्या
621	*Divyavigraha*	दिव्यविग्रहा
195	*Doshavarjitā*	दोषवर्जिता
744	*Dourbhāgyatoolavātoolā*	दौर्भाग्यतूलवातूला
650	*Drushyarahitā*	दृश्यरहिता

No.	Name in English	Name in Samskrit
191	*Du:khahantree*	दु:खहन्त्री
194	*Durācārashamanee*	दुराचारशमनी
772	*Durādharshā*	दुराधर्षा
771	*Durārādhyā*	दुराराध्या
190	*Durgā*	दुर्गा
189	*Durgamā*	दुर्गमा
188	*Durlabhā*	दुर्लभा
193	*Dushṭadoorā*	दुष्टदूरा
668	*Dvaitavarjitā*	द्वैतवर्जिता
423	*Dvijavrundanishevitā*	**द्विजवृन्दनिषेविता**
768	*Dyutidharā*	द्युतिधरा
712	*Ĕ*	ई
665	*Ekākinee*	एकाकिनी
855	*Gaganāntasthā*	गगनान्तस्था
854	*Gambheerā*	गम्भीरा
857	*Gānalolupā*	गानलोलुपा
636	*Gandharvasevitā*	गन्धर्वसेविता
719	*Gaŋāmbā*	गणाम्बा
856	*Garvitā*	गर्विता
420	*Gāyatree*	गायत्री
69	*Geyachakrarathārooḍhamantrinee -parisevitā*	गेयचक्ररथारूढमन्त्रिणी –परिसेविता
605	*Gomātā*	गोमाता
42	*Gooḍhagulphā*	गूढगुल्फा
266	*Goptree*	गोप्त्री
635	*Gouree*	गौरी
267	*Govindaroopiŋee*	गोविन्दरूपिणी
501	*Guḍānnapreetamānasā*	गुडान्नप्रीतमानसा
606	*Guhajanmabhoo*:	गुहजन्मभू:
706	*Guhāmbā*	गुहाम्बा
624	*Guhyā*	गुह्या
720	*Guhyakārādhyā*	गुह्यकाराध्या
707	*Guhyaroopiŋee*	गुह्यरूपिणी
604	*Guŋanidhi*:	गुणनिधि:

No.	Name in English	Name in Samskrit
961	*Guŋāteetā*	गुणातीता
713	*Gurumaŋḍalaroopiŋee*	गुरुमण्डलरूपिणी
603	*Gurumoorti*:	गुरुमूर्तिः
722	*Gurupriyā*	गुरुप्रिया
527	*Hākineeroopadhārinee*	हाकिनीरूपधारिणी
525	*Hamsavateemukhyashaktisamanvitā*	हंसवतीमुख्यशक्तिसमन्विता
456	*Hamsinee*	हंसिनी
84	*Haranetrāgnisamdagdha-kāmasamjeevanoushadhi*:	हरनेत्राग्निसंदग्ध–कामसंजीवनौषधिः
297	*Haribrahmendrasevitā*	हरिब्रह्मेन्द्रसेविता
526	*Haridrānnaikarasikā*	हरिद्रान्नैकरसिका
304	*Heyopādeyavarjitā*	हेयोपादेयवर्जिता
302	*Hreematee*	ह्रीमती
301	*Hreemkāree*	ह्रींकारी
595	*Hrudayasthā*	हृदयस्था
303	*Hrudyā*	हृद्या
658	*Icchāshaktijnānashaktikriyāshakti svaroopiŋee*	इच्छाशक्तिज्ञानशक्तिक्रियाशक्ति–स्वरूपिणी
594	*Indradhanu:prabhā*	इन्द्रधनुःप्रभा
41	*Indragopaparikshipta-smaratoonābhajanghikā*	इन्द्रगोपपरिक्षिप्त–स्मरतूणाभजङ्घिका
271	*Ishvaree*	ईश्वरी
418	*Jadashakti*:	जडशक्तिः
419	*Jadātmikā*	जडात्मिका
935	*Jagaddhātree*	जगद्धात्री
257	*Jāgarinee*	जागरिणी
325	*Jagateekandā*	जगतीकन्दा
378	*Jālandharasthitā*	जालन्धरस्थिता
823	*Jananee*	जननी
851	*Janmamrutyu Jarātapta Janavishrāntidāyinee*	जन्ममृत्यु जरातप्त जनविश्रान्तिदायिनी
766	*Japāpushpa Nibhākruti*:	जपापुष्प निभाकृतिः
745	*Jarādhvāntaraviprabhā*	जराध्वान्तरविप्रभा
377	*Jayā*	जया

No.	Name in English	Name in Samskrit
788	*Jayatsenā*	जयत्सेना
643	*Jnānadā*	ज्ञानदा
980	*Jnānagamyā*	ज्ञानगम्या
981	*Jnānajneyasvaroopiņee*	ज्ञानज्ञेयस्वरूपिणी
979	*Jnānamudrā*	ज्ञानमुद्रा
644	*Jnānavigrahā*	ज्ञानविग्रहा
71	*Jwālāmālinikākshipta-vahniprākāramadhyagā*	ज्वालामालिनिकाक्षिप्त–वह्निप्राकारमध्यगा
323	*Kadambakusumapriyā*	कदम्बकुसुमप्रिया
21	*Kadambamanjareekluptakarnapoora-manoharā*	कदम्बमंजरीक्लृप्तकर्णपूर–मनोहरा
330	*Kādambareepriyā*	कादम्बरीप्रिया
60	*Kadambavanavāsinee*	कदंबवनवासिनी
625	*Kaivalyapadadāyinee*	कैवल्यपददायिनी
513	*Kākineeroopadhārinee*	काकिनीरूपधारिणी
557	*Kālahantree*	कालहन्त्री
464	*Kālakaņţhee*	कालकण्ठी
328	*Kalālāpā*	कलालापा
794	*Kalāmālā*	कलामाला
612	*Kalānāthā*	कलानाथा
797	*Kalānidhi:*	कलानिधिः
491	*Kālarātryādishaktyoughavrutā*	कालरात्र्यादिशक्त्यौघवृता
611	*Kalātmikā*	कलात्मिका
327	*Kalāvatee*	कलावती
555	*Kalikalmashanāshinee*	कलिकल्मषनाशिनी
858	*Kalpanārahitā*	कल्पनारहिता
903	*Kalyā*	कल्या
324	*Kalyānee*	कल्याणी
63	*Kāmadāyinee*	कामदायिनी
795	*Kāmadhuk*	कामधुक्
322	*Kāmakalāroopā*	कामकलारूपा
863	*Kāmakelitarangitā*	कामकेलितरङ्गिता
589	*Kāmakoţikā*	कामकोटिका
62	*Kāmākshee*	कामाक्षी

No.	Name in English	Name in Samskrit
558	*Kamalāksha Nishevitā*	कमलाक्ष निषेविता
375	*Kāmapoojitā*	कामपूजिता
796	*Kāmaroopiŋee*	कामरूपिणी
586	*Kāmasevitā*	कामसेविता
30	*Kāmeshabaddhamāngalyasootra-Shobhitakandharā*	कामेशबद्धमाङ्गल्यसूत्र–शोभितकन्धरा
39	*Kāmeshajnātasoubhāgya-Mārdavorudvayānvitā*	कामेशज्ञातसौभाग्य–मार्दवोरुद्वयान्विता
373	*Kāmeshvaraprāŋanādee*	कामेश्वरप्राणनाडी
33	*Kāmeshvarapremaratnamaŋiprathi-Paŋastanee*	कामेश्वरप्रेमरत्नमणिप्रथि–पणस्तनी
77	*Kāmeshwaramukhālokakalpita-Śreegaŋeshvarā*	कामेश्वरमुखालोककल्पित–श्रीगणेश्वरा
82	*Kāmeshwarāstranirdagdhasabhaŋḍā -surashoonyakā*	कामेश्वरास्त्रनिर्दग्धसभण्डा –सुरशून्यका
321	*Kāmyā*	काम्या
31	*Kanakāngadakeyoorakamaneeya-Bhujānvitā*	कनकाङ्गदकेयूरकमनीय–भुजान्विता
864	*Kanatkanakatāṭankā*	कनत्कनकताटङ्का
329	*Kāntā*	कान्ता
861	*Kāntārdhavigrahā*	कान्तार्धविग्रहा
86	*Kanṭhādhakaṭiparyantamadhya-kooṭasvaroopiŋee*	कण्ठाधकटिपर्यन्तमध्य–कूटस्वरूपिणी
449	*Kānti:*	कान्तिः
465	*Kāntimatee*	कान्तिमती
793	*Kapardinee*	कपर्दिनी
80	*Karāngulinakhotpannanārāyaŋa -dashākruti:*	करांगुलिनखोत्पन्ननारायण –दशाकृतिः
26	*Karpooraveeṭikāmodasamākarshi -digantarā*	कर्पूटबीटिकामोदसमाकर्षि –दिगन्तरा
320	*Karuŋārasa Sāgarā*	करुणारस सागरा
862	*Kāryakāraŋanirmukta*	कार्यकारणनिर्मुक्ता
859	*Kāshṭhā*	काष्ठा
590	*Kaṭāksha Kinkaree Bhootakamalākoṭisevitā*	कटाक्ष किङ्करी भूतकमलाकोटिसेविता

No.	Name in English	Name in Samskrit
556	*Kātyāyanee*	कात्यायनी
798	*Kāvyakalā*	काव्यकला
613	*Kāvyālāpavinodinee*	काव्यालापविनोदिनी
623	*Kevalā*	केवला
478	*Khaṭvāngādipraharanā*	खट्वाङ्गादिप्रहरणा
70	*Kiricakrarathārooḍhadaŋḍanāthā-puraskrutā*	किरिचक्ररथारूढदण्डनाथा–पुरस्कृता
622	*Kleemkāree*	क्लींकारी
437	*Komalākārā*	कोमलाकारा
721	*Komalāngee*	कोमलाङ्गी
43	*Koormaprushṭhajayishnu-Prapadānvitā*	कूर्मपृष्ठजयिश्णु–प्रपदान्विता
896	*Kooṭasthā*	कूटस्था
690	*Koshanāthā*	कोशनाथा
441	*Koulamārgatatparasevitā*	कौलमार्गतत्परसेविता
94	*Koulinee*	कौलिनी
925	*Koulinee Kevalā*	कौलिनी केवला
9	*Krodhākārānkushojvalā*	क्रोधाकाराङ्कुशोज्वला
169	*Krodhashamanee*	क्रोधशमनी
374	*Krutajnā*	कृतज्ञा
757	*Ksharāksharātmikā*	क्षराक्षरात्मिका
867	*Kshayavinirmuktā*	क्षयविनिर्मुक्ता
344	*Kshayavruddhivinirmuktā*	क्षयवृद्धिविनिर्मुक्ता
343	*Kshetrakshetrajnapālinee*	क्षेत्रक्षेत्रज्ञपालिनी
345	*Kshetrapālasamarchitā*	क्षेत्रपालसमर्चिता
341	*Kshetrasvaroopā*	क्षेत्रस्वरूपा
342	*Kshetreshee*	क्षेत्रेशी
869	*Kshipraprasādinee*	क्षिप्रप्रसादिनी
466	*Kshobhiŋee*	क्षोभिणी
440	*Kulakuŋḍālayā*	कुलकुण्डालया
90	*Kulāmrutaikarasikā*	कुलामृतैकरसिका
92	*Kulānganā*	कुलाङ्गना
93	*Kulāntasthā*	कुलान्तस्था
897	*Kularoopiŋee*	कुलरूपिणी

No.	Name in English	Name in Samskrit
91	*Kulasanketapālinee*	कुलसङ्केतपालिनी
95	*Kulayoginee*	कुलयोगिनी
439	*Kuleshvaree*	कुलेश्वरी
714	*Kulotteerŋā*	कुलोत्तीर्णा
442	*Kumāragaŋanāthāmbā*	कुमारगणनाथाम्बा
110	*Kunḍalinee*	कुन्डलिनी
438	*Kurukullā*	कुरुकुल्ला
14	*Kuruvindamaŋishreneekanat-koṭeeramanḍitā*	कुरुविन्दमणिश्रेणीकनत्–कोटीरमण्डिता
436	*Kushalā*	कुशला
740	*Lajjā*	लज्जा
503	*Lākinyambāsvaroopiŋee*	लाकिन्यम्बास्वरूपिणी
35	*Lakshyaromalatādhāratāsamunneya-madhyamā*	लक्ष्यरोमलताधारतासमुन्नेय–मध्यमा
1000	*Lalitāmbikā*	ललिताम्बिका
738	*Lāsyapriyā*	लास्यप्रिया
739	*Layakaree*	लयकरी
865	*Leelā Vigrahadhārinee*	लीला विग्रहधारिणी
648	*Leelākluptabrahmaŋḍamaŋḍalā*	लीलाक्लुप्तब्रह्माण्डमण्डला
966	*Leelāvinodinee*	लीलाविनोदिनी
171	*Lobhanāshinee*	लोभनाशिनी
960	*Lokāteetā*	लोकातीता
664	*Lokayātrāvidhāyinee*	लोकयात्राविधायिनी
454	*Lolāksheekāmaroopiŋee*	लोलाक्षीकामरूपिणी
647	*Lopāmudrārchitā*	लोपामुद्रार्चिता
432	*Madaghoorŋitaraktākshee*	मदघूर्णितरक्ताक्षी
159	*Madanāshinee*	मदनाशिनी
433	*Madapāṭalagaŋḍabhoo:*	मदपाटलगण्डभू:
431	*Madashālinee*	मदशालिनी
717	*Madhumatee*	मधुमती
510	*Madhupreeta*	मधुप्रीता
575	*Mādhveepānālasā*	माध्वीपानालसा
370	*Madhyamā*	मध्यमा
222	*Mahābalā*	महाबला

No.	Name in English	Name in Samskrit
231	*Mahābhairavapoojitā*	महाभैटबपूजिता
219	*Mahābhogā*	महाभोगा
223	*Mahābuddhi:*	महाबुद्धि:
237	*Mahācatu:shashṭikoṭiyogineegaŋa-Sevitā*	महाचतु:षष्टिकोटियोगिनीगन–सेविता
209	*Mahādevee*	महादेवी
78	*Mahāgaŋeshanirbhinnavighna -yantrapraharshitā*	महागणेशनिर्भिन्नविघ्न –यन्त्रप्रहर्षिता
752	*Mahāgrāsā*	महाग्रासा
220	*Mahaishvaryā*	महैश्वर्या
578	*Mahākailāsanilayā*	महाकैलासनिलया
751	*Mahākālee*	महाकाली
233	*Mahākāmeshamahishi*	महाकामेशमहिषी
403	*Mahākāmeshanayanakumudāhlāda-koumudee*	महाकामेशनयनकुमुदाह्लाद–कौमुदी
210	*Mahālakshmee*	महालक्ष्मी
48	*Mahālāvaŋyashevadhi:*	महालावण्यशेवधि:
227	*Mahāmantra*	महामन्त्रा
215	*Mahāmāyā*	महामाया
580	*Mahaneeyā*	महनीया
59	*Mahāpadmāṭaveesamsthā*	महापद्माटवीसंस्था
81	*Mahāpāshupatāstrāgninirdhagdhā-Surasainikā*	महापाशुपतास्त्राग्निनिर्धग्धा–सुरसैनिका
214	*Mahāpātakanāshinee*	महापातकनाशिनी
213	*Mahāpoojyā*	महापूज्या
571	*Mahāpralayasākshinee*	महाप्रलयसाक्षिणी
218	*Mahārati:*	महारति:
212	*Mahāroopā*	महारूपा
109	*Mahāshakti:*	महासक्ति:
582	*Mahāsāmrājyashālinee*	महासाम्राज्यशालिनी
229	*Mahāsanā*	महासना
216	*Mahāsatvā*	महासत्वा
217	*Mahāshakti:*	महाशक्ति:
753	*Mahāshanā*	महाशना

No.	Name in English	Name in Samskrit
224	*Mahāsiddhi:*	महासिद्धिः
226	*Mahātantra*	महातन्त्रा
774	*Mahatee*	महती
234	*Mahātripurasundaree*	महात्रिपुरसुन्दरी
493	*Mahāveerendravaradā*	महावीरेन्द्रवरदा
221	*Mahāveeryā*	महावीर्या
584	*Mahāvidyā*	महाविद्या
230	*Mahāyāgakramāyādhyā*	महायागक्रमाराध्या
228	*Mahāyantrā*	महायन्त्रा
225	*Mahāyogesvareshvaree*	महायोगेस्वरेश्वरी
718	*Mahee*	मही
932	*Maheshee*	महेशी
232	*Maheshvaramahākalpamahā -tānḍavasākshinee*	महेश्वरमहाकल्पमहा –ताण्डवसाक्षिणी
750	*Maheshvaree*	महेश्वरी
208	*Māheshvaree*	माहेश्वरी
570	*Maitryādivāsanālabhyā*	मैत्र्यादिवासनालभ्या
524	*Majjāsamsthā*	मज्जासंस्था
458	*Malayāchalavāsinee*	मलयाचलवासिनी
455	*Mālinee*	मालिनी
165	*Mamatāhantree*	ममताहन्त्री
500	*Māmsanishṭā*	माम्सनिष्ठा
930	*Manasvinee*	मनस्विनी
931	*Mānavatee*	मानवती
776	*Mandārakusumapriyā*	मन्दारकुसुमप्रिया
28	*Mandasmitaprabhāpoora -majjatkāmeshamānasā*	मन्दस्मितप्रभापूर –मज्जत्कामेशमानसा
933	*Mangalākruti:*	मङ्गलाकृतिः
40	*Mānikyamukuṭākārajānudvaya -virājitā*	माणिक्यमुकुटाकारजानुद्वय –विराजिता
941	*Manomayee*	मनोमयी
207	*Manonmanee*	मनोन्मनी
10	*Manorupekshukodaŋḍā*	मनोरुपेक्षुकोदण्डा
415	*Manovāchāmagocharā*	मनोवाचामगोचरा

No.	Name in English	Name in Samskrit
846	*Mantrasārā*	मन्त्रसारा
786	*Mantrineenyastarājyadhoo:*	मन्त्रिणीन्यस्तराज्यधू:
75	*Mantrinyambāvirachitavishanga -vadhatoshitā*	मन्त्रिण्यम्बाविरचितविषङ्ग –वधतोषिता
238	*Manuvidyā*	मनुविद्या
495	*Maŋipoorābjanilayā*	मणिपूराब्जनिलया
101	*Maŋipoorāntaruditā*	मणिपूरान्तरुदिता
47	*Marāleemandagamanā*	मरालीमन्दगमना
785	*Mārtānḍa Bhairavārādhyā*	मार्तण्ड भैटबाराध्या
457	*Mātā*	माता
445	*Mati:*	मति:
577	*Matrukāvarŋaroopiŋee*	मातृकावर्णरूपिणी
576	*Mattā*	मत्ता
716	*Māyā*	माया
538	*Medhā*	मेधा
509	*Medonishṭhā*	मेदोनिष्ठा
775	*Merunilayā*	मेरुनिलया
735	*Mithyājagadadhishṭhānā*	मिथ्याजगदधिष्ठाना
565	*Mitraroopiŋee*	मित्ररूपिणी
163	*Mohanāshinee*	मोहनाशिनी
562	*Mohinee*	मोहिनी
99	*Moolādhāraikanilayā*	मूलाधारैकनिलया
514	*Moolādhārāmbujārooḍhā*	मूलाधाराम्बुजारूढा
89	*Moolakooṭatrayakalebarā*	मूलकूटत्रयकलेबरा
88	*Moolamantratmikā*	मूलमन्त्रात्मिका
397	*Moolaprakruti:*	मूलप्रकृति:
840	*Moolavigraharoopiŋee*	मूलविग्रहरूपिणी
813	*Moortā*	मूर्ता
564	*Mruḍānee*	मृडानी
211	*Mruḍapriyā*	मृडप्रिया
561	*Mrugākshee*	मृगाक्षी
579	*Mrunālamrududorlatā*	मृणालमृदुदोर्लता
749	*Mrutyudāruguṭhārikā*	मृत्युदारुगुठारिका
181	*Mrutyumathanee*	मृत्युमथनी

No.	Name in English	Name in Samskrit
519	*Mudgoudanāshakachittā*	मुद्गौदनासक्तचित्ता
868	*Mugdhā*	मुग्धा
16	*Mukhachandrakalannkābha-mruganābhivisheshakā*	मुखचन्द्रकलन्ङ्काभ– मृगनाभिविशेषका
563	*Mukhyā*	मुख्या
736	*Muktidā*	मुक्तिदा
839	*Muktinilayā*	मुक्तिनिलया
737	*Muktiroopiɳee*	मुक्तिरूपिणी
838	*Mukundā*	मुकुन्दा
816	*Munimānasa Hamsikā*	मुनिमानस हंसिका
34	*Nābhyālavālaromālilatāphala -kuchadvayee*	नाभ्यालवालरोमालिलताफल –कुचद्वयी
299	*Nādaroopā*	नादरूपा
901	*Nādaroopiɳee*	नादरूपिणी
900	*Naishkarmyā*	नैष्कर्म्या
44	*Nakhadeedhitisamchannanamajjana Tamoguɳā*	नखदीधितिसंछन्ननमज्जन –तमोगुणा
460	*Nalinee*	नलिनी
732	*Nāmapārāyaɳapreetā*	नामपारायणप्रीता
300	*Nāmaroopavivarjitā*	नामरूपविवर्जिता
450	*Nandinee*	नन्दिनी
733	*Nandividyā*	नन्दिविद्या
298	*Nārāyaɳee*	नारायणी
734	*Naṭeshvaree*	नटेश्वरी
19	*Navachampakapushpābhanāsā -daɳḍavirājitā*	नवचम्पकपुष्पाभनासा –दण्डविराजिता
24	*Navavidrumabimba Shreenyakkāridashanaccadā*	नवविद्रुमबिम्ब श्रीन्यक्कारिदशनच्छदा
185	*Neelachikurā*	नीलचिकुरा
156	*Neerāgā*	नीरागा
172	*Ni.samshayā*	निःसंशया
287	*Nijāgnāroopanigamā*	निजाज्ञारूपनिगमा
12	*Nijārunaprabhāpooramajjad Brahmaɳḍamaɳḍalā*	निजारुणप्रभापूरमज्जद् ब्रह्माण्डमण्डला

No.	Name in English	Name in Samskrit
27	*Nijasallāpamādhuryavinirbhartsita -kacchapee*	निजसल्लापमाधुर्यविनिर्भर्त्सित –कच्छपी
569	*Nikhileshvaree*	निखिलेश्वरी
177	*Nirābādhā*	निराबाधा
132	*Nirādhārā*	निराधारा
161	*Nirahamkārā*	निरहंकारा
137	*Nirākārā*	निराकारा
138	*Nirākulā*	निराकुला
877	*Nirālambā*	निरालम्बा
876	*Nirāmayā*	निरामया
133	*Niranjanā*	निरन्जना
151	*Nirantarā*	निरन्तरा
186	*Nirapāyā*	निरपाया
147	*Nirāshrayā*	निराश्रया
187	*Niratyayā*	निरत्यया
150	*Niravadyā*	निटबद्या
174	*Nirbhavā*	निर्भवा
178	*Nirbhedā*	निर्भेदा
667	*Nirdvaitā*	निर्द्वैता
155	*Nireeshvarā*	निरीश्वरा
139	*Nirguŋā*	निर्गुणा
134	*Nirlepā*	निर्लेपा
170	*Nirlobhā*	निर्लोभा
158	*Nirmadā*	निर्मदा
135	*Nirmalā*	निर्मला
164	*Nirmamā*	निर्ममा
162	*Nirmohā*	निर्मोहा
180	*Nirnāshā*	निर्नाशा
154	*Nirupādhi*:	निरुपाधि:
389	*Nirupamā*	निरुपमा
143	*Nirupaplavā*	निरुपप्लवा
390	*Nirvāŋasukhadāyinee*	निर्वाणसुखदायिनी
176	*Nirvikalpā*	निर्विकल्पा
145	*Nirvikārā*	निर्विकारा

No.	Name in English	Name in Samskrit
160	*Nishcintā*	निश्चिन्ता
140	*Nishkalā*	निष्कला
153	*Nishkalamkā*	निष्कलंका
142	*Nishkāmā*	निष्कामा
152	*Nishkāraŋā*	निष्कारणा
182	*Nishkriyā*	निष्क्रिया
168	*Nishkrodhā*	निष्क्रोधा
166	*Nishpāpā*	निष्पापा
183	*Nishparigrahā*	निष्परिग्रहा
146	*Nishprapajnchā*	निष्प्रपञ्चा
429	*Nisseemamahimā*	निस्सीममहिमा
789	*Nistraiguŋyā*	निस्त्रैगुण्या
184	*Nistulā*	निस्तुला
136	*Nityā*	नित्या
149	*Nityabuddhā*	नित्यबुद्धा
388	*Nityaklinnā*	नित्यक्लिन्ना
144	*Nityamuktā*	नित्यमुक्ता
73	*Nityāparākramāṭopanireekshaŋa -samutsukā*	नित्यापराक्रमाटोपनिरीक्षण –समुत्सुका
391	*Nityāshoḍashikāroopā*	नित्याषोडशिकारूपा
148	*Nityashuddhā*	नित्यशुद्धा
566	*Nityatruptā*	नित्यतृप्ता
430	*Nityayouvanā*	नित्ययौवना
568	*Niyantree*	नियन्त्री
379	*Oḍyānapeeṭhanilayā*	ओड्याणपीठनिलया
767	*Ojovatee*	ओजोवती
45	*Padadvayaprabhājālaparākruta -saroruhā*	पदद्वयप्रभाजालपराकृत –सरोरुहा
280	*Padmanābhasahodaree*	पद्मनाभसहोदरी
247	*Padmanayanā*	पद्मनयना
248	*Padmarāgasamaprabha*	पद्मरागसमप्रभा
23	*Padmarāgashilādarshaparibhāvi -kapolabhoo:*	पद्मरागशिलादर्शपरिभावि –कपोलभूः
278	*Padmāsanā*	पद्मासना

No.	Name in English	Name in Samskrit
949	*Pajnchabhooteshee*	पञ्चभूतेशी
58	*Pajnchabrahmasanasthitā*	पञ्चब्रह्मासनस्थिता
428	*Pajnchakoshāntarasthitā*	पञ्चकोशान्तरस्थिता
948	*Pajnchamee*	पञ्चमी
947	*Pajnchapretamajnchādhishāyinee*	पञ्चप्रेतमञ्चाधिशायिनी
950	*Pajnchasankhyopachārinee*	पञ्चसंख्योपचारिणी
833	*Pajnchāshatpeeṭharoopiŋee*	पञ्चाशत्पीठरूपिणी
11	*Pajnchatanmātrasāyakā*	पञ्चतन्मात्रसायका
946	*Pajnchayajnapriyā*	पञ्चयज्ञप्रिया
250	*Panchabrahmasvaroopiŋee*	पन्चब्रह्मस्वरूपिणी
274	*Panchakrutyaparāyanā*	पन्चकृत्यपरायणा
249	*Panchapretāsanāseenā*	पन्चप्रेतासनासीना
515	*Panchavaktrā*	पन्चवक्त्रा
167	*Pāpanāshinee*	पापनाशिनी
743	*Pāpāraŋyadavānalā*	पापारण्यदवानला
366	*Parā*	परा
369	*Paradevatā*	परदेवता
782	*Parākāshā*	पराकाशा
618	*Paramā*	परमा
252	*Paramānandā*	परमानन्दा
812	*Paramantravibhedinee*	परमन्त्रविभेदिनी
808	*Paramānu:*	परमाणु:
396	*Parameshvaree*	परमेश्वरी
806	*Paramjyoti:*	परंज्योति:
940	*Parāmodā*	परामोदा
939	*Paramodārā*	परमोदारा
807	*Parandhāma*	परंधाम
573	*Parānishthā*	परानिष्ठा
790	*Parāparā*	परापरा
572	*Parāshakti:*	पराशक्ति:
809	*Parātparā*	परात्परा
246	*Pārvatee*	पार्वती
811	*Pāshahantree*	पाशहन्त्री
810	*Pāshahastā*	पाशहस्ता

No.	Name in English	Name in Samskrit
482	*Pashulokabhayankaree*	पशुलोकभयङ्करी
354	*Pashupāshavimochanee*	पशुपाशविमोचनी
368	*Pashyantee*	पश्यन्ती
773	*Pāṭaleekusumapriyā*	पाटलीकुसुमप्रिया
619	*Pāvanākruti:*	पावनाकृतिः
480	*Pāyasānnapriyā*	पायसान्नप्रिया
507	*Peetavarŋā*	पीतवर्णा
803	*Poojyā*	पूज्या
292	*Poorŋā*	पूर्णा
975	*Poorvajā*	पूर्वजा
394	*Prabhāroopā*	प्रभारूपा
393	*Prabhāvatee*	प्रभावती
827	*Prachaŋḍā*	प्रचण्डा
938	*Pragalbhā*	प्रगल्भा
574	*Prajnānaghanaroopiŋee*	प्रज्ञानघनरूपिणी
261	*Prajnātmikā*	प्रज्ञात्मिका
830	*Prakaṭākruti:*	प्रकटाकृतिः
783	*Prāŋadā*	प्राणदा
832	*Prāŋadātree*	प्राणदात्री
784	*Prāŋaroopiŋee*	प्राणरूपिणी
831	*Prāŋeshvaree*	प्राणेश्वरी
826	*Prasavitree*	प्रसवित्री
395	*Prasiddhā*	प्रसिद्धा
610	*Pratipanmukhyarākāntatithi -maŋḍalapoojitā*	प्रतिपन्मुख्यराकान्ततिथि –मण्डलपूजिता
829	*Pratishṭhā*	प्रतिष्ठा
781	*Pratyagroopā*	प्रत्यग्रूपा
367	*Pratyakchiteeroopā*	प्रत्यक्चितीरूपा
730	*Premaroopā*	प्रेमरूपा
731	*Priyamkaree*	प्रियंकरी
770	*Priyavratā*	प्रियव्रता
545	*Pulomajārchitā*	पुलोमजार्चिता
542	*Puŋyakeertti:*	पुण्यकीर्त्तिः
543	*Puŋyalabhyā*	पुण्यलभ्या

No.	Name in English	Name in Samskrit
288	*Puŋyāpuŋyaphlapradā*	पुण्यापुण्यफलप्रदा
544	*Puŋyashravaŋakeerttanā*	पुण्यश्रवणकीर्त्तना
802	*Purātanā*	पुरातना
291	*Purushārthapradā*	पुरुषार्थप्रदा
804	*Pushkarā*	पुष्करा
805	*Pushkarekshaŋā*	पुष्करेक्षणा
801	*Pushṭā*	पुष्टा
444	*Pushṭi:*	पुष्टिः
157	*Rāgamathanee*	रागमथनी
8	*Rāgasvaroopapāshāḍhyā*	रागस्वरूपपाशाढ्या
382	*Rahastarpaŋatarpitā*	रहस्तर्पणतर्पिता
381	*Rahoyāgakrmārādhyā*	रहोयागक्रमाराध्या
688	*Rājapeeṭhaniveshitanijāshritā*	राजपीठनिवेशितनिजाश्रिता
305	*Rājarājārchitā*	राजराजार्चिता
684	*Rājarājeshvaree*	राजराजेश्वरी
687	*Rājatkrupā*	राजत्कृपा
308	*Rājeevalochanā*	राजीवलोचना
306	*Rājnee*	राज्ञी
309	*Rajnjanee*	रञ्जनी
685	*Rājyadāyinee*	राज्यदायिनी
689	*Rājyalakshmee:*	राज्यलक्ष्मीः
686	*Rājyavallabhā*	राज्यवल्लभा
314	*Rākenduvadanā*	राकेन्दुवदना
494	*Rākinyambāsvaroopiŋee*	राकिण्यम्बास्वरूपिणी
317	*Rakshākaree*	रक्षाकरी
318	*Rākshasaghnee*	राक्षसघ्नी
499	*Raktavarŋā*	रक्तवर्णा
313	*Ramā*	रमा
319	*Rāmā*	रामा
320	*Ramaŋalampaṭā*	रमणलम्पटा
310	*Ramaŋee*	रमणी
741	*Rambhādi Vanditā*	रम्भादिवन्दिता
307	*Ramyā*	रम्या
312	*Raŋatkinkiŋimekhalā*	रणत्किङ्किणिमेखला

No.	Name in English	Name in Samskrit
799	*Rasajnā*	रसज्ञा
800	*Rasashevadhi:*	रसशेवधि:
311	*Rasyā*	रस्या
316	*Ratipriyā*	रतिप्रिया
315	*Ratiroopā*	रतिरूपा
32	*Ratnagraiveyachintākalola -muktāphalānvitā*	रत्नग्रैवेयचिन्ताकलोल –मुक्ताफलान्विता
38	*Ratnakimkiŋikāramyarashanā -dāmabhooshitā*	रत्नकिंकिणिकारम्यरशना –दामभूषिता
596	*Raviprakhyā*	रविप्रख्या
748	*Rogaparvatadambholi:*	रोगपर्वतदम्भोलि:
490	*Rudhirasamsthitā*	रुधिरसंस्थिता
104	*Rudragranthivibhedinee*	रुद्रग्रन्थिविभेदिनी
269	*Rudraroopā*	रुद्ररूपा
700	*Saccidānandaroopiŋee*	सच्चिदानन्दरूपिणी
614	*Sachāmararamāvāŋee -savyadakshiŋasevitā*	सचामटटमावाणी –सव्यदक्षिणसेविता
356	*Sadācārapravarttikā*	सदाचारप्रवर्त्तिका
661	*Sadasadroopadhāriŋee*	सदसद्रूपधारिणी
272	*Sadāshivā*	सदाशिवा
911	*Sadāshivakuṭumbinee*	सदाशिवकुटुम्बिनी
709	*Sadāshivapativratā*	सदाशिवपतिव्रता
921	*Sadātushṭā*	सदातुष्टा
201	*Sadgatipradā*	सद्गतिप्रदा
711	*Sādhu*	साधु
128	*Sādhvee*	साध्वी
920	*Saditā*	सदोदिता
383	*Sadya: Prasādinee*	सद्य: प्रसादिनी
694	*Sāgaramekhalā*	सागरमेखला
528	*Sahasradalapadmasthā*	सहस्रदलपद्मस्था
283	*Sahasrākshee*	सहस्राक्षी
284	*Sahasrapāt*	सहस्रपात
105	*Sahasrārāmbujārooḍhā*	सहस्राराम्बुजारूढा
282	*Sahasrasheershavadanā*	सहस्रशीर्षवदना

No.	Name in English	Name in Samskrit
290	*Sakalāgamasamdohashakti -samputamouktikā*	सकलागमसंदोहशुक्ति –संपुटमौक्तिका
520	*Sākinyambāsvaroopiŋee*	साकिन्यम्बास्वरूपिणी
385	*Sākshivarjitā*	साक्षिवर्जिता
909	*Sāmagānapriyā*	सामगानप्रिया
198	*Samānādhikavarjitā*	समानाधिकवर्जिता
792	*Sāmarasyaparāyaŋā*	सामरस्यपरायणा
502	*Samastabhaktasukhadā*	समस्तभक्तसुखदा
98	*Samayācāratatparā*	समयाचारतत्परा
97	*Samayāntasthā*	समयान्तस्था
268	*Samhāriŋee*	संहारिणी
355	*Samhrutāsheshapāshaŋḍā*	संहृताशेशपाशण्डा
66	*Sampatkareesamārooḍha sindhuravrajasevitā*	सम्पत्करीसमारूढ –सिन्धुटब्रजसेविता
710	*Sampradāyeshvaree*	सम्प्रदायेश्वरी
692	*Sāmrājyadāyinee*	साम्राज्यदायिनी
880	*Samsāra Panka Nirmagna Samuddharaŋa Paŋḍitā*	संसारपङ्कनिर्मग्न समुद्धरण पण्डिता
173	*Samshayaghnee*	संशयघ्नी
726	*Sanakādi Samārādhyā*	सनकादि समाराध्या
422	*Sandhyā*	सन्ध्या
197	*Sāndrakaruŋā*	सान्द्रकरुणा
704	*Sarasvatee*	सरस्वती
51	*Sarvābharaŋabhooshitā*	सर्वाभरणभूषिता
659	*Sarvādhārā*	सर्वाधारा
702	*Sarvagā*	सर्वगा
196	*Sarvajnā*	सर्वज्ञा
697	*Sarvalokavashankaree*	सर्वलोकवशंकरी
758	*Sarvalokeshee*	सर्वलोकेशी
200	*Sarvamangalā*	सर्वमंगला
204	*Sarvamantrasvaroopiŋee*	सर्वमन्त्रस्वरूपिणी
203	*Sarvamayee*	सर्वमयी
703	*Sarvamohinee*	सर्वमोहिनी
552	*Sarvamrutyunivāriŋee*	सर्वमृत्युनिवारिणी

No.	Name in English	Name in Samskrit
819	*Sarvāntaryāmiŋee*	सर्वान्तर्यामिणी
995	*Sarvānullanghyashāsanā*	सर्वानुल्लङ्घ्यशासना
913	*Sarvāpadvinināriŋee*	सर्वापद्विनिवारिणी
698	*Sarvārthadātree*	सर्वार्थदात्री
49	*Sarvāruŋā*	सर्वारुणा
199	*Sarvashaktimayee*	सर्वशक्तिमयी
206	*Sarvatantraroopā*	सर्वतन्त्ररूपा
724	*Sarvatantreshee*	सर्वतन्त्रेशी
962	*Sarvāteetā*	सर्वातीता
532	*Sarvatomukhee*	सर्वतोमुखी
529	*Sarvavarŋopashobhitā*	सर्ववर्णोपशोभिता
263	*Sarvāvasthāvivarjitā*	सर्वावस्थाविवर्जिता
645	*Sarvavedāntasamvedyā*	सर्ववेदान्तसंवेद्या
551	*Sarvavyādhiprashamanee*	सर्वव्याधिप्रशमनी
205	*Sarvayantrātmikā*	सर्वयन्त्रात्मिका
530	*Sarvāyudhadharā*	सर्वायुधधरा
202	*Sarveshvaree*	सर्वेश्वरी
708	*Sarvopādhivinirmuktā*	सर्वोपाधिविनिर्मुक्ता
852	*Sarvopanishadudghushṭā*	सर्वोपनिषदुद्घुष्टा
533	*Sarvoudanapreetacittā*	सर्वौदनप्रीतचित्ता
820	*Satee*	सती
791	*Satyajnānānandaroopā*	सत्यज्ञानानन्दरूपा
646	*Satyānandasvaroopiŋee*	सत्यानन्दस्वरूपिणी
818	*Satyaroopā*	सत्यरूपा
693	*Satyasandhā*	सत्यसन्धा
817	*Satyavratā*	सत्यव्रता
699	*Sāvitree*	सावित्री
912	*Savyāpasavyamārgasthā*	सव्यापसव्यमार्गस्था
991	*Shaḍadhvāteetaroopiŋee*	षडध्वातीतरूपिणी
523	*Shaḍānanā*	षडानना
386	*Shaḍangadevatāyuktā*	षडङ्गदेवतायुक्ता
387	*Shāḍguŋyaparipooritā*	षाड्गुण्यपरिपूरिता
634	*Shailendratanayā*	शैलेन्द्रतनया
87	*Shaktikooṭaikatāpannakatyadho*	शक्तिकूटैकतापन्नकट्यधो

No.	Name in English	Name in Samskrit
	-bhāgadhāriŋee	–भागधारिणी
963	*Shamātmikā*	शमात्मिका
122	*Shāmbhavee*	शाम्भवी
954	*Shambhumohinee*	शम्भुमोहिनी
126	*Shānkaree*	शान्करी
141	*Shāntā*	शान्ता
447	*Shānti:*	शान्ति:
131	*Shāntimatee*	शान्तिमती
853	*Shāntyateetakalātmikā*	शान्त्यतीतकलात्मिका
129	*Sharaccandranibhānanā*	शरच्चन्द्रनिभानना
123	*Shāradārādhyā*	शारदाराध्या
953	*Sharmadā*	शर्मदा
125	*Sharmadāyinee*	शर्मदायिनी
124	*Sharvāŋee*	शर्वाणी
952	*Shāshvataishvaryā*	शाश्वतैश्वर्या
951	*Shāshvatee*	शाश्वती
705	*Shāstramayee*	शास्त्रमयी
845	*Shāstrasārā*	शास्त्रसारा
108	*Shaṭchakroparisamsthitā*	षट्चक्रोपरिसंस्थिता
130	*Shātodaree*	शातोदरी
591	*Shira:sthitā*	शिर:स्थिता
412	*Shishṭapoojitā*	शिष्टपूजिता
411	*Shishṭeshṭā*	शिष्टेष्टा
53	*Shivā*	शिवा
405	*Shivadootee*	शिवदूती
727	*Shivajnnānapradāyinee*	शिवज्ञानप्रदायिनी
52	*Shivakāmeshvarānkasthā*	शिवकामेश्वराङ्कस्था
408	*Shivamkaree*	शिवंकरी
407	*Shivamoortti:*	शिवमूर्त्ति:
410	*Shivaparā*	शिवपरा
409	*Shivapriyā*	शिवप्रिया
406	*Shivārādhyā*	शिवाराध्या
999	*Shivashaktyaikyaroopiŋee*	शिवशक्त्यैक्यरूपिणी
462	*Shobhanā*	शोभना

No.	Name in English	Name in Samskrit
683	*Shobhanā Sulabhā Gati*:	शोभना सुलभा गतिः
506	*Shoolādhyāyudha Sampannā*	शूलाद्यायुध संपन्ना
376	*Shrungārarasasampoorŋā*	श्रृंगाटटससम्पूर्णा
682	*Shubhakaree*	शुभकरी
765	*Shuddhā*	शुद्धा
973	*Shuddhamānasā*	शुद्धमानसा
25	*Shuddhavidyānkurākāradvijapankti -dwayojjwalā*	शुद्धविद्याङ्कुराकारद्विजपंक्ति –द्वयोज्ज्वला
531	*Shuklasamsthitā*	शुक्लसंस्थिता
522	*Shuklavarŋā*	शुक्लवर्णा
486	*Shyāmābhā*	श्यामाभा
473	*Siddhamātā*	सिद्धमाता
472	*Siddhavidyā*	सिद्धविद्या
471	*Siddheshvaree*	सिद्धेश्वरी
46	*Sijnjānamaŋimanjeeramaŋḍita -Śreepadāmbujā*	सिञ्जानमणिमंजीरमण्डित –श्रीपदांबुजा
632	*Sindooratilakājncitā*	सिन्दूरतिलकाञ्चिता
540	*Smruti*:	स्मृतिः
492	*Snigdoudana Priyā*	स्निग्दौदनप्रिया
910	*Somyā (Soumyā)*	सोम्या (सौम्या)
467	*Sookshmaroopiŋee*	सूक्ष्मरूपिणी
998	*Śree Shivā*	श्री शिवा
996	*Śreechakrarājanilayā*	श्रीचक्रराजनिलया
392	*Śreekanṭhārdhashareeriŋee*	श्रीकण्ठार्धशरीरिणी
127	*Śreekaree*	श्रीकरी
85	*Śreemadvāgbhavakooṭaika -svaroopamukhapamkajā*	श्रीमद्वाग्भवकूटैकस्व –रूपमुखपंकजा
2	*Śreemahārājnee*	श्रीमहाराडी
56	*Śreemannagaranāyikā*	श्रीमन्नगरनायिका
1	*Śreemātā*	श्रीमाता
997	*Śreematripurasundaree*	श्रीमत्त्रिपुरसुन्दरी
3	*Śreematsimhāsaneshwaree*	श्रीमत्सिंहासनेश्वरी
587	*Śreeshoḍashākshareevidyā*	श्रीषोडशाक्षरीविद्या
585	*Śreevidyā*	श्रीविद्या

No.	Name in English	Name in Samskrit
264	*Srushṭikartree*	सृष्टिकर्त्री
539	*Sruti:*	श्रुतिः
929	*Srutisamstutavaibhavā*	श्रुतिसंस्तुतवैभवा
289	*Srutiseemantasindoorikrutapādābja- -dhoolikā*	श्रुतिसीमन्तसिन्दूरिकृतपादाब्ज –धूलिका
36	*Stanabhāradalanmadhyapaṭṭa -Bandhavalitrayā*	स्तनभारदलन्मध्यपट्ट –बन्धवलित्रया
927	*Stotrapriyā*	स्तोत्रप्रिया
928	*Stutimatee*	स्तुतिमती
761	*Subhagā*	सुभगा
461	*Subhroo:*	सुभ्रूः
61	*Sudhāsāgaramadhyasthā*	सुधासागरमध्यस्था
106	*Sudhāsārābhivarshiṇee*	सुधासाराभिवर्षिणी
879	*Sudhāsruti:*	सुधास्रुतिः
968	*Sukhakaree*	सुखकरी
192	*Sukhapradā*	सुखप्रदा
681	*Sukhārādhyā*	सुखाराध्या
967	*Sumangalee*	सुमङ्गली
55	*Sumerumadhyasrungasthā*	सुमेरुमध्यश्रुङ्गस्था
459	*Sumukhee*	सुमुखी
660	*Supratishṭhā*	सुप्रतिष्ठा
260	*Suptā*	सुप्ता
463	*Suranāyikā*	सुरनायिका
970	*Suvāsinee*	सुवासिनी
971	*Suvāsinyarchanapreetā*	सुवासिन्यर्चनप्रीता
969	*Suveshāḍhyā*	सुवेषाढ्या
915	*Svabhāvamadhurā*	स्वभावमधुरा
536	*Svadhā*	स्वधा
54	*Svādheenavallabhā*	स्वाधीनवल्लभा
504	*Svādhishṭānāmbujagatā*	स्वाधिष्टानांबुजगता
535	*Svāhā*	स्वाहा
258	*Svapantee*	स्वपन्ती
414	*Svaprakāshā*	स्वप्रकाशा
764	*Svargāpavargadā*	स्वर्गापवर्गदा

No.	Name in English	Name in Samskrit
638	*Svarŋagarbhā*	स्वर्णगर्भा
914	*Svasthā*	स्वस्था
448	*Svastimatee*	स्वस्तिमती
723	*Svatantra*	स्वतन्त्रा
365	*Svātmānandalavee Bhootabrahmadyānanda Santati:*	स्वात्मानन्दलवी भूतब्रह्माद्यानन्द सन्ततिः
878	*Svātmārāmā*	स्वात्मारामा
107	*Taḑillatāsamaruchi:*	तडिल्लतासमरुचिः
259	*Taijasātmikā*	तैजसात्मिका
847	*Talodaree*	तलोदरी
559	*Tāmboolapooritamukhee*	ताम्बूलपूरितमुखी
361	*Tamopahā*	तमोपहा
360	*Tanumadhyā*	तनुमध्या
359	*Tāpasārādhyā*	तापसाराध्या
357	*Tāpatrayāgnisantaptasamāhlādana -chandrikā*	तापत्रयाग्निसन्तप्तसमाह्लादन –चन्द्रिका
20	*Tārākāntitiraskāri - Nāsābharaŋabhāsurā*	ताराकान्तितिरस्कारि– नासाभरणभासुरा
922	*Taruŋādityapāṭalā*	तरुणादित्यपाटला
358	*Taruŋee*	तरुणी
425	*Tat*	तत्
22	*Tāṭankayugaleebhootatapanodupa-maŋḑalā*	ताटङ्कयुगलीभूततपनोडुप –मण्डला
363	*Tatpadalakshyārthā*	तत्पदलक्ष्यार्था
906	*Tatvādhikā*	तत्वाधिका
908	*Tatvamarthasvaroopiŋee*	तत्वमर्थस्वरूपिणी
907	*Tatvamayee*	तत्वमयी
424	*Tatvāsanā*	तत्वासना
452	*Tejovatee*	तेजोवती
270	*Tirodhānakaree*	तिरोधानकरी
872	*Trayee*	त्रयी
630	*Triaksharee*	त्र्यक्षरी
762	*Triambakā*	त्र्यम्बका
629	*Tridasheshvaree*	त्रिदशेश्वरी

No.	Name in English	Name in Samskrit
984	*Triguŋā*	त्रिगुणा
763	*Triguŋātmikā*	त्रिगुणात्मिका
627	*Trijagadvandyā*	त्रिजगद्वन्द्या
983	*Trikhaŋḍeshee*	त्रिखण्डेशी
986	*Trikoŋagā*	त्रिकोणगा
597	*Trikoŋāntaradeepikā*	त्रिकोणान्तरदीपिका
588	*Trikooṭā*	त्रिकूटा
477	*Trilochanā*	त्रिलोचना
628	*Trimoortti:*	त्रिमूर्त्तिः
453	*Trinayanā*	त्रिनयना
626	*Tripurā*	त्रिपुरा
875	*Tripuramālinee*	त्रिपुरमालिनी
976	*Tripurāmbikā*	त्रिपुराम्बिका
978	*Tripurāshreevashankaree*	त्रिपुराश्रीवशन्करी
787	*Tripureshee*	त्रिपुरेशी
874	*Tristhā*	त्रिस्था
760	*Trivargadhātree*	त्रिवर्गधात्री
873	*Trivarganilayā*	त्रिवर्गनिलया
262	*Turyā*	तुर्या
443	*Tushṭi:*	तुष्टिः
481	*Tvaksthā*	त्वक्स्था
426	*Tvam*	त्वम्
848	*Udārakeerti:*	उदारकीर्तिः
849	*Uddhāma Vaibhavā*	उद्धाम वैभवा
6	*Udyadbhānusahasrābhā*	उद्यद्भानुसहस्राभा
633	*Umā*	उमा
281	*Unmeshanimishotpannavipanna -bhuvanāvalee*	उन्मेषनिमिषोत्पन्नविपन्न –भुवनावली
487	*Vadanadvayā*	वदनद्वया
479	*Vadanaikasamanvitā*	वदनैकसमन्विता
17	*Vadanasmaramāngalyagruhatoraŋa -cillikā*	वदनस्मरमाङ्गल्यगृहतोरण –चिल्लिका
496	*Vadanatrāyasamyutā*	वदनत्रयसम्युता

No.	Name in English	Name in Samskrit
640	*Vāgadheeshvaree*	वागधीश्वरी
350	*Vāgvādinee*	वाग्वादिनी
352	*Vahnimaŋḍalavāsinee*	वह्निमण्डलवासिनी
371	*Vaikhareeroopā*	वैखरीरूपा
892	*Vaishŋavee*	वैष्णवी
989	*Vājnchitārthapradāyinee*	वाञ्छितार्थप्रदायिनी
497	*Vajrādikāyudhopetā*	वज्रादिकायुधोपेता
468	*Vajreshvaree*	वज्रेश्वरी
944	*Vajriŋee*	वज्रिणी
18	*Vaktralakshmeepareevāha-chalanmeenābhalochanā*	वक्त्रलक्ष्मीपरीवाह –चलन्मीनाभलोचना
469	*Vāmadevee*	वामदेवी
351	*Vāmakeshee*	वामकेशी
945	*Vāmakeshvaree*	वामकेश्वरी
332	*Vāmanayanā*	वामनयना
349	*Vandārujanavatsalā*	वन्दारुजनवत्सला
348	*Vandyā*	वन्द्या
331	*Varadā*	वरदा
518	*Varadādinishevitā*	वरदादिनिषेविता
850	*Varŋaroopiŋee*	वर्णरूपिणी
286	*Varŋāshramavidhāyinee*	वर्णाश्रमविधायिनी
333	*Vāruŋee Madavihvalā*	वारुणी मदविह्वला
670	*Vasudā*	वसुदा
470	*Vayo'vasthāvivarjitā*	वयोऽवस्थाविवर्जिता
338	*Vedajananee*	वेदजननी
335	*Vedavedyā*	वेदवेद्या
652	*Vedyavarjitā*	वेद्यवर्जिता
899	*Veerā*	वीरा
898	*Veeragoshṭheepriyā*	वीरगोष्ठीप्रिया
836	*Veeramātā*	वीरमाता
777	*Veerārādhya*	वीराराध्या
904	*Vidagdhā*	विदग्धा
337	*Vidhātree*	विधात्री
549	*Vidhyā*	विद्या

No.	Name in English	Name in Samskrit
402	*Vidhyā'vidhyāsvaroopiŋee*	विद्याऽविद्यास्वरूपिणी
891	*Vidrumābhā*	विद्रुमाभा
451	*Vighnanāshinee*	विघ्ननाशिनी
346	*Vijayā*	विजया
253	*Vijnānaghanaroopiŋee*	विज्ञानघनरूपिणी
902	*Vijnānakalanā*	विज्ञानकलना
651	*Vijnātree*	विज्ञात्री
340	*Vilāsinee*	विलासिनी
347	*Vimalā*	विमला
943	*Vimānasthā*	विमानस्था
548	*Vimarsharoopiŋee*	विमर्शरूपिणी
336	*Vindhyāchalanivāsinee*	विन्ध्याचलनिवासिनी
887	*Viprapriyā*	विप्रप्रिया
888	*Vipraroopā*	विप्ररूपा
778	*Virāḓroopā*	विराड्रूपा
937	*Virāgiŋee*	विरागिणी
779	*Virajā*	विरजा
936	*Vishālākshee*	विशालाक्षी
102	*Vişhŋugranthivibhedinee*	विष्णुग्रन्थिविभेदिनी
339	*Vişhŋumāyā*	विष्णुमाया
893	*Vişhŋuroopiŋee*	विष्णुरूपिणी
834	*Vishrunkhalā*	विश्रृङ्खला
475	*Vishuddhicakra Nilayā*	विशुद्धिचक्र निलया
76	*Vishukraprāŋaharaŋavārāhee Veeryananditā*	विशुक्रप्राणहरणवाराही –वीर्यनंदिता
889	*Vishvabhramaŋakāriŋee*	विश्वभ्रमणकारिणी
759	*Vishvadhāriŋee*	विश्वधारिणी
334	*Vishvādhikā*	विश्वाधिका
637	*Vishvagarbhā*	विश्वगर्भा
890	*Vishvagrāsā*	विश्वग्रासा
934	*Vishvamātā*	विश्वमाता
256	*Vishvaroopā*	विश्वरूपा
384	*Vishvasākshiŋee*	विश्वसाक्षिणी
780	*Vishvatomukhee*	विश्वतोमुखी

No.	Name in English	Name in Samskrit
401	*Vividhākārā*	विविधाकारा
835	*Viviktasthā*	विविक्तस्था
550	*Viyadādijagatprasoo:*	वियदादिजगत्प्रसू:
837	*Viyatprasoo:*	वियत्प्रसू:
671	*Vruddhā*	वृद्धा
421	*Vyāhruti:*	व्याहृति:
399	*Vyaktāvyaktasvaroopiŋee*	व्यक्ताव्यक्तस्वरूपिणी
400	*Vyāpinee*	व्यापिनी
942	*Vyomakeshee*	व्योमकेशी
769	*Yagnyaroopā*	यज्ञयरूपा
883	*Yajamānasvaroopiŋee*	यजमानस्वरूपिणी
882	*Yajna Kartree*	यज्ञकर्त्री
881	*Yajnayapriyā*	यज्ञयप्रिया
534	*Yākinyambāsvaroopiŋee*	याकिन्यम्बास्वरूपिणी
474	*Yashasvinee*	यशस्विनी
654	*Yogadā*	योगदा
656	*Yogānandā*	योगानन्दा
653	*Yoginee*	योगिनी
655	*Yogyā*	योग्या
982	*Yonimudrā*	योनिमुद्रा
895	*Yoninilayā*	योनिनिलया
657	*Yugamdharā*	युगंधरा

*****

Appendix 2

All the words in Samskrit cannot be translated into English to provide complete meaning. An attempt has been made to describe the words in the below table;

#	Samskrit word	Description
1.	*Agni*	Fire
2.	*Ākāśā*	Space, ether
3.	*Apāna*	The seat and field of activity of *Apāna* is from the navel to the soles of the feet It is characterised by heaviness and has a downward movement Its function is elimination It eliminates stool, urine, semen and menses It helps in the process of childbirth When this energy is not regulated one feels lazy, dull, heavy and confused It is yellow in colour
4.	*Ashṭānga Sankalpa*	During any *sankalpa* it is usual to describe the place, the time and the intention In time, the description is eight level viz., 1 year, 2 *ayanam* [half of the year], 3 *ritu*, 4 month, 5 *paksha* [bright or dark half of lunar month], 6 day, 7 star of the day and 8 *thithi* [counting from previous new or full moon day] Hence it is called *Ashṭānga*)
5.	*Bhāga*	Part
6.	*Brahma*	The God responsible for creation
7.	*Chakra*	A wheel
8.	*Deekshā*	Initiation
9.	*Deva*	Deity, Godhead
10.	*Devees*	Feminine form of *Devas*
11.	*Dhyāna*	Meditation
12.	*Graha*	House
13.	*Guru*	Teacher
14.	*Indrā*	King of *Devas*
15.	*Jala*	Water
16.	*Japa*	Pious repetition of a holy name or sacred *mantra*, practiced as a spiritual discipline
17.	*Jeevā*	The soul
18.	*Kalasam*	A holy pot with water, coconut, mango leaves, etc.
19.	*Katikā*	One sixtieth part of the day – 22 minutes – also called as *Nāzhikai*
20.	*Krişhŋapaksha*	Dark half of the lunar month
21.	*Kunḍalinee*	The coiled power or energy
22.	*Mahābhāratha*	One of the two epics of Hindu religion The other

#	Samskrit word	Description
		one is *Rāmāyana*
23.	*Manmatha*	God of Love – Equivalent of Greek god Cupid – He has a bow made of sugarcane and arrows made of flowers
24.	*Mantra*	Sacred chant - 3 types of measurement A mystical verse as a prayer or form of exorcism
25.	*Nāḍis*	Pulse in the human body
26.	*Nama*:	Salutations or bow to
27.	*Nyāsā*	Mental appropriation
28.	*Parvā*	Either full or new moon
29.	*Pathivrathai*	One who is loyal to her husband by virtue
30.	*Pooja*	Offering prayers
31.	*Poorva*	First or initial
32.	*Prāna*	The seat and field of activity of *Prana* is from the heart to the throat Its main function is respiration It moves between the nostrils and the heart during inhalation/ exhalation It controls and regulates all the activities of the sense organs It helps in sound production, swallowing and regulates the body temperature It is golden in colour, light in weight and has an upward movement
33.	*Praṇavam*	The word *Om*
34.	*Prithvi*	Earth
35.	*Pūrāṇā*	A legendary tale containing accounts of gods, *Devas*, etc.
36.	*Rishi*	Sage
37.	*Sahasranāma*	1000 names
38.	*Shakti*	Energy
39.	*Samāna*	The seat and filed of activity of *Samana* is from the navel to the heart. Its function is digestion and assimilation. It therefore nourishes the whole body and gives glowing health. It is white in color and cool in nature.
40.	*Sankalpa*	Resolute, wish, intention Prior to initiating any ritualistic endeavor such as *pooja*, it is proper and traditional to state to God what it is that we are about to do, why, the geographical description of the place where we do *pooja* the astronomical time when we do *pooja* (sankalpa)
41.	*Saraswathee*	Goddess of learning
42.	*Sāstra*	A Hindu religious book as laid down and considered

#	Samskrit word	Description
		of divine origin or authority
43.	*Siddha*	One of the eighteen classes of supernal or demigods inhabiting the middle air or region between the earth and the Sun embracing several sub divisions
44.	*Sloka*	Verse, poem
45.	*Shiva*	God responsible for destruction
46.	*Śree*	Normally *Śree* stands for *Lakshmee*, the goddess of wealth It is also prefixed with names instead of Mr
47.	*Stotram*	A prayer
48.	*Suklapaksha*	Bright half of the lunar month
49.	*Sumangali*	Ladies with living husband Antonym of widow
50.	*Tantra*	Trick – 3 types of bodies
51.	*Trishatee*	300 names
52.	*Udāna*	The seat and filed of activity of *Udāna* is from the throat to the head It keeps the body lifted upwards and does not allow it to fall down while running or turning in different directions It helps in vomiting It also helps in sound production, speaking, singing, etc. By regulating this energy the body can be made very light It is green in colour After death a portion of this energy remains in the body This energy then decomposes the physical body reverting the physical matter of the body to its elemental forms
53.	*Vāyu*	Wind/ Air
54.	*Veda*	The holy book of Hindus
55.	*Veena*	A string instrument
56.	*Vidyā*	Education
57.	*Viṣhṇu*	God responsible for protection
58.	*Vyāna*	This energy pervades the whole body Its major function is circulation It co-ordinates all activities of the nervous system It helps in maintaining co-ordination and balance It is sky-blue in colour
59.	*Vyāsā*	The sage who compiled all the *Vedas*
60.	*Yama*	Lord of death
61.	*Yantra*	Talisman – 3 types of energies - A plate (normally of copper) where some drawing is made in a specific design to the concerned god Ardent devotees do *pooja* with the *Yantra* instead of idols

*****

Bibilography

The important other books, which helped in writing this book are listed below;

#	Book/ site	Author/ Remarks
1.	*Soubhāgya Bhāskaram*	The detailed commentaries of *Śree Bhāskararāya*in Samskrit This is fundamental base for the entire book
2.	*Soundaryalaharee*	Alongwith the 9 commentaries published by *Śree Kānchi* Mutt further with the meanings of Śree GV *Gaŋesaiyer* and *Tetiyoor Brahmaśree Subramaŋia Sāstrigal*
3.	*Śree Durgā saptashatee* alias *Chaŋḍi or Devee Mahātmeeyam*	The meanings of *Śree Bhāskararāya* and others
4.	*Śreemad Bhagavad Geeta*	
5.	*Śree Varivasyā Rahasyam*	
6.	*Śree Lalitā Trishatee*	Commentary by *Śree Ādi Śaṇkara*
7.	*Śree Vişhŋu Sahasranāma*	Commentary by *Śree Ādi Śaṇkara*
8.	*Mahā Shoḍanyāsam*	
9.	*Nityā Shoḍashikārnavam*	Including books on other *tantra sāstrās* like *Tantrarājatantram, Kulārnavam, Gnānārnavam*
10.	*Shiva Sūtras*	
11.	*Pratyabhignāhrutayam*	
12.	*Sānkyakārikai*	
13.	*Śree Lalitopākyānam*	
14.	*Brahma Sūtram*	
15.	*Upanishads*	
16.	*Śreevidyāsaparyāpaddhati*	
17.	*Devee Bhāgavatam*	
18.	*Lalitā Sahasranāma*	Tamil meaning of Śree GV Gaŋesaiyer
19.	*Lalitā Sahasranāma*	Tamil meaning of Śree SV Radha Krişhŋa Sāstrigal
20.	*Lalitā Sahasranāma*	English Translation of Śree Ananda Krişhŋa Sāstrigal
21.	*Patanjaliyoga Sutrās*	

#	Book/ site	Author/ Remarks
22.	*Speeches on Lalitā Sahasranāma*	*Brahma Śree Godā Venkateshvara Sāstrigal* at *Gnānabhāskara Sangam* – every Sunday for nearly five years

Further the below sites and books were referred for translating into English;

#	Book/ site	Author/ Remarks
23.	http://wwwindiadivine.org	
24.	http://sanskritinriafr/DiCO/indexhtml	
25.	http://wwwtamildict.com	
26.	Tamil English Dictionary	Asian Educational Services Publications
27.	*Śreemad Bhagavad Geeta*	Commentary in English by *Swami Chidbhavananda* published by *Śree Ramakrişhŋa Tapovanam*
28.	The concise Sanskrit-English Dictionary	Motilal Banarsidass Publishers
29.	*Soundaryalaharee*	
30.	*Śree Lalitā Trishatee*	
31.	*Devee Bhāgavatam*	
32.	*Vişhŋu Sahasranāma*	

*****

About the Author

http://ramamurthy.jaagruti.co.in/

Ramamurthy is a versatile personality having experience and expertise in various areas of Banking, related IT solutions, Information Security, IT Audit, Vedas, Samskrit and so on.

His thirst for continuous learning does not subside even at the age of late fifties. He is also pursuing research on Information Technology and Samskrit and has submitted his dissertation for Ph.D. degree. He is into a project of developing a Samskrit based compiler.

It is his passion to spread his knowledge and experience through conducting classes, training programmes and writing books.

He has already published books:

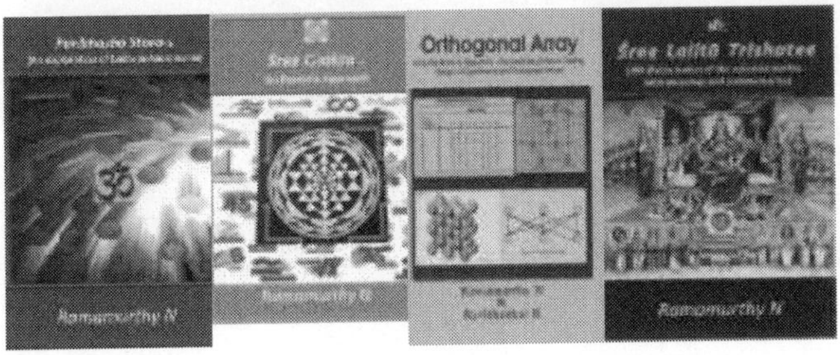

His other books are being published:

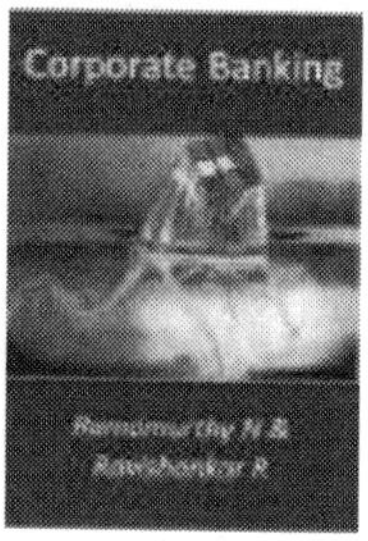

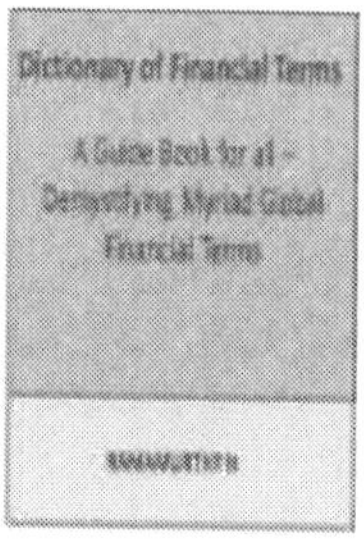

Books being penned: Pranic Healing, Corporate Finance, Information Security in Banks and more.

Let him be wished with a long and healthy life so that he could continue his services.

*****

22078142R00406

Printed in Great Britain
by Amazon